A BASIC BIBLIOGRAPHY
FOR THE STUDY OF
THE SEMITIC LANGUAGES

VOLUME I

EDITED BY

J. H. HOSPERS

LEIDEN
E. J. BRILL
1973

ISBN 90 04 03623 7

A BASIC BIBLIOGRAPHY
FOR THE STUDY OF
THE SEMITIC LANGUAGES

VOLUME I

CONTENTS

A. LANGUAGES OF THE ANCIENT NEAR EAST AND THEIR HISTORICAL RELATIONSHIP

B. COMPARATIVE SEMITICS

PREFACE

This Basic Bibliography for the Study of the Semitic Languages is the result of material brought together by the teaching staff of the Institute for Semitic Studies and Archaeology of the Near East at the State University in Groningen during the 1967/68 course for the purpose of delivering a number of bibliography lectures to their students during that academic year. Because the collectors of that material thought that the fruits of their labours might be useful to a wider circle of students, they decided to supplement their material so as to make it up to date with a view to publishing it, hoping that it might serve as a guide for Semitists. [1]

The publisher E.J. Brill proved to be willing to undertake the publication of such a work. After consultations with the publisher it was decided to widen the original scope of the work so as to let it include the few fields of study not covered by the Groningen teaching staff. For this purpose a few scholars from outside were asked to co-operate. Both the publisher and the compilers are convinced that it might be useful for students of the Semitic languages to have a bibliography which includes publications in those fields of study bordering on Semitic Languages. This first volume does not include the Arabic. In a forthcoming second volume this field of study will be treated.

The character of the Bibliography is didactic-selective, which means that it is in no way exhaustive, in the sense of the exhaustiveness claimed by other bibliographical works in view of their set-up. [2] Our Bibliography aims at a different kind of exhaustiveness: to list as completely as possible and in the relevant contexts everything really needed by students in the Semitic languages, and other persons interested in these studies, in such a way that they can use the bibli-

---

[1] An earlier effort in this direction is W. S. LaSor, A Basic Semitic Bibliography (Annotated), Wheaton, Ill., 1950, but this work is very concise and in any case by now out of date.

[2] Cf. e.g. periodicals such as the "Annual Egyptological Bibliography compiled by M. S. G. H. HEERMA VAN VOSS and J. J. JANSEN, Leiden 1948 sqq. and the "International Bibliography of the History of Religions" compiled by C. J. BLEEKER and others, Leiden 1948 sqq. and occasional bibliographical works such as W. LESLAU, Modern South Arabic Languages. A Bibliography, New York, 1946 and W. LESLAU, An annotated Bibliography of the Semitic Languages of Ethiopia, The Hague, 1965.

ographic information as an aid to discover for themselves more detailed material.

The selective character of the Bibliography naturally includes some measure of subjectivity. The compilers have constantly been aware of this, knowing that the proof of the pudding is in the eating and that the practical use will make out wether they have selected wisely. In view of its didactic character the compilers tried to give as completely as possible a list of bibliographical works, handbooks, grammars, lexica and text editions in every field of study. As for selection of monographs and articles in periodicals the compilers paid designedly much attention to more recent publications, becouse earlier publications can usually be found in all kinds of handbooks to which the reader is referred, as said above, at the very beginning of the survey in each field of study. The way in which the bibliographic material is arranged, speaks for itself.

The bibliography has not been annotated. The publisher and the compilers have felt that they have to abstain from giving an evaluation of any kind in a bibliography which has a didactic-selective character.

The individual compiler has been given every freedom, so far as was possible of course within the limits of a certain uniformity in presenting the material. The compilers did not try to prevent double listing of publications, because they believe that the true character of a publication can only be assessed when it appears in all the contexts where it belongs. With regard to certain text editions it will be clear that a separation e.g. between Hebrew and Aramaic, especially in Section B "Literature", would be unnatural, since many texts contain both Hebrew and Aramaic.

In some respects the individual compilers had their own way of presenting their material. But this will in no way detract from the usefulness of the Bibliography. To give one example: the compiler of the rubric "Mishnaic and Talmudical Hebrew" uses Hebrew characters to indicate that the relevant book or article is written in modern Hebrew. The compiler of the rubrics "Hebrew of the Middle Ages" and "New and Modern Hebrew", however, gives English titles in such cases, where the book itself has an English translation of the Hebrew title page, but otherwise transcriptions of the Hebrew titles.

At the end of the book the reader can find a list of Periodicals and abbreviations. These abbreviations are mostly the same as those occuring in the list of K. DELLER [1] and of W. VON SODEN in his "Ak-

---

[1] K. DELLER, Keilschriftbibliographie, 24, Or 32, 1963, 1-14.

kadisches Handwörterbuch" [1] Where necessary these lists have been supplemented. In some cases the compilers have chosen other, in their opinion better, abbreviations, which can be found in the list at the end of our Bibliography. There are also some individual compilers who have added short lists of particular abbreviations which are only relevant to their own contributions.

Groningen 1-11-1972   J. H. HOSPERS

---

[1] W. VON SODEN, Akkadisches Handwärterbuch unter Benutzung des lexikalischen Nachlasses von B. Meissner (1868-1947), Wiesbaden 1959-, (especially Lief. 1, 1959, X-XVI; 6, 1965, 567-568; the frontcovers in Lief. 7, 1966; 8, 1967; 9, 1969; 10, 1971).

A

LANGUAGES OF THE ANCIENT NEAR EAST AND THEIR HISTORICAL RELATIONSHIP

I. AKKADIAN *

COMPILED BY

W. H. Pʜ. RÖMER

General Works

R. Borger, Handbuch der Keilschriftliteratur 1, Berlin, 1967.
A. Deimel, Übersicht über die Keilschrift-Literatur, Or Nr. 27, Rome, 1927.
É. Laroche, Littérature suméro-akkadienne, CTH, Paris, 1971, 145-148 (also H. G. Güterbock, ibid. 47-53).
S. A. Pallis, The antiquity of Iraq. A handbook of Assyriology, Copenhagen, 1956.
A. Pohl, K. H. Deller, Or. 9 ff., Keilschriftbibliographie.
E. F. Weidner (a.o.), AfO 1926 ff. Bibliographie: Mesopotamien.

A good deal of bibliographic references is also found in periodicals as ZA; RA; BiOr; from time to time surveys are being published a.o. in ArOr; BiOr; OLZ of publications in Slavonic languages (s. also V. J. Avdiev, L'étude de l'Ancien Orient en U.R.S.S., 1917-1957, Moscow, 1958). See further:
I. A. Pratt, Assyria and Babylonia, a list of references in the New York Public Library, compiled under the direction of R. Gottheil, enl. sep. ed., New York 1918.

E. F. Weidner, Die Assyriologie 1914-22, Berlin, 1922.

Not continued up to now:
L. van den Berghe, H. F. Mussche, Bibliographie analytique de l'assyriologie et de l'archéologie du Proche Orient; published:
I A: L'archéologie 1954-55, Leyden, 1956.
I Ph: La philologie 1954-56, Leyden, 1957.
II A: L'archéologie 1956-57, Leyden, 1960.

---

* See also continuously Bibliography of Sumerian, p. 38 ff.

Encyclopaedic:

E. EBELING, B. MEISSNER, E. F. WEIDNER, W. VON SODEN, Real-
    lexikon der Assyriologie 1 ff., Berlin; Leipzig, 1932 ff.

See also:

E. A. W. BUDGE, Rise and progress of Assyriology, London, 1925.
D. J. WISEMAN, The expansion of Assyrian studies, London, 1962.

Some catalogues of certain text collections and lists of text-"joins":

C. BEZOLD, Catalogue of the cuneiform tablets ... of the British Mu-
    seum, London, 1889-1899 + Supplement by L. W. KING, London,
    1914.
W. G. LAMBERT; A. R. MILLARD, Catalogue of the cuneiform tablets
    in the Kouyunjik collection of the British Museum, Second
    Supplement, London, 1968.
C. A. BATEMAN; J. PARSLEY, A list of fragments rejoined in the
    Kuyunjik collection in the British Museum (revised and enlarged),
    London, 1960.
M. DIETRICH, Verzeichnis der erwähnten und chronologisch ein-
    geordneten Museumsnummern unveröffentlichter Briefe, WO 4,
    1967, 102-103; 5, 1969, 54-56 (s. WO 4, 1967, 61-103; 1968,
    183-251).
H. H. FIGULLA, Catalogue of the Babylonian tablets in the British
    Museum 1, London, 1961.
D. A. KENNEDY, Nouveaux "Joins" dans la collection de Kuyunjik,
    RA 56, 1962, 153-156.
E. LEICHTY, A bibliography of the cuneiform tablets of the Kouyunjik
    collection in the British Museum, London, 1964 (s. K. DELLER,
    Or. 33, 1964, 476-478; R. BORGER, HKL 1, 651-659).

A. PHILOLOGY

1. GRAMMARS

a. *Ordinary grammars*

F. DELITZSCH, Assyrische Grammatik mit Übungstücken und kurzer
    Literatur-Übersicht², Porta Linguarum Orientalium 10, Berlin,
    1906.

W. von Soden, Grundriss der akkadischen Grammatik, AnOr 33, Rome, 1952 (s. I. J. Gelb, BiOr 12, 1955, 93-111).

W. von Soden, Ergänzungsheft zum Grundriss der akkadischen Grammatik, AnOr 47, Rome, 1969 (s. W. G. Lambert, JSS 17, 1972, 130-131).

In both works detailed bibliographic information on grammatical and syntactic studies can be found. Based on W. von Soden's grammar:

R. Borger, Babylonisch-assyrische Lesestücke 1, Rome, 1963 (III-XXXV: Elemente der Grammatik; I-II: Bibliographic references of dictionaries, grammars, sign-lists, and chrestomathies; s.R. Borger, HKL 1, 30-31; for some special chrestomathies we refer to W. J. Hinke, Selected Babylonian kudurru inscriptions, Semitic Study Series 14, Leyden, 1911; S. Langdon, The Annals of Ashurbanapal (V Rawlinson Pl. I-X), id. 2, Leyden, 1903; J. D. Prince, The Abu Habba cylinder of Nabuna' id (V Rawlinson Pl. 64), id. 5, Leyden, 1905; A. Ungnad, Selected Babylonian business and legal documents of the Ḫammurabi period, id. 9, Leyden, 1907; A. Ungnad, Selected business documents of the Neo-Babylonian period, id. 10, Leyden, 1908).

A. Lancellotti, Grammatica della Lingua accadica, Analecta Hierosolymitana 1, Jerusalem, 1962.

K. K. Riemschneider, Lehrbuch des Akkadischen, Lehrbücher für das Studium der orientalischen und afrikanischen Sprachen 16, Leipzig, 1969.

A. Ungnad; L. Matouš, Grammatik des Akkadischen[4], Munich, 1964.

In part also:

G. Rijckmans, Grammaire accadienne[4], Louvain, 1960.

Cf. finally:

B. Meissner; K. Oberhuber, Die Keilschrift[3], Berlin, 1968.

S. A. Pallis, Akkadisk og Sumerisk, Festskr. udg. af Københavns Universitet i anl. af H. M. Kongens fødselsdag, Copenhagen, 1958, 1-71.

b. *Historical grammars*

Properly speaking not available for Akkadian. Provisionally can be consulted, apart from the book by:

I. J. GELB, Sequential reconstruction of Proto-Akkadian, AS 18, Chicago, 1969 (s. W. von Soden, JNES 29, 1970, 202-207)

the older works:

H. ZIMMERN, Vergleichende Grammatik der semitischen Sprachen. Elemente der Laut- und Formenlehre, Berlin, 1898.

C. BROCKELMANN, Grundriss der vergleichenden Grammatik der semitischen Sprachen 1; 2; Berlin, 1908; 1913

and now the recent works:

S. MOSCATI; A. SPITALER; E. ULLENDORFF; W. VON SODEN, An introduction to the comparative grammar of the Semitic languages. Phonology and Morphology, Porta Linguarum Orientalium NS 6, Wiesbaden, 1964 (cf. M. DAHOOD; K. DELLER; R. KÖBERT, Or 34, 1965, 35-44; H. HIRSCH, WZKM 61, 1967, 17-21).

I. M. DIAKONOFF, Semito-Hamitic languages, an essay in classification, Moscow, 1965 (s. D. O. Edzard, RA 61, 1967, 137-149).

c. *Syntaxes*

To be consulted the above-mentioned grammars by W. VON SODEN (with Ergänzungsheft) and by A. UNGNAD; L. MATOUŠ.

2. LEXICA

The two modern dictionaries:

I. J. GELB; TH. JACOBSEN; B. LANDSBERGER; A. L. OPPENHEIM a.o., The Assyrian Dictionary of the Oriental Institute of Chicago, Glückstadt, 1956 ff. (11 volumes published).

W. VON SODEN, Akkadisches Handwörterbuch unter Benutzung des lexikalischen Nachlasses von B. Meissner (1868-1947), Wiesbaden, 1959 ff. (11 parts published).

For lexical entries not yet treated in the modern dictionaries cf. provisionally:

C. BEZOLD, Babylonisch-assyrisches Glossar, Heidelberg, 1926 (without references).

A. DEIMEL; P. GÖSSMANN, Šumerisches Lexikon, Rome, 1928-1950 (s. for the different editions R. BORGER, HKL 1, 74; in those cases where A. DEIMEL cites false text quotations, it may be useful to consult the older works by R. BRÜNNOW, A classified list etc., Leyden, 1897 (s. R. BORGER, o.c. 36) and by B. MEISSNER,

Seltene assyrische Ideogramme, Leipzig, 1910 (s. R. BORGER, o.c. 344), worked up by him).

F. DELITZSCH, Assyrisches Handwörterbuch, Leipzig, 1896.

G. HOWARDY, Clavis cuneorum, sive Lexicon signorum Assyriorum linguis Latina, Brittannica, Germanica ... compositum, London; Leipzig; Copenhagen, 1904-1933.

B. MEISSNER, Supplement zu den assyrischen Wörterbüchern, Leyden, 1898.

W. MUSS-ARNOLT, Assyrisch-English-Deutsches Handwörterbuch, Berlin, 1905.

N.B. For the history of Akkadian lexicography see:

R. BORGER, BiOr 14, 1957, 113-122.

I. J. GELB, CAD A₁, Glückstadt, 1964, VII-XXIII.

See also:

W. VON SODEN, Benno Landsberger (1890-1968), ZDMG 119, 1969, 1-14.

3. PHILOLOGIC MONOGRAPHS AND IMPORTANT ARTICLES

The reader is referred to the (list of) quotations by W. VON SODEN, GAG + Ergänzungsheft and by A. UNGNAD; L. MATOUŠ, Grammatik des Akkadischen[4]. Cf. further:

G. G. GIACUMAKIS, The Akkadian of Alalakh, The Hague-Paris, 1970.

K. HECKER, Grammatik der Kültepe-Texte, AnOr 44, Rome, 1968. (s. C. SAPORETTI, OrAnt 9, 1970, 264-270).

W. MAYER, Untersuchungen zur Grammatik des Mittelassyrischen AOATS 2, Kevelaer; Neukirchen-Vluyn 1971.

G. G. SWAIM, A grammar of the Akkadian tablets found at Ugarit (doct. diss. Brandeis Univ.), Waltham, Mass., 1963.

In course of preparation or planned are:

K. DELLER, Neo-Assyrian grammar (still unpublished: K. DELLER, Lautlehre des Neuassyrischen, Vienna 1959; but s. K. Deller, Lautwerte des Typs KVKV im Neuassyrischen, Or 31, 1962, 7-26; 186-196).

M. DIETRICH, Neo-Babylonian grammar.

M. DIETRICH; O. LORETZ, Grammar of Alalaḫ Akkadian.

Cf. further:

J. Aro, Remarks on the language of the Alalakh texts, AfO 17, 1956, 361-365.

——, Parallels to the Akkadian stative in the West Semitic languages, AS 16, Chicago, 1965, 407-411.

G. Buccellati, An interpretation of the Akkadian stative as a nominal sentence, JNES 27, 1968, 1-12.

——, On the use of the Akkadian infinitive after Ša or construct state, JSS 17, 1972, 1-29.

V. Christian, "Energicus" oder "Ventiv" im Akkadischen?, ZA 36, 1925, 71-73.

K. Deller, Assyrisches Sprachgut by Tukulti-Ninurta II. (888-884), Or 26, 1957, 268-272.

D. O. Edzard, Grammatik, RlA 3/8, 1971, 610-616.

H. Fleisch, Phrase relative en Accadien, MUSJ 42, 1966, 247-284.

I. J. Gelb, Morphology of Akkadian, Chicago, 1952.

——, The origin of the West Semitic qatala morpheme, Symbolae Linguisticae in honorem G. Kuryłowicz, Kraków, 1965, 72-80.

A. Goetze, Some observations on Nuzu Akkadian, Language 14, 1938, 134-143.

C. H. Gordon, Nouns in the Nuzi Tablets, Babyloniaca 16, 1936, 1-153.

——, Numerals in the Nuzi tablets, RA 31, 1934, 53-60.

——, The pronoun in the Nuzi tablets, AJSL 51, 1934-'35, 1-21.

W. Heimpel; G. Guidi, Der Koinzidenzfall im Akkadischen, ZDMG Spl. 1/1, Wiesbaden, 1969, 148-152.

Th. Jacobsen, The Akkadian ablative accusative, JNES 22, 1963, 18-29 (also published in Th. Jacobsen, Toward the image of Tammuz and other essays on Mesopotamian history and culture, Cambridge, Mass., 1970, 271-292).

Ch. F. Jean, Étude sur deux caractères du style assyro-babylonien, Les lettres de Ḫammurapi à Sin-idinnam, Paris 1913, 1-56.

B. Kienast, Das dativische [š] im akkadischen Pronominalsystem, Or 26, 1957, 260.

——, Akkadisch iparras-äthiopisch jəqattəl, Or 26, 1957, 262-267.

——, Der Präfixvokal u im Kausativ und im D- Stamm des Semitischen, MSS 11, 1957, 104-108.

——, Zu den Vokalklassen beim akkadischen Verbum, HSAO, Wiesbaden, 1967, 63-85.

V. Kinnier Wilson, "Desonance" in Accadian, JSS 13, 1968, 93-103.

S. N. KRAMER, The verb in the Kirkuk tablets, AASOR 11, 1931, 62-119.

F. R. KRAUS, Eine Besonderheit der älteren akkadischen Orthographie, RSO 32, 1957, 103-108.

W. G. LAMBERT, The language of Mari, RAI 15, Paris, 1967, 29-38.

——, Literary style in first millennium Mesopotamia, JAOS 88, 1968, 123-132.

J. LEWY, On some Akkadian expressions for "afterwards" and related notions, WO 2, 1959, 432-437.

M. LIVERANI, Antecedenti del diptotismo arabo nei testi accadici di Ugarit, RSO 38, 1963, 131-160.

A. L. OPPENHEIM, Idiomatic Accadian, JAOS 61, 1941, 251-271.

——, The Neo-Babylonian Preposition LA, JNES 1, 1942, 369-372.

Th. G. PINCHES, The infinitive of verbs פ״ו, BOR 2, 1887-'88, 39.

E. REINER, The phonological interpretation of a sub-system in the Akkadian syllabary, StOpp, Chicago, 1964, 167-180.

O. RÖSSLER, Die Präfixkonjugation Qal der Verba I^ae Nûn im Althebräischen und das Problem der sogenannten Tempora, ZAW 74, 1962, 125-141 (s. also A. BLOCH, ZDMG 113, 1964, 41-50).

A. SCHOTT, "Man kann hören", "man kann sehen" im Akkadischen, ZA 44, 1938, 290-296.

——, Verbalideogramm + meš als Wiedergabe von -t-n-Formen in astrologischen Keilschrifttexten, ZA 44, 1938, 296-298.

J. SEIDMANN, Zur Grammatik (der Inschriften Adadnirâris II.), MAOG 9/3, 1935, 46-55.

S. H. SIEDL, Gedanken zum Tempussystem im Hebräischen und Akkadischen, Wiesbaden, 1971.

W. VON SODEN, dakāku I und II und die Wurzelvariabilität beim schwachen Verbum im Akkadischen, WZKM 55, 1959, 54-55.

——, n als Wurzelaugment im Semitischen, WZH 17, 1968, G, H. 2/3, 175-184.

F. THUREAU-DANGIN, Observations sur la graphie des sifflantes dans l'écriture cunéiforme, RA 30, 1933, 93-96.

A. UNGNAD, Die Partikel -ma im Babylonisch-Assyrischen, BA 5, 1906, 713-716.

——, Zur Aussprache des Spätbabylonischen, MAOG 4, 1928/29, 220-225.

——, Sprachellipsen im Akkadischen, Or 6, 1937, 347-357.

G. WILHELM, Untersuchungen zum Hurro-Akkadischen von Nuzi, AOAT 9, Kevelaer; Neukirchen-Vluyn, 1970.

J. M. ZINKAND, A study of the morphology of Ugaritic and Akkadian (doct. diss. Brandeis Univ.), Waltham, Mass., 1958.

For cuneiform writing and the Akkadian syllabary see:

G. A. BARTON, The origin and development of Babylonian writing, BA 9, Leipzig, 1913.

R. BORGER, Akkadische Zeichenliste, AOATS 6, Kevelaer; Neukirchen-Vluyn, 1971.

A. DEIMEL, P. GÖSSMANN, ŠL 1³, Rome, 1947.

Ch. FOSSEY, Manuel d'Assyriologie 2, Évolution des cunéiformes, Paris, 1926.

R. LABAT, Manuel d'Épigraphie akkadienne⁴, Paris, 1963.

S. A. B. MERCER, A Sumero-Babylonian sign list, New York, 1918 (repr. 1966).

W. RÖLLIG, Die Keilschrift und die Anfänge der Alphabetschrift, StGen 18/12, Berlin; Heidelberg; New York, 1965, 729-742.

W. VON SODEN; W. RÖLLIG, Das akkadische Syllabar², AnOr 42, Rome, 1967 (cf. J. RENGER, ZA 61, 1971, 23-43).

F. THUREAU-DANGIN, Recherches sur l'origine de l'écriture cunéiforme. Iᵉ partie: Les formes archaïques et leurs équivalents modernes, Paris 1898.

For a special question we refer to:

A. SCHOTT, Vorarbeiten zur Geschichte der Keilschriftliteratur, I, Die assyrischen Königsinschriften vor 722, a) der Schreibgebrauch, BOS 13, Stuttgart, 1936.

Further we call attention here for the lexicography of Akkadian to a number of special glossaries on certain groups of texts and to monographs or articles on certain words belonging together according to their significance:

J. ARO, Glossar zu den mittelbabylonischen Briefen, StOr 22, Helsinki, 1957.

K. BALKAN, Contributions to the understanding of the idiom of the Old Assyrian merchants of Kanish, Or 36, 1967, 393-415.

W. BAUMGARTNER, Untersuchungen zu den akkadischen Bauausdrücken, ZA 36, 1925, 29-40; 123-138; 219-253.

E. BILGIÇ, Die einheimischen Appellativa der kappadokischen Texte und ihre Bedeutung für die anatolischen Sprachen, Ankara, 1954.

J. BOTTÉRO; A. FINET, Archives royales de Mari 15. Répertoire analytique des tomes I à V, Paris, 1954.

É. DHORME, L'emploi métaphorique des noms de parties du corps en Hébreu et en Akkadien, Paris, 1963.

M. DIETRICH; O. LORETZ, Die soziale Struktur von Alalaḫ und Ugarit 1, WO 3, 1966, 188-205; 2, WO 5, 1969, 57-93; 4, ZA 60, 1970, 88-123; 5, UF 1, 1969, 37-64.

G. R. DRIVER, Letters of the first Babylonian dynasty, OEC 3, Oxford, 1924.

——; J. C. MILES, The Assyrian Laws, Oxford 1935.

——; ——, The Babylonian Laws 2, Oxford, 1955.

E. EBELING, Glossar zu den neubabylonischen Briefen, Munich, 1955.

W. EILERS, Iranische Beamtennamen in der keilschriftlichen Überlieferung, AKM 25/5, Leipzig, 1940, Nendeln, 1966.

I. J. GELB, Glossary of Old Akkadian, MAD 3, Chicago, 1957.

W. W. HALLO, Early Mesopotamian royal titles, AOS 43, New Haven, 1957.

A. FALKENSTEIN, Kontakte zwischen Sumerern und Akkadern auf sprachlichem Gebiet, Genava n.s. 8, Geneva, 1960, 301-314.

W. J. HINKE, A new boundary stone of Nebuchadrezzar I, BER 4, Philadelphia, 1907.

H. HOLMA, Die Namen der Körperteile im Assyrisch-Babylonischen, eine lexikalisch-etymologische Studie, Leipzig, 1911 (also: AASF B 7, Helsinki, 1913).

——, Kleine Beiträge zum assyrischen Lexikon, AASF B 7/2, Helsinki, 1913.

——, Die assyrisch-babylonischen Personennamen der Form quttulu mit besonderer Berücksichtigung der Wörter für Körperfehler, AASF B 13/2-4, Helsinki, 1914.

——, Weitere Beiträge zum assyrischen Lexikon, AASF B 15/1, Helsinki 1921.

——, Zum akkadischen Wörterbuch, Or 13, 1944, 102-115; 14, 1945, 242-258.

B. HROZNÝ, Das Getreide im alten Babylonien 1, Vienna, 1913.

A. KAMMENHUBER, Die Arier im Vorderen Orient, Heidelberg, 1968, 252-285.

R. LABAT, L'Akkadien de Boghaz-Köi, Bordeaux, 1932.

E. LACHEMAN, Epigraphic evidences of the material culture of the Nuzians, Nuzi 1, Cambridge, Mass., 1939, 528-544.

(Cf. further for Akkadian words in cuneiform-Hittite texts:

J. FRIEDRICH, Hethitisches Wörterbuch, Heidelberg, 1952-54; 3 Ergänzungshefte, Heidelberg, 1957/66)).

B. LANDSBERGER, Das gute Wort, MAOG 4, 1928-'29, 294-321.

——, Die Fauna des alten Mesopotamien nach der 14. Tafel der Serie Ḫar-ra = ḫubullu, ASAW 42/6, Leipzig, 1934.

——, The date palm and its by-products according to the cuneiform sources, AfOBeih 17, Graz, 1967.

P. LEANDER, Über die sumerischen Lehnwörter im Assyrischen, Uppsala, 1903.

M. MAYRHOFER, Die Indo-Arier im alten Vorderasien, Wiesbaden, 1966, 129-145.

W. L. MORAN, Some Akkadian names of the stomachs of ruminants, JCS 21, 1969, 178-182.

O. NEUGEBAUER, Astronomical cuneiform texts 2, London, 1955.

J. NOUGAYROL, Rapports paléobabyloniens d'haruspices, JCS 21, 1969, 219-235.

A. L. OPPENHEIM, Lexikalische Untersuchungen zu den kappadokischen Briefen, AfO 12, 1937-'39, 342-362.

A. SALONEN, The studies mentioned by R. Borger, HKL 1, 434-435. Further:

——, Das Rad der altmesopotamischen Wagen, RAI 2, Paris, 1951, 59-62.

——, Die Öfen der alten Mesopotamier, BagM 3, Berlin, 1964, 100-124.

——, Bemerkungen zur sumerisch-akkadischen Brennholz-Terminologie, JEOL 18, Leyden, 1965, 331-338.

——, Die Hausgeräte der alten Mesopotamier nach sumerisch-akkadischen Quellen 1, AASF B 139, Helsinki, 1965; 2, Gefässe, AASF B 144, 1966.

——, Agricultura mesopotamica nach sumerisch-akkadischen Quellen, AASF B 149, Helsinki, 1968.

——, Die Fussbekleidung der alten Mesopotamier nach sumerisch-akkadischen Quellen, AASF B 157, 1969.

——, Die Fischerei im Alten Mesopotamien, AASF B 166.

——, Die Ziegeleien im Alten Mesopotamien, AASF B 171, Helsinki, 1972.

E. SALONEN, Die Waffen der alten Mesopotamier, StOr 33, Helsinki, 1966.

——, Die Gruss- und Höflichkeitsformeln in babylonisch-assyrischen Briefen, StOr 38, Helsinki, 1967.

——, Über das Erwerbsleben im Alten Mesopotamien. Untersuchungen zu den akkadischen Berufsnamen, StOr 41, Helsinki, 1970.

C. SAPORETTI, Onomastica medio-assira 1, I nomi di persona; 2, Studi, vocabolari ed elenchi, StP 6, Rome, 1970.

A. SCHOTT, Die Vergleiche in den akkadischen Königsinschriften, MVAeG 30/2, Leipzig, 1926.

A. VAN SELMS, De babylonische termini voor zonde en hun beteekenis voor onze kennis van het babylonische zondebesef, Wageningen, 1933.

M.-J. SEUX, Épithètes royales akkadiennes et sumériennes, Paris, 1967.

W. VON SODEN, Zum Wortschatz des hymnisch-epischen Dialekts, ZA 41, 1933, 160-173.

——, Aramäische Wörter in neuassyrischen und neu- und spätbabylonischen Texten. Ein Vorbericht, I (agâ-mūš), Or 35, 1966, 1-20; II (n-z und Nachträge), Or 37, 1968, 261-271.

J. J. STAMM, Die akkadische Namengebung, MVAeG 44, Leipzig, 1939.

J. N. STRASSMAIER, Alphabetisches Verzeichnis der assyrischen und akkadischen Wörter der Cuneiform Inscriptions of Western Asia vol. II, ..., AB 4, Leipzig, 1886 (s. R. BORGER, HKL 1, 507).

R. C. THOMPSON, A dictionary of Assyrian chemistry and geology, Oxford, 1936.

——, A dictionary of Assyrian botany, London, 1949.

K. TALLQVIST, Die Sprache der Kontrakte Nabû-nâ'ids (555-538 v. Chr.), mit Berücksichtigung der Contracte Nebukadrezars und Cyrus', Helsingfors, 1890.

——, Sumerisch-akkadische Namen der Totenwelt, StOr 5/4, Helsingfors, 1934.

——, Akkadische Götterepitheta, StOr 7, Helsingfors, 1938.

K. R. VEENHOF, Aspects of Old Assyrian trade, Leyden, 1972.

C. J. M. WEIR, A lexicon of Accadian prayers in the rituals of expiation, Oxford; London, 1934.

H. ZIMMERN, Akkadische Fremdwörter als Beweis für babylonischen Kultureinfluss, Leipzig, 1917.

On Greek personal names in seleucid texts s. R. A. BOWMAN, AJSL 56, 1939, 231-243; W. RÖLLIG, Or 29, 1960, 376-391.

The lists of occurring and/or treated words and expressions and/or the commentaries in the following studies are likewise to be consulted:

AASOR 16; ABIM; AbB 1-5; AC; ACC; AfOBeih 6; AGS; AlT; AM; AND; AnOr 43; AOAT 1; 2; 3/1; 5/1; 7; 8; 12; AOATT;

AOB; ARDēr; ARM 1-9; 11-13; ATHE; Atr; ATR; BAP;
BBEA; BBR; BBS; BEC, *Bîtrimki*; BKBM; BR 8/7; BR 6;
BRAD; BVW; CA; CBSM; CCK; Comm; DM; EAK; EL; Erra;
FAI; GDBT; Genava n.s. 8, 241-314; Gilg; HBA; HMA; HSAO;
Idr; Iraq 7, 22-61; Iščâlî; ITn; Izbu; JCS 7, 145-146; KTBl;
KTH; KTK; Kud; KUG; Larsa; LE; LFBD; LHS; LKU;
LSSNF 1; 2; Lugalb.; Maqlû; MAWNR 28/6; 29/5; MCT;
MDP 34; MKJ; MKT; MP; MSL 1-10; 12; 13; MVAeG 36/1; 40/2;
41/3; 44; NARG; NBB; NBD; NBDMich; NPN; NRVGl; NRET;
Nuzi 1; OACP; OAIC; ÖB; OEC 3; 6; OIP 27; 79; PBC; PKT;
PL; PRT; PRU 3; 4; 6; RCA 4; RMA; SD 1; 3; 5; 6; Sg 8;
SGL 1; 2; SgWi; ShT; SKIZ; SLB 1/1; 1/2; 1/3; Ššmk; StOr 8/1;
StP 1;3; Šurpu; SVAT; SWU; Tākultu; TBP; TCS 2; TDP;
TEBA; Tigl III; TJAUB; TJDB; TMB; TTC; Ugar 5, 349-351;
VAB 2; 3; 4; 5; 6; 7; Wilb; YNER 1; 2; 3; 4; YOS 10; ZA 42,
1934, 167-169; ZA 56, 1964, 142-149.

In numerous articles in the periodicals (s. below D) studies and remarks
on Akkadian words and expressions are found which cannot be enumerated here. Cf. particularly articles by the following authors:

J. ARO; R. D. BIGGS; R. BORGER; J. A. BRINKMAN; E. CASSIN;
K. DELLER; M. DIETRICH; J. VAN DIJK; G. DOSSIN; E. EBELING;
D. O. EDZARD; A. FALKENSTEIN; J. J. FINKELSTEIN; C. FRANK;
H. FREYDANK; C. J. GADD; P. GARELLI; I. J. GELB; A. GOETZE;
E. I. GORDON; O. R. GURNEY; K. HECKER; H. HIRSCH; H. HOL-
MA; H. HUNGER; Ch. F. JEAN; P. JENSEN; B. KIENAST; F.
KÖCHER; P. KOSCHAKER; F. R. KRAUS; J. KRECHER; J.-R. KUP-
PER; R. LABAT; E. R. LACHEMAN; J. LAESSØE; W. G. LAMBERT;
B. LANDSBERGER; W. F. LEEMANS; H. LEWY; J. LEWY; O.
LORETZ; G. MEIER; B. MEISSNER; E. W. MOORE; J. NOUGAYROL;
A. L. OPPENHEIM; F. E. PEISER; A. F. RAINEY; E. REINER;
J. RENGER; W. H. PH. RÖMER; A. SALONEN; M. SAN NICOLÒ;
V. SCHEIL; M.-J. SEUX; W. VON SODEN; E. A. SPEISER; M.
STRECK; K. TALLQVIST; R. C. THOMPSON; F. THUREAU-DANGIN;
A. UNGNAD; K. R. VEENHOF; Ch. VIROLLEAUD; E. F. WEIDNER;
C. WILCKE; H. ZIMMERN (cf. also R. BORGER, HKL 1).

In this connection we call attention to the following bibliographies and
indices:

Bibliographie A. FALKENSTEIN 1931-1966, HSAO, Wiesbaden, 1967, 1-11.

Bibliographie Th. JACOBSEN, Toward the image of Tammuz and other essays on Mesopotamian history and culture (W. L. MORAN ed.), Cambridge, Mass., 1970, 471-474.

A. L. OPPENHEIM a.o., B. Landsbergers lexicographical contributions, JCS 4, 1950, 3-62 (in preparation an up to date bibliography by J. RENGER).

J. A. BRINKMAN, Bibliography of publications by A. L. Oppenheim, StOpp, Chicago, 1964, 195-200.

W. RÖLLIG, Schriftenverzeichnis W. von Soden (up to 1.3.1968), AOAT 1, Kevelaer; Neukirchen-Vluyn, 1969, XI-XXVIII.

É. DHORME, Liste des publications de F. Thureau-Dangin, MVEOL 8, Leyden, 1946, 19-35.

F. H. WEISSBACH, Zimmern-Bibliographie, ZA 40, 1931, 144-162 and the following indices on periodicals:

E. H. SCHAFER; I. DYEN; H. E. FERNALD; H. W. GLIDDEN, Index to the Journal of the American Oriental Society, Vol. 21-60, New Haven, 1955.

A. SPYCKET, Revue d'Assyriologie, Tables des matières des volumes XXI à XLIII, 1924-1949, Paris, 1951.

The indices in ZA 45 (1939) and ever since 49 (1950).

Some recent lexicographical articles of a more general kind:

J. ARO, Gemeinsemitische Ackerbauterminologie, ZDMG 113, 1963, 471-480.

I. J. GELB, The word for dragoman in the Ancient Near East, Glossa 2/1, 1968, 93-104.

M. HELD, mḫṣ/*mḫš in Ugaritic and other Semitic languages, JAOS 79, 1959, 169-176.

——, Studies in comparative semitic lexicography, AS 16, Chicago, 1965, 395-406.

——, The root ZBL/SBL in Akkadian, Ugaritic, and Biblical Hebrew, JAOS 88, 1968, 90-96.

B. LANDSBERGER, Akkadisch-hebräische Wortgleichungen, Hebräische Wortforschung, VT S 16, Leyden, 1967, 176-204 (+ Nachtr. zu S. 199).

——, Über Farben im Sumerisch-Akkadischen, JCS 21, 1969, 139-173.

W. LESLAU, Southeast Semitic cognates of the Akkadian vocabulary, I, JAOS 82, 1962, 1-4; II, JAOS 84, 1964, 115-118; III, JAOS 89, 1969, 18-22.

W. von Soden, Vedisch *magham*, "Geschenk" - Neuarabisch *maǧǧā-nīja*, "Gebührenfreiheit". Der Weg einer Wortsippe, JEOL 18, Leyden, 1964, 339-344 (+ Nachtr. zu S. 340).

——, Beiträge zum Ugaritischen und Hebräischen, Hebräische Wortforschung, VT S 16, Leyden, 1967, 291-300.

——, Zur Herkunft von hebr. 'ebjōn "arm", MIO 15, 1969, 322-326.

——, Mirjām-Maria "(Gottes-)geschenk", UF 2, 1970, 269-272.

——, Hurritisch *sil(l)*- "alt", WO 6, 1972, 255-256.

For the lexicographical material the old Mesopotamians themselves left to us and which is still basic for all modern lexicographical research we refer to:

M. Çiǧ; H. Kizilyay; B. Landsberger, Zwei altbabylonische Schulbücher aus Nippur, TTKY 7/35, Ankara, 1959.

A. Draffkorn Kilmer, The first tablet of *malku* = *šarru* together with its explicit version, JAOS 83, 1963, 421-446 (s. also 85, 1965, 208).

A. Falkenstein; L. Matouš, Zur 3. Tafel der Serie d i r i = DIR = *siₐaku* = *watru*, ZA 42, 1934, 144-151.

A. Goetze, The vocabulary of the Princeton theological seminary, JAOS 65, 1945, 223-237.

——, The 38th Tablet of the series á-A-nâqu, JCS 13, 1959, 120-127.

R. T. Hallock, The Chicago syllabary and the Louvre syllabary AO 7661, AS 7, Chicago, 1940.

L. F. Hartman; A. L. Oppenheim, On beer and brewing techniques in Ancient Mesopotamia, JAOS Spl. 10, Baltimore, 1950.

F. Köcher, Keilschrifttexte zur assyrisch-babylonischen Drogen- und Pflanzenkunde, Berlin, 1955.

——, Zum Assur-Fragment der Serie i g i. d u ḫ . a = *tāmartu*, AfO 18, 1957-'58, 86-88.

B. Landsberger, Die Liste der Menschenklassen im babylonischen Kanon, ZA 41, 1933, 184-192.

——, Die angebliche babylonische Notenschrift, AfOBeih 1, 1933, 170-178.

——, a.o., Materialien zum sumerischen Lexikon 1-10; 12; 13, Rome, 1937-1971.

——, O. R. Gurney, Practical vocabulary of Assur, AfO 18; 1957-'58, 328-341.

——, ——, i g i - d u ḫ - a = *tāmartu*, short version, AfO 18, 1957-'58, 81-86.

——, The seventh tablet of the series e a-*nâqu*, JCS 13, 1959, 128-131.

——, The third tablet of the series Ea A Nâqu, JAOS 88, 1968, 133-147.

L. MATOUŠ, Die lexikalischen Tafelserien der Babylonier und Assyrer in den Berliner Museen 1 : Gegenstandslisten (Serie ḪAR-*ra* = *ḫubullu*), Berlin, 1933 (LTBA 1).

P. VAN DER MEER, Syllabaries A, B[1] and B with miscellaneous lexicographical texts from the Herbert Weld collection, OEC 4, Oxford; London, 1938.

B. MEISSNER, many publications: Assyriologische Studien 2-6, MVAG 9, Leipzig, 1904, 196-220; 10, 1905, 233-256; 12, 1907, 143-150; 15, 1910, 501-514; 18/2, 1913, 10-47; Assyriologische Forschungen 1, AOTU 1/1, Leyden, 1917, 18-43; 2/1, Breslau, 1920, 25-47: Neue Fragmente der Serie ana ittiš; 52-72; Beiträge zum assyrischen Wörterbuch 1, AS 1/1, Chicago, 1931 (s. B. LANDSBERGER, ZA 41, 1933, 184-192; STT 373); 2, AS 4, 1932; Studien zur assyrischen Lexikographie 1-4, MAOG 1/2, Leipzig, 1925, 3-34; 3/3, 1929, 3-22; 11/1-2, 1937, 84-98; 13/2, 1940, 31-50.

J. NOUGAYROL, "Vocalisés" et "syllabes en liberté" à Ugarit, AS 16, Chicago, 1965, 29-39.

——, Nouveau "Silbenvokabular A" d'Ugarit (RS 29103), RA 63, 1969, 83-85.

H. OTTEN, W. VON SODEN, Das akkadisch-hethitische Vokabular KBo I 44 + KBo XIII 1, StBoT 7, Wiesbaden, 1968.

G. A. REISNER, The Berlin Vocabulary V.A.Th. 244, ZA 9, 1894, 149-164.

H. S. SCHUSTER, Die nach Zeichen geordneten sumerisch-akkadischen Vokabulare, ZA 44, 1938, 217-270.

W. VON SODEN, Die akkadischen Synonymenlisten, Berlin, 1933 (LTBA 2).

——, Die akkadische Synonymenliste D, ZA 43, 1936, 233-250.

——, Leistung und Grenze sumerischer und babylonischer Wissenschaft, Darmstadt 1965.

——, Zweisprachigkeit in der geistigen Kultur Babyloniens, SÖAW, 235/1, Vienna 1960.

E. SOLLBERGER, A three-column Silbenvokabular A, AS 16, Chicago, 1965, 21-28.

R. C. THOMPSON, Cuneiform texts from Babylonian tablets (, etc.) in the British Museum, 11 (London 1900); 12 (1901); 14 (1902); 18 (1904); 19 (1904).

B. ZIMOLONG, Das sumerisch-assyrische Vokabular Ass. 523, Leipzig, 1922.

Further lexicographical material must be found by means of reading the cuneiform sources. Many books on personal names in general or on personal names of certain groups of texts or periods and publications of texts or treatments of texts (s. A3; below B 1; 3 and the materials quoted by J. J. STAMM, MVAeG 44, Leipzig, 1939, 6-8; R. BORGER, HKL 1 and by W. VON SODEN, AHw; GAG; AnOr 47) contain lists of personal (and divine names and geographical) names. We here only refer to:

E. BILGIÇ, Die Ortsnamen der "kappadokischen" Urkunden im Rahmen der alten Sprachen Anatoliens, AfO 15, 1945-'51, 1-37.

A. BOUDOU, Liste des noms géographiques, Or Nr. 36-38, Rome, 1929.

A. DEIMEL, Pantheon babylonicum[1], Rome, 1914.

——, Panth. bab.[2], ŠL 4/1, Rome, 1950.

M. FALKNER, Studien zur Geographie des alten Mesopotamien, AfO 18, 1957-'58, 1-37.

F. GÖSSMANN, Planetarium babylonicum, oder: Die sumerisch-babylo-nischen Sternnamen, ŠL 4/2, Rome, 1950.

H. HIRSCH, Untersuchungen zur alt-assyrischen Religion, AfOBeih 13/14, Graz, 1961 (s. P. GARELLI, RA 56, 1962, 191-210).

S. PARPOLA, Neo-Assyrian Toponyms, AOAT 6 Kevelaer; Neukirchen-Vluyn, 1970.

J. J. STAMM, Die akkadische Namengebung, MVAeG 44, Leipzig, 1939.

Finally we refer for two special questions to:

W. VON SODEN, Aufgabe und Methode des akkadischen Sprach-unterrichts, OLZ 1942, 345-353

and to the remarks of:

A. L. OPPENHEIM, Can these bones live? An essay on translating Akkadian texts, Letters from Mesopotamia, Chicago, 1967, 54-67.

B. LITERATURE etc.

1. TEXT EDITIONS

The Akkadian texts are published in a number of series, books and periodicals (s. below D). As it is impossible to give a survey of the immense material we possess today we can only refer to R. BORGER, HKL 1, to W. VON SODEN, AHw; AnOr 47; GAG, and to CAD.

In publications on archaeology too here and there Akkadian (and
Sumerian) texts can be found. We now give here a list of series of
Akkadian (and partially also Sumerian) text publications:
AB; AbB; ABL; ACT; ADD; ARM; BAM; BE; BIN; BRM; CCT;
CT; GCCI; HSS (5; 9; 10; 13; 14; 15; 16; 19); ICK; JEN; KAH;
KAJ; KAR; KAV; KBo; KUB; LKA; MAD; MDP 2; 4; 6;
10; 14; 18; 21; 22; 23; 24; 27; 28; 32; 34; 36; PRAK; PRU
(3; 4; 6); R; OEC; SACTI; STT; TCL; TIM; TLB; TMH (NS);
UET; UM; VS; YOS.

2. Histories of literature

C. Bezold, Kurzgefasster Überblick über die babylonisch-assyrische
Literatur, Leipzig, 1886.
F. M. Th. (de Liagre) Böhl, Babylonisch-Assyrische Letterkunde, in:
H. Wagenvoort, Algemene Literatuur-Geschiedenis 1, Utrecht,
1943, 15-26.
H. A. Brongers, De literatuur der Babyloniërs en Assyriërs, The
Hague, w.y.
A. Deimel, Übersicht über die Keilschrift-Literatur, Or Nr. 27, Rome,
1927.
É. Dhorme, La littérature babylonienne et assyrienne, Paris, 1937.
R. F. Harper, Assyrian and Babylonian literature, selected trans-
lations, with a critical introduction by R. F. Harper, New York,
1904.
Ch. F. Jean, Le milieu biblique avant Jésus-Christ. II. La littérature,
Paris, 1923.
——, La littérature des Babyloniens et des Assyriens, Paris, 1924.
B. Meissner, Die babylonisch-assyrische Literatur, Handbuch der
Literaturwissenschaft, Wildpark-Potsdam, 1928.
L. L. Orlin, Ancient Near Eastern literature. On thousand themes
on the cuneiform literatures of the ancient world, Ann Arbor, 1969.
G. Rinaldi, Storia della letteratura dell'antica Mesopotamia (sumerica
e assiro-babilonese)[2], Milan, 1961.
O. Weber, Die Literatur der Babylonier und Assyrer, Leipzig, 1907.

For all these books is to be consulted the article by:

W. von Soden, Das Problem der zeitlichen Einordnung akkadischer
Literaturwerke, MDOG 85, 1953, 14-26.

See further:

J. van Dijk, UVB 18, Berlin, 1962, 44-52.
W. W. Hallo, New viewpoints on cuneiform literature, IEJ 12, 1962,
    13-26.
H. Hunger, Babylonische und assyrische Kolophone, AOAT 2,
    Kevelaer; Neukirchen-Vluyn, 1968 (cf. R. Borger, WO 5, 1970,
    165-171).
W. G. Lambert, Ancestors, authors, and canonicity, JCS 11, 1957,
    1-14; additions and corrections: JCS 11, 112.
— —, A catalogue of texts and authors, JCS 16, 1962, 59-77.
W. von Soden, Zweisprachigkeit in der geistigen Kultur Babyloniens,
    SÖAW 235/1, Vienna, 1960.

3. Monographs on literature etc.

Here a number of studies may be mentioned which contain transcriptions, and/or translations (and commentaries) on Akkadian texts, or
parts thereof — part of which contain the publication of the cuneiform
texts as well — and we also refer to the data in R. Borger, HKL 1
and W. von Soden, AHw; GAG; AnOr 47; CAD, and to the list of
publications above sub A3:

AASOR 16; AbB 1-5; ABIM; ABPh; ACC; ACh; ACT; ADB;
    AGH; AGS; AKA; AIT; AM; AND; AOAT 1; 2; 5/1; 7; 8; 12;
    AOATT; AOB; AOS 6; AOTU 1/4; AR; ARM 1-9; 11-13; AS 5;
    Ash; AssLaws; ATHE; ATR; BabLaws; BabMen; BagM 2;
    BBEA; BBR; BBS; BDHP; BEC; BER 4; BHT; *Bîtrimki*;
    BKBM; BL; BoSt 8; 9; BR 8/7; BR 6; BRAD; BVW; BW;
    BWL; CA; CahTD; CBSM; CCEBK; CCK; CDSmith; ChDiv;
    ChTRAB; CHJ; CN; Comm; Dilbat; Dreams; EAK; Ee (R. Labat,
    PBC; S. Langdon, BEC), EG; EL; Era; Erra (s. now L. Cagni,
    StP 5, Rome, 1970); FAI; Gilg; HBA; Hém; HGŠ; IAsb; Idr;
    IKT; ITn; KB 3; 6/1; 6/2; KTBl; KTH; Kud; KUG; Larsa;
    LE; LFBD; LHS; LSS 1/6; 2/4; 3/4; MAOG 1/1; 5/3; 6/1; 9/3;
    10/1; 12/2; 14/2; 15; 16; Maqlû; MCT; MDP, a.o. 14; 21; 22; 23;
    27; 28; 34; MKT; MLVS; Mold; MVA(e)G 23/1; 23/2; 35/2;
    36/1; 40/2; 41/3; NARG; NBD; NBDMich; NBr; NKRA; NRV;
    OAIC; ÖB; OEC; PBC; PEA; PKT; PL; PRT; PRU 3; 4; 6;
    Racc; RCA; RMA; SAHWSR; SAKF; SBP; SCT; SgLie;

SgWi; Sg 8; ShT; SLB; Sn; SSA; StrKT; SVAT; SWU; Ššmk;
Šurpu; Tākultu; TCS 2; TDP; Tigl III; TJAUB; TJDB; TMB;
Tn II; Tn-Ep; TuL; UCP 9/4; 9/8; 10/1; UDBD; Ugar 5,1-
446; Unger, Bab.; UVB 1; VAB 1; 2; 3; 4; 5; 6; 7.

Cf. further the following text translations by:

F. M. Th. DE LIAGRE BÖHL, Het Gilgamesj Epos[3], Amsterdam, 1958.
G. CASTELLINO, Sapienza babilonese, Turin, 1962.
G. CONTENAU, L'épopée de Gilgamesh, poème babylonien[4], Paris, 1939.
E. EBELING, in: H. GRESSMANN, Altorientalische Texte zum Alten
    Testament[2], Berlin; Leipzig, 1926.
A. FALKENSTEIN; W. VON SODEN, Sumerische und akkadische Hymnen
    und Gebete, Zürich; Stuttgart, 1953.
R. HAASE, Die keilschriftlichen Rechtssammlungen in deutscher Über-
    setzung, Wiesbaden, 1963.
A. HEIDEL, The Gilgamesh epic and old Testament parallels[2], Chicago,
    1949.
——, The Babylonian Genesis[2], Chicago, 1954.
J. KOHLER; F. E. PEISER, Aus dem babylonischen Rechtsleben 1-4,
    Leipzig, 1890-1898.
J. KOHLER; P. KOSCHAKER; A. UNGNAD, Hammurabi's Gesetz 1-6,
    Leipzig, 1909-1923.
J. KOHLER; A. UNGNAD, Hundert ausgewählte Rechtsurkunden aus
    der Spätzeit des babylonischen Schrifttums von Xerxes bis
    Mithridates II, 485-93 v. Chr., Leipzig, 1911.
D. D. LUCKENBILL, Ancient records of Assyria and Babylonia 1; 2,
    Chicago, 1926; 1927 (reprint 1968).
A. L. OPPENHEIM, Letters from Mesopotamia, Chicago, 1967 (s. F. R.
    KRAUS, JESHO 12, 1969, 200-211).
A. SCHOTT, W. VON SODEN, Das Gilgamesch-Epos[3], Stuttgart, 1970.
E. SOLLBERGER; J, R, KUPPER, Inscriptions royales sumériennes et
    akkadiennes, Paris 1971.
E. A. SPEISER; TH. J. MEEK; A. L. OPPENHEIM; A. SACHS; F. J. STEP-
    HENS; R. H. PFEIFFER; W. F. ALBRIGHT in: J. B. PRITCHARD,
    ANET[2], Princeton, 1955 (also editio minor, Princeton, 1958).
    See now third edition (1970) with revisions and supplement
    (s. next item).
A. K. GRAYSON; J. J. FINKELSTEIN; E. REINER; A. L. OPPENHEIM;
    R. D. BIGGS; W. L. MORAN in: J. B. PRITCHARD, Ancient Near
    East. Supplementary Texts and Pictures relating to the Old

Testament, Princeton; New Jersey, 1969, 65-82; 90-92; 95-111;
120-131; 156-171; 187-196; Addenda 235 ff.
A. UNGNAD, Die Religion der Babylonier und Assyrer, Jena, 1921.

Finally we refer to the following special bibliographies:

J. A. BRINKMAN, A preliminary catalogue of written sources for a
political history of Babylonia: 1160-722 B.C., JCS 16, 1962, 83-109
(s. also J. A. BRINKMAN, A political history of post-Kassite
Babylonia 1158-722 B.C., AnOr 43, Rome, 1968, 3-36; the same,
StOpp, Chicago 1964, 41-53).

P. GARELLI, Les Assyriens en Cappadoce, Paris, 1963, 391-405
(bibliography of Old Assyrian texts; s. also K. HECKER, Grammatik der Kültepe-Texte, AnOr 44, Rome, 1968, 2-11).

I. J. GELB, Old Akkadian writing and grammar, MAD 2², Chicago,
1961, 1-19 (Old Akkadian bibliography).

W. J. HINKE, A new boundary stone of Nebuchadrezzar I. from
Nippur, BER 4, Philadelphia, 1907, XIV-XXV Bibliography of
the Babylonian Kudurru inscriptions (s. also L. W. KING, BBS
and U. SEIDL, Die bablyonischen Kudurru-Reliefs, BagM 4,
Berlin, 1968, 7-220 (; F.X. STEINMETZER, Kud. S.1-92).

H. HIRSCH, Die Inschriften der Könige von Agade, AfO 20, 1963, 1-33.

K. JARITZ, Quellen zur Geschichte der Kaššû-Dynastie, MIO 6, 1958,
187-265.

G. JUCQOIS, Phonétique comparée des dialectes moyens-babyloniens
du nord et de l'ouest, Louvain, 1966, 31-57. (bibliography of
northern and western Akkadian texts).

L. DE MEYER in: CahTD 1, Paris, 1960, 1-30 (Gilgameš).

W. MAYER, Untersuchungen zur Grammatik des Mittelassyrischen,
AOATS 2, Kevelaer; Neukirchen-Vluyn, 1971, 1-3 (bibliography
of Middle Assyrian texts).

L. L. ORLIN, Assyrian colonies in Cappadocia, The Hague; Paris,
1970, 248-264 (bibliography of Old Assyrian texts).

S. PARPOLA, Neo-Assyrian Toponyms, AOAT 6, Kevelaer; Neukirchen-
Vluyn, 1970, XVII-XXVI (texts from the Neo-Assyrian period).

R. H. PFEIFFER, State letters of Assyria, AOS 6, New Haven, 1935,
254-260 (ever since to be completed with a.o. articles by K. DEL-
LER (and S. PARPOLA) in Or 30 (1961) ff.; s. also K. DELLER,
The Neo-Assyrian epigraphical remains of Nimrud, [Or 35, [1966,
179-194).

A. F. Rainey, El Amarna tablets 359-379. Supplement to J. A.
Knudtzon, Die El-Amarna-Tafeln, AOAT 8, Kevelaer; Neu-
kirchen-Vluyn, 1970 (concordance p. 4-5; cf. also D. O. Edzard
in: D. O. Edzard; R. Hachmann; P. Maiberger; G. Mansfeld,
Kamid el-Loz-Kumidi, Saarbr. Beitr. zur Altertumskunde 7,
Bonn, 1970, 55-62).

C. Saporetti, Bibliografia delle lettere private medio-assire, AION
NS 20/2, 1970, 141-152.

A. Spycket, Bibliographie de Mari, StMar, Leyden, 1950, 127-138.

R. F. G. Sweet, Bibliography of Old Babylonian letters, MCS 7, 1957,
29-48.

G. Wilhelm, AOAT 9, Kevelaer; Neukirchen-Vluyn, 1970, 1-8 gives
a bibliography of Nuzi texts; 95-104 of Nuzi subjects.

F. el-Wailly, Synopsis of royal sources of the Kassite period, Sumer
10, 1954, 43-54.

C. SOME BOOKS AND ARTICLES ON (CULTURAL) HISTORY,
RELIGION, AND HISTORY OF ART OF
THE AKKADIANS AND MESOPOTAMIA.
AMORITES

1. History; Geography (s. also Bibliography of Sumerian)

S. S. Aḥmed, Southern Mesopotamia in the time of Ashurbanipal,
The Hague, 1968.

J. Bottéro, Le problème des Ḫabiru, Paris, 1954.

A. Boudou, Liste de noms géographiques, OrNr 36-38, Rome 1929.

J. A. Brinkman, Merodach-Baladan II, StOpp, Chicago, 1964, 6-53.

———, A political history of post-Kassite Babylonia, AnOr 43, Rome,
1968.

R. T. O'Callaghan, Aram Naharaim, AnOr 26, Rome, 1948.

M. Dietrich, Neue Quellen zur Geschichte Babyloniens I, WO 4, 1967,
61-103; II, WO 4, 1968, 183-251; II. Indizes, WO 5, 1969, 51-56;
III, WO 5, 1970, 176-190; IV, WO 6, 1971, 157-162.

———, Die Aramäer Südbabyloniens in der Sargonidenzeit (700-648),
AOAT 7, Kevelaer; Neukirchen-Vluyn, 1970.

D. O. Edzard, Die "Zweite Zwischenzeit" Babyloniens, Wiesbaden,
1957.

A. Falkenstein; D. O. Edzard; J. Bottéro; E. Cassin; R. Labat, a.o., Fischer Weltgeschichte 2-4, Die altorientalischen Reiche 1-3, Frankfurt a.M., 1965-1967.

H. FINE, Studies in Middle-Assyrian chronology and religion, Cincinnati, 1955.

P. GARELLI, Le Proche-Orient asiatique des origines aux invasions des peuples de la mer, Nouvelle Clio 2, Paris, 1969 (important bibliography: 15-40).

——, Les Assyriens en Cappadoce, Paris, 1963.

I. J. GELB, Hurrians and Subarians, SAOC 22, Chicago, 1944.

——, New light on Hurrians and Subarians, Studi Orientalistici in onore di G. Levi della Vida 1, Rome, 1956, 378-392 (s. also W. H. Ph. RÖMER, WO 4, 1967, 15-20; J. VAN DIJK, VS 17, p. 8-9).

M. GREENBERG, The Ḫab/piru, New Haven, 1955.

H. G. GÜTERBOCK, Die historische Tradition und ihre Gestaltung bei Babyloniern und Hethitern bis 1200, ZA 42, 1934, 1-91; 44, 1938, 45-149.

H. KLENGEL, Geschichte Syriens im 2. Jahrtausend v. u.Z., 1, Nordsyrien, Berlin, 1965; 2, Mittel- und Südsyrien, 1969; 3, Historische Geographie und allgemeine Darstellung, 1970.

——, Lullubum. Ein Beitrag zur Geschichte der altvorderasiatischen Gebirgsvölker, MIO 11, 1965, 349-371.

F. R. KRAUS, Sumerer und Akkader. Ein Problem der altmesopotamischen Geschichte, MAW NR 33/8, Amsterdam; London, 1970.

J.-R. KUPPER, Les nomades en Mésopotamie au temps des rois de Mari, Paris, 1957.

J. LAESSØE, People of ancient Assyria, London, 1963.

——, Det første Assyriske imperium. Et aspekt, Festskr. udg. af Københavns Universitet i anl. af Universitetets Årsfest, Copenhagen, 1966, 1-110.

M. LIVERANI, Storia di Ugarit nell' età degli archivi politici, SS 6, Rome, 1962.

——, Introduzione alla storia del'Asia anteriore antica, Rome, 1963.

A. MOORTGAT, Geschichte Vorderasiens bis zum Hellenismus, in: A. SCHARFF and A. M., Ägypten und Vorderasien im Altertum, Munich, 1950.

D. OATES, Studies in the ancient history of Northern Iraq, London, 1958.

L. L. ORLIN, Assyrian colonies in Cappadocia, The Hague-Paris, 1970.

H. SCHMÖKEL, Geschichte des alten Vorderasien, HO 2/3, Leyden, 1957. (This book at the same time contains cultural-historical data).

——, Hammurabi von Babylon. Die Errichtung eines Reiches, Munich, 1958.

W. VON SODEN, Herrscher im Alten Orient, Berlin; Göttingen; Heidelberg, 1954.

——, Aufstieg und Untergang der Grossreiche des Zweistromgebietes (Sumerer, Babylonier, Assyrer) in: W. F. MUELLER, Aufstieg und Untergang der Grossreiche des Altertums², Stuttgart, 1958.

——, Der Nahe Osten im Altertum, Propyläen-Weltgeschichte 1, 1961, 525-609.

——, Sumer, Babylon und Hethiter bis zur Mitte des zweiten Jahrtausends v. Chr., Propyläen-Weltgeschichte 2, 1962, 41-133.

——, Aššuretililāni, Sînšarriškun, Sînšum(u)-lišer und die Ereignisse im Assyrerreich nach 635 v. Chr., ZA 58, 1967, 241-255.

E. A. SPEISER, Mesopotamian origins, Philadelphia, 1930.

F. M. TOCCI, La Siria nell'età di Mari, SS 3, Rome, 1960.

A. UNGNAD, Subartu, Berlin-Leipzig, 1936.

K. VEENHOF, Kanisj-Kültepe. Een assyrische handelskolonie in Klein-Azië uit het begin van het 2e mill. v. Chr., Phoenix 15/2, 1969, 284-304.

E. VON VOIGTLÄNDER, A survey of Neobabylonian history, Microfilm, Ann Arbor, U.S.A., 1969.

P. WALCOT, Hesiod and the Near East, Cardiff, 1966, esp. 27-54.

The Cambridge Ancient History, many parts, see e.g. the backcover of CAH², Vol. 2, Ch. XXV, J. M. MUNN-RANKIN, Assyrian military power 1300-1200 B.C., Cambridge, 1967.

2. CULTURAL HISTORY (s. also Bibliography of Sumerian)

A. AABOE, Some lunar auxiliary tables and related texts from the Late Babylonian Period, Kong. Danske Vid. Selsk., Mat. fys. Medd. 36, 12, Copenhagen 1968.

K. BALKAN, Babilde feodalizm araştırmaları, Kas'lar devrinde Babil [Untersuchungen zum Feudalsystem in Babylonien: Babylonien in der Kassiten-Zeit], Fak. Derg. 2/1, 1943, 45-55 (s. H. G. GÜTERBOCK, AfO 15, 1945-'51, 130-131).

——, Kassiten-studien. 1. Die Sprache der Kassiten, AOS 37, New Haven, 1954.

R. D. BIGGS, Medicine in Ancient Mesopotamia, History of Science 8, 1969, 94-105.

R. Borger, Ausstrahlungen des Zweistromlandes, JEOL 18, 1965, 317-330.

G. Boyer, Introduction bibliographique à l'histoire du droit suméro-akkadien, AHDO 2, 1938, 81-91.

E. M. Bruins, Interpretation of cuneiform mathematics, Physis 4/4, Florence, 1962.

G. Cardascia, Droits cunéiformes. Introduction bibliographique à l'histoire du droit et à l'ethnologie juridique A/2, Brussels, 1966.

——, Les lois assyriennes, Paris, 1969.

D. Cocquerillat, Palmeraies et cultures de l'Eanna d'Uruk (559-520), ADFU 8, Berlin, 1968.

M. Duchesne-Guillemins, La harpe à plectre iranienne: son origine et sa diffusion, JNES 28, 1969, 109-115.

——, Note complémentaire sur l'instrument a l - g a r , JNES 29, 1970, 200-201.

R. J. Forbes, Studies in ancient technology 1-9, Leyden, 1955-1964.

H. Freydank, Spätbabylonische Wirtschaftstexte aus Uruk, Berlin, 1971.

C. J. Gadd, Teachers and students in the oldest schools, London, 1956.

I. J. Gelb, Approaches to the study of ancient society, JAOS 87, 1967, 1-8.

O. R. Gurney, An Old Babylonian treatise on the tuning of the harp, Iraq 30, 1968, 229-233.

H. G. Güterbock, Musical notation in Ugarit, RA 64, 1970, 45-52.

R. Haase, Einführung in das Studium keilschriftlicher Rechtsquellen, Wiesbaden, 1965.

A. Kammenhuber, Die Arier im vorderen Orient, Heidelberg, 1968.

A. D. Kilmer, The strings of musical instruments. Their names and significance, AS 16, 1965, 261-272.

——, The discovery of an ancient Mesopotamian theory of music, PAPS 115, 1971, 131-149.

V. Korosec, Keilschriftrecht, HO, Erg. Bd. 3, Orientalisches Recht, Leyden-Cologne, 1964, 49-219 (also separately available).

F. R. Kraus, Viehhaltung im altbabylonischen Lande Larsa, MAW NR 29/5, Amsterdam 1966.

H. M. Kümmel, Zur Stimmung der babylonischen Harfe, Or 39, 1970, 252-263.

J. Laessøe, Literacy and oral tradition in Ancient Mesopotamia, Studia Orientalia I. Pedersen ... dicata, Copenhagen, 1953, 205-218.

B. LANDSBERGER, Die Eigenbegrifflichkeit der babylonischen Welt, Darmstadt, 1965.

——, Jungfräulichkeit, SymDav 2, 1968, 41-105.

W. F. LEEMANS, The Old-Babylonian merchant; his business and his social position, SD 3, Leyden, 1950.

——, Economische gegevens in Sumerische en Akkadische teksten, en hun problemen, JEOL 15, 1957-'58, 197-214.

——, Foreign trade in the Old Babylonian period as revealed by texts from southern Mesopotamia, SD 6, Leyden, 1960.

——, Old Babylonian letters and economic history, JESHO 11, 1968, 171-226.

M. MAYRHOFER, Die Indo-Arier im alten Vorderasien mit einer analytischen Bibliographie, Wiesbaden, 1966.

B. MEISSNER, Babylonien und Assyrien 1; 2, Heidelberg, 1920-'25.

W. NAGEL, Frühe Tierwelt in Südwestasien I, Festschrift O. F. GANDERT, BBV 2, 1959, 106-118; (II), ZA 55, 1963, 169-236.

A. L. OPPENHEIM, The seafaring merchants of Ur, JAOS 74, 1954, 6-17.

——, Mesopotamian medecine, BHM 36, 1962, 97-108.

——, Ancient Mesopotamia. Portrait of a dead civilization, Chicago, 1964.

——, A note on the scribes in Mesopotamia, AS 16, Chicago, 1965, 253-256.

——, Letters from Mesopotamia, Chicago, 1967, 1-53.

——, Essay on overland trade in the first millennium B.C., JCS 21, 1969, 236-254.

W. RÖLLIG, Das Bier im alten Mesopotamien, Berlin, 1970.

G. ROUX, Ancient Iraq, London, 1964.

A. and E. SALONEN, many books and articles, s. above A 3.

H. SCHMÖKEL, Mesopotamien, in: Kulturgeschichte des Alten Orient, Kröner, Stuttgart, 1961, 2-310.

P. SCHNABEL, Berossos und die babylonisch-hellenistische Literatur, Leipzig; Berlin, 1923.

W. VON SODEN, Leistung und Grenze sumerischer und babylonischer Wissenschaft, Darmstadt, 1965.

W. STAUDER, Die Musik der Sumerer, Babylonier und Assyrer, HO 1, Erg. Bd. 4, Leyden-Cologne, 1970, 171-243.

——, Die Harfen und Leiern Vorderasiens in babylonischer und assyrischer Zeit, Frankfurt a.M., 1961.

E. SZLECHTER, Les lois d'Ešnunna. Transcription -- Traduction et commentaire, Paris, 1954.

F. Thureau-Dangin, Esquisse d'une histoire du système sexagésimal, Paris, 1932.

A. Ungnad, Subartu. Beiträge zur Kulturgeschichte und Völkerkunde Vorderasiens, Berlin; Leipzig, 1936.

K. R. Veenhof, Aspects of Old Assyrian trade and its terminology, Leyden 1972.

K. Vogel, Die Mathematik der Babylonier, Vorgriechische Mathematik 2, Hannover; Paderborn, 1959.

E. F. Weidner, Handbuch der babylonischen Astronomie 1, AB 23, Leipzig, 1915.

——, Die Bibliothek Tiglatpilesers I., AfO 16, 1952-'53, 197-215.

——, Amts- und Privatarchive aus mittelassyrischer Zeit, Vorderasiatische Studien. Festschrift für Prof. Dr. V. Christian, Vienna, 1956, 111-118.

——, Gestirn-Darstellungen auf babylonischen Tontafeln, SÖAW 254/2, Vienna, 1967.

M. Weitemeyer, Babylonske og Assyriske Arkiver og Biblioteker, Copenhagen, 1955.

D. Wulstan, The tuning of the Babylonian harp, Iraq 30, 1968, 215-228.

3. Religion (s. also Bibliography of Sumerian)

F. M. Th. de Liagre Böhl, Das Menschenbild in babylonischer Schau, Numen Spl. 2, 1955, 28-48.

J. Bottéro, Les divinités sémitiques anciennes en Mésopotamie, in: Le antiche divinità semitiche, SS 1, Rome, 1958, 17-63.

E. Cassin, La splendeur divine. Introduction à l'étude de la mentalité mésopotamienne, Paris, 1968 (s. W. von Soden, ZA 61, 1971, 312-314).

G. Contenau, La divination chez les Assyriens et les Babyloniens, Paris, 1940.

É. Dhorme, Les religions de Babylonie et d'Assyrie, "Mana" 2, Paris, 1949.

G. van Driel, The cult of Aššur, Assen, 1969.

D. O. Edzard, Wörterbuch der Mythologie 1/1, Stuttgart, 1965.

H. Fine, Studies in Middle-Assyrian chronology and religion, Cincinnati, 1955, 98-116.

C. Frank, Studien zur babylonischen Religion 1, Strassburg, 1911.

H. Frankfort, Kingship and the gods, Chicago, 1948.

P. Garelli ed., Gilgameš et sa légende, CahTD 1, Paris, 1960.

W. HELCK, Betrachtungen zur grossen Göttin und den ihr verbundenen
    Gottheiten, Religion und Kultur der alten Mittelmeerwelt in
    Parallelforschungen 2, Munich; Vienna, 1971.
H. HIRSCH, Untersuchungen zur altassyrischen Religion, AfOBeih13/
    14, Graz, 1961.
Th. JACOBSEN, Ancient Mesopotamian religion: the central concerns,
    PAPS 107/6, 1963, 473-484 (also published in: Th. JACOBSEN,
    Toward the immage of Tammuz, Cambridge, Mass., 1970, 39-46).
——, Mesopotamia, in: H. and H. A. FRANKFORT, a.o., The intellectual
    adventure of ancient man², Chicago, 1948, 123-219.
F. R. KRAUS, Altmesopotamisches Lebensgefühl, JNES 19, 1960, 117-
    132.
H. M. KÜMMEL, Der Ersatzkönigritus in Mesopotamien, StBoT 3,
    Wiesbaden, 1967, 169-187.
J. LAESSØE, Babylonsk og assyrisk religion, Illustreret Religions-
    historie², red. af J. P. Asmussen og J. Laessøe, Copenhagen,
    1968, 437-463, (s. now German edition; below p. 79: J. VAN
    DIJK).
W. G. LAMBERT; A. R. MILLARD, Atra-ḫasīs. The Babylonian story
    of the flood, Oxford, 1969.
B. MEISSNER, Babylonien und Assyrien 2, Heidelberg, 1925, 1-323;
    419-438.
J. C. DE MOOR, Mondelinge overlevering in Mesopotamië, Ugarit en
    Israël, Leyden, 1965.
J. NOUGAYROL a.o., La divination en Mésopotamie ancienne et dans
    les régions voisines, Paris, 1966.
——, La divination babylonienne, in : La divination. Études recueillies
    par A. CACQUOT et M. LEIBOVICI, Paris, 1968, 25-81.
——, La religion babylonienne, in : H. Ch. PUECH (ed.), Encyclopédie
    de la Pléiade. Histoire des religions 1, Paris, 1970, 203-249.
A. L. OPPENHEIM, "Mesopotamian religion", Ancient Mesopotamia,
    Chicago, 1964, 171-227; 385-386.
——, Divination and celestial observation in the last Assyrian
    empire, Centaurus 14/1, Copenhagen, 1969, 97-135.
G. PETTINATO, Die Ölwahrsagung bei den Babyloniern 1; 2, SS 21;
    22, Rome, 1966.
J. RENGER, Götternamen in der altbabylonischen Zeit, HSAO, Wies-
    baden, 1967, 137-171.
——, Untersuchungen zum Priestertum in der altbabylonischen Zeit 1,
    ZA 58, 1967, 110-188; 2, ZA 59, 1969, 104-230.

K. K. RIEMSCHNEIDER, Babylonische Geburtsomina in hethitischer
    Übersetzung, StBoT 9, Wiesbaden, 1970 (cf. also H. G. GÜTER-
    BOCK, AfO 18, 1957-'58, 78-80).
W. H. Ph. RÖMER, Religion of ancient Mesopotamia, in: C. J. BLEEKER;
    G. WIDENGREN, Historia Religionum 1, Leyden, 1969, 115-194.
I. SEIBERT, Hirt, Herde, König. Zur Herausbildung des Königtums in
    Mesopotamien, Berlin, 1969.
W. VON SODEN, Gebet II (babylonisch und assyrisch), RlA 3/2; 3/3,
    Berlin, 1959-'64, 160-170.
——, Akkadische Gebete an Göttinnen, RA 52, 1958, 131-136.
——, Das Fragen nach der Gerechtigkeit Gottes im alten Orient,
    MDOG 96, 1965, 41-59.
E. VON WEIHER, Der babylonische Gott Nergal, AOAT 11, Kevelaer;
    Neukirchen-Vluyn, 1971.

4. ARCHAEOLOGY AND HISTORY OF ART
(s. also Bibliography of Sumerian)

R. McC. ADAMS, Land behind Baghdad. A history of settlement on
    the Diyala plains, Chicago; London, 1965.
P. AMIET, La glyptique mésopotamienne archaïque, Paris, 1961, and
    many articles by the same author in RA; Syria.
W. ANDRAE, Das wiedererstandene Assur, Leipzig, 1938.
R. D. BARNETT, Assyrische Palastreliefs, Prague, w.y.
M. Th. BARRELET, Figurines et reliefs en terre cuite de la Mésopotamie
    antique 1, Potiers, termes de métier, procédés de fabrication et
    production, Paris, 1968.
F. BASMADSCHI, Landschaftliche Elemente in der mesopotamischen
    Kunst des IV. und III. Jahrtausends, Basel, w.y.
M. A. BEEK, Bildatlas der assyrisch-babylonischen Kultur, Gütersloh,
    1961 (s. B. HROUDA, ZA 57, 1965, 312-314).
Th. BERAN, Assyrische Glyptik des 14. Jahrhunderts, ZA 52, 1957,
    141-215.
——, Die babylonische Glyptik der Kassitenzeit, AfO 18, 1957-'58,
    255-278.
R. M. BOEHMER, Die Entwicklung der Glyptik während der Akkad-
    Zeit, Unters. z. Assyriol. u. vorderas. Arch. 4, Berlin, 1965.
B. BUCHANAN, Catalogue of ancient Near Eastern Seals in the Ash-
    molean Museum, Vol. 1, cylinder seals, Oxford, 1966.
E. D. VAN BUREN, Foundation figurines and offerings, Berlin, 1931,

and many articles by the same author in i.a. Or; Iraq; ZA; RA (s. also R. Borger, HKL 1, 39 f.).

T. A. Busink, Sumerische en babylonische tempelbouw. Bijdrage tot de geschiedenis der sacrale bouwkunst in Oud-Babylonië, Batavia, 1940.

——, De babylonische tempeltoren. Een archaeologische en stijl-critische studie, Leyden, 1949.

——, L'origine et l'évolution de la ziggurat babylonienne, JEOL 21, 1970, 91-142.

V. Christian, Altertumskunde des Zweistromlandes 1, 2 vol., Leipzig, 1940.

G. Contenau, Manuel d'archéologie orientale, 4 vol., Paris, 1927-1947.

H. Frankfort, Cylinder seals. A documentary essay on the art and religion of the ancient Near East, London, 1939 ([2]1966).

——, The art and architecture of the Ancient Orient, The Pelican History of Art, Z 7, Harmondsworth, 1954.

——, The birth of civilization in the Near East, Garden City, N. Y., 1956.

——, The last predynastic period in Babylonia, rev. and re-arr. by L. Davies, CAH[2] 1, Ch. XII, Cambridge, 1958.

C. J. Gadd, The stones of Assyria. The surviving remains of Assyrian sculpture, their recovery, and their original positions, London, 1936.

B. L. Goff, Symbols of prehistoric Mesopotamia, New Haven; London, 1963.

A. R. al-Haik, Key lists of archaeological excavations in Iraq 1842-1965, Field research projects, Coconut Grove, 1968.

D. Homès-Fredericq, Les cachets mésopotamiens protohistoriques, DMOA 14, Leyden, 1970.

B. Hrouda, Die Kulturgeschichte des assyrischen Flachbildes, Saarbr. Beitr. zur Altertumskunde 2, Bonn, 1965.

——, Die Grundlagen der bildenden Kunst in Assyrien, ZA 57, 1965, 274-297.

——, Vorderasien 1, Mesopotamien, Babylonien, Iran und Anatolien, Handbuch der Archäologie, Munich, 1971.

A. J. Jawad, The advent of the era of townships in Northern Meso-potamia, Leyden, 1965.

R. Koldewey, Das wiederstehende Babylon[4], Leipzig, 1925.

H. Lenzen, Die Entwicklung der Zikurrat von ihren Anfängen bis zur Zeit der III. Dynastie von Ur, ADFU 4, Leipzig, 1941.

——, Mesopotamische Tempelanlagen von der Frühzeit bis zum zweiten Jahrtausend, ZA 51, 1955, 1-36.

T. A. Madhloom, The chronology of Neo-Assyrian art, London, 1970.

M. E. L. Mallowan, Nimrud and its remains 1; 2, London, 1966.

——, The early dynastic period in Mesopotamia, CAH² 1, Ch. XVI, Cambridge, 1968, and many articles by the same author and by D. Oates in Iraq.

P. van der Meer, The chronology of Ancient Western Asia and Egypt², Leyden, 1955.

A. Moortgat, Die bildende Kunst des Alten Orients und die Bergvölker, Berlin, 1932.

——, Assyrische Glyptik des 13. Jahrhunderts, ZA 47, 1942, 50-88.

——, Assyrische Glyptik des 12. Jahrhunderts, ZA 48, 1944, 23-44.

——, Tammuz, Der Unsterblichkeitsglaube in der altorientalischen Bildkunst, Berlin, 1949 (cf. the same author, RAI 3, 1954, 18-41).

——, Altvorderasiatische Malerei, Berlin, 1959.

——, Vorderasiatische Rollsiegel. Ein Beitrag zur Geschichte der Steinschneidekunst², Berlin, 1966.

——, Die Kunst des Alten Mesopotamien. Die klassische Kunst Vorderasiens, Cologne, 1967.

U. Moortgat-Correns, Beiträge zur mittelassyrischen Glyptik, Vorderasiatische Archäologie (Moortgat-Festschr.), Berlin, 1964, 165-177.

W. Nagel, Die Bauern- und Stadtkulturen im vordynastischen Vorderasien, Berlin, 1964.

——, Djamdat Nasr-Kulturen und frühdynastische Buntkeramiker, BBV 8, Berlin, 1964.

——, Der mesopotamische Streitwagen und seine Entwicklung im ostmediterranen Bereich, BBV 10, Berlin, 1966.

——, Die neuassyrischen Reliefstile unter Sanherib und Assurbanaplu, BBV 11, Berlin, 1967.

H. J. Nissen, Zur Datierung des Königsfriedhofes von Ur, Bonn, 1966 (cf. M. E. L. Mallowan; B. Parker, Iraq 32, 1970, 214-218).

R. North, Status of the Warka Excavation, Or 26, 1957, 185-256.

R. Opificius, Das altbabylonische Terrakottarelief, Unters. z. Assyriol. u. vorderas. Arch. 2, Berlin, 1961.

A. Parrot, Mari, une ville perdue ...², Paris, 1945.

——, Archéologie mésopotamienne, 2 vol., Paris, 1946-'53.

——, Tello. Vingt campagnes de fouilles (1877-1933), Paris, 1948.

——, Ziggurats et Tour de Babel, Paris, 1949.

——, Mari. Documentation photographique de la mission archéologique de Mari, Collection des ides photographiques 7, Neuchâtel; Paris, 1953.

——, Babylone et l'Ancien Testament, Cahiers d'archéologie biblique 8, Neuchâtel; Paris, 1956, and many articles by the same author i.a. in RA and Syria.

——, Assur², Munich, 1972.

A. L. PERKINS, The comparative archeology of Early Mesopotamia², SAOC 25, Chicago, 1957.

U. SEIDL, Die babylonischen Kudurru-Reliefs, BagM 4, Berlin, 1968, 7-220.

T. SOLYMAN, Die Entstehung und Entwicklung der Götterwaffen im alten Mesopotamien und ihre Bedeutung, Beirut, 1968.

E. STROMMENGER, Das Menschenbild in der altmesopotamischen Rundplastik von Mesilim bis Hammurapi, BagM 1, Berlin, 1960, 1-103.

——, Die neuassyrische Rundskulptur, Abh. DOG 15, Berlin, 1970.

E. UNGER, Babylon, die heilige Stadt², Berlin, 1970.

J. WIESNER, Die Kunst des Alten Orients, Ullstein Kunstgeschichte 2, Frankfurt a.M.; Berlin, 1963.

D. J. WISEMAN, Götter und Menschen im Rollsiegel Westasiens, Prague, 1958.

Sir L. WOOLLEY, Excavations at Ur. A record of twelve year's work, London, 1954.

——, A forgotten kingdom, being a record of the results obtained from the excavations of two mounds Atchana and el-Mina in the Turkish Hatay², London, 1959.

For techniques and methods of excavation and archaeological research cf. a.o.:

B. HROUDA; K. KARSTENS, Zur inneren Chronologie des Friedhofes "A" in Ingharra/Chursagkalama bei Kiš, ZA 58, 1967, 256-298.

W. NAGEL, Vorderasiatische Archäologie (Moortgat-Festschr.), Berlin, 1964, 7-11 on the scientific method of A. Moortgat and his pupils (s. ibid., 12-17: P. CALMEYER, Bibliographie A. Moortgat 1923-1963).

A. PARROT, Archéologie mésopotamienne 2 (s. above) 11-103, Technique.

Sir M. WHEELER, Moderne Archäologie. Methoden und Technik der Ausgrabung, Rowohlts Deutsche Enzyklopädie, Bd. 111/112, Hamburg, 1960.

The above (c 4) mentioned studies contain a good deal of literature on archaeology of Mesopotamia and adjacent territories; cf. further the periodicals, particularly AfO; AnSt; BagM; Belleten; ILN; Iraq; MDOG; Mesopotamia; Or; Sumer; Syria (s. also below, D), in which partly also regularly provisional accounts of current and new excavations can be found.

5. AMORITES

As nowadays one is frequently concerned with problems relative to the Amorites, it may be useful to mention here some books and articles on the subject:

Th. BAUER, Die Ostkanaanäer, Leipzig, 1926.
G. BUCCELLATI, The Amorites of the Ur III period, Naples, 1966 (s. G. PETTINATO, AION 18, 1968, 1-7).
A. T. CLAY, The empire of the Amorites, YOSR 6, New Haven, 1919.
É. DHORME, Les Amorrhéens. A propos d'un livre récent, Recueil É. Dhorme, Paris, 1951, 81-165.
D. O. EDZARD, Die "Zweite Zwischenzeit" Babyloniens, Wiesbaden, 1957, 30-43.
J. J. FINKELSTEIN, The genealogy of the Hammurapi dynasty, JCS 20, 1966, 95-118.
I. J. GELB, La lingua degli Amoriti, ANLA Rendiconti, Classe di Scienze morali, storiche et filologiche 13/3-4, Rome, 1958, 143-164.
——, The early history of the West Semitic peoples, JCS 15, 1961, 27-47.
——, An Old Babylonian list of Amorites, JAOS 88, 1968, 39-46.
C. H. J. DE GEUS, The Amorites in the archaeology of Palestine, UF 3, 1971, 41-60.
——, Amorieten en Kanaanieten, Phoenix 16/1, 1970, 328-336.
A. GOETZE, Amurrite names in Ur III and early Isin texts, JSS 4, 1959, 193-203.
J. C. GREENFIELD, Amurrite, Ugaritic, and Canaanite, Proceedings of the International Conference on Semitic Studies, Jerusalem, 1969, 92-101.
A. HALDAR, Who were the Amorites?, Leyden, 1971.
H. B. HUFFMON, Amorite personal names in the Mari texts. A structural and lexical study, Baltimore, 1965 (s. M. DIETRICH; O. LORETZ, OLZ 1966, 235-244).

K. M. KENYON, Amorites and Canaanites, The Schweich Lectures of the British Academy 1963, London, 1966.

Ch. KRAHMALKOV, The Amorite enclitic particle TA/I, JSS 14, 1969, 201-204.

F. R. KRAUS, Ein Edikt des Königs Ammi-ṣaduqa von Babylon, SD 5, Leyden, 1958, 188-189 (s. now J. J. FINKELSTEIN, RA 63, 1969, 45-64; 189-190).

J. R. KUPPER, Les nomades en Mésopotamie au temps des rois de Mari, Paris, 1957, 147-247 (cf. the same author, L'iconographie du dieu Amurru dans la glyptique de la Ire dynastie babylonienne, Brussels, 1961).

W. G. LAMBERT, Babylonian Wisdom Literature, Oxford, 1960, 225 : B. Landsberger (s. R. BORGER, HKL 1, 267).

——, Another look at Hammurabi's ancestors, JCS 22, 1968, 1-2.

S. J. LIEBERMANN, Booty from the land of Mardu, JCS 22, 1969, 53-62.

M. B. ROWTON, The Abu Amurrim, Iraq 31, 1969, 68-73.

W. VON SODEN, Zur Einteilung der semitischen Sprachen, WZKM 56, 1960, 177-191 (cf. the same author, WO 3, 1966, 178-181).

C. WILCKE, Zur Geschichte der Amurriter in der Ur III-Zeit, WO 5, 1969, 1-31 (s. also the same, ZA 60, 1970, 54-69).

Shortly a book by O. LORETZ and generally also J. HENNINGER, Über Lebensraum und Lebensformen der Frühsemiten, Cologne; Opladen, 1968.

D. THE MORE IMPORTANT PERIODICALS OR SERIES WHICH CAN CONTAIN PUBLICATIONS ON AKKADIAN

(s. again R. BORGER, HKL 1; W. VON SODEN, AHw; AnOr 47) are:

AAA; AASOR; AB; AcOr; AK; AfO (Beih); AHDO (+RIDA); AIPO; AJA; AJSL; Anatolica; AnBi; AnSt; AnOr; ArOr; 'Atiqôt; AS; BA; Babyloniaca; BagM; BASOR; Belleten; BiOr; BOR; BSOAS; ErIs; HUCA; IEJ; IrAnt; Iraq; JA; JAOS; JCS; JEOL; JESHO; JJP; JKF; JNES; JRAS (CSpl); JSOR; JSS; JTVI; LSS(NF); MAOG; MCS; MDOG; MIO; MVA(e)G; MVEOL; OLZ; Or; OrNr ...; OrS; PAPS; PSBA; RA; RB; RÉS; RHA; RSO; RT; SD; Semitica; Sumer; Syria; UF; WO; WZJ; WZKM; ZA; ZDMG; ZDPV.

E.

Finally we mention the very useful "Rencontres assyriologiques internationales", organized annually by the Groupe François Thureau-Dangin. The papers read on the occasion are published partly in RAI, partly in other books and periodicals.

F. ABBREVIATIONS

See the list of abbreviations at the end of the present vol. 1 (mainly based on the list proposed by K. DELLER, Or 37, 1968, 1*-14*) and the lists in W. VON SODEN, Akkadisches Handwörterbuch, Lief. 1, 1959, X-XVI; 6, 1965, 567-568; 11 (1972); the frontcovers in Lief. 7, 1966; 8, 1967; 9, 1969; 10, 1971. In addition the following abbreviations are used:

ACC	= L. L. ORLIN, Assyrian colonies in Cappadocia. The Hague; Paris, 1970.
AOATT	= K. R. VEENHOF, Aspects of Old Assyrian trade and its terminology, Leyden, 1972.
BAP	= B. GEMSER, Babylonisch-Assyrische persoonsnamen, Wageningen, 1924.
BEC	= S. LANGDON, The Babylonian epic of creation, Oxford, 1923.
BOS	= Bonner Orientalistische Studien.
ChTRAB	= P. DHORME, Choix de textes religieux assyro-babyloniens, Paris, 1907.
CN	= E. B. SMICK, A cylinder of Nebuchadrezzar II, Ringwood, 1953.
Comm	= R. LABAT, Commentaires assyro-babyloniens sur les présages, Bordeaux, 1933.
CTH	= E. LAROCHE, Catalogue des textes hittites, Paris 1971.
DM	= A. VAN PRAAG, Droit matrimonial assyro-babylonien, Amsterdam, 1945.
HKL	= R. BORGER, Handbuch der Keilschriftliteratur 1, Berlin, 1967.
Iščâlî	= M. SEIF, Über die altbabylonischen Rechts- und Wirtschaftsurkunden aus Iščâlî, Berlin; Charlottenburg, 1938.

Kud	= F. X. STEINMETZER, Die babylonischen Kudurru (Grenzsteine) als Urkundenform untersucht, Paderborn, 1922 (reprint New York, 1968).
Larsa	= Ch. F. JEAN, Larsa d'après les textes cunéiformes *2187 à *1901, Paris, 1931.
LHS	= Ch. F. JEAN, Lettres de Hammurabi à Sinidinnam, Paris, 1913.
MP	= D. CROSS, Movable property in the Nuzi documents, AOS 10, New Haven, 1937 (repr. New York, 1967).
NBD	= E. W. MOORE, Neo-Babylonian business and administrative documents with transliteration, translation, and notes, Ann Arbor, 1935.
NRET	= F. R. STEELE, Nuzi real estate transactions, AOS 25, New Haven, 1943.
PBC	= R. LABAT, le poème babylonien de la création, Paris, 1935.
SACTI	= Sumerian and Akkadian Cuneiform Texts in the collection of the World Heritage Museum of the University of Illinois, Urbana, 1971 ff.
SAHWSR	= M. WEITEMEYER, Some aspects of the hiring of workers in the Sippar region at the time of Hammurabi, Copenhagen, 1962.
StP	= Studia Pohl, Rome.
SWU	= H. FREYDANK, Spätbabylonische Wirtschaftstexte aus Uruk, Berlin, 1971.

II. SUMERIAN

COMPILED BY

W. H. Ph. RÖMER

General Works

The reader is referred to the Bibliography of Akkadian (general works).

A. PHILOLOGY

1. Grammars

a. *Ordinary grammars*

See the materials mentioned by A. Falkenstein, Das Sumerische, HO 1/2, 1-2/1, Leyden, 1959, 61-62, and by E. Sollberger, Le système verbal dans les inscriptions "royales" présargoniques de Lagaš, Geneva, 1952, 5-6 (s. A. Falkenstein, AfO 18, 1957-'58, 89-96; J. van Dijk, ZA 52, 1957, 309-324).

See particularly:

A. Falkenstein, Grammatik der Sprache Gudeas von Lagaš 1; 2, AnOr 28; 29, Rome, 1949; 1950.
——, Das Sumerische, HO 1/2, 1-2/1, Leyden, 1959, 14-62.
A. Poebel, Grundzüge der sumerischen Grammatik, Rostock, 1923.
S. A. Pallis, Akkadisk og Sumerisk, Festskrift udg. af Københavns Universitet i anl. af H. M. Kongens fødselsdag, Copenhagen, 1958.

b. *Historical grammars*

One could only mention, apart from below, A3, end:
K. Schildmann, Compendium of the historical grammar of Sumerian, HGS. Including the related material contained in Proto-Semitic and Proto-Egyptian, Acta et Studia 2, Bonn, 1964 ff. (publ. 3 parts; to be expected probably 11 parts as a whole).

c. *Syntaxes*

The reader is referred to the books of A. FALKENSTEIN, I. KÄRKI, and A. POEBEL mentioned above/below, A 3.

2. LEXICA

The reader is referred to the materials mentioned in Bibliography of Akkadian A 2 and by A. FALKENSTEIN, Das Sumerische 62; E. SOLLBERGER, SV 4-5.

See further:

M. LAMBERT, Contribution au Thésaurus de la langue sumérienne 1 : GAR, Paris, 1954.

R. JESTIN; M. LAMBERT, Contribution ... 2: AK, Paris, 1955.

3. PHILOLOGIC MONOGRAPHS AND IMPORTANT ARTICLES

The reader is referred to the books and articles on grammar quoted by A. FALKENSTEIN, Das Sumerische 61-62, and by E. SOLLBERGER, SV 5-11.

See further:

E. BERGMANN, Untersuchungen zu syllabisch geschriebenen sumerischen Texten, ZA 56, 1964, 1-43; ZA 57, 1965, 31-42.

M. BIELITZ, Melismen und ungewöhnliche Vokal- und Silbenwiederholung, bzw. Alternanz in sumerischen Kulttexten der Seleukidenzeit, Or 39, 1970, 152-156.

M. CIVIL; R. D. BIGGS, Notes sur des textes sumériens archaïques, RA 60, 1966, 1-16.

D. O. EDZARD, Fragen der sumerischen Syntax, ZDMG 109, 1959, 235-252.

——, Sumerische Komposita mit dem 'Nominalpräfix' n u - , ZA 55, 1963, 91-112.

——, Das sumerische Verbalmorphem / e d / in den alt- und neusumerischen Texten, HSAO, Wiesbaden, 1967, 29-62.

——, Grammatik, RlA 3/8, 1971, 610-616.

——, *ḫamṭu, marû* und freie Reduplikation beim sumerischen Verbum I, ZA 61, 1971, 208-232. ; II, ZA 62, 1972, 1-34.

A. FALKENSTEIN, Das Potentialis- und Irrealissuffix - e - š e des Sumerischen, IF 60, 1950, 113-130.

——, Zur Grammatik der altsumerischen Sprache, AfO 18, 1957-'58, 89-96 (s. also J. VAN DIJK, ZA 52, 1957, 309-324).

——, Kontakte zwischen Sumerern und Akkadern auf sprachlichem Gebiet, Genava, n.s. 8, Geneva, 1960, 301-314.

G. GRAGG, The syntax of the copula in Sumerian, The verb 'be' and its synonyms, philosophical and grammatical studies ed. by J. W. M. VERHAAR, 3, Foundations of language, supplementary series, vol. 8, Dordrecht, 1968, 86-109.

W. HEIMPEL, Tierbilder in der sumerischen Literatur, StP 2, Rome, 1968.

P. HULIN, A table of reciprocals with Sumerian spellings, JCS 17, 1963, 72-76.

Th. JACOBSEN, About the Sumerian verb, AS 16, Chicago, 1965, 71-102 (also published in Th. JACOBSEN, Toward the image of Tammuz and other essays on Mesopotamian history and culture, Cambridge, Mass., 1970, 245-270 (s. also the same, MSL 4, Rome, 1956, 1*-50*).

R. JESTIN, Übungen im Edubba, ZA 51, 1955, 37-44.

——, Le sens emphatique de la particule sumérienne u-, École des langues orientales anciennes de l'Institut catholique de Paris. Mémorial du cinquantenaire (1914-1964), Paris, 1964, 33-36.

——, Notes de graphie et de phonétique sumériennes, Paris, 1965.

——, Notes sur quelques particules sumériennes, Anatolica 1, 1967, 78-82.

——, Sur les particules verbales sumériennes, RA 61, 1967, 45-50.

——, La rime sumérienne, BiOr 24, 1967, 9-12.

——, La rime interne en Sumérien, RA 63, 1969, 115-120.

I. T. KANYEVA, Conjugation of the Sumerian verb (according to the data of the heroic epics), Peredne'aziatskiy Sbornik 2, Moscow, 1966, 165-168.

I. KÄRKI, Die Sprache der sumerischen Königsinschriften der frühalt-babylonischen Zeit, StOr 35, Helsinki, 1967 (s. J. KRECHER, WO 5, 1969, 127-129; W. H. Ph. RÖMER, BiOr 27, 1970, 160-167; D. O. EDZARD, OLZ 1970, 347 ff.).

S. N. KRAMER, Studies in Sumerian phonetics, ArOr 8, 1936, 18-33.

——, Sumerian similes: panoramic view of man's oldest literary images, JAOS 89, 1969, 1-17.

F. R. KRAUS, DLZ 1955, 260 ff.: BVW, Berlin, 1951, 36 ff. an exercise for translating into Sumerian (s. R. BORGER, HKL 1, 94).

J. Krecher, Zur sumerischen Grammatik, ZA 57, 1965, 12-30.

——, Die sumerischen Texte in "syllabischer" Orthographie, ZA 58, 1967, 16-65; WO 4, 1968, 252-277.

——, Zum Emesal-Dialekt des Sumerischen, HSAO, Wiesbaden, 1967, 87-110.

——, Zur Aussprache und Transkription des Sumerischen, ZDMG Spl. 1, Wiesbaden, 1969, 220-225.

——, Verschlusslaute und Betonung im Sumerischen, AOAT 1, Neukirchen-Vluyn, 1969, 157-197.

M. Lambert, Phonétique sumérienne. A propos d'un livre récent, RA 44, 1950, 147-152.

——, Cités et dialectes sumériens, RAI 1, Leyden, 1951, 2-4.

——, Formule šu-ba-ti et "Bon d'achat", RA 57, 1963, 97-98.

——, L'infixe pronominal - m a - en sumérien, RA 53, 1959, 147-149.

——, Le préfixe sumérien ḫé-, indice de l'inéluctable, RA 55, 1961, 35-40.

B. Landsberger; R. Hallock; Th. Jacobsen; A. Falkenstein, MSL 4, Rome 1956.

G. Meier, Zweisprachige Weihinschrift mit Aussprache-Angabe des Sumerischen, AfO 11, 1936-'37, 364-365.

J. D. Prince, The Sumerian numerals, P. Haupt Anniversary Volume, Baltimore; Leipzig, 1926, 272-277.

W. H. Ph. Römer, Einige Bemerkungen zu einer Grammatik der frühaltbabylonisch-sumerischen Königsinschriften, BiOr 27, 1970, 160-167.

H. Sauren, Untersuchungen zur Schrift- und Lautlehre der neusumerischen Urkunden aus Nippur, ZA 59, 1969, 11-64.

——, Zur poetischen Struktur der sumerischen Literatur, UF 3, 1971, 327-334.

——, Beispiele sumerischer Poesie, JEOL 22, 1971-'72, 255-306 (on Sumerian metrics).

V. Scheil, Quelques particularités du sumérien en Élam, RA 22, 1925, 45-53.

N. Schneider, Das Verbalafformativ e š (é š) in den Ur III-Urkunden, Or 12, 1943, 85-90.

——, Einige bemerkenswerte Schreibvarianten von Ortsnamen in den Ur III-Urkunden, Muséon 62, 1949, 1-10.

A. Shaffer, ta ša kīma a ītenerrubu: a study in native Babylonian philology, Or 38, 1969, 433-446.

P. Siro, Über die Symmetrie des sumerischen Satzes, StOr 16/4, Helsinki, 1951.

W. von Soden, Das akkadische t-Perfekt in Haupt- und Nebensätzen und sumerische Verbalformen mit den Präfixen b a - , i m m a - und u - , AS 16, Chicago, 1965, 103-110.

C. Wilcke, Das modale Adverb i - g i₄ - i n - z u im Sumerischen, JNES 27, 1968, 229-242.

M. Witzel, Zum sumerischen Strophenbau, Or 2, 1933, 224-231.

M. Yoshikawa, On the grammatical function of the Sumerian verbal suffix - e - d è / - e - d a (m) , JNES 27, 1968, 251-261.

——, The *marû ḫamṭu* aspects in the Sumerian system, Or 37, 1968, 401-417.

On lexicography of Sumerian see further:

B. Alster, Sum. nam-en, nam-lagar, JCS 23, 1970, 116-117.

M. Th. Barrelet, Le problème du nom sumérien du potier, RA 58, 1964, 1-8.

R. D. Biggs, ašgi (*ašširgi) in Pre-Sargonic texts, JCS 24, 1971, 1-2.

M. Civil, La lecture de muš croisé, JCS 15, 1961, 125-126.

——, Bloc-notes, RA 60, 1966, 92.

——, Notes on Sumerian lexicography I, JCS 20, 1966, 119-124.

——, Notes lexicographiques sur suhur/ka, RA 61, 1967, 63-68.

——, Notes brèves 13, RA 63, 1969, 179-180.

V. Christian, Sumerische Miszellen, AfO 19, 1959-'60, 128-131; AfO 20, 1963, 149-152.

J. van Dijk, è š - g a l oder i r i₁₀-₁₁ - g a l ? , AfO 20, 1963, 162-163.

A. Falkenstein, s ù - u d - á g a , ZA 52, 1957, 304-307.

——, Sumerische Bauausdrücke, Or 35, 1966, 229-246.

——, Zum sumerischen Lexikon, ZA 58, 1967, 5-15.

T. Fish; M. Lambert, "Vérification" dans la bureaucratie sumérienne, RA 57, 1963, 93-97.

A. Goetze, The meaning of Sumerian k i s l a ḫ and its Akkadian equivalents, AJSL 52, 1935-'36, 143-159.

W. W. Hallo, Early Mesopotamian royal titles: a philologic and historical analysis, AOS 43, New Haven, 1957.

E. Huber, Die Personennamen in den Keilschrifturkunden aus der Zeit der Könige von Ur und "Nisin", AB 21, Leipzig, 1907.

Th. Jacobsen, Some Sumerian city-names, JCS 21, 1969, 100-103.

A. D. Kilmer, Notes brèves, RA 61, 1967, 190.

V. Kinnier Wilson, Notes brèves, RA 61, 1967, 189-190.

J. KLEIN, Sum. GA-RAŠ = Akk. *PURUSSÛ*, JCS 23, 1971, 118-122.

F. R. KRAUS, Die sumerische Entsprechung der Phrase *ana ittišu*, SD 2, Leyden 1939, 50-60.

J. KRECHER, Die pluralischen Verba für "gehen" und "stehen" im Sumerischen, WO 4, 1967, 1-11.

——, Glossen. A. In sumerischen und akkadischen Texten, RlA 3, Berlin, 1969, 431-440.

M. LAMBERT, Le signe b u r 5 et sa signification "moineau", RA 48, 1954, 29-32.

——, La lecture de PA-TE-si, RA 50, 1956, 140 (see also M. LAMBERT, RA 49, 1955, 160).

——, Les noms du père en Sumérien, Proc. of the 22nd Congr. of Orientalists held in Istanbul, Vol. 2, Leyden, 1957, 27-29.

——, Deux termes techniques de l'économie sumérienne: LAL-Lí "récession", DIRIG "expansion", RA 56, 1962, 39-44.

——, Les deux noms personnels: m a - a n - s u m et m a - a n - s u m - n a , RA 57, 1963, 203-204.

——, Notes brèves, RA 62, 1968, 96.

B. LANDSBERGER, Einige unerkannt gebliebene oder verkannte Nomina des Akkadischen 4. *anzû*, (mythischer) Riesenvogel (Adler), WZKM 57, 1961, 1-23.

——, Über Farben im Sumerisch-akkadischen, JCS 21, 1969, 139-173.

P. LEANDER, Über die sumerischen Lehnwörter im Assyrischen, Uppsala, 1903.

H. LIMET, "zabar-dib", RA 47, 1953, 175-180.

——, Le travail du métal au pays de Sumer au temps de la IIIe dynastie d'Ur, Paris, 1960.

——, L'anthroponymie sumérienne dans les documents de la 3e dynastie d'Ur, Paris, 1968 (s. G. PETTINATO, OrAnt 10, 1971, 1-19).

L. MATOUŠ, Zu den Ausdrücken für „Zugaben" in den vorsargonischen Grundstückkaufurkunden, ArOr 22, 1954, 434-443.

A. POEBEL, Die sumerischen Personennamen zur Zeit der Dynastie von Larsam und der ersten Dynastie von Babylon, Breslau, 1910.

——, *Murnisqu* and *nisqu* in cylinder A of Gudea, AS 14, Chicago, 1947, 43-87.

I. M. PRICE, The great cylinder inscriptions A and B of Gudea, 2, transliteration, translation, notes, full vocabulary and sign-lists, AB 26, Leipzig, 1927.

A. SALONEN, E 2 - k u 6 - n u - k u 2, "Das Haus, das Fische nicht frisst", StOr 19/2, Helsinki, 1953.

——, še+suḫur, Polydactylos tetradaktylus, AfO 23, 1970, 51 and other lexicographical studies by the same author: bibliography of Akkadian A3.

M. J. Seux, Épithètes royales akkadiennes et sumériennes, Paris, 1967.

Å. Sjöberg, g i r i$_x$ (= ka) - z a l , ZA 55, 1963, 1-10.

——, Beiträge zum sumerischen Wörterbuch, AS 16, Chicago, 1965, 63-70; Or 39, 1970, 75-98.

——, Bloc-notes, RA 60, 1966, 91-92.

——, Zu einigen Verwandtschaftsbezeichnungen im Sumerischen, HSAO, Wiesbaden, 1967, 201-231 (vgl. D. O. Edzard, Genava n.s. 8, Geneva, 1960, 253-258; M. Lambert, Proc. 22nd Congr. of Orient. 2, Leyden, 1957, 27-29).

——, Contributions to the Sumerian lexicon, JCS 21, 1969, 275-278.

E. Sollberger, ki.en.gi= Šumer, RA 45, 1951, 114-115.

——, Bloc-notes, RA 60, 1966, 90.

F. J. Stephens, Sumerian ka.tab, JCS 13, 1959, 12-14.

K. Tallqvist, Sumerisch-akkadische Namen der Totenwelt, StOr 5/4, Helsingfors, 1934.

C. Wilcke, k u - l i , ZA 59, 1969, 65-99.

Further lexicographical material can be found by means of reading the cuneiform sources (s. below B1) and consulting the numerous books and articles on Sumerian texts, esp. by A. Falkenstein and his pupils (s. below B3 and the book by W. Heimpel quoted above). See further I. Abusch; J. Durham; S. Lieberman, Lexical index to Jacobsen's writings in: Th. Jacobsen, Toward the image of Tammuz, Cambridge, Mass., 1970, 475-482.

For the Sumerian syllabary and signs see bibl. of Akkadian and :

R. Borger, Akkadische Zeichenliste, AOATS 6, Kevelaer; Neukirchen-Vluyn, 1971.

A. Goetze, JCS 23, 1970, 55-56.

Y. Rosengarten, Répertoire commenté des signes présargoniques sumériens de Lagaš, Paris, 1967.

V. Scheil, Recueil de signes archaïques de l'écriture cunéiforme, Paris, 1898.

E. Sollberger, Le syllabaire présargonique de Lagaš, ZA 54, 1961, 1-50 (s. also J. Bauer, Notes brèves 9, RA 64, 1970, 188-189).

and shortly the book prepared by M. Civil, Sumerian graphemics.

For the comparison of Sumerian with other languages see the studies quoted by E. SOLLBERGER, SV 10-11; further:

I. BOBULA, Sumerian Affiliations: a plea for reconsideration, Washington, 1951.
M. VON TSERETHELI, Das Sumerische und das Georgische, Bedi Karthlisa 32-33, Paris, 1959, 77-104.

B. LITERATURE, etc.

1. TEXT EDITIONS

(The texts are often treated in the same book or article; cf. B3). For archaic Sumerian texts see, apart from the book by G. BUCCELLATI; R. D. BIGGS, AS 17 (s. B3): W. J. Ph. RÖMER, JAOS 87, 1967, 643[97] (s. also J. BOTTÉRO, UVB 22, Berlin, 1966, 45-68; H. J. NISSEN, UVB 23, 1967, 37-39; 24, 1968, 39-42).

R. D. BIGGS, JCS 20, 1966, 73-88 (s. B3).
E. BURROWS, Archaic Texts, UET 2, London, 1935.
A. DEIMEL, Schultexte aus Fara, in Umschrift herausgegeben und bearbeitet, WVDOG 43, Leipzig, 1923.
——, Wirtschaftstexte aus Fara, in Umschrift herausgegeben und bearbeitet, WVDOG 45, Leipzig, 1924.
J. VAN DIJK, UVB 16, Berlin, 1960, 57-59; 18 (1962), 39 (s. below).
A. FALKENSTEIN, Archaische Texte aus Uruk, ADFU 2, Berlin, 1936.
A. GOETZE, JCS 23, 1970, 39-56 (s. B3).
R. JESTIN, Tablettes sumériennes de Šuruppak conservées au Musée de Stamboul, Paris, 1937.
——, Nouvelles tablettes sumériennes de Šuruppak au Musée d'Istanbul, Paris, 1957.
S. LANGDON, Pictographic inscriptions from Jemdet Nasr OEC 7, London, 1928.
E. SOLLBERGER, Notes on the early inscriptions from Ur and el-'Obēd, Iraq 22, 1960, 69-89 (bibliography).
See for further archaic texts and records W. H. Ph. RÖMER, JAOS 87, 1967, 643[97]; R. BORGER, HKL 1, 11; 12; 14; 40; 92; 115; 117; 118; 143; 170; 203; 224; 232; 247; 268; 280; 281; 303; 306; 307; 318; 327; 373; 379; 400; 433; 437; 441; 456; 461; 466; 499; 501; 502; 562; 565; 567; 604; 606.

For Old Sumerian texts and Sargonic Sumerian texts:

E. Sollberger, Corpus des inscriptions "royales" présargoniques de
Lagaš, Geneva, 1956 (with bibliography).

J. Bauer, Altsumerische Wirtschaftstexte aus Lagasch, Würzburg,
1967, 25-26 (with bibliography).

Further (apart from G. Buccellati; R. D. Biggs, AS 17, s. B3):

D. O. Edzard; F. Basmachi, Statue of a son of Enannatum I in the
Iraq Museum, Sumer 14, 1958, 109-113.

T. Fisch, Miscellaneous texts, MCS 4, 1954, 12.

I. J. Gelb, Sargonic texts in the Louvre Museum, MAD 4, Chicago
1970, nr. 14-15; 17-170.

M. Lambert, Deux étiquettes de panier, RA 63, 1969, 97-100.

K. Oberhuber, Sumerische und akkadische Keilschriftdenkmäler des
archäologischen Museums zu Florenz, Innsbruck, 1960, Nr. 1;
2; 3.

A. Pohl, Vorsargonische und sargonische Wirtschaftstexte TMH 5,
Leipzig, 1935.

A. P. Riftin, Die altsumerischen Wirtschaftstexte, Publications de
la Société Égyptologique à l'Université de l'État de Leningrad 1,
Leningrad, 1929, 13 ff. (s. R. Borger, HKL 1, 427).

E. Sollberger, Royal inscriptions, part II, UET 8, London, 1965,
Nr. 1-15 (s. A. Falkenstein, BiOr 23, 1966, 164-168; G. Pettinato, Or 36, 1967, 450-458; J. Krecher, ZA 60, 1970, 195-199).

——, Pre-Sargonic and Sargonic economic texts, Cuneiform texts
from Babylonian tablets in the British Museum 50, London 1972.

See for further Old Sumerian and Sargonic Sumerian records and other
texts R. Borger, HKL 1, 74; 81; 127; 149; 193; 275; 301; 401;
451; 496.

For Neo-Sumerian texts cf. the bibliographies:

A. L. Oppenheim, Catalogue of the cuneiform tablets of the Wilber-
force Eames Babylonian collection in the New York Public
Library. Tablets of the time of the Third Dynasty of Ur, AOS 32,
New Haven, 1948, 215-225.

T. B. Jones; J. W. Snyder, Sumerian economic texts from the Third
Ur Dynasty. A catalogue and discussion of documents from
various collections, Minneapolis, 1961, 347-352.

W. W. Hallo, HUCA 33, 1962, 23-43 (about royal inscriptions of
the Ur III period) (s. also M. Lambert, RA 64, 1970, 70-71; 91).

See further:

A. AMIAUD *apud* E. DE SARZEC, Découvertes en Chaldée, partie épi-
   graphique, Paris, 1884-1912, Pl. IV-XXVIII; LVIII-LX.
G. BUCCELLATI, The Amorites of the Ur III period, Naples 1966,
   Pl. I-XIV.
M. ÇIĞ; H. KIZILYAY, Neusumerische Rechts- und Verwaltungs-
   urkunden aus Nippur 1, Ankara, 1965 (s. D. O. EDZARD, BiOr 25,
   1968, 354-356).
V. A. CRAWFORD, Texts and fragments 16, JCS 8, 1954, 46.
J. VAN DIJK, The archives of Nūršamaš and other loans, TIM 3,
   Wiesbaden, 1966, Nr. 145-151 (s. F. RESCHID, HSAO 1967, 126-
   129).
——, Old Babylonian contracts and related material, TIM 5, Wies-
   baden, 1968 (s. preface).
D. O. EDZARD, Texts and fragments 43; 45; 47; 48, JCS 16, 1962, 78-81.
A. FALKENSTEIN, Die neusumerischen Gerichtsurkunden 3, Munich,
   1957, Tf. 1-21.
T. FISCH, Unpublished Lagash texts, MCS 5, 1955, 27-32.
——, A copy of the Umma tablet BM 106055, and copies of other
   tablets relating to its subject-matter, MCS 8, 1959, 84-98.
H. DE GENOUILLAC, Tablettes d'Ur, Hilprecht anniversary volume,
   Leipzig, 1909, 137-141.
A. GOETZE, Texts and fragments 34, JCS 11, 1957, 71; 61, JCS 22,
   1968, 51-52.
W. W. HALLO, Account texts bearing on the livestock industry under
   the Third Dynasty of Ur; archival texts of various kinds chiefly
   from the Ur III period, TLB 3, Leyden, 1963.
S. T. KANG, Sumerian economic texts from the Drehem archive,
   SACTI 1, Urbana, 1971.
C. E. KEISER, Neo-Sumerian account texts from Drehem, BIN 3,
   New Haven, 1971.
K. OBERHUBER, Innsbrucker Keilschrifttexte, Innsbruck, 1956, Nr. 1.
——, Sumerische und akkadische Keilschriftdenkmäler des Archä-
   ologischen Museums zu Florenz, Innsbruck, 1958-60, Nr. 4-105;
   108-127.
F. RESCHID, Administrative texts from the Ur III dynasty, TIM 6,
   Baghdad, 1971.
E. VON SCHULER, Texts and fragments 35, JCS 13, 1959, 104.
S. SIMMONS, Texts and fragments 49, JCS 17, 1963, 32.
E. SOLLBERGER, UET 8, London, 1965, 19 ff.

F. Thureau-Dangin, Tablettes et inscriptions diverses provenant
des nouvelles fouilles de Tello, *apud* C. Cros, Nouvelles fouilles
de Tello, Paris, 1910 (1911), 183-185.

——, Les cylindres de Goudéa, TCL 8, Paris, 1925 (for a bibliography
of Gudeainscriptions s. W. H. Ph. Römer, BiOr 26, 1969, 157-
169; A. Falkenstein, RlA 3/9, 1971, 676-679).

See for further Ur III records R. Borger, HKL 1, 23; 33; 46; 51(?);
60; 69; 70 f.; 72 f.; 92; 111; 125; 126; 129; 132; 146; 153; 158;
160; 172; 191; 199; 214; 215; 252 f.; 265; 300 f.; 315; 316;
322(?); 369; 372; 386; 395; 401; 411; 417; 419; 439; 440; 450;
451; 452; 459; 463; 469(!); 470; 496; 499; 504; 518; 524; 561;
576; 578; 601; 619; 641.

For a bibliography of the Sumerian royal inscriptions of the early
Old Babylonian period:

W. W. Hallo, BiOr 18, 1961, 4-14.
I. Kärki, StOr 35, Helsinki, 1967, 326-337 (s. further W. H. Ph. Römer, BiOr 27, 1970, 167; C. B. F. Walker, A new inscription
of Sîn-kāšid, AfO 23, 1970, 88-89; also B. Kienast, JCS 19,
1965, 41, 60; A. Falkenstein, UVB 22, 1966, 29-30; S. Levy;
P. Artzi, ᶜAtiqôt, Engl. ser. 4, 1965, nr. 85; D. I. Owen; G. D.
Young, JCS 23, 1970, 72-73, nr. 5).

For further Old Bal. Sum. texts cf.:

V. E. Crawford, Sumerian economic texts from the first dynasty
of Isin, BIN 9, New Haven, 1954.
T. Fisch, kuš texts of the Isin period, MCS 5, 1955, 115-124.
From the Sumerian records from the Old Babylonian period we further
only mention the book of G. G. R. Hunter, Sumerian contracts from
Nippur, OEC 8, Oxford, 1930.

Literary etc. texts in (early) Old Babylonian Sumerian and from later
times (treatments of the text partially in the same volumes!):

G. A. Barton, Miscellaneous Babylonian Inscriptions, New Haven,
1918.
E. Chiera, Lists of personal names from the temple school of Nippur,
UM 11/1 (Philadelphia, 1916); 11/3 (1919).
——, Sumerian religious texts, Upland, Pa., 1924 (s. S. N. Kramer,
ZA 52, 1957, 76-90 for collations).

——, Sumerian lexical texts from the temple school of Nippur, OIP 11, Chicago, 1929 (s. R. BORGER, HKL 1, 48; this volume also contains some literary texts).

——, Sumerian epics and myths, OIP 15, Chicago, 1934.

——, Sumerian texts of varied contents, OIP 16, Chicago, 1934.

M. ÇIĞ; H. KIZILYAY; S. N. KRAMER, New Sumerian literary fragments, TAD 8/2, Ankara, 1959, 3-4 + 12 pl.

——; ——; ——, Istanbul Arkeoloji Müzelerinde Bulunan Sumer Edebî Tablet ve Parçaları-I, TTKY 6/13, Ankara, 1969 (s. S. N. KRAMER, RA 64, 1970, 95-96; 95[1]; W. W. HALLO, JCS 24, 1971, 38-40; M. CIVIL, Or 41, 1972, 83-90).

A. T. CLAY, Epics, myths, omens, and other texts, BRM 4, New Haven, 1923, Nr. 8; 9; 10; 11; 17; 43; 44; 45; 46; 53.

J. VAN DIJK, Textes divers du musée de Baghdad I, Sumer 11, 1955, 110 + Pl. I-XVI; II, Sumer 13, 1957, 65-133; III, Sumer 15, 1959, 5-14 + Pl. 1-15.

——, Textes divers, TLB 2, Leyden, 1957.

——, Nicht-kanonische Beschwörungen und sonstige literarische Texte, VS 17 (NF 1), Berlin, 1971.

G. DOSSIN, Autres textes sumériens et accadiens, MDP 18, Paris, 1927.

E. EBELING, Keilschrifttexte aus Assur religiösen Inhalts, 1, WVDOG 28, Leipzig, (1915-)1919; 2, WVDOG 34, (1920-)1923, Nr. 4; 8; 9; 12; 13; 14; 15/16; 17; 18; 24; 40; 41; 54; 73; 95; 97; 99; 100; 101; 111; 113; 128/129; 131; 161; 251; 296; 297 b; 305; 308; 309; 333; 337 b; 346; 359; 363; 370; 375.

——; F. KÖCHER, Literarische Keilschrifttexte aus Assur, Berlin, 1953, Nr. 9; 21; 22; 23; 33; 34; 65; 76.

D. O. EDZARD, Texts and fragments 44; 46, JCS 16, 1962, 78-81.

A. FALKENSTEIN, Literarische Keilschrifttexte aus Uruk, Berlin 1931.

H. H. FIGULLA, Cuneiform texts from Babylonian tablets (, etc.) in the British Museum 42, London, 1959 (s. A. FALKENSTEIN, OLZ 1961, 368-374; Å. SJÖBERG, Or 33, 1964, 108-111 and for collations S. N. KRAMER, JCS 18, 1964, 35-48; JCS 23, 1970, 10-16).

C. FRANK, Strassburger Keilschrifttexte in Sumerischer und babylonischer Sprache, Berlin-Leipzig, 1928, Nr. 1; 2; 3; 4; 21; 43.

C. J. GADD, Cuneiform texts from Babylonian tablets (, etc.) in the British Museum 36, London, 1921, Pl. 26-50 (to Pl. 47-50 s. now S. N. KRAMER, RA 65, 1971, 181-183).

——; L. LEGRAIN, Royal Inscriptions, UET 1, London, 1928.

——, Fragments of Assyrian scholastic literature, BSOAS 20, 1957, 255-265.

——; S. N. KRAMER, Literary and religious texts 1, UET 6/1, London, 1963 (s. A. FALKENSTEIN, BiOr 22, 1965, 279-283; W. W. HALLO, JCS 20, 1966, 89-93; J. KRECHER, ZA 58, 1967, 315-320); 2, UET 6/2, London, 1966 (s. S. N. KRAMER, Iraq 25, 1963, 171-176; Å. SJÖBERG, Or 37, 1968, 232-241; D. O. EDZARD, AfO 23, 1970, 91-95; J. KRECHER, ZA 60, 1970, 199-205).

H. DE GENOUILLAC, Premières recherches archéologiques à Kich 1, Paris, 1924; 2, 1925.

——, Textes religieux sumériens du Louvre 1, TCL 15, Paris, 1930; 2, TCL 16, 1930 (s. S. N. KRAMER, JAOS 54, 1934, 407-420 for collations).

A. GOETZE, Texts and fragments 9-10, JCS 4, 1950, 137-139; 24-30, JCS 8, 1954, 144-148, Nr. 29.

——, Early Dynastic dedication inscriptions from Nippur, JCS 23 1970, 39-56.

H. G. GÜTERBOCK, Keilschrifttexte aus Boghazköi 14, Vermischte Texte, WVDOG 79, Berlin, 1963, Nr. 51.

O. R. GURNEY, Sumer 9, 1953, 25 nr. 29 + Pl.

—; P. HULIN, The Sultantepe tablets 2, London, 1964, Nr. 150-219; 230; 373; 395; 398; 399 (s. M. CIVIL, JNES 26, 1968, 200-211).

P. HAUPT, Akkadische und sumerische Keilschrifttexte nach den Originalen im Britischen Museum copirt und mit einleitenden Zusammenstellungen sowie erklärenden Anmerkungen herausgegeben, AB 1, Leipzig, (1881-)1882.

Th. JACOBSEN, Texts and fragments 17-23, JCS 8, 1954, 82-86.

L. W. KING, Cuneiform texts from Babylonian tablets (, etc.) in the British Museum 15, London, 1902, Pl. 7-30 (s. S. N. KRAMER, RA 65, 1971, 23-26 for collations).

S. N. KRAMER, Sumerian literary texts from Nippur in the Museum of the Ancient Orient at Istanbul, AASOR 23, New Haven, 1944 (s. A. FALKENSTEIN, ZA 49, 1950, 324-328; Th. JACOBSEN, BASOR 102, 1946, 12-17).

——, Bulletin University Museum 16/2, Philadelphia, 1951, 21-39; 17/2, 1952, 5-42.

——; M. ÇIĞ; H. KIZILYAY, Five new Sumerian literary texts, Belleten 16, 1952, 355-365 + Pl. LIX-LXXIV (mostly repeated in ISET 1).

——; M. ÇIĞ; H. KIZILYAY, Selected Sumerian literary texts, Or 22, 1953, 190-193 + Pl. XXIX-LVI (partly repeated in ISET 1).

——, From the tablets of Sumer. Twenty-five firsts in man's recorded history, Indian Hills, 1956, *passim*.

——; I. BERNHARDT, Sumerische literarische Texte aus Nippur 1, Mythen, Epen, Weisheitsliteratur und andere Literaturgattungen, TMHNF 3, Berlin, 1961 (s. A. FALKENSTEIN, OLZ 1962, 366-373; Å. SJÖBERG, BiOr 20, 1963, 44-47); 2, Hymnen, Klagelieder, Weisheitstexte und andere Literaturgattungen, TMHNF 4, Berlin, 1967 (s. Å. SJÖBERG, Or 38, 1969, 354-355).

S. LANGDON, Babylonian liturgies, Paris, 1913.

——, Historical and religious texts from the temple library of Nippur, BE 31, Munich, 1914 (s. S. N. KRAMER, JAOS 60, 1940, 234-257 for collations).

——, Sumerian liturgical texts, UM 10/2, Philadelphia, 1917 (s. for collations E. CHIERA, AJSL 36, 1919-'20, 233-244).

——, Sumerian grammatical texts, UM 12/1, Philadelphia, 1917.

——, Sumerian liturgies and psalms, UM 10/4, Philadelphia, 1919.

——, Le poème sumérien du paradis, du déluge, et de la chute de l'homme, Paris; London, 1919 (s. also S. LANGDON, UM 10/1, Philadelphia, 1915).

——, Sumerian and Semitic religious and historical texts, OEC 1, Oxford, 1923.

——, Babylonian penitential psalms, to which are added fragments of the Epic of Creation from Kish in the Weld Collection of the Ashmolean Museum excavated by the Oxford-Field Museum expedition, OEC 6, Paris, 1927.

L. LEGRAIN, Historical fragments, UM 13, Philadelphia, 1922.

——, Royal inscriptions and fragments from Nippur and Babylon, UM 15, Philadelphia, 1926.

H. F. LUTZ, Selected Sumerian and Babylonian texts, UM 1/2, Philadelphia, 1919.

K. D. MACMILLAN, Some cuneiform tablets bearing on the religion of Babylonia and Assyria, BA 5/5, Leipzig, 1906, 531-712.

Th. J. MEEK, Cuneiform bilingual hymns, prayers, and penitential psalms, BA 10/1, Leipzig, 1913 (s. F. DELITZSCH, BA 10/1, 129-146).

——, Some Babylonian religious texts, AJSL 35, 1918-'19, 134-144.

P. E. VAN DER MEER, Textes scolaires de Suse, MDP 27, Paris, 1935.

D. W. MYHRMAN, Babylonian hymns and prayers, UM 1/1, Philadelphia, 1911.

J. B. NIES; C. E. KEISER, Historical, religious, and economic texts

and antiquities, BIN 2, New Haven; London; Oxford, 1920, Nr. 1;
3; 4; 5; 6; 7; 8; 9; 10; 11; 12; 14; 16; 17; 22; 23; 24; 25; 26; 30.

J. NOUGAYROL, Textes suméro-accadiens des Archives privées d'Ugarit,
Ugaritica 5, Paris, 1968, 1-446, Nr. 15; 17; 164; 165; 169.

Th. G. PINCHES, The cuneiform inscriptions of Western Asia IV²:
a selection from the miscellaneous inscriptions of Assyria, prepared ... by ... Sir H. C. RAWLINSON, London, 1891.

——, Cuneiform texts from Babylonian tablets (, etc.) in the British
Museum 44, London, 1963, Nr. 10-19; 24-34 (s. M. CIVIL, JNES 28,
1969, 70-72; RA 63, 1969, 179).

A. POEBEL, Historical and grammatical texts, UM 5, Philadelphia,
1914.

H. RADAU, Miscellaneous Sumerian texts, Hilprecht anniversary
volume, Leipzig, 1909, 374-457 + Pl. 1-30; I-XV.

——, Sumerian hymns and prayers to god Nin-ib from the temple
library of Nippur, BE 29/1, Philadelphia, 1911.

——, Sumerian hymns and prayers to god Dumuzi, or: Babylonian
lenten songs, from the temple library of Nippur, BE 30/1,
Munich, 1913.

G. A. REISNER, Sumerisch-babylonische Hymnen nach Thontafeln
griechischer Zeit, Berlin, 1896.

V. SCHEIL, Mémoires de la Délégation en Perse 2, Paris, 1900 (s.
R. BORGER, HKL 1, 443).

——, MDP 4, Paris, 1902 (s. R. BORGER, HKL 1, 443-444).

——, MDP 6, Paris, 1905 (s. R. BORGER, HKL 1, 444).

——, MDP 10, Paris, 1908 (s. R. BORGER, HKL 1, 445).

——, MDP 14, Paris, 1913 (s. R. BORGER, HKL 1, 445).

——, MDP 28, Paris, 1939 (s. R. BORGER, HKL 1, 447).

E. SOLLBERGER, Selected texts from American collections, JCS 10,
1956, 27, 13 (s. p. 24).

——, Royal inscriptions II, UET 8, London, 1965 (s. above).

R. C. THOMPSON, Cuneiform texts from Babylonian tablets (, etc.) in
the British Museum 16, London, 1903; 17, London, 1903.

F. H. WEISSBACH, Babylonische Miscellen, WVDOG 4, Leipzig, 1903,
Nr. I; XI; XIII (s. R. BORGER, HKL 1, 624).

D. J. WISEMAN, The Alalakh Tablets, London, 1953, Nr. 453; 453 a.

H. ZIMMERN, Sumerische Kultlieder aus altbabylonischer Zeit 1,
VS 2, Leipzig, 1912; 2, VS 10, Leipzig, 1913.

See for further literary texts and conjurations (also bilingual), letters,
legal texts, literary catalogues, and votive texts from different periods

R. Borger, HKL 1, 12; 20; 24; 25; 36; 37; 38; 59; 60; 61; 67; 69;
   75; 77; 85; 86; 87; 92; 93; 108 f.; 111; 112; 141 ff.; 149; 153;
   155; 156; 169; 170; 172; 176; 202; 203; 215; 225; 232; 234;
   241; 242; 248; 251; 252; 255; 268; 275; 280; 281; 291; 292;
   293; 299; 301; 303; 306; 318; 330; 335; 338; 339; 346; 350;
   364; 370; 371; 382; 383; 387; 389; 396; 397; 400; 407; 414;
   433; 437; 441; 444; 447; 455; 461; 470; 483; 488; 494; 496;
   497; 498; 501 f.; 505; 506; 518; 545; 560; 563; 565; 567; 569;
   574 f.; 576; 580; 583; 600; 618; 621; 624; 629; 630; 634; 639;
   641; 648.

2. Histories of literature

Here we can only mention G. Rinaldi, Storia della letteratura dell'
antica Mesopotamia (sumerica e assiro-babilonese)², Milan, 1961.
Cf. also the articles by A. Falkenstein, RAI 2, Paris, 1951, 12-27;
MDOG 85, 1953, 1-13 and W. W. Hallo, JAOS 83, 1963, 167-176
and the book of S. N. Kramer, Sumerian Mythology², New York,
1961 (s. B3).

3. Monographs on literature etc.

(For Ur III-materials s. again Wilb 215-224; SET 347-352!) (the texts
are often published in the same book or article) (cf. also B1).

F. A. Ali, Sumerian letters: two collections from the Old Babylonian
   Schools, Philadelphia, 1964 (Univ. Microfilms Ltd., High Wy-
   combe, England, nr. 64-10, 343, xerocopy).
——, Blowing the horn for official announcement, Sumer 20, 1964,
   66-68.
——, Two collections of Sumerian letters, ArOr 33, 1965, 529-540.
——, Dedication of a dog to Nintinugga, ArOr 34, 1966, 289-293
   (cf. M. Civil, RA 63, 1969, 180).
B. Alster, Notes brèves 12; 13; 14, RA 64, 1970, 189-190; notes
   brèves 7, RA 65, 1971, 179.
——, On the Sumerian lullaby, RA 65, 1971, 170-171.
——, Who is Dumuzi's friend (ku-li)?, AcOr (K) 33, 1971, 335-346.
——, Dumuzi's dream. Aspects of oral poetry in a Sumerian myth.
   Mesopotamia 1, Copenhagen, 1972.
P. Amiet (and M. Lambert), Masse d'armes présargonique de la collec-
   tion M. Foroughi, RA 64, 1970, 9-16.

54   LANGUAGES OF THE ANCIENT NEAR EAST

J. M. AYNARD, Les clous d'argile du Musée du Louvre, RA 54, 1960, 11-18.

A. BAER, Goudéa, cylindre B, colonnes XVIII à XXIV. Essai de restauration, RA 65, 1971, 1-14.

G. A. BARTON, The royal inscriptions of Sumer and Akkad, New Haven, 1929.

J. BAUER, Altsumerische Beiträge (1-3), WO 6, 1972, 143-152.

C. A. BENITO, "Enki and Ninmah" and "Enki and the World Order", Philadelphia, 1969 (University Microfilms Ltd., High Wycombe, England, nr. 70-16, 124, xerocopy).

J. BERNHARDT; S. N. KRAMER, Sumerische literarische Texte in der Hilprecht-Sammlung, WZJ 5, Jena, 1955-'56, 753-763.

——; S. N. KRAMER, Götter-Hymnen und Kult-Gesänge der Sumerer auf zwei Keilschrift-"Katalogen" in der Hilprecht-Sammlung, WZJ 6, 1956-'57, 389-395 + 2 Pl.

——; S. N. KRAMER, Enki und die Weltordnung. Ein sumerischer Keilschrifttext über die "Lehre von der Welt" in der Hilprecht-Sammlung und im University Museum of Pennsylvania, WZJ 9, 1959-'60, 231-256 + 16 Pl. (s. A. FALKENSTEIN, ZA 56, 1964, 44-113; the book by C. A. BENITO, s. above).

R. D. BIGGS, The Abū Ṣalābīkh tablets. A preliminary survey, JCS 20, 1966, 73-88.

——, An archaic Ṣumerian version of the Kesh temple hymn from Tell Abu Ṣalābīkh, ZA 61, 1972, 193-207.

F. M. Th. DE LIAGRE BÖHL, Eine zweisprachige Weihinschrift Nebukadnezars I, BiOr 7, 1950, 42-46.

J. BÖLLENRÜCHER, Gebete und Hymnen an Nergal, LSS 1/6, Leipzig 1904, 21-50.

R. BORGER, Einige altbabylonische Königsinschriften aus Kiš, Or 27, 1958, 407-408.

——, Die erste Tafel der z i - p à - Beschwörungen (ASKT 11), AOAT 1, Kevelaer; Neukirchen-Vluyn, 1969, 1-22 (s. also R. BORGER, WO 5, 1970, 172-175).

——, Das dritte "Haus" der Serie bīt rimki, JCS 21, 1969, 1-17.

——, Zum Handerhebungsgebet an Nanna-Sin IV R 9, ZA 61, 1971, 81-83.

——, Weiteres Material zu V R 50-51 (JCS 21, S. 1-17), ZA 61, 1971, 84-88.

L. CAGNI, Tavoletta economica neo-sumerica di proprietà privata, Or 39, 1970, 496-499.

D. Calvot, Deux documents inédits de Šelluš-Dagan, RA 63, 1969, 102-114 (s. H. Limet, RA 65, 1971, 94-95).

G. Buccellati; R. D. Biggs, Cuneiform texts from Nippur. The eighth and ninth seasons, AS 17, Chicago 1969.

G. Castellino, Inno alla dea Inanna e a Išmedagan (SRT 36), RSO 32, 1957, 13-30.

——, Urnammu/Three religious texts, ZA 52, 1957, 1-57 (s. now S. N. Kramer, JCS 21, 1969, 104-122); ZA 53, 1959, 106-132.

——, Incantation to Utu, OrAnt 8, 1969, 1-57.

——, Un mattone di Kurigalzu, OrAnt 10, 1971, 175-176.

E. Chiera, Sumerian religious texts, Upland, 1924, p. 14-23: the compositions "Marriage of Martu"; p. 26-32: "Ewe and Grain".

M. Çığ; H. Kizilyay; A. Falkenstein, Neue Rechts- und Gerichtsurkunden der Ur III-Zeit aus Lagaš aus den Sammlungen der Istanbuler archäologischen Museen, ZA 53, 1959, 51-92.

M. Civil, Prescriptions médicales sumériennes, RA 54, 1960, 57-72.

——, Une nouvelle prescription médicale sumérienne, RA 55, 1961, 91-94.

——, The home of the Fish, Iraq 23, 1961, 154-175.

——, A hymn to the Beer Goddess and a drinking song, StOpp, Chicago, 1964, 67-89.

——, The "message of Lú-dingir-ra to his mother" a group of Akkado-Hittite "proverbs", JNES 23, 1964, 1-11 (s. J. Nougayrol, Ugaritica 5, Paris, 1968, 310-319; J. S. Cooper, JBL 90, 1971, 157-162).

——, New Sumerian law fragments, AS 16, Chicago, 1965, 1-12.

——, Remarks on "Sumerian and bilingual texts", JNES 26, 1968, 200-211.

——, Išme-Dagan and Enlil's chariot, JAOS 88, 1968, 3-14 (cf. M. Civil, RA 63, 1969, 179-180; M. de J. Ellis, JAOS 90, 1970, 266-269).

——, Šū-Sîn's historical inscriptions collection B, JCS 21, 1969, 24-38.

——, The Sumerian flood story, in: W. G. Lambert; A. R. Millard, Atra-ḫasīs. The Babylonian story of the Flood, Oxford, 1969, 138-145; 167-172.

——, Notes brèves 11, Sur un texte sumérien d'Ugarit, RA 63, 1969, 179.

——, Notes brèves 14, Le chien de Nintinugga, RA 63, 1969, 180.

In future the book prepared by M. Civil, Sumerian debates and dialogues, TCS 5.

J. S. Cooper, A Sumerian š u - í l - l a from Nimrud with a prayer for Sin-šar-iškun, Iraq 32, 1970, 51-67.

——, Bilinguals from Boghazköi I, ZA 61, 1971, 1-22.

Shortly ——, a new edition of A n - g i m - d í m - m a (AnOr).

J. van Dijk, La sagesse suméro-accadienne. Recherches sur les genres littéraires des textes sapientiaux, avec choix de textes, Leyden, 1953 (s. E. I. Gordon, BiOr 17, 1960, 121-152).

——, La fête du nouvel an dans un texte de Šulgi, BiOr 11, 1954, 83-88.

——, Sumerische Götterlieder 2, AHAW, Phil.-hist. Kl., 1960/1, Heidelberg, 1960.

——, Le dénouement de "Gilgames au bois de cèdres" selon LB 2116, CahTD 1, Paris, 1960, 69-81.

——, Inschriftliche Funde, UVB 16, Berlin, 1960, 57-60.

——, Die Inschriftfunde, UVB 18, Berlin, 1962, 39-61.

——, Textes divers du Musée de Bagdad III, Sumer 15, 1959, 5-14 + Pl. 1-15.

——, Textes divers du Musée de Bagdad IV. Restitution des tablettes IV et V de L u g a l - e , Sumer 18, "1962", 19-32 + Pl. 1.

——, Neusumerische Gerichtsurkunden in Bagdad, ZA 55, 1963, 70-90 (s. on IM 28051 J. van Dijk, Or 39, 1970, 99-102; S. Greengus, HUCA 40/41, 1969-'70, 33-44; Å. Sjöberg, Or 39, 1970, 92-93).

——, Le motif cosmique dans la pensée sumérienne, AcOr (K) 28, 1964, 1-59.

——, Une insurrection générale au pays de Larša avant l'avènement de Nūr-Adad, JCS 19, 1965, 1-25.

——, L'hymne à Marduk avec intercession pour le roi Abi'ešuḫ, MIO 12, 1966, 57-74.

——, VAT 8382. Ein zweisprachiges Königsritual, HSAO, Wiesbaden, 1967, 233-268.

——, "Vert comme Tišpak", Or 38, 1969, 539-547.

——, Les contacts ethniques dans la Mesopotamie et les syncrétismes de la religion sumérienne, in: Syncretism, Scripta Instituti Donneriani Aboensis 3, Stockholm, 1969, 171-206 (+ corr. et add.).

——, La "confusion des langues". Note sur le lexique et sur la morphologie d'Enmerkar, 147-155, Or 39, 1970, 302-310.

G. Dossin, L'inscription de Mesanepada, apud A. Parrot, Le trésor d'Ur, Mission archéologique de Mari 4, Paris, 1968, 53-59 (cf. E. Sollberger, RA 63, 1969, 169-170).

E. Ebeling, Sammlungen von Beschwörungsformeln, teils in sumerisch-akkadischer, teils in sumerischer oder akkadischer Sprache, ArOr 21, 1953, 357-423 (part. 361-403) (s. W. G. LAMBERT, JSS 10, 1972, 123-124).

D. O. EDZARD, Die Königsinschriften des Iraq-Museums, Sumer 13, 1957, 172-189; 15, 1959, 19-28.

——, Die "zweite Zwischenzeit" Babyloniens, Wiesbaden 1957.

——, Enmebaragesi von Kiš, ZA 53, 1959, 9-26.

——, Neue Inschriften zur Geschichte von Ur III unter Sūsuen, AfO 19, 1959-'60, 1-32.

——, Eine Inschrift Aššuretelilānis aus Nippur, AfO 19, 1959-'60, 143.

——, Eine Inschrift des Kudurmabuk von Larsa aus Nippur, AfO 20, 1963, 159-161.

——, Sumerische Rechtsurkunden des III. Jahrtausends aus der Zeit vor der III. Dynastie vor Ur, ABAW NF 67, Munich, 1968.

——, Ein umstrittener Passus bei Entemena: Ent 28 III 1, AfO 23, 1970, 31.

M. DE J. ELLIS, A note on the "chariot's crescent", JAOS 90, 1970, 266-269.

A. FALKENSTEIN, Die Haupttypen der sumerischen Beschwörung literarisch untersucht, LSS NF 1, Leipzig, 1931.

——, Archaische Texte aus Uruk, ADFU 2, Berlin; Leipzig, 1936.

——, Ein sumerischer "Gottesbrief", ZA 44, 1938, 1-25.

——, Sumerische Beschwörungen aus Boğazköy, ZA 45, 1939, 8-41.

——, Zu "Inannas Gang zur Unterwelt", AfO 14, 1941-'44, 113-138.

——, Eine Hymne auf Šūšin von Ur, WO 1, 1947, 43-50 (s. also Th. JACOBSEN, JCS 7, 1953, 46-47).

——, Der "Sohn des Tafelhauses", WO 1, 1948, 172-186 (s. also A. FALKENSTEIN, Die babylonische Schule, Saeculum 4, Freiburg i.B., 1953, 125-137).

——, Ein sumerisches Kultlied auf Samsu'iluna, ArOr 17/1, 1949, 212-226.

——, Die Ibbisîn-Klage, WO 1, 1950, 377-387 (s. also S. N. KRAMER, Iraq 25, 1963, 171-172; UET 6/2, London, 1966, p. 1; *apud* J. B. PRITCHARD, The Ancient Near East. Supplementary texts and pictures relating to the Old Testament, Princeton-New Jersey, 1969, 175-183).

——, Das Gesetzbuch Lipit-Ištars von Isin. I, Philologisches zum Gesetzbuch, Or 19, 1950, 103-111 (s. also A. FALKENSTEIN, JCS 5, 1951, 75).

——, Ibbîsîn-Išbi'erra, ZA 49, 1950, 59-79 (with remarks by M. B. ROWTON).

——, Sumerische religiöse Texte 1, ZA 49, 1950, 80-150; 2, ZA 50, 1952, 61-91; 3, ZA 52, 1957, 58-75; 4, ZA 55, 1963, 11-67; 5; 6, ZA 56, 1964, 44-129.

——, Zur Chronologie der sumerischen Literatur, RAI 2, Paris, 1951, 12-27.

——, 'Inannas Erhöhung', BiOr 9, 1952, 88-92.

——, Zu einem syllabisch geschriebenen Emesal-Text, AfO 16, 1952-'53, 60-64.

——, Zur Chronologie der sumerischen Literatur. Die nachaltbabylonische Stufe, MDOG 85, 1953, 1-13.

——, W. VON SODEN, Sumerische und akkadische Hymnen und Gebete, Die Bibliothek der alten Welt, Reihe der Alte Orient, Zürich/Stuttgart, 1953 (s. S. N. KRAMER, BiOr 11, 1954, 170-176).

——, Appendix on S. N. Kramer, Ur-Nammu law code, Or 23, 1954, 49-51.

——, publication of a Sumerian stela from the Kassite period: UVB 12/13, Berlin, 1956, 43-44.

——, Die neusumerischen Gerichtsurkunden 1-3, ABAW NF 39; 40; Munich, 1956-'57.

——, recension of M. ÇIĞ; H. KIZILYAY; A. SALONEN, PDT, OLZ 1958, 135-143.

——, Sumerische Götterlieder 1, AHAW, Phil.-Hist. Kl. 1959/1, Heidelberg, 1959.

——, Ein sumerischer Brief an den Mondgott, AnBi 12, Rome, 1959, 69-77 (s. Å. SJÖBERG, MNS 1, Stockholm, 1960, 104-107).

——, Zwei Rituale aus seleukidischer Zeit, UVB 15, Berlin, 1959, 36-44.

——, Zur Überlieferung des Epos' von Gilgameš und Ḫuwawa, JNES 19, 1960, 65-71.

——, Ein Lied auf Šulgi, Iraq 22, 1960, 139-150.

——, Ein d i t i l l a - Fragment, ZA 55, 1963, 68-69.

——, Zu den Inschriftenfunden der Grabung in Uruk-Warka, 1960-1961, BagM 2, Berlin, 1963, 1-82, part. 50-82.

——, Eine Inschrift Waradsîns aus Babylon, BagM 3, Berlin, 1964, 25-40.

——, Fluch über Akkade, ZA 57, 1965, 43-124 (vgl. VAN DIJK, OLZ 1967, 234-235).

——, Zu 'Gilgameš und Agga', AfO 21, 1966, 47-50.

——, publication of two "Tonpilze": UVB 22, Berlin, 1966, 29-30.

——, Der sumerische und der akkadische Mythos von Inannas Gang zur Unterwelt, Festschrift W. Caskel, Leyden, 1968, 96-110.

——, Gilgameš. A. Nach sumerischen Texten, RlA 3/5, Berlin, 1968, 357-363.

——, Die Inschriften Gudeas von Lagaš. I. Einleitung, AnOr 30/1, Rome, 1966 (s. W. H. Ph. RÖMER, BiOr 26, 1969, 159-171).

A. J. FERRARA, The itinerary of Nanna-Su'en's journey to Nippur, Or 41, 1972, 1-4.

J. J. FINKELSTEIN, Sex offenses in Sumerian laws, JAOS 86, 1966, 355-372.

——, The laws of Ur-Nammu, JCS 22, 1968-'69, 66-82 (cf. also M. CIVIL, RA 60, 1966, 92).

T. FISCH, Harvard 6318, MCS 1, 1951, 54-55; Harvard 7058, MCS 1, 1951, 56.

——, A Sumerian exorcism text, MCS 2, 1952, 59-60.

——, Hymn to Marduk, MCS 2, 1952, 61-62.

——, Towards a study of Lagash "mission" or "messenger" texts, MCS 4, 1954, 78-105; 5, 1955, 1-26.

——; M. LAMBERT, "Vérification" dans la bureaucratie sumérienne, RA 57, 1963, 93-97.

A. H. AL-FOUADI, Enki's journey to Nippur: the journeys of the gods, Philadelphia, 1969 (University Microfilms Ltd., High Wycombe, England, nr. 70-7772, xerocopy).

C. FRANK, Zu kalū und kurgarrū und ihren Kultgeräten, ZA 29, 1914-'15, 197-201 (cf. Th. JACOBSEN, AnBi 12, Rome, 1959, 142-143).

——, Ein Klagelied der Muttergöttin aus Uruk, ZA 40, 1931, 81-94.

——, Die Anu-Hymne AO 6494 (TU Nr. 53), ZA 41, 1933, 193-199.

——, Kultlieder aus dem Ischtar-Tamūz-Kreis, Leipzig, 1939.

C. J. GADD, A Sumerian reading-book, Oxford, 1924 (s. shortly a Sumerian reader by E. SOLLBERGER).

——, Epic of Gilgamesh, tablet XII, RA 30, 1933, 127-143.

——, En-an-e-du, Iraq 13, 1951, 27-39.

——, Teachers and students in the oldest schools, London, 1956 (s. also BSOAS 20, 1957, 255-265).

——, Rim-Sin approaches the grand entrance, Iraq 22, 1960, 157-165.

——, The second lamentation for Ur, Hebrew and Semitic studies presented to G. R. DRIVER, London, 1961, 59-71 (s. also S. N. KRAMER, Iraq 25, 1963, 171-172; UET 6/2, London, 1966, p. 1; *apud*

J. B. PRITCHARD, The Ancient Near East. Supplementary texts
and pictures relating to the Old Testament, Princeton; New Jersey,
1969, 175-183).

I. J. GELB, Growth of a herd of cattle in ten years, JCS 21, 1969,
64-69.

S. GELLER, Die sumerisch-assyrische Serie Lugal-e ud me-lam-bi
nir-gál, AOTU 1/4, Leyden, 1917 (cf. also J. V. KINNIER WILSON,
ZA 54, 1961, 71-89; J. VAN DIJK, Sumer 18, "1962", 19-32).

H. DE GENOUILLAC, Hymnologie sumérienne. Hymnes en l'honneur
des rois d'Isin, JA 1928, 125-138.

A. GOETZE, Two Ur Dynasty tablets dealing with labor, JCS 16, 1962,
13-16.

——, Šakkanakus of the Ur III empire, JCS 17, 1963, 1-31.

——, Early Dynastic dedication inscriptions from Nippur, JCS 23,
1970, 39-56.

E. I. GORDON, Sumerian proverbs. Glimpses of everyday life in Ancient
Mesopotamia, Museum monographs, Philadelphia, 1959 (s. Å. SJÖ-
BERG, AfO 20, 1963, 172-175; O. LORETZ, Eine sumerische Paral-
lele zu Ez 23, 20, BZ (NF) 14, 1970, 126).

——, Sumerian proverbs: "collection four", JAOS 77, 1957, 67-79.

——, Sumerian proverbs and fables, JCS 12, 1958, 1-21; 43-75.

——, A new look at the wisdom of Sumer and Akkad, BiOr 17, 1960,
121-152.

——, Animals as represented in the Sumerian proverbs and fables;
a preliminary study, Drevniy Mir (Struwe volume),Moscow,
1962, 226-249.

J. P. GRÉGOIRE, À propos d'un passage des Lamentations sur Ur
(ll. 331-341), RA 55, 1961, 96-100.

——, La province méridionale de l'état de Lagash, Paris, 1962.

——, Archives administratives sumériennes, Paris, 1970.

H. G. GÜTERBOCK, Die sumerische historische Literatur, ZA 42, 1934,
24-47.

——, Vocabulaires, apud E. LAROCHE, CTH, Paris, 1971, 47-53.

O. R. GURNEY; S. N. KRAMER, Two fragments of Sumerian laws,
AS 16, Chicago, 1965, 13-19.

W. W. HALLO, Contributions to Neo-Sumerian, HUCA 29, 1958,
69-107 + 27 Pl.

——, The last years of the kings of Isin, three new royal inscriptions
from Isin, JNES 18, 1959, 54-72.

——, The royal inscriptions of Ur: a typology, HUCA 33, 1962, 1-43.

——, Royal hymns and Mesopotamian unity, JCS 17, 1963, 112-118.

——, On the antiquity of Sumerian literature, JAOS 83, 1963, 167-176.

——, The coronation of Urnammu, JCS 20, 1966, 133-141.

——, New hymns to the kings of Isin, BiOr 23, 1966, 239-247.

——, Individual prayer in Sumerian: the continuity of a tradition, JAOS 88, 1968, 71-89.

——; J. VAN DIJK, The exaltation of Inanna, YNER 3, New Haven; London, 1968 (s. H. SAUREN, BiOr 27, 1970, 38-41; W. HEIMPEL, JNES 30, 1971, 232-236 and shortly W. H. Ph. RÖMER in UF 4, 1972).

——, The lame and the halt, ErIs 9, 1969, 66-70.

——, New texts from the reign of Sin-iddinam, JCS 21, 1969, 95-99.

——, The Neo-Sumerian letter-orders, BiOr 26, 1969, 171-176.

——, The cultic setting of Sumerian poetry, RAI 17, 1970, 116-134.

——, Antediluvian cities, JCS 23, 1971, 57-67.

——, The house of Ur-Meme, JNES 31, 1972, 87-95.

A. W. HANSON, Fieldplans, MCS 2, 1952, 21-26 (cf. A. W. HANSON, MCS 2, 1952, 1-3).

J. HEHN, Hymnen und Gebete an Marduk, BA 5, 1906, 332-347; 374; 380-384.

W. HEIMPEL, Tierbilder in der sumerischen Literatur, StP 2, Rome, 1968 (s. J. S. COOPER, JNES 30, 1971, 147-152).

F. HROZNÝ, Sumerisch-babylonische Mythen von dem Gotte Ninrag (Ninib), MVAG 8/5, Berlin, 1903 (s. shortly a new edition by J. S. COOPER in AnOr).

B. HRUŠKA, Das spätbabylonische Lehrgedicht "Inannas Erhöhung", ArOr 37, 1969, 473-522.

TH. JACOBSEN, New texts of the third Ur period, AJSL 55, 1938, 419-421.

——, The Sumerian king list, AS 11, Chicago, 1939 (s. also W. G. LAMBERT, Atra-ḫasīs, p. 25, with ref.; S. N. KRAMER, BUM 17/2, Philadelphia, 1952, Fig. 9; M. CIVIL, RA 63, 1969, 179; E. SOLLBERGER, JCS 8, 1954, 135-136; 21, 1969, 279-291).

Th. JACOBSEN, Parerga Sumerologica, JNES 2, 1943, 117-121.

——, Translations contributed to H. FRANKFORT, Kingship and the gods, Chicago, 1948; A. L. OPPENHEIM, The interpretation of dreams in the ancient Near East, Philadelphia, 1956).

——, The reign of Ibbī-Suen, JCS 7, 1953, 36-47 (also published in Th. JACOBSEN, Toward the image of Tammuz and other essays on Mesopotamian history and culture, Cambridge, Mass., 1970, 173-186).

——; S. N. KRAMER, The myth of Inanna and Bilulu, JNES 12, 1953, 160-188 + Pl. LXVI-LXVIII (also published in Th. JACOBSEN, Toward the image of Tammuz, Cambridge, Mass., 1970, 52-71).

——, An ancient Mesopotamian trial for homicide, AnBi 12, Rome, 1959, 130-150 (also published in Th. JACOBSEN, Toward the image of Tammuz, Cambridge, Mass., 1970, 193-214).

——, Notes on selected sayings, in: E. I. GORDON, Sumerian proverbs, Philadelphia, 1959, 447-487; on Gilgameš and Agga': AJA 53, 1949, 16-18.

Ch. F. JEAN, L'origine des choses d'après une tradition sumérienne de Nippur, RA 26, 1929, 33-38.

R. JESTIN, Textes économiques sumériens de la IIe dynastie d'Ur (transcription et traduction) avec étude grammaticale de ces textes, Paris, 1935.

——, Textes économiques de Mari (IIIe Dynastie d'Ur), RA 46, 1952, 185-202.

——, Textes religieux sumériens, RA 35, 1938, 158-173; 39, 1942-'44, 83-97; 40, 1945-'46, 49-54; 41, 1947, 55-66; 44, 1950, 45-71; 52, 1958, 193-202.

——, Sur un passage des statues de Gu-de-a, RA 64, 1970, 161-162.

A. KAPP, Ein Lied auf Enlilbāni von Isin, ZA 51, 1955, 76-87.

I. KÄRKI, Die sumerischen Königsinschriften der frühaltbabylonischen Zeit in Umschrift und Überzetzung (Textband zu StOr 35, s. above A3), Helsinki, 1968.

B. KIENAST, Eine neusumerische Gerichtsurkunde, ZA 53, 1959, 93-96.

J. M. KIENTZ; M. LAMBERT, L'élevage du gros bétail à Lagash au temps de Lugalanda et d'Urukagina, RSO 38, 1963, 93-117; 198-218.

J. V. KINNIER WILSON, Lugal ud melambi nirgal: new texts and fragments, ZA 54, 1961, 71-89.

E. E. KNUDSEN, An incantation tablet from Nimrud, Iraq 21, 1959, 54-61.

——, Two Nimrud incantations of the Utukku type, Iraq 27, 1965, 160-170.

G. KOMORÓCZY, Zum sumerischen Epos "Enmerkar und der Herr von Aratta", Acta antiqua Academiae Scientiarum Hungaricae 16/1-4, Budapest, 1968, 15-20.

——, "Fenylö Ölednik Édes Örömeben ...". A Sumer irodalom kistükre (Anthologie der sumerischen Literatur), Budapest, 1970.

——, A Tilmuni kereskedelem himnusza, Kululenyomat az antik Tanulmányok 1971. Evi XVIII/1. Számából, Budapest, 1972.

S. N. KRAMER, Inanna's descent to the Nether World, RA 34, 1937, 93-134.

——, Gilgamesh and the ḫuluppu-tree, a reconstructed Sumerian text, AS 10, Chicago, 1938.

——, Additional material to "Inanna's descent to the Nether World", RA 36, 1939, 68-80.

——, Lamentation over the destruction of Ur, AS 12, Chicago, 1940 (s. A. FALKENSTEIN, ZA 49, 1950, 320-324; SAGH sum. 38; Th. JACOBSEN, AJSL 58, 1941, 219-224).

——, Ishtar in the Nether World according to a new Sumerian text, BASOR 79, 1940, 18-27.

——, The oldest literary catalogue. A Sumerian list of literary compositions compiled about 2000 B.C., BASOR 88, 1942, 10-19.

——, The death of Gilgamesh, BASOR 94, 1944, 2-12 (s. A. FALKENSTEIN, RlA 3/5, Berlin, 1968, 363).

——, Enki and Ninḫursag, a Sumerian "paradise" myth, BASOR, Supplementary Studies 1, New Haven, 1945 (s. M. LAMBERT; R. TOURNAY, RA 43, 1949, 105-136).

——, Gilgamesh and the Land of the Living, JCS 1, 1947, 3-46 (s. A. FALKENSTEIN, JNES 19, 1960, 65-71; J. VAN DIJK, CahTD 1, Paris, 1960, 69-81).

——, Fragments of a diorite statue of Kurigalzu in the Iraq Museum, Sumer 4, 1948, 1-38 (together with S. LEVY and T. BAQIR).

——, Schooldays: a Sumerian composition relating to the education of a scribe, Museum monographs, Philadelphia, 1949 (also published in JAOS 69, 1949, 199-215).

——, A blood-plague motif in Sumerian mythology, ArOr 17/1, 1949, 399-405.

——, Gilgamesh and Agga. With comments by Th. JACOBSEN, AJA 53, 1949, 1-18 (s. Th. JACOBSEN, ZA 52, 1957, 116-118; A. FALKENSTEIN, AfO 21, 1966, 47-50).

——, "Inanna's descent to the Nether World" continued and revised. First part, JCS 4, 1950, 199-214 + Addendum by Th. JACOBSEN (p. 211); second part, JCS 5, 1951, 1-17.

——, Enmerkar and the lord of Aratta, Museum monographs, Philadelphia, 1952.

——; Th. JACOBSEN, Enmerkar and Ensukušširanna, Or 23, 1954, 232-234.

——, Ur-Nammu law code, Or 23, 1954, 40-48 (+ Appendix: notes by A. FALKENSTEIN, 49-51).

S. N. KRAMER, Forty-eight proverbs and their translation, RAI 3, Leyden, 1954, 75-83.

——, Translations of Sumerian texts in J. B. PRITCHARD, ANET², Princeton, 1955, 37-59; 159-161; 382; 455-463; 480-481; 496 and in J. B. PRITCHARD, The Ancient Near East. Supplementary texts and pictures relating to the Old Testament, Princeton; New Jersey, 1969, 137-155; 175-183.

——, From the tablets of Sumer, twenty-five firsts of man's recorded history, Indian Hills, 1956 (also published as History begins at Sumer², London, 1961).

——, Hymn to the Ekur, RSO 32, 1957, 95-102.

——, A father and his perverse son, the first example of juvenile delinquency in the recorded history of man, National Probation and Parole Association Journal 3, 1957, 169 ff.

——, Love, hate, and fear: psychological aspects of Sumerian culture, ErIs 5, 1958, 66-74.

——, Sumerian literature and the Bible, AnBi 12, Rome, 1959, 185-204.

——, A Sumerian document with microscopic cuneiform, Expedition 1/3, Philadelphia, 1959, 2-3.

——, Two elegies on a Pushkin Museum tablet. A new Sumerian literary genre, Moscow, 1960.

——, Gilgamesh: some new Sumerian data, CahTD 1, Paris, 1960, 59-68.

——, "Man and his god". A Sumerian variation on the "Job" motif, VT S 3, Leyden, 1960, 170-182.

——, Sumerian mythology², New York, 1961 (s. Th. JACOBSEN, JNES 5, 1946, 128-152; A. FALKENSTEIN, BiOr 5, 1948, 163-167).

——, Mythology of Sumer and Akkad, Mythologies of the ancient World, Garden City, 1961, 93-137.

——, New literary catalogue from Ur, RA 55, 1961, 169-176.

——, Sumerian literature, a general survey, The Bible and the Ancient Near East, essays in honor of W. F. Albright, London, 1961, 249-266.

——, The Sumerians and the world about them, Drevniy Mir (Struwe volume), Moscow, 1962, 291-299.

——, Cuneiform studies and the history of literature: the Sumerian sacred marriage texts, PAPS 107, Philadelphia, 1963, 485-525.

——, Dumuzi's annual resurrection: an important correction to Inanna's descent, BASOR 183, 1966, 31.

——, Šulgi of Ur. Royal hymn and divine blessing, JQR 75, 1967, 369-380.

S. N. Kramer, Inanna and Šulgi: a Sumerian fertility song, Iraq 31, 1969, 18-23.

——, Lamentation over the destruction of Nippur, ErIs 9, 1969, 89-93.

——, The Sacred Marriage rite. Aspects of faith, myth, and ritual in Ancient Sumer, Bloomington, 1969 (vgl. S. N. Kramer, MIO 15, 1969, 262-274; RAI 17, 1970, 135-141).

——, The death of Ur-Nammu and his descent to the Netherworld, JCS 21, 1969, 104-122.

——, Sumerian similes: panoramic view of man's oldest literary images, JAOS 89, 1969, 1-17.

——, The "Babel of tongues": a Sumerian version, JAOS 88, 1969, 108-111 (s. also S. N. Kramer, Or 39, 108-109; J. van Dijk, ibid., 302-310).

——, Notes brèves 6, RA 64, 1970, 95-96.

J. Krecher, Sumerische Kultlyrik, Wiesbaden, 1966.

——, Schreiberschulung in Ugarit: Die Tradition von Listen und sumerischen Texten, UF 1, 1969, 131-158.

R. Kutscher, a - a b - b a ḫ u - l u ḫ - ḫ a : the history of a Sumerian congregational lament (unpubl. doct. diss., Yale, 1966, s. W. W. Hallo, JAOS 88, 1968, 75[22]; RAI 17, 1970, 119[10]).

——, Apillaša, governor of Kazallu, JCS 22, 1968-'69, 63-65.

L. J. Krušina-Černý, Two Prague collections of the Sumerian tablets of the Third Dynasty of Ur, 1, ArOr 25, 1957, 547-562; 2, 27, 1959, 357-378.

S. Lackenbacher, Note sur l'ardat-lilî, RA 65, 1971, 119-154.

J. Laessøe, Studies on the Assyrian ritual and series bît rimki, Copenhagen, 1955.

M. Lambert, Le rêve de Gudéa et le cylindre BM. N° 89115, RA 41, 1947, 185-200.

——, Notes d'archéologie et d'épigraphie sumérienne, RA 42, 1948, 189-210.

——; R. Tournay, Le cylindre A de Gudéa, RB 55, 1948, 403-457; Le cylindre B de Gudéa, 520-543.

——; R. Tournay, Poésie et art sumériens, Cahiers d'Art 24/1, Paris, 1949.

——, Nouveaux documents concernant la ville d'Ur, RA 44, 1950, 73-87.

——; R. Tournay, La statue B de Gudéa, RA 45, 1951, 49-66.

——, Épigraphie présargonique I, RA 46, 1952, 57-58; II, 112-115; III, 163-164; IV, 215-216; V, RA 47, 1953, 84-86; VI, 142-144;

VII, 188-191; VIII, RA 48, 1954, 89-93; IX, 207-210; X, RA 50, 1956, 95-100; XI, 204-209; XII, RA 51, 1957, 110-113.

——; R. TOURNAY, Les statues D, G, E et H de Gudéa, RA 46, 1952, 75-85 (+ Excursus by M. LAMBERT, 86).

——, Textes commerciaux de Lagash, 1, RA 47, 1953, 57-69; 2, 105-120; 3, ArOr 23, 1955, 557-574.

——, Deux textes de Gudéa, RA 47, 1953, 83-84.

——, Sur un passage de Gudéa (Cyl. A 20, 26), RA 47, 1953, 34; (CB 18, 6 !-7 !, SB 7, 42-43), RA 48, 1954, 148-149; (CB 3, 14), RA 49, 1955, 153; (CB 17, 17 = SB 7 !, 29), 206-207.

——, Les réformes d'Urukagina, RA 50, 1956, 169-184.

——, Une énigme du roi d'Uruk, Enmerkar, RA 50, 1956, 37-39.

——, Documents pour le § 3 des "Réformes" d'Urukagina, RA 51, 1957, 139-144.

——, Une amulette au nom de Gudéa, RA 51, 1957, 147-149.

——, Sur deux textes d'Ur-Nazi, RA 53, 1959, 149-153.

——, De quelque proverbes sumériens, RA 53, 1959, 100-102.

——, Les archives de Urabba, fils de Bazig I, RA 54, 1960, 113-130; II, RA 58, 1964, 97-110.

——, La littérature sumérienne, RA 55, 1961, 177-196; RA 56, 1962, 81-90; 214.

——, L'usage de l'argent-métal à Lagash, RA 57, 1963, 79-92; 193-200.

——, Formule šu-ba-ti et "bon d'achat", RA 57, 1963, 97-98.

——, La vie économique à Umma à l'époque d'Agadé, RA 59, 1965, 61-72; 115-126.

——, Le pontife de la cité de In^{ki}, ArOr 35, 1967, 521-523.

——, Recherches sur les proverbes sumériens de la collection 1, RSO 42, 1967, 75-99; id. de la collection 2, RSO 45, 1970, 29-58.

——, Tablettes économiques de Lagash (époque de la IIIe dynastie d'Ur), copiées en 1900 au Musée Ottoman par Ch. VIROLLEAUD, Cah. de la Société asiatique 19, Paris, 1968.

——, Sur une ligne du cône d'Entemena, JCS 22, 1968, 3.

——, Deux étiquettes de panier, RA 63, 1969, 97-100.

——, Notes brèves 1, RA 64, 1970, 94.

——, Objets inscrits du Musée du Louvre, RA 64, 1970, 69-72.

——, Quatre nouveaux contracts de l'époque de Shuruppak, In memoriam E. UNGER (ed. M. LURKER), Baden-Baden, 1971, 27-49.

——, Deux textes de l'époque d'Agadé, RA 65, 1971, 167-169.

——, Notes brèves 1, RA 65, 1971, 94.

W. G. LAMBERT, Babylonian wisdom literature, Oxford, 1960, 118-120; 190; 222-275.

——, Ancestors, authors, and canonicity, JCS 11, 1957, 1-14; additions and corrections, 112.

——, An eye-stone of Esarhaddon's queen and other similar gems, RA 63, 1969, 65-71.

——, Enmeduranki and related matters, JCS 21, 1969, 126-138.

——, The reading of the name Uru.KA. gi-na, Or 39, 1970, 419.

——, Fire incantations, AfO 23, 1970, 39-45.

——, A Cassite seal with Sumerian inscription, AfO 23, 1970, 49.

——, Inscribed Pazuzu heads from Babylon, Staatliche Museen zu Berlin, Forschungen und Berichte 12, Archäologische Berichte, Berlin 1970, 41-47 + Tf. 4-5.

——, The converse tablet: a litany with musical instructions, Near Eastern Studies in Honor of W. F. ALBRIGHT, Baltimore, 1971, 335-353.

S. LANGDON, Sumerian and Babylonian psalms, Paris, 1909.

——, A bilingual tablet from Erech of the first century B.C., RA 12, 1915, 73-84.

——, Three new hymns in the cults of deified kings, PSBA 40, 1918, 30 ff.; 45 ff.; 69 ff.

——, Unidentified duplicates of part of the Sumerian liturgy e - l u m - g u d - s u n. The titular liturgy, AnOr 12, Rome 1935, 202 ff.

——, The liturgical series "From the assembly wisdom is departed", a Nabû liturgy, Gaster anniversary volume - Occident and Orient, London, 1936, 335-348 (s. now W. G. LAMBERT, The converse tablet: a litany with musical instructions, Near Eastern Studies in Honor of W. F. ALBRIGHT, Baltimore, 1971, 335-353.

E. LAROCHE, Littérature Suméro-Akkadienne, CTH, Paris, 1971, 145-148 (for Sumerian in Boğazköy).

——, Un hymne trilingue à Iškur-Adad, RA 58, 1964, 69-78.

W. F. LEEMANS, Cuneiform texts in the collection of Dr. Ugo Sissa, JCS 20, 1966, 34-47.

——, Le faux témoin, RA 64, 1970, 63-66.

C. F. LEHMANN, Šamaššumukîn, König von Babylonien, 2, AB 8/2, Leipzig, 1892, 6-9 (s. Tf. I-IV).

B. A. LEVINE; W. W. HALLO, Offerings to the temple gates at Ur, HUCA 38, 1967, 17-58.

S. LEVY; P. Artzi, Sumerian and Akkadian documents from public and private collections in Israel, ᶜAtiqôt, Engl. ser. 4, 1965.

S. J. Lieberman, An Ur III text from Drēhem recording 'booty from the land of Mardu', JCS 22, 1968-'69, 53-62.

H. Limet, Un texte lexicographique datant de la IIIᵉ dynastie d'Ur, RA 58, 1964, 37-40 (s. also R. Borger, HKL 1, 90 for a school tablet from Byblos (Ur III).

——, Tablettes inédites du Musée du Louvre, RA 62, 1968, 1-15.

——, Contribution à l'établissement du texte de l'élégie sur la destruction d'Ur, RA 63, 1969, 5-10.

——, Au début du règne de Šulgi, RA 65, 1971, 15-21.

——, Notes brèves 3, RA 65, 1971, 94-95.

J. Makkay, The Tartaria tablets, Or 37, 1968, 272-289 (cf. also H. Hirsch, AfO 22, 1968-'69, 203).

J. A. Maynard, A lamentation to Aruru, JSOR 3, 1919, 14-20.

G. Meier, Zweisprachige Weihinschrift mit Aussprache-Angabe des Sumerischen, AfO 11, 1936-'37, 364-365.

S. A. B. Mercer, Some Babylonian cones, JSOR 10, 1926, 281-286.

F. Nötscher, Ellil in Sumer and Akkad, Hannover, 1927.

J. Nougayrol, Petites inscriptions de Lagaš, RA 41, 1947, 26-29.

——, Conjuration ancienne contre Samana, ArOr 17/2, 1949, 213-226.

——, Un fragment du Code (en) sumérien, RA 46, 1952, 53-55 (with remarks by A. Falkenstein).

——, Une amulette de Syrie et un nouvel "œil", RA 64, 1970, 67-68.

——, Textes religieux (I), RA 65, 1971, 155-158.

K. Oberhuber, Eine Hymne an Nippur (UET VI 118), ArOr 35, 1967, 262-270.

H. Otten; W. von Soden, Das akkadisch-hethitische Vokabular KBo I 44 + KBo XIII 1, StBoT 7, Wiesbaden, 1968.

D. I. Owen, Ur III letter-orders from Nippur in the University Museum, Or 40, 1971, 386-400.

——, Incomplete year formulae of Iddin-Dagān again, JCS 24, 1971, 17-19.

——; G. D. Young, Cuneiform texts in the Museum of Fine Arts, Boston, JCS 23, 1971, 68-75 (+ corr., s. offprint).

——; ——, Ur III texts in the Sion Research Library, Boston, JCS 23, 1971, 95-115 (+ corr.).

A. Parrot, Taureau androcéphale au nom de Gudéa (AO 20152), RA 46, 1952, 203-204.

G. Perry, Hymnen und Gebete an Sin, LSS 2/4, Leipzig 1908, 1-12; 16-22; 33-46.

G. Pettinato, Texte zur Verwaltung der Landwirtschaft in der Ur III-Zeit, AnOr 45, Rome, 1969.

——, Unveröffentlichte Texte des Königs Sînkāšid von Uruk, OrAnt 9, 1970, 97-112.

——, Das altorientalische Menschenbild und die sumerischen und akkadischen Schöpfungsmythen, AHAW Phil.-hist. Kl. 1971/1, Heidelberg, 1971.

Th. G. Pinches, The legend of the divine lovers: Enlil and Ninlil, JRAS 1919, 185-205 (s. also Th. G. Pinches, PSBA 33, 1919, 77-93).

J. Pinckert, Hymnen und Gebete an Nebo, LSS 3/4, Leipzig, 1920, 22-27.

A. Poebel, Historical texts, UM 4/1, Philadelphia, 1914.

——, Zum Ruhmeslied der Ištar SK 199 III 8-41, ZA 35, 1923, 52-56.

——, Eine sumerische Inschrift Samsuilunas über die Erbauung der Festung Dur-Samsuiluna, AfO 9, 1933-'34, 241-292 (s. also F. Thureau-Dangin, La chronologie de la première dynastie babylonienne, Académie des Inscriptions et Belles-Lettres, Paris, 1942, 15-21).

——, Miscellaneous Studies, AS 14, Chicago, 1947.

H. Radau, Nin-ib, the determiner of fates according to the great Sumerian epic Lugal-u ŭg me-lám-bi ner-gál from the Temple Library of Nippur, BER 5/2, Philadelphia, 1910.

E. Reiner, Šurpu. A collection of Sumerian and Akkadian incantations, AfO Beih 11, Graz, 1958, 30-39; 45-49; 52-53.

——, The etiological myth of the "Seven Sages", Or 30, 1961, 1-11.

——, Thirty pieces of silver, JAOS 88, 1968, 186-190.

D. Reisman, Ninurta's journey to Eridu, JCS 24, 1971, 3-10.

F. Reschid, Verträge aus der Ur III- und der altbabylonischen Zeit, HSAO, Wiesbaden, 1967, 121-135.

W. H. Ph. Römer, Sumerische 'Königshymnen' der Isin-zeit, Leyden, 1965 (s. Å. Sjöberg, Or 35, 1966, 286-304; W. W. Hallo, BiOr 23, 1966, 239-247; G. Pettinato, ZA 60, 1970, 206-214).

——, 'Königshymnen' der Isinzeit und Königsinvestitur, ZDMG Spl. 1, Wiesbaden, 1969, 130-147.

——, Einige Beobachtungen zur Göttin Nini(n)sina auf Grund von Quellen der Ur III-Zeit und der altbabylonischen Periode, AOAT 1, Kevelaer; Neukirchen-Vluyn, 1969, 279-305.

——, Eine sumerische Hymne mit Selbstlob Inannas, Or 38, 1969, 97-114.

——, Zum heutigen Stande der Gudeaforschung, BiOr 26, 1969, 159-171).

Y. ROSENGARTEN, Le concept sumérien de consommation dans la vie économique et religieuse. Étude linguistique et sociale d'après les textes présargoniques de Lagaš, Paris, 1960.

——, Au sujet d'un théatre religieux sumérien, RHR 174, 1968, 117-160.

A. SALONEN, Georgica Sumerica, AgrM, AASF B 149, Helsinki, 1968, 202-212 (s. S. N. KRAMER, The Sumerians², Chicago, 1964, 340-342; UET 6/2, p. 3: nr. 172).

H. SAUREN, Une conjuration sumérienne et ses rapports avec le culte, Genava n.s. 16, Geneva, 1968, 109-117.

——, Wirtschaftsurkunden aus der Zeit der III. Dynastie von Ur im Besitz des Musée d'Art et d'Histoire in Genf. 1. Umschrift und Übersetzung, Indizes, Naples, 1969.

——, Zwei Arbeitstexte aus Umma, OLP 1, 1970, 39-41.

——, Zum Bürgsschaftsrecht in neusumerischer Zeit, ZA 60, 1970, 70-87.

——, Zwei Duplikate zur Ur-Klage des Musée d'Art et d'Histoire, JNES 29, 1970, 42-44.

——, Zu den Wirtschaftsurkunden des Musée d'Art et d'Histoire-II, AION 31, 2, 1971, 165-182.

V. SCHEIL, Nouveau chant sumérien en l'honneur d'Ištar et de Tamūz, RA 8, 1911, 161-171.

——, La déesse Nina et ses poissons, RA 15, 1918, 127-134.

——, Complainte à la déesse Aruru, RA 17, 1920, 45-50.

——, Conjuration du Grand Serpent, RA 23, 1926, 42-44.

N. SCHNEIDER, Die Siegellegenden der Geschäftsurkunden der Stadt Ur in Chaldäa. Siegelrecht und Siegelpraxis in Südmesopotamien im 20. Jahrhundert vor Chr., Med. Kon. Vlaamse Ac. v. Wetensch., Kl. d. Lett. 12/6, Brussels, 1950.

A. SCHOLLMEYER, Der Ištarhymnus K. 41 nebst seinen Duplikaten, MVAG 13, Berlin, 1908, 206-230.

——, Sumerisch-babylonische Hymnen und Gebete an Šamaš, Paderborn, 1912 (reprint New York, 1968).

A. SHAFFER, Sumerian sources of Tablet XII of the Epic of Gilgameš, Microfilm ... 1966 (cf. V. SCHNEIDER, Gilgamesch, Zürich, 1967, 171-186).

W. SCHRAMM, Ein Bruchstück einer zweisprachigen Beschwörung gegen Totengeister, Or 39, 1970, 405-408.

E. von Schuler, Inschrift König Šulgis, BJV 7, 1967, 293-295.

Å. Sjöberg, Der Mondgott Nanna-Suen in der sumerischen Überlieferung, 1. Teil: Texte, Stockholm, 1960.

——, Ein syllabisch geschriebener Urnammu-Text, OrS 10, 1961, 3-12.

——, Ein Selbstlob des Königs Ḫammurabi von Babylon, ZA 54, 1961, 51-70.

——, Hymns to Meslamtaea, Lugalgirra, and Nanna-Suen in honour of King Ibbīsuen (Ibbisîn) of Ur, OrS 19-20, 1970-'71, 140-178.

——; E. Bergmann †, The collection of the Sumerian temple hymns and G. B. Gragg, The Keš temple hymn, TCS 3, Locust Valley, New York, 1969 (s. C. Wilcke, JNES 31, 1972, 37-42).

E. Sollberger, Šulgi, an 41 ?, RA 44, 1950, 89-90.

——, Miscellanea Sumerica, RA 45, 1951, 105-116.

——, Un "état néant" sous la IIIᵉ dynastie d'Ur, RA 45, 1951, 116.

——, Deux pierres de seuil d'Entemena, ZA 50, 1952, 3-28.

——, Le galet B d'Ennanatumu Iᵉʳ, Or 24, 1955, 16-19.

——, Selected texts from American collections, JCS 10, 1956, 11-31.

——, Sumerica, ZA 53, 1959, 1-8.

——, La frontière de Šara, Or 28, 1959, 336-350.

——, Notes on the early inscriptions from Ur and el-'Obēd, Iraq 22, 1960, 69-89.

——, The Tummal inscription, JCS 16, 1962, 40-47.

——, Three Ur-Dynasty documents, JCS 19, 1965, 26-30.

——, The business and administrative correspondence under the kings of Ur, TCS 1, Locust Valley, N. Y., 1966 (s. G. Pettinato, OrAnt 7, 1968, 165-179; 278-288; W. W. Hallo, BiOr 26, 1969, 171-176; J. Krecher, ZA 60, 1970, 182-188; see for further Ur III letters R. Borger, HKL 1, 92; 140).

——, Two Kassite votive inscriptions, JAOS 88, 1968, 191-197.

——, The rulers of Lagaš, JCS 21, 1969, 279-291.

——, Old-Babylonian worshipper figurines, Iraq 31, 1969, 90-93.

——, La perle de Mari, RA 63, 1969, 169-170.

——, Samsu-ilūna's bilingual inscriptions C and D, RA 63, 1969, 29-43.

——, Notes brèves 16, RA 63, 1969, 180.

——; J. R. Kupper, Inscriptions royales sumériennes et akkadiennes, Paris 1971.

F. R. Steele, The code of Lipit-Ishtar, Museum monographs, Phila-

delphia, 1948 (also published in AJA 52, 1948, 425-450; s. M. SAN
NICOLÒ; A. FALKENSTEIN, Or 19, 1950, 103-117; A. FALKENSTEIN,
JCS 5, 1951, 75).

——, An additional fragment of the Lipit-Ishtar code tablet from
Nippur, ArOr 18/1-2, 1950, 489-493.

F. J. STEPHENS, Sumerian KA.TAB, JCS 13, 1959, 13-14.

É. SZLECHTER, A propos du code d'Urnammu, RA 47, 1953, 1-10.

——, Le code d'Urnammu, RA 49, 1955, 169-177.

——, Le code de Lipit-Ištar I, RA 51, 1957, 57-82; II, 177-196;
III, RA 52, 1958, 74-90.

——, Quatre textes administratifs de Lagaš, RA 59, 1965, 111-114.

——, Trois textes administratifs de l'époque d'Ur III, RA 59, 1965,
145-148.

——, Nouveaux textes législatifs sumériens (I), RA 61, 1967, 105-126;
II, RA 62, 1968, 147-160.

F. THUREAU-DANGIN, Die sumerischen und akkadischen Königsinschriften, VAB 1, Leipzig, 1907.

——, La fin de la domination Gutienne, RA 9, 1912, 111-120 (s. also
F. THUREAU-DANGIN, RA 10, 1913, 98-100).

——, L'exaltation d'Ištar, RA 11, 1914, 141-158.

——, La passion du dieu Lillu, RA 19, 1922, 175-185.

——, Une lamentation sur la dévastation du temple d'Ištar, RA 33,
1936, 103-111.

——, L'inscription bilingue B de Samsuiluna, RA 39, 1942-'44, 5-17.

R. J. TOURNAY, Inscription d'Anam, roi d'Uruk et successeur de
Gilgamesh, Near Eastern Studies in honor of W. F. ALBRIGHT,
Baltimore, 1971, 453-457.

E. UNGER, Kalksteinstatue des Gudea von Lagasch in Paris und
Istanbul, RA 51, 1957, 169-176.

A. UNGNAD, Die zweite Tafel der Serie bît mēseri, AfO 14, 1941-'44,
139-152.

H. WAETZOLDT, Zwei unveröffentlichte Ur III-Texte über die Her-
stellung von Tongefässen, WO 6, 1971, 7-41.

——, Untersuchungen zur neusumerischen Textilindustrie, Rome 1972.

C. WILCKE, Einige Erwägungen zum § 29 des Codex Lipiteštar,
WO 4, 1968, 153-162.

——, Das Lugalbandaepos, Wiesbaden, 1969.

——, Zur Geschichte der Amurriter in der Ur III-Zeit, WO 5, 1969,
1-31.

——, Eine Schicksalsentscheidung für den toten Urnammu, RAI 17, 1970, 81-92.

——, Drei Phasen des Niedergangs des Reiches von Ur III, ZA 60, 1970, 54-69 m. Nachtr.

——, Die akkadischen Glossen in TMH NF 3 Nr. 25 und eine neue Interpretation des Textes, AfO 23, 1970, 84-87.

M. WITZEL, Der Drachenkämpfer "Ninib", KSt 2, Fulda, 1920.

——, Der Gudea-Zylinder A in neuer Übersetzung mit Kommentar. Anhang: Eridu-Hymnus, KSt 3, Fulda, 1922.

——, Perlen sumerischer Poesie in Transcription und Übersetzung mit Kommentar, KSt 5, Fulda, 1925; id. Neue Folge, KSt 6, Jerusalem, 1929; id., Dritte Folge: Die grosse Ischmedagan-Liturgie, KSt 7, Jerusalem, 1930.

——, Texte zum Studium sumerischer Tempel und Kultzentren, AnOr 4, Rome, 1932.

——, Tammuz-Liturgien und Verwandtes, AnOr 10, Rome, 1935.

——, Auswahl sumerischer Dichtungen I, AnOr 15, Rome, 1938.

——, Übung 47-53, in: A. DEIMEL, ŠGr², Rome, 1939, 236-284. S. also many articles by M. WITZEL in Or.

H. ZIMMERN, Sumerisch-babylonische Tamūzlieder, BSGW 59/4, Leipzig, 1907.

——, Der babylonische Gott Tamūz, ASGW 27/20, Leipzig, 1909.

——, König Lipit-Ištar's Vergöttlichung, BSGW 68/5, Leipzig, 1916.

——, Das Nergallied Berl. VAT 603 = Philad. CBM 11344 = Lond. Sm. 526, ZA 31, 1917-'18, 111-121.

——, Ein Zyklus altsumerischer Lieder auf die Haupttempel Babyloniens, ZA 39, 1930, 245-276 (s. now Å. SJÖBERG; E. BERGMANN †; G. B. GRAGG, TCS 3, s. above).

C. SOME BOOKS AND ARTICLES ON (CULTURAL) HISTORY, RELIGION, GEOGRAPHY, AND ARCHAEOLOGY OF THE SUMERIANS

1. HISTORY

(See also bibliography of Akkadian).

J. BOTTÉRO, Le problème des Habiru, Cah. de la Société asiatique 12, Paris, 1954, 3-7; 12-18 (with comm. by A. FALKENSTEIN and A. GOETZE).

V. CHRISTIAN, Die Herkunft der Sumerer, SÖAW 236/1, Vienna, 1961.

M. CIVIL, Un Nouveau synchronisme Mari-IIIᵉ dynastie d'Ur, RA 56, 1962, 213.

——, Šū-Sîn's historical inscriptions: collection B, JCS 21, 1969, 24-38.

——, Sur le nom d'un roi de Kiš, RA 63, 1969, 179.

F. CORNELIUS, Zur sumerischen Geschichte, AfO 19, 1959-'60, 132-138.

G. DOSSIN, L'inscription de Mesanepada, in: A. PARROT, Le trésor d'Ur, Mission archéologique de Mari 4, Paris, 1968, 53-59.

D. O. EDZARD, Enmebaragesi von Kiš, ZA 53, 1959, 9-26.

——, Neue Inschriften zur Geschichte von Ur III unter Šūsuen, AfO 19, 1959-'60, 1-32.

——, Sumerer und Semiten in der frühen Geschichte Mesopotamiens, Genava n.s. 8, Geneva, 1960, 241-258.

——, Die frühdynastische Zeit, Fischer Weltgeschichte 2, Frankfurt a.M., 1965, 57-90; Das Reich der III. Dynastie von Ur und seine Nachfolgestaaten, ibid., 129-164.

A. FALKENSTEIN, La cité-temple sumérienne, CHM 1/4, Paris, 1954, 784-814.

——, Die Ur- und Frühgeschichte des Alten Vorderasien, Fischer Weltgeschichte 2, Frankfurt a.M., 1965, 13-56.

——, Zur Geschichte Gudeas und der II. Dynastie von Lagaš, AnOr 30/1, Rome, 1966, 1-54.

T. FISH, Lagash and Umma in Ur III, MCS 5, 1955, 56-58.

I. J. GELB, Sumerians and Akkadians in their ethno-linguistic relationship, Genava n.s. 8, Geneva, 1960, 258-271.

A. GOETZE, The chronology of Šulgi again, Iraq 22, 1960, 151-156.

——, Early kings of Kish, JCS 15, 1961, 105-111.

E. I. GORDON, Mesilim and Mesannepadda - are they identical?, BASOR 132, 1953, 27-30.

M. GREENBERG, The Ḫab/piru, AOS 39, New Haven, 1955, 15-17 (with comm. by A. GOETZE and S. N. KRAMER).

A. HALDAR, Woher kamen die Sumerer?, BiOr 22, 1965, 131-140 (139: comm. by G. KURTH).

H. HIRSCH, Eannatum von Lagaš und Sargon von Agade, StOpp Chicago, 1964, 136-139.

——, *Mesilim, König von Kiš, AfO 22, 1968-'69, 78-79.

Th. JACOBSEN, The Sumerian King list, AS 11, Chicago, 1939 (s. above, B3).

——, The assumed conflict between Sumerians and Semites in early Mesopotamian history, JAOS 59, 1939, 485-495 (also published

in Th. JACOBSEN, Toward the image of Tammuz and other
essays on Mesopotamian history and culture, Cambridge, Mass.,
1970, 187-192).

——, The reign of Ibbī-Suen, JCS 7, 1953, 36-47 (also published in
Th. JACOBSEN, Toward the image of Tammuz, Cambridge, Mass.,
1970, 173-186).

——, Early political development in Mesopotamia, ZA 52, 1957,
91-140 (also published in Th. JACOBSEN, Toward the image of
Tammuz, Cambridge, Mass., 1970, 132-156).

T. B. JONES, The Sumerian problem, New York; London; Sydney;
Toronto, 1969.

S. N. KRAMER, The Sumerians², History: Heroes, Kings, and Ensi's,
Chicago, 1964, 33-72.

F. R. KRAUS, Sumerer und Akkader. Ein Problem der altmesopotamischen Geschichte, MAW NR 33/8, Amsterdam; London, 1970.

M. LAMBERT, L'intronisation de Lugalanda, RA 50, 1956, 85.

——, Une histoire du conflit entre Lagaš et Umma, RA 50, 1956,
141-146.

——, L'infiltration nomade dans l'empire d'Ur III, RA 54, 1960, 44.

——, La guerre entre Lugal-zaggesi et Urukagina: ses incidences
sur l'économie de Lagash, Iraq 25, 1963, 192-193.

B. LANDSBERGER, Die Sumerer, RFLHGA 1, 1943, 97-102.

——, Die Anfänge der Zivilisation in Mesopotamien, RFLHGA 2,
1944, 431-437.

M. E. L. MALLOWAN, Early Mesopotamia and Iran, London, 1965.

A. PARROT, Mari et Ur, Iraq 22, 1960, 124-126; Le trésor d'Ur, Mission
archéologique de Mari 4, Paris, 1968, 45-52.

A. POEBEL, Der Konflikt zwischen Lagaš und Umma zur Zeit Enanna-
tums I und Entemenas, P. Haupt anniversary volume, Baltimore;
Leipzig, 1926, 220-267.

H. SAUREN, Der Feldzug Utuḫengals gegen Tirigan und das Siedlungs-
gebiet der Gutäer, RA 61, 1967, 75-79.

——, Zur Datierung Gudeas von Lagaš, ZDMG Spl. 1/1, Wiesbaden,
1969, 115-129.

N. SCHNEIDER, Die Zeitbestimmungen der Wirtschaftsurkunden von
Ur III, AnOr 13, Rome, 1936.

E. SOLLBERGER, Remarks on Ibbīsîn's reign, JCS 7, 1953, 48-50.

——, Sur la chronologie des rois d'Ur et quelques problèmes connexes,
AfO 17, 1954-'56, 10-48.

——, Byblos sous les rois d'Ur, AfO 19, 1959-'60, 120-122.

——, Notes sur Gudéa et son temps, RA 62, 1968, 137-145.

——, The rulers of Lagaš, JCS 21, 1969, 279-291.

——, Ladies of the Ur III empire, RA 61, 1967, 69-70.

E. A. SPEISER, The Sumerian problem reviewed, HUCA 23, 1950-'51, 339-355.

A. SPYCKET, La rivalité entre Umma et Lagaš à l'époque néo-sumérienne, RA 54, 1960, 153-154.

F. J. STEPHENS, Notes on some economic texts of the time of Urukagina, RA 49, 1955, 129-136.

C. WILCKE, Zur Geschichte der Amurriter in der Ur III-Zeit, WO 5, 1969, 1-31.

——, Drei Phasen des Niedergangs des Reiches von Ur III, ZDMG Spl. 1, Wiesbaden, 1969, 218-219.

2. CULTURAL HISTORY

(See also bibliography of Akkadian).

R. D. BIGGS, Le lapis-lazuli dans les textes sumériens archaïques, RA 60, 1966, 175-176.

J. B. CURTIS; W. W. HALLO, Money and merchants in Ur III, HUCA 30, 1959, 103-139.

A. DEIMEL, many studies (s. R. BORGER, HKL 1, 72 ff.).

I. M. DIAKONOV, Sale of Land in Pre-Sargonic Sumer, Papers presented by the Soviet delegation at the XXIIIth International Congress of Orientalists, assyriology, Moscow, 1954, 19-29.

——, Some remarks on the "reforms" of Urukagina, RA 52, 1958, 1-15.

——, Obščestvenniy i gosudarstvenniy stroy drewnego dvurec'ya-Šumer (Sumer: Society and state in Ancient Mesopotamia-Sumer), Moscow, 1959 (cf. M. LAMBERT, RA 59, 1965, 133-135).

J. VAN DIJK, La sagesse suméro-accadienne. Recherches sur les genres littéraires des textes sapientiaux, avec choix de textes, Leyden, 1953.

A. FALKENSTEIN, Die babylonische Schule, Saeculum 4, Freiburg i.B., 1953, 125-137.

N. W. FORDE, The Sumerian DAM-KÀR-E-NE, Microfilm, ..., 1969.

I. FUHR, Ein sumerischer Tierarzt, ArOr 34, 1966, 570-573.

C. J. GADD, Teachers and students in the oldest schools, London, 1956.

I. J. GELB, The Philadelphia onion archive, AS 16, Chicago, 1965, 57-62.

——, The Ancient Mesopotamian ration system, JNES 24, 1965, 230-243.

——, Growth of a herd of cattle in ten years, JCS 21, 1969, 64-69.

——, On the alleged temple and state economies in Ancient Mesopotamia, Studi in onore di Edoardo Volterra, vol. VI, Rome, 1969, 137-154.

E. I. GORDON, A new look at the wisdom of Sumer and Akkad, BiOr 17, 1960, 121-152.

H. HARTMANN, Die Musik der sumerischen Kultur, Frankfurt a.M., 1960.

G. HERRMANN, Lapis lazuli: the early phases of its trade, Iraq 30, 1968, 21-57.

Th. JACOBSEN, Primitive democracy in Ancient Mesopotamia, JNES 2, 1943, 159-172 (also published in Th. JACOBSEN, Toward the image of Tammuz and other essays on Mesopotamian history and culture, Cambridge, Mass., 1970, 157-170).

——, Mesopotamia, in: H. and H. A. FRANKFORT a.o., The intellectual adventure of ancient man[2], Chicago, 1948, 123-219 (s. S. N. KRAMER, JCS 2, 1948, 39-70).

——, Note sur le rôle de l'opinion publique dans l'ancienne Mésopotamie d'après un passage du poème d'Enmerkar, RA 58, 1964, 157-158.

S. N. KRAMER, The Sumerians, their history, culture, and character[4], Chicago, 1970 (s. W. H. Ph. RÖMER, JAOS 87, 1967, 637-643).

——, "Vox populi" and the Sumerian literary documents, RA 58, 1964, 149-156.

——, "Biblical parallels from Sumerian literature", Special exhibit in honor of the American-Jewish tercentenary 1654-1954, The University Museum, Philadelphia, 1954.

F. R. KRAUS, Le rôle des temples depuis la troisième dynastie d'Ur jusqu'à la première dynastie de Babylone, CHM 1/3, 1954, 518-545.

M. LAMBERT, La période présargonique, Sumer 8, 1952, 57-77; 9, 1953, 198-213; 10, 1954, 150-190.

——, À propos du bain des brebis, RA 54, 1960, 88.

——, La vie économique d'un quartier de Lagash, RA 55, 1961, 77-146.

——, Recherches sur la vie ouvrière, ArOr 29, 1961, 422-443.

——, Les finances de Lagash sous la IIIe dynastie d'Ur, RA 56, 1962, 146-152.

B. LANDSBERGER, Die geistigen Leistungen der Sumerer, RFLHGA 3, 1945, 150-158.

H. LENZEN, Die Sumerer, Berlin, 1948.

H. LIMET, La clause du double en droit néo-sumérien, Or 38, 1969, 520-532.

J. MAHONEY, A study in Sumerian administrative history of the Third Ur Dynasty, Ann Arbor, 1970 (University Microfilms Ltd., High Wycombe, England, xerocopy).

J. DE MENASCE, Sumero-Iranica, RA 51, 1957, 145-147.

G. OFFNER, Jeux corporels en Sumer, RA 56, 1962, 31-38.

W. VAN OS, Wie haben die Sumerer ihre Statuen angefertigt ?, BiOr 18, 1961, 3-4.

G. PETTINATO, Untersuchungen zur neusumerischen Landwirtschaft 1. Die Felder, 2 pts., Naples, 1967 (s. J. BAUER, WO 5, 1970, 341-346; on 1/1 s. H. LIMET, Or 38, 1969, 349-353).

——, Il binomio tempio-stato e l'economia della seconda dinastia di Lagaš, OrAnt 7, 1968, 39-50.

Y. ROSENGARTEN, Le concept sumérien de consommation dans la vie économique et religieuse. Étude linguistique et sociale d'après les textes présargoniques de Lagash, Paris, 1960.

M. SAN NICOLÒ, Das Gesetzbuch Lipit-Ištars von Isin. II Rechtsgeschichtliches zum Gesetzbuch, Or 19, 1950, 111-118.

H. SCHMÖKEL, Das Land Sumer. Die Wiederentdeckung der ersten Hochkultur der Menschheit[3], Urban-Bücher 13, Stuttgart, 1962 (s. J. VAN DIJK, BiOr 16, 1959, 141-143).

A. SCHNEIDER, Die Anfänge der Kulturwirtschaft, die sumerische Tempelstadt, Plenge, Staatswissenschaftliche Beiträge 4, Essen, 1920.

N. SCHNEIDER, Das Drehem- und Djoḫaarchiv 1-5, Rome, 1924-1930 (s. R. BORGER, HKL 1, 469).

W. VON SODEN, Zweisprachigkeit in der geistigen Kultur Babyloniens, SÖAW, 235/1, Vienna, 1960.

W. STAUDER, Die Harfen und Leiern der Sumerer, Frankfurt a.M., 1957.

W. W. STRUWE, Accounts of work-team overseers on a royal estate under the third dynasty of Ur, Papers ... (s. above sub I. M. DIAKONOFF) 43-"51".

3. RELIGION

(See also above B 3 and bibliography of Akkadian).

J. BAUER, Zum Totenkult im altsumerischen Lagasch, ZDMG Spl. 1/1, Wiesbaden, 1969, 107-114.

G. CASTELLINO, Il concetto sumerico di "me" nella sua accezione concreta, AnBi 12, Rome, 1959, 25-32.

——, Mitologia Sumerico-Accadica, Turin, 1967.

J. VAN DIJK, Gott. A. Nach sumerischen Texten, RlA 3/7, Berlin, 1969, 532-543.

——, Einige Bemerkungen zu sumerischen religionsgeschichtlichen Problemen, OLZ 1967, 229-244.

——, Le motif cosmique dans la pensée sumérienne, AcOr (K) 28, Copenhagen, 1964, 1-59.

——, Sumerisk religion, in: Illustreret Religionshistorie³, redigeret af J. P. ASMUSSEN of J. LAESSØE (G.E.C. Gads Forlag), Copenhagen, 1968, 377-435 (see now the German edition of this article in: Handbuch der Religionsgeschichte 1 (ed. by J. P. ASMUSSEN; J. LAESSØE; C. COLPE), Göttingen 1971, 431 ff.).

——, Les contacts ethniques dans la Mésopotamie et les syncrétismes de la religion sumerienne, Syncretism, Scripta Instituti Donneriani Aboensis 3, Stockholm, 1969, 171-206 (+ corr. et add.).

A. FALKENSTEIN, Tammūz, RAI 3, Leyden, 1954, 41-65.

——, Enḫedu'anna, die Tochter Sargons von Akkade, RA 52, 1958, 129-131.

——, akiti und akiti-Festhaus, Festschrift J. Friedrich zum 65. Geburtstag, Heidelberg, 1959, 147-182.

——, Gebet I. Das Gebet in der sumerischen Überlieferung, RlA 3/2, Berlin, 1959, 156-160.

——, Die Anunna in der sumerischen Überlieferung, AS 16, Chicago, 1965, 127-140.

——, Zum Pantheon des Stadtstaates von Lagaš und zur Kulttopographie, AnOr 30/1, Rome, 1966, 55-170.

——, Wahrsagung in der sumerischen Überlieferung, La divination en Mésopotamie ancienne et dans les régions voisines, Paris, 1966, 45-68.

——, Gilgameš. A. Nach sumerischen Texten, RlA 3/5, Berlin, 1968, 357-363.

T. FISH, (d)Ha-ni, MCS 1, 1951, 57.

——, d. GÌR, MCS 7, 1957, 13-14.

P. Garelli, Les conceptions religieuses sumériennes, Le Proche-Orient asiatique des origines aux invasions des peuples de la mer, Paris, 1969, 288-301.

S. Greengus, Old Babylonian marriage ceremonies and rites, JCS 20, 1966, 55-72.

O. R. Gurney, Tammuz reconsidered: some recent developments, JSS 7, 1962, 147-160.

W. W. Hallo, A Sumerian Amphiktyony, JCS 14, 1960, 88-114.

——; J. van Dijk, The exaltation of Inanna, YNER 3, New Haven; London, 1968 (s. above, B 3).

Th. Jacobsen, Sumerian mythology, a review article, JNES 5, 1946, 128-152 (also published in Th. Jacobsen, Toward the image of Tammuz, and other essays on Mesopotamian history and culture, Cambridge, Mass., 1970, 104-131).

——, Formative tendencies in Sumerian religion, The Bible and the Ancient Near East, Essays in honor of W. F. Albright, London, 1961, 267-278 (also published in Th. Jacobsen, Toward the image of Tammuz, Cambridge, Mass., 1970, 1-15).

——, Ancient Mesopotamian religion: the central concerns, PAPS 107, 1963, 473-484 (also published in Th. Jacobsen, Toward the image of Tammuz, Cambridge, Mass., 1970, 39-46).

——, Toward the image of Tammuz, in: Th. Jacobsen, Toward the image of Tammuz, Cambridge, Mass., 1970, 73-103.

——, Mesopotamian gods and pantheons, in: Th. Jacobsen, Toward the image of Tammuz, Cambridge, Mass., 1970, 16-38.

Ch. F. Jean, La religion sumérienne d'après les documents sumériens antérieurs à la dynastie d'Isin (—2186), Paris, 1931.

——, Le dieu AN à Lagaš sous Entemena, RA 44, 1950, 127-133.

R. Jestin, La religion sumérienne, in: H. Ch. Puech (ed.), Encyclopédie de la Pléiade. Histoire des religions 1, Paris, 1970, 154-202.

S. N. Kramer, Sumero-Akkadian interconnections: religious ideas, Genava n.s. 8, Geneva, 1960, 272-283.

——, Death and nether world according to the Sumerian literary texts, Iraq 22, 1960, 59-68.

——, Enki and his inferiority complex, Or 39, 1970, 103-110.

M. Lambert, La lune chez les Sumériens, in: La lune, mythes et rites, Sources Orientales 6, Paris, 1962, 71-91.

W. G. Lambert, The creation of man in Sumero-Babylonian Myth, RAI 11, 1964, 101-102.

H. Limet, L'organisation de quelques fêtes mensuelles à l'époque néo-sumérienne, RAI 17, 1970, 59-74.

K. Oberhuber, Der numinose Begriff me im Sumerischen, Innsbruck, 1963.

J. Renger, Untersuchungen zum Priestertum in der altbabylonischen Zeit, 1, ZA 58, 1967, 110-188; 2, ZA 59, 1969, 104-230.

Y. Rosengarten, Le régime des offrandes dans la société sumérienne d'après les textes présargoniques de Lagaš, Paris, 1960.

——, Trois aspects de la pensée religieuse sumérienne, Paris, 1971.

H. Sauren, Besuchsfahrten der Götter in Sumer, Or 38, 1969, 214-236.

——, Les fêtes néo-sumériennes et leur périodicité, RAI 17, 1970, 11-29.

N. Schneider, Die Götternamen von Ur III, AnOr 19, Rome, 1939 (s. A. Falkenstein, OLZ 1943, 350-355; Th. Jacobsen, Or 16, 1947, 391-398).

——, Die Religion der Sumerer und Akkader, in: F. König, Christus und die Religionen der Erde 2, Vienna, 1951, 383-439.

Å. Sjöberg, Götterreisen. A. Nach sumerischen Texten, RlA 3/6; 3/7, Berlin, 1969, 480-483.

A. Spycket, Les statues de culte dans les textes mésopotamiens des origines à la Ire dynastie de Babylone, CahRB 9, Paris, 1968 (s. H. Sauren, JSS 14, 1969, 116-119).

E. M. Yamauchi, Additional notes on Tammuz, JSS 11, 1966, 10-15.

H. Zimmern, Der babylonische Gott Tamūz, ASGW 27/20, Leipzig, 1909.

4. Geography

V. Crawford, The location of Bad-tibira, Iraq 22, 1960, 197-199.

J. van Dijk, Le site de Gutium et d'Ak-s[a? - a] kᵏⁱ, AfO 23, 71-72.

A. Falkenstein, ⁱ7dur.kib= ⁱ7naran= Nahrauān, ZA 45, 1939, 69-70.

——, Zur Lage des südbabylonischen Dūrum, AfO 21, 1966, 50-51.

——, Der Machtbereich der II. Dynastie von Lagaš und die auswärtigen Beziehungen, AnOr 30/1, Rome, 1966, 17-54.

T. Fish, List of CITY/TOWN names on Ur III tablets, MCS 6, 1956, 114-130.

——, A-pi₄-šál.ki, MCS 6, 1956, 78-84.

——, Some place names and their contexts, MCS 7, 1959, 15-24.

C. J. Gadd, Geographical history of the Mesopotamian plains, RA 48, 1954, 28-29.

I. J. GELB, Makkan and Meluḫḫa in early Mesopotamian sources, RA 64, 1970, 1-8.

J. P. GRÉGOIRE, La province méridionale de l'état de Lagash, Paris, 1962.

H. HELBAEK, Ecological effects of irrigation in Ancient Mesopotamia, Iraq 22, 1960, 186-196.

Th. JACOBSEN, La géographie et les voies de communications du pays de Sumer, RA 52, 1958, 127-129.

——, The waters of Ur, Iraq 22, 1960, 174-185 (also published in: Th. JACOBSEN, Toward the image of Tammuz and other essays on Mesopotamian history and culture, Cambridge, Mass., 1970, 231-243).

——, Some Sumerian city-names, JCS 21, 1969, 100-103.

F. R. KRAUS, Provinzen des neusumerischen Reiches von Ur, ZA 51, 1955, 45-75.

M. LAMBERT, La ville d'Urusagrig, RA 47, 1953, 11-15.

——, Le quartier Lagash, RSO 32, 1957, 123-143.

G. M. LEES; N. L. FALCON, The geographical history of the Mesopotamian plains, Geographical Journal 118, 1952, 24-39.

S. LEVY, Harmal geographical list, Sumer 3, 1947, 50-63 (with appendix by S. N. KRAMER, Nippur geographical list, 64-83).

J. RENGER, Zur Lokalisierung von Karkar, AfO 23, 1970, 73-78.

H. SAUREN, Topographie der Provinz Umma nach den Urkunden der Zeit der III. Dynastie von Ur, Heidelberg, 1966.

E. SOLLBERGER, Garaš-ana(k), AfO 18, 1957-'58, 104-108.

——, La frontière de Šara, Or 28, 1959, 336-350.

E. F. WEIDNER, Simurrum und Zaban, AfO 15, 1945-'51, 75-80.

5. ARCHAEOLOGY

(See also bibliography of Akkadian C 4).

P. AMIET, Les éléments sumériens et akkadiens du répertoire iconographique de Mésopotamie, Genava n.s. 8, Geneva, 1960, 297-300.

M. Th. BARRELET, Peut-on remettre en question la "Restitution matérielle de la Stèle des Vautours"?, JNES 29, 1970, 233-258.

R. BOEHMER, Die Entwicklung der Hörnerkrone von ihren Anfängen bis zum Ende der Akkad-Zeit, BJV 7, 1967, 273-292.

J. BOESE, Altmesopotamische Weihplatten, Unters. z. Assyriol. u. vorderas. Arch. 6, Berlin; NewYork, 1971.

E. Heinrich, Bauwerke in der altsumerischen Bildkunst, Wiesbaden, 1957.

B. Hrouda, Vorderasien 1, Mesopotamien, Babylonien, Iran und Anatolien, Handbuch der Archäologie, Munich, 1971.

A. Moortgat, Frühe Bildkunst in Sumer, MVAeG 40/3, Leipzig, 1935.

——, Die Entstehung der sumerischen Hochkultur, AO 43, Leipzig, 1945.

——, Tammuz. Der Unsterblichkeitsglaube in der altorientalischen Bildkunst, Berlin, 1949.

——, Der Bilderzyklus des Tammuz, RAI 3, Leyden, 1954, 18-41.

H. J. Nissen, Zur Datierung des Königsfriedhofes von Ur, Bonn, 1966 (cf. M. E. L. Mallowan; B. Parker, Iraq 32, 1970, 214-218).

A. Parrot, Le cycle iconographique de Tammouz, RAI 3, Leyden, 1954, 66-67.

——, Sumer³, Munich, 1970. Suppl., Munich, 1970.

D.

For periodicals and series containing studies on Sumerology cf. Bibliography of Akkadian D and above B1.

E. ABBREVIATIONS

See the list of abbreviations at the end of the present vol. 1 (mainly based on the list proposed by K. Deller, Or 37, 1968, 1*-14*) and the lists in A. Falkenstein, Analecta Orientalia 28, Rome, 1949, XI-XV; 29, 1950, IX-XVI; 30/1, 1966, XI-XVIII and in W. von Soden, Akkadisches Handwörterbuch, Lief. 1, 1959, X-XVI; 6, 1965, 567-568; 11, 1972; the front covers in Lief. 7, 1966; 8, 1967; 9, 1969; 10, 1971.

ISET = Istanbul ... Sumer Edebî Tablet ve Parçaları, Istanbul, 1970 ff.

OLP = Orientalia Lovaniensia Periodica, Louvain, 1970 ff.

RFLHGA = Revue de la Faculté de Langues, d'Histoire et de Géographie/Université d'Ankara.

SACTI = Sumerian and Akkadian Cuneiform Texts in the collection of the World Heritage Museum of the University of Illinois, Urbana, 1971 ff.

III. ANATOLIAN LANGUAGES

COMPILED BY

Philo H. J. HOUWINK TEN CATE

A. BIBLIOGRAPHY

G. Contenau, Éléments de Bibliographie Hittite, Paris, 1922.

——, Supplément aux Éléments de Bibliographie Hittite, Extrait de Babyloniaca X 1-3, Paris, 1927.

B. Schwartz, The Hittites. A List of References in the New York Public Library, New York, 1939.

E. Laroche, Dix ans d'études asianiques, Conférences de l'Institut de Linguistique de l'Université de Paris IX, 1949, Paris (1950), 79-93.

——, Periodical Bibliographies in RHA.

E. Weidner, Bibliographie [III. Kleinasien], AfO III, 1926, and following volumes.

A. Pohl, Keilschriftbibliographie, Or IX, 1940 - XXXI, 1962.

K. Deller (and H. Klengel), Keilschriftbibliographie, 24 ff., Or XXXII, 1963, and following volumes.

B. SOURCES

1. Cuneiform Tablets

KBo	= Keilschrifttexte aus Boghazköi, I-VI, Leipzig, 1916-1921. VII-..., Berlin, 1954 and following years.
KUB	= Keilschrifturkunden aus Boghazköi, I-XXXII, Berlin, Staatliche Museen, Vorderasiatische Abteilung, 1921-1942. XXXIII-XXXIV, Deutsche Orient-Gesellschaft zu Berlin, 1943-1944. XXXV-..., Deutsche Akademie der Wissenschaften zu Berlin, Institut für Orientforschung.

BoTU	=	Die Boghazköi-Texte in Umschrift, Leipzig, WVDOG 41-42, 1922, 1926.
1 BoTU	=	E. FORRER, Die Keilschrift von Boghazköi, 1922.
2.1 BoTU	=	E. FORRER, Geschichtliche Texte aus dem alten Chatti-Reich, 1926.
2.2 BoTU	=	E. FORRER, Geschichtliche Texte aus dem neuen Chatti-Reich, 1926 (reprints of all three volumes: Osnabrück, 1969).
HT	=	L. W. KING and S. SMITH, Hittite Texts in the Cuneiform Character from Tablets in the British Museum, London, 1920.
VBoT	=	A. GÖTZE, Verstreute Boghazköi-Texte, Marburg, 1930.
FHG	=	E. LAROCHE, Fragments hittites de Genève, RA XLV, 1951, 131-138, 184-194; RA XLVI, 1952, 42-50.
IBoT	=	Istanbul Arkeoloji Müzelerinde Bulunan Boğazköy Tabletlerinden Seçme Metinler, I-III, Istanbul, 1944, 1947, 1954.
ABoT	=	Ankara Arkeoloji Müzesinde Bulunan Boğazköy Tabletleri, Istanbul, 1948.
Bo	=	Catalog numbers of Boghazköy tablets from excavations 1906-12, in the Museums of Istanbul and/or Berlin.
.../a, .../b, etc.	=	Catalog numbers of Boghazköy tablets from excavations since 1931, letters indicating campaigns (/a = first campaign = 1931, up to z = 1967; there after Bo 68/..., Bo 69/... etc.), in the Museum of Ankara.

2. HIEROGLYPHIC MONUMENTS AND SEALS

For a convenient bibliography see E. LAROCHE, Les Hiéroglyphes Hittites I, Paris, 1960, XXI-XXXV and more recently RHA XXVII Fasc. 84-85 (1969), 110-131.

L. MESSERSCHMIDT, Corpus Inscriptionum Hettiticarum, MVAeG V 4-5, VII 3, XI 5, Berlin, 1900, 1902, 1906.

B. B. CHARLES, A. T. OLMSTEAD, J. E. WRENCH, Travels and Studies in the nearer East (The Cornell Expedition I 2), Hittite Inscriptions, Ithaca N. Y., 1911.

Carchemish, Report on the Excavations at Djerabis/Jerablus on
Behalf of the British Museum, Part I, D. G. HOGARTH, London, 1914;
II, C. L. WOOLLEY, London, 1922; III, Sir L. WOOLLEY and R. D.
BARNETT, London, 1952. An important review article on the last
volume was published by H. G. GÜTERBOCK, Carchemish, JNES XIII,
1954, 102-114. (reprints of all three volumes : London, 1969).

D. G. HOGARTH, Hittite Seals with particular reference to the Ashmolean Collection, Oxford, 1920.

W. ANDRAE, Hettitische Inschriften auf Bleistreifen aus Assur,
WVDOG 46, Leipzig, 1924; see now, too, the Kululu lead strips
as published by T. ÖZGÜÇ, Kültepe and its Vicinity in the Iron
Age, Türk Tarih Kurumu Yayinlarindan V. Seri 29, Ankara,
1971, 111-116, Pl. L-LII.

I. J. GELB, Inscriptions from Alishar and Vicinity, OIP XXVII,
Chicago, 1935, Nos. 67-89, pp. 73-75, Pl. LII-LVII.

——, Hittite Hieroglyphic Monuments, OIP XLV, Chicago, 1939.

——, in H. GOLDMAN, Excavations at Gözlü Kule, Tarsus II, Princeton,
1956, 242-254, Pl. 401-408 (see, too, E. LAROCHE, Syria XXXV,
1958, 252-260).

H. G. GÜTERBOCK, Siegel aus Boğazköy I-II, AfO Beih. 5, 7, Berlin,
1940, 1942 (reprint: Osnabrück, 1967).

H. Th. BOSSERT, Karatepe 1-55 = Oriens I, 1948, 171-173; 56-128 =
Oriens II, 1949, 91-97; 1-158 = Symb. Hrozný IV (1950) =
ArOr XVIII 3, 18-28; 159-216 = JKAF I, 1951, 270-272; 217-
260 = JKAF II, 1952, 178-179; 261-302 = JKAF III, 1953,
306-308; 303-330 = MNHMHΣ XAPIN, Gedenkschrift P. Kretschmer I, 1956, 41-44.

R. D. BARNETT, Hittite Hieroglyphic Texts in Aleppo, Iraq X, 1948,
122-139.

D. A. KENNEDY, The Inscribed Hittite Seals in the Ashmolean Museum, RHA fasc. 63, 1958, 65-84.

——, Sceaux hittites conservés à Paris, RHA fasc. 65, 1959, 147-172.

E. LAROCHE, Documents hiéroglyphiques provenant de Palais d'Ugarit, in: C. F. A. SCHAEFFER, Ugaritica III, Paris, 1956, 97-160.

Th. BERAN, Die hethitische Glyptik von Bogazköy I, WVDOG 76,
Berlin, 1967.

C. LINGUISTICS

1. GRAMMARS AND READINGBOOKS

J. FRIEDRICH, Hethitisches Elementarbuch: 1. Teil Kurzgefasste Grammatik (Indogerm. Bibliothek, I. Abt., 1. Reihe: Grammatiken, Bd. 23[1]), Heidelberg, 1940; Zweite, verbesserte und erweiterte Auflage, Heidelberg, 1960; 2. Teil Lesestücke in Transkription, mit Erläuterungen und Wörterverzeichnissen (———, Bd. 23[2]), Heidelberg, 1946; Zweite, verbesserte Auflage, Heidelberg, 1967.

———, Hethitisches Keilschrift-Lesebuch (Indogerm. Bibliothek, 1. Reihe: Lehr- und Handbücher): Teil I, Lesestücke; Teil II, Schrifttafel und Erläuterungen, Heidelberg, 1960.

H. KRONASSER, Vergleichende Laut- und Formenlehre des Hethitischen, Heidelberg, 1956.

———, Etymologie der Hethitischen Sprache: I 1, Zur Schreibung und Lautung des Hethitischen; II 2-5/6, Wortbildung des Hethitischen, Wiesbaden, 1962-1966.

E. H. STURTEVANT, A Comparative Grammar of the Hittite Language, Linguistic Society of America, Philadelphia, 1933; Revised edition 1951, 1964[2], Yale University Press, New Haven and London.

———, G. BECHTEL, A Hittite Chrestomathy, Linguistic Society of America, Philadelphia, 1935; Second Printing, corrected, 1952.

So far there is no historical grammar in the strict sense, but in a number of recent articles and monographs various scholars have used an "historical approach":

A. KAMMENHUBER, Studien zum hethitischen Infinitivsystem (see below sub 8).

———, Die hethitischen Vorstellungen von Seele und Leib, Herz- und Leibesinnerem, Kopf und Person, ZA LVI, N.F. 22, 1964, 150-212; ZA LVII, N.F. 23, 1965, 177-222.

O. CARRUBA, V. SOUČEK, R. STERNEMANN, Kleine Bemerkungen zur jüngsten Fassung der hethitischen Gesetze, ArOr XXXIII, 1965, 1-18.

O. CARRUBA, Die Verbalendungen auf -wani und -tani und das relative Alter der heth. Texte, Sprache XII, 1966, 79-89.

———, Die Chronologie der heth. Texte und die heth. Geschichte der Grossreichszeit, ZDMG Suppl. I, 1969, 226-249.

J. FRIEDRICH, Zur Frage alter und junger Sprachformen im Keil-
hethitischen, JCS XXI (1967), 49-50, in a longer article: Keil-
hethitisches und hieroglyphenhethitisches, ibidem, 49-51.

Ph. H. J. HOUWINK TEN CATE, The Records of the Early Hittite
Empire, Ned. Hist.-Arch. Instituut te Istanbul, XXVI, 1970.

2. GLOSSARIES AND DICTIONARIES

J. FRIEDRICH, Hethitisches Wörterbuch, Kurzgefasste kritische Sammlung der Deutungen hethitischer Wörter (Indogerm. Bibliothek,
I. Abt., 2. Reihe: Wörterbücher), Heidelberg, 1952; 1., 2., 3. Erg.,
1957, 1961, 1966.

P. REICHERT, Glossaire inverse de la langue hittite, RHA fasc. 73,
1963, 61-143.

H. A. HOFFNER, An English-Hittite Glossary, RHA fasc. 80, 1967,
7-99.

3. GENERAL WORKS

Altkleinasiatische Sprachen, Handbuch der Orientalistik, Erster Abt.,
Zweiter Abschn., Lieferung 2, Leiden-Köln, 1969 (contributions by
J. FRIEDRICH, E. REINER, A. KAMMENHUBER, G. NEUMANN and A.
HEUBECK). The history of Hittite studies is dealt with by A. KAMMEN-
HUBER on pp. 127-141. Three important "landmarks" are:

J. A. KNUDTZON, Die zwei Arzawa-Briefe. Die ältesten Urkunden in
indogerm. Sprache. Mit Bemerkungen v. S. BUGGE und A. TORP,
Leipzig, 1902.

F. HROZNÝ, Die Lösung des hethitischen Problems, MDOG 56, 1915,
17-50.

——, Die Sprache der Hethiter, ihr Bau und ihr Zugehörigkeit zum
indogermanischen Sprachstamm; ein Entzifferungsversuch, Boghazköi-Studien 1-2, Leipzig, 1917.

4. ANATOLIAN LANGUAGES IN GENERAL

F. HROZNÝ, Über die Völker und Sprachen des alten Chatti-Landes,
Boghazköi-Studien 5, Leipzig, 1920.

E. FORRER, Die acht Sprachen der Boghazköi-Inschriften, Sitzb. d.
Preuss. Akad. d. Wiss., Philol. Kl., 1919, 1029-1041.

——, Die Inschriften und Sprachen des Ḫatti-Reiches, ZDMG LXXVI, 1922, 174-269.

J. FRIEDRICH, Hethitisch und "Kleinasiatische" Sprachen (Grundriss der indogerm. Sprach- und Altertumskunde; Geschichte der indogerm. Sprachwissenschaft II, Bd. 5, Lief. 1), Berlin, 1931.

5. SCRIPT, LIBRARY AND SCRIBE

Th. V. GAMKRELIDZE, The Akkado-Hittite Syllabary and the problem of the origin of the Hittite script, ArOr XXIX, 1961, 406-418.

H. G. GÜTERBOCK, OLZ LI, 1956, cols. 515-516, JAOS LXXXIV, 1964, 108-110.

E. LAROCHE, La bibliothèque de Hattusa, Symb. Hrozný II (1949) = ArOr XVII 2, 7-23.

——, Catalogue des textes hittites, Klincksieck, Études et Commentaires 15, Paris, 1971.

H. OTTEN, Bibliotheken im alten Orient, Altertum I, 1955, 67-81.

——, Hethitische Schreiber in ihren Briefen, MIO IV, 1956, 179-189.

——, Schrift, Sprache und Literatur der Hethiter in: G. WALSER, Neuere Hethiterforschung, 1964, 11-22.

CHR. RÜSTER, Hethitische Keilschrift-Paläographie, Stud. zu den Boğ.-T. 20, Wiesbaden, 1972.

6. SPECIFIC ANATOLIAN LANGUAGES

a. *Hattic*

I. M. DUNAJEVSKAJA, Principles of the Verbal Structure in Hattic (Proto-Hittite), PASb, 1961, 57-159 (Russian), 583-586 (English summary).

A. KAMMENHUBER, Das Hattische, in Altkleinasiatische Sprachen, 428-546 (the history of the research is described on pp. 438-442), cf. above 3.

——, Hattische Studien, RHA fasc. 70, 1962, 1-29.

E. LAROCHE, Études "proto-hittites", RA XLI, 1947, 67-98.

H. S. SCHUSTER, Die protoḫattisch-hethitischen Bilinguen, 2 Teile, Leiden, 1973. (?)

b. *Palaic*

The history of the research is described by A. KAMMENHUBER in altkleinasiatische Sprachen, 141-143, cf. above 3.

A. KAMMENHUBER, Das Palaische: Texte und Wortschatz, RHA
fasc. 64, 1959, 1-92.
——, Esquisse de grammaire palaïte, BSLP LIV, 1959, 18-45.
O. CARRUBA, Das Palaische. Texte, Grammatik, Lexikon, Studien zu
den Boğ.-T. 10, Wiesbaden, 1970 (continued in Beiträge zum
Palaischen, Ned. Hist.-Arch. Instituut te Istanbul, XXXI, 1972).

c. *Cuneiform Luwian*

The history of the research is described by A. KAMMENHUBER, Altkleinasiatische Sprachen, 143-147.

B. ROSENKRANZ, Beiträge zur Erforschung des Luvischen, Wiesbaden,
1952.
H. OTTEN, Luvische Texte in Umschrift, Berlin, 1953.
——, Zur grammatikalischen und lexikalischen Bestimmung des
Luvischen, Berlin, 1953.
E. LAROCHE, Dictionnaire de la langue louvite, Paris, 1959 (Addenda
et Corrigenda, RHA fasc. 76, 1965, 44-50). A Sketch of the Luwian
grammar can be found on pp. 131-145 of Laroche's book.

The following reviews of the books by ROSENKRANZ and OTTEN (next
to LTU and Bestimmung also KUB XXXV, Luvische und Palaische
Texte) were of great importance:
E. LAROCHE, BiOr XI, 1954, 121-124.
A. KAMMENHUBER, OLZ L, 1955, cols. 352-378.
H. G. GÜTERBOCK, Or XXV, 1956, 113-140.
For the so-called "Glossenkeil" words see B. ROSENKRANZ, JKAF I,
1950, 189-198 and ZA LI, N.F. 17, 1955, 252-254; H. G. GÜTERBOCK,
Or XXV, 1956, 113-140.

d. *Hieroglyphic Luwian (formerly called Hieroglyphic Hittite)*
The history of the research is described by A. KAMMENHUBER, Alt-
kleinasiatische Sprachen, 148-161.
The following studies are of bibliographical interest:
P. MERIGGI, Die hethitische Hieroglyphenschrift. Eine Vorstudie zur
Entzifferung, ZA XXXIX, N.F. 5, 1929, 165-212.
——, Die kürzeren Votiv- und Bauinschriften, WZKM XL, 1933,
233-280.
——, Die längeren Votiv- und Bauinschriften, WZKM XLI, 1934,
1-42.
——, Die längsten Bauinschriften in "hethitischen" Hieroglyphen

nebst Glossar zu sämtlichen Texten, MVAeG XXXIX 1, Leipzig, 1934 (= MERIGGI, Glossar).

——, Listes des hiéroglyphes hittites, RHA fasc. 27, 1937, 69-114 and 29, 1937, 157-200.

H. Th. BOSSERT, Šantaš und Kupapa. Neue Beiträge zur Entzifferung der kretischen und hethitischen Bilderschrift, MAOG VI 3, Leipzig, 1932.

——, Ein hethitisches Königssiegel, Istanb. Forschungen XVII, Berlin, 1944.

——, Asia, Istanbul, 1946.

E. FORRER, Die hethitische Bilderschrift, SAOC 3, Chicago, 1932 = AJSL XLVIII, 1932, 137-169.

I. J. GELB, Hittite Hieroglyphs I-III, SAOC 2, 14 and 21, Chicago, 1931, 1935 and 1942.

F. HROZNÝ, Les inscriptions hittites hiéroglyphiques I-III, Praha, 1933, 1934 and 1937.

Still to be consulted are:

H. G. GÜTERBOCK, Siegel aus Bogazköy I-II, AfO Beih. 5, 7, Berlin, 1940, 1942 (reprint: Osnabrück, 1967).

S. ALP, Zur Lesung von manchen Personennamen auf den hieroglyphenhethitischen Siegeln und Inschriften, Ankara, 1950.

The most important handbooks of the moment are:

E. LAROCHE, Les Hiéroglyphes Hittites I (L'écriture), Paris, 1960.

P. MERIGGI, Hieroglyphisch-Hethitisches Glossar, Wiesbaden, 1962 (completely revised edition of MERIGGI's book of 1934). Important articles by H. MITTELBERGER should be used alongside of MERIGGI's Glossar (Bemerkungen zu Meriggis hieroglyphisch-hethitischem Glossar, Sprache IX, 1963, 69-106, and, Zur Schreibung und Lautung des Hieroglyphen-hethitischen, Sprache X, 1964, 50-98).

——, Manuale di Eteo Geroglifico: Part I, Grammatica; Parte II, Testi, Incunabula Graeca XIII and XIV, Roma, 1966 and 1967.

e. *Alphabetic Luwian (Lycian)*

The history of the research is described by G. NEUMANN, Altkleinasiatische Sprachen, 361-366.

E. H. Sturtevant, Some Nouns of relationship in Lycian and Hittite, TAPA LIX, 1928, 48-56.
H. Pedersen, Lykisch und Hittitisch, Det Kgl. Danske Videnskabernes Selskab Hist.-fil. Meddelelser XXX 4, 1945, København.
F. J. Tritsch, Lycian, Luwian and Hittite, Symb. Hrozný III (1950), ArOr XVIII 1-2, 494-518.
E. Laroche, Comparaison du louvite et du lycien I, II, [III], IV, BSLP LIII, 1957-58, 159-197; BSLP LV, 1960, 155-185; [BSLP LVIII, 1963, 58-79]; BSLP LXII, 1967, 46-64.
Ph. H. J. Houwink ten Cate, The Luwian Population Groups of Lycia and Cilicia Aspera during the Hellenistic Period, Leiden, 1961 (reprint: 1965), 51-100.
G. Neumann, Lykisch in Altkleinasiatische Sprachen, 358-396.

f. *Lydian*

The history of the research is described by A. Heubeck, Altkleinasiatische Sprachen, 401-403.

R. Gusmani, Lydisches Wörterbuch mit grammatischer Skizze und Inschriftensammlung, Wiesbaden, 1964.
O. Carruba, Lydisch und Lyder, MIO VIII, 1961, 383-408.
A. Heubeck, Lydisch in Altkleinasiatische Sprachen, 397-427.
O. Carruba, Zur Grammatik des Lydischen, Studi in Onore di P. Meriggi, Athen. XLVII, 1969, 39-83.

7. Hittite and Indo-European

The history of the research is described by A. Kammenhuber, Altkleinasiatische Sprachen, 134-141.

C. J. S. Marstrander, Caractère indo-européen de la langue hittite, Christiania, 1919.
E. H. Sturtevant, A Comparative Grammar of the Hittite Language, see above 1.
H. Pedersen, Hittitisch und die andere Indoeuropäischen Sprachen, Det Kgl. Danske Videnskabernes Selskab, Hist.-fil. Meddelelser XXV 2, 1938, København.
F. Sommer, Hethiter und Hethitisch, Stuttgart, 1947.
E. Benveniste, Hittite et Indo-européen. Études comparatives, Paris, 1962.

A. Kammenhuber, Zur hethitisch-luvischen Sprachgruppe, KZ LXXVI, 1959, 1-26, and, Zur Stellung des Hethitisch-Luvischen innerhalb der indogermanischen Gemeinsprache, KZ LXXVII, 1961, 31-75.

——, Hethitisch, Palaisch, Luwisch und Hieroglyphenluwisch in Altkleinasiatische Sprachen, 119-357 (and along the same lines, Die Sprachen des vorhellenistischen Kleinasien in ihrer Bedeutung für die heutige Indogermanistik, MSS 24, 1968, 55-123).

B. Rosenkranz, Die Struktur der hethitischen Sprache, ZDMG Suppl. I, 1969, 164-169.

See also:

W. Porzig, Die Stellung des Hethitischen in his book Die Gliederung des indogermanischen Sprachgebietes, Heidelberg, 1954, 187-192.

J. Puhvel, Dialectal Aspects of the Anatolian Branch of Indo-European in: H. Birnbaum and J. Puhvel (editors), Ancient Indo-European Dialects, Berkeley-Los Angeles, 1966, 235-247.

R. Gusmani, Il Lessico Ittito, Napoli, 1968.

For literature on the so-called laryngal theory, see:

A. Kammenhuber, Altkleinasiatische Sprachen, 136.

8. Linguistical Monographs and Articles

N. van Brock, Dérivés nominaux en L du hittite et du louvite, RHA fasc. 71, 1962, 69-168.

——, Les thèmes verbaux à redoublement du hittite et le verbe indo-européen, RHA fasc. 75, 1964, 119-165.

F. Josephson, Pronominal Adverbs of Anatolian: Formation and Function, RHA fasc. 79, 1966, 133-154.

G. Bechtel, Hittite Verbs in -sk-. A Study of verbal Aspect, Ann Arbor, Mich., 1936.

W. Dressler, Studien zur verbalen Pluralität, Österr, Akad. d. Wiss., Phil.-hist. Klasse, Sitzungsber. 259. Band, 1. Abh., Wien, 1968, 157-236 (Die hethitischen šk-Formen).

B. Rosenkranz, Die hethitische hi-Konjugation, JKAF II, 1953, 339-349.

E. Neu, Interpretation der hethitischen mediopassiven Verbalformen, Studien zu den Boğ.-T. 5, Wiesbaden, 1968, and, Das hethitische Mediopassiv und seine indogermanischen Grundlagen, Studien zu den Boğ.-T. 6, Wiesbaden, 1968.

F. Ose, Supinum und Infinitiv im Hethitischen, MVAeG XLVII 1, Leipzig, 1944.

A. Kammenhuber, Studien zum hethitischen Infinitivsystem, MIO II, 1954, 44-77, 245-265, 403-444; MIO III, 1955, 31-57, 345-377; MIO IV, 1956, 40-60.

A. Götze, Über die Parikeln -za, -kan und -šan der hethitische Satz-verbindung, ArOr V, 1933, 1-38. See also: the discussion be-tween B. Schwartz and A. Goetze in JAOS LXX, 1950, 18-24, 173-178 and 179.

E. Laroche, Notes de linguistique anatolienne: ... 3. Hittite -kan et louvite -ta, RHA fasc. 68, 1961, 30-36.

O. Carruba, Hethitisch -(a)sta, -(a)pa und die anderen "Ortsbezugs-partikeln", Or XXXIII, 1964, 405-436.

——, Die satzeinleitenden Partikeln in den indogermanischen Sprachen Anatoliens, Incunabula Graeca XXXII, Roma, 1969.

H. A. Hoffner, On the Use of Hittite -za in Nominal Sentences JNES XXVIII, 1969, 225-230.

F. Josephson, The Function of the Sentence Particles in Old and Middle Hittite, Uppsala, 1972.

L. Zuntz, Die hethitischen Ortsadverbien arḫa, para, piran als selb-ständige Adverbien und in ihrer Verbindung mit Nomina und Verba, München, 1936.

J. Friedrich, Zum hethitischen Irrealis und Potentialis, KlF I, 1929, 286-296.

A. Hahn, The Shift of a Hittite Conjunction from the Temporal to the Conditional Sphere, Language XX, 1944, 91-107.

R. Sternemann, Temporale und konditionale Nebensätze des Hethi-tischen, MIO XI, 1965, 231-274 and 377-415.

W. H. Held, The Hittite Relative Sentence, Supplement Language Dissertation No. 55, Baltimore, 1957.

D. LITERATURE

1. Text editions

a. *Anthologies*

F. Hrozný, Hethitische Keilschrifttexte aus Boghazköi in Umschrift mit Übersetzung und Komentar, Boghazköi-Studien 3, Leipzig, 1919.

M. Witzel, Hethitische Keilschrift-Urkunden (= Keilschriftliche Studien IV), Fulda, 1924.

A. Götze, Ausgewählte hethitische Texte historischen und juristischen Inhalts, transkribiert (Kleine Texte für Vorlesungen und Übungen No. 153), Bonn, 1926.

J. Friedrich, Kleinasiatische Sprachdenkmäler (Kleine Texte für Vorlesungen und Übungen No. 163), Berlin, 1932.

b. *Historical Texts* (*in chronological order*)

E. Forrer, 2 BoTU, Geschichtliche Texte aus dem alten und neuen Chatti-Reich, WVDOG 42, 1-2, 1926 (reprint: Osnabrück, 1969).

F. Sommer, A. Falkenstein, Die hethitisch-akkadische Bilingue des Ḫattušili I (Labarna II), Abh. d. Bayr. Akademie d. Wiss., Phil.-Hist. Abt., N.F. 16, München, 1938.

A. Götze, Madduwattaš, MVAeG XXXII 1, Leipzig, 1928 (reprint: Darmstadt, 1968). See now, H. Otten, Sprachliche Stellung und Datierung des Madduwatta-Textes, Studien zu den Boğ.-T. 11, Wiesbaden, 1969.

H. G. Güterbock, The Deeds of Šuppiluliuma as Told by His Son Muršili II, JCS X, 1956, 41-68, 75-98, 107-130.

A. Götze, Die Annalen des Muršiliš, MVAeG XXXIX, Leipzig, 1933 (reprint: Darmstadt, 1967). See, too, H. Otten, Neue Fragmente zu den Annalen des Muršili, unter Mitarbeit von K. K. Riemschneider und W. Scholze, MIO III, 1955, 153-175, and, Ph. H. J. Houwink ten Cate, Mursilis' Northwestern Campaigns Additional Fragments of His Comprehensive Annals, JNES XXV, 1966, 162-191; A. Kammenhuber, Or 39, 1970, 548-549.

——, Ḫattušiliš. Der Bericht über seine Thronbesteigung nebst den Paralleltexten, MVAeG XXIX 3, Leipzig, 1925 (reprint: Darmstadt, 1967), and idem, Neue Bruchstücke zum grossen Text des Ḫattušiliš und den Paralleltexten, MVAeG XXIV 2, Leipzig, 1930 (reprint: Darmstadt, 1970).

R. Stefanini, KBo IV 14 = VAT 13049, Atti della Accademia Nazionale dei Lincei, Rendiconti, Classe di Scienze morali storiche e filologiche XX, 1965, Roma, 39-79 (see also: idem, Ancora sull' attribuzione di KBo IV 14, Atti e Memorie dell' Accademia Toscana di Scienze e Lettere, La Colombaria XXXI, N.S. 17, 1966, Firenze, 105-111).

See also: F. Sommer, Die Aḫḫijavā-Urkunden, München, 1932 (below E 4a).

c. *Treaties (in chronological order)*

H. OTTEN, Ein althethitischer Vertrag mit Kizzuwatna, JCS V, 1951, 129-132.

A. KEMPINSKI, S. KOŠAK, Der Išmeriga-Vertrag, Welt des Orients V 2, 1970, 191-217.

E. VON SCHULER, Die Kaškäer. Ein Beitrag zur Ethnographie des alten Kleinasien, Berlin, 1965.

H. FREYDANK, Eine hethitische Fassung des Vertrages zwischen dem Hethiter-König Šuppiluliuma und Aziru von Amurru, MIO VII, 1959-60, 356-381.

J. FRIEDRICH, Staatsverträge des Ḫatti-Reiches in hethitischer Sprache I-II, MVAeG XXXI 1 and XXXIV 1, Leipzig, 1926 and 1930.

C. KÜHNE, H. OTTEN, Der Šaušgamuwa-Vertrag, Studien zu den Boǧ.-T. 16, Wiesbaden, 1971.

See, too, the Akkadian treaties edited by:

E. F. WEIDNER, Politische Dokumente aus Kleinasien, Boghazköi-Studien 8-9, Leipzig, 1923 (reprint: Hildesheim-New York, 1970).

d. *State documents*

K. K. RIEMSCHNEIDER, Die hethitischen Landschenkungsurkunden, MIO VI, 1958, 321-381.

V. SOUČEK, Die hethitischen Feldertexte I-II, ArOr XXVII, 1959, 5-43 and 379-396.

E. H. STURTEVANT, A Hittite Text on the Duties of Priests and Temple Servants, JAOS LIV, 1934, 363-406 (= American Oriental Society Series No. 4 = E. H. STURTEVANT and G. BECHTEL, A Hittite Chrestomathy, 127-174; cf. above C 1).

L. (JAKOB-)ROST, Beiträge zum hethitischen Hofzeremoniell (IBoT I 36), MIO XI, 1965, 165-225.

S. ALP, Military Instructions of the Hittite King Tutḫaliya IV, Belleten fasc. 43, 1947, 383-414.

E. VON SCHULER, Hethitische Dienstanweisungen, AfO Beih. 10, Graz, 1957 (reprint: Osnabrück, 1967). See also: H. OTTEN, Bemerkungen zu den hethitischen Instruktionen für die LÚ.MEŠ SAG, AfO XVIII, 1957-58, 387-390, and, A. GOETZE, The Beginning of the Hittite Instructions for the Commander of the Border Guards, JCS XIV, 1960, 69-73.

——, Die Würdenträgereide des Arnuwanda, Or XXV, 1956, 209-240.

J. FRIEDRICH, Die hethitischen Gesetze, Leiden, 1959. (reprint with new preface by A. KAMMENHUBER: 1971). See also:

F. IMPARATI, Le Leggi Ittiti, Incunabula Graeca VII, Roma, 1964. Important reviews and review articles were devoted to Friedrich's text edition: H. G. GÜTERBOCK, JCS XV, 1961, 62-78 and XVI, 1962, 17-23; A. KAMMENHUBER, BiOr XVIII, 1961, 77-82 and 124-127; O. CARRUBA, Kratylos VII, 1962, 155-160. Important new material has been added by H. OTTEN and V. SOUČEK, Neue hethitische Gesetzefragmente aus dem Grossen Tempel, AfO XXI, 1966, 1-12; H. OTTEN, Ein Fragment zu Tafel II der hethitischen Gesetze, ZA LXI 2, 1971, 239-241.

R. WERNER, Hethitische Gerichtsprotokolle, Studien zu den Boğ.-T. 4, Wiesbaden, 1967.

Related material:

A. KAMMENHUBER, Hippologia Hethitica, Wiesbaden, 1961.

H. OTTEN, V. SOUČEK, Das Gelübde der Königin Pudeḫepa an die Göttin Lelwani, Studien zu den Boğ.-T. 1, Wiesbaden, 1965.

e. *Epical and Mythological texts*

J. FRIEDRICH, Die hethitischen Bruchstücke des Gilgameš-Epos, ZA XXXIX, N.F. 5, 1930, 1-82; H. OTTEN, Zur Überlieferung des Gilgameš-Epos nach den Boğazköy-Texten in: P. GARELLI (ed.), Gilgameš et sa légende, CRAI VII, 1958, Paris, 1960, 139-143, and, Idem, Die erste Tafel des hethitischen Gilgamesch-Epos, IM VIII, 1958, 93-125.

——, Der churritische Mythus vom Schlangendämon Ḫedammu in hethitischer Sprache, Symb. Hrozný I (1949) = ArOr XVII 1, 230-254.

——, Churritische Märchen und Sagen in hethitischer Sprache, ZA XLIX, N.F. 15, 1950, 213-255.

H. G. GÜTERBOCK, Kumarbi Efsanesi, Türk Tarih Kurumu Yayinlarindan VII. Seri - No. 11 and 11 a, Ankara, 1945 and 1947 (= Idem, Kumarbi. Mythen vom Churritischen Kronos aus den hethitischen Fragmenten zusammengestellt, übersetzt und erklärt, Istanbuler Schriften 16, Zürich-New York, 1946).

——, The Song of Ullikummi. Revised text of the Hittite version of a Hurrian Myth, JCS V, 1951, 135-161 and JCS VI, 1952, 8-42.

H. OTTEN, Mythen vom Gotte Kumarbi, Berlin, 1950.

——, Die Überlieferungen des Telipinu-Mythus, MVAeG XLVI 1, 1942, Leipzig.

E. Laroche, Textes mythologiques hittites en transcription I: Mythologie anatolienne, RHA fasc. 77, 1965, 61-178; and II: Mythologie d'origine étrangère, RHA fasc. 82, 1968, 121-204.

J. Siegelová, Appu-Märchen und Ḫedammu-Mythus, Studien zu den Boğ.-T. 14, Wiesbaden, 1971.

f. *Prayers*

J. Friedrich, Ein hethitisches Gebet an die Sonnengöttin der Erde, RSO XXXII, 1957, 217-224.

A. Götze, Die Pestgebete des Muršiliš, KlF I, 1929, 161-251.

O. R. Gurney, Hittite Prayers of Muršili II, AAA XXVII, 1940, 3-163.

g. *Rituals (alphabetical order based on the name of the editor)*

O. Carruba, Das Beschwörungsritual für die Göttin Wišurijanza, Studien zu den Boğ.-T. 2, Wiesbaden, 1966.

J. Friedrich, Der hethitische Soldateneid, ZA XXXV, N.F. 1, 1923, 161-192.

A. Götze, H. Pedersen, Muršiliš Sprachlähmung, Det Kgl. Danske Videnskabernes Selskab, Hist.-fil. Meddelelser XXI 1, 1934, København.

A. Goetze, E. H. Sturtevant, The Hittite Ritual of Tunnawi, American Oriental Series No. 14, New Haven, Conn., 1938.

H. Kronasser, Die Umsiedelung der schwarzen Gottheit. Das hethitische Ritual XXIX 4 (des Ulippi), Österreich. Akad. d. Wiss., Philos.-hist. Kl. 241.3, 1963, Wien.

H. M. Kümmel, Ersatzrituale für den hethitischen König, Studien zu den Boğ.-T. 3, Wiesbaden, 1967.

E. Neu, Ein althethitisches Gewitterritual, Studien zu den Boğ.-T. 12, Wiesbaden, 1970.

H. Otten, Hethitische Totenrituale, Berlin, 1958.

——, Eine Beschwörung des Unterirdischen aus Boğazköy, ZA LIV, N.F. 20, 1961, 114-157.

——, V. Souček, Ein althethitisches Ritual für das Königspaar, Studien zu den Boğ.-T. 8, Wiesbaden, 1969.

H. Otten, Ein hethitisches Festritual (KBO XIX 128), Studien zu den Boğ.-T. 13, Wiesbaden, 1971.

L. (Jakob-)Rost, Ein hethitisches Ritual gegen Familienzwist, MIO I, 1953, 345-379.

B. Schwartz, The Hittite and Luwian Ritual of Zarpiya of Kezzuwatna. KUB IX 31 = HT 1, JAOS LVIII, 1958, 334-353.

————, A Hittite Ritual Text (KUB XXIX 1 = 1780/c), Or XVI, 1947, 23-55.

G. Szabó, Ein hethitisches Entsühnungsritual für das Königspaar Tuthalija und Nikalmati. Texte der Hethiter 1, Heidelberg, 1971.

F. Sommer, H. Ehelolf, Das hethitische Ritual des Papanikri von Komana, Boghazköi-Studien 10, Leipzig, 1924.

E. H. Sturtevant, A Hittite Tablet in the Yale Babylonian Collection, TAPA LVIII, 1927, 5-31 (= E. H. Sturtevant and G. Bechtel, A Hittite Chrestomaty, 100-126 (The Ritual of Anniwiyaniš)).

L. Zuntz, Un Testo Ittita di Scongiuri, Atti del Reale Istituto Veneto di Scienze, Lettere ed Arti XCVI, 1936-37, 477-546.

h. *Translations of Hittite Texts*

J. Friedrich, Aus dem hethitischen Schrifttum: Der Alte Orient XXIV 2-3 and XXV 2, Leipzig, 1925, 1. Heft (Historische Texte, Staatsverträge, Königliche Erlasse, Briefe, Gesetze, Wirtschaftliche Texte), 2. Heft (Religiöse Texte).

A. Goetze in J. B. Pritchard (editor), ANET[1], 120-128 (Myths, Epics and Legends), 201-206 (Treaties), 207-211 (Instructions), 318-319 (Historical Texts), 346-361 (Rituals, Incantations and Festival Texts), 393-401 (Prayers), 497-498 (Omen); Suppl., 1969, 519 (Myth), 529-530 (treaty).

i. *Series*

Boghazköi-Studien 1-10, Leipzig, 1917-1924.

Hethitische Texte in Umschrift, mit Übersetzung und Erläuterungen (MVAeG publications) 1-8, Leipzig, 1924-1943.

Studien zu den Boğazköy-Texten 1-..., Wiesbaden, 1965 and following years.

Texte der Hethiter I-..., Heidelberg, 1971 and Following years.

2. Literary Studies

H. G. Güterbock, Die historische Tradition und ihre literarische

Gestaltung bei Babyloniern und Hethitern bis 1200; ... Zweiter
Teil: Hethiter, ZA XLIV, N.F. 10, 1938, 45-149.

——, The Hittite Version of the Hurrian Kumarbi Myths; Oriental
Forerunners of Hesiod, AJA LII, 1948, 123-134.

——, Muršilli's Accounts of Šuppiluliuma's dealings with Egypt,
RHA fasc. 66-67, 1960, 57-63.

——, The Composition of Hittite Prayers to the Sun, JAOS LXXVIII,
1958, 237-245.

——, A View on Hittite Literature, JAOS LXXXIV, 1964, 107-115.

A. Kammenhuber, Die hethitische Geschichtsschreibung, Saeculum
IX, 1958, 136-155.

A. Archi, La storiographia ittita, Athen. XLVII, 1969, 7-20.

E. HISTORY

1. Chronology

F. Hrozný, Hethitische Könige, Boghazköi-Studien 6, Leipzlg, 1920,
49-53.

E. Forrer, Forschungen I-II, Erkner bei Berlin, 1926.

A. Götze, Zur Chronologie der Hethiterkönige, KlF I, 1927, 115-119.

A. Goetze, The Problem of Chronology and Early Hittite History,
BASOR 122, 1951, 18-25, and, The Predecessors of Šuppiluliumaš
of Hatti, JAOS LXXII, 1952, 67-72.

——, Alalakh and Hittite Chronology, BASOR 146, 1957, 20-26, and,
On the Chronology of the Second Millennium B.C., JCS XI,
1957, 53-61 and 63-73.

F. Cornelius, Chronology, eine Erwiderung, JCS XII, 1958, 101-104.

O. Carruba, Hattusili II, Studi Micenei ed Egeo-Anatolici XIV,
1971, 75-94.

H. G. Güterbock, The Predecessors of Šuppiluliuma again, JNES
XXIX, 1970, 73-77.

A. Kammenhuber, Die Vorgänger Šuppiluliumaš I. Untersuchungen
zu einer neueren Geschichtsdarstellung H. Ottens, Or XXXIX,
1970, 278-301.

H. Otten, Die hethitischen "Königslisten" und die altorientalische
Chronologie, MDOG 83, 1951, 47-71.

——, Die hethitischen historischen Quellen und die altorientalische
Chronologie, Akad. d. Wiss. u. d. Lit. in Mainz, Abh. Geistes-

und Sozialwiss. Kl., 1968. 3, Wiesbaden (see, too, ZA LXI 2, 1971, 233-238).

E. LAROCHE, Šuppiluliuma II, RA XLVII, 1953, 70-78.

——, Chronologie hittite: état des questions, Anadolu II, 1955, 1-22.

2. GENERAL WORKS AND STUDIES
(Mainly dealing with political history)

L. DELAPORTE, Les Hittites, Paris, 1936.

A. A. KAMPMAN, Schets der Hethietische Geschiedenis en Beschaving, Leiden, 1939 (= offprints from JEOL 3, 1935 (11-117), 4, 1936 (212-231), 5, 1937-38 (384-400), 6, 1939 (177-201)).

E. CAVAIGNAC, Les Hittites, Paris, 1950.

H. OTTEN, Das Hethiterreich in H. Schmökel, Kulturgeschichte des alten Orient, Stuttgart, 1961, 331-441.

——, Hethiter, Churriter und Mitanni, Die Altorientalische Reiche II (Fischer Weltgeschichte 3), Frankfurt, 1966, 102-176.

E. and H. KLENGEL, Die Hethiter. Geschichte und Umwelt, Leipzig and Wien-München, 1970.

3. STUDIES DEALING WITH SPECIFIC PERIODS

a. *The Period of the Cappadocian texts*

H. OTTEN, Zu den Anfängen der hethitischen Geschichte, MDOG 83, 1951, 33-45.

P. GARELLI, Les Assyriens en Cappadoce, Paris, 1963.

H. LEWY, Anatolia in the Old Assyrian Period, CAH fasc. 40, Cambridge, 1965.

W L. ORLIN, Assyrian Colonies in Cappadocia, Studies in Ancient History 1, The Hague-Paris, 1970.

b. *The Old Hittite Kingdom*

R. S. HARDY, The Old Hittite Kingdom, AJSL LVIII, 1941, 177-216.

H. OTTEN, Der Weg des hethitischen Staates zum Grossreich, Saeculum XV, 1964, 115-124.

O. R. GURNEY, Anatolia c. 1750-1600 B.C., CAH fasc. 11, Cambridge, 1962, and, Anatolia c. 1600-1380 B.C., CAH fasc. 44, Cambridge, 1966.

c. *The New Hittite Empire*

A. Goetze, a) The Struggle for the Domination of Syria (1400-1300 B.C.); b) Anatolia from Shuppiluliumash to the Egyptian War of Muwatallish; c) The Hittites and Syria (1300-1200 B.C.), CAH fasc. 37, Cambridge, 1965.

d. *The End of the Hittite Empire*

E. Laroche, Šuppiluliuma II, RA XLVII, 1953, 70-78.

H. Otten, Neue Quellen zum Ausklang des hethitischen Reiches, MDOG 94, 1963, 1-23.

G. Steiner, Neue Alašiya-Texte, Kadmos I, 1962, 130-138.

H. G. Güterbock, The Hittite Conquest of Cyprus reconsidered, JNES XXVI, 1967, 73-81.

e. *Anatolia* (1200-500 *B.C.*)

P. Naster, L'Asie Mineure et l'Assyrie aux VIIIe et VIIe siècles av. J.-C. d'après les Annales des Rois Assyriens, Louvain, 1938.

M. Kalaç, Die Ausbreitung des assyrischen Grossreiches nach Anatolien in seiner Blütezeit, 745-620 v. Chr., Sumeroloji Araştirmalari, Istanbul, 1941 (= Sumeroloji Enstitüsü Neşriyati 1), 982-1019 (in Turkish).

B. Landsberger, Sam'al. Studien zur Entdeckung der Ruinenstätte Karatepe, Veröffentlichungen der Türkischen Historischen Gesellschaft, VII. Serie, No. 16, Ankara, 1948.

Ph. H. J. Houwink ten Cate, Kleinasien zwischen Hethitern und Persen, Die Altorientalischen Reiche III (Fischer Weltgeschichte 4), Frankfurt, 1967, 112-134.

R. D. Barnett, Phrygia and the Peoples of Anatolia in the Iron Age, CAH fasc. 56, Cambridge, 1967.

W. Orthmann, Untersuchungen zur späthethitischen Kunst, Saarbrücker Beiträge zur Altertumskunde 8, Bonn, 1971, Kapitel V (Auswertung der schriftlichen Quellen).

4. Studies dealing with Specific Problems

a. *The Ahhiyawa Question* (a selective list)

E. Forrer, Vorhomerische Griechen in den Keilschrifttexten von Boghazköi, MDOG 63, 1924, 1-21 (see also Forrer, Forschungen I, 95-261, above E I).

J. FRIEDRICH, Werden in den hethitischen Keilschrifttexten die Griechen erwähnt?, KlF I, 1927, 87-107.

F. HROZNÝ, Hethiter und Griechen, ArOr I, 1929, 323-343.

P. KRETSCHMER, Zur Frage der griechischen Namen in den hethitischen Texten, Glotta XVIII, 1930, 161-170.

F. SOMMER, Die Aḫḫijavā-Urkunden, Abh. d. Bayr. Akademie d. Wiss., Phil.-Hist. Abt., N.F. 6, München, 1932 (see also H. G. GÜTERBOCK, Neue Aḫḫijavā-Texte, ZA XLIII, N.F. 9, 1936, 321-327).

——, Aḫḫijavā-Frage und Sprachwissenschaft, Abh. d. Bayr. Akademie d. Wiss., Phil.-Hist. Abt., N.F. 9, München, 1934.

——, Aḫḫijavā und kein Ende?, IF LV, 1937, 169-297.

F. SCHACHERMEYR, Hethiter und Achäer, MAOG IX 1-2, Leipzig, 1935.

G. HUXLEY, Achaeans and Hittites, Oxford, 1960.

G. STEINER, Die Aḫḫijawa-Frage heute, Saeculum XV, 1964, 365-392.

b. *Indo-Aryans in Hittite Texts* (a selective list)

M. MAYRHOFER, Die Indo-Arier im alten Vorderasien, Wiesbaden, 1966.

A. KAMMENHUBER, Die Arier im Vorderen Orient, Heidelberg, 1968.

c. *The Amarna Age* (a selective list)

J. STURM, Zur Datierung der El-Amarna-Briefe, Klio XXVI, 1932, 1-28.

J. VERGOTE, Toutankhamon dans les archives hittites, Ned. Hist.-Arch. Instituut te Istanbul, XII, 1961.

W. HELCK, Die Beziehungen Ägyptens zu Vorderasien im 3. und 2. Jahrtausend v.Chr., Wiesbaden, 1962 (2nd enbarged edition, 1971).

K. A. KITCHEN, Suppiluliuma and the Amarna Pharaohs, Liverpool, 1962.

E. F. CAMPBELL, The Chronology of the Amarna Letters, Baltimore, 1964.

H. KLENGEL, Aziru of Amurru and his Position in the History of the Amarna Age, MIO X, 1964, 57-84.

d. *Political Relations in the 13th Century*

Egypt

J. STURM, Der Hettiterkrieg Ramses' II., WZKM Beiheft 4, Wien, 1939.

A. Goetze, JCS I, 1947, 241-251.

E. Edel in numerous articles especially on the political correspondence, JNES VII, 1948, 11-24; JNES VIII, 1949, 44-47; IF LX,
1950, 72-85; ZA XLIX, N.F. 15, 1950, 195-212; JKAF II, 1953,
262-273; Festschrift A. Alt, 1953, 29-63; JCS XII, 1958, 130-133;
MDOG 92, 1960, 15-20; ZÄS XL, 1963, 31-35.

W. Helck, Urḫi-Tešup in Ägypten, JCS XVII, 1963, 87-97.

M. B. Rowton, The Background of the Treaty between Ramesses II
and Hattusilis III, JCS XIII, 1959, 1-11.

Assur

H. Otten, Korrespondenz mit Tukulti-Ninurta aus Boğazköy in
E. Weidner, Die Inschriften Tukulti-Ninurtas I, AfO Beih. 12,
1959, 64-68.

——, Ein Brief aus Hattusa an Bâbu-aḫu-iddina, AfO XIX, 1959-60,
39-46.

Babylon

A. L. Oppenheim, A Letter from the Hittite King (passages from
KBo I 10 in translation) in: Letters from Mesopotamia, Chicago,
1967, 139-146.

5. Books mainly dealing with Cultural History

A. Goetze, Kleinasien, Handbuch der Altertumswissenschaft Abt. 3,
Teil 1, Bd. 3, Abschnitt 2, Unterabschnitt 1, München, 1933;
Zweite, neubearbeite Auflage, München, 1957.

G. Walser (editor), H. Otten, A. Goetze, E. von Schuler, H. G.
Güterbock, E. Akurgal and K. Bittel together reviewed the
continuation of Hittitological research in Neuere Hethiterforschung, Historia Einzelschriften 7, Wiesbaden, 1964.

A. Goetze, Hethiter, Churriter und Assyrer. Hauptlinien der vorderasiatischen Kulturentwicklung im II. Jahrtausend v. Chr. Geb.,
Oslo, 1936.

G. Contenau, La Civilisation des Hittites et des Mitanniens, Paris,
1934.

G. Furlani, Saggi sulla Civiltà degli Hittiti, Udine, 1939.

O. R. Gurney, The Hittites, Pelican A 259, Hammondsworth, 1952[1]
etc.; Revised edition, 1961 etc.

The following books are still of some interest:

E. MEYER, Reich und Kultur der Chetiter, Berlin, 1914.

J. GARSTANG, The Hittite Empire being a Survey of the History, Geography and Monuments of Hittite Asia Minor and Syria, London, 1929 (particularly useful in respect to the description of geographical features and archaeological monuments).

6. IMPORTANT STUDIES

H. G. GÜTERBOCK, The Hurrian Element in the Hittite Empire, CHM II, 1954, 383-394.

——, Towards a Definition of the Term "Hittite", Oriens X, 1957, 233-239.

7. STUDIES ON SOCIAL HISTORY

I. M. DIAKONOFF, Die hethitische Gesellschaft, MIO XIII, 1967, 313-366 (review article of E. A. MENABDE, Chettskoe Obščestvo Ekonomika, sobstvennost', sem'ja i nasledovanie, Tbilisi, 1965).

S. ALP, Die Soziale Klasse der NAM.RA-Leute und ihre hethitische Bezeichnung, JKAF I, 1950, 113-135.

K. K. RIEMSCHNEIDER, Zum Lehnwesen bei den Hethitern, ArOr XXXIII, 1965, 333-340.

V. SOUČEK, Randnotizen zu den hethitischen Feldertexten, MIO VIII, 1963, 368-382.

H. KLENGEL, Die Rolle der "Ältesten" (LÚ.MEŠŠU.GI) in Kleinasien der Hethiterzeit, ZA LVII, N.F. 23, 1965, 223-236.

H. OTTEN, Aufgaben eines Bürgermeisters in Hattusa, BM III, 1964, 91-95.

K. K. RIEMSCHNEIDER, Die Thronfolgeordnung im althethitischen Reich in H. KLENGEL (ed.), Beiträge zur sozialen Struktur des alten Vorderasiens, Schriften zur Geschichte und Kultur des alten Orients 1, Berlin, 1971, 79-102.

8. THE POSITION OF THE HITTITE KING

H. G. GÜTERBOCK, Authority and Law in the Hittite Kingdom in Authority and Law in the Ancient Orient, JAOS Supplement 17, 1954, 16-24.

O. R. Gurney, Hittite Kingship in: S. H. Hooke (editor), Myth,
Ritual, and Kingship, Oxford, 1958, 105-121.
E. von Schuler, Hethitische Königserlasse als Quellen der Rechts-
findung und ihr Verhältniss zum kodifizierten Recht, Festschrift
Friedrich, Heidelberg, 1959, 435-472.

9. International Law and Warfare

V. Korošec, Hethitische Staatsverträge. Ein Beitrag zur ihrer juris-
tischen Wertung, Leipziger rechtswissenschaftlicher Studien 60,
Leipzig, 1931 (reprint: Leipzig, 1970; new edition forthcoming).
E. von Schuler, Sonderformen hethitischer Staatsverträge, Anadolu
Araştirmalari II 1-2, 1965, 445-464.
A. Goetze, Warfare in Asia Minor, Iraq XXV, 1963, 124-130.
V. Korošec, The Warfare of the Hittites - From the Legal point of
view, Iraq XXV, 1963, 159-166.

10. The Geography of Hittite Asia Minor

A. Götze, Kleinasien zur Hethiterzeit. Eine geographische Unter-
suchung, Heidelberg, 1924.
A. Goetze, Kizzuwatna and the Problem of Hittite Geography,
Yale Oriental Series, Researches XXII, New Haven, 1940.
E. Forrer, Forschungen I-II, Erkner bei Berlin, 1926.
——, Ḫayaša-Azzi, Caucasica IX, 1931, 1-24.
——, Kilikien zur Zeit des Hatti-Reiches, Klio XXX, 1937, 135-186.
E. Bilgiç, Die Ortsnamen der "kappadokischen" Urkunden im
Rahmen der alten Sprachen Anatoliens, AfO XV, 1945-51, 1-53.
F. Cornelius, Geographie des Hethiterreiches, Or XXVII, 1958,
225-251 and 373-397.
J. Garstang, O. R. Gurney, The Geography of the Hittite Empire,
London, 1959.
H. G. Güterbock, The North-Central Area of Hittite Anatolia,
JNES XX, 1961, 85-97.
——, Das dritte Monument am Karabel, IM XVII, 1967, 63-71.
E. Laroche, Notes de toponymie anatolienne, ΜΝΗΜΗΣ ΧΑΡΙΝ
Gedenkschrift P. Kretschmer II 1957, 1-7.
——, Études de toponymie anatolienne, RHA fasc. 69, 1961, 57-98.
H. Otten, Zur Lokalisierung von Arzawa und Lukka, JCS XV, 1961,
112-113.

J. G. MacQueen, Geography and History in Western Asia Minor in
the Second Millennium B.C., AnSt XVIII, 1968, 169-185; See
also: J. Mellaart, Anatolian Trade with Europe and Anatolian
Geography and Culture Provinces in the Late Bronze Age, AnSt
XVIII, 1968, 187-202.

E. von Schuler, Die Kaškäer. Ein Beitrag zur Ethnographie des
alten Kleinasien, Berlin, 1965.

11. Personal Names in Hittite Texts

E. Laroche, Les Noms des Hittites, Paris, 1966. See also, for the
period of the Cappadocian Texts, P. Garelli, Les Assyriens en
Cappadoce, Chapitre III, Les populations en présence, 127-168
(see above E 3 a).

F. RELIGION

1. General Works

E. Laroche, Recherches sur les noms des dieux hittites, RHA fasc. 46,
1946-47, 1-139.

H. G. Güterbock, Hittite Religion in V. Ferm (editor), Forgotten
Religions, New York, 1949, 83-109.

——, Hittite Mythology in S. N. Kramer (editor), Mythologies of
the Ancient World, Garden City, New York, 1961, 139-179.

H. Otten, Die Religionen des alten Kleinasien in Handbuch der
Orientalistik Bd. VIII: Religion, 1. Abschn., Lief. 1, Leiden, 1964.

E. von Schuler, Kleinasien. Die Mythologie der Hethiter und Hur-
riter in H. W. Haussig, Wörterbuch der Mythologie I (Götter
und Mythen im vorderen Orient), Stuttgart, 1965, 141-215.

V. Haras, Der Kult von Nerik. Ein Beitrag zur hethitischen Religionsgeschichte, Studia Pohl 4, Roma, 1970.

2. Special Studies

S. Alp, Untersuchungen zu den Beamtennamen im hethitischen
Festzeremoniell, Sammlung Orientalistischer Arbeiten 5, Leipzig,
1940.

E. Laroche, La prière hittite: vocabulaire et typologie, École pratique des Hautes Études, Vᵉ Section, Sciences Religieuses; Annuaire T. LXXII, 1964-65, 3-29.

M. KALAÇ, Das Pantheon der hieroglyphen-luwischen Inschriften, Or XXXIV, 1965, 401-427.

K. K. RIEMSCHNEIDER, Babylonische Geburtsomina in hethitischer Übersetzung, Studien zu den Boğ.-T. 9, Wiesbaden, 1970.

For the description of Hittite Cult Statues in Cuneiform texts, see:

C. G. VON BRANDENSTEIN, Götterbilder in hethitischen Texten, MVAeG XLVI 2, 1943, Leipzig (review by H. G. GÜTERBOCK in: Or XV, 1946, 482-496).

H. G. GÜTERBOCK, Hethitischer Götterdarstellungen und Götternamen, Belleten fasc. 26, 1943, 295-317.

L. (JAKOB-)ROST, Zu den hethitischen Bildbeschreibungen, MIO VIII, 1961, 161-217; IX, 1963, 175-239.

For the Hittite Sanctuary at Yazilikaya, see (in chronological order):

K. BITTEL, R. NAUMANN and H. OTTO, Yazilikaya, WVDOG 61, Leipzig, 1941 (reprint: Osnabrück, 1967).

E. LAROCHE, Le panthéon de Yazilikaya, JCS VI, 1952, 115-123.

H. G. GÜTERBOCK, Yazilikaya, MDOG 86, 1953, 65-76.

H. OTTEN, Die Götter Nupatik Pirinkir, Ḫešue und Ḫatni-Pišaisapḫi in den hethitischen Felsrelief von Yazilikaya, Anatolia IV, 1959, 27-37.

H. G. GÜTERBOCK, The God Suwaliyat reconsidered, RHA fasc. 68, 1961, 1-18.

Th. BERAN, Zur Datum des Felsrelief von Yazilikaya, ZA LVII, N.F. 23, 1965, 258-273.

Th. BERAN, Die Siegel der hethitischen Grosskönige, IM XVII, 1967, 72-77.

H. OTTEN, Zur Datierung und Bedeutung des Felsheiligtums von Yazilikaya. Eine Entgegnung, ZA LVIII, N.F. 24, 1967, 223-240.

E. LAROCHE, Les dieux de Yazilikaya, RHA XXVII Fasc. 84-85, 1969, 61-109.

G. HITTITE ART

H. Th. BOSSERT, Altanatolien (Die ältesten Kulturen des Mittelmeerkreises, 2. Band), Berlin, 1942.

R. NAUMANN, Architektur Kleinasiens von ihren Anfängen bis zum

Ende der hethitischen Zeit, Tübingen, 1955 (2nd enlarged edition: 1971).

M. Vieyra, Hittite Art 2300-750 B.C., London, 1955.

E. Akurgal, Die Kunst der Hethiter, München Hirmer Verlag, 1961 (see also: E. Akurgal in: G. Walser, Neuere Hethiterforschung, 74-118, cf. E 5).

W. Orthmann, Untersuchungen zur späthethitischen Kunst, Saarbrücker Beiträge zur Altertumskunde 8, Bonn, 1971.

IV. HURRIAN

COMPILED BY

Philo. H. J. HOUWINK TEN CATE

A. SOURCES

J. Friedrich, Churritisch in Altkleinasiatische Sprachen, 1-30 (the history of the research is described on pp. 6-10).

For an enumeration of the available Hurrian material, see Friedrich, l. c., pp. 2-5 and add E. Laroche, Documents en langue hourrite provenant de Ras Shamra, Chapitre II in Ugaritica V, Paris, 1968, 447-544.

For the Hurrian Personal Names of Boğazköy and Ras Shamra, see now:

E. Laroche, Les Noms de Hittites, 343-362 (Les noms hourrites).
Fr. Gröndahl, Die Personennamen der Texte aus Ugarit, Studia Pohl 1, Roma, 1967, II. Kap.: Die hurritischen Namen.
Hurrian names in the Capadocian Tablets have been collected anew by:

P. Garelli, Les Assyriens en Cappadoce, 155-158 (see above III E 3 a).

B. LINGUISTICS

1. Grammars

E. A. Speiser, Introduction to Hurrian, AASOR XX (1940-1941), 1941, New Haven (reviewed by J. Friedrich, Die erste Gesamtdarstellung der churritischen Grammatik, Or XII, 1943, 199-225).
F. W. Bush, A Grammar of the Hurrian Language, Brandeis University 1964, available in Xerography from University Microfilms Limited Tylers Green, High Wycombe, England.
E. Laroche, Le hourrite de Ras Shamra, Ugaritica V, 527-533 (see above).

2. GLOSSARIES

J. FRIEDRICH, Hethitisches Wörterbuch, 1952, 1957, 1961, 1966 (cf. Anatolian Languages, C 2).

E. LAROCHE, Lexique hourrite (de Ras Shamra), Ugaritica V, 533-540 (see above).

3. GRAMMATICAL STUDIES

To the material given by Friedrich may be added:

A. KAMMENHUBER, Hurrische Nomina, Gedenkschrift für W. BRAN-DENSTEIN, Innsbruck 1968, 247-258, and Morphologie hurrischer Nomina, MSS 23, 1968, 49-80.

W. FARBER, Zu einigen Enklitika im Hurrischen, Or XL, 1971, 29-66.

On the relationship between Urartian and Hurrian, see:

W. C. BENEDICT, Urartians and Hurtians, JAOS LXXX, 1960, 100-104.

I. M. DIAKONOFF, A Comparative Survey of the Hurtian and Urartean Languages, PASb, 1961, 369-423 (Russian), 598-602 (English Summary).

——, Hurrisch und Urartäisch, MSS Beihefte N. F. 6, München, 1971.

C. HISTORY

A. UNGNAD, Subartu. Beiträge zur Kulturgeschichte und Völker-kunde Vorderasiens, Berlin-Leipzig, 1936.

I. J. GELB, Hurrians and Subarians, Chicago, 1944.

——, New Light on Hurrians and Subarians, Studi Orientalistici in Onore di G. Levi della Vida, Publicazioni dell' Istituto per L'Oriente LII, Vol. I, 1956, 378-392.

——, Hurrians at Nippur in the Sargonic Period, Festschrift Friedrich, Heidelberg, 1959, 183-194.

F. IMPARATI, I Hurriti, Firenze, 1964 (with extensive bibliography).

Hurrian influence on neighbouring countries:

E. A. SPEISER, The Hurrian Participation in the Civilization of Meso-potamia, Syria and Palestine, CHM I, 1953, 311-327

H. G. Güterbock, The Hurrian Element in the Hittite Empire, CHM II, 1954, 383-394.

D. RELIGION

See above Anatolian Languages F, and add:
E. Laroche, Notes sur le panthéon hourrite de Ras Shamra, JAOS LXXXVIII, 1968, 148-150.

E. IMPORTANT JOURNALS

Anadolu. Revue des études d'archéologie et d'histoire en Turquie (Paris, 1951-   ).
Anatolia. Revue annuelle de l'Institut d'Archéologie de l'Université d'Ankara (Ankara, 1956-   ).
Anatolica. Annuaire international pour les civilisations de l'Asie antérieure publiée sous les auspices de l'Institut historique et archéologique néerlandais à Istanbul (Leiden, 1967-   ).
Anatolian Studies. Journal of the British Institute of Archaeology at Ankara.
Belleten. Türk Tarih Kumuru (Belleten) (Ankara, 1937-   ).
Istanbuler Mitteilungen (Berlin, 1950-   ).
Jahrbuch für Kleinasiatische Forschung (Heidelberg, 1950-1953), continued under the name of Anadolu Araştirmalari. Istanbul Universitesi Edebiyat Fakültesi ... (Ankara, 1955; Istanbul, 1959-   ).
Revue hittite et asianique. Organe de la Société des études hittites (Paris, 1930-   ).

N.B. The publications of the German Oriental Society are of special importance for Hittite studies:

MDOG   = Mitteilungen der Deutschen Orient-Gesellschaft (Berlin, 1899-   ).
WVDOG = Wissenschaftliche Veröffentlichungen der Deutschen Orient-Gesellschaft (Leipzig, 1900-   ).
See, too, Studien zu den Boğazköy-Texten, herausgegeben von der Kommission für den Alten Orient der Akademie der Wissenschaften

und der Literatur, Mainz (in Zusammenarbeit mit der Deutschen
Orient-Gesellschaft) (Wiesbaden, 1965-   ).

KlF   = This abbreviation refers to the Kleinasiatische Forschun-
             gen (Weimar, 1927-1930: I 1-3).

V. URARTIAN

COMPILED BY

L. DE MEYER

General Works

In general the reader is referred to:

Keilschriftbibliographie appearing in Orientalia.
E. F. WEIDNER, Bibliographie, AfO.

The Soviet researches have been summed up in:

G. A. MELIKISHVILI, G. G. GIORGADZE, Urartology and Hittitology,
Fifty Years of Soviet Oriental Studies (Brief Reviews), Moscow,
1968.

The latest status quaestionis was presented by:

J. FRIEDRICH, Urartäisch, Handbuch der Orientalistik II, 1/2, 2,
Leiden-Köln, 1969, 31-53.

A. PHILOLOGY

1. GRAMMARS

a. *Based essentially on* J. FRIEDRICH, Einführung ins Urartäische,
MVAG 37, 3, Leipzig, 1933, *are:*

W. C. BENEDICT, Urartian Phonology and Morphology, Ann Arbor,
1958.
G. A. MELIKISHVILI, Die urartäische Sprache, Rome, 1971 (with an
appendix by M. SALVINI).
I. I. MESHCHANINOV, The Grammatical Structure of the Urartian
Language, Moscow-Leningrad, 1958 (Part I) and 1962 (Part II)
(in Russian).

b. *A new presentation* of the grammatical features was given by FRIEDRICH in 1969, cf. supra.

2. LEXICA

a. V. A. GVAKHARIYA, A Dictionary-Symphony of the Urartian Language, Moscow, 1963 (in Russian).

b. Also in the text editions, infra sub B 1, by KÖNIG and MELIKISHVILI and, sub B 3, by ARUTYUNIAN and DYAKONOV.

3. SOME PHILOLOGIC ARTICLES

a. *Grammatical Studies*

J. FRIEDRICH, Urartäisches, WZKM 47, 1940, 187-201.
——, Zwei Berichtigungen zum Urartäischen, Or 37, 1968, 346.
T. V. GAMKRELIDZE, Some Problems of the Structure of Urartean, VDI 4/1956, 138-145 (in Russian).
A. GOETZE, Indefinites and Negations, Prohibitive and Imperative in the Urartean Language, RHA 3, 1936, 179-198.
——, On some Urartean Verbal Forms, RHA 3, 1936, 266-282.
M. SALVINI, Studi sul verbo urarteo, Studi micenei ed egeo-anatolici 5, 1968, 97-127.

b. *Comparative Studies*

W. C. BENEDICT, Urartians and Hurrians, JAOS 80, 1960, 100-104.
I. M. DYAKONOV, Hurrisch und Urartäisch, Munich 1971.
G. B. JAHUKYAN, The Urartean and Indo-European Languages, Erevan, 1963 (in Russian).

B. LITERATURE

1. TEXT EDITIONS

a. F. W. KÖNIG, Handbuch der chaldischen Inschriften, AfO Beih. 8, Graz, 1955-1957.

G. A. MELIKISHVILI, Urartean Cuneiform Inscriptions, Moscow[2], 1960 (in Russian).

b. For a list of texts published after KÖNIG, cf. FRIEDRICH, Handbuch der Orientalistik II, 1/2, 2, 32-33 and SALVINI *apud* MELIKISH-VILI, Die urartäische Sprache, 91-92 and 105.

2. HISTORY OF LITERATURE

For a brief survey cf. L. DE MEYER, Oerarteïsche Literatuur, Moderne Encyclopedie der Wereldliteratuur 5, Gent, 1970, 64.

3. SOME MONOGRAPHS ON TEXTS

N. V. ARUTYUNIAN, The Annals of Argisti, EV 7, 1953, 81-119 (in Russian).

——, New Urartian Inscriptions from Karmir Blur, Erevan, 1966 (in Russian).

M. SALVINI, Neue urartäische Inschriften aus Karmir-Blur, Or 36, 1967, 437-449.

I. M. DYAKONOV, Urartian Letters and Records, Moscow-Leningrad, 1963 (in Russian).

J. FRIEDRICH, Neue urartäische Inschriften, ZDMG 105, 1955, 53-73.

A. GOETZE, Zur Kelischin-Stele, ZA 39, 1930, 99-128.

W. C. BENEDICT, The Urartian-Assyrian Inscription of Kelishin, JAOS 81, 1961, 359-385.

M. VON TSERETHELI, Die neuen haldischen Inschriften des Königs Sardurs von Urartu (um 750 v. Chr.), Heidelberg, 1928.

——, Études ourartéennes, RA, from 1933 to 1959 (irregular).

C. SOME BOOKS ON (CULTURAL) HISTORY

E. AKURGAL, Urartäische und altiranische Kunstzentren, Ankara, 1968.

G. AZARPAY, Urartian Art and Artifacts. A Chronological Study, Berkeley-Los Angeles, 1968.

Th. BERAN, Urartu, H. SCHMÖKEL (ed.), Kulturgeschichte des alten Orient, Stuttgart, 1961, 606-657.

I. M. DYAKONOV e.a., Assyrian and Babylonian Sources for the History of Urartu, Supplement to the VDI, 1951, No. 2, 255-356, No. 3, 205-252, Index, No. 4, 283-305 (in Russian).

A. GOETZE, Kleinasien, Handbuch der Altertumswissenschaft III, 1, 3, München², 1957, 187-200.

M. N. VAN LOON, Urartian Art: its Distinctive Traits in the Light of New Excavations, Istanbul, 1966.

B. B. PIOTROVSKY, P. N. SCHULTZ, V. A. GOLOVKINA, S. P. TOLSTOV, Ourartou, Néapolis des Scythes Kharezm, Paris, 1954.

B. B. PIOTROVSKIJ, Urartu: the Kingdom of Urartu and its Art (translated and edited by P. S. GELLING), London, 1967.

——, Il regno di Van: Urartu (translated by M. SALVINI), Incunabula Graeca XII, Rome, 1966.

M. SALVINI, Nairi e Ur(u)aṭri. Contributo alla storia della formazione del regno di Urarṭu, Incunabula Graeca XVI, Rome, 1967.

D. PERIODICALS

For periodicals containing studies on Urartology cf. Bibliography of Akkadian D and the Soviet journals such as EV, IFŽ, VDI and further:

Anadolu, Revue des études d'archéologie et d'histoire en Turquie (Paris, 1951-   ).

Anatolia, Revue annuelle de l'Institut d'Archéologie de l'Université d'Ankara (Ankara, 1956).

Istanbuler Mitteilungen (Berlin, 1950-   ). (IM),

VI. ELAMITIC

L. DE MEYER

General Works

In general the reader is referred to:

Keilschriftbibliographie appearing in Orientalia.
E. F. WEIDNER, Bibliographie, AfO.
H. H. PAPER, The Phonology and Morphology of Royal Achaemenid
    Elamite, Ann Arbor, 1955, 112-119 (*Selected Bibliography*).

An excellent status quaestionis was presented by:

E. REINER, The Elamite Language, Handbuch der Orientalistik II,
    1/2, 2, Leiden-Köln, 1969, 54-118.

A. PHILOLOGY

1. GRAMMARS

a. *Surveys*

F. BORK, Elam (Sprache), RLV 3, 1925, 70-83.
I. M. DYAKONOV, The Elamite Language, *Idem*, The Languages of
    the Ancient Near East, Moscow, 1967, 85-112 and 439-442 (in
    Russian).
R. LABAT, Structure de la langue élamite: état présent de la question,
    Conférences de l'Institut de Linguistique de l'Université de
    Paris 10, 1951, 23-42.
P. MERIGGI, L'elamico, ANLA 76, Rome, 1966, 559-567.

b. *RAE*

H. H. PAPER, The Phonology and Morphology of Royal Achaemenid
    Elamite, Ann Arbor, 1955.

c. *A New Presentation*

E. REINER, The Elamite Language, *supra*.

2. LEXICA

Complete glossaries are only found in the text editions, *infra sub* B 1, by König, Stève, Cameron and *infra sub* B 3, by Yusifov.

W. HINZ, Zum elamischen Wortschatz, ZA 50, 1952, 237-252.
——, Elamisch *hu-sa*, Or 31, 1962, 34-44.
——, Elamica II, Or 36, 1967, 323-333.
M. LAMBERT, Epigraphie élamite: I, RA 49, 1955, 42-45; II, RA 49, 1955, 149-153; III, RA 56, 1962, 91-94.

For other contributions to lexicon in periodicals by CAMERON, FRIE-DRICH, HALLOCK, HINZ, LABAT, LAMBERT, REINER, see the bibliographies.

3. SOME PHILOLOGIC ARTICLES

a. *Grammatical studies*

F. BORK, Die elamischen Klammer, AfO 9, 1933-34, 292-300.
J. FRIEDRICH, Die Partikeln der zitierten Rede im Achämenidisch-Elamischen, Or 12, 1943, 23-30.
——, Altpersisches und Elamisches, Or 18, 1949, 1-29.
R. T. HALLOCK, Notes on Achaemenid Elamite, JNES 17, 1958, 256-262.
——, The Finitive Verb in Achaemenid Elamite, JNES 18, 1959, 1-19.
——, The Pronominal Suffixes in Achaemenid Elamite, JNES 21, 1962, 53-56.
——, The Verbal Nouns in Achaemenid Elamite, AS 16, Chicago, 1965, 121-126.
W. HINZ, Elamisches, ArOr 18, 1950, 282-306.
——, Zur Entzifferung der elamischen Strichschrift, IrAnt 2, 1962, 1-21.
P. MERIGGI, Zur Lesung und Deutung der proto-elamischen Königs-inschriften, BiOr 26, 1969, 176-177.
E. REINER, Calques sur le vieux perse en élamite achéménide, BSLP 55, 1960, 222-227.

J. B. Yusifov, On the Grammatical Forms of the Economic Documents of Susa, VDI 84, ²/1963, 204-209 (in Russian).

b. *Comparative studies*

Th. Kluge, Das Elamische: ein Versuch zu einer sprachlichen Eingliederung, Mus 46, 1933, 111-156.
Dyakonov, *supra sub* A la, 107-112.

B. LITERATURE

1. Text Editions

a. *General*

Most of the Elamite texts are published in the *MDP*. W. Hinz (contributions by R. Borger and G. Gropp), Altiranische Funde und Forschungen, Berlin, 1969, contains some new text edition.

b. *Old and Middle Elamite Texts*

E. Reiner, Corpus of Old and Middle Elamite Texts, forthcoming, will include also a critical bibliography.
F. W. König, Die elamischen Königsinschriften, AfO Beih. 16, Graz, 1965.
M.-J. Steve, Textes élamites et accadiens de Tchoga Zanbil, MDP 41, Paris, 1967.

c. *Achaemenid Elamite Texts*

R. G. Kent, Old Persian: Grammar, Texts, Lexicon, New Haven, ²1953 (repr. 1961) contains a complete bibliography of editions of Achaemenid texts, including the Elamite versions.
F. H. Weissbach, Die Keilinschriften der Achämeniden, VAB 3, Leipzig, 1911.
G. G. Cameron, Persepolis Treasury Tablets, OIP 65, Chicago, 1948.
——, Persepolis Treasury Tablets Old and New, JNES 17, 1958, 161-176.
——, New Tablets from the Persepolis Treasury, JNES 24, 1965, 167-192.
R. T. Hallock, Persepolis Fortification Tablets, OIP 92, Chicago, 1970.

2. History of Literature

For a brief survey cf. L. De Meyer, Elamitische Literatuur, Moderne Encyclopedie der Wereldliteratuur 2, Gent, 1964, 496-497, with bibliography.

3. Some Articles on Texts

R. Borger, W. Hinz, Eine Dareios-Inschrift aus Pasargadae, ZDMG 109, 1959, 117-127.

F. Bork, Die Zeughausurkunden von Susa: Teil I. Schrift, Sprache, Chronologie, Altkaukasische Studien III, Leipzig, 1941.

G. G. Cameron, The Elamite Version of the Bisitun Inscriptions, JCS 14, 1960, 59-68.

——, The "Daiva" Inscription of Xerxes in Elamite, WO 2, 1959, 470-476.

W. Hinz, Elams Vertrag mit Narām-Sin von Akkade, ZA 58, 1967, 66-96.

——, Die elamischen Inschriften des Hanne, A Locust's Leg. Studies in Honour of S. H. Taqizadeh, London, 1962, 105-116.

——, The Elamite Version of the Record of Darius' Palace at Susa, JNES 9, 1950, 1-7.

——, Die untere Grabinschrift des Dareios, ZDMG 115, 1965, 229-241.

M. Lambert, Les inscriptions élamites de Tchogha-Zanbil, IrAnt 5, 1965, 18-38.

E. Reiner, The Earliest Elamite Inscription?, JNES 24, 1965, 337-340.

M.-J. Steve, Fragmenta Elamica, Or 37, 1968, 290-303.

Y. B. Yusifov, The Elamite Economic Documents from Susa, VDI 84, 2/1963, 191-222 and 85, 3/1963, 200-261 (in Russian).

C. SOME BOOKS ON (CULTURAL) HISTORY

P. Amiet, Elam, Auvers-sur Oise, 1966.

L. Van den Berghe, Archéologie de l'Iran ancien, DMOA 6, Leiden, 1959 (repr. 1966), with forthcoming supplement.

G.G. Cameron, History of Early Iran, Chicago, 1936 (repr. 1968).

W. Hinz, Das Reich Elam, Stuttgart, 1964.

——, Persia c. 2400-1800 B.C., CAH² I, 23, Cambridge, 1963.

——, Persia c. 1800-1550 B.C., CAH² II, 7, Cambridge, 1964.

R. LABAT, Elam c. 1600-1200 B.C., CAH² II, 29, Cambridge, 1963.

——, Elam and Western Persia c. 1200-1000 B.C., CAH² II, 32, Cambridge, 1964.

E. PORADA, The Art of Ancient Iran. Pre-Islamic Cultures, New York, 1965 (with the collaboration of R. H. DYSON and C. K. WILKINSON).

Y. B. YUSIFOV, Elam. Social and Economic History, Moscow, 1968 (in Russian).

D. PERIODICALS

For periodicals containing studies on Elamitology cf. Bibliography of Akkadian D.

VII. ANCIENT PERSIAN

L. DE MEYER

General Works

In general the reader is referred to:
Keilschriftbibliographie appearing in Orientalia.
E. F. WEIDNER, Bibliographie, AfO.
M. MAYRHOFER, W. DRESSLER, Indogermanische Chronik, Die Sprache
(Zeitschrift für Sprachwissenschaft) since 1967.

A. PHILOLOGY

1. GRAMMARS

W. BRANDENSTEIN, M. MAYRHOFER, Handbuch des Altpersischen,
Wiesbaden, 1964.
R. G. KENT, Old Persian: Grammar, Texts, Lexicon, AOS 33, New
Haven, ²1953 (repr. 1961).
A. MEILLET, E. BENVENISTE, Grammaire du Vieux-Perse, Paris, ²1931.

2. LEXICA

a. W. HINZ, Altpersischer Wortschatz, Leipzig, 1942 (repr. 1966).
W. WÜST, Altpersische Studien. Sprach- und kulturgeschichtliche
Beiträge zum Glossar der Achämeniden-Inschriften, München,
1966.

b. Also in the handbooks sub A 1.

c. For Old Persian words in other languages, see:

K. HOFFMANN, Handbuch der Orientalistik I, IV, 1, Leiden, 1958, p. 5,
note 1.
E. BENVENISTE, Titres et noms propres en iranien ancien, Paris, 1966.

3. SOME PHILOLOGIC ARTICLES

a. *Grammatical studies*

W. COWGILL, The Aorists and Perfects of Old Persian, ZVS 82, 1968,
259-268.

W. EILERS, Zum altpersischen Relativpronomen, ZVS 82, 1968, 62-88.

E. A. HAHN, On Alleged Anacolutha in Old Persian, JAOS 85, 1965,
48-58.

M. MAYRHOFER, Altpersische Späne, Or 33, 1964, 72-87.

R. SCHMITT, Medisches und persisches Sprachgut bei Herodot, ZDMG
117, 1967, 119-145.

K. STRUNK, Wortstruktur und Pronomen im Altpersischen, ZVS 81,
1967, 265-275.

——, Wortstellung und Univerbierung altpersischer Korrelativver-
bindungen, ZVS 83, 1969, 49-58.

b. *Comparative studies*

J. DUCHESNE-GUILLEMIN, L'étude de l'iranien ancien au vingtième
siècle, Kratylos 7, 1962, 1-44.

K. HOFFMANN, Altiranisch, Handbuch der Orientalistik I, IV, 1,
Leiden, 1958, 1-19.

M. MAYRHOFER, Die Rekonstruktion des Medischen, Sonderabdruck
aus dem Anzeiger der phil.-hist. Klasse der Österreichischen
Akademie der Wissenschaften, Jahrgang 1968, 1-22.

c. *The Old Persian Cuneiform Script*

I. M. DYAKONOV, The Origin of the 'Old Persian' Writing System and
the Ancient Oriental Epigraphic and Annalistic Tradition,
W. B. Henning Memorial Volume, London, 1968, 98-124.

W. HINZ, Die Entstehung der altpersischen Keilschrift, AMI NF 1,
1968, 95-98.

J. HARMATTA, The Bisitun Inscription and the Introduction of the
Old Persian Cuneiform Script, AcAn 14, 1966, 255-283.

J. KURYŁOWICZ, Zur altpersischen Keilschrift, Zeitschrift für Phonetik, Sprachwissenschaft und Kommunikationsforschung 17, 6,
1964, 563-569.

B. LITERATURE

1. Text Editions

Awaiting the planned volume on Old Persian in the *Corpus Inscriptionum Iranicarum*, the reader is referred to Kent, *Old Persian*, supra sub A 1, for a comprehensive edition of all the epigraphical material.

Older editions are:

F. H. Weissbach, Die Keilinschriften der Achämeniden, Leipzig, 1911.

E. Herzfeld, Altpersische Inschriften, Berlin, 1938.

W. Hinz, Altiranische Funde und Forschungen, Berlin, 1969, contains some new text edition (contributions of R. Borger and G. Gropp).

2. History of Literature

I. Gershevitch, Old Iranian Literature, Handbuch der Orientalistik, I, IV, 2, Leiden, 1968, 5-10.

R. Rocher, Oud- en Middel-Iraanse Literatuur, Moderne Encyclopedie der Wereldliteratuur 6 (Gent, 1970), 321-322.

3. Some Articles on Texts

G. G. Cameron, The Old Persian Text of the Bisitun Inscription, JCS 5, 1951, 47-54.

R. G. Kent, Cameron's Old Persian Readings at Bisitun. Restorations and Notes, JCS 5, 1951, 55-57.

E. Herzfeld, A New Inscription of Xerxes from Persepolis, SAOC 5, Chicago, 1932.

W. Hinz, Die untere Grabinschrift des Dareios, ZDMG 115, 1965, 227-241.

F. W. König, Der Burgbau zu Susa, Leipzig, 1930.

——, Relief und Inschrift des Königs Dareios I. am Felsen von Bagistan, Leiden, 1938.

C. SOME BOOKS ON (CULTURAL) HISTORY

H. BENGSTON (ed.), Griechen und Perser, Fischer Weltgeschichte 5, Frankfurt, 1967.

L. VAN DEN BERGHE, Archéologie de l'Iran ancien, DMOA 6, Leiden, 1959 (repr. 1966) with forthcoming supplement.

A. CHRISTENSEN, Die Iranier, Handbuch der Altertumswissenschaft III, I, 3, 3, 1, München, 1933, 201-310.

W. CULICAN, The Medes and Persians, Ancient Peoples and Places 42, London, 1965.

——, Imperial Cities of Persia. Persepolis, Susa and Pasargadae, London, 1970.

J. DUCHESNE-GUILLEMIN, La religion de l'Iran ancien, Mana 1/III, Paris, 1962.

I. M. DYAKONOV, History of Media, Moscow-Leningrad, 1956 (in Russian).

R. GHIRSHMAN, Perse (Proto-Iraniens, Mèdes, Achéménides), L'univers des Formes, Paris, 1963.

E. HERZFELD, The Persian Empire. Studies in Geography and Ethnography of the Ancient Near East, Wiesbaden, 1968.

W. HINZ, Persis, RE Suppl. 12, Stuttgart, 1970, 1022-1038.

F. W. KÖNIG, Älteste Geschichte der Meder und Perser, Leipzig, 1934.

O. LEUZE, Die Satrapieneinteilung in Syrien und im Zweistromenlande von 520-320, Halle/S, 1935.

A. T. OLMSTEAD, History of the Persian Empire, Chicago, 1948 (5th impr. 1966).

H. H. VON DER OSTEN, Die Welt der Perser, Grosse Kulturen der Frühzeit, Stuttgart, 1966 (6th impr.).

G. WALSER, Die Völkerschaften auf den Reliefs von Persepolis. Historische Studie über den sog. Tributzug an der Apadana-Treppe, Teheraner Forschungen 2, Berlin, 1966.

D. PERIODICALS

For periodicals containing studies on Old Persian cf. Bibliography of Akkadian D and the journals on linguistics or on Iranian studies (e.g. the list of abbreviations in BRANDENSTEIN-MAYRHOFER, supra sub A 1).

VIII. UGARITIC *

J. P. LETTINGA

General Works

This section contains the available bibliographical material.

W. BAUMGARTNER, Ras Schamra und das Alte Testament, ThRsch 12, 1940, 163-188; 13, 1941, 1-20, 85-102, 157-183.

M. DIETRICH, O. LORETZ, Ugaritistische Bibliographie der Jahre **1928-1966**: I. Titelband, II. Indizes der Titel, III. Indexbände (AOAT 20/1-3 ff.) (in the press).

A. HERDNER, Corpus des tablettes en cunéiformes alphabétiques découvertes à Ras Shamra-Ugarit de 1929 à 1939 (MRS X), Paris, 1963, 293-339: Bibliographie générale [**1939-1961**].

R. DE LANGHE, Les textes de Ras Shamra-Ugarit et leurs rapports avec le milieu biblique de l'Ancien Testament I, Gembloux-Paris, 1945, XV-LVII: Index bibliographique.

C. F. A. SCHAEFFER, Ugaritica I (MRS III), Paris, 1939, 147-322: Bibliographie de Ras Shamra (années **1929-1938**).

A. PHILOLOGY

1. GRAMMARS

J. AISTLEITNER, Untersuchungen zur Grammatik des Ugaritischen (BSAW 100, Heft 6), Berlin, 1954 (in fact a complete grammar of Ugaritic).

F. C. FENSHAM, 'n Beknopte Ugaritiese Grammatika, Annale Universiteit van Stellenbosch Vol. 32, Serie B No. 1, 1970.

H. GOESEKE, Die Sprache der semitischen Texte Ugarits und ihre

---

* I.e. the language of the alphabetic cuneiform texts discovered at Ras Shamra (Ugarit) and belonging to the 14th and 13th centuries B.C.

Stellung innerhalb des Semitischen, Wissenschaftl. Zeitschr. der
Martin   Luther-Universität   Halle-Wittenberg   [Ges.-Sprachw.
Reihe] VII/3, Juni 1958, 623-652.

C. H. GORDON, Ugaritic Grammar. The Present Status of the Linguistic
Study of the Semitic Alphabetic Texts from Ras Shamra (AnOr
20), Roma, 1940.

——, Ugaritic Handbook. Revised Grammar, Paradigms, Texts in
Transliteration, Comprehensive Glossary (AnOr 25), Roma, 1947.

——, Ugaritic Manual. Newly Revised Grammar, Texts in Transliteration, Cuneiform Selections, Paradigms, Glossary, Indices
(AnOr 35), Roma, 1955.

——, Ugaritic Textbook. Grammar, Texts in Transliteration, Cuneiform Selections, Glossary, Indices (AnOr 38), Roma, 1965. Photo-
mechanical Reprint with Supplement (8 p.), Roma, 1967.

2. LEXICONS AND CONCORDANCES

J. AISTLEITNER, Wörterbuch der ugaritischen Sprache[3], hrsg. von
O. EISSFELDT (BSAW 106, Heft 3), Berlin, 1967.

M. DIETRICH, O. LORETZ, Ugaritisches Handwörterbuch (in preparation).

G. D. YOUNG, Concordance of Ugaritic (AnOr 36), Roma, 1956.

See also AISTLEITNER and GORDON sub A 1.

3. LINGUISTIC MONOGRAPHS AND IMPORTANT ARTICLES

This section includes articles on the linguistic position of Ugaritic.

J. AISTLEITNER, Studien zur Frage der Sprachverwandtschaft des
Ugaritischen, AcOr (Bud) 7, 1957, 251-307; 8, 1958, 51-98.

H. BAUER, Entzifferung der Keilschrifttafeln von Ras Schamra,
Halle, 1930.

——, Das Alphabet von Ras Schamra, seine Entzifferung und seine
Gestalt, Halle, 1932.

J. BLAU, On Problems of Polyphony and Archaism in Ugaritic Spelling,
JAOS 88, 1968, 523-526.

——, S. E. LOEWENSTAMM, Zur Frage der scriptio plena im Ugaritischen und Verwandtes, UF 2, 1970, 19-33.

C. BROCKELMANN, Zur Syntax der Sprache von Ugarit, Or 10, 1941,
223-240.

———, Kanaanäische Miscellen, Festschrift Otto Eissfeldt, Halle, 1947, 61-67.

———, Die kanaanäischen Dialekte mit dem Ugaritischen, HO I, iii/1, Leiden, 1953, 40-58.

J. Cantineau, La langue de Ras Shamra, Syria 13, 1932, 164-170.

———, La langue de Ras Shamra, Syria 21, 1940, 38-61.

———, La langue de Ras Shamra, Sem 3, 1950, 21-34.

F. M. Cross, The Canaanite Cuneiform Tablet from Taanach, BASOR 190, 1968, 41-46.

———, Th. O. Lambdin, A Ugaritic Abecedary and the Origins of the Proto-Canaanite Alphabet, BASOR 160, 1960, 21-26.

M. Dahood, Some Aphel Causatives in Ugaritic, Bibl 38, 1957, 62-73.

———, The Linguistic Position of Ugaritic in the Light of Recent Discoveries, Sacra Pagina I, Paris-Gembloux, 1959, 269-279.

———, Ugaritic-Hebrew Philology (Biblica et orientalia 17), Rome, 1965. See also Pope.

———, Ugaritic-Hebrew Syntax and Style, UF 1, 1969, 15-36. See also Martinez.

M. Dietrich, O. Loretz, Untersuchungen zur Schrift- und Lautlehre des Ugaritischen (I), Der ugaritische Konsonant ġ, WO 4/2, 1968, 300-315.

T. L. Fenton, The Ugaritic Verbal System (typewritten doctoral thesis), Oxford, 1963.

———, Command and Fulfilment in Ugaritic — "tqtl : yqtl" and "qtl : qtl", JSS 14, 1969, 34-38.

———, The Absence of a Verbal Formation *yaqattal from Ugaritic and North-west Semitic, JSS 15, 1970, 31-41.

P. Fronzaroli, La fonetica Ugaritica, Roma, 1955.

G. Garbini, Il semitico di Nord-Ovest, Napoli, 1960.

H. L. Ginsberg, The Classification of the North-West Semitic Languages, Akten des 24. Internat. Orientalisten-Kongresses München 1957, Wiesbaden, [1957], 256-257.

A. Goetze, The Tenses of Ugaritic, JAOS 58, 1938, 266-309.

———, Is Ugaritic a Canaanite Dialect?, Language 17, 1941, 127-138.

———, Ugaritic Negations, Studia orientalia Ioanni Pedersen, 1953, 115-123.

C. H. Gordon, New Data on Ugaritic Numerals, Studia semitica Ioanni Bakoš dicata, Bratislava, 1965, 127-130.

J. C. Greenfield, Amurrite, Ugaritic and Canaanite, Proceedings of the International Conference on Semitic Studies held in Jerusalem, 19-23 July 1965, Jerusalem, 1969, 92-101.

A. GUÉRINOT, Remarques sur la phonétique de Ras Shamra, Syria 19, 1938, 38-46.

E. HAMMERSHAIMB, Das Verbum im Dialekt von Ras Schamra. Eine morphologische und syntaktische Untersuchung des Verbums in den alphabetischen Keilschrifttexten aus dem alten Ugarit, Kopenhagen, 1941.

M. HELD, Studies in Ugaritic Lexicography and Poetic Style (unpublished doctoral thesis, John Hopkins University), Baltimore, 1957.

——, The YQTL-QTL (QTL-YQTL) Sequence of Identical Verbs in Biblical Hebrew and in Ugaritic, Studies and Essays in Honor of A. A. Neuman, Leiden, 1962, 281-290.

——, The Action-Result (Factitive-Passive) Sequence of Identical Verbs in Biblical Hebrew and Ugaritic, JBL 84, 1965, 272-282.

——, Rhetorical Questions in Ugaritic and Biblical Hebrew, ErIs 9 [= W. F. Albright Volume], 1969, 71-79.

H. D. HUMMEL, Enclitic *mem* in Early Northwest Semitic, especially Hebrew, JBL 76, 1957, 85-107.

A. JIRKU, Zum Infinitivus absolutus im Ugaritischen, JKAF 3, 1953, 111-115 (= Von Jerusalem nach Ugarit, 363-367).

——, Eine 'Afʿel-Form im Ugaritischen?, AfO 18, 1957, 129-130.

——, Der Buchstabe Ghain im Ugaritischen, ZDMG 113, 1963, 481-482.

——, Die Umschrift ugaritischer Laryngale durch den akkadischen Buchstaben ú, ArOr 38, 1970, 129-130.

Ch. KRAHMALKOV, A Letter in Ugaritic Dialect, JNES 28, 1969, 262-264.

R. DE LANGHE, De taal van Ras Sjamra-Ugarit, Nijmegen-Utrecht, 1948.

S. E. LOEWENSTAMM, On Ugaritic Pronouns in the Light of Canaanitic [Hebrew], Lešonenu 23, 1958-59, 72-84.

——, The Numerals in Ugaritic, Proceedings of the International Conference on Semitic Studies held in Jerusalem, 19-23 July 1965, Jerusalem, 1969, 172-179.

——, Matres Lectionis in Ugaritic [Hebrew], Lešonenu 32 (1967-68), 369-373; reply by E. Y. KUTSCHER, ibid., 374-375.

——, Yod as Mater Lectionis in Ugaritic [Hebrew], Lešonenu 33 (1968-69), 2-3.

D. MARCUS, The Three Alephs in Ugaritic, JANES 1/1, 1968, 50-60.

——, Studies in Ugaritic Grammar I [infinitive absolute], JANES 1/2, 1969, 55-61.

——, The *qal* Passive in Ugaritic, JANES 3/2, 1970-71, 102-111.

E. R. MARTINEZ, Hebrew-Ugaritic Index to the Writings of Mitchell J. Dahood. A Bibliography with Indices of Scriptural Passages, Hebrew and Ugaritic Words and Grammatical Observations (Scripta Pontificii Instituti Biblici 116), Roma, 1967.

G. E. MENDENHALL, The Verb in Early Northwest Semitic Dialects (unpublished doctoral thesis, John Hopkins University), Baltimore, 1947.

S. MOSCATI, Plurali interni in Ugaritico?, RSO 32, 1957, 329-352.

——, Il semitico di Nord-ovest, Studi orientalistici in onore di Giorgio Levi della Vida II, Roma, 1956, 202-221.

——, On Semitic Case-Endings, JNES 17, 1957, 142-144.

M. POPE, Ugaritic Enclitic -*m*, JCS 5, 1951, 123-128.

——, 'Pleonastic' Waw before Nouns in Ugaritic and Hebrew, JAOS 73, 1953, 95-98.

——, Marginalia to M. Dahood's Ugaritic-Hebrew Philology, JBL 85, 1966, 455-466.

A. F. RAINEY, Observations on Ugaritic Grammar, UF 3, 1971, 151-172.

J. A. REIF, The Loss of Consonantal Aleph in Ugaritic, JSS 4, 1959, 16-20.

O. RÖSSLER, Ghain im Ugaritischen, ZA 54, 1961, 158-172.

J. SANMARTÍN ASCASO, Notizen zur ugaritischen Orthographie, UF 3, 1971, 173-180.

S. SEGERT, Ugaritisch und Aramäisch, Studia semitica Ioanni Bakoš dicata, Bratislava, 1965, 215-226.

——, Recent Progress in Ugaritology, AnOr 36, 1968, 443-467.

——, Le rôle de l'ugaritique dans la linguistique sémitique comparée, in: Ugaritica VI (MRS XVII), Paris, 1969, 461-477.

——, L. ZGUSTA, Indogermanisches in den alphabetischen Texten aus Ugarit, ArOr 21, 1953, 272-275.

A. VAN SELMS, Pa'yāl Formations in Ugaritic and Hebrew Nouns, JNES 26, 1967, 289-295.

A. D. SINGER, The 'final -*m*' (= *ma*?) in the Ugaritic Tablets, BJPES 10, 1943, 54-62.

——, The Vocative in Ugaritic, JCS 2, 1949, 1-12.

E. A. SPEISER, The Terminative-Adverbial in Canaanite-Ugaritic and Akkadian, IEJ 4, 1954, 108-115.

——, The Syllabic Transcription of Ugaritic [h] and [ḫ], BASOR 175, 1964, 42-47.

R. R. Stieglitz, The Ugaritic Cuneiform and Canaanite Linear Alphabets, JNES 30, 1971, 135-139.

E. Ullendorff, The Position of Ugaritic within the Framework of the Semitic Languages [Hebrew], Tarbiz 24, 1954-55, 121-125.

W. A. Ward, Comparative Studies in Egyptian and Ugaritic, JNES 20, 1961, 31-40.

M. Weippert, [Archäologischer Jahresbericht. II. Minutia quaedam epigraphica] 4. Tell Taʻannek: Eine neue 'ugaritische' Keilschrift-tafel und das Problem der alphabetischen Keilschrift des Typs B, ZDPV 82, 1966, 311-328 (see also ZDPV 83, 1967, 82-83).

G. L. Windfuhr, The Cuneiform Signs of Ugarit, JNES 29, 1970, 48-51.

G. D. Young, The Present Status of Ugaritic Studies, JKAF 2, 1952-53, 225-245.

J. M. Zinkand, A Study of the Morphology of Ugaritic and Akkadian (unpublished doctoral thesis, Brandeis University), Waltham, Mass., 1958.

4. Lexicographical Studies

K. Aartun, Beiträge zum ugaritischen Lexikon, WO 4/2, 1968, 278-299.

——, Die Partikeln des Ugaritischen (AOAT 21) (in the press).

M. J. Dahood, Hebrew-Ugaritic Lexicography, I-X, Bibl 44, 1963, 289-303; 45, 1964, 393-412; 46, 1965, 311-332; 47, 1966, 403-419; 48, 1967, 421-438; 49, 1968, 355-369; 50, 1969, 337-356; 51, 1970, 391-404; 52, 1971, 337-356; 53, 1972, 386-403.

——, Ugaritic Lexicography (= a review-article of J. Aistleitner, Wörterbuch der ugaritischen Sprache[1], Berlin 1963), Mélanges Eugène Tisserant I, 1964, 81-104.

——, Ugaritic-Hebrew Philology (Biblica et orientalia 17), Rome, 1965.

M. Dietrich, O. Loretz, Zur ugaritischen Lexikographie I, BiOr 23, 1966, 127-133; II, OLZ 62, 1967, 533-552; III, BiOr 25, 1968, 100-101; IV, UF 3, 1971, 372.

——, Das Ugaritische in den Wörterbüchern von L. Köhler und W. Baumgartner (I), BZ NF 13, 1969, 187-207.

G. R. Driver, Ugaritic and Hebrew Words, in: Ugaritica VI (MRS XVII), Paris 1969, 181-184.

F. C. Fensham, Ugaritic and the Translation of the O. T., The Bible Translator 18, 1967, 71-74.

M. C. Fisher, The Lexical Relationship between Ugaritic and Ethiopic (unpublished doctoral thesis, Brandeis University), Waltham, Mass., 1969.

J. Friedrich, 'Hethitisch-Ugaritisches', ZDMG 96, 1942, 471-494.

J. C. Greenfield, Ugaritic Lexicographical Notes, JCS 21, 1967, 89-93.

F. Gröndahl, Die Personennamen der Texte aus Ugarit (Studia Pohl. Dissertationes Scientificae de Rebus Orientis Antiqui, 1), Rom, 1967 (review article: P. R. Berger, WO 5/2, 1970, 271-282).

B. Hartmann, Mögen die Götter dich behüten und unversehrt bewahren, VTS 16, 1967, 102-105.

M. Held, Studies in Ugaritic Lexicography and Poetic Style (unpublished doctoral thesis, John Hopkins University), Baltimore, 1957.

———, Studies in Comparative Semitic Lexicography, Studies in Honor of Benno Landsberger (AS 16), Chicago, 1965, 395-406.

A. Jirku, Ugaritische Eigennamen als Quelle des ugaritischen Lexikons, ArOr 37, 1969, 8-11.

O. Kaiser, Zum Formular der in Ugarit gefundenen Briefe, ZDPV 86, 1970, 10-23.

D. Kinlaw, The Personal Names of the Syllabic Texts from Ugarit (unpublished doctoral thesis, Brandeis University), Waltham, Mass., 1967.

E. Koffmahn, Sind die altisraelitischen Monatsbezeichnungen mit den kanaanäisch-phönikischen identisch?, BZ NF 10, 1966, 197-219.

W. Leslau, Observations on Semitic Cognates in Ugaritic, Or 37, 1968, 347-366 [a supplement to Gordon's glossary of Ugaritic].

S. E. Loewenstamm, Ugaritic Formulas of Greeting, BASOR 194, 1969, 52-54.

J. C. de Moor, Frustula Ugaritica, JNES 24, 1965, 355-364.

———, Murices in Ugaritic Mythology, Or 37, 1968, 212-215.

J. P. J. Olivier, Notes on the Ugaritic Month Names [I], JNSL 1, 1971, 39-45; II, JNSL 2, 1972, 53-59.

A. F. Rainey, Some Prepositional Nuances in Ugaritic Administrative Texts, Proceedings of the International Conference on Semitic Studies held in Jerusalem, 19-23 July 1965, Jerusalem, 1969, 205-211.

——, Notes on the Syllabic Ugaritic Vocabularies, IEJ 19, 1969, 107-109.

——, Linguistic Method — May they Preserve it [Hebrew], Lešonenu 35, 1970, 11-15.

W. VON SODEN, Kleine Beiträge zum Ugaritischen und Hebräischen, VTS 16, 1967, 291-300.

P. SUÁREZ, Praepositio *'al = coram* in Litteratura Ugaritica et Hebraica-Biblica, VD 42, 1964, 71-80.

E. ULLENDORFF, Ugaritic Marginalia I, Or 20, 1951, 270-274; II, JSS 7, 1962, 339-351.

W. A. WARD, Comparative Studies in Egyptian and Ugaritic, JNES 20, 1961, 31-40.

A. A. WIEDER, Ugaritic-Hebrew Lexicography, JBL 84, 1965, 160-164.

I. AL-YASIN, The Lexical Relation between Ugaritic and Arabic, New York, 1952 (review article: W. L. MORAN, JBL 73, 1954, 263-264).

B. LITERATURE

1. TEXT EDITIONS

a. Texts with/in Transliteration

H. BAUER, Die alphabetischen Keilschrifttexte von Ras Schamra (Lietzmann's Kleine Texte 168), Berlin, 1936.

C. H. GORDON, Ugaritic Textbook, II. Texts in Transliteration ... (AnOr 38), Roma, 1965.

A. HERDER, Corpus des tablettes en cunéiformes alphabétiques découvertes à Ras Shamra-Ugarit de 1929 à 1939 (MRS X), Paris, 1963.

Ch. VIROLLEAUD, Le Palais royal d'Ugarit II. Textes alphabétiques des Archives Est, Ouest et Centrales (MRS VII), Paris, 1957 (review article: H. DONNER, BiOr 17, 1960, 179-181; see also O. EISSFELDT, JSS 5, 1960, 1-49 = Kleine Schriften II, 375-415).

——, Le Palais royal d'Ugarit V. Textes alphabétiques des Archives Sud, Sud-Ouest et du Petit-Palais (MRS XI), Paris, 1965 (review article: M. DAHOOD, Or 34, 1965, 482-484).

——, Les nouveaux textes mythologiques et liturgiques de Ras Shamra (XXIVe Campagne, 1961), in: J. NOUGAYROL, E. LAROCHE, Ch. VIROLLEAUD, e.a., Ugaritica V (MRS XVI), Paris, 1968, 545-606.

b. *Texts in Transliteration and Translation*

K. H. BERNHARDT, Anmerkungen zur Interpretation des KRT-Textes von Ras Schamra-Ugarit, Wissenschaftl. Zeitschr. der ... Univ. Greifswald [Ges.-Sprachw. Reihe Nr. 2/3] 5, 1955-56, 101-121.

G. R. DRIVER, Canaanite Myths and Legends, Edinburgh, 1956 (review article: H. CAZELLES, VT 7, 1957, 420-430).

L. R. FISHER, The Claremont Ras Shamra Tablets (AnOr 48), Roma, 1971.

P. FRONZAROLI, Leggenda di Aqhat. Testo Ugaritico, Florence, 1955.

H. L. GINSBERG, כתבי אוגרית (The Ugarit Texts), Jerusalem, 1936.

——, The Legend of King Keret (BASOR SS 2-3), New Haven, 1946.

J. GRAY, The KRT Text in the Literature of Ras Shamra. A Social Myth of Ancient Canaan², Leiden, 1964 (review article: J. HOFT-IJZER, BiOr 24, 1967, 65-68).

W. HERRMANN, Yariḫ und Nikkal und der Preis der Kuṯarāt-Göttinen. Ein kultisch-magischer Text aus Ras Schamra (BZAW 106), Berlin, 1968 (see also ZAW 83, 1971, 97-98).

R. LARGEMENT, La naissance de l'Aurore. Poème mythologique de Ras Shamra-Ugarit, Gembloux-Louvain, 1949.

J. PEDERSEN, Die KRT-Legende, Berytus 6, 1941, 63-105.

SVI RIN, SHIFRA RIN, עֲלִילוֹת הָאֵלִים / Acts of the Gods. The Ugaritic Epic Poetry Transliterated, Transcribed and Interpreted [Hebrew], Jerusalem, 1968.

H. SAUREN, G. KESTEMONT, Keret, roi de Ḫubur, UF 3, 1971, 181-221.

Ch. VIROLLEAUD, La légende phénicienne de Danel (MRS I), Paris, 1936.

——, La légende de Kéret, roi des Sidoniens (MRS II), Paris, 1936.

——, La déesse 'Anat. Poème de Ras Shamra (MRS IV), Paris, 1938.

c. *Translations*

J. AISTLEITNER, Die mythologischen und kultischen Texte aus Ras Schamra², Budapest, 1964.

A. CAQUOT, M. SZNYCER, Les textes ougaritiques, in: Les religions du Proche-Orient asiatique (collection Le trésor spirituel de l'humanité), Paris, 1970, 351-458.

Th. H. GASTER, Thespis. Ritual, Myth, and Drama in the Ancient Near East² (Anchor Book A 230), Garden City, 1961.

H. L. GINSBERG, Ugaritic Myths, Epics, and Legends, ANET³, Princeton, 1969, 129-155.

——, Ugaritic Myths and Epics, in: I. MENDELSOHN e.a., Religions of the Ancient Near East, New York, 1955, 221-279.
C. H. GORDON, Ugaritic Literature. A Comprehensive Translation of the Poetic and Prose Texts, Roma, 1949.
——, Ugarit and Minoan Crete, New York, 1966, 40-143.
J. GRAY, Texts from Ras Shamra, in: D. WINTON THOMAS (ed.), Documents from Old Testament Times, London, 1958, 118-133.
A. HERDNER, Les Cananéens. La légende de Kéret. La légende d'Aqhat, fils de Danel, in: Les Écrivains célèbres. L'Orient Ancien, Paris, 1961, 139-151.
A. JIRKU, Kanaanäische Mythen und Epen aus Ras Schamra-Ugarit, Gütersloh, 1962.

2. MONOGRAPHS AND IMPORTANT ARTICLES

J. BLAU, J. C. GREENFIELD, Ugaritic Glosses, BASOR 200, 1970, 11-17 (with an Additional Note by D. R. HILLERS, p. 18).
U. CASSUTO, האלה ענת / The Goddess Anath. Canaanite Epics of the Patriarchal Age[2] [Hebrew], Jerusalem, 1953 (review article of the first edition : M. POPE, JCS 6, 1952, 133-146).
U. CASSUTO, The Goddess Anath. Canaanite Epics of the Patriarchal Age. Transl. from the Hebrew by I. ABRAHAMS, Jerusalem, 1970.
M. DIETRICH, O. LORETZ, Beschriftete Lungen- und Lebermodelle aus Ugarit, in: Ugaritica VI (MRS XVII), Paris, 1969, 165-179.
——, Konkordanz der ugaritischen Textzählungen (AOAT 19), Kevelaer-Neukirchen, 1972.
O. EISSFELDT, Bestand und Benennung der Ras Schamra-Texte, ZDMG 96, 1942, 507-539 (== Kleine Schriften II, 330-355).
——, Die keilschriftalphabetischen Texte aus der zehnten und elften Ausgrabungskampagne in Ras Schamra, AfO 14, 1941-44, 371-375 (= Kleine Schriften II, 356-364).
——, Die keilschriftalphabetischen Texte der Kampagnen 1948/51, AfO 16, 1952-53, 116-122 (= Kleine Schriften II, 365-374).
——, The Alphabetical Cuneiform Texts from Ras Shamra published in "Le Palais Royal d'Ugarit", Vol. II, 1957, JSS 5, 1960, 1-49 (= Kleine Schriften II, 375-415).
——, Mesopotamische Elemente in den alphabetischen Texte von Ugarit, Syria 39, 1962, 36-41 (= Kleine Schriften IV, 39-43).
——, Neue keilalphabetische Texte aus Ras Schamra-Ugarit (SDAW 1965, Heft 6), Berlin, 1965.

——, Sohnespflichten im Alten Orient, Syria 43, 1966, 39-47.

F. C. FENSHAM, Remarks on certain difficult Passages in Keret, JNSL 1, 1971, 11-22.

——, Remarks on Keret 26-43, JNSL 2, 1972, 37-52.

L. R. FISHER, F. B. KNUTSON, An Enthronement Ritual at Ugarit, JNES 28, 1969, 157-167.

T. H. GASTER, A Canaanite Ritual Drama. The Spring Festival at Ugarit, JAOS 66, 1946, 49-76.

C. H. GORDON, Sabbatical Cycle or Seasonal Pattern?, Or 22, 1953, 79-81.

J. GRAY, Ba'al's Atonement, UF 3, 1971, 61-70.

J. C. GREENFIELD, Some Glosses on the Keret Epic, ErIs 9 [= W. F. Albright Volume], 1969, 60-65.

A. JIRKU, Doppelte Überlieferungen im Mythus und im Epos von Ugarit?, ZDMG 110, 1960, 20-25 (= Von Jerusalem nach Ugarit, 387-392).

A. S. KAPELRUD, The Number Seven in Ugaritic Texts, VT 18, 1968, 494-499.

——, Baal and the Devourers, in: Ugaritica VI (MRS XVII), Paris, 1969, 319-332.

K. KOCH, Die Sohnesverheissung an den ugaritischen Daniel, ZA 58, 1967, 211-221.

H. KOSMALA, Mot and the Vine: The Time of the Ugaritic Fertility Rite, ASTI 3, 1964, 147-151.

J. KRECHER, Schreiberschulung in Ugarit: Die Tradition von Listen und sumerischen Texten, UF 1, 1969, 131-158.

R. DE LANGHE, Myth, Ritual, and Kingship in the Ras Shamra Tablets, in: S. H. HOOKE (ed.), Myth, Ritual, and Kingship, Oxford, 1960, 122-148.

B. LEVINE, Ugaritic Descriptive Rituals, JCS 17, 1963, 105-111.

M. LICHTENSTEIN, A Note on the Text of I Keret, JANES 2/2, 1970, 94-100.

E. LIPIŃSKY, Recherches ugaritiques, Syria 44, 1967, 253-287.

——, Banquet en l'honneur de Baal: CTA 3 (V AB), A, 4-22, UF 2, 1970, 75-88.

——, Épiphanie de Baal-Haddu: RS 24.245, UF 3, 1971, 81-92.

F. LØKKEGAARD, A Plea for El, the Bull, and other Ugaritic Miscellanies, Studia orientalia Ioanni Pedersen, 1953, 219-235.

S. E. LOEWENSTAMM, The Seven Day-Unit in Ugaritic Epic Literature, IEJ 15, 1965, 121-133.

——, Prostration from Afar in Ugaritic, Accadian and Hebrew, BASOR 188, 1967, 41-43.

——, Eine lehrhafte ugaritische Trinkburleske, UF 1, 1969, 71-77.

J. C. DE MOOR, Studies in the New Alphabetic Texts from Ras Shamra [published in Ugaritica V], UF 1, 1969, 167-188; 2, 1970, 303-327.

——, The Seasonal Pattern in the Ugaritic Myth of Ba'lu according to the Version of Ilimilku (AOAT 16), Kevelaer-Neukirchen, 1971.

H. P. MÜLLER, Magisch-mantische Weisheit und die Gestalt Daniels, UF 1, 1969, 79-94.

J. OBERMANN, Ugaritic Mythology. A Study of Its Leading Motifs, New Haven, 1948.

M. H. POPE, J. H. TIGAY, A Description of Baal, UF 3, 1971, 117-130.

A. F. RAINEY, The Scribe at Ugarit: His Position and Influence, Proceedings of The Israel Academy of Sciences and Humanities 3, 1969, 126-147.

G. SAUER, Bemerkungen zu 1965 edierten ugaritischen Texten [PRU V = MRS XI], ZDMG 116, 1967, 235-241.

J. F. A. SAWYER, J. STRANGE, Notes on the Keret-Text, IEJ 14, 1964, 96-98.

S. SEGERT, Die Schreibfehler in den ugaritischen literarischen Keilschrifttexten in Anschluss an das textkritische Hilfsbuch von Friedrich Delitzsch klassifiziert, Von Ugarit nach Qumran [= Festschrift O. Eissfeldt] (BZAW 77), Berlin, 1958, 193-212.

——, Die Schreibfehler in den ugaritischen nichtliterarischen Keilschrifttexten, ZAW 71, 1959, 23-32.

A. VAN SELMS, Yammu's Dethronement by Baal, UF 2, 1970, 251-268.

——, The Fire in Yammu's Palace, UF 3, 1971, 249-252.

R. E. WHITAKER, Formulaic Analysis of Ugaritic Poetry (unpublished doctoral thesis, Harvard University) Cambridge, Mass., 1969.

P. J. VAN ZIJL, Baal. A Study of Texts in Connection with Baal in the Ugaritic Epics (AOAT 10), Kevelaer-Neukirchen, 1972.

C. HISTORY AND CIVILIZATION OF UGARIT

This section includes articles on the theme Ugarit and the Greek World.

A. ALT, Ein phönikisches Staatswesen des frühen Altertums, FF 18, 1942, 207-209.

——, Ägyptisch-Ugaritisches, AfO 15, 1945-51, 69-75.

——, Hohe Beamte in Ugarit, Studia orientalia Ioanni Pedersen, 1953, 1-11.

——, Bemerkungen zu den Verwaltungs- und Rechtsurkunden von Ugarit und Alalach, WO 2/1, 1954, 7-18; 2/3, 1956, 234-243; 2/4, 1957, 338-342; 3/1-2, 1964, 3-18.

M. C. Astour, New Evidence on the Last Days of Ugarit, AJA 69, 1965, 253-258.

——, Hellenosemitica. An Ethnic and Cultural Study in West Semitic Impact on Mycenaean Greece, Leiden, 1965.

——, The Partition of the Confederacy of Mukiš-Nuḫašše-Nii by Šuppiluliuma. A Study in Political Geography of the Amarna-Age, Or 38, 1969, 381-414.

——, Ma'ḫadu, the Harbor of Ugarit, JESHO 13, 1970, 113-127.

A. F. Campbell, Homer and Ugaritic Literature, AbN 5, 1964-65, 29-56.

M. Dietrich, O. Loretz, Die soziale Struktur von Alalaḫ und Ugarit I: WO 3/3, 1966, 188-205; II: WO 5/1, 1969, 57-93; III: in preparation; IV: ZA 60, 1970, 88-123; V: UF 1, 1969, 37-64.

——, Der Vertrag zwischen Šuppiluliuma und Niqmandu. Eine philologische und kulturhistorische Studie, WO 3/3, 1966, 206-245.

M. S. Drower, Ugarit (CAH II, Chapter XXI b), Cambridge, 1968.

O. Eissfeldt, Baal Zaphon, Zeus Kasios und der Durchzug der Israeliten durchs Meer, Halle, 1932.

——, Ras Schamra und Sanchuniaton, Halle, 1939.

——, Taautos und Sanchunjaton (SDAW 1952, Heft 1), Berlin, 1952.

——, Sanchunjaton von Berut und Ilumilku von Ugarit, Halle, 1952.

F. C. Fensham, Widow, Orphan, and the Poor in Ancient Near Eastern Legal and Wisdom Literature, JNES 21, 1962, 129-139.

——, Iron in the Ugaritic Texts, OA 8, 1969, 209-213.

R. Follet, Sanchuniaton, personnage mythique ou personne historique ?, Bibl 34, 1953, 81-90.

C. H. Gordon, Homer and Bible. The Origin and Character of East Mediterranean Literature, HUCA 26, 1955, 43-108.

——, The Common Background of Greek and Hebrew Civilizations, New York, 1965.

——, Ugarit and Minoan Crete. The Bearing of their Texts on the Origins of Western Culture, New York, 1966.

J. Gray, The Canaanites², London, 1965.

——, Ugarit: a Canaanite Metropolis of the Bronze Age, ET 66, 1955, 326-330.

——, Ugarit, in: D. WINTON THOMAS (ed.), Archaeology and Old Testament Study, Oxford, 1967, 145-167.

H. HAAG, Homer, Ugarit und das Alte Testament (Biblische Beiträge NF, Heft 2), Einsiedeln, 1962.

——, Der gegenwärtige Stand der Erforschung der Beziehungen zwischen Homer und dem Alten Testament, JEOL 19, 1965-66, 508-518.

B. HARTMANN, De herkomst van de goddelijke ambachtsman in Oegarit en Griekenland, Leiden, 1964.

A. M. HONEYMAN, The Tributaries of Ugarit. A Toponymic Study, JKAF 2, 1951-53, 74-87.

H. KLENGEL, Geschichte Syriens im 2. Jahrtausend v.u.Z., 3 Teile, Berlin 1965-1970 (especially Teil II, Berlin, 1969, 326-421 = 7. Abschnitt: Ugarit).

J. P. LETTINGA, Oegarit (rās esj-sjamra). Een nieuwe Phoenicische stad uit de Oudheid, Den Haag, 1948.

M. LIVERANI, Storia di Ugarit nell'età degli archivi politici, Roma, 1962 (review article: H. KLENGEL, OLZ 57, 1962, 453-462).

L. M. MUNTINGH, Die sosiale struktuur binne die woongebied van die Kanaäniete gedurende die Laat-Bronstijdperk (typewritten doctoral thesis), Stellenbosch, 1963.

——, The Social and Legal Status of a Free Ugaritic Female, JNES 26, 1967, 102-112.

J. NOUGAYROL, Guerre et paix à Ugarit, Iraq 25, 1963, 110-123.

A. F. RAINEY, The Social Stratification of Ugarit (unpublished doctoral thesis, Brandeis University, 1962), Grand Rapids, Michigan, 1963.

——, A Canaanite at Ugarit, IEJ 13, 1963, 43-45.

——, Business Agents at Ugarit, IEJ 13, 1963, 313-321.

——, Ugarit and the Canaanites Again, IEJ 14, 1964, 101.

——, Family Relationships in Ugarit, Or 34, 1965, 10-22.

——, The Military Personnel of Ugarit, JNES 24, 1965, 17-27.

——, The Kingdom of Ugarit, BiAr 28, 1965, 102-125.

——, A Social Structure of Ugarit. A Study of West Semitic Social Stratification during the Late Bronze Age [Hebrew with English Summary], Jerusalem, 1967.

G. SAADÉ, Ras-Shamra. Ruines d'Ugarit. Guide, Beyrouth, 1954.

J. M. SASSON, Canaanite Maritime Involvement in the Second Millenium B.C., JAOS 86, 1966, 126-138.

C. F. A. SCHAEFFER, Ugaritica. Études relatives aux découvertes de Ras Shamra I (MRS III), Paris, 1939.

——, The Cuneiform Texts of Ras Shamra (Schweich Lectures 1936), London, 1939.

——, Ugaritica II. Nouvelles études relatives aux découvertes de Ras Shamra (MRS V), Paris, 1949.

——, Une industrie d'Ugarit: La pourpre, AAS 1, 1951, 188-192.

——, Ugarit und die Hethiter nach den im Süd-Archiv des Palastes 1953 entdeckten Keilschrifttexten, AfO 17, 1954-55, 93-99.

S. SEGERT, Ugarit und Griechenland, Altertum 4, 1958, 67-80.

A. VAN SELMS, Marriage and Family Life in Ugaritic Literature, London, 1954.

P. WALCOT, The Comparative Study of Ugaritic and Greek Literatures, UF 1, 1969, 111-118; 2, 1970, 273-275.

D. RELIGION

This section includes articles on the theme Ugarit and the Old Testament*.

W. F. ALBRIGHT, Yahweh and the Gods of Canaan. A Historical Analysis of Two Contrasting Faiths, London, 1968.

M. C. ASTOUR, Some New Divine Names from Ugarit, JAOS 86, 1966, 277-284.

W. BAUMGARTNER, Ugaritische Probleme und ihre Tragweite für das Alte Testament, ThZ 3, 1947, 81-100.

K. H. BERNHARDT, Aschera in Ugarit und im Alten Testament, MIO 13, 1967, 163-174.

C. H. W. BREKELMANS, Ras Sjamra en het Oude Testament, Nijmegen-Utrecht, 1962.

——, Some Considerations on the Translation of the Psalms by M. Dahood: I. The Preposition b = 'from' in the Psalms according to M. Dahood, UF 1, 1969, 5-14.

D. CONRAD, Der Gott Reschef, ZAW 83, 1971, 157-183.

J. COPPENS, Les Parallèles du Psautier avec les textes de Ras Shamra-Ugarit, Louvain, 1946.

M. J. DAHOOD, Ancient Semitic Deities in Syria and Palestine, in:

---

* An Ugaritic and Hebrew Parallels Project is underway at the Institute for Antiquity and Christianity, Claremont Graduate School, Claremont, California (cf. Or 37, 1968, 141-142; NTSt 16, 1970, 190-191; UF 3, 1971, 25-31). See FISCHER.

S. Moscati (ed.), Le antiche divinità semitiche, Roma, 1958, 65-94.

——, Ugaritic Studies and the Bible, Greg 43, 1962, 55-79.

——, Proverbs and Northwest Semitic Philology, Rome, 1963.

——, Vocative Lamedh in the Psalter, VT 16, 1966, 299-311.

——, Congruity of Metaphors, VTS 16, 1967, 40-49.

——, Ugaritic and the Old Testament, in: H. Cazelles (éd.), De Mari à Qumrân [= Donum natalicium J. Coppens, Vol. I], Gembloux-Paris, 1969, 14-33.

H. Donner, Art und Herkunft des Amtes der Königinmutter im Alten Testament, Festschrift Joh. Friedrich, Heidelberg, 1959, 105-145.

——, Ugaritismen in der Psalmenforschung, ZAW 79, 1967, 322-350.

R. Dussaud, Les Découvertes de Ras Shamra (Ugarit) et l'Ancien Testament², Paris, 1941.

——, Les origines cananéennes du sacrifice israélite², Paris, 1941.

——, Les religions des Hittites et des Hourrites, des Phéniciens et des Syriens² (MANA I/2), Paris, 1949.

O. Eissfeldt, Ras Schamra und Sanchuniaton, Halle, 1939.

——, El im ugaritischen Pantheon (BSAW 98, Heft 4), Berlin, 1951.

——, El and Yahweh, JSS 1, 1956, 25-37.

——, Ba'al Ṣaphon von Ugarit und Amon von Ägypten, FF 36, 1962, 338-340.

——, Kanaanäisch-ugaritische Religion, HO I, viii/1, Leiden, 1964, 76-91.

T. L. Fenton, Ugaritica-Biblica, UF 1, 1969, 65-70.

L. R. Fisher (ed.), Ras Shamra Parallels : The Texts from Ugarit and the Hebrew Bible, Vol. I (AnOr 49), Roma 1972 (the first volume resulting from the Ugaritic and Hebrew Parallels Project).

H. Gese, Die Religionen Altsyriens, in: C. M. Schröder (Hrsg.), Die Religionen der Menschheit, Band 10/2, Stuttgart, 1970, 3-232.

J. Gray, Cultic Affinities between Israel and Ras Shamra, ZAW 62, 1949-50, 207-220.

——, The Legacy of Canaan. The Ras Shamra Texts and their Relevance to the Old Testament², VTS 5, Leiden, 1965.

——, Social Aspects of Canaanite Religion, VTS 15, 1966, 170-192.

H. S. Haddad, Baal-Hadad: A Study of the Syrian Storm-god (type-written doctoral thesis University of Chicago), 1960.

B. Hartmann, De herkomst van de goddelijke ambachtsman in Oegarit en Griekenland, Leiden, 1964.

W. HERRMANN, Götterspeise und Göttertrank in Ugarit und Israel, ZAW 72, 1960, 205-216.

——, Aštart, MIO 15, 1969, 6-51.

R. HILLMANN, Wasser und Berg. Kosmische Verbindungslinien zwischen dem kanaanäischen Wettergott und Jahwe (typewritten doctoral thesis), Halle, 1965.

F. F. HVIDBERG, Weeping and Laughter in the Old Testament. A Study of Canaanite-Israelite Religion, Leiden-København, 1962.

J. W. JACK, The Ras Shamra Tablets, their Bearing on the Old Testament, Edinburgh, 1935.

E. JACOB, Ras Shamra et l'Ancien Testament, Neuchâtel, 1960.

A. JIRKU, Der Mythus der Kanaanäer, Bonn, 1966.

O. KAISER, Die mythische Bedeutung des Meeres in Ägypten, Ugarit und Israel² (BZAW 78), Berlin, 1962.

A. S. KAPELRUD, Baal in the Ras Shamra Texts, Kopenhagen, 1952.

——, Ras Sjamra-funnene og det Gamle Testament, Oslo, 1953.

——, The Ras Shamra Discoveries and the O. T. [Engl. Transl., G. W. ANDERSON], Oxford, 1955.

——, Die Ras-Schamra-Funde und das A. T. [deutsche Übers. von F. CORNELIUS], München, 1967.

——, The Violent Goddess. Anat in the Ras Shamra Texts, Oslo, 1969 (review article: J. C. DE MOOR, UF 1, 1969, 223-227).

R. DE LANGHE, Les textes de Ras Shamra-Ugarit et leurs rapports avec le milieu biblique de l'Ancien Testament, 2 vols., Gembloux-Paris, 1945 (review article: J. P. LETTINGA, BiOr 5, 1948, 107-113).

——, La Bible et la littérature ugaritique, L'Ancien Testament et l'Orient, Louvain, 1957, 65-87.

S. E. LOEWENSTAMM, The Ugaritic Myth of the Sea and its Biblical Counterparts [Hebrew], ErIs 9 [= W. F. Albright Volume], 1969, 96-101 (English summary p. 136).

O. LORETZ, Götter und Frauen (Gen 6, 1-4). Ein Paradigma zu: Altes Testament-Ugarit, Bibel und Leben 8, 1967, 120-127.

V. MAAG, Syrien-Palästina, in: H. SCHMÖKEL (Hrsg.), Kulturgeschichte des alten Orients, Stuttgart, 1961, 447-604 (especially IX. Ugaritische und hebräische Literatur ...; XI. Die syro-kanaanäische Religion).

J. C. DE MOOR, The Semitic Pantheon of Ugarit, UF 2, 1970, 187-228.

——, New Year with Canaanites and Israelites. Part One: Description; Part Two: The Canaanite Sources (Kamper Cahiers 21 and 22), Kampen, 1972.

H. P. Müller, Magisch-mantische Weisheit und die Gestalt Daniels, UF 1, 1969, 79-94.

M. J. Mulder, Kanaänitische goden in het Oude Testament (Exegetica IV/4-5), Den Haag, 1965 (review article: R. Frankena, ThLZ 93, 1968, col. 335-336).

——, Accentverschuiving bij de karakterisering van enige Kanaänitische goden, NTT 24, 1969/70, 401-420.

D. Nielsen, Ras Šamra Mythologie und biblische Theologie, Leipzig, 1936.

U. Oldenburg, The Conflict between El and Baʿal in Canaanite Religion, Leiden, 1969 (review article: M. J. Mulder, UF 2, 1970, 359-366).

J. H. Patton, Canaanite Parallels to the Book of Psalms, Baltimore, 1944.

J. Pedersen, Kanaʿanaeisk Religion, Illustreret Religionshistorie, København, 1948, 191-212.

C. F. Pfeiffer, Ras Shamra and the Bible, Grand Rapids, 1962.

M. Pope, El in the Ugaritic Texts, VTS 2, Leiden, 1955.

——, The Goddesses Anat and Kali, 20th Intern. Congress of Orientalists, Summaries, New Delhi, 1964, 15-16.

——, W. Röllig, Syrien. Die Mythologie der Ugariter und Phönizier, in: H. W. Haussig (Hrsg.), Wörterbuch der Mythologie I, Stuttgart, 1965, 219-312.

A. F. Rainey, Organized Religion at Ugarit, Christian News from Israel 15, 1964, 16-24.

R. Rendtorff, El, Baʿal und Jahwe. Erwägungen zum Verhältnis von kanaanäischer und israelitischer Religion, ZAW 78, 1966, 277-292.

H. Ringgren, The Religion of Ancient Syria, in: C. J. Bleeker, G. Widengren, Historia Religionum I, Leiden, 1969, 193-222.

G. Sauer, Die Sprüche Agurs (BWANT 84), Stuttgart, 1963.

W. Schmidt, Königtum Gottes in Ugarit und Israel² (BZAW 80), Berlin, 1966 (review article: J. C. de Moor, BiOr 24, 1967, 207-209).

A. Soggin, Der offiziell geförderte Synkretismus in Israel während des 10. Jahrhunderts, ZAW 78, 1966, 179-204.

R. Stadelmann, Syrisch-palästinensische Gottheiten in Ägypten, Leiden, 1967.

R. de Vaux, El et Baal, le Dieu des pères et Yahweh, in: Ugaritica VI (MRS XVII), Paris, 1969, 501-517.

K. L. VINE, The Establishment of Baal at Ugarit (unpublished doctoral thesis, University of Michigan), Ann Arbor, 1965.
P. J. VAN ZIJL, Baal. A Study of Texts in Connection with Baal in the Ugaritic Epics (AOAT 10), Kevelaer-Neukirchen, 1972.

E. SERIES AND PERIODICALS

AAS 1, 1951-...; AfO 5, 1928-29-...; BASOR 46, 1932-...; CRAIBL 1929-...; MRS; PRU; Syria 10, 1929 - 20, 1939; 28, 1951-...; UF 1, 1969-...

IX. PHOENICIAN-PUNIC

COMPILED BY

K. R. VEENHOF

Introductory remark

Phoenician, the language of inscriptions from Phoenicia proper, Syria, Asia Minor, Cyprus and in general the eastern part of the Mediterranean (ranging from the 11/10th century B.C. to the first century B.C. or perhaps A.D.) is traditionally distinguished from Punic, the language of inscriptions from Carthago and its colonial empire in North Africa, Spain, the islands and coastal regions of the western Mediterranean (9th century B.C. to 2nd century A.D.). Though the older Punic inscriptions from the linguistic point of view could nearly as well be called Phoenician, this distinction makes sense, as later Punic texts show an increasing number of changes in orthography, phonology and morphology, due partly to later developments, partly to the influence of the various native tongues. Moreover, the later Punic texts are written in a rather cursive type of script. Some scholars also distinguish between Punic and Neopunic, the latter being applied to the inscriptions dating from after the fall of Carthago (146 B.C.). This distinction is a rather mechanical and not a linguistic one, though it is true that Punic texts from the last centuries show a great number of deviations from standard Punic. Friedrich called them "vulgärpunisch", but this creates the problem of distinguishing between Punic and Vulgar Punic forms and writings within one and the same text.

A. PHILOLOGY

1. GRAMMARS

A. VAN DEN BRANDEN, Grammaire phénicienne, Bibliothèque de l'Université Saint-Esprit, t. II, Beyrouth, 1969. This grammar uses the old Phoenician script throughout.

J. FRIEDRICH, Phönizisch-Punische Grammatik (Anhang: Skizze der Sprache von Ja'udi im nördlichen Syrien), AnOr 32, Roma, 1951.

——, W. RÖLLIG, Phönizisch-Punische Grammatik, AnOr 46, Roma, 1970. Revised edition of Friedrich's grammar from 1951.

Z. S. HARRIS, Grammar of the Phoenician Language, American Oriental Series 8, New Haven, 1936. Contains bibliographical material and on p. 73-156 a large glossary (reprint: 1964).

P. SCHRÖDER, Die phönizische Sprache. Entwurf einer Grammatik nebst Sprach- und Schriftproben, Halle, 1869.

Comparative material is to be found in:

C. BROCKELMANN, Die Kanaanäische Dialekte mit dem Ugaritischen, HO Bd. 3, I. Abschn., Leiden, 1953, 40-58.

G. GARBINI, Il Semitico di Nord-Ovest, AIUON 1, Napoli, 1960.

Z. S. HARRIS, Development of the Canaanite Dialects. An investigation of linguistic history, American Oriental Series 16, New Haven, 1939 (reprint New York, 1967).

2. DICTIONARIES, GLOSSARIES, CONCORDANCES

Charles-F. JEAN, Jacob HOFTIJZER, Dictionnaire des inscriptions sémitiques de l'Ouest, Leiden, 1965. Normally abbreviated DISO. On p. 337 ff. a concordance between numbers and designations in DISO, CIS, KAI and RÉS (for the abbreviations see *sub* B, 1, a, and List of Abbreviations).

M. A. LEVY, Phönizisches Wörterbuch, Breslau, 1864 (includes personal names).

Glossaries are moreover appended to several important text editions, like LIDZBARSKI, Handbuch (cf. below sub A, 3), 204-388; COOK, Textbook (cf. below *sub* B, 1, a), 363-377; DONNER, RÖLLIG, KAI (cf. below *sub* B, 1, a) vol. III; and AMADASI, Iscrizioni (cf. below *sub* B, 1, a), 185 ff. Also HARRIS, Grammar (cf. above sub A, 1) contains a glossary. BENZ, Personal Names (see below), ch. IV (255-432) is a long "Glossary of Name Elements". These glossaries normally include personal and geographical names and names of gods.

Special studies of the *onomasticon* are:

Frank L. BENZ, Personal Names in the Phoenician-Punic Inscriptions, Studia Pohl 8, Roma, 1972.

A. DIETRICH, Phönizische Ortsnamen in Spanien, Leipzig, 1936.

G. Halff, L'Onomastique punique de Carthage, Karthago 12, 1963-64, 61-146.

3. Monographs and Articles of Linguistic Nature

a. *Grammar and orthography*

Remark. Monographs and even articles on problems of Phoenician and Punic grammar are not very numerous. These questions are more often dealt with in the philological commentary accompanying text editions than in separate studies. We list mainly articles published after 1950 (cf. now the bibliography in Friedrich, Röllig, Grammatik (above *sub* A,1).

L. A. Bange, A Study of the Use of Vowel-Letters in Alphabetic Consonantal Writing, München, 1971, ch. V-VI.

F. L. Benz, Personal Names (cf. above *sub* A, 2), ch. III (199-254), "Grammatical Study of the Names".

F. M. Cross, D. N. Freedman, The pronominal suffixes of the third person singular in Phoenician, JNES 10, 1951, 228-230.

M. Dahood, G. R. Driver and the enclitic *mem* in Phoenician, Bibl 49, 1968, 89-90.

R. Degen, Die Genitivverbindung aus zwei Regentes und einem Rectum im Phönizischen, ZDMG 120, 1970, 1-5.

A. Dotan, Vowel Shift in Phoenician and Punic, AbN 12, 1971-72, 1 ff.

——, Phoenician *a>o* Shift in Some Greek Transcriptions, UF 3, 1972, 293-297.

J. G. Février, Le waw conversif en punique, in: Hommages à André Dupont-Sommer, Paris, 1971, 191-194.

J. Friedrich, Zum Phönizisch-Punischen, ZS 2, 1924, 2-5.

——, Zur Einleitungsformel der ältesten phönizischen Inschriften aus Byblos, Mélanges Syriens offerts à M. R. Dussaud, Paris, 1939, 39-47.

——, Punische Studien, ZDMG 107, 1957, 282-298.

G. Garbini, Note Semitiche, AIUON-L. 4, 1962, 85 ff. 3. La seconda coniugazione a prefix in punico.

S. Gevirtz, On the Etymology of the Phoenician particle שׁא, JNES 16, 1957, 124-127.

J. Hoftijzer, The nota accusativi *'t* en phénicien, Mus 76, 1963, 195-200.

A. M. Honeyman, Canaanite Pronominal Suffixes at Byblos and Elsewhere, JRAS, 1941, 31-36.

Ch. Kramalkov, Studies in Phoenician and Punic Grammar, JSS 15, 1970, 181-188 (the pron. suff. 3 masc. plur. in Phoen.; the poss. pron. 3 masc. sing. in Punic).

——, Observations to the affixing of possessive pronouns in Punic, RSO 44, 1969, 181-186.

——, Comments on the Vocalization of the Suffix Pronoun of the Third Feminine Singular in Phoenician and Punic, JSS 17, 1972, 68-75.

E. Y. Kutscher, Canaanite - Hebrew - Phoenician - Aramaic - Mishnaic - Hebrew - Punic, Lešonenu 33, 1969, 83-110.

G. Levi della Vida, Punico mu, pronome interrogativo e relativo, in: Mélanges Marcel Cohen..., réunis par David Cohen, The Hague, 1970, 274-76.

J. Oberman, Phoenician yqtl 'nk, JNES 9, 1950, 94-100.

A. Poebel, Das appositionell bestimmte Pronomen der 1e Pers. sing. in den westsemitischen Inschriften, Assyriological Studies 3, Chicago, 1932.

H. S. Schuster, Der Relativsatz im Phönizischen und Punischen. Exkurs: Der Gebrauch des Artikels in den älteren phönizischen Inschriften, Studies in Honor of Benno Landsberger, Assyriological Studies 16, Chicago, 1965, 431-448.

J. M. Solá-Solé, Sur les parties du discours en phénicien, BiOr 14, 1957, 64-68.

J. Teixidor, Bulletin d'épigraphie sémitique 1971, no. 11, "Le suffixe phénicien", Syria 48, 1971, 454-456.

J. W. Wevers, The Infinitive Absolute in the Phoenician Inscription of Azitawadd, ZAW 62, 1949-50, 316-317.

b. *Problems of dialects, position of the so called Ja'udic*

J. Friedrich, Kleinigkeiten zum Phönizischen, Punischen und Numidischen, ZDMG 114, 1964, 225 ff., 1. Zur Orthographie der phön. Inschrift des Jeḥaumilk von Byblos.

——, Zur Stellung des Jaudischen in der nordwestsemitischen Sprachgeschichte, Studies in Honor of Benno Landsberger, Assyriological Studies 16, Chicago, 1965, 425-429.

G. Garbini, L'Aramaico Antico, ANLM ser. 8, vol. 7, fasc. 5, Roma, 1956, 280-282.

——, Studi Aramaici, AIUON 19, 1969, 1-8.

H. L. GINSBERG, The Classification of the North-West Semitic Languages, Akten des XXIV. Internationalen Orientalisten-Kongresses, München, 1958, Wiesbaden, 1959, 256-267.

J. HOFTIJZER, Kanttekeningen bij het onderzoek van de west-semitische epigrafie, JEOL 15, 1957-58, 112-125 (especially 113-119).

W. R. LANE, The Phoenician Dialect of Larnax Lapethou (Cyprus), BASOR 194, 1969, 39-45.

S. SEGERT, Aramäische Studien. III. Zum Problem der altaramäischen Dialekte, ArOr 26, 1958, 561-572.

M. L. WAGNER, Die Punier und ihre Sprache in Sardinien, Sprache 3, 1954 ff., 27 ff., 78 ff. Cf. J. FRIEDRICH, ibidem, 221 ff.

c. *More general investigations and varia*

J. FERRON, Paralipomena punica, V-VII, Cahiers de Byrsa 8, 1958-59, 25-36.

J. G. FÉVRIER, Remarques sur l'épigraphie néopunique, OA 2, 1963, 257-267.

J. FRIEDRICH, Griechisches und römisches in phönizischem und punischem Gewande, in: Festschrift für Otto Eissfeldt zum 60. Geburtstag (ed. J. FÜCK), Halle, 1947, 109-124.

——, Vulgärpunisch und Vulgärlatein in den neupunischen Inschriften, Cahiers de Byrsa 3, 1953, 99-111.

G. GARBINI, Note di epigrafia punica. I, RSO 40, 1965, 205-213; II, RSO 42, 1967, 1-13; III, RSO 43, 1968, 5-17. Discusses linguistic problems and comments on the text of several inscriptions.

Ch. KRAHMALKOV, The Punic Speech of Hanno, OrNS 39, 1970, 52-74.

G. LEVI DELLA VIDA, Parerga Neopunica, OA 4, 1965, 59-70.

M. LIDZBARSKI, Handbuch der Nordsemitischen Epigraphik, Weimar 1898. Band I Text. Contains inter alia an extensive bibliography of text editions and literature (on p. 4-84 and 493-498), and a linguistic and typological analysis of the inscriptions.

D. NEIMAN, Phoenician Place Names, JNES 24, 1965, 113-115.

S. SEGERT, Some Phoenician Etymologies of North African Toponyms, OA 5, 1966, 19-25.

J. M. SOLÁ-SOLÉ, Ensayo de antroponimia feno-púnica de la Hispania antigua, RSO 42, 1967, 305-322.

——, Semitic Elements in Ancient Hispania, CBQ 29, 1967, 487 ff.
J. Sznycer, Les passages puniques en transcription latine dans le 'Poenulus' de Plaute, Paris, 1967.

B. TEXTS AND LITERATURE

1. Text editions

a. *The great compendia in chronological order*

Corpus Inscriptionum Semiticarum. Pars Prima Inscriptiones Phoenicias Continens, Paris, 1881 ff. Abbreviated CIS. Tomus I, 1881, Nos. 1-437; Tomus II, 1890, Nos. 438-3251; Tomus III, 1962, No. 3252-6068. Apart from the first half of the first volume, the main body of the texts consists of inscriptions from Carthage and Africa.

M. Lidzbarski, Handbuch der Nordsemitischen Epigraphik, nebst ausgewählte Inschriften, Weimar, 1898, I. Text, II Tafeln. Contains the more important Phoenician and Punic inscriptions known by then.

G. A. Cook, A Textbook of North-semitic Inscriptions, Oxford, 1903. Phoenician and Punic Inscription from no. 3 onwards.

M. Lidzbarski, Ephmeris für Semitische Epigraphik. Band I-III. Giessen, 1902-1915. Publishes and discusses inter alia the Phoenician and Punic inscriptions discovered between 1898 and 1915.

Répertoire d'Épigraphic Sémitique, publié par la Commission du Corpus Inscriptionum Semiticarum, Paris, 1900 ff., t. I-IV. Abbreviated RÉS, normally quoted after number. A concordance of RÉS and CIS numbers in DISO, 339-342.

M. Lidzbarski, Kanaanäische Inschriften. Altsemitische Texte I, Giessen, 1907.

J.-B. Chabot, Punica, JA série 11, tome 7, 1916, 77-109, 443-467; 8, 1916, 483-520; 9, 1917, 145-166; 10, 1917, 1-79; 11, 1918, 249-302 (I-XXV).

N. Slouschz, Thesaurus of Phoenician Inscriptions, Tell Aviv, 1942 (in Hebrew).

W. R. Lane, A Handbook of Phoenician Inscriptions. Unpublished Dissertation John Hopkins University, 1962.

H. Donner, W. Röllig, Kanaanäische und Aramäische Inschriften,

Band I-III (Texte; Kommentar; Glossare-Indizes-Bibliographie-Tafeln), Wiesbaden, 1962-64. Revised edition (adding the 'Pyrgi-inscription' as no. 277) 1966-1969. Abbreviated KAI. The Phoenician-Punic material treated by W. RÖLLIG covers nos. 1-181 (with extensive bibliographical material and concordances between CIS, RÉS, COOK and KAI numbers). Cf. vol. II², 338 ff. and the reviews by G. LEVI DELLA VIDA in RSO 39, 1964, 295-314, and by R. DEGEN in ZDMG 121, 1971, 121 ff. for additions and corrections.

M. G. G. AMADASI, Le iscrizioni fenicie e puniche delle Colonie in Occidente, Studi Semitici 28, Roma, 1967. Contains inscriptions from Malta, Sicily, Sardinia, Spain, Italy and France (abbreviated ICO).

b. *Smaller collections, groups of miscellaneous inscriptions*

W. F. ALBRIGHT, The Phoenician Inscriptions of the Tenth Century B.C., JAOS 67, 1947, 153-160.

A. BERTHIER, R. CHARLES, Le Sanctuaire Punique d'El-Hofra à Constantine, Paris, 1955, 2 vols., text and plates. Contains the texts of many inscribed Punic stelae (concordance: KAI III, p. 68).

M. DUNAND, Byblia Grammata, Beyrouth, 1945.

——, R. DURU, Oumm el-'Amed, une ville de l'époque hellénistique aux échelles de Tyr. I., Paris, 1962. Contains on p. 181-194 the text of 16 inscriptions (concordance: KAI III, p. 66).

J. G. FÉVRIER, Les découvertes épigraphiques puniques et néopuniques depuis la guerre, SOLDV 1, Roma, 1956, 274-286.

——, Inscriptions Puniques et Néopuniques, in: Inscriptions Antiques du Maroc, publié par le Centre de Recherche sur l'Afrique Méditerranée, Paris, 1966, 81-132.

G. GARBINI, Catalogo delle iscrizioni fenicie conservate nel Museo Archeologico di Palermo, *Κωκαλος*, XIII, 1967, 66-72.

M. LIDZBARSKI, Phönizische und aramäische Kruginschriften aus Elephantine. Anhang zu den APAW, Berlin, 1912.

W. MARTIN, A Preliminary report after re-examination of the Byblian Inscriptions, OrNS 30, 1961, 46-78.

A. MENTZ, Beiträge zur Deutung der phönizischen Inschriften, |Abh. f. d. Kunde des Morgenlandes XXIX, 2, Leipzig, 1944.

J. NAVEH, Phoenician and Punic Inscriptions, Lešonenu 30, 1965, 232-239. Survey of 18 recently published inscriptions.

Th. C. Vriezen, J. H. Hospers, Palestine Inscriptions, Textus Minores XVII, Leiden, 1951. Contains inscriptions also published as KAI nos. 1, 4, 5, 6 and 7.

c. *New editions of and comments on previously published inscriptions*

We list mainly contributions not yet mentioned in the bibliographical notes in KAI II², 338 ff., and III², 63 ff. *sub* VII; the texts are, when possible, identified by their KAI numbers. ICO = M. G. G. Amadasi, listed *sub* B, 1, a; DLPS = J. B. Peckham, listed *sub* C, 3, f.; BÉS = J. Teixidor, Bulletin d'épigraphie sémitique, published in Syria.

CIS I, 145	= J. Ferron, WZKM 62, 1969, 62-75 (Nora II).
CIS II, 75, 3914	= M. Sznycer, AEPHEH, 101, 1968, 93 ff.
KAI 1	= H. Tawil, ANES 3, 1970-71, 32-36.
KAI 5	= J. G. Février, Africa 1, 1966, 13-17.
KAI 14	= BÉS 1971 nos. 102-103.
KAI 15	= J. T. Milik, Bibl 48, 1967, 597 ff.
KAI 17	= ibidem, 572 ff.
KAI 24	= T. Collins, WO 6, 1971, 181-188.
KAI 26	= BÉS 1971, nos. 97-98.
KAI 27	= F. M. Cross, R. J. Saley, BASOR 197, 1970, 42-49; L. A. Bange, A Study... (cf. above *sub* A, 3, 1), 137 f.; A. Caquot, R. du Mesnil du Buisson, Syria 48, 1971, 391-406 (with pl. I-II); BÉS 1971 no. 101.
KAI 30, 31, 38, 39, 41	= DLPS, 13-24.
KAI 37	= J. B. Peckham, OrNS 37, 1968, 304 ff.
KAI 38	= D. Kellerman, ZDPV 86, 1970, 24-37.
KAI 42, 43	= W. R. Lane, BASOR 194, 1969, 39-45.
KAI 46	= M. Delcor, Syria 45, 1968, 322 f.; BASOR 180, 1966, 42; ICO, 83-87.
KAI 47	= ICO, 15-17.
KAI 61	= G. Garbini, RSO 43, 1968, 5 ff.
KAI 62	= ICO, 23-25.
KAI 64	= ICO, 101-102.
KAI 66	= ICO, 91-93.
KAI 70	= J. Ferron, Studi Maghrebini 2, 1967, 89 ff.

KAI 73	= J. FERRON, Mus 81, 1968, 255-261; DLPS, 119-124.
KAI 89	= A. VAN DEN BRANDEN, MUSJ 45, 1969, 307-318.
KAI 175	= I. Š. ŠIFMAN, Semitskie jazyki, Moskva 1963, 166-170.
KAI² 277	= (Pyrgi inscription) AMADASI, ICO, Appendice 2 (with bibliography); W. RÖLLIG, WO 5, 1969, 108 ff., no. 1; TEIXIDOR, BÉS, 1967, no. 52; 1969, no. 104.
RÉS 453	= D. KELLERMAN, ZDPV 86, 1970, 24 ff.
RÉS 1214	= A. CAQUOT, O. MASSON, Syria 45, 1968, 295 ff.
"Parahyba Inscription"	= edited as an authentic Phoenician inscription by C. H. GORDON, OrNS 37, 1968, 75 ff.; cf. L. DELEKAT, Phönizier in Amerika, Bonn, 1969. Rejected as a fake by: J. HOFTIJZER, Phoenix 14, 1968, 182 ff.; J. FRIEDRICH, OrNS 37, 1968, 421 ff.; F. M. CROSS, ibidem, 437 ff.; M. G. G. AMADASI, OA 7, 1968, 245 ff.

d. *New inscriptions not yet or only partly contained in the great compendia (CIS, KAI)*

It is impossible to record here the rich and continuous harvest of new, mainly Punic, inscriptions, discovered all over the Mediterranean area at sites of former Phoenician or Punic settlements. Only the more important or isolated inscriptions are mentioned here. Cf. for full information, apart from the bibliographies in KAI III², 64-78, BENZ, Personal Names, ch. I (above sub A, 2), and in AMADASI, ICO (quoted *sub* a), especially the entries in J. TEIXIDOR, BÉS (cf. below *sub* D, 1, c), where the new material is recorded and discussed.

α. Phoenicia

J. T. MILIK, Flèches à inscriptions phéniciennes au Musée National Libanais, BMB 16, 1961, 103-108.

M. DUNAND, Nouvelles inscriptions phéniciennes du Temple d'Echmoun à Bostan ech-Cheikh près de Sidon, BMB 18, 1965, 105-109. Cf. W. RÖLLIG, WO 5, 1969, 121-124: 3. Eine neue phönizische Dynastie in Sidon.

A. Vanel, Six ostraca phéniciens trouvés au temple d'Echmoun, près de Saida, BMB 20, 1967, 45-95.

——, Le septième ostracon phénicien trouvé au temple d'Echmoun, MUSJ 45, 1969, 343-364.

J. Starckey, Une inscription phénicienne de Byblos, MUSJ 45, 1969, 257-274.

β. Cyprus

A. Caquot, O. Masson, Deux inscriptions phéniciennes de Chypre, Syria 45, 1968, 295-321 (no. 1 = RÉS 1214; no. 2 is a new inscription from Idalion, mentioning *ršp-mkl*).

A. Dupont-Sommer, Une inscription phénicienne archaique récemment trouvée à Kition (Chypre), Extrait des Mémoires de l'Académie des Inscriptions et des Belles Lettres, t. 44, 1970, Paris, 1970.

γ. Carthage

J. Ferron, Inscription punique archaique à Carthage, Mélanges de Carthage (Cahiers de Byrsa 10), 1964-65, 55 ff.

——, Inscription dite bilingue des disques en plomb de Carthage, ibidem, 65 ff.

A. Mahjoubi, M. H. Fantar, Une nouvelle inscription carthaginoise, ANL Rend., Ser. VIII, 21, 1966, 201 ff.

C. Saumagne, J. Ferron, Une inscription commémorative de la *consecratio* de Carthage, CRAIBL, 1966, 61-78.

A. Dupont-Sommer, Une nouvelle inscription punique à Carthage, CRAIBL, 1968, 116-132 (cf. also G. Garbini, RSO 43, 1968, 11-13).

δ. Tripolitania (Leptis Magna)

(Cf. for Trip. nos. 1-37 DISO p. xxviii *sub* 'Trip.'; and KAI nos. 118-132 and 178 and vol. III² p. 77 f. for Trip. nos. 1-51).

G. Levi della Vida, Frustuli neopuniche tripolitani, ANL Rend., Ser. VIII, 18, 1963, 463 ff. (Trip. nos. 41-50).

——, Sulle iscrizioni 'latino-libiche' della Tripolitania, OA 2, 1963, 64-94.

——, Le iscrizioni neopuniche di Wadi el-'Amud (Trip. 38-40), LibAnt 1, 1964, 57-63.

——, Ostracon Neopunica dalla Tripolitania, OrNS 33, 1964, 1 ff. (Trip. 51).

156   LANGUAGES OF THE ANCIENT NEAR EAST

——, Una inedita iscrizione neopunica da Leptis Magna, WZHalle 17, 1968, 127-132 (Trip. 52).
——, Qualche osservazione a AION, n.s. 16, AIUON 17, 1967, 256-266.
F. VATTIONI, Appunti sull'iscrizioni puniche tripolitani, AIUON 16, 1966, 37-55.

ε. Spain

J. M. SOLA-SOLÉ, Miscelánea Punico-Hispana, I, Sefarad 16, 1956, 325 ff.; II, Sefarad 17, 1957, 18 ff.; III, Sefarad 25, 1965, 27 ff.; IV, Sefarad 27, 1967, 12 ff. (Hisp. 11 ff.).
——, Nueva inscripción fenicia de España, RSO 41, 1966, 97-108 (Hisp. 14); cf. also J. FERRON. Ampurias 28, 1966, 246 ff.; G. GARBINI, RSO 42, 1967, 1 ff.; M. HELTZER, OA 6, 1967, 265 ff.; F. VATTIONI, OrNS 36, 1967, 178 ff.; A. VAN DEN BRANDEN, RSO 44, 1969, 103 ff.; M. DELCOR, MUSJ 45, 1969, 319-342; F. M. CROSS, HTR 64, 1971, 189-196; BÉS 1971, no. 106.
——, Assaig d'interpretació d'algunes inscripcions "ibériques" mitjançant el fenici i punic, OA 7, 1968, 223-244.
J. FERRON, L'inscription carthaginoise peinte sur l'urne cinéraire d'Almuñécar, Mus 83, 1970, 249-265.

ζ. Mozia (Sicily)

G. GARBINI, in: Mozia, Rapporto preliminare della Missione congiunta con la Soprintendenza all'Antichità della Sicilia Occidentale, II, Roma, 1966 (Pubbl. d. Centro di Studio per la Civiltá Fenicia e Punica; series: Studi Semitici), 109-115, with pl. LXXVIII, 1-3 (nos. 1-2).
——, in: Mozia ... III, Roma, 1967, 71-81 with pl. XLI-XLIII (nos. 1-3).
——, in: Mozia ... IV, Roma, 1968, 96-102 with pl. XLVI-XLIX (nos. 1-6).
M. G. G. AMADASI, in: Mozia ... V, Roma, 1969, 115-116 with pl. LVIII, 1 (no. 1).
——, in: Mozia ... VI, 1970, 95-116 with pl. LXIX-LXXIX (nos. 1-21). (Almost exclusively inscriptions on stelae from the tophet of Mozia, containing dedications to 'dn bʿl ḥmn).
B. ROCCO, L'iscrizione punica di Mozia, BibOr 9, 1967, 209 ff.
——, Iscrizioni fenicie di Mozia, AIUON 20, 1970, 105-116.

η. Antas (Sardinia)

S. Moscati, Antas, A new Punic Site in Sardinia, BASOR 196, 1969, 23-36.

G. Garbini, Le iscrizioni puniche di Antas, AIUON 19, 1969, 317-331.

M. Fantar, in: E. Acquaro et al., Ricerche puniche ad Antas, Roma, 1969 (Studi Semitici 30), ch. II, 'Les inscriptions puniques', 47-93 (nos. 1-21) with pl. 23-38. Cf. BÉS 1970 no. 73.

θ. Various inscriptions

R. D. Barnett, Layard's Bronzes and their Inscriptions, ErIs 8, 1967, 1* ff.

F. Barreca, Nuove iscrizioni fenicie da Sulcis, OA 4, 1965, 53 ff.

F. M. Cross, Jar Inscriptions from Shiqmona, IEJ 18, 1968, 226-233.

J. Ferron, Textes puniques et néopuniques relatifs aux testaments, Sem 11, 1961, 3-8.

——, Épigraphie funéraire punique, OA 5, 1966, 197-201.

——, A propos d'une expression employée sur les stèles funéraires néopuniques de Mactar, Cahiers de Tunisie 15, 1967, 33-37.

J. G. Février, M. Fantar, Les nouvelles inscriptions monumentales néopuniques de Mactar, Karthago 12, 1963-64, 45-59.

G. Garbini, L'iscrizione punica, in: Monte Sirai II, Roma, 1965, 79-92.

S. Gevirtz, A Spindle Whorl with Phoenician Inscription, JNES 26, 1967, 13-16.

J. Hoftijzer, Liste des pierres et moulages à textes phéniciens/puniques du Musée des Antiquités à Leyde, OML 44, 1963, 89-98.

L. Karpinski, Phoenician Stelae from the National Museum in Krakow, Études et Travaux, Centre d'Arch. Médit. de l'Acad. Pol. d. Sciences, 3, 1966, 23-31 (3 inscribed stelae; no. 3 = CIS I, 180).

G. Levi della Vida, Iscrizione punica da Sabratha, Lib.Ant. 3/4, 1966-67, 1 ff.

O. Masson, Recherches sur les Phéniciens dans le monde hellénistique, BCH 93, 1969, 694-699 (three bilingual funerary stelae, two of them unpublished; cf. Teixidor, BÉS, 1970, nos. 70-72).

W. Röllig, Eine neue Harpokrates-Statuette mit Phönizischer Inschrift, WO 5, 1969, 118-121, no. 2 (study of the text published by R. D. Barnett, BMQ 27, 1963-64, p. 85 with pl. XLI; bilingual inscription, from Egypt).

W. Röllig, Alte und neue phönizische Inschriften aus dem ägäischen Raum, NESE a, 1972, 1-8.

2. LITERATURE

Of the Phoenician-Punic literature, in the sense of "belles lettres", practically nothing has been preserved. Understanding literature as "written heritage", it can be said to consist mainly of votive, sepulchral, building and commemorative inscriptions (the latter especially from Phoenicia proper, giving some historical information), beside a small number of texts of religious nature (the so called sacrificial tariffs, an incantation, a *tabula devotionis*, etc.). Some literary works have been preserved in partial Greek or Latin versions or extracts.

Separate studies on Phoenician-Punic literature accordingly are extremely seldom. Most books about Phoenician civilisation have a chapter or paragraph on literature or written remains. Compendia of inscriptions, like KAI, ICO etc., normally contain translations of the more important inscriptions.

The discoveries in Ugarit have revealed a corpus of religious literature, part of which will undoubtedly have been passed on in some form to the later Phoenicians.

T. COLLINS, The Kilamuwa Inscription — a Phoenician Poem, WO 6, 1971, 181-188.

M. DAHOOD, The Phoenician Contribution to Biblical Wisdom Literature, in: W. A. WARD (ed.), The Role of the Phoenicians in the Interaction of Mediterranean Civilizations. Centennial Publication of the American University of Beirut. Beirut, 1968, 123-152 (cf. by the same author, Bibl 33, 1952, 30 ff. and 191 ff.).

——, The Phoenician Background of Qoheleth, Bibl 47, 1966, 403-419.

J. C. GREENFIELD, Scripture and Inscriptions. The literary and rhetorical elements in some early Phoenician inscriptions, in: H. GOEDICKE (ed), Near Eastern Studies in Honor of F. W. Albright, Baltimore, 1970, 253-368.

G. GERMAIN, Qu'est-ce que le Périple d'Hannon? Document, amplification littéraire ou faux intégral?, Hespéris 44, 1957, 205 ff.

S. SEGERT, The Phoenician Background of Hanno's Periplus, MUSJ 45, 1969, 499-520.

M. SZNYCER, Les passages puniques en transcription latine dans le "Poenulus" de Plaute, Paris, 1967.

——, La littérature punique, in: Archéologie Vivante, 1, 1968, 141-148.

F. ROSENTHAL, Canaanite and Aramaic Inscriptions, in: J. B. PRIT-

CHARD, ANET³, 1969, 653-662 (= The Ancient Near East. Supplementary Texts and Pictures Relating to the Old Testament, Princeton, 1969, 217-226), contains the translation, with short introductory and bibliographical notes, of KAI nos. 1, 4, 10, 14, 24-27, 61, 69 and 74.

C. HISTORY AND CULTURE

1. GENERAL WORKS ON PHOENICIAN HISTORY AND CULTURE

D. BARAMKI, Phoenicia and Phoenicians, Beirut, 1961; German edition: Die Phönizier, Stuttgart, 1965 (Urban Bücher).
D. HARDEN, The Phoenicians, London, 1962 (Ancient Peoples and Places).
M. DUNAND, Article 'Phénicie', Dictionnaire de la Bible, Suppl. VII, 1966, col. 1142-1203.
O. EISSFELDT, Philister und Phönizier, Der Alte Orient 34, 1936.
S. MOSCATI, The World of the Phoenicians, London, 1968.
F. K. MOVERS, Die Phönizier, Bonn, 1841-1856, 3 vols. Reprint, 1967.
R. PIETSCHMAN, Geschichte der Phönizier, Berlin, 1889.
G. RAWLINSON, The Story of the Nations: Phoenicia, London, 1889.

2. HISTORY OF THE PHOENICIANS AND THEIR COLONIES

a. *General*

W. F. ALBRIGHT, Syria, the Philistines and Phoenicia, CAH², vol. II, ch. 33 (fasc. 51), Cambridge, 1966.
J. P. BROWN, The Lebanon and Phoenicia. Ancient texts illustrating their physical geography and native industries. Vol. 1. The physical setting and the forest, Beirut, 1969.
FISCHER WELTGESCHICHTE, Band 4, 1967, 135 ff. (W. CASKEL); Band 5, 1965, 371 ff. (H. BENGTSON); Band 6, 1965, 244 ff. (M. SMITH).
E. MEYER, Geschichte des Altertums II, 2, 2, Stuttgart-Berlin, 1931, 61-186.
A. T. OLMSTEAD, History of Palestine and Syria, 1941.

b. *Byblos, Sidon and Tyre*

W. Herrmann, Der historische Ertrag der altbyblischen Königs-inschriften, MIO VI, 1958, 14-32.

N. Jidejian, Byblos through the Ages, Beirut, 1968.

H. Klengel, Geschichte Syriens im 2. Jahrtausend v. u.Z., II, Berlin, 1969, 8. Abschnitt, 'Gubla/Byblos', 422-440; III, Berlin, 1970, 4-29.

E. J. Wein, R. Opificius, 7000 Jahre Byblos, Nürnberg, 1963.

P. Montet, Byblos et l'Égypte, Paris, 1928.

F. C. Eiselen, Sidon. A Study in Oriental History, New York, 1907.

K. Galling, Eschmunazar und der Herr der Könige, ZDPV 79, 1963, 140-151.

W. Röllig, Eine neue phönizische Dynastie in Sidon, WO 5, 1969, 121 ff., *sub* 3.

W. B. Fleming, History of Tyre, New York, 1915.

N. Jidejian, Tyre through the Ages, Beirut, 1969.

M. J. Katzenstein, The History of Tyre from the beginning of the Second Millennium until the rise of the Assyrian Empire. Un-published dissertation, Jerusalem, 1965.

J. Liver, The Chronology of Tyre at the Beginning of the First Millennium B.C., IEJ 3, 1953, 113-120.

B. Mazar, The Philistines and the Rise of Israel and Tyre, Proc. Israel Acad. of Sciences and Hum., I, 1964, no. 7, 1-22.

H.-P. Müller, Phönizien und Juda in exilisch-nachexilischer Zeit, WO 6, 1971, 189-204.

R. de Vaux, Les Phéniciens et les peuples de la mer, MUSJ 45, 1969, 479-498.

c. *Colonisation and expansion*

W. F. Albright, New Light on the Early History of Phoenician Colonization, BASOR 83, 1941, 14 ff.

F. Barreca (et alii), Ricerche puniche nel Mediterraneo Centrale, Roma, 1970 (Studi Semitici 36; with good maps of Punic settle-ments in Sardinia, Sicily and North-Africa).

J. M. Blazquez, Tartessos y los origines de la Colonizacion Fenicia en Occidente, Salamanca, 1968.

P. Bosch-Gimpera, Phéniciens et Grecs dans l'Extrême-Occident, La Nouvelle Clio 3, 1951, 269-296.

R. Carpenter, The Phoenicians in the West, AJA 62, 1958, 35-53.

W. Culican, Aspects of Phoenician Settlement in the West Mediterranean, AbN 1, 1961, 36-55.

——, Almuñecar, Assur and the Phoenician Penetration of the Western Mediterranean, Levant 2, 1970, 28-36.

L'Espansione Fenicia nel Mediterranea. Relazioni di Colloquio in Roma, 4-5 Maggio 1970, (Studi Semitici 38) Roma, 1971.

K. Galling, Der Weg der Phöniker nach Tarsis in literarischer und archäologischer Sicht, I (Fortsetzung folgt), ZDPV 88, 1972, 1-18.

G. Garbini, I Fenici in Occidente, Studi Etruschi 34, 1966, 111-147.

D. Y. Gordon, The Historical Background of Phoenician Expansion into the Mediterranean in the Early First Millennium B.C. Unpublished dissertation, 1970 (cf. Dissertation Abstracts 31, 1970, 1173A).

O. Masson, Recherches sur les Phéniciens dans le monde hellénistique, BCH 93, 1969, 694-799.

d. *Carthage*

Carthage, sa naissance, sa grandeur, = Archéologie Vivante I, 1968, no. 2 (special number with 15 articles about history and civilisation of Carthage, 156 p., 64 pl.).

E. Frézouls, Une nouvelle hypothèse sur la fondation de Carthage, BCH 79, 1955, 153-176.

S. Gsell, Histoire ancienne de l'Afrique du Nord, I-IV, Paris, 1951².

G. G. Lapeyre, A. Pellegrin, Carthage punique, Paris, 1942.

C. Picard, Carthage, Paris, 1951.

G. and C. Picard, Life and Death of Carthago, London, 1968.

B. H. Warmington, Carthage, London, 1964² (Pelican A 598); revised edition, London, 1969.

e. *Colonies in the West*

S. Chiappisi, Il Melqart di Sciacca e la questione fenicia in Sicilia, Roma, 1961.

P. Cintas, Contribution à l'étude de l'expansion carthaginois au Maroc, Paris, 1954.

——, Tarsis, Tartessos, Gadès, Sem 16, 1966, 5-35.

S. Moscati, Antas. A new Punic Site in Sardinia, BASOR 196, 1969, 23-36.

——, La penetrazione fenicia in Sardegna, ANL Mem. Ser. VIII, 12, 1966, 217-250.

——, Sulle più antica storia dei Fenici in Sicilia, OA 7, 1968, 165 ff.
——, Fenici e Cartaginesi in Sardegna, Milano, 1968.
R. Menendez Pidal, Historia de España, Madrid, 1960, I, 2, 281-492.
G. Pesce, Sardegna Punica, Cagliari, 1961.
A. di Vita, Les phéniciens de l'Occident d'après les découvertes
     archéologiques de Tripolitanie, in: W. Ward (ed.), The Role of the
     Phoenicians ... (cf. sub C, 3, 1 below), 77-98.

Only the most important items, especially under c), d), and e), could
be mentioned. For a rich bibliography on these subjects see S. Moscati, The World of the Phoenicians, London, 1968, 264-271, Bibliography, and G. and C. Picard, The Life and Death of Carthage
(cf. sub d), 347-352, Bibliography.

3. Phoenician-Punic Culture

a. *General surveys of the Phoenician culture*

W. F. Albright, The Role of the Canaanites in the History of Civili-
     zation, in: G. E. Wright (ed.), The Bible and the Ancient Near
     East, New York, 1961, 328 ff.
J. M. Chami, De la Phénicie, Beirut, 1968.
G. Contenau, La civilisation phénicienne, Paris, 1949 (with a rich
     bibliography).
W. A. Ward (ed.), The Role of the Phoenicians in the Interaction of
     Mediterranean Civilizations. Centennial Publication American
     University of Beirut, 1866-1966. Beirut, 1968. A collection of
     ten articles about different aspects of Phoenician culture.

b. *Archaeology of Phoenicia*

J. Ch. Assmann, Zur Baugeschichte der Königsgruft von Sidon,
     AA 1963, col. 690-715.
M. Dunand, Fouilles de Byblos I, II, Paris, 1939-1958 (BAH XXIV).
——, Byblos, son histoire, ses ruines, Beyrouth, 1963.
G. Contenau, Mission archéologique à Sidon, Paris, 1921-24.
R. Hachmann, Das Königsgrab V von Jebeil (Byblos), IM 17, 1967,
     93-114.
L. Hennequin, Fouilles en Phénicie, Dict. de la Bible, Suppl. III,
     Paris, 1936, col. 436-470.
A. Poidebard, Tyr, un grand port disparu, Paris, 1939.

——, J. LAUFFRAY, Sidon. Aménagements antiques au port de Saida, Beyrouth, 1951.

P. THOMPSON, articles 'Byblos', 'Sidon', and 'Tyrus' in: M. EBERT, Reallexikon der Vorgeschichte, 2, 1926, 246 ff.; 12, 1928, 77 ff.; 13, 1929, 516 ff.

C. WATZINGER, Phönikien und Palestina: die Blütezeit, in: W. OTTO, Handbuch der Archäologie, I, München, 1939, 797 ff.

Reports on the current excavations by M. DUNAND at Byblos and Sidon (temple of Eshmun) are to be found in the Bulletin du Musée de Beyrouth (Beyrouth, 1937 ff.) especially vol. 18 ff.

c. *Carthago and its colonies*

Cf. the books and their bibliographies mentioned *sub* C, 2, d and e, which give good information about the many archeological undertakings on sites of Punic settlement all over the Western Mediteranean. Some works of archaeological nature are moreover mentioned below *sub* g (Religion) ḥ (Temples and Cults). Here I mention only the most important books:

A. M. BISI, La ceramica punica. Aspetti e problemi. Napoli, 1970.

P. CINTAS, Manuel d'archéologie punique, t, I. Histoire et archéologie comparées. Chronologie des temps archaiques de Carthage et des villes phéniciennes de l'Ouest, Paris, 1970.

P. GAUCKLER, Nécropoles puniques I-II, Paris, 1915.

C. and G. C. PICARD, La vie cotidienne à Carthage au temps d'Hannibal, Paris, 1964².

M. PONSICH, Nécropoles phéniciennes de la région de Tanger, Paris, 1969 (Études et travaux d'archéologie marocaine 3).

d. *Art*

E. ACQUARO, Note su una classe di amuleti punici, AO 9, 1970, 65-73.

——, I rasoi punici, (Studi Semitici 41) Roma, 1971.

R. D. BARNETT, The Nimrud Ivories and the Art of the Phoenicians, Iraq 2, 1935, 179 ff.

——, A Catalogue of Nimrud Ivories in the British Museum, London, 1957.

A. BISI, Le stele puniche, Roma, 1967 (Studi Semitici 27).

M. CHÉHAB, Le sarcophage d'Ahiram, MUSJ 46, 1971, 107 ff.

——, Les terres cuites de Kharayeb, Paris, 1951-54.

P. CINTAS, Céramique punique, Paris, 1950.

——, Amulettes puniques, Tunis, 1946.

W. CULICAN, Aperçus sur les ateliers phéniciens, Syria 45, 1968, 275-293.

——, The Iconography of some Phoenician Seals and Seal Impressions, Australian Journal of Bibl. Archaeology 1, 1968, 50-103.

C. DECAMPS DE MERTZENFELD, Inventaire commenté des ivoires phéniciens découverts dans le Proche-Orient, Paris, 1954.

M. DUNAND, La statuaire de la favissa du temple d'Echmoun à Sidon, in: Archäologie und Altes Testament, Festschrift K. Galling, Tübingen, 1970, 61-68.

R. DUSSAUD, L'art phénicien du IIe millénaire, Paris, 1949.

M. P. FOUCHET, L'art à Carthage, Paris, 1962.

G. GARBINI, Maschere Puniche, AIUON 18, 1968, 319-330.

M. HARAN, The Bas-Reliefs on the Sarcophagus of Ahiram in the Light of Archaeological and Literary Parallels from the Ancient Near East, IEJ 8, 1958, 15-25.

M. HOURS-MEIDAN, Les représentations figurés sur les stèles de Carthage, Cahiers de Byrsa 1, 1951, 15-160.

E. KUKAHN, Anthropoide Sarkophage in Beyrouth, Berlin, 1955.

J. LECLANT, Les talismans égyptiens dans les nécropoles (de Carthage), Archéologie Vivante 1, 1968, nr. 2, 95-113.

A. LÉZINE, Architecture punique. Recueil de documents. Paris, 1962.

S. MOSCATI, Art phénicien d'Occident, MUSJ 45, 1969, 381-390.

——, New Light on Punic Art, in: W. WARD (ed.), The Role of the Phoenicians ... (see sub C, 3, a), 65-76.

——, Stèles puniques de Nora, in: Hommages à André Dupont-Sommer, Paris, 1971, 95-116.

——, M. L. UBERTI, Le stele puniche di Nora nel Museo Nazionale di Cagliari, Roma, 1970 (Studi Semitici 35).

G. PERROT, C. CHIPIEZ, Histoire de l'art dans l'antiquité, III, Phénicie-Chypre, Paris, 1885.

J. VERCOUTTER, Les objets égyptiens et égyptisants du mobilier funéraire carthaginois, Paris, 1945.

e. *Trade and economy*

M. ASTOUR, The origin of the terms 'Canaan', 'Phoenician' and 'Purple', JNES 24, 1964, 346-350.

R. D. BARNETT, Early Shipping in the Near East, Antiquity 32, 1958, 220-230.

R. CARPENTER, Navigateurs puniques sur les routes de la mer, Archéol. Vivante 1, 1968, 31 ff.

W. CULICAN, The First Merchant Venturers, London, 1965, ch. IV: 'Phoenicia and Israel'.

J.-G. FÉVRIER, L'ancienne marine phénicienne et les découvertes récentes. La Nouvelle Clio, I-II, 1949-50, 128-143.

L. B. JENSEN, Royal Purple of Tyre, JNES 22, 1963, 104-118.

J. LECLANT, Les relations entre l'Égypte et la Phénicie du voyage d'Ounamon à l'expédition d'Alexandre, in: W. WARD (ed.), The Role of the Phoenicians ... (see above sub C, 3, a).

A. L. OPPENHEIM, Essay on Overland Trade in the First Millennium B.C., JCS 21, 1967 (published 1969), 236-254.

J. PIRENNE, A propos du droit commercial phénicien antique, Bull. Acad. Roy. de Belgique, Vᵉ série, 41, 1955, 586-614.

f. Alphabet and script

F. M. CROSS Jr., The Origin and Early Evolution of the Alphabet, ErIs 8, 1967, 8*-24*.

D. DIRINGER, Problems of the Present Day on the Origin of the Phoenician Alphabet, CHM 4, 1957-58, 40-58.

M. F. MARTIN, A Twelfth Century Bronse Palimpsest, RSO 37, 1962, 175-193.

J. NAVEH, The Development of the Aramaic Script, Proc. of the Israel Acad. of Sciences and Hum., V/1, Jerusalem, 1970, ch. II and VII.

W. RÖLLIG, Alphabetschrift, in: Handbuch der Archäologie. Grundlagen, München 1968, 289-302.

J. B. PECKHAM, The Development of the Late Phoenician Script, Cambridge Mass., 1968 (Harvard Semitic Series 20).

g. Religion

α. General works

F. W. ALBRIGHT, Yahweh and the Gods of Canaan, London, 1968 (Jordan Lectures, 1965), ch. 5, 181 ff.: 'The religious cultures of Israel and Phoenicia in periodic tension'.

C. CLEMEN, Die phönikische Religion nach Philo von Byblos, MVAeG 42/3, Leipzig, 1939.

R. DUSSAUD, La religion des Hittites et des Hourites, des Phéniciens et des Syriens, Paris, 1949².

O. Eissfeldt, Art und Aufbau der phönizischen Geschichte des Philo von Byblos, Syria 33, 1956, 81-90.

——, Ras Schamra und Sanchunjaton, Halle, 1939.

H. Gese, in: H. Gese, M. Höfner, K. Rudolph, Die Religionen Altsyriens, Altarabiens und der Mandäer, Stuttgart, 1970, ch. VI, 162-215.

J. P. Lettinga, De godsdiensten van Kanaänieten en Arameeërs, in: G. van der Leeuw (ed.), De Godsdiensten der Wereld, II³, Amsterdam, 1956, 308 ff.

S. Moscati, The World of the Phoenicians, London, 1968, part I, ch. 3 and part II, ch. 10.

J. Pedersen, Kanaanäische Religion, in: Handbuch der Religionsgeschichte, Band 2, Göttingen 1972.

G. C. Picard, Les Religions de l'Afrique antique, Paris, 1954 (Carthage).

M. H. Pope, W. Röllig, Syrien. Die Mythologie der Ugariter und Phönizier, in: H. W. Haussig, Wörterbuch der Mythologie, Stuttgart, 1962 ff., vol. I, 217-312.

β. The gods

The gods are discussed by Röllig in Pope-Röllig (mentioned *sub* g, α) in alphabetical order. We here mention a number of studies, mainly those published since 1962.

A. Alt, Die Götter in den phönikischen Inschriften von Karatepe, TLZ 74, 1949, 513-522.

M. G. G. Amadasi, Note sul deo Sid, in: Ricerche puniche ad Antas, Studi Semitici 30, Roma, 1969, 95-104.

W. W. Baudissin, Adonis und Esmun, Leipzig, 1911.

E. Bresciani, Rešef-MKL, OA 1, 1962, 215-217.

A. Caquot, Chadrafa, Syria 29, 1952, 74-88.

——, O. Masson, Nouvel dédicace d'Idalion à Reshef-MKL, Syria 45, 1968, 295 ff., no. 2.

——, Milkaštart d'après les inscriptions d'Umm el 'Amed, Semitica 15, 1965, 29 ff.

P. Cintas, Le signe de Tanit, Archéologie Vivante 1, 1968, 4-10.

S. Chiappisi, Il Melqart di Sciacca e la questione fenicia in Sicilia, Roma, 1961.

W. Culican, Dea Tyria Gravida, Australian Journ. of Bibl. Arch., 1, 1968, 35-50.

R. Dussaud, Melqart d'après des récents travaux, RHR 158, 1957, 1-21.

O. Eissfeldt, Ba'alšamen und Jahwe, ZAW 57, 1939, 1-31.

J. Ferron, Le caractère solaire du dieu de Carthage, Africa 1, 1965, 41 ff.

L. Foucher, Les représentations de Baal Hammon, Archéologie Vivante, 1, 1968, 131-140.

J. G. Février, A propos de Ba'al Addir, Sem 2, 1949, 21-28.

É. Lipinski, La fête de l'ensevelissement et de la résurrection de Melqart, Actes de la XVIIᵉ Rencontre Assyriologique International, Ham-sur-Heure, 1970, 30-58.

P. Matthiae, Note sul dio siriano Rešef, OA 2, 1963, 27-43.

R. du Mesnil du Buisson, Origine et évolution du Panthéon de Tyr, RHR 164, 1963, 133-163.

R. du Mesnil du Buisson, Études sur les dieux phéniciens hérités par l'empire romain, Leiden, 1970.

E. Meyer, Untersuchungen zur phönikischen Religion. Die Inschriften von Maᶜṣub und Umm el-'Awamid und die Inschrift der Bodostor von Sidon, ZAW 49, 1931, 1-15.

P. Naster, Le Ba'al de Sidon, Festschrift Bossert (Anadolu Araştir-malari II, 1-2), Istanbul, 1965, 327-332.

C. and G. C. Picard, Hercule et Melqart, in: Mélanges J. Bayet, Collection Latomus 70, Brussels, 1964, 569 ff.

W. Röllig, El als Gottesbezeichnung im Phönizischen, Festschrift J. Friedrich, 1959, 403 ff.

H. Seyrig, Les grands dieux de Tyr à l'époque grecque et romaine, Syria 40, 1963, 19-30.

J. M. Sola-Solé, hgd 'ršf y el panteón fenicio-punico de España, Sefarad 16, 1956, 341-355.

F. Vattioni, Il dio Resheph, AIUON 15, 1965-66, 39-74.

M. Weipert, Elemente phönikischer und kilikischer Religion in den Inschriften vom Karatepe, ZDMG Suppl. 1, XVII. Deutscher Orientalistentag, Vorträge, Teil I, Wiesbaden, 1969, 191-217.

γ. Temples and cults

N. Aimé-Giron, Un naos phénicien de Sidon, BIFAO 34, 1934, 31-42.

D. van Berchem, Sanctuaires d'Hercule-Melqart. Contribution à l'étude de l'expansion phénicien en Mediteranée, Syria 44, 1967, 73-109.

A. BERTHIER, R. CHARLIER, Le Sanctuaire punique d'El-Hofra à Constantine, Paris, 1955 (2 vols).

A. VAN DEN BRANDEN, Lévitique 1-7 et le Tarif de Marseille (CIS I, 165), RSO 40, 1965, 107-130.

Th. A. BUSINK, Der Tempel von Jerusalem von Salomo bis Herodes, Leiden, 1970, vol. I, part IV: Tempel in Altkanaan, Phönikien und Ugarit, 527 ff.

L. CARTON, Un sanctuaire punique découvert à Carthage, Paris, 1929.

R. CHARLIER, La nouvelle série de stèles puniques de Constantine et la question des sacrifices dits 'molchomor', en relation avec l'expression 'BSRM BTM', Karthago 4, 1953, 1-48.

P. CINTAS, Le sanctuaire punique de Sousse, Rev. Africaine 90, 1947, 1-80.

M. DUNAND, Les sculptures de la favissa du temple d'Amrit, BMB 7, 1944-45, 99-107; 8, 1946-48, 81-107.

——, Nouvelles fouilles au temple d'Eschmoun à Bostan ech-Cheikh près Sidon, BMB 18, 1965, 103 ff.; 20, 1967, 27 ff. (excavations since 1963; for older excavations in this temple, see the literature in W. RÖLLIG, WO 5, 1969, p. 121, n. 51).

R. DUSSAUD, Les origines cananéennes du sacrifice israélite, Paris, 1941².

——, Précisions épigraphiques touchant les sacrifices puniques d'enfants, CRAIBL, 1946, 371 ff.

O. EISSFELDT, Molk als Opferbegriff im Punischen und Hebräischen und das Ende des Gottes Moloch, Halle, 1935.

M. FANTAR, Eschatologie phénicienne-punique, Tunis, 1970.

J. G. FÉVRIER, Essai de reconstitution du sacrifice molek, JA 248, 1960, 167-187.

——, Molchomor, RHR 143, 1953, 8-18.

——, Remarques sur le Grand Tarif dit de Marseille, Cahiers de Byrsa 8, 1958-59, 35-43.

——, Le rite de substitution dans les textes de N'gaous, JA 250, 1962, 1-10.

——, Les sacrifices d'enfants, Archéologie Vivante I, 1968, 114-118.

——, Le vocabulaire sacrificiel punique, JA 243, 1955, 49-63.

J. HOFTIJZER, Eine Notiz zum punischen Kinderopfer, VT 8, 1958, 288 ff.

S. MOSCATI, Il sacrificio dei fanciulli, Rend. d. Pont. Accad. Romana di Arch. 38, 1965-66, 1-8.

E. OLAVARRI, El calendario cultico de Karatepe y el Zebaḥ Hayyamym

en I Sam., EstBib 29, 1970, 311-325 (cf. BÉS 1971, no. 97 and
M. HARAN, VT 19, 1969, 372 f.).
G. PESCE, Il tempio punica di Tharros, Monum. Antichi d. Accad.
Naz. d. Lincei, 45, 1961, col. 333-440.
C. PICARD, Les installations cultuelles retrouvées au Tophet de Sa-
lammbo, RSO 42, 1967, 189-199.
L. POINSSOT, R. LANTIER, Une sanctuaire de Tanit à Carthage,
RHR 87, 1923, 32-68.
A. VERGER, Sur una caratteristica formale delle tariffe sacrificali
puniche, OA 7, 1968, 123-126.

D. BIBLIOGRAPHY

There exists no special journal devoted to Phoenician studies, nor
a separate bibliography of Phoenician-Punic. Material is to be found
in bibliographies covering the (old) Semitic Languages in general or
North-Western Semitic. Moreover, the main books dealing with
culture, language and inscriptions often contain much bibliographical
material.

1. LANGUAGE AND INSCRIPTIONS

a. *Older bibliographies*

M. LIDZBARSKI, Handbuch (see above *sub* B, 1, a), 1898, 4-84 and
    493-498; continued in the same author's Ephemeris, I-III,
    Giessen, 1902-1915 (see above *sub* B, 1, a).
Z. HARRIS, Grammar, 1936 (see above *sub* A, 1), *sub* 'Bibliography';
    continues, where Lidzbarski ended.
G. GARBINI, Il Semitico di Nord-Ovest, 1960 (see above *sub* A, 1);
    contains most of the later material on the language.

b. *Recent bibliographies in books*

H. DONNER, W. RÖLLIG, KAI (see above *sub* B, 1, a), revised edition,
    1966-1969, vol II (Kommentar): bibliographical material is
    mentioned in the introduction to each inscription; vol. III,
    p. 63 ff., VII. Bibliographie der kanaanäischen Inschriften, A.
    Phönizisch; B. Punish und Neupunish (67-76); vol. II², 338-341,
    Literaturnachträge und Ergänzungen. Cf. the review by R. DEGEN
    in ZDMG 121, 1971, 121 ff.

J. Friedrich, W. Röllig, Phönizisch-Punische Grammatik, 1970 (see above *sub* A, 1); bibliographic material in the introduction.

Charles-F. Jean, Jacob Hoftijzer, DISO (see above *sub* A, 2); bibliographic material on p. XIII ff. 'Liste des abréviations'.

F. L. Benz, Personal Names (cf. above *sub* A, 2) contains in ch. I, 14-52 a detailed list and bibliography of inscriptions, and on 468-511 an extensive bibliography of books and articles.

c. *Current bibliographies*

Bibliographie Sémitique, published every two to four years in the journal Orientalia (Nova Series), Roma, since vol. 16, 1947. Last instalment: no. 9 in vol. 33, 1964.

Bulletin d'épigraphie sémitique (= BÉS), published annually by Javier Teixidor in the journal Syria, from vol. 44, 1967 onwards. Contains material on script, language, onomasticon, seals, inscriptions, and indexes.

Elenchus Bibliographicus Biblicus, published annually, originally as an appendix to the journal Biblica, but since 1968 separately. Contains material on Phoenician and Punic language and inscriptions *sub* XVI, 'Philologia Biblica', and elsewhere also material on history, religion and archaeology.

Internationale Zeitschriftenschau für Bibelwissenschaft und Grenzgebiete, Düsseldorf. Contains the relative information under the heading: 'Sprache-Epigraphik'; gives also information about history, culture and archaeology.

Neue Ephemeris für Semitische Epigraphik (NESE) by R. Degen, W. W. Müller, and W. Röllig (1, Wiesbaden, 1972) will include treatments of old and new Phoenician-Punic inscriptions.

Other current bibliographies contain important references, like the bibliography in the Archiv für Orientforschung and the Keilschrift-bibliographie in Orientalia, without however striving for completeness in this field.

2. History and Civilisation

Beside the material contained in some of the bibliographies mentioned *sub* 1, I refer to some bibliographies appended to articles in dictionaries and to books. Especially:

G. Contenau, La civilisation phénicienne, 1949, 296-310.

M. Dunand, article 'Phénicie', Dict. de la Bible, Suppl. VII, 1966, cols. 1142 ff.

O. Eissfeldt, article 'Phoiniker, Phoinikia', Pauly-Wissowa 20, 1941, cols. 350-380.

L. Hennequin, article 'Fouilles en Phénicie', Dict. de la Bible, Suppl. III, 1936, cols. 436 ff.

S. Moscati, The World of the Phoenicians, 1968, 264-271.

G. and C. Picard, Life and Death of Carthage, 1968, 347-352.

3. Journals

Publications of new texts and articles about all aspects of Phoenician and Punic history and civilisation may be found from time to time in all the leading orientalistic journals, and even in some journals in the field of Old Testament Studies (Biblica, Catholic Biblical Quarterly, Zeitschrift für die Alttestamentliche Wissenschaft, Vetus Testamentum). More often we meet them in the following periodicals (P in brackets means: primarily Punic studies): Africa (Tunis, 1, 1965 ff.; P); Annali dell'Istituto Universitario Orientale, Napoli (AIUON); Atti dell'Accademia Nazionale dei Lincei (Classe di Scienze morali, storiche e filologiche), Rendiconti/Memorie (ANL Rend./Mem.); Berytus (Copenhagen); Bulletin du Musée de Beyrouth (BMB); Cahiers de Byrsa (1, 1951 ff.; P); Comptes Rendus de la Académie des Inscriptions et Belles Lettres (CRAIBL); Journal of Near Eastern Studies (JNES); Journal of North-West Semitic Languages (JNSL; 1, Leiden, 1971 f); Karthago, Revue d'archéologie africaine (P); Libya Antiqua (1, 1964 ff.; P); Mélanges de l'Université Saint-Joseph, Beyrouth(MUSJ); Neue Ephemeris für Semitische Epigraphik (NESE; 1, Wiesbaden, 1972); Orientalia, Nova Series (OrNS); Oriens Antiquus (OA); Rivista degli Studi Orientali (RSO); Semitica; Studi Maghrebini (1, 1966 ff.; P); Syria; Ugarit-Forschungen (1, 1969 ff.; UF).

X. AMARNA-CANAANITE *

J. P. LETTINGA

Works about the El-Amarna Letters

1. TEXT EDITIONS

a. *Cuneiform Texts*

C. BEZOLD, E. A. W. BUDGE (eds.), The Tell el-Amarna Tablets in the British Museum, London, 1892. Reprint Framingham, Mass., [1962].

G. DOSSIN, Une nouvelle lettre d'El-Amarna, RA 31, 1934, 127 [**EA 369**].

C. H. GORDON, The New Amarna Tablets, Or 16, 1947, 15-21 [**EA 370-377**].

H. V. HILPRECHT, Old Babylonian Inscriptions chiefly from Nippur (BE 1), Part II, Philadelphia, 1896, Pl. LXIV, No. 147 [**EA 333**].

A. R. MILLARD, A Letter from the Ruler of Gezer, PEQ 97, 1965, Pl. XXV [**EA 378**].

A. H. SAYCE *apud* W. M. FLINDERS PETRIE, Tell el Amarna, London, 1894, Tab. XXXI-XXXIII.

V. SCHEIL, Tablettes d'El-Amarna de la collection Rostovicz, Mémoires publiés par les membres de la Mission archéologique française au Caire 6/II, Paris, 1892, 298-309.

——, Deux nouvelles lettres d'El Amarna, Bulletin de l'Institut français d'archéologie orientale du Caire 2, 1902, 113 sqq. [**EA 15, 153**].

O. SCHROEDER, Die Tontafeln von El-Amarna (VS XI-XII), Leipzig, 1914-1915. Reprint Framingham, Mass. [1962].

S. SMITH, C. J. GADD, A Cuneiform Vocabulary of Egyptian Words, JEA 11, 1925, 253 [**EA 368**].

F. THUREAU-DANGIN, Nouvelles lettres d'El-Amarna, RA 19, 1922, 101-108 [**EA 209, 362-367**].

H. WINCKLER, L. ABEL, Der Thontafelfund von El Amarna, I-III (Mittheilungen aus den orientalischen Sammlungen der königlichen Museen zu Berlin, 1-3), Berlin, 1889-1890.

b. *Transliterations and Translations*

J. A. KNUDTZON, Die El-Amarna Tafeln (VAB 2), Leipzig, 1915. Reprint Aalen 1964 [**EA 1-358**] (review article: A. UNGNAD, OLZ 19, 1916, 180-187).

S. A. B. MERCER, The Tell el-Amarna Tablets, 2 vols., Toronto, 1939 [**EA 1-358** +

---

* I.e. the language of the Canaanite glosses in the El-Amarna letters (14th cent. B.C.) which are written in an Akkadian showing many Canaanite peculiarities.

359-361; NB! MERCER 354a = **EA 379**] (review article: C. J. GADD, PEQ 72, 1940, 116-123).

A. F. RAINEY, El Amarna Tablets 359-379. Supplement to J. A. KNUDTZON, Die El-Amarna-Tafeln (AOAT 8), Kevelaer-Neukirchen, 1970 [**EA 359-379**].

c. *Translations*

W. F. ALBRIGHT, Akkadian Letters. The Amarna Letters, ANET[3], Princeton, 1969, 483-490 [EA 137, 147, 367, 234, 244, 245, 365, 250, 252, 254, 256, 270, 271, 36₆, 280, 366, 286, 287, 288, 289, 290, 292, 297, 298, 320, 333].

R. BORGER, in: K. GALLING, Textbuch zur Geschichte Israels[2], Tübingen, 1968, 24-28 [EA 369, 286, 366, 365].

C. J. MULLO WEIR, Letters from Tell El-Amarna, in: D. WINTON THOMAS (ed.), Documents from O. T. Times, London, 1958, 28-35 [EA 287, 288].

2. MONOGRAPHS AND IMPORTANT ARTICLES

W. F. ALBRIGHT, The Amarna Letters from Palestine (CAH II, Chapter XX), Cambridge, 1966 (with bibliography; I. The Tablets and their Chronology; II. Political Organization of Palestine in the Amarna Age; III. Palestine: Demography and Society).

P. ARTZI, 'Vox populi' in the Amarna Tablets, RA 58, 1964, 159-166.

——, The Exact Number of the Published Amarna Documents, Or 36, 1967, 432.

M. C. ASTOUR, The Partition of the Confederacy of Mukiš-Nuḫašše-Nii by Šuppiluliuma. A Study in Political Geography of the Amarna-Age, Or 38, 1969, 381-414.

R. BORGER, Handbuch der Keilschriftliteratur I, Berlin, 1967, 237-240 (especially the articles of W. F. ALBRIGHT and W. L. MORAN).

F. F. BRUCE, Tell el-Amarna, in: D. WINTON THOMAS (ed.), Archaeology and Old Testament Study, Oxford, 1967, 3-20.

J. BOTTÉRO, Le problème des Ḫabiru (Cahiers de la Société asiatique XII), Paris, 1954 (review article: R. DE VAUX, RB 63, 1956, 261-267).

E. F. CAMPBELL, The Chronology of the Amarna Letters, Baltimore, 1964.

P. DHORME, Amarna (Lettres d'el-Amarna), DBS, Paris, 1928, 207-222.

I. J. GELB, The Early History of the West Semitic Peoples, JCS 15, 1961, 27-47.

M. P. GRAY, The Ḫâbirū-Hebrew Problem in the Light of the Source Material Available at Present, HUCA 29, 1958, 135-202.

M. GREENBERG, The Ḫab/piru (AOS 39), New Haven, 1955.

K. A. KITCHEN, Suppiluliuma and the Amarna Pharaohs. A Study in Relative Chronology, Liverpool, 1962 (review article: Ph. H. J. HOUWINK TEN CATE, BiOr 20, 1963, 270-276).

H. KLENGEL, Geschichte Syriens im 2. Jahrtausend v.u. Z. I. Nordsyrien, Berlin, 1965; II. Mittel- und Südsyrien, Berlin, 1969; III, Historische Geographie und allgemeine Darstellung, Berlin, 1970.

J. DE KONING, Studiën over de El-Amarnabrieven en het O. T. inzonderheid uit historisch oogpunt (doctoral thesis, Free University, Amsterdam), Delft, 1940 (review articles: W. F. ALBRIGHT, JNES 6, 1947, 58-59; A. ALT, AfO 14, 1941-44, 349-352; M. NOTH, ZDPV 64, 1941, 115-117).

C. Kühne, Die Chronologie der internationalen Korrespondenz von El-Amarna (AOAT 17) (in the press).

M. Liverani, Contrasti e confluenze di concezioni politiche nell'età di El-Amarna, RA 61, 1967, 1-18.

——, Le lettere del Faraone a Rib-Adda, OA 10, 1971, 253-268.

R. de Vaux, Le Pays de Canaan, JAOS 88, 1968, 23-30.

——, Le problème des Ḫapiru après quinze années, JNES 27, 1968, 221-228.

A. LANGUAGE

1. Grammars

F. M. Th. Böhl, Die Sprache der Amarnabriefe mit besonderer Berücksichtigung der Kanaanismen (LSS V/2), Leipzig, 1909. Reprint Leipzig, 1968.

E. Dhorme, La langue de Canaan, RB 22, 1913, 369-393; 23, 1914, 37-59, 344-372. Reprinted in Recueil Édouard Dhorme, Paris, 1951, 405-487. See also E. Dhorme, Les nouvelles tablettes d'El-Amarna, RB 33, 1924, 5-32.

2. Lexicon

Ch. F. Jean, J. Hoftijzer, Dictionnaire des inscriptions sémitiques de l'Ouest, Leiden, 1965 („toutes les glosses cananéennes sont rassemblées sous le *siglum* Can[anéen] Anc[ien]").

3. Linguistic Monographs and Important Articles

P. Artzi, The 'Glosses' in the El-Amarna Tablets. A Contribution to the Study of Cultural and Writing Traditions among the Scribes of Canaan before the Israelite Conquest [Hebrew], Bar-'Îlan 1, 1963, 24-57; English Summary, XIV-XVII.

——, Evidence of Lexical Knowledge in the Amarna Documents, Bar-'Îlan 6, 1968, 105-108.

——, Some Unrecognized Syrian Amarna Letters (EA 260, 317, 318), JNES 27, 1968, 163-171.

M. Burchardt, Die altkanaanäischen Fremdworte und Eigennamen im Ägyptischen, Leipzig, 1909-1910.

E. Ebeling, Das Verbum der El-Amarna-Briefe, BA VIII/2, 1910, 39-79.

J. J. FINKELSTEIN, Three Amarna Notes, ErIs 9 [= W. F. Albright
    Volume], 1969, 14-19.
J. FRIEDRICH, Kanaanäisch und Westsemitisch, Scientia 84, 1949,
    220-223.
Z. S. HARRIS, Development of the Canaanite Dialects (AOS 16),
    New Haven, 1939.
M. HELD, Studies in Comparative Semitic Lexicography, Studies in
    Honor of Benno Landsberger (AS 16), Chicago, 1965, 395-406.
A. HERDNER, Une particularité grammaticale commune aux textes
    d'el-Amarna et de Ras-Shamra: t-préfixe pronominale de la
    troisième personne masculin pluriel, RÉS 3, 1938, 76-83.
Ch. KRAHMALKOV, Northwest Semitic Glosses in Amarna Letter
    no. 64: 22-23, JNES 30, 1971, 140-143.
W. L. MORAN, A Syntactical Study of the Dialect of Byblos as Re-
    flected in the Amarna Tablets (unpublished doctoral thesis,
    John Hopkins University), Baltimore, 1950.
——, The Use of the Canaanite Infinitive Absolute as a Finite Verb
    in the Amarna Letters from Byblos, JCS 4, 1950, 169-172 (see also
    JCS 5, 1951, 58-61 and 6, 1952, 76-80).
——, New Evidence on Canaanite taqtulū(na), JCS 5, 1951, 33-35.
——, Early Canaanite yaqtula, Or 29, 1960, 1-19.
——, The Hebrew Language in its Northwest Semitic Background,
    The Bible and the Ancient Near East (Essays in Honor of William
    Foxwell Albright), Garden City, 1961, 54-72.
R. F. YOUNGBLOOD, The Amarna Correspondence of Rib Haddi,
    Prince of Byblos (EA 68-98) (unpublished doctoral thesis, Dropsie
    College), Philadelphia, 1961.
——, Amorite Influence in a Canaanite Amarna Letter (EA 96),
    BASOR 168, 1962, 24-27.

B. PERIODICALS

BASOR; JCS; PJB; ZDPV.

XI. HEBREW

EDITED BY

J. H. HOSPERS AND C. H. J. DE GEUS

I. BIBLICAL AND EPIGRAPHICAL HEBREW

COMPILED BY

J. H. HOSPERS

General Works

A. BIBLIOGRAPHICAL MATERIAL

1. Publications with many Bibliographical References

P. R. Ackroyd (ed.), Booklist of the Society for Old Testament Study. An annual bibliographical aid (last number: Leeds, 1972).

G. W. Anderson, A Decade of Bible Bibliography (Reprint of the above named Booklists, 1957-1966), Oxford, 1967.

C. Brockelmann, Das Hebräische, B. Spuler, Handbuch der Orientalistik III, 1, Leiden, 1953, 59-69.

H. Cazelles, Hébreu, G. Levi della Vida, Linguistica Semitica: Presente e Futuro, Roma, 1961, 91-113.

F. M. Cross, D. N. Freedman, Early Hebrew Orthography. A Study of the epigraphic evidence, New Haven, 1952 (especially pp. 45-57 and 71-77).

M. Dahood, Ugaritic-Hebrew Philology, Roma, 1965.

Dictionary Catalogue of Cincinnati Library of the Hebrew Union College, Boston, 1963.

D. Diringer, Le iscrizioni antico-ebraiche palestinesi, Firenze, 1934.

H. Donner, W. Röllig, Kanaanäische und Aramäische Inschriften², 3 vols., Wiesbaden, 1966-1969.

H. Fleisch, Introduction à l'étude des langues sémitiques, Paris, 1947 (especially pp. 51-56).

G. Garbini, Il Semitico di nord-ovest, Napoli, 1960.

M. Haran, Biblical Research in Hebrew, Jerusalem, 1970.

Z. S. Harris, Development of the Canaanite Dialects. An investigation of linguistic history, New Haven, 1939. (Reprint: New York, 1967).

J. Hoftijzer, Kanttekeningen bij het onderzoek van de westsemitische epigrafie, JEOL 15, 1957-1958, 112-124.

Internationale Zeitschriftenschau für Bibelwissenschaft und Grenzgebiete, Vol. XIII, Düsseldorf, 1967.

Ch.-F. Jean, J. Hoftijzer, Dictionaire des inscriptions sémitiques de l'Ouest (DISO), Leiden, 1965.

Kirjath Sepher, Bibliographical quarterly of the Jewish National and University Library, Index to studies, notes and reviews, vol. 1-40 (Suppl. to Kirjath Sepher, vol. 41), Jerusalem, 1967.

J. H. Kramers, De Semietische Talen, Leiden, 1949.

B. Landsberger, Prinzipienfragen der semitischen speziell der hebräischen Grammatik, OLZ XXIX, 1926, cols. 967-979.

Linguistic Bibliography for the year ... published by the Permanent International Committee of Linguistics under the auspices of the International Council for Philosophy and Humanistic Studies with the financial assistance of UNESCO, Utrecht-Antwerpen, 1951-   (since the second world war 19 numbers).

A. Malamat, H. Reviv, A Bibliography of the Biblical Period. (With emphasis on publications in Modern Hebrew), Jerusalem, 1968.

H. Michaud, Sur la pierre et l'argile. Inscriptions hébraiques et Ancient Testament, Neuchâtel-Paris, 1958.

S. Moscati, L'epigrafia ebraica antica 1935-1950, Rome, 1951.

——, Lezioni di linguistica semitica, Roma, 1959, 169-172.

—— (ed.), An Introduction to the Comparative Grammar of the Semitic Languages, Wiesbaden, 1964 (especially pp. 172-174).

P. Nober, Elenchus Bibliographicus Biblicus, Vol. 51, Roma, 1970.

J. van der Ploeg, Vijf en twintig jaar Hebreeuwse Lexicographie, JEOL 9, 1944, 89-98.

Ch. Rabin, Hebrew, in: Th. A. Sebeok (ed.), Current Trends in

Linguistics, vol. 6, Linguistics in South West Asia and North Africa. The Hague-Paris, 1970, 304-346.

H. H. ROWLEY, Eleven years of Bible Bibliography, Indian Hills, 1957.

P. THOMSEN, Die Palästina-Literatur, Leipzig, 1953-1960; Band VII, 1940-1945, Lieferung IV (O. EISSFELDT and L. ROST ed.), Berlin, 1972.

K. R. VEENHOF, Nieuwe Palestijnse Inscripties, Phoenix XI, 1965, 243-260.

Th. C. VRIEZEN and J. H. HOSPERS, Palestine Inscriptions, Leiden, 1951.

2. PERIODICALS WITH MANY BIBLIOGRAPHICAL REFERENCES IMPORTANT FOR THE STUDY OF THE OLD-HEBREW

Bibliotheca Orientalis (BiOr), Leiden, 1944.
Orientalistische Literaturzeitung (OLZ), Berlin, 1898.
Vetus Testamentum (VT), Leiden, 1951.
Zeitschrift für die Alttestamentliche Wissenschaft (ZAW), Berlin, 1888.

3. WORKS ON THE HISTORY OF THE STUDY OF HEBREW

W. CHOMSKY, David Kimhi's grammar, New York, 1952.

L. KUKENHEIM, Contributions à l'histoire de la grammaire hébraïque à l'époque de la Renaissance, Leiden, 1951.

D. MIEROWSKY, Hebrew Grammar and Grammarians throughout the Ages, Johannesburg, 1955.

S. L. SKOSS, Saadia Gaon, the earliest Hebrew grammarian, Philadelphia, 1955.

S. STEIN, The Beginnings of Hebrew Studies at University College, London, 1952.

P. WECHTER, Ibn Barūn's Arabic Works on Hebrew Grammar and Lexicography, Philadelphia-London, 1964.

4. WORKS ON HEBREW PALAEOGRAPHY

C. BERNHEIMER, Paleografia ebraica, Firenze, 1924.

S. A. BIRNBAUM, The Hebrew Scripts. 2 parts. 1. Texts (1971) 2. Plates (1954-1957), Leiden, 1971.

B. PHILOLOGY

1. GRAMMARS

a. *"Normal" grammars*

A. BERTSCH, Kurzgefasste Hebräische Sprachlehre², Stuttgart, 1961.

. B. DAVIDSON, J. MAUCHLINE, An Introductory Hebrew Grammar²⁶, Edinburgh, 1966.

B. GEMSER, Hebreeuwse Spraakkuns. Vormleer, Sinsleer en Oefeninge, Pretoria, 1953.

M. GREENBERG, Introduction to Hebrew², Englewood Cliffs N.J., 1969.

O. GRETHER, Hebräische Grammatik für den akademischen Unterricht³, München, 1962.

R. K. HARRISON, Biblical Hebrew² (Teach Yourself Books), London, 1971.

B. S. J. ISSERLIN, A Hebrew Work-Book for Beginners, Leeds, 1971.

P. JOÜON, L. SEMKOWSKI, Grammaire de l'hébreu biblique. Deuxième éd. anastat. corrigée de la première éd. de Roma 1923, Roma, 1947 (Reprint: Roma, 1962).

M. LAMBERT, Traité de grammaire hebraïque. 3 vols., Paris, 1931-1938.

J. P. LETTINGA, Grammatica van het Bijbels Hebreeuws. 7de druk van NAT-KOOPMANS' Grammatica geheel opnieuw bewerkt, Leiden, 1972.

——, Hulpboek bij de grammatica van het Bijbels Hebreeuws. Oefeningen, Stukken uit het O.T. en Woordenlijsten, 5de druk van NAT-KOOPMANS' Oefeningen bij de Hebreeuwse Grammatica, Leiden, 1972.

——, Biblisch-Hebräische Grammatik. Auf der Grundlage von NAT-KOOPMANS' Hebreeuwse Grammatica mit Hilfsbuch zur biblisch-hebräischen Grammatik. Übungsstücke, Lesestücke aus dem A.T. und Vokabulare, Leiden, in prep.

J. MAUCHLINE, Key to the Exercises in the Late Professor A. B. DAVIDSON's Introductory Hebrew Grammar with Explanatory Notes³, Edinburgh, 1969.

R. MEYER, Hebräische Grammatik. 4 Bde. I: Einleitung, Schrift und Lautlehre³, Berlin, 1966; II: Formenlehre, Flexionstabellen³, Berlin, 1969; III: Satzlehre, Berlin, 1972; IV: Register, Berlin, 1972. (New ed. of G. BEER, R. Meyer's Hebräische Grammatik, Berlin, 1952-1955).

——, Hebräisches Textbuch zu G. Beer-R. Meyer, Hebräische Grammatik, Berlin, 1960.

A. MURTONEN, Concise Grammar for Biblical Hebrew, Melbourne, 1962.

A. SPERBER, Grammar of Masoretic Hebrew, Leiden, 1972.

C. STEUERNAGEL, Hebräische Grammatik[14], Leipzig, 1962.

H. L. STRACK, A. JEPSEN, Hebräische Grammatik mit Übungsbuch[15], München, 1952.

J. WEINGREEN, A Practical Grammar for Classical Hebrew[2], Oxford, 1959.

b. *Historical grammars of Biblical Hebrew*

H. BAUER, P. LEANDER, Historische Grammatik der hebräischen Sprache des A.T., Halle, 1922 (Reprint: Hildesheim, 1965).

G. BERGSTRÄSSER, Hebräische Grammatik: W. Gesenius-Kautzsch' Hebräische Grammatik 29. Auflage. 2 vols., Leipzig, 1918-1929 (Reprint: Hildesheim, 1962).

K. BEYER, Althebräische Grammatik, Göttingen, 1969.

A. E. COWLEY, Gesenius's Hebrew Grammar. As edited and enlarged by the late E. KAUTZSCH and revised by A. E. COWLEY[2], Oxford, 1910 (Reprint: London, 1966).

F. E. KÖNIG, Historisch-Kritisches Lehrgebäude der hebräischen Sprache. 2 vols., Leipzig, 1881-1897.

J. MALFROY, Index Volume to Alexander Sperber's Historical Grammar of Biblical Hebrew and his Grammar of Masoretic Hebrew, Leiden, 1972.

A. MURTONEN, Materials for a Non-Masoretic Hebrew Grammar, I, II and III, Helsinki, 1958-1960-1964.

A. SPERBER, A Historical Grammar of Biblical Hebrew. A presentation of problems with suggestions to their solution, Leiden, 1966.

c. *Syntaxes with regard to the Hebrew of the whole Old Testament*

C. BROCKELMANN, Hebräische Syntax, Neukirchen, 1956.

A. B. DAVIDSON, Hebrew Syntax[3], Edinburgh, 1901 (Reprint: Edinburgh, 1924).

P. JOÜON, L. SEMKOWSKI, Grammaire de l'hébreu biblique[2], Roma, 1947 (Reprint: 1962) (especially pp. 289-536).

E. KÖNIG, Syntax der hebräischen Sprache, Leipzig, 1897.

R. MEYER, Hebräische Grammatik, III: Satzlehre, Berlin, 1972.

C. Rabin, Taḥbor lešon hammiqrā, Jerusalem, 1967.
J. W. Watts, A Survey of Syntax in the Hebrew Old Testament, Nashville Tennessee, 1951 (Reprint: Grand Rapids, 1964).
R. J. Williams, Hebrew Syntax. An outline, Toronto, 1967.

d. *Syntaxes of parts of the Old Testament and of separate inscriptions*

F. I. Andersen, Moabitic Syntax, Or 35, 1966, 81-119.
——, The Hebrew Verbless Clause in the Pentateuch, Nashville-New York, 1970.
K. Beyer, Althebräische Syntax in Prosa und Poesie, Festgabe für K. G. Kuhn, Göttingen, 1972, 76-96.
A. M. Honeyman, The Syntax of the Gezer Calendar, JRAS, 1953, 53-58.
A. Kropat, Syntax des Autors der Chronik, Giessen, 1909.
E. Kuhr, Die Ausdrucksmittel der Konjunktionslosen Hypotaxe in der ältesten hebräischen Prosa, Leipzig, 1929 (Reprint: Hildesheim, 1968).
Th. F. McDaniel, Philological Studies in Lamentations, Bibl 49, 1968, I, 27-53; II, 199-220 (in II Syntactical Elements).
H. Striedl, Untersuchungen zur Syntax und Stilistik des hebräischen Buches Esther, ZAW 1937, 73-107.

2. Lexica

F. Brown, S. R. Driver, C. A. Briggs, A Hebrew and English Lexicon of the Old Testament based on the Thesaurus of Gesenius as translated by E. Robinson², Oxford, 1929 (Reprint: Oxford, 1968).
F. Buhl, Wilhelm Gesenius' Handwörterbuch über das Alte Testament. Unveränderter Neudruck der 1915 erschienenen 17. Auflage, Berlin, 1962.
B. Davidson, The Analytical Hebrew and Chaldee Lexicon. (Reprint: London, 1963).
G. Fohrer, Hebräisches und Aramäisches Wörterbuch zum Alten Testament, Berlin, 1970.
J. Fürst, Hebräisches Wörterbuch über das Alte Testament, Berlin, 1920 (Reprint: Berlin, 1960).
R. A. Grossmann, Compendious Hebrew-English Dictionary comprising a complete vocabulary of biblical, mishnaic, medieval and

modern Hebrew. Compiled in collaboration with H. Sachs. Revised and edited by M. H. Segal, Tel-Aviv, 1968.

W. L. Holladay, A concise Hebrew and Aramaic Lexicon of the O.T., Leiden, 1971.

Ch.-F. Jean, J. Hoftijzer, Dictionnaire des Inscriptions sémitiques de l'ouest (DISO), Leiden, 1965.

E. ben Jehuda, Thesaurus totius Hebraitatis et veteris et recentioris, VIII vols., New York-London, 1960.

L. Koehler, W. Baumgartner, Lexicon in Veteris Testamenti Libros. Editio photomechanica iterata, Leiden, 1958.

——, Supplementum ad Lexicon in Veteris Testamenti Libros, Leiden, 1958.

——, Hebräisches und Aramäisches Lexikon zum Alten Testament. Dritte Auflage neubearbeitet von W. Baumgartner unter Mitarbeit von B. Hartmann und E. Y. Kutscher, Leiden, 1967-   .

E. König, Hebräisches und Aramäisches Wörterbuch zum Alten Testament. Neudruck der 6.-7. Ausgabe, Leipzig, 1936. (Reprint: Wiesbaden, 1968).

S. E. Loewenstamm, J. Blau, Thesaurus of the Language of the Bible. 2 vols., Jerusalem, 1957-1959.

F. Zorell, L. Semkowski, Lexicon Hebraicum et Aramaicum Veteris Testamenti, Roma, 1940-1954 (Reprint: Roma, 1968).

Wordlists

F. Baumgärtel, Hebräisches Wörterbuch zur Genesis. Einzelwörterbücher zum Alten Testament I, Berlin, 1961.

J. Barton Payne, Hebrew Vocabularies, Michigan, 1956.

J. Hempel, Hebräisches Wörterbuch zu Jesaja. Einzelwörterbücher zum A.T. II, Giessen, 1924.

J. Herrmann, Hebräisches Wörterbuch zu den Psalmen. Einzelwörterbücher zum A.T. IV, Giessen, 1924.

C. H. Peisker, Hebräische Wortkunde. Ein didaktisch durchdachtes Lerh- und Wiederholungsbuch², Göttingen, 1967.

J. D. W. Watts, List of Words Occurring frequently in the Hebrew Bible, Hebrew-English Edition², Leiden, 1967.

Old Testament Concordances

J. Comay, Who's who in the Old Testament together with the Apocrypha, London, 1971.

E. JENNI, C. WESTERMANN (eds), Theologisches Handwörterbuch zum Alten Testament (THAT). Zwei Bände, München, 1971.

G. LISOWSKY, Konkordanz zum hebräischen Alten Testament. Unter verantwortlicher Mitwirkung von L. ROST, Stuttgart, 1958.

S. MANDELKERN, Veteris Testamenti Concordantiae Hebraicae atque Chaldaicae, Leipzig, 1937 (Reprint: Graz, 1967).

H. H. ROWLEY, Dictionary of Bible Personal Names, London, 1968.

3. IMPORTANT LINGUISTIC MONOGRAPHS AND ARTICLES

K. AARTUN, Althebräische Nomina mit konserviertem kurzem Vokal in der Hauptdrucksilbe, ZDMG 117, 1967, 247-265.

——, Moabitisch 'l, BiOr XXVIII, 1971, 125.

——, Hebräisch 'āni und ᵒānāw, BiOr XXVIII, 1971, 125-126.

P. R. ACKROYD, The Meaning of Hebrew דּוֹד considered, JSS 13, 1968, 3-10.

——, B. LINDARS (eds.), Words and Meanings. Essays presented to David WINTON THOMAS, Cambridge, 1968.

Y. AHARONI, The Samaria Ostraca, an additional note, IEJ XII, 1962, 67-69.

——, The Use of Hieratic Numerals in Hebrew Ostraca and the Shekel Weights, BASOR 184, 1966, 13-19.

——, Three Hebrew Ostraca from Arad, BASOR 197, 1970, 16-42.

——, The Incense Altar of Lakiš, Lešonénu XXXV, 1970, 3-6.

——, Khirbet Raddana and its Inscription IEJ XXI, 1971, 130-135.

B. ALFRINK, La prononciation "Jehova" du Tétragramme, OTS V, 1948, 43-62.

J. M. ALLEGRO, Uses of the Semitic Demonstrative Element z in Hebrew, VT V, 1955, 309-312.

J. D. AMUSIN, M. L. HELTZER, The Inscription from Meṣad Ḥashavyahu. Complaint of a Reaper of the seventh century B.C., IEJ, XIV, 1964, 148-160.

F. I. ANDERSEN, A Short Note on Construct K in Hebrew, Bibl 50, 1969, 68-69.

J. ARO, Parallels to the Akkadian Stative in the West Semitic Language; H. G. GÜTERBOCK, Th. JACOBSEN, Studies in honor of Benno Landsberger on his 75th birthday, Chicago, Illin., 1965, 407-411.

N. AVIGAD, The Seal of Abigad, IEJ XVIII, 1968, 52-53.

——, A Sculptured Hebrew Stone Weight, IEJ XVIII, 1968, 181-187.

——, Ammonite and Moabite Seals, J. A. SANDERS, Essays in horon of Nelson Glueck, Garden City, New York, 1970, 284-298.

M. AZAR, Analyse morphologique du texte hébreu de la Bible. 2 vol., Nancy, 1970.

O. L. BARNES, A New Approach to the Problem of the Hebrew Tenses and its Solution without Recourse to the waw-Consecutive, Oxford, 1965.

J. BARR, The Semantics of Biblical Language[3], London, 1962.

——, Hypostatization of Linguistic Phenomena in modern Theological Interpretation, JSS 7, 1962, 85-94.

——, Old and New in Interpretation. A Study of the Two Testaments, London, 1966.

——, St. Jerome and the Sounds of Hebrews, JSS 12, 1967, 1-36.

——, Vocalization and the Analysis of Hebrew among the Ancient Translators, Hebräische Wortforschung, Festschrift W. Baumgartner, VTS XVI, Leiden, 1967, 1-11.

——, Comparative Philology and the Text of the Old Testament, Oxford, 1968.

——, Biblical Words for Time, Revised Edition, London, 1969.

——, The Symbolism of Names in the Old Testament, BJRL LII, 1970, 11-29.

J. R. BARLETT, The Use of the Word ראש as a Title in the Old Testament, VT XIX, 1969, 1-10.

W. BAUMGARTNER, Das hebräische Nominalpräfix mi-, ThZ 9, 1953, 154-157.

——, Was wir heute von der hebräischen Sprache und ihrer Geschichte wissen, zum A.T. und seiner Umwelt. Ausgewählte Aufsätze von W. BAUMGARTNER, 208-239, Leiden, 1959.

Z. BEN HAYYIM, Studies in the traditions of the Hebrew Language, Madrid-Barcelona, 1954.

——, Observations on the Hebrew and Aramaic Lexicon from the Samaritan Tradition, Hebräische Wortforschung, Festschrift W. Baumgartner, VTS XVI, Leiden, 1967, 12-24.

H. BIRKELAND, Akzent und Vokalismus im Althebräischen, Oslo, 1940.

F. R. BLAKE, The Apparent Interchange between a and i in Hebrew, JNES 9, 1950, 76-83.

——, Pretonic Vowels in Hebrew, JNES 10, 1951, 243-255.

——, A Resurvey of Hebrew Tenses. With an appendix: Hebrew Influence on Biblical Aramaic, Roma, 1951 (Reprint: Roma, 1968).

J. Blau, Zum angeblichen Gebrauch von 't vor dem Nominativ, VT IV, 1954, 7-19.

——, Gibt es ein emphatisches 't in Bibel-Hebräisch?, VT VI, 1956, 211-212.

——, Adverbia als psychologische und grammatische Subjecte/ Praedikate im Bibelhebraeisch, VT IX, 1959, 130-138.

——, Reste des i-Imperfekts von zkr qal, VT XI, 1961, 81-86.

——, Bibelhebräische Nomina die auf pataḥ-ʿayin enden, ZDMG 118, 1968, 257-258.

——, Some Difficulties in the Reconstruction of "Proto-Hebrew" and "Proto-Canaanite", M. Black, G. Fohrer, In Memoriam Paul Kahle, BZAW 103, 29-43, Berlin, 1968.

P. A. H. de Boer, An Inquiry into the Meaning of the Term משא, OTS V, 1948, 197-214.

——, Étude sur le sens de la racine QWH, OTS X, 1954, 225-246.

——, Gedenken und Gedächtnis in der Welt des Alten Testaments. Vorlesungen zur Bedeutung der Wurzel zkr, Leiden, 1962.

M. Bogaert, Les suffixes verbaux non accusativs dans le sémantique nord-occidental et particulièrement en hébreu, Bibl 45, 1964, 220-247.

B. Bonder, Mesha's Rebellion against Israel, JANES III, 1970-1971, 83-88.

W. Borée, Die alten ortsnamen Palästinas² Hildesheim 1968.

M. M. Bravmann, Notes on the Forms of the Imperative in Hebrew and Arabic, JQR 42, 1961, 51-56.

——, The West-Semitic Conditional Conjunction 'im, 'in and some Related Particles of Arabic and Akkadian, Mus 84, 1970, 241-248.

—, The Hebrew Perfect Forms: qatᵉlā, qatᵉlū, JAOS 91, 1971, 429-430.

Ch. Brekelmans, Pronominal Suffixes in the Hebrew Book of Psalms, JEOL 17, 1963, 202-206.

——, Some Translation Problems. Judges V 29, Psalm CXX 7, Jona IV 9, OTS XV, 1969, 170-176.

C. Brockelmann, Neuere Theorien zur Geschichte des Akzents und des Vokalismus im Hebräischen und Aramäischen, ZDMG 94, 1940, 332-371.

H. A. Brongers, Bemerkungen zum Gebrauch des adverbialen Weʿattāh im Alten Testament (ein lexikologischer Beitrag), VT XV, 1965, 289-299.

——, Merismus, Synekdoche und Hendiadys in der Bibel-Hebräischen Sprache, OTS XIV, 1965, 100-114.

——, Die Wendung bešēm jhwh im Alten Testament, ZAW 77, 1965, 1-20.

E. BRØNNO, Studien über hebräische Morphologie und Vokalismus auf Grundlage der mercatischen Fragmente der 2. Kolumne der Hexapla des Origenes, Leipzig, 1943 (Reprint: Nendeln, 1966).

——, Die Aussprache der hebräischen Laryngale nach Zeugnissen des Hieronymus, Aarhus, 1970.

J. CANTINEAU, De la place de l'accent de mot en hébreu et en araméen biblique, BÉO I, 1931, 81-98.

——, Élimination des syllabes brèves en hébreu et en araméen biblique, BÉO II, 1932, 125-144.

——, Essai de phonologie de l'hébreu biblique, BSLP 46, 1950, 82-122.

A. CAQUOT, Hébreu siyyîm, Grec Aithiopes, D. COHEN, Mélanges M. Cohen, Den Haag, 1970, 219-223.

H. CAZELLES, Note sur l'origine des temps convertis hébreux d'après quelques textes ugaritiques, RB LIV, 1947, 388-393.

——, La mimation nominale en ouest-sémitique, GLECS 5, 1951, 79-81.

——, 'al tḫws 'yn 'l, GLECS 13, 1968-1969, 132-134.

W. CHOMSKY, The Ambiguity of the Prefixed Prepositions ב״למ in the Bible, JQR LXI, 1970, 87-89.

——, The Pronunciation of the Shewa, JQR LXII, 1971, 88-94.

V. CHRISTIAN, Untersuchungen zur Laut- und Formenlehre des Hebräischen, Wien, 1953.

W. T. CLAASSEN, The Role of /ṣ/ in the North-West Semitic Languages, AION 31, 1971, 285-302.

——, On a recent proposal as to a distinction between Piʻel and Hiphʻil JNSL I, 1971, 3-10.

——, The declarative-estimative Hiphʻil, JNSL II, 1972, 5-16.

G. W. COATS, Self-abasement and Insult Formulas, JBL 89, 1970, 14-26.

A. CODY, A New Inscription from Tell-al Rimāh and King Jehoash of Israel, CBQ XXXII, 1970, 325-340.

Ch. COHEN, Hebrew tbh: proposed etymologies, JANES IV, 1972, 36-51.

M. B. COHEN, The Masoretic accents as a Biblical Commentary, JANES IV, 1972, 2-11.

J. S. CROATTO, 'Abrek "Intendant" dans Gén XLI, 41, 43, VT XVI, 1966, 113-115.

F. M. CROSS, The Discovery of the Samaria Papyri, BiAr XXVI, 1963, 110-121.

——, Epigraphic Notes on the Ammān Citadel Inscription, BASOR 193, 1969, 13-19.

——, D. N. Freedman, Early Hebrew Orthography. A study of the epigraphic evidence, New Haven, Conn., 1952.

——, ——, An Inscribed Jar Handle from Raddana, BASOR 201, 1971, 19-22.

——, The Name of Ashdod, BASOR 175, 1964, 48-50.

——, The Cave Inscriptions from Khirbet Beit Lei, J. A. Sanders, Essays in honor of Nelson Glueck, Garden City, New York, 1970, 299-306.

M. Dahood, Ugaritic-Hebrew Philology, Roma, 1965.

——, Vocative Lamedh in the Psalter, VT XVI, 1966, 299-311.

——, Ugaritic-Hebrew Syntax and Style, UF I, 1969, 15-36.

——, The Independent Personal Pronoun in the Oblique Case in Hebrew, CBQ XXXII, 1970, 86-160.

R. Degen, Zur neueren hebraistischen Forschung, WO VI, 1971, 47-79.

M. Delcor, Two Special Meanings of the Word יד in Biblical Hebrew, JSS XII, 1967, 230-240.

L. Delekat, Zum hebräischen Wörterbuch, VT XIV, 1964, 7-67.

——, Yáhō-Yahwáe und die allttestamentlichen Gottesnamenkorrekturen, G. Jeremias, H.-W. Kuhn, H. Stegemann, Tradition und Glaube, Göttingen, 1972, 23-75.

A. Demsky, The Genealogy of Gibeon (I Chronicles 9:35-44): Biblical and Epigraphic Considerations, BASOR 202, 1971, 16-23.

W. G. Dever, Iron Age Epigraphic Material from the Area of Khirbet El-Kôm, HUCA XL-XLI, 1969-1970, 139-204.

B. W. W. Dombrowski, Some Remarks on the Hebrew Hitpaʾel and Inversative -t- in the Semitic Languages, JNES 21, 1962, 220-223.

J. C. C. van Dorssen, De derivata van de stam ʾmn in het Hebreeuws van het O.T., Amsterdam, 1951.

G. R. Driver, Problems of the Hebrew Verbal System, Edinburgh, 1936.

——, Supposed Arabisms in the Old Testament, JBL LV, 1936, 101-120.

——, Gender in Hebrew Numerals, JSS I, 1948, 90-104.

——, Hebrew Homonyms, Hebräische Wortforschung, Festschrift W. Baumgartner, VTS XVI, Leiden, 1967, 50-64.

——, Colloquialisms in the Old Testament, D. Cohen, Mélanges M. Cohen, Den Haag 1970, 232-239.

S. R. DRIVER, A Treatise on the Use of the Tenses in Hebrew, London, 1892 (Reprint: 1970).

H. J. VAN DIJK, A Neglected Connotation of Three Hebrew Verbs (nātan, šîm, šît), VT XVIII, 1968, 16-30.

——, Does Third Masculine Singular *TAQTUL Exist in Hebrew?, VT XIX, 1969, 440-447.

W. EISENBEIS, Die Wurzel שלם im Alten Testament, BZAW 113, Berlin, 1969.

O. EISSFELDT, Etymologische und archäologische Erklärung alt-testamentlicher Worte, OA V, 1966, 165-176.

M. ELLENBOGEN, Foreign Words in the Old Testament: Their origin and etymology, London, 1962.

K. ELLIGER, Der Sinn des hebräischen wortes šᵉfî, ZAW 83, 1971, 317-329.

J. A. EMERTON, Were Greek transliterations of the Hebrew Old Testament Used by Jews before the Time of Origin?, JTS XXI, 1970, 17-31.

J. H. EYBERS, The Root Ṣ-L in Hebrew words, JNSL II, 1972, 23-36.

Z. W. FALK, Hebrew Legal Terms, I, JSS V, 1960, 350-354; II, JSS XII, 1967, 241-244; III, JSS XIV, 1969, 39-44.

T. L. FENTON, The Absence of a Verbal Formation *yaqattal from Ugaritic and North-West Semitic, JSS XV, 1970, 31-41.

A. FITZGERALD, A Note on G-Stem ynṣr forms in the Old Testament, ZAW 84, 1972, 90-92.

Ch. FONTINOY, Les noms de lieux en — ayim dans la Bible, UF 3, 1971, 33-40.

R. FRANKENA, Einige Bemerkungen zum Gebrauch des Adverbs 'al ken im Hebräischen, Studia Biblica et Semitica Th. C. Vriezen dedicata, Wageningen, 1966, 94-99.

D. N. FREEDMAN, The Orthography of the Arad Ostraca, IEJ XIX, 1969, 52-56.

J. FRIEDRICH, Kanaanäisch und Westsemitisch, Scientia 84, 1949, 220-223.

J. FÜCK, Gedanken zur Methodik des hebräischen Unterrichts, J. FÜCK, Festschrift O. Eissfeldt, Halle/S, 1947, 125-140.

G. GARBINI, Il semitico di nord-ovest, Napoli, 1960.

——, La lingua degli Ammoniti, AION XX, 1970, 249-258.

——, The Phonetic Shift of Sibilants in North-Western Semitic in the First Millennium B.C., JNSL I, 1971, 32-38.

——, Note Epigrafiche, AION XXII, 1972, 95-102.

I. J. GELB, La lingua degli Amoriti, ANLA VIII, 13, 1958, 143-164.

B. GEMSER, Die merkwaardigste verskijnsel in die Hebreeuwse taal en sy verklaring, Tijdskrif vir Wetenskap en Kuns, Bd. 2, 2de afl., Pretoria, 1941.

G. GERLEMAN, Bemerkungen zum alttestamentlichen Sprachstil, Studia Biblica et Semitica Th. C. Vriezen dedicata, Wageningen, 1966, 108-114.

M. GERTNER, Terms of Scriptural Interpretation: a Study in Hebrew Semantics, BSOAS XXV, 1962, 1-27.

J. C. L. GIBSON, Hebrew Writing as a Subject of Linguistic Investigation, GlasgOrTrans XX, 1963-1964, Leiden, 1965, 49-62.

——, On the Linguistic Analysis of Hebrew Writing, ArchLing 17, 1969, 131-160.

H. L. GINSBERG, Lexicographical Notes, Hebräische Wortforschung, Festschrift W. Baumgartner, VTS XVI, Leiden, 1967, 71-82.

J. GLÜCK, 'ªri and lavî' (labî')- an Etymological Study, ZAW 81, 1969, 232-235.

——, Paronomasia in Biblical Literature, Semitics I, 1970, 50-78.

A. GOETZE, Accent and Vokalism in Hebrew, JAOS 59, 1939, 431-459.

R. GORDIS, Studies in Hebrew Roots of Contrasted Meanings, JQR XXVII, 1936/1937, 33-58.

M. H. GOSHEN-GOTTSTEIN, Der Qumrân-Typus yᵉqotlehu und das hebräische Verbalsystem, RQum II, 1959-1960, 43-46.

——, Afterthought and the Syntax of Relative Clauses in Biblical Hebrew, Text and language in Bible and Qumran, Jerusalem-Tel Aviv, 1960, 143-155.

——, Semitic Morphological Structures. The basic morphological structure of Biblical Hebrew, Studies in Egyptology and Linguistics in honour of H. J. Polotsky, Jerusalem, 1964, 104-116.

D. E. GOWAN, The use of ya'an in Biblical Hebrew, VT XXI, 1971, 168-185.

J. C. GREENFIELD, The "Periphrastic Imperative" in Aramaic and Hebrew, IEJ 19, 1969, 199-210.

A. GUILLAUME, Hebrew and Arabic Lexicography: a comparative study, Leiden, 1965.

E. HAMMERSHAIMB, On the so-Called Infinitivus Absolutus in Hebrew, Hebrew and Semitic Studies presented to G. R. Driver, Oxford, 1963, 85-94.

Z. S. HARRIS, The Linguistic Structure of Hebrew, JAOS 61, 1941, 143-167.

——, Componential Analysis of a Hebrew Paradigm, Language XXIV, 1948, 87-91.

——, Development of the Canaanite Dialects, New Haven, 1939 (Reprint: New York, 1967).

M. HELD, The YQTL-QTL (QTL-YQTL) Sequence of Identical Verbs in Biblical Hebrew and Ugaritic, A. A. Neuman Festschrift, Leiden, 1962, 281-290.

——, The Action-Result (Factitive Passive) Sequence of Identical Verbs in Biblical Hebrew and Ugaritic, JBL 84, 1965, 272-282.

——, Studies in Biblical Homonyms in the Light of Akkadian, JANES III, 1970-1971, 47-55.

M. HELTZER, Some North-West Semitic Epigraphic Gleanings from the XI-VI Centuries B.C., AION XXI, 1971, 183-198.

D. R. HILLERS, Delocutive Verbs in Biblical Hebrew, JBL 86, 1967, 320-324.

J. HOFTIJZER, Remarks Concerning the Use of the Particle 't in Classical Hebrew, OTS XIV, 1965, 1-99.

W. L. HOLLADAY, The Root sûbh in the Old Testament, with particular reference to its usages in covenantal texts, Leiden, 1958.

S. H. HORN, The Amman Citadel Inscription, BASOR 193, 1969, 2-13.

J. H. HOSPERS, De Hebreeuwse taalwetenschap in de laatste dertig jaar, JEOL 14, 1955-1956, 42-44.

——, Some Observations about the Teaching of Old Testament Hebrew, M. A. BEEK, A. A. KAMPMAN, C. NIJLAND, J. RIJCKMANS, Symbolae Biblicae et Mesopotamicae F. M. Th. de Liagre Böhl Dedicatae, Leiden, 1972, 188-198.

J. HUESMAN, Finite Uses of the Infinitive Absolute, Bibl 37, 1956, 271-295.

——, The Infinitive Absolute and the Weak waw Perfect, Bibl 37, 1956, 410-434.

H. B. HUFFMON, Amorite Personal Names in the Mari Texts. A structural and lexical study, Baltimore, 1965.

J. A. HUGHES, Another Look at the Hebrew Tenses, JNES 29, 1970, 12-24.

A. R. HULST, Old Testament Translation Problems. In co-operation with other scholars, Leiden, 1960.

——, Is het Oude Testament vertaalbaar?, NedTT XVIII, 1963, 81-93.

——, De betekenis van het woord menūḫā, Schrift en Uitleg aangeboden aan W. H. Gispen, Kampen, 1970, 62-78.

H. D. Hummel, Enclitic mem in Early North-west Semitic, especially
Hebrew, JBL LXXVI, 1957, 85-108.

A. Hurvitz, The Chronological Significance of the „Aramaisms" in
Biblical Hebrew, IEJ 18, 1968, 234-241.

T. Jansma, Vijf teksten in de tora met een dubieuze constructie,
NedTT XII, 1958-1959, 161-179.

G. Janssens, De werkwoordelijke tijden in het Semietisch en in het
bijzonder in het Hebreeuws, JEOL 15, 1957-1958, 97-103.

——, Het Hebreeuws van de tweede Kolom van Origenes' Hexapla,
JEOL 15, 1957-1958, 103-112.

——, Bijdrage tot de geschiedenis der werkwoorden ע"ע in het
Hebreeuws, OrGand I, 1964, 131-156.

E. Jenni, Faktitiv und Kausativ von אבד "zugrunde gehen",
Hebräische Wortforschung, Festschrift W. Baumgartner, VTS
XVI, Leiden, 1967, 143-157.

——, Das Hebräische Pi'el. Syntaktisch semasiologische Untersuchung
einer Verbalform im Alten Testament, Zürich, 1968.

——, „Wollen" und „Nicht Wollen" im Hebräischen, Hommages à
Dupont-Sommer, Paris, 1971, 202-207.

——, Zur Verwendung von 'attā „jetzt" im Alten Testament, ThZ 28,
1972, 5-12.

A. Jepsen, Kanaanäisch und Hebräisch, Akten des Moskauer Orientalistenkongresses 1960, Moskau, 1962, 316-321.

——, Warum? Eine lexikalische und theologische Studie, F. Maasz,
Festschrift L. Rost, Berlin, 1967, 106-113.

——, Kleine Bemerkungen zu drei Westsemitischen Inschriften, MIO
XV, 1969, 1-5.

B. Jongeling, Jeux de mots en Sophonie III 1 et 3?, VT XXI, 1971,
541-547.

P. Kahle, Pre-Masoretic Hebrew, Textus II, 1962, 1-7.

D. J. Kamhi, The Term to'ar in Hebrew and its Status as a Grammatical Category, BSOAS XXXIV, 1971, 256-272.

——, The Gentilicial Adjective in Hebrew, JRAS, 1971, 2-8.

P. Katz, Hebräische Grundkenntnisse für jeden Theologen — warum,
wozu und wie?, ZAW 84, 1972, 220-242.

C.-A. Keller, Probleme des hebräischen Sprachunterrichts, VT XX,
1970, 278-286.

M. A. Klopfenstein, Scham und Schande nach dem Alten Testament.

Eine begriffsgeschichtliche Untersuchung zu den hebräischen wurzeln bôs, klm und ḫpr, Zürich, 1972.

L. KÖHLER, Syntactica, VT III, 1953, 84-87 and 299-305.

L. KOPF, Arabische Etymologien und Parallelen zum Bibelwörterbuch, VT IX, 1959, 247-288.

J. KÖRNER, Die Bedeutung der Wurzel bārā im Alten Testament, OLZ LXIV, 1969, 533-540.

K. KOSKINEN, Kompatibilität in den dreikonsonantigen hebräischen Wurzeln, ZDMG 114, 1964, 16-58.

H. KOSMALA, The Term geber in the Old Testament and in the Scrolls, Congress Volume Roma 1968, VTS XVII, Leiden, 1969, 159-169.

E. Y. KUTSCHER, Contemporary Studies in North-Western Semitics, JSS X, 1965, 21-51.

——, Yeminite Hebrew and Ancient Promunication, JSS XI, 1966, 217-266.

——, Isaiah of the Dead Sea Scrolls (Its language and linguistic background). Transl. from the first (1959) one vol. ed. in Hebrew, 2 vols., vol. I, Leiden, 1970.

C. J. LABUSCHAGNE, Teraphim, A new proposal for its etymology, VT XVI, 1966, 115-117.

——, The Emphasizing Particle gam and its Connotations, Studia Biblica et Semitica Th. C. Vriezen dedicata, Wageningen, 1966, 193-203.

——, Original Shaphʻel-forms in Biblical Hebrew, Old Testament Studies, Pretoria, 1971, 51-64.

I. LANDE, Formelhafte Wendungen der Umgangssprache im Alten Testament, Leiden, 1949.

B. LANDSBERGER, Akkadisch-Hebräische Wortgleichungen, Hebräische Wortforschung, Festschrift W. Baumgartner, VTS XVI, Leiden, 1967, 176-204.

A. LEMAIRE, L'ostracon de Meṣad Ḥashavyahu (Yavneh-Yam) re-placé dans son contexte, Semitica XXI, 1971, 57-79.

W. LESLAU, Ethiopic and South Arabic Contributions to the Hebrew Lexicon, Berkeley-Los Angeles, 1958.

J. P. LETTINGA, De „Tale Kanaäns". Enkele beschouwingen over het Bijbels Hebreeuws, Groningen, 1971.

G. LEVI DELLA VIDA, The Shiloaḥ Inscription Reconsidered, M. BLACK, G. FOHRER, In Memoriam P. Kahle, Berlin, 1968, 162-166.

K. LEVY, Zur masoretischen Grammatik. Texte und Untersuchungen, Stuttgart, 1936.

F. M. Th. DE LIAGRE BÖHL, Wortspiele im Alten Testament, Opera Minora, Groningen, 1953, 11-25.

E. LIPIŃSKI, באחרית הימים dans les textes préexiliques, VT XX, 1970, 445-450.

——, Psalm 68:7 and the Role of the Košarot, AION XXI, 1971, 532-537.

——, Etymological and Exegetical Notes on the Meša' Inscription, Or 40, 1971, 325-340.

O. LORETZ, Die hebräische Nominalform qattāl, Bibl 41, 1960, 411-416.

J. MACDONALD, The Particle 't in Classical Hebrew, VT XIV, 1964, 264-275.

J. L. MALONE, Wave Theory, Rule Ordering, and Hebrew-Aramaic Segolation, JAOS 91, 1971, 44-66.

D. MARCUS, The Stative and the *waw* Consecutive, JANES II, 1969, 37-40.

T. J. MEEK, The co-Ordinate Adverbial Clause in Hebrew, AJSL 47, 1930-1931, 51-52.

——, The Hebrew Accusative of Time and Place, JAOS 60, 1940, 224-233.

——, Again the Accusative of Time in Amos 1: 1, JAOS 61, 1941, 190-191.

——, The Syntax of the Sentence in Hebrew, JBL LXIV, 1945, 1-13.

——, Archaeology and a Point in Hebrew Syntax, BASOR 122, 1951, 31-34.

——, Result and Purpose Clauses in Hebrew, JQR XLVI, 1955-1956, 40-43.

T. N. D. MESSINGER, The Nominal Pattern „qᵉtulla" in Biblical Hebrew, JSS XVI, 1971, 2-14.

R. MEYER, Probleme der hebräischen Grammatik, ZAW 63, 1951, 221-235.

——, Zur Geschichte des hebräischen Verbums, VT III, 1953, 225-235.

——, Das hebräische Verbalsystem im Lichte der gegenwärtigen Forschung, Congress Volume Oxford 1959, VTS VII, Leiden, 1960, 309-317.

——, Spuren eines westsemitischen Präsens-Futur in den Texten von Chirbet Qumran, J. HEMPEL, L. ROST, Von Ugarit nach Qumran, Eissfeldt Festschrift², BZAW 77, Berlin, 1961, 118-128.

——, Aspekt und Tempus im alt-Hebräischen Verbalsystem, OLZ 59, 1964, 117-126.

D. MICHEL, Tempora und Satzstellung in den Psalmen, Bonn, 1960.

J. T. MILIK, F. M. CROSS, Inscribed Javelin Heads from the Period of Judges, BASOR 134, 1954, 5-14.

A. R. MILLARD, "Scriptio Continua" in Early Hebrew: Ancient practice or modern surmise ?, JSS XV, 1970, 2-15.

C. H. MILLER, The Infinitive Construct in the Lawbooks of the O.T., CBQ XXXII, 1970, 222-226.

P. D. MILLER, A Note on the Meša' Inscription, Or 38, 1969, 461-464.

S. MORAG, The Vocalization Systems of Arabic, Hebrew and Aramaic, Den Haag, 1962.

W. L. MORAN, New Evidence on Canaanite taqtulu (na), JCS 5 1951, 33-35.

——, Early Canaanite yaqtula, Or XXIX, 1960, 1-19.

——, The Hebrew Language in its North-West Semitic Background, BANE, New York, 1961, 54-72.

——, *taqtul — Third Masculin Singular, Bibl XLV, 1964, 80-82.

S. MOSCATI, Preistoria e storia del consonantismo ebraico antico, ANLA VIII, 5, 8, Roma, 1954.

——, Il Semitico di nord-ovest, Studi orientalistici in onore di G. Levi della Vida II, Roma, 1956, 202-221.

——, Sulla posizione linguistica del semitico nord-occidentale, RSO 31, 1956, 229-234.

S. MOWINCKEL, Zum Problem der hebraischen Metrik, Festschrift A. Bertholet, Tübingen, 1950.

M. J. MULDER, Versuch zur Deutung von Sokènèt in I Kön. I, 2, 4, VT XXII, 1972, 43-54.

H.-P. MÜLLER, Notizen zu althebräischen Inschriften I, UF II, 1970, 229-242.

——, Die Wurzeln עיק, יעק und עוק, VT XXI, 1971, 556-564.

T. MURAOKA, Emphasis in Biblical Hebrew, Oxford 1969.

R. E. MURPHY, A Fragment of an Early Moabite Inscription from Dibon, BASOR 125, 1952, 20-23.

A. MURTONEN, Prolegomena to a Comparative Description of non-Masoretic Hebrew Dialects and Traditions, M. BLACK, G. FOHRER, In Memoriam Paul Kahle, Berlin, 1968, 180-187.

J. NAVEH, A Palaeographic Note on the Distribution of the Hebrew Scripts, HThR 61, 1968, 68-74.

——, The Scripts in Palestine and Transjordan in the Iron Age, J. A. SANDERS, Essays in honor of N. Glueck, Garden City, New York, 1970, 277-283.

E. A. NIDA, Implications of Contemporary Linguistics for Biblical Scholarship, JBL 91, 1972, 73-89.

M. NOTH, Die israelitischen Personennamen im Rahmen der gemeinsemitischen Namengebung, Stuttgart, 1928 (Reprint: Hildesheim, 1965).

B. OBED, ,,The Amman Theater Inscription", RSO 44, 1969, 187-189.

G. S. OGDEN, Time and the Verb הָיָה in O.T. Prose, VT XXI, 1971, 451-469.

J. L. PALACHE, Over beteekenisverandering der woorden in het Hebreeuwsch (Semietisch) en andere talen, Sinai en Paran, Opera Minora van J. L. Palache, Leiden, 1959, 101-132.

——, Semantic Notes on the Hebrew Lexicon, Leiden, 1959.

C. H. PEISKER, Hebräische Wortkunde, Berlin, 1962.

J. VAN DER PLOEG, Vijf en twintig jaar hebreeuwse lexicographie, JEOL 9, 1944, 89-98.

J. PRIGNAUD, Notes d'épigraphie hébraïque, RB 77, 1970, 50-67.

E. PUECH, Sur la racine slḥ en hébreu et en araméen, Semitica XXI, 1971, 5-19.

C. RABIN, The Hebrew Development of Proto-Semitic ā, Tarbiz 30, 1960, 99-111.

——, L with Imperative (Gen. XXIII), JSS XIII, 1968, 113-124.

——, Towards a Descriptive Semantics of Biblical Hebrew, Proceedings of the 26th International Congress of Orientalists 1964, New Delhi, 1968, 51.

——, La correspondence d'hébreu -ḏ arabe, D. COHEN, Mélanges M. Cohen, Den Haag, 1970, 290-297.

A. RAHLFS, Zur Setzung der Lesemütter im Alten Testament, NGWG 1916, Göttingen, 1916, 315-347.

A. F. RAINEY, Private Seal-Impressions: a note on semantics, IEJ XVI, 1966, 187-190.

——, Semantic Parallels to the Samaria Ostraca, PEQ CII, 1970, 45-51.

——, A Hebrew ,,Receipt" from Arad, BASOR 202, 1971, 23-29.

S. C. REIF, A Note on a Neglected Connotation of NTN, VT XX, 1970, 114-116.

——, A Note on גָּעַר, VT XXI, 1971, 241-244.

A. REIFENBERG, Ancient Hebrew Seals, London, 1952.

M. REISEL, Observations on the Tetragrammaton in Connection with the Names of Ehyeh ašer ehyeh-huha and Šem hammephoras, Assen, 1957.

D. Robertson, The Morphemes -Y (-ī) and -W (-ō) in Biblical Hebrew, VT XIX, 1969, 211-223.

H. B. Rosén, Remarques au sujet de la phonologie de l'hébreu biblique, RB LX 1953, 30-40.

——, Zur Vorgeschichte des Relativsatzes im Nordwestsemitischen, ArOr 27, 1959, 186-198.

——, A Marginal Note on Biblical Hebrew Phonology, JNES 20, 1961, 124-126.

——, The Comparative Assignment of Certain Hebrew Tense Forms, Proceedings of the International Conference on Semitic Studies in Jerusalem 1965, Jerusalem, 1969, 212-234.

——, Les successivités, D. Cohen, Mélanges M. Cohen, Den Haag, 1970, 113-129.

O. Rössler, Eine bisher unbekannte Tempusform im Althebräischen, ZDMG 111, 1960, 445-451.

——, Die Präfixkonjugation Qal der Verba I^{ae} Nûn im Althebräischen und das Problem der sogenannten Tempora, ZAW 74, 1962, 125-141.

A. Rubinstein, A Finite Verb continued by an Infinitive Absolute in Biblical Hebrew, VT II, 1952, 362-367.

F. Rundgren, Das althebräische Verbum. Abriss der Aspektlehre, Stockholm, 1961.

N. M. Sarna, The Interchange of the Prepositions beth and min in Biblical Hebrew, JBL 78, 1959, 310-316.

J. F. A. Sawyer, Root-Meanings in Hebrew, JSS XII, 1967, 37-50.

——, Semantics in Biblical Research. New Methods of Defining Hebrew Words for Salvation, London, 1972.

P. P. Saydon, The Use of Tenses in Deutero-Isaiah, Roma, 1959.

——, The Conative Imperfect in Hebrew, VT XII, 1962, 124-126.

——, Meanings and Uses of the Particle 't, VT XIV, 1964, 192-210.

J. Scheiden, Observations sur la prononciation antique de l'hébreu, Mus LXX, 1957, 349-352.

G. Schmuttermayr, Ambivalenz und Aspektdifferenz. Bemerkungen zu den hebräischen Präpositionen B, L und MIN, BZ 15, 1971, 29-51.

W. Schottroff, Der altisraelitische Fluchspruch, Neukirchen-Vluyn, 1969.

G. M. Schramm, The Graphemes of Tiberian Hebrew, Berkeley-Los Angeles, 1964.

R. B. Y. Scott, The n-ṣ-p weights from Judah, BASOR 200, 1970, 62-66.

S. Segert, Die Sprache der moabitischen Königinschrift, ArOr 29, 1961, 197-268.

——, Aspekte des althebräischen Aspekt-Systems, ArOr 33, 1965, 93-104.

——, Hebrew Bible and Semitic Comparative Lexicography, Congress Volume Roma 1968, VTS XVII, Leiden, 1969, 204-211.

J. Severino Croatto, L'article hébreu et les particules emphatiques dans le sémitique de l'ouest, ArOr 39, 1971, 389-400.

K. Seybold, Zwei Bemerkungen zu גמל/גמול, VT XXII, 1971, 112-117.

S. H. Siedl, Gedanken zum Tempussystem im Hebräischen und Akkadischen, Wiesbaden, 1971.

E. Sievers, Studien zur hebräischen Metrik I, Untersuchungen, Leipzig, 1901.

J. F. K. Skeehan, Egypto-Semitic Elucidation of the waw Conversive, Bibl 52, 1971, 39-43.

W. von Soden, Tempus and Modus im Semitischen, XXIV. Int. Or. Kongr. 1959, Wiesbaden, 1959, 263-265.

——, Zur Herkunft von hebr. 'ebjōn "arm", MIO XV, 1969, 322-326.

J. Soisalon-Soininen, Der Infinitivus constructus mit ל im Hebräischen, VT XXII, 1972, 82-90.

E. A. Speiser, The "Elative" in West-Semitic and Akkadian, JCS 6, 1952, 81-92.

A. Sperber, Hebrew Based upon Greek and Latin Transliterations, HUCA XII-XIII, 1937-1938, 103-274.

——, Hebrew Grammar: a new approach, JBL 62, 1943, 137-262.

D. Sperling, ḫgr I and ḫgr II, JANES III, 1970-1971, 121-128.

J. J. Stamm, Hebräische Ersatznamen, H. G. Güterbock, Th. Jacobsen, Studies in honor of Benno Landsberger, Chicago, Illin., 1965, 413-424.

——, Hebräische Frauennamen, Hebräische Wortforschung, Festschrift W. Baumgartner, VTS XVI, Leiden, 1967, 301-339.

G. J. Thierry, The Pronunciation of the Tetragrammaton, OTS V, 1948, 30-42.

M. Tsevat, A Study of the Language of the Biblical Psalms, Philadelphia, 1955.

E. Ullendorff, The Contribution of South Semitic to Hebrew Lexicography, VT VI, 1956, 190-198.

——, The Knowledge of the Languages in the Bible, J. M. GRINTZ,
    J. LIVER, Studies in the Bible presented to M. H. Segal, Jeru-
    salem, 1964.
——, C'est de l'hébreu pour moi ?, JSS 13, 1968, 125-135.
——, Is Biblical Hebrew a Language ?, BSOAS XXXIV, 1971,
    241-255.
D. VETTER, J. WALTHER, Sprachtheorie und Sprachvermittlung,
    Erwägungen zur Situation des hebräischen Sprachstudiums,
    ZAW 83, 1971, 73-96.
E. VOGT, Zur Geschichte der hebräischen Sprache, Bibl 52, 1971, 72-78.
Th. C. VRIEZEN, De betekenis van de semasiologie voor exegese en
    schriftbeschouwing, VoxTheol XX, 1950, 89-100.
——, Einige Notizen zur Übersetzung des Bindewortes kï, J. HEMPEL,
    L. ROST, Von Ugarit nach Qumran, Eissfeldt Festschrift², BZAW
    77, Berlin, 1961, 266-273.
——, Das Hiphil von 'āmar in Deut. 26, 17.18, JEOL 17, 1963,
    207-210.
——, Enkele opmerkingen over het woordonderzoek, Schrift en Uitleg
    aangeboden aan W. H. Gispen, Kampen, 1970, 237-247.
L. WÄCHTER, Reste von Šafʿel-Bildungen im Hebräischen, ZAW 83,
    1971, 380-389.
M. WAGNER, Die lexikalischen und grammatikalischen Aramaismen
    im alttestamentlichen Hebräisch, BZAW 96, Berlin, 1966.
——, Beiträge zur Aramaismenfrage im alttestamentlichen Hebräisch,
    Hebräische Wortforschung, Festschrift W. Baumgartner, VTS
    XVI, Leiden, 1967, 355-371.
N. WALKER, Concerning the function of 't, VT V, 1955, 314-315.
W. WATSON, Shared consonants in Northwest Semitic, Bibl 50, 1969,
    525-533.
——, More on Shared Consonants, Bibl 52, 1971, 44-50.
G. WEHMEYER, Der Segen im Alten Testament. Eine semasiologische
    Untersuchung der wurzel brk, Basel, 1970.
W. WEINBERG, Transliteration and Transcription of Hebrew, HUCA
    XL-XLI, 1969-1970, 1-32.
J. WEINGREEN, The Construct-Genitive Relation in Hebrew Syntax,
    VT IV, 1954, 50-59.
——, Classical Hebrew Composition, Oxford, 1957 (Reprint: London,
    1962).
D. WEISBERG, The Rare Accents of the Twenty-one Books, JQR LVII,
    1966, 57-71.

G. J. Wenham, Beṯûlāh "a girl of marriageable age", VT XXII, 1972, 326-348.

P. Wernberg-Møller, "Pleonastic" *waw* in Classical Hebrew, JSS 3, 1958, 321-326.

———, Observations on the Hebrew particle, ZAW 71, 1959-1960, 54-67.

S. B. Wheeler, The Infixed -t- in Biblical Hebrew, JANES III, 1970-1971, 21-31.

C. F. Whitley, Some Functions of the Hebrew Particles beth and lamedh, JQR LXXII, 1972, 199-206.

———, The Positive Force of the Hebrew Particle בל, ZAW 84, 1972, 213-219.

J. R. Wilch, Time and Event. An exegetical study of the use of 'ēth in the Old Testament in comparison to other temporal expressions in clarification of the concept of time, Leiden, 1969.

H. Wildberger, "Glauben". Erwägungen zu האמין, Hebräische Wortforschung, Festschrift W. Baumgartner, VTS XVI, Leiden, 1967, 372-386.

D. Winton Thomas, The Language of the Old Testament, H. Wheeler Robinson, Record and Revelation, Oxford, 1938, 374-402.

———, The Recovery of the Ancient Hebrew language, Cambridge, 1939.

———, A Consideration of some Unusual Ways of Expressing the Superlative in Hebrew, VT III, 1953, 209-224.

———, Documents from Old Testament Times, London, 1958.

———, Again "the prophet" in the Lachish Ostraca, J. Hempel, L. Rost, Von Ugarit nach Qumran, Eissfeldt Festschrift², BZAW 77, Berlin, 1961, 244-249.

———, Some Further Remarks on Unusual Ways of Expressing the Superlative in Hebrew, VT XVIII, 1968, 120-124.

A. S. van der Woude, De mal'ak Jahweh: een Godsbode, NedTT XVIII, 1964, 1-13.

———, Das hebräische Pronomen demonstrativum als hinweisende Interjektion, JEOL 18, 1964, 307-313.

Y. Yadin, A further Note on the Samaria Ostraca, IEJ XII, 1962, 64-67.

———, A Further Note on the Lamed in the Samaria Ostraca, IEJ XVIII, 1968, 50-51.

A. S. Yahuda, Die Sprache des Pentateuch in ihrem Beziehungen zum Aegyptischen I, Berlin-Leipzig, 1929.

H. Yallon, The Kamaeṣ in Babylonian Phonetics and in Yemen, Tarbiz XXXIII, 1963-1964, 97-108.

K. ZIMMERLI, Die Weisung des A.T. zum Geschäft der Sprache,
W. SCHNEEMELCHER, Das Problem der Sprache in Theologie und
Kirche, Berlin, 1959, 1-20.

F. ZIMMERMANN, Folk Etymology of Biblical Names, VTS XV,
Congress Volume Genève 1965, Leiden, 1966, 311-326.

A. H. VAN ZYL, The Moabites², Leiden, 1970.

C. LITERATURE

1. TEXT EDITIONS (See also A 1)

H. BARDTKE, Hebräische Konsonantentexte, Leipzig, 1954.

Corpus Inscriptionum Semiticarum I, II, V, Paris, 1947-1963.

G. A. COOKE, A Textbook of North-Semitic Inscriptions, Oxford, 1903.

D. DIRINGER, Le iscrizioni anticho-ebraiche palestinesi, Firenze, 1934.

H. DONNER, W. RÖLLIG, Kanaanäische und aramäische Inschriften
mit einem Beitrag von O. RÖSSLER², 3 vols: I (Texts 1966, II
(Commentary) 1968, III (Plates) 1969, Wiesbaden, 1966-1969.

K. ELLIGER, W. RUDOLPH, Biblia Hebraica Stuttgartensia. Editio
funditus renovata, Stuttgart, 1968-   .

J. C. L. GIBSON, Textbook of Syrian Semitic Inscriptions. Vol. I:
Hebrews and Moabite Inscriptions, London, 1971.

R. KITTEL, Biblia Hebraica³. Textum Masoreticum curavit P. Kahle,
Stuttgart, 1937 (Reprint: Ed. Septima, 1953, with slight alter-
ations in the apparatus criticus).

I. LÉVI, The Hebrew Text of the Book of Ecclesiasticus. Edited with
Brief Notes and a Selected Glossary. Reprint of the 1904 ed.,
Leiden, 1969.

M. LIDZBARSKI, Handbuch der nordsemitischen Epigraphik, nebst
ausgewählten Inschriften, 2 vols., Weimar, 1898 (Reprint: Hildesheim, 1962).

——, Altsemitische Texte I, Kanaanäische Inschriften, Giessen,
1907.

——, Ephemeris für semitische Epigraphik, 3 vols., Giessen, 1900-
1915 (Reprint: Berlin, 1962).

H. MICHAUD, Sur la pierre et l'argile. Inscriptions hébraïques et
Ancient Testament, Neuchâtel-Paris, 1958.

S. MOSCATI, L'epigrafia ebraica antica 1935-1950, Roma, 1951.

Répertoire d'Épigraphie sémitique, Paris, 1900-1950.

E. J. Revell, Hebrew Texts with Palestinian vocalization, Toronto, 1970.

A. Sperber, The Hebrew Bible. With pre-Masoretic Tiberian vocalization. The prophets according to the Codex Reuchlinianus (in a critical analysis), Leiden, 1970.

H. Torczyner, Lachish I, The Lachish Letters (Tell ed Duweir), London, 1938.

Th. C. Vriezen, J. H. Hospers, Palestine Inscriptions, Leiden, 1951.

2. Handbooks, monographs and articles on the text of the Old Testament

a. *Handbooks*

D. R. Ap-Thomas, A Primer of Old Testament Text Criticism[2], Oxford, 1964.

W. Bloemendaal, De tekst van het Oude Testament, Baarn, 1966.

E. C. Colwell, The Study of the Bible[3], Chicago, 1964.

E. E. Flack, B. M. Metzger a.o., The Text, Canon and Principal Versions of the Bible, Michigan, 1956.

F. Kenyon, Our Bible and the Ancient Manuscripts, London, 1958.

B. J. Roberts, The Old Testament Text and Versions, Cardiff, 1951.

E. Würthwein, Der Text des Alten Testamentes[3], Stuttgart, 1966.

b. *Monographs and articles*

S. Baer, H. L. Strack, Die Dikduke ha-Te'amim des Ahron ben Mosche ben Ascher und andere alte grammatisch-massoretische Lesestücke zur Feststellung eines richtigen Textes der hebräischen Bibel, Leipzig, 1879 (Reprint: Jerusalem, 1970).

J. Barr, Comparative Philology and the Text of the Old Testament, Oxford, 1968.

D. Barthélemy, Les Tiqquné Sopherim et la critique textuelle de l'Ancien Testament, Congress Volume Bonn 1962, VTS IX, Leiden, 1963, 185-304.

——, Les devanciers d'Aquila. Première publication intégrale du texte des fragments du Dodecapropheton trouvés dans le désert de Juda, Leiden, 1963.

G. Bertram, Das Problem der griechischen Umschrift des hebräischen Alten Testaments, WO V, 1970, 237-264.

J. A. Bewer, Textkritische Bemerkungen zum Alten Testament, Festschrift A. Bertholet, Tübingen, 1950.

E. Birnbaum, The Michigan Codex. An important Hebrew Bible manuscript discovered in the University of Michigan Library, VT XVII, 1967, 373-415.

L. Blau, Masoretische Untersuchungen, Strassbourg, 1891.

R. Butin, The Ten Nequdoth of the Tora or the Meaning and Purpose of the Extraordinary Points of the Pentateuch. Prolegomenon by S. Talmon, New York, 1906 (Reprint: New York, 1969).

F. Chénique, Principes et méthodes de l'étude de la Bible massorétique sur les calculateurs électroniques — Exemples des ordinateurs IBM 1134, Strasbourg, 1967.

F. M. Cross, The Contribution of the Qumrân Discoveries to the Study of the Biblical text, IEJ XVI, 1966, 81-95.

A. ben David, The Differences between Ben Asher and Ben Naphtali, Tarbiz XXVI, 1957, 384-409.

F. Delitzsch, Die Lese- und Schreibfehler im Alten Testament nebst den dem Schrifttexte einverleibten Randnoten klassifiziert, Berlin-Leipzig, 1920.

M. Dietrich, Neue palästinisch punktierte Bibelfragmente veröffentlicht und auf Text und Punktation hin untersucht, Massorah II, 1, Leiden, 1968.

A. Diez Macho, Importants manuscripts hébreux et araméens aux États-Unies, Congress Volume Strasbourg 1956, VTS IV, Leiden, 1957, 27-46.

——, A New List of So-Called "Ben Naftali" Manuscripts, Preceded by an Inquiry into the True Character of these Manuscripts, Hebrew and Semitic Studies presented to G. R. Driver, Oxford, 1963, 16-52.

G. R. Driver, Abbreviations in the Massoretic text, Textus I, 1960, 112-131.

——, Once again Abbreviations, Textus IV, 1964, 76-94.

E. Ehrentreu, Untersuchungen über die Massora, ihre geschichtliche Entwicklung und ihren Geist, Hannover, 1925 (Reprint: Hildesheim, 1968).

A. B. Ehrlich, Randglossen zur hebräischen Bibel. Textkritisches, Sprachliches und Sachliches, 7 vols., Leipzig, 1908-1914 (Reprint: Hildesheim, 1968).

S. Frendsdorff, The Massorah Magna. Part One. Massoretic Dic-

tionary or the Massorah in Alphabetical, Prolegomenon by
G. E. Weil, New York, 1968.

M. Gertner, The Masora and the Levites. An essay in the history of
a concept, VT X, 1960, 241-272.

C. D. Ginsburg, Introduction to the Massoretico-Critical Edition of
the Hebrew Bible. Prolegomena by H. M. Orlinski, The Masoretic text, a critical evaluation, New York, 1966.

D. W. Goodwin, Text-Restoration Methods in Contemporary U.S.A.
Biblical Scholarship, Napoli, 1969.

M. H. Goshen-Gottstein, Text and Language in Bible and Qumran,
Jerusalem-Tel Aviv, 1960.

——, Theory and Practice of Textual Criticism, Textus III, 1963,
130-158.

——, The Book of Isaiah. Sample edition with introduction, The
Hebrew University Bible Project, Jerusalem, 1966.

——, Hebrew Biblical Manuscripts. Their history and their place
in the Hebrew University Bible Project Edition, Bibl 48, 1967,
243-290.

H. G. G. Herklots, How our Bible Came to Us. Its texts and versions,
New York, 1954.

G. Howard, Frank Cross and the Recensional Criticism, VT XXI,
1971, 440-450.

T. Jansma, Inquiry into the Hebrew Text and the Ancient Versions
of Zachariah IX-XIV, Leiden, 1949.

S. Jellicoe, The Septuagint and Modern Study, London, 1968.

A. Jepsen, Von den Aufgaben der Alttestamentlichen Textkritik,
VTS IX, Congress Volume Bonn 1962, Leiden, 1963, 332-341.

P. E. Kahle, Masoreten des Ostens. Die ältesten punktierten Handschriften des Alten Testaments und der Targume, Leipzig, 1913.
(Reprint: Hildesheim, 1966).

——, Aus der Geschichte der ältesten hebräischen Bibelhandschrift,
Baudissin Festschrift, BZAW 33, Berlin, 1918, 247-260.

——, Die überlieferte Aussprache des Hebräischen und die Punktation
der Masoreten, ZAW 39, 1921, 230-239.

——, Die Punktation der Masoreten, Marti Festschrift, BZAW 41,
Berlin, 1925, 167-172.

——, Masoreten des Westens, 2 vols., Stuttgart, 1927-1930 (Reprint:
Hildesheim, 1967).

——, Die hebräischen Handschriften aus der Höhle, Stuttgart, 1951.

——, Opera Minora, Leiden, 1956.

——, The Cairo Geniza[2], Oxford, 1959.

——, Die Kairoer Genisa, Berlin, 1962.

——, Der hebräische Bibeltext seit Franz Delitzsch, Stuttgart, 1961.

E. Y. KUTSCHER, Yemenite Hebrew and Ancient Pronunciation, JSS 11, 1966, 217-225.

P. LEANDER, Bemerkungen zur palästinischen Überlieferung des Hebräischen, ZAW 13, 1936, 91-99.

I. O. LEHMANN, A Forgotten Principle of Biblical Textual Tradition Rediscovered, JNES 26, 1967, 93-101.

K. LEVY, Zur masoretischen Grammatik. Texte und Untersuchungen, Stuttgart, 1936.

M. MANSOOR, The Massoretic Text in the Light of Qumran, Congress Volume Bonn 1962, VTS IX, Leiden, 1963, 305-321.

M. L. MARGOLIS, La formation de la Bible hébraïque, Paris, 1953.

M. J. MULDER, Het meisje van Sodom. De targumin op Gen. 18: 20, 21 tussen Bijbeltekst en Haggada, Kampen, 1970.

A. MURTONEN, Spoken Hebrew from the Tenth Century, ABN III, 1961-1962, 45-60.

H. M. ORLINSKY, The Origin of the kethib-qere System: a new approach, Congress Volume Oxford 1959, VTS VII, Leiden, 1960, 184-192.

——, The Textual Criticism of the O.T., BANE, New York, 1961, 113-132.

C. PERROT, Petuhot et Setumot, Étude sur les alinéas du Pentateuque, RB LXXXVI, 1969, 50-91.

B. J. ROBERTS, The Hebrew Bible since 1937, JTS 15, 1964, 253-264.

H. P. RÜGER, Ein Fragment der bisher ältesten datierten hebräischen Bibelhandschrift mit babylonischer Punktation, VT XVI, 1966, 65-73.

——, Text und Textform im hebräischen Sirach. Untersuchungen zur Textgeschichte und Textkritik der hebräischen Sirachfragmente aus der Kairoer Geniza, BZAW 112, Berlin, 1969.

P. SACCHI, Per una edizione critica del testo dell' Antico Testamento, OA IX, 1970, 221-233.

S. SHAKED, A Tentative Bibliography of Geniza Documents, Paris-Den Haag, 1964.

P. W. SKEHAN, The Biblical Scrolls from Qumran and the Text of the Old Testament, BiAr XXVIII, 1965, 87-100.

A. SPERBER, The Hebrew Bible with pre-Masoretic Vocalization.

The Prophets. Hebrew text based on the Codex Reuchlinianus with pre-Masoretic Tiberian vocalization, Leiden, 1970.

S. TALMON, Double Readings in the Masoretic Text, Textus I, 1960, 144-184.

G. E. WEIL, Élie Lévita, Humaniste et masorète (1469-1549), Leiden, 1963.

——, La nouvelle édition de la Massorah (BHK IV) et l'histoire de la Massorah, VTS IX, Congress Volume Bonn 1962, Leiden, 1963, 266-284.

——, Massorah Gedolah selon le manuscrit B 19a de Léningrad. Édition critique en IV volumes. Vol. I. Les listes, Roma, 1971.

——, F. CHÉNIQUE, Prolégomènes à l'utilisation des méthodes de statistique linguistique pour l'étude historique et philologique de la Bible hébraïque et des paraphrases, VT XIV, 1964, 344-366.

I. YEIVIN, The New Edition of the Biblia Hebraica — Its text and massorah, Textus VII, 1969, 114-123.

3. LITERARY HISTORIES

G. FOHRER, Einleitung in das alte Testament, Heidelberg, 1965.

H. GUNKEL, Die israelitische Literatur, Leipzig, 1925 (Reprint: Darmstadt, 1963).

J. HEMPEL, Die althebräische Literatur und ihr hellenistisch-jüdisches Nachleben, Wildpark-Potsdam, 1930 (Reprint: Berlin, 1968).

E. JACOB, L'Ancien Testament, Paris, 1967.

O. KAISER, Einleitung in das Alte Testament. Eine Einführung in ihre Ergebnisse und Probleme, Gütersloh, 1969.

A. LODS, Histoire de la littérature hébraïque et juive depuis les origines jusqu'à la ruine de l'État juif (135 après J.-C.), Paris, 1950.

A. RAVENNA, Letteratura cananea, O. BOTTA (ed.), Storia delle letterature d'Oriente I, Milano, 1969, 661-667.

L. ROST, Einleitung in die alttestamentlichen Apokryphen und Pseudepigraphen einschliesslich der grossen Qumranhandschriften, Heidelberg, 1971.

Th. C. VRIEZEN, De literatuur van Oud-Israël, Den Haag, 1961.

4. COMMENTARIES

Biblischer Kommentar, Altes Testament, Neukirchen-Vluyn.

Das Alte Testament Deutsch, Göttingen.

Die Botschaft des Alten Testaments, Stuttgart.
Göttinger Handkommentar zum Alten Testament, Göttingen (GHKAT).
Handbuch zum Alten Testament, Tübingen (HAT).
Kommentar zum Alten Testament, Leipzig (KAT).
Old Testament Library, London (OTL).
The Anchor Bible, New York.
The International Critical Commentary, Edinburgh (ICC).
Züricher Bibelkommentar, Zürich.

5. MONOGRAPHS AND ARTICLES WITH REGARD TO LITERARY QUESTIONS

L. BLANKSTEIN, Hebrew Proverbs. Their origin with parallels from other languages, Jerusalem, 1964.

D. R. BLUMENTHAL, A Play on Words in the Nineteenth Chapter of Job, VT XVI, 1966, 497-501.

H. A. BRONGERS, Die Wendung "bᵉšēm Jhwh" im Alten Testament, ZAW 77, 1965, 1-20.

D. J. A. CLINES, X, X Ben Y, Ben Y; Personal Names in Hebrew Narrative Style, VT XXII, 1972, 266-287.

F. CRÜSEMANN, Studien zur Formgeschichte von Hymnus und Danklied in Israel, Neukirchen-Vluyn, 1969.

M. DAHOOD, Congruity of Metaphors, Hebräische Wortforschung, Festschrift W. Baumgartner, VTS XVI, Leiden, 1967, 40-49.

E. DHORME, L'emploi métaphorique des noms des parties du corps en hébreu et en akkadien, Paris, 1923 (Reprint: Paris, 1963).

T. DONALD, The Semantic Field of Rich and Poor in the Wisdom Literature of Hebrew and Accadian, OA 3, 1964, 27-41.

O. EISSFELDT, Der Beutel der Lebendigen. Alttestamentliche Erzählungs- und Dichtungsmotive im Lichte neuer Nuzi-Texte, Berlin, 1960.

J. H. EYBERS, Some Examples of Hyperbole in Biblical Hebrew, Semitics I, 1970, 38-49.

S. GEVIRTZ, Patterns in the Early Poetry of Israel, Chicago, 1963.

E. M. GOOD, Irony in the Old Testament, Philadelphia, 1965.

J. HEMPEL, Pathos und Humor in der israelitischen Erziehung, J. HEMPEL, L. ROST, Von Ugarit nach Qumran, Eissfeldt Festschrift², BZAW 77, Berlin, 1961, 63-81.

——, Geschichten und Geschichte im Alten Testament bis zur persischen Zeit, Gütersloh, 1964.

H. KOSMALA, Form and Structure in Ancient Hebrew Poetry, VT XIV, 1964, 423-445 and XVI, 1966, 152-180.

B. O. LONG, The Problem of Ethiological Narrative in the Old Testament, BZAW 108, Berlin, 1968.

O. LORETZ, Qohelet und der Alte Orient. Untersuchungen zu Stil und theologischer Thematik des Buches Qohelet, Freiburg, 1964.

——, Studien zur althebräischen Poesie I: Das althebräische Liebeslied. Untersuchungen zur Stichometrie und Redaktionsgeschichte des Hohenliedes und des 45. Psalms, Neukirchen-Vluyn, 1971.

H.-P. MÜLLER, Der Aufbau des Deboraliedes, VT XVI, 1966, 446-459.

——, Der Begriff "Rätsel" im Alten Testament, VT XX, 1970, 465-489.

E. NIELSEN, Die Zehn Gebote. Eine traditionsgeschichtliche Skizze, Kopenhagen, 1965.

J. L. PALACHE, Het karakter van het Oud-Testamentische verhaal, Sinai en Paran, Opera Minora van J. L. PALACHE, Leiden, 1959, 15-36.

D. F. PAYNE, Characteristic word-play in "Second Isaiah". A reappraisal, JSS 12, 1967, 207-229.

B. PORTEN, The Structure and Theme of the Solomon Narrative, HUCA XXXVIII, 1967, 93-128.

D. F. RAUBER, Literary Values in the Bible: the Book of Ruth, JBL 89, 1970, 27-37.

W. RICHTER, Exegese als Literaturwissenschaft. Entwurf einer alttestamentlichen Literaturtheorie und Methodologie, Göttingen, 1971.

N. H. RIDDERBOS, Kenmerken der Hebreeuwse poëzie, GTT 55, 1955, 171-183.

H. RINGGREN, A Law of Stylistic Balance in Hebrew, Horae Soederblomianae, Lund, 1964, 9-15.

W. M. W. ROTH, Numerical Sayings in the Old Testament, Leiden, 1965.

J. F. A. SAWYER, Context of Situation and Sitz im Leben, Proceedings of the University of Newcastle upon Tyne, Philosophical Society, Vol 1, 11, 1967, 137-147.

H. H. SCHMIDT, Wesen und Geschichte der Weisheit. Eine Untersuchung zur altorientalischen und israelitischen Weisheitsliteratur, BZAW 101, Berlin, 1966.

S. Segert, Zur literarischen Form und Funktion der fünf Megilloth, ArOr 33, 1965, 451-467.

——, Versbau und Sprachbau in der althebraischen Poesie, MIO XV, 1969, 312-321.

P. B. Yoder, A-B pairs and oral composition in Hebrew Poetry, VT XXI, 1971, 470-489.

D. THE MOST IMPORTANT WORKS AND ARTICLES ON (CULTURAL) HISTORY

P. R. Ackroyd, Exile and restauration, London, 1968.

——, D. F. Evans (ed.), The Cambridge History of the Bible. From the Beginnings to Jerome, Cambridge, 1970.

Y. Aharoni, The Land of the Bible. A historical geography. Translated from the Hebrew by A. F. Rainey, London, 1966.

G. W. Anderson, The History and Religion of Israel, Oxford, 1966.

M. Avi-Yonah, The Holy Land from the Persian to the Arab Conquests (536 B.C. to A.D. 640). A historical geography, ..., 19... .

H. Bardtke, Bibel, Spaten und Geschichte², Göttingen, 1971.

R. D. Barnett, Illustrations of Old Testament History, London, 1966.

M. A. Beek, Geschiedenis van Israel², Zeist, 1960.

——, Geschichte Israels³, Stuttgart, 1970.

K.-H. Bernhardt, Die Umwelt des Alten Testaments, I: Die Quellen und ihre Erforschung, Gütersloh, 1967.

J. Boulos, Les peuples et les civilisations du Proche Orient. Essai d'une histoire comparée des origines à nos jours, 5 vols., Den Haag, 1961-1968.

G. Cansdale, Animals of Bible Lands, Exeter, 1970.

E. L. Ehrlich, A Concise History of Israel from the Earliest Times to the Destruction of the Temple in A.D. 70. Translated by J. Barr, New York, 1965.

——, Geschichte Israëls. Von den Anfängen bis zur Zerstörung des Tempels (70 n. Chr.)², Berlin, 1967.

O. Eissfeldt, Syrien und Palästina vom Ausgang des 11. bis zum Ausgang des 6. Jahrhunderts, Fischer Weltgeschichte 3, Die Altorientalischen Reiche, III: Die erste Hälfte des 1. Jahrtausends, Frankfurt a.M., 1967, 135-203.

G. Fohrer, Das Alte Testament, Einführung in Bibelkunde und

Literatur des Alten Testaments und in Geschichte und Religion Israels, I, Gütersloh, 1969.

——, Geschichte der israelitischen Religion, Berlin, 1969.

K. GALLING, Studien zur Geschichte Israels im persischen Zeitalter, Tübingen, 1964.

——, Textbuch zur Geschichte Israels², Tübingen, 1968.

C. H. GORDON, Geschichtliche Grundlagen des Alten Testaments², Zürich, 1961.

——, Before the Bible. The common background of Greek and Hebrew civilisations, New York, 1962.

J. GRAY, Archaeology and the Old Testament Word, London, 1962.

——, The Canaanites², London, 1965.

H. GRESSMANN, Altorientalische Texte zum Alten Testament. 2. Nachdruck der 2. Aufl. von 1926, Berlin, 1970.

E. W. HEATON, Everyday life in Old Testament times, London, 1956.

——, The Hebrew Kingdoms, Oxford, 1968.

A. JIRKU, Geschichte Palästina-Syriens im orientalischen Zeitalter, Aalen, 1963.

——, The World of the Bible, London, 1967.

K. M. KENYON, Amorites and Canaanites, London, 1966.

H. J. KRAUS, Gottesdienst in Israel. Grundriss einer Geschichte des alttestamentlichen Gottesdienstes², München, 1962.

J. LIVER, The Military History of the Land of Israel in Biblical Times, Tel-Aviv, 1965.

A. MALAMAT, Syrien-Palästina in der zweiten Hälfte des 2. Jahrtausends, Fischer Weltgeschichte 3, Die Altorientalischen Reiche, II: Das Ende des 2. Jahrtausends, Frankfurt a.M., 1966, 177-221.

——, The last kings of Judah and the fall of Jerusalem. An historical-chronological study, IEJ 18, 1968, 137-156.

B. MAZAR (ed.), The World History of the Jewish People. Vol. II Patriarchs, London, 1971.

A. NEHER, R. NEHER, Histoire biblique du peuple d'Israel, 2 vols., Paris, 1962.

M. NOTH, Geschichte Israels, Göttingen, 1950.

——, Die Welt des Alten Testamentss, Berlin, 1962.

——, The Old Testament World, London, 1966.

H. M. ORLINSKY, Ancient Israel², Ithaca, New York, 1960.

P. PARAF, La vie quotidienne en Israel, Paris, 1971.

J. B. PRITCHARD, Archaeology and the Old Testament, Princeton N.J., 1958.

——, Die Archäologie und das Alte Testament, Wiesbaden, 1964.

——, Culture and history, Archaeology and the future of biblical studies, J. Ph. HYATT, The Bible in modern scholarship, Nashville-New York, 1965, 313-324.

——, The Ancient Near East in Pictures Relating to the Old Testament[2] (ANEP), London, 1969.

——, Ancient Near Eastern Texts Relating to the Old Testament[3], (ANET), London, 1969.

J. B. PRITCHARD, The Ancient Near East. Supplementary Texts and Pictures relating to the Old Testament[2], Princeton N.J., 1969.

H. RINGGREN, Israelitische Religion, Stuttgart, 1963.

——, La religion d'Israel, Paris, 1966.

J. A. SOGGIN, Das Königtum in Israel. Ursprünge, Spannungen, Entwicklung, BZAW 104, Berlin, 1967.

R. DE VAUX, Les Institutions de l'Ancient Testament, 2 vols., Paris, 1959.

——, Le pays de Canaan, JAOS 88, 1968, 23-30.

——, Histoire Ancienne d'Israel, Paris, 1971.

Th. C. VRIEZEN, The Study of the Old Testament and the History of Religion, Congress Volume Roma 1968, VTS XVII, Leiden, 1969, 1-24.

E. WERNER, Hebräische Musik, Köln, 1961.

G. WIDENGREN, Israelite-Jewish Religion, C. J. BLEEKER, G. WIDENGREN, Historia Religionum. Handbook for the history of religions. Vol. I: Religions of the past, Leiden, 1969, 223-317.

D. WINTON THOMAS (ed.), Archaeology and Old Testament Study, Oxford, 1967.

D. WOHLENBERG, Kultmusik in Israel, Hamburg, 1967.

E. ATLASES

Y. AHARONI, M. AVI-YONA, The Macmillan Bible Atlas, New York-London, 1968.

Atlas of Israel, Amsterdam, 1969.

L. H. GROLLENBERG, Bildatlas zur Bibel[2], Gütersloh, 1958.

——, Kleine atlas van de Bijbel, Amsterdam-Brussel, 1959.

H. G. MAY, Oxford Bible Arlas, Oxford, 1962.

J. H. NEGENMAN, Grosser Bildatlas zur Bibel, German edition by C. RIETZSCHEL, Gütersloh, 1969.

——, New Atlas of the Bible, London, 1969.

H. H. Rowley, Atlas zur Bibel, Wuppertal, 1965.

G. E. Wright, F. V. Filson, The Westminster Historical Atlas to the Bible, London, 1946.

II. SAMARITAN HEBREW

COMPILED BY

J. H. HOSPERS

General

PUBLICATIONS WITH MANY BIBLIOGRAPHICAL REFERENCES

J. Macdonald, The Leeds School of Samaritan Studies, AnLeeds III, 1961-1962, 115-118.

L. A. Mayer, D. Broadribb, Bibliography of the Samaritans, Supplements to Abr Nahrain I, Leiden, 1964.

J. A. Montgomery, The Samaritans, New York, 1968.

A. LINGUISTICS

1. GRAMMARS

R. Macuch, Grammatik des samaritanischen Hebräisch, Studia Samaritana I, Berlin, 1969.

A. Murtonen, Materials for a non-masoretic Hebrew Grammar III: A grammar of the Samaritan Dialect of Hebrew, Helsinki, 1964.

H. Petermann, Versuch einer hebräischen Formenlehre nach der Aussprache der heutigen Samaritaner nebst einer darnach gebildeten Transcription der Genesis und einer Beilage enth. die von d. recipirten Texte des Pentateuchs abweichenden Lesarten der Samaritaner, Leipzig, 1868 (Reprint: Nendeln, 1966).

2. Important linguistic monographs and articles

Z. Ben Ḥayyim, The literary and oral tradition of Hebrew and
Aramaic amongst the Samaritans, 3 vols., Jerusalem, 1957-1967
(Hebrew with English foreword).

——, Observations on the Hebrew and Aramaic Lexicon from the
Samaritan tradition, Hebräische Wortforschung, Festschrift W.
Baumgartner, VTS XVI, Leiden, 1967, 12-24.

——, The contribution of the Samaritan Inheritance to Research into
the History of Hebrew, Proceedings of the Israel Academy of
Sciences and Humanities III, Jerusalem, 1969, 162-174.

——, Some Problems of a Grammar of Samaritan Hebrew, Bibl 52,
1971, 229-252.

E. Brønno, Samaritan Hebrew and Origen's Secunda, JSS XIII,
1968, 192-201.

F. Diening, Das Hebräische bei den Samaritanern. Ein Beitrag zur
vormasoretischen Grammatik des Hebräischen, Bonner Orien-
talistischen Studien 24, Stuttgart, 1938.

P. Kahle, Zur Aussprache des Hebräischen bei den Samaritanern,
P. Kahle, Opera Minora, Leiden, 1956, 180-185.

R. Macuch, Der liquide Apikal und die apikale Liquide des samaritanischen Hebräisch, R. Stiehl, H. E. Stier, Beiträge zur alten
Geschichte und deren Nachleben, Bd. II, Berlin, 1970, 169-175.

A. Murtonen, The pronunciation of Hebrew by the Samaritans as
recorded at Nāblus in 1917 by H. Ritter and H. Schaade, P. E.
Kahle, The Cairo Geniza², Appendix II, Oxford, 1959, 318-335.

——, An etymological vocabulary to the Samaritan Pentateuch,
Materials for a non-masoretic grammar II, Helsinki, 1960.

B. LITERATURE

1. Text editions

M. Baillet, Deux inscriptions samaritaines de la région de Naplouse,
RB LXXI, 1964, 57-72.

I. Ben-Zvi, A lamp with a Samaritan inscription, IEJ 11, 1961,
139-142.

A. von Gall, Der Hebräische Pentateuch der Samaritaner, Berlin,
1914-1918 (Reprint: Berlin, 1966).

J. KAPLAN, Two Samaritan amulets, IEJ 17, 1967, 138-162.

H. G. KIPPENBERG, Ein Gebetbuch für den Samaritanischen Synagogen Gottesdienst aus dem 2. Jh. n. Chr., ZDPV LXXXV, 1969, 76-103.

J. MACDONALD, The Samaritan Chronicle II (or: Sepher Ha-Yamim). From Joshua to Nebuchadnezzar, BZAW 107, Berlin, 1969.

J. H. PETERMANN, Brevis linguae samaritanae grammatica, litteratura, chrestomathia cum glossario, Berlin, 1873.

2. MONOGRAPHS AND ARTICLES WITH REGARD TO LITERARY QUESTIONS

R. T. ANDERSON, Le Pentateuque samaritain CW 2473, RB LXXVII, 1970, 68-75.

——, Le Pentateuque samaritain CW 2478a, RB LXXVII, 1970, 550-560.

A. D. CROWN, Second thoughts on the age of the anonymous portions of the Samaritan Burial Liturgy, E. C. B. MACLAURIN, Essays in honor of G. W. Thatcher, Sydney, 1967, 63-83.

J. G. FRASER, Ussher's sixth copy of the Samaritan Pentateuch, VT XXI, 1971, 100-107.

K. HAACKER, Assumptio Mosis — Eine Samaritanische Schrift?, ThZ 25, 1969, 385-405.

Z. SHUNNAR, Zweisprachiges samaritanisches Lobpreisgedicht auf Moses, R. STIEHL, H. E. STIER, Beiträge zur alten Geschichte und deren Nachleben, Bd. II, Berlin, 1970, 176-191.

C. THE MOST IMPORTANT WORKS AND ARTICLES ON (CULTURAL) HISTORY

Z. BEN-ḤAYYIM, Einige Bemerkungen zur samaritanischen Liturgie, ZDPV 86, 1970, 87-89.

J. BOWMAN, The exegesis of the Pentateuch among the Samaritans and among the Rabbis, OTS VIII, 1950, 220-262.

——, The importance of Samaritan researches, AnLeeds I, 1958-1959, 43-54.

——, Samaritanische Probleme. Studien zum Verhältnis von Samaritanertum, Judentum und Urchristentum, Stuttgart, 1967.

M. GASTER, The Samaritans. Their history, doctrines and literature, London, 1925.

H. G. KIPPENBERG, Garizim und Synagoge. Traditionsgeschichtliche Untersuchungen zur samaritanischen Religion der aramäischen Periode, Berlin, 1971.

J. MACDONALD, The theology of the Samaritans, Philadelphia, 1965.

S. NOJA, Erklärung der 72 Lehren der Samaritaner, ZDMG 118, 1968, 270-273.

J. D. PURVIS, The Samaritan Pentateuch and the origin of the Samaritan Sect, Cambridge, Mass., 1968.

III. QUMRAN, MURABBA'AT, MASADA, ETC.

COMPILED BY

B. JONGELING

Introductory Remark

Publications from 1948 up to 1957 are systematically listed in the 'Bibliography of the Dead Sea Scrolls 1948-1957' by W. S. LASOR, Pasadena, Calif., 1958. By way of exception only we insert here basic works from that period. As for the studies that appeared since 1958 we had to make a selection: the second volume of the well-known alphabetical 'Bibliographie zu den Handschriften vom Toten Meer' by Chr. BURCHARD, Berlin, 1965, which includes the years 1956-1962, in fact lists almost 3000 publications and has nearly 300 pages! Such a selection shows always a certain arbitrariness. Perhaps another composer would have made another choice here or there. Nevertheless we expect that this bibliography will be a useful help for the study of the finds from the Judaean Desert.

Division:
A. Bibliographical Material.
B. General Publications. History of the Discoveries.
C. Linguistic Studies. Concordances. Dictionary.
D. Text-Editions.
E. Translations and Commentaries.
F. Studies on Various Manuscripts.
G. Archaeology and History.

H. Religion and Cult. Organization. Theology. The Messiah(s). The Teacher of Right-
eousness.
I. Qumran and the Old Testament.
J. Apocryphal and Pseudepigraphical Literature.
K. Qumran and Judaism. The Calendar.
L. Qumran and the New Testament. Qumran and Christianity.
M. Important Monographs. Collective Works.

A. BIBLIOGRAPHICAL MATERIAL

G. W. ANDERSON (ed.), A Decade of Bible Bibliography, Oxford, 1967.
[A volume of the Book Lists for 1957-1966].

H. BRAUN, Qumran und das Neue Testament, I, II, Tübingen, 1966.

Chr. BURCHARD, Bibliographie zu den Handschriften vom Toten Meer,
Berlin, I 1959², II 1965.

——, W. S. LASOR, J. CARMIGNAC, Bibliographie, RQum from I,
1958-1959, p. 149 onwards.

R. BUSA, Index of all Non Biblical Dead Sea Scrolls published up
to December 1957, RQum I, 1958-1959, 187-198. See also: Sacra
Pagina. Miscellanea biblica Congressus Internationalis Catholici
de re biblica II, Paris-Gembloux, 1959, 7-12.

J. A. FITZMYER, A Bibliographical Aid to the Study of the Qumrân
Cave IV, Texts 158-186, CBQ 31, 1969, 59-71.

G. GLANZMAN, J. A. FITZMYER, An Introductory Bibliography for
the Study of Scripture, Westminster Md., 1961. [pp. 105-111:
The Dead Sea Scrolls].

E. HAAPA, The Dead Sea Discoveries in the Research of the Fifties,
Porvoo-Helsinki, 1960.

A. M. HABERMANN, Bibliography on the Research into the Scrolls
from the Judaean Desert and the other Discoveries made there,
Beth Miqra', from 1, 1955-1956 onwards.

B. JONGELING, De vondsten in de woestijn van Juda 1962-1969.
(Een beknopt overzicht), VoxTheol 39, 1969, 305-321; 40, 1970,
29-44; 176-197.

——, A Classified Bibliography of the Finds in the Desert of Judah
1958-1969, STDJ VII, Leiden, 1971.

W. S. LASOR, Bibliography of the Dead Sea Scrolls 1948-1957, Pasadena, Calif., 1958.

P. NOBER, Elenchi Volumen Separatum 47 (1966). Complectens
Elenchum Bibliographicum Biblicum, e Biblica 47 (1966), et

Elenchum Suppletorium (sect. XI-XIII) e *Verbum Domini* 44 (1965), Romae, 1967.

J. VAN DER PLOEG, De in 1947 in de woestijn van Juda gevonden oude handschriften in het kader van gelijktijdige schriftelijke documenten, JEOL IV, 1949-1954, 41-71.

——, De in 1947 bij de Dode Zee gevonden oude handschriften, JEOL IV, 1949-1954, 221-248.

——, Les manuscrits trouvés depuis 1947 dans le désert de Juda III, JEOL V, 1955-1958, 85-116.

——, Les manuscrits du Désert de Juda. Études et découvertes récentes, BiOr 11, 1954, 145-160.

——, Les manuscrits du Désert de Juda. Publications et études, BiOr 14, 1957, 122-126.

——, Les manuscrits du Désert de Juda. Livres récents, BiOr 16, 1959, 162-176.

——, Six années d'études des manuscrits du désert de Juda (1952-1958), La secte de Qumrân et les origines du christianisme (Rech Bib 4), Bruges, 1959, 11-84.

——, Les manuscrits du Désert de Juda. Publications récentes, BiOr 20, 1963, 200-228.

——, Les manuscrits du Désert de Juda. Publications récentes importantes, BiOr 23, 1966, 133-142.

S. SEGERT, Some Trends in Qumran Research, ArOr 35, 1967, 128-144.

A. S. VAN DER WOUDE, De vondsten in de woestijn van Juda I-III, VoxTheol 32, 1961-1962, 1-9; 83-90; 159-168.

M. YIZHAR, Bibliography of Hebrew Publications on the Dead Sea Scrolls 1948-1964, Cambridge, 1967.

Periodicals regularly offering more or less ample bibliographical material:

Archiv für Orientforschung, Graz (Österreich).

Archiv Orientální, Prague.

Beth Miqra', Jerusalem.

Biblica, Rome (Elenchus bibliographicus biblicus, published separately from vol. 49, 1968).

Bibliographie der deutschen Zeitschriftenliteratur mit Einschluss von Sammelwerken, Osnabrück.

Bibliographie der fremdsprachigen Zeitschriftenliteratur, Osnabrück.

Bibliotheca Orientalis, Leiden.

Book List (The Society for Old Testament Studies Book List), Manchester.

Bulletin de Littérature Ecclésiastique, Toulouse.

Elenchus bibliographicus biblicus, vide *sub* Biblica.

Ephemerides Theologicae Lovanienses, Louvain.

Internationale Zeitschriftenschau für Bibelwissenschaft und Grenzgebiete, Düsseldorf.

New Testament Abstracts, Weston (Mass.).

Kiryat Sepher, Jerusalem.

Revue de Qumrân, Paris.

Theologische Literaturzeitung, Berlin.

Theologische Rundschau, Tübingen.

Zeitschrift für die Alttestamentliche Wissenschaft, Berlin.

In addition much bibliographical material is presented in general works and in various translations (and commentaries), e.g. in J. CARMIGNAC e.a., Les textes de Qumrân traduits et annotés, Paris, I 1961, II 1963.

B. GENERAL PUBLICATIONS.
HISTORY OF THE DISCOVERIES

J. M. ALLEGRO, The Dead Sea Scrolls, London-Melbourne-Baltimore, 1956; American edition: The Dead Sea Scrolls and the Origins of Christianity, New York, 1957; German edition: Die Botschaft vom Toten Meer, Frankfurt a.M., 1957.

——, The People of the Dead Sea Scrolls in Text and Pictures, London, 1959.

——, The Dead Sea Scrolls: A Re-appraisal, Harmondsworth, 1964. [2nd (revised) edition of 'The Dead Sea Scrolls'].

H. BARDTKE, Die Handschriftenfunde am Toten Meer, Berlin, 1953.

——, Die Handschriftenfunde am Toten Meer, Band II: Die Sekte von Qumran, Berlin, 1958, 1961².

——, Die Handschriftenfunde in der Wüste Juda (= Die Handschriftenfunde am Toten Meer, Band III), Berlin, 1962.

—— (ed.), Qumran-Probleme. Vorträge des Leipziger Symposions über Qumran-Probleme 1961, Berlin, 1963.

F. F. BRUCE, Second Thoughts on the Dead Sea Scrolls, Revised and enlarged edition, London, 1961, Grand Rapids, 1961.

M. BURROWS, The Dead Sea Scrolls, New York, 1955; British edition: London, 1956; French edition: Les manuscrits de la Mer Morte,

Paris, 1957; German edition: Die Schriftrollen vom Toten Meer, München, 1957.

——, More Light on the Dead Sea Scrolls. New Scrolls and New Interpretations, New York, 1958; British edition: London, 1958; German edition: Mehr Klarheit über die Schriftrollen. Neue Rollen und neue Deutungen nebst Übersetzung wichtiger jüngst entdeckter Texte, München, 1959; French edition: Lumières nouvelles sur les manuscrits de la Mer Morte, Paris, 1959.

F. M. CROSS Jr., The Ancient Library of Qumrân and Modern Biblical Studies, London, 1958.

——, Die antike Bibliothek von Qumran und die moderne biblische Wissenschaft, Neukirchen, 1967. [German edition of 'The Ancient Library :...' revised and enlarged].

G. R. DRIVER, The Judaean Scrolls. The Problem and a Solution, Oxford, 1965.

A. DUPONT-SOMMER, Les écrits esséniens découverts près de la Mer Morte, Paris, 1959; German edition: Die essenischen Schriften vom Toten Meer, Tübingen, 1960; English edition: The Essene Writings from Qumran, Oxford, 1961; New York, 1962.

O. EISSFELDT, Einleitung in das Alte Testament, Tübingen, 1943; [Qumrân, 864-906]; English translation: Oxford, 1965.

A. N. GILKES, The Impact of the Dead Sea Scrolls, London, 1962.

H. HAAG, Die Handschriftenfunde aus der Wüste Juda, Zürich, 1958, Stuttgart, 1966².

R. K. HARRISON, The Dead Sea Scrolls. An Introduction, New York, 1961.

J. HEMPEL, Die Texte von Qumran in der heutigen Forschung. Weitere Mitteilungen über Text und Auslegung der am Nordwestende des Toten Meeres gefundenen hebräischen Handschriften, Göttingen, 1962.

E. M. LAPERROUSAZ, Les manuscrits de la Mer Morte, Paris, 1961.

A. R. C. LEANEY, R. P. C. HANSON, J. POSEN, A Guide to the Scrolls. Nottingham Studies on the Qumran Discoveries, London, 1958.

M. MANSOOR, The Dead Sea Scrolls. A College Textbook and a Study Guide, Leiden, 1964.

H. E. DEL MEDICO, L'énigme des manuscrits de la Mer Morte. Étude sur la date, la provenance et le contenu des manuscrits découverts dans la grotte I de Qumrân, Paris, 1957; English edition: The Riddle of the Scrolls, London, 1958.

J. T. MILIK, Dix ans de découvertes dans le Désert de Juda, Paris,

1957; English edition: Ten Years of Discovery in the Wilderness of Judaea, London, 1959.

J. VAN DER PLOEG, Vondsten in de woestijn van Juda. De Rollen der Dode Zee, Utrecht-Antwerpen, 1970⁴; English edition: The Excavations at Qumran. A Survey of the Judaean Brotherhood and its Ideas, London-New York-Toronto, 1958/1959; German edition: Funde in der Wüste Juda. Die Schriftrollen vom Toten Meer und die Brüderschaft von Qumrân, Köln, 1959.

——, e.a., La secte de Qumrân et les origines du christianisme. Communications aux IXᵉˢ Journées bibliques, Louvain, septembre 1957, éditées par J. VAN DER PLOEG, RechBib 4, Bruges, 1959.

Ch. RABIN, Qumran Studies, Oxford, 1957.

——(ed.), Essays on the Dead Sea Scrolls in Memory of E. L. Sukenik, Jerusalem, 1961. [Modern Hebrew].

——, Y. YADIN (edd.), Aspects of the Dead Sea Scrolls, ScrHier 4.

K. H. RENGSTORF, Ḥirbet Qumrân und die Bibliothek vom Toten Meer, Stuttgart, 1960.

C. ROTH, The Dead Sea Scrolls. A New Historical Approach, New York, 1965.

H. H. ROWLEY, The Dead Sea Scrolls from Qumran. The second Montefiore Memorial Lecture, University of Southampton, 1958.

——, Les manuscrits de Qumran. Bulletin de la faculté des lettres de Strasbourg 39, no. 3, 4, 1960/1961.

A. Y. SAMUEL, Treasure of Qumran: My Story of the Dead Sea Scrolls, Philadelphia (Pa.), 1966.

J. A. SANDERS, Palestinian Manuscripts 1947-1967, JBL 86, 1967, 431-440.

J. SCHREIDEN, Les Énigmes des Manuscrits de la Mer Morte, Wetteren (Belgium), 1961.

E. F. SUTCLIFFE, The Monks of Qumran as Depicted in the Dead Sea Scrolls, London, 1960.

F. M. TOCCI, I manoscritti del Mar Morto, Bari, 1967.

J. C. TREVER, The Untold Story of Qumran, Westwood (N.J.), 1965; German edition: Das Abenteuer von Qumran, Kasel, 1967. [A detailed description of the history of the first discoveries].

W. TYLOCH, Rekopisy z Qumran nad Morzem Martwym, Warszawa, 1963.

G. VERMES, Les manuscrits du Désert de Juda, Paris-Tournai-Rome-New York, 1953, 1954², 1953³; English edition: Discovery in the Judean Desert. The Dead Sea Scrolls and their Meaning, New York-Tournai-Paris-Rome, 1956.

D. WINTON-THOMAS, The Dead Sea Scrolls: What may we believe?, AnLeeds 6, 1966-1968 (Dead Sea Scroll Studies, 1969), 7-20.

Y. YADIN, The Hidden Scrolls from the Judaean Desert, Jerusalem, 1957; 2nd edition revised and enlarged, Jerusalem, 1957. [Modern Hebrew].

——, The Message of the Scrolls, London, 1957. [English edition of preceding work].

——, The Temple Scroll, BiAr 30, 1967, 135-139.

C. LINGUISTICA

1. GENERAL STUDIES. LINGUISTIC HISTORY.

Z. BEN ḤAYYIM, Traditions in the Hebrew Language, with Special Reference to the Dead Sea Scrolls, ScrHier 4, 200-214.

——, La tradition samaritaine et sa parenté avec les autres traditions de la langue hébraïque, MélPhLJ 3, 4, 5, 1958-1962, 89-128.

M. H. GOSHEN-GOTTSTEIN, Die Qumran-Rollen und die hebräische Sprachwissenschaft, 1948-1958, RQum I, 1958-1959, 103-112.

——, Linguistic Structure and Tradition in the Qumran Documents, ScrHier 4, 101-137.

——, Philologische Miszellen zu den Qumrantexten, RQum II, 1959-1960, 43-51.

——, The Qumran Scrolls and their Linguistic Status. Studies in Hebrew and Biblical Philology I, Jerusalem-Tel Aviv, 1959. [Modern Hebrew].

——, Text and Language in Bible and Qumran, Jerusalem-Tel Aviv, 1960. [Photographic reproduction of eleven articles published during the years 1949-1960].

J. M. GRINTZ, Hebrew as the Spoken and Written Language in the Last Days of the Second Temple, JBL 79, 1960, 32-47.

A. HURVITZ, Observations on the Language of the Third Apocryphal Psalm of Qumran, RQum V, 1964-1966, 225-232.

——, The Language and Date of Psalm 151 from Qumran, Eretz-Israel 8, Jerusalem, 1967, 82-87. [Modern Hebrew].

E. Y. KUTSCHER, The Language and Linguistic Background of the Complete Isaiah Scroll, Jerusalem, 1959. [Modern Hebrew].

E. Y. Kutscher, The Language of the Genesis Apocryphon. A
Preliminary Study, ScrHier 4, 1-35.
——, The Language and Linguistic Background of the Complete
Isaiah Scroll, Jerusalem, 1959. [Modern Hebrew].
——, Isaiah of the Dead Sea Scrolls. Its Language and its Linguistic
Background (STDJ VI), Leiden, in the press. [Translation of
preceding work].
M. Mansoor, Some Linguistic Aspects of the Qumran Texts, JSS 3,
1958, 40-54.
M. Martin, The Scribal Character of the Dead Sea Scrolls, I, II,
Louvain, 1958.
R. Meyer, Bemerkungen zu den hebräischen Aussprachetraditionen
von Chirbet Qumrân, ZAW 70, 1958, 39-48.
Ch. Rabin, The Historical Background of Qumran Hebrew, ScrHier 4,
144-161.
J. Schreiden, Les caractéristiques linguistiques de l'hébreu qumrânien
et leur inférence sur le problème historique, Mus 72, 1959, 153-157.
S. Segert, Zur Orthographie und Sprache der aramäischen Texte
von Wadi Murabba'at, ArOr 31, 1963, 122-137.
——, Sprachliche Bemerkungen zu einigen aramäischen Texten von
Qumran, ArOr 33, 1965, 190-206. [11QtgJob, 1QGenAp].
——, Bedeutung der Handschriftenkunde am Toten Meer für die
Aramaistik, Bibel und Qumran (Festschrift H. Bardtke), Berlin,
1968, 183-187.

2. Palaeography. Orthography

N. Avigad, The Palaeography of the Dead Sea Scrolls and Related
Documents, ScrHier 4, 56-87.
H. Bardtke, Zur Paläographie und zur Handschriftenkunde von
Qumrân, ThRsch 30, 1965, 296-315.
F. M. Cross, The Development of the Jewish Scripts, The Bible and
the Ancient Near East. Essays in Honor of W. F. Albright,
Garden City (N.Y.)-London, 1961, 133-202.
D. N. Freedman, The Massoretic Text and the Qumran Scrolls:
a Study in Orthography, Textus 2, 1962, 87-102.
R. S. Hanson, Palaeo-Hebrew Script in the Hasmonean Age, BASOR
no. 175, 1964, 26-42.
J. Leveen, The Orthography of the Hebrew Scroll of Isaiah; A,

Proceedings of the 22nd Congress of Orientalists (Istanbul, 1951), Leiden, 1957, 577-583.

S. SEGERT, Zur Orthographie und Sprache der aramäischen Texte von Wadi Murabbaʻat, ArOr 31, 1963, 122-137.

P. WERNBERG-MØLLER, Studies in the Defective Spellings in the Isaiah Scroll of St. Mark's Monastery, JSS 3, 1958, 244-264.

3. GRAMMATICAL STUDIES

Z. BEN ḤAYYIM, Traditions in the Hebrew Language, with Special Reference to the Dead Sea Scrolls, ScrHier 4, 200-214.

——, La tradition samaritaine et sa parenté avec les autres traditions de la langue hébraïque, MélPhLJ 3, 4, 5, 1958-1962, 89-128.

J. CARMIGNAC, Le temps des verbes dans les "interprétations" de la grotte 4, RQum III, 1961-1962, 533-538.

——, Un aramaïsme biblique et qumrânien: l'infinitif placé après son complément d'objet, RQum V, 1964-1966, 503-520.

B. JONGELING, Les formes QṬWL dans l'hébreu des manuscrits de Qumrân, RQum I, 1958-1959, 483-494.

T. LEAHY, Studies in the Syntax of 1 QS, Bibl 41, 1960, 135-157.

M. MARTIN, The Use of Second Person Singular Suffixes in 1 QIs[a], Mus 70, 1957, 127-144.

R. MEYER, Spuren eines westsemitischen Präsens-Futur in den Texten von Chirbet Qumran, Von Ugarit nach Qumran (Festschrift O. Eissfeldt), Berlin, 1961[2], 118-128.

——, Hebräische Grammatik, I. Einleitung, Schrift- und Lauthlehre, Berlin, 1966; II. Formenlehre, Flexionstabellen, Berlin, 1969 (Sammlung Göschen 763/764).

J. VAN DER PLOEG, L'usage du parfait et de l'imparfait comme moyen de datation dans le commentaire d'Habacuc, Les manuscrits de la Mer Morte. Colloque de Strasbourg, 25-27 mai 1955, Paris, 1957, 25-35, 131.

O. RÖSSLER, Eine bisher unbekannte Tempusform im Althebräischen, ZDMG 111, 1961, 445-451.

A. SPERBER, A Grammar of Masoretic Hebrew. A General Introduction to the Pre-Masoretic Bible, Copenhagen, 1959.

S. J. DE VRIES, The Syntax of Tenses and Interpretation in the Hodayoth, RQum V, 1964-1966, 375-414.

——, Consecutive Constructions in the 1Q Sectarian Scrolls, Dōrōn. Hebraic Studies in Honor of A. I. Katsh, New York, 1965, 75-87.

P. Wernberg-Møller, The Noun of the Qᵉṭōl Class in the Massoretic Text, RQum II, 1959-1960, 448-450.

H. Yalon, Studies in the Dead Sea Scrolls, Philological Essays (1949-1952), Jerusalem, 1967. [Modern Hebrew].

4. Lexicographical Studies

A. A. Anderson, The Use of "Ruaḥ" in 1QS, 1QH and 1QM, JSS 7, 1962, 293-303.

J. P. Asmussen, Das iranische Lehnwort naḥšir in der Kriegsrolle von Qumran (1QM), AcOr(K) 26, 1961, 3-20.

H. A. Brongers, Das Wort NPŠ in den Qumranschriften, RQum IV, 1963-1964, 407-415.

A. M. Denis, Les thèmes de connaissance dans le Document de Damas, Louvain, 1967.

B. M. Dombrowski, HYḤD in 1QS and tò koinón: An Instance of Early Greek and Jewish Synthesis, HThR 59, 1966, 293-307.

J. C. Greenfield, Lexicographical Notes I, HUCA 29, 1958, 203-228; II, HUCA 30, 1959, 141-151.

——, The Root "GBL" in Mishnaic Hebrew and in the Hymnic Literature from Qumran, RQum II, 1959-1960, 155-162.

M. Z. Kaddari, The Root TKN in the Qumran Texts, RQum V, 1964-1966, 219-224.

E. Katz, Die Bedeutung des hapax legomenon der Qumraner Handschriften, HUAHA, Bratislava, 1967.

H. Kosmala, The Three Nets of Belial. A Study in the Terminology of Qumran and the New Testament, ASTI 4, 1965, 91-113.

M. R. Lehmann, Talmudic Material Relating to the Dead Sea Scrolls, RQum I, 1958-1959, 391-404.

——, Identification of the Copper Scroll based on its Technical Terms, RQum V, 1964-1966, 97-105.

J. C. de Moor, Lexical Remarks concerning Yaḥad and Yaḥdaw, VT 7, 1957, 350-355.

R. E. Murphy, Šaḥat in the Qumran Literature, Bibl 39, 1958, 61-66.

——, Yeṣer in the Qumran Literature, Bibl 39, 1958, 334-344.

——, BŚR in the Qumrân Literature, Sacra Pagina. Miscellanea biblica Congressus Internationalis Catholici de re biblica II, Paris-Gembloux, 1959, 60-76.

——, GBR and GBWRH in the Qumran Writings, Lex Tua Veritas (Fetsschrift H.Junker), Trier, 1961, 137-143.

J. Neusner, The Fellowship (ḤBWRH) in the Second Jewish Common-
wealth, HThR 53, 1960, 125-142.
——, ḤBR and N'MN, RQum V, 1964-1966, 119-122.
I. Rabinowitz, The Qumran Authors' SPR HHGW/Y, JNES 20,
1961, 109-114.
K. H. Rengstorf, The Concept "Goral" in the Dead Sea Scrolls,
Tarbiz 35, 1965-1966, 108-121. [Modern Hebrew].
G. Rinaldi, La particella uBeKēN in 1QSa I, 11, StBFranc, LA 13,
1962-1963, 101-109.
L. H. Silbermann, Unriddling the Riddle. A Study in the Structure
and Language of the Habakkuk Pesher, RQum III, 1961-1962,
323-364.
R. S. Sirat, Évolution sémantique de la racine "'TQ" en hébreu,
RÉNLO 3, 1966, 35-62.
D. Sperber, An Early Meaning of the Word ŠAPUD, RÉJ 4 (= 124),
1965, 179-184.
S. Wagner, YD' in den Lobliedern von Qumran, Bibel und Qumran
(Festschrift H. Bardtke), 232-252.
M. Wallenstein, Some Aspects of the Vocabulary and Morphology
of the Hymns Scroll with special Reference to the Interpretation
of Related Obscure Passages, VT 9, 1959, 101-107.
H. Yalon, Studies in the Dead Sea Scrolls, Philological Essays (1949-
1952), Jerusalem, 1967. [Modern Hebrew].
W. Zimmerli, ḤSD im Schrifttum von Qumran, Hommages à André
Dupont-Sommer, Paris, 1971, 439-449.

Moreover there are many articles in the Theologisches Wörterbuch
zum Neuen Testament by G. Kittel (û) e.a., Stuttgart, 1935-
(from vol. V onwards) containing a section on the occurrence and the
significance of words in Qumran literature. Vide RQum I, 1958-1959,
477-478; II, 1959-1960, 125; V, 1964-1966, 466-467; VII, 1969-1971,
135.

5. Concordances. Dictionary.

J. Carmignac, Concordance de la "Règle de la guerre", RQum I,
1958-1959, 7-49.
Bilhah Habermann, Concordance on 1QpH, CD, 1QSa, 1QM, 1QH, in:
A. M. Habermann, Megilloth Midbar Yehudah. The Scrolls
from the Judean Desert, Jerusalem, 1959. [Modern Hebrew].

K. G. Kuhn (ed.), Konkordanz zu den Qumrantexten, Göttingen, 1960.

———, Nachträge zur "Konkordanz zu den Qumrantexten", RQum IV, 1963-1964, 163-234.

———, Rückläufiges Hebräisches Wörterbuch, Göttingen, 1958.

H. Lignée, Concordance de "1Q Genesis Apocryphon", RQum I, 1958-1959, 163-186.

Several text-editions contain also indexes of words.

D. TEXT-EDITIONS

1. Major Publications

J. M. Allegro, (with the collaboration of Arnold A. Anderson), Qumrân Cave 4, vol. I (4Q 158 - 4Q 186), DJD V, Oxford, 1968. [Review Article by J. Strugnell in RQum VII, 1969-1971, 163-276].

N. Avigad, Y. Yadin, A Genesis Apocryphon. A Scroll from the Wilderness of Judaea, Jerusalem, 1956.

M. Baillet, J. T. Milik, R. de Vaux O.P., (avec une contribution de H. W. Baker), Les "Petites Grottes" de Qumrân: Les grottes 2Q, 3Q, 5Q, 6Q, 7Q à 10Q, le rouleau de cuivre. Vol. I: Textes, Vol. II: Planches, DJD III, Oxford, 1962.

D. Barthélemy O.P., J. T. Milik, (with contributions by R. de Vaux O.P., G. M. Crowfoot, H. J. Plenderleith, G. L. Harding), Qumrân Cave I, DJD I, Oxford, 1955.

P. Benoit O.P., J. T. Milik, R. de Vaux O.P., (avec des contributions de † Mrs. G. M. Crowfoot et Miss E. Crowfoot, A. Grohmann), Les grottes de Murabba'at. Vol. I Texte, Vol. II Planches, DJD II, Oxford, 1961.

M. Burrows, (with the assistance of John C. Trever and William H. Brownlee), The Dead See Scrolls of St. Mark's Monastery. Volume I: The Isaiah Manuscript and the Habakkuk Commentary, New Haven, 1950.

———, (with the assistance of John C. Trever and William H. Brownlee), The Dead Sea Scrolls of St. Mark's Monastery. Volume II, Fascicle 2: Plates and Transcription of the Manual of Discipline, New Haven, 1951. [Publication not continued].

J. Carmignac, La Règle de la Guerre des Fils de Lumière contre les Fils de Ténèbres. Texte restauré, traduit et commenté, Paris, 1958.

M. Delcor, Les Hymnes de Qumrân (Hodayot). Texte hébreu, Intrc-duction, Traduction, Commentaire, Paris, 1962.

A. M. Habermann, Megilloth Midbar Yehudah. The Scrolls from the Judean Desert, Jerusalem, 1959. [The Commentary on Habakkuk, the Rule of the Community, the Damaskus Document, the War Scroll, the Psalms of Thanksgivings, and supplements; edited with vocalization, introduction and notes; modern Hebrew].

E. Koffmahn, Die Doppelurkunden aus der Wüste Juda, STDJ V, Leiden, 1968.

J. Licht, The Thanksgiving Scroll. A Scroll from the Wilderness of Judaea. Text, Introduction, Commentary and Glossary, Jeru-salem, 1957. [Modern Hebrew].

——, The Rule Scroll. A Scroll from the Wilderness of Judaea. 1QS-1QSa-1QSb. Text, Introduction and Commentary, Jerusalem, 1965. [Modern Hebrew].

E. Lohse, Die Texte aus Qumran hebräisch und deutsch mit maso-retischer Punktation, Übersetzung, Einführung und Anmerkun-gen, München, 1964.

J. van der Ploeg O.P., A. S. van der Woude (avec la collaboration de B. Jongeling), Le Targum de Job de la grotte XI de Qumrân, Leiden, 1971.

Chaim Rabin, The Zadokite Documents. I: The admonition, II: The laws. Second revised edition, Oxford, 1958.

J. A. Sanders, The Psalms Scroll of Qumrân Cave 11 (11QPsᵃ). DJD IV, Oxford, 1965.

——, The Dead Sea Psalms Scroll, New York, 1967.

S. Schechter, Fragments of a Zadokite Work; Fragments of the Book of the Commandments of Anan. Documents of Jewish Sectaries I and II. Prolegomenon by J. A. Fitzmyer, S.J. Reprint. Ktav Publ. House, New York, 1970.

E. L. Sukenik, 'Oṣar ha-Megilloth ha-Genuzoth šè-bi-yᵉdēy ha-Universitah ha-Ivrith (N. Avigad ed.), Jerusalem, 1954. [Modern Hebrew].

——, The Dead Sea Scrolls of the Hebrew University (Prepared for the press by N. Avigad), Jerusalem, 1955. [== Preceding work in English].

Y. Yadin, Megillath Milḥemet Bᵉnēy 'Or bi-Bᵉnēy Ḥošek mi-Megilloth Midbar Yehudah, Jerusalem, 1955, 1957². [Modern Hebrew].

——, The Scroll of the War of the Sons of Light Against the Sons
of Darkness, edited with Commentary and Introduction by
Yigael YADIN, translated from the Hebrew by Batya and Chaim
RABIN, Oxford, 1962. [= Preceding work].
——, The Ben Sira Scroll from Masada. With Introduction, Emen-
dations and Commentary, Jerusalem, 1965.
——, The Ben Sira Scroll from Masada, Eretz-Israel VIII. E. L. Suke-
nik Memorial Volume, Jerusalem, 1967, 1-45. [= Preceding work
in modern Hebrew].
——, Tefillin from Qumran (xQPhyl 1-4), Jerusalem, 1969. [= Modern
Hebrew edition in Eretz-Israel IX. W. F. Albright Volume,
Jerusalem, 1969, Hebrew Section, 60-85].
S. ZEITLIN, The Zadokite Fragments. Facsimile of the Manuscripts
in the Cairo Genizah Collection in the Possession of the University
Library, Cambridge, England. With an Introduction by Solomon
ZEITLIN, Philadelphia, 1952.

2. MINOR PUBLICATIONS

The following studies are mostly preliminary editions published in
various periodicals. In the meanwhile a number of these texts have been
published in the official edition: Discoveries in the Judaean Desert,
Oxford, 1955-   . It is, however, of great interest to mention these
preliminary publications, since a more or less ample commentary
is usually added to them.

J. M. ALLEGRO, A Newly Discovered Fragment of a Commentary on
Psalm XXXVII from Qumran, PEQ 86, 1954, 69-75.
——, Further Light on the History of the Qumrân Sect, JBL 75,
1956, 89-95. [4QpNah, 4QPs 37, 4QpHos, 4QFlor].
——, Further Messianic References in Qumran Literature, JBL 75,
1956, 174-187.
——, More Isaiah Commentaries from Qumran's Fourth Cave, JBL 77,
1958, 215-221. [4QpIs^b, 4QpIs^c, 4QpIs^d].
——, Fragments of a Qumran Scroll of Eschatological Midrāšîm,
JBL 77, 1958, 350-354.
——, A Recently Discovered Fragment of a Commentary on Hosea
from Qumran's Fourth Cave, JBL 78, 1959, 142-147. [4QpHos^b].
——, An Unpublished Fragment of Essene Halakhah (4QOrdinances),
JSS 6, 1961, 71-73.

——, More Unpublished Pieces of a Qumran Commentary on Nahum (4QpNah), JSS 7, 1962, 304-308.

——, Some Unpublished Fragments of Pseudepigraphical Literature from Qumran's Fourth Cave, AnLeeds 4, 1962-1963, 3-5.

——, The Wiles of the Wicked Woman. A Sapiential Work from Qumran's Fourth Cave, PEQ 96, 1964, 53-55.

——, An Astrological Cryptic Document from Qumran, JSS 9, 1964, 291-294.

M. BAILLET, Fragment araméen de Qumran 2. Description de la Jérusalem Nouvelle, RB 62, 1955, 222-245.

——, Fragments du Document de Damas, Qumrân grotte 6, RB 63, 1956, 513-523.

——, Un recueil liturgique de Qumrân, grotte 4: "Les Paroles des Luminaires", RB 68, 1961, 195-250 et planches XXIV-XXVIII.

——, Débris de textes sur papyrus de la grotte 4 de Qumrân, RB 71, 1964, 353-371. [a. Textes liturgiques; b. Textes sapientiels et prophétiques; c. Règle de la Guerre des Fils de Lumière contre les Fils de Ténèbres. Certitudes et Problèmes; d. Textes d'un genre mal reconnu; e. Déchets].

D. BARTHÉLEMY, Les devanciers d'Aquila. Première publication intégrale du texte des fragments du Dodécaprophéton trouvés dans le désert de Juda, précédée d'une étude sur les traductions et recensions grecques de la Bible réalisées au premier siècle de notre ère sous l'influence du rabbinat palestinien. Supplements to VT 10, Leiden, 1963.

F. M. CROSS Jr., The Ancient Library of Qumran and Modern Biblical Studies, Garden City (N.Y.)-London, 1961[2]. [pp. 188, 191: 4Q-Sam[a]: 2 Sam. 4:1s; 24:16s.].

——, Die antike Bibliothek von Qumran, Neukirchen, 1967. [pp. 175, 177: 4QSam[a]: 2 Sam.4:1s; 24:16s.].

R. DEICHGRÄBER, Fragmente einer Jubiläen-Handschrift aus Höhle 3 von Qumran, RQum V, 1964-1966, 415-422.

J. A. FITZMYER, The Aramaic "Elect of God" Text from Qumran Cave IV, CBQ 27, 1965, 348-372.

M. DE JONGE, A. S. VAN DER WOUDE, 11QMelchizedek and the New Testament, NTSt 12, 1965-1966, 301-326.

B. JONGELING, Publication provisoire d'un fragment provenant de la grotte 11 de Qumrân (11Q JérNouv ar), JSJ 1, 1970, 58-64.

——, Note additionnelle, JSJ 1, 1970, 185-186.

K. G. KUHN, Phylakterien aus Höhle 4 von Qumran, Heidelberg, 1957.

E. M. Laperrousaz, Publication des cinq chapitres découverts à Masada et d'un autre passage, provenant de Qumrân, de l'Ecclésiastique en hébreu, RHR 169, 1966, 235-237.

J. T. Milik, Le Testament de Lévi en araméen. Fragment de la grotte 4 de Qumrân, RB 62, 1955, 398-406.

——, "Prière de Nabonide" et autres écrits d'un cycle de Daniel. Fragments araméens de Qumrân 4, RB 63, 1956, 408-415.

——, Deux Documents inédits du Désert de Juda, Bibl 38, 1957, 245-268. [4QPs 31: 24s; 33: 1-18; 35: 4-20 and an Aramaic Deed of Sale].

——, Fragment d'une source du Psautier (4QPs 89) et fragments des Jubilés, du Document de Damas, d'un Phylactère dans la grotte 4 de Qumrân, RB 73, 1966, 94-106.

——, 4Q Visions de 'Amram et une citation d'Origène, RB 79, 1972, 77-97.

J. van der Ploeg, Le Psaume XCI dans une recension de Qumrân, RB 72, 1965, 210-217.

——, Fragments d'un manuscrit de Psaumes de Qumrân (11 QPs^b), RB 74, 1967, 408-412.

——, Lév. IX, 23-X, 2 dans un texte de Qumran, Bibel und Qumran (Festschrift Bardtke), 153-155.

——, Un petit rouleau de psaumes apocryphes (11QPsAp^a), Tradition und Glaube. Festgabe für K. G. Kuhn, Göttingen, 1971, 128-139.

I. Rabinowitz, The Alleged Orphism of 11QPss 28,3-12, ZAW 76, 1964, 193-200.

A. Rofe (Roifer), Further Manuscript Fragments of the Jubilees in the Third Cave of Qumran, Tarbiz 34, 1964-1965, 333-336. [Modern Hebrew].

J. A. Sanders, The Scroll of Psalms (11QPss) from Cave 11. A Preliminary Report, BASOR no. 165, 1962, 11-15.

——, Ps 151 in 11QPss, ZAW 75, 1963, 73-86.

——, Two Non-Canonical Psalms in 11QPs^a, ZAW 76, 1964, 57-75.

P. W. Skehan, The Apocryphal Psalm 151, CBQ 25, 1963, 407-409.

——, A Psalm Manuscript from Qumran (4QPs^b), CBQ 26, 1964, 313-322.

J. Starcky, Un texte messianique araméen de la grotte 4 de Qumrân, Mémorial du cinquantenaire de l'École des Langues Orientales Anciennes de l'Institut Catholique de Paris, 1914-1964, Paris, 1964, 51-66.

———, Psaumes apocryphes de la grotte 4 de Qumran (4QPsᶠ VII-X), RB 73, 1966, 353-371.

H. STEGEMANN, Der pešer Psalm 37, RQum IV, 1963-1964, 235-270.

———, Weitere Stücke von 4QPsalm 37, von 4QPatriarchal Blessings und Hinweis auf eine unedierte Handschrift aus Höhle 4Q mit Exzerpten aus dem Deuteronomium, RQum VI, 1967-1969, 193-227.

J. STRUGNELL, The Angelic Liturgy at Qumrân, 4QSerek Širôt 'Olat Haššabât, Congress Volume Oxford 1959, Supplements to VT 7, Leiden, 1960, 318-345.

———, More Psalms of "David", CBQ 27, 1965, 207-216.

S. TALMON, The Order of Prayers of the Sect from the Judaean Desert, Tarbiz 29, 1959-1960, 1-20. [Modern Hebrew].

J. C. TREVER, Completion of the Publication of Some Fragments from Qumran Cave I, RQum V, 1964-1966, 323-344.

———, A Further Note about 1QPrayers, RQum VI, 1967-1969, 137-138. [1QPrayers compared with 4Q181 (vide J. M. ALLEGRO, Some Unpublished Fragments ...)].

A. S. VAN DER WOUDE, Melchisedek als himmlische Erlösergestalt in den neugefundenen Midraschim aus Qumran Höhle XI, OTS 14, Leiden, 1965, 354-373.

———, Ein neuer Segensspruch aus Qumran (11QBer), Bibel und Qumran (Festschrift Bardtke), 253-258.

———, Fragmente des Buches Jubiläen aus Qumran Höhle XI, Tradition und Glaube. Festgabe für K. G. Kuhn, Göttingen, 1971, 140-146 + plates.

———, vide M. DE JONGE.

Y. YADIN, Another Fragment (E) of the Psalms Scroll from Qumran Cave 11 (11 QPsᵃ), Textus 5, 1966, 1-10.

E. TRANSLATIONS AND COMMENTARIES

For translations and commentaries see also section IV, Text-editions. It is superfluous to list here again all the translations and commentaries presented in that section. See also the sections VIh, j, k: Fragments from Qumrân Cave 1, Texts from Qumrân Cave 4, Other Texts especially from Cave 11.

J. M. ALLEGRO, The Treasure of the Copper Scroll, Garden City (N.Y.)-

London, 1960; Revised Edition, Garden City (N.Y.), 1964.

J. D. Amusin, The Texts of Qumran. Part I (Monuments of Oriental Literature XXXIII, 1), Moscow, 1971 [Russian].

M. Baillet, Remarques sur le manuscrit du livre des Jubilés de la grotte 3 de Qumrân, RQum V, 1964-1966, 423-433.

R. Bergmeier, H. Pabot, Ein Lied von der Erschaffung der Sprache. Sinn und Aufbau von 1QHodayot I, 27-31, RQum V, 1964-1966, 435-439.

H. A. Brongers, De Gedragsregels der Qumrangemeente, Amsterdam, 1958.

——, De rol van de strijd, Amsterdam, 1960.

J. Cantera Ortiz de Urbina, El Comentario de Habacuc de Qumran (Textos y Estudios del Seminario filológico Cardenal Cisneros), Madrid-Barcelona, 1960.

J. Carmignac, La Règle de la Guerre des Fils de Lumière contre les Fils de Ténèbres. Texte restauré, traduit et commenté, Paris, 1958.

——, P. Guilbert, Les textes de Qumrân traduits et annotés. I, La Règle de la Communauté, La Règle de la Guerre, Les Hymnes, Paris, 1961.

——, É. Cothenet, H. Lignée, Les textes de Qumrân traduits et annotés. II, Règle de la Congrégation, Recueil de bénédictions, Interprétations de prophètes et de psaumes, Document de Damas, Apocryphe de la Genèse, Fragments des grottes 1 et 4, Paris, 1963.

——, Le Recueil de prières liturgiques de la grotte 1, RQum IV, 1963-1964, 271-276.

——, La forme poétique du Psaume 151, RQum IV, 1963-1964, 371-378.

——, Les horoscopes de Qumrân, RQum V, 1964-1966, 199-217.

——, Un texte messianique araméen, RQum V, 1964-1966, 206-217.

——, Précisions sur la forme poétique du Psaume 151, RQum V, 1964-1966, 249-252.

——, Poème allégorique sur la secte rivale ("The Wiles of the Wicked Woman"), RQum V, 1964-1966, 361-374.

R. Deichgräber, Fragmente einer Jubiläen-Handschrift aus Höhle 3 von Qumran, RQum V, 1964-1966, 415-422.

M. Delcor, Les Hymnes de Qumrân. Texte hébreu, Introduction, Traduction et Commentaire, Paris, 1962.

——, Recherches sur un horoscope en langue hébraïque provenant de Qumrân, RQum V, 1964-1966, 521-542.

——, L'hymne à Sion du rouleau des Psaumes de la grotte 11 de Qumrân (11QPsa), RQum VI, 1967-1969, 71-88.

A. Dupont-Sommer, Les écrits esséniens découverts près de la Mer Morte, Paris, 1959; German edition: Die essenischen Schriften vom Toten Meer, Tübingen, 1960; English edition: The Essene Writings from Qumran, Oxford, 1961.

——, Le Commentaire de Nahum découvert près de la Mer Morte (4QpNah), Sem 13, 1963, 55-88.

——, Deux documents horoscopiques esséniens découverts à Qoumrân, près de la Mer Morte, CRAIBL 1965, 239-253.

J. A. Fitzmyer, The Genesis Apocryphon of Qumran Cave I. A Commentary, Rome, 1966; 1971².

——, Further Light on Melchizedek from Qumran Cave 11, JBL 16, 1966, 25-41.

H. Goedhart, De slothymne van het Manual of Discipline. A theological-exegetical study of 1QS, X 9-XI 22, Rotterdam, 1965.

J. G. Harris, The Commentary on Habakkuk. An Introduction to the Study of the Qumrân Commentary on Habakkuk for the General Reader, London, 1966.

S. Holm-Nielsen, Hodayot. Psalms from Qumrân (Acta Theologica Danica, vol. II), Aarhus, 1960.

M. de Jonge, A. S. van der Woude, 11Q Melchizedek and the New Testament, NTSt 12, 1965-1966, 301-326.

B. Jongeling, Le rouleau de la Guerre des manuscrits de Qumrân. Commentaire et Traduction, Assen, 1962.

E. Koffmahn, Die Doppelurkunden aus der Wüste Juda, STDJ V, Leiden, 1968.

A. R. C. Leaney, The Rule of Qumran and its Meaning. Introduction, Translation and Commentary, London, 1966.

M. R. Lehmann, Studies in the Murabba'at and Naḥal Ḥever Documents, RQum IV, 1963-1964, 53-81.

——, Identification of the Copper Scroll based on its Technical Terms, RQum V, 1964-1966, 97-105.

J. Licht, The Thanksgiving Scroll. A Scroll from the Wilderness of Judaea. Text, Introduction, Commentary and Glossary, Jerusalem, 1957. [Modern Hebrew].

——, The Rule Scroll. A Scroll from the Wilderness of Judaea. 1QS-1QSa-1QSb. Text, Introduction and Commentary, Jerusalem, 1965. [Modern Hebrew].

E. Lohse, Die Texte aus Qumran. Hebräisch und deutsch mit maso-retischer Punktation, Übersetzung, Einführung und Anmerkungen, Darmstadt-München, 1964.

J. MAIER, Die Texte vom Toten Meer. I, Übersetzung. II, Anmerkungen, München-Basel, 1960.

——, Weitere Stücke zum Nahumkommentar aus der Höhle 4 von Qumran, Judaica 18, 1962, 215-250.

M. MANSOOR, The Thanksgiving Hymns, STDJ III, Leiden/Grand Rapids, 1961.

R. MEYER, Das Gebet des Nabonid. Eine in den Qumranhandschriften wiederentdeckte Weisheitserzählung, Berlin, 1962.

J. T. MILIK, Le rouleau de cuivre de Qumrân (3Q 15). Traduction et commentaire topographique, RB 66, 1959, 321-357.

——, The Copper Document from Cave III of Qumran: Translation and Commentary, ADAJ 4/5, 1960, 137-155.

G. MOLIN, Lob Gottes aus der Wüste. Lieder und Gebete aus den Handschriften vom Toten Meer, Freiburg i.Br./München, 1957.

E. NIELSEN, B. OTZEN, Dødehavsteksterne. Skrifter fra den Jødiske Menighed i Qumran i Oversættelse og med Noter, København, 1959.

J. VAN DER PLOEG, Le rouleau de la Guerre, STDJ II, Leiden/Grand Rapids, 1959.

Ch. RABIN, The Zadokite Documents. I, The admonition. II, The laws. Edited with a translation and notes. Second revised edition, Oxford, 1958.

J. A. SANDERS, The Dead Sea Psalms Scroll, New York, 1967.

O. J. R. SCHWARZ, Der erste Teil der Damaskusschrift und das Alte Testament, Diest, 1966.

A. VAN SELMS, De rol der lofprijzingen. Een der Dode-Zeerollen vertaald en toegelicht, Baarn, 1957.

H. STEGEMANN, Der Pešer Psalm 37 aus Höhle 4 von Qumran, RQum IV, 1963-1964, 235-270.

——, Weitere Stücke von 4QPsalm 37, von 4QPatriarchal Blessings und Hinweis auf eine unedierte Handschrift aus Höhle 4 mit Exzerpten aus dem Deuteronomium, RQum VI, 1967-1969, 193-227.

G. VERMES, The Dead Sea Scrolls in English (Pelican Books A 551), Harmondsworth, Middlesex, 1962.

P. WERNBERG-MØLLER, The Manual of Discipline, translated and annotated, with an introduction, STDJ I, Leiden, 1957/Grand Rapids 1958.

A. S. VAN DER WOUDE, De dankpsalmen, Amsterdam, 1957.

——, Bijbelcommentaren en Bijbelse verhalen, Amsterdam, 1958.

—— —, Melchisedek als himmlische Erlösergestalt in den neugefundenen eschatologischen Midraschim aus Qumran Höhle XI, OTS 14, Leiden, 1965, 354-373.

——, Ein neuer Segensspruch aus Qumran (11QBer), Bibel und Qumran (Festschrift Bardtke), 253-258.

——, vide M. DE JONGE.

Y. YADIN, The Scroll of the War of the Sons of Light against the Sons of Darkness, edited with Commentary and Introduction by Yigael YADIN, translated from the Hebrew by Batya and Chaim RABIN, Oxford, 1962.

——, The Ben Sira Scroll from Masada, with Introduction, Emendations and Commentary, Jerusalem, 1965.

R. YARON, The Murabba'at Documents, JJS 11, 1960, 157-171.

F. STUDIES ON VARIOUS MANUSCRIPTS

In this section we do not mention again all the Translations and Commentaries enumerated above.

a. *The Damaskus Document* (CD)

J. CARMIGNAC, Comparaison entre les manuscrits "A" et "B" du Document de Damas, RQum II, 1959-1960, 53-67.

R. DEICHGRÄBER, Zur Messiaserwartung der Damaskusschrift, ZAW 78, 1966, 333-343.

A. M. DENIS, Les thèmes de connaissance dans le Document de Damas, Louvain, 1967.

H. W. HUPPENBAUER, Der Mensch zwischen zwei Welten. Der Dualismus der Texte von Qumran (Höhle I) und der Damaskusfragmente. Ein Beitrag zur Vorgeschichte des Evangeliums, Zürich, 1959. [= Diss. Basel, 1958, partly abridged].

A. JAUBERT, "Le pays de Damas", RB 65, 1958, 214-248.

Ch. RABIN, The Zadokite Documents. I, The admonition. II, The laws. Edited with a translation and notes. Second revised edition, Oxford, 1958.

O. J. R. SCHWARZ, Der erste Teil der Damaskusschrift und das Alte Testament, Diest, 1966.

b. *The Isaiah Scrolls from Qumran Cave* 1 (1QIsᵃ, 1QIsᵇ)

S. A. Birnbaum, The Date of the Incomplete Isaiah Scroll from
Qumrân, PEQ 92, 1960, 19-26.

W. H. Brownlee, The Meaning of the Qumrân Scrolls for the Bible
with Special Attention to the Book of Isaiah, Oxford, 1964.

J. Carmignac, Six passages d'Isaïe éclairés par Qumran, Bibel und
Qumran (Festschrift Bardtke), 37-46.

D. Flusser, The Text of Isaiah 49:17 in the Dead Sea Scrolls, Textus 2,
1962, 140-142.

F. D. James, A Critical Examination of the Text of Isaiah based on
the Dead Sea Scroll of Isaiah, the Masoretic Text, the Septuagint
and the Isaiah Texts of Clement of Alexandria, Origen and
Eusebius, diss., Boston, 1959. [Micro-film, no. 59-3466].

E. J. Kissane, The Qumrân Text of Isaiah IX, 7-9, Sacra Pagina.
Miscellanea biblica Congressus Internationalis Catholici de re
biblica I, Paris-Gembloux, 1959, 413-418.

B. J. Roberts, The Second Isaiah Scroll from Qumrân, BJRL 42,
1959-1960, 132-144.

J. R. Rosenbloom, The Dead Sea Isaiah Scroll: A Literary Analysis.
A Comparison with the Masoretic Text and the Biblia Hebraica,
Grand Rapids, Mich., 1970.

P. Sacchi, Il Rotolo A di Isaia (Problemi di storia del testo), Atti e
Memorie 30 (Nuova Serie 16), 1965, 27-111.

I. L. Seeligmann, Isaiah 53,11 according to the Septuagint, 1Q-
Isaiahᵃ and 1QIsaiahᵇ, Tarbiz 27, 1957-1958 (Presented to
Gershom Sholem in Honour of his sixtieth Birthday), 127-141.
[Modern Hebrew].

S. Talmon, DSIa as a witness to ancient exegesis of the Book of
Isaiah, ASTI 1, 1962, 62-72.

J. Ziegler, Die Vorlage der Isaias-Septuagint (LXX) und die erste
Isaias-Rolle von Qumran (1QIsᵃ), JBL 78, 1959, 34-59.

c. *The Habakkuk Commentary* (1QpHab)

J. D. Amusin, The Qumran Commentaries and their Significance for
the History of the Qumran Community, Moscow, 1967.

——, Bemerkungen zu den Qumran-Kommentaren, Bibel und Qumran
(Festschrift Bardtke), 9-19.

K. M. T. Atkinson, The Historical Setting of the Habakkuk Commentary, JSS 4, 1959, 238-263.

W. H. BROWNLEE, The Text of Habakkuk in the Ancient Commentary from Qumran, Philadelphia (Pa.), 1959.
F. F. BRUCE, The Dead Sea Habakkuk Scroll, AnLeeds 1, 1958-1959, 5-24.
——, Biblical Exegesis in the Qumran Texts, Exegetica III, 1, The Hague, 1959; British edition, completely reset, London, 1960.
A. DÍEZ-MACHO, El texto biblico del comentario de Habacuc de Qumran, Lex Tua Veritas (Festschrift H. Junker), Trier, 1961, 59-64.
J. G. HARRIS, The Commentary on Habakkuk. An Introduction to the Study of the Qumrân Commentary on Habakkuk for the General Reader, London, 1966.
G. JEREMIAS, Der Lehrer der Gerechtigkeit, Göttingen, 1963.
S. LOWY, Some Aspects of Normative and Sectarian Interpretation of the Scriptures, AnLeeds 6, 1966-1968, 98-163.
H. E. DEL MEDICO, L'identification des Kittim avec les Romains, VT 10, 1960, 448-453.
L. M. MUNTINGH, Enige variante bij die werkwoord in die Habakkuk-kommentaar, HTS 14, 1958-1959, 79-82.
J. VAN DER PLOEG, L'usage du parfait et de l'imparfait comme moyen de datation dans le commentaire d'Habacuc, Les manuscrits de la Mer Morte, Colloque de Strasbourg, mai 1955, Paris, 1957, 25-35.
J. A. SANDERS, Habakkuk in Qumran, Paul and the Old Testament, JRel 39, 1959, 232-244.
H. J. SCHOEPS, Beobachtungen zum Verständnis des Habakuk-kommentars von Qumran, RQum II, 1959-1960, 75-80.
L. H. SILBERMAN, Unriddling the Riddle. A Study in the Structure and Language of the Habakkuk Pesher, RQum III, 1961-1962, 323-364.
G. VERMES, The Qumran Interpretation of Scripture in its Historical Setting, AnLeeds 6, 1966-1968, 85-97.

d. *The Rule of the Community* (1QS). *The Rule of the Congregation* (1QSa). *The Rule of the Blessings* (1QSb).

Y. BAER, Serek ha-Yaḥad (The Manual of Discipline, a Jewish-Christian Document from the Beginning of the Second Century C.E.), Zion 29, 1964, 1-60. [Modern Hebrew].
G. BAUMBACH, Qumrân und das Johannes-Evangelium. Eine ver-

gleichende Untersuchung der dualistischen Aussagen der Ordensregel von Qumrân und des Johannes-Evangeliums mit Berücksichtigung der spätjüdischen Apokalypsen, Berlin, 1958. [Sum-
mary of dissertation, Berlin, 1956].

J. CARMIGNAC, Quelques détails de lecture dans la "Règle de la Congrégation", le "Recueil de Bénédictions" et les "Dires de Moïse",
RQum IV, 1963-1964, 83-96.

E. ETTISCH, Eschatologisch-astrologische Vorstellungen in der Gemeinderegel (X, 1-8), RQum II, 1959-1960, 3-19.

——, Antwort auf drei Fragen zu der eschatologisch-astrologischen
Erklärung der Gemeinderegel X, 1-8, RQum III, 1961-1962,
453-456.

H. GOEDHART, De slothymne van het Manual of Discipline. A Theological-Exegetical Study of 1QS X, 9-XI, 22, Rotterdam, 1965.

P. GUILBERT, Le plan de la Règle de la Communauté, RQum I, 1958-
1959, 323-344.

R. G. JONES, The Manual of Discipline (1QS), Persian Religion, and
the Old Testament, The Teacher's Yoke (Studies in Memory
of H. Tranham), Waco, Texas, 1964, 94-108.

J. T. MILIK, [Texte des variantes des dix manuscrits de la Règle de
la Communauté trouvés dans la grotte 4, RB 67, 1960, 411-416].
[This list is to be found in a recension of P. WERNBERG-MØLLER,
The Manual of Discipline, translated and annotated, Leiden,
1957].

S. H. SIEDL, Qumran, eine Mönchsgemeinde im alten Bund. Studie
über Serek ha-Yaḥad, Rome, 1963.

E. F. SUTCLIFFE, The Rule of the Congregation II, 11-12: Text and
Meaning, RQum II, 1959-1960, 541-547.

M. WEISE, Kultzeiten und kultischer Bundesschluss in der "Ordensregel" vom Toten Meer, SP-B III, Leiden, 1961.

P. WERNBERG-MØLLER, Waw and Yod in the Rule of the Community
(1QS), RQum II, 1959-1960, 223-236.

——, A Reconsideration of the two Spirits in the Rule of the Community (1QSerek III, 13-IV, 26), RQum III, 1961-1962, 413-441.

——, The nature of the Yaḥad according to the Manual of Discipline
and related documents, AnLeeds 6, 1966-1968, 56-81.

Y. YADIN, A Crucial Passage in the Dead Sea Scrolls (1QSa II, 11-17),
JBL 78, 1959, 238-241.

e. *Hodayoth* (1QH)

J. DE CAEVEL, La connaissance religieuse dans les hymnes d'action de grâces de Qumrân, ETL 38, 1962, 435-460.

J. CARMIGNAC, Remarques sur le texte des Hymnes de Qumrân, Bibl 39, 1958, 139-155.

——, Localisation des fragments 15, 18 et 22 des Hymnes, RQum I, 1958-1959, 425-430.

——, Compléments au texte des Hymnes de Qumrân?, RQum II, 1959-1960, 267-276; 549-558.

——, Les éléments historiques des Hymnes de Qumrân, RQum II, 1959-1960, 205-222.

——, Les citations de l'Ancien Testament et spécialement des Poèmes du Serviteur dans les Hymnes de Qumrân, RQum II, 1959-1960, 357-394.

——, Étude sur les procédés poétiques des Hymnes, RQum II, 1959-1960, 515-532.

——, La théologie de la souffrance dans les Hymnes de Qumrân, RQum III, 1961-1962, 365-386.

H. W. KUHN, Enderwartung und gegenwärtiges Heil. Untersuchungen zu den Gemeindeliedern von Qumran, Göttingen, 1966.

M. MANSOOR, The Thanksgiving Hymns and the Massoretic Text, RQum III, 1961-1962, 259-266; 387-394.

G. MORAWE, Vergleich des Aufbaus der Danklieder und hymnischen Bekenntnislieder (1QH) von Qumran mit dem Aufbau der Psalmen im Alten Testament und im Spätjudentum, RQum IV, 1963-1964, 323-356.

B. THIERING, The Poetic Forms of the Hodayot, JSS 8, 1963, 189-209.

S. J. DE VRIES, The Syntax of Tenses and Interpretation in the Hodayoth, RQum V, 1964-1966, 375-414.

S. WAGNER, YDᶜ in den Lobliedern von Qumran, Bibel und Qumran (Festschrift Bardtke), 232-252.

P. WERNBERG-MØLLER, The Contribution of the Hodayot to Biblical Textual Criticism, Textus 4, 1964, 133-175.

f. *Milḥamah* (1QM)

J. P. ASMUSSEN, Das iranische Lehnwort naḥšir in der Kriegsrolle von Qumrân, AcOr(K) 26, 1961, 3-20.

K. M. T. ATKINSON, The Historical Setting of the "War of the Sons of Light and the Sons of Darkness", BJRL 40, 1957-1958, 272-297.

A. M. Gazov-Ginsberg, The Structure of the Army of the Sons of Light, RQum V, 1964-1966, 163-176.

J. van der Ploeg, La guerre sainte dans la "Règle de la Guerre" de Qumrân, Mélanges bibliques rédigés en l'honneur de A. Robert, Paris, 1957, 326-333.

——, La composition littéraire de la "Règle de la Guerre" de Qumrân, Sacra Pagina. Miscellanea biblica Congressus Internationalis Catholici de re biblica, II, Paris-Gembloux, 1959, 13-19.

——, Zur literarischen Komposition der Kriegsrolle, Qumran-Probleme, 293-298.

M. H. Segal, The Qumran War Scroll and the Date of its Composition, ScrHier 4, 138-143.

B. Sveinar, Om bruken av særæk og te'udah i Qumrans krigsrull, NTT 60, 1959, 233-244.

M. Treves, The Date of the War of the Sons of Light, VT 8, 1958, 419-424.

g. *The Genesis Apocryphon* (1 QGenAp ar)

Although the Genesis Apocryphon is written in Aramaic we mention here some studies dealing with this scroll.

J. Coppens, Allusions historiques de la Genèse apocryphe, La secte de Qumrân et les origines du christianisme (RechBib 4), Bruges, 1959, 109-112.

J. A. Fitzmyer, Some Observations on the Genesis Apocryphon, CBQ 22, 1960, 277-292. [Includes a good bibliography].

——, The Genesis Apocryphon of Qumran Cave I. A Commentary, Rome, 1966; 1971². [With much bibliographical material].

M. R. Lehmann, 1Q Genesis Apocryphon in the Light of Targumim and Midrashim, RQum I, 1958-1959, 249-263.

H. Lignée, Concordance de 1Q Genesis Apocryphon, RQum I, 1958-1959, 163-186.

E. Osswald, Beobachtungen zur Erzählung von Abrahams Aufenthalt in Ägypten im "Genesis-Apocryphon", ZAW 72, 1960, 7-25.

H. H. Rowley, Notes on the Aramaic of the Genesis Apocryphon, Hebrew and Semitic Studies presented to G. R. Driver, Oxford, 1963, 116-129.

h. *Fragments from Qumran Cave 1*

J. CARMIGNAC, Notes sur les Peshârîm, RQum III, 1961-1962, 505-538.
[1QpMichée, 1QpSophonie, 1QpPs 68].
——, Le recueil de Prières liturgiques de la grotte 1 (1 Q **34** et **34** bis),
RQum IV, 1963-1964, 271-276.
R. MEYER, Die Fragmente der Höhle I, ThLZ 82, 1957, 21-28.
S. TALMON, The "Manual of Benedictions" of the Sect of the Judaean
Desert, RQum II, 1959-1960, 475-500.
J. C. TREVER, Completion of the Publication of Some Fragments
from Qumran Cave I, RQum V, 1964-1966, 323-344.

i. *The Copper Scroll from Qumran Cave 3* (cu3Q **15**)

J. M. ALLEGRO, The Treasure of the Copper Scroll, Garden City (N.Y.)-
London, 1960; Revised Edition, Garden City (N.Y.), 1964.
A. DUPONT-SOMMER, Les rouleaux de cuivre trouvés à Qumrân,
RHR 151, 1957, 22-36.
J. JEREMIAS, J. T. MILIK, Remarques sur le rouleau de cuivre de
Qumrân, RB 67, 1960, 220-223.
E. M. LAPERROUSAZ, Remarques sur l'origine des rouleaux de cuivre
découverts dans la grotte 3 de Qumrân, RHR 159, 1961, 157-172.
M. R. LEHMANN, Identification of the Copper Scroll based on its
Technical Terms, RQum V, 1964-1966, 97-105.
J. T. MILIK, Le rouleau de cuivre de Qumrân (3Q **15**). Traduction
et commentaire topographique, RB 66, 1959, 321-357.
——, The Copper Document from Qumran Cave III of Qumran:
Translation and Commentary, ADAJ 4/5, 1960, 137-155.
F. NÖTSCHER, Die Kupferrolle von Qumran (3Q **15**), BZ 5, 1961, 292-
297.

j. *Texts from Qumran Cave 4*

J. D. AMUSIN, Bemerkungen zu den Qumrân-Kommentaren, Bibel
und Qumran (Festschrift Bardtke), 9-19.
D. S. ATTEMA, Het gebed van Nabonidus, Schrift en Uitleg. Studies
aangeboden aan Prof. Dr. W. H. GISPEN, Kampen, 1970, 7-20.
J. CARMIGNAC, Notes sur les Peshârîm (4Q Pésher Isaïe A, Fragments
B, C, D; 4Q Pésher Psaume 37), RQum III, 1961-1962, 511-515;
521-526.
——, Les horoscopes de Qumrân, RQum V, 1964-1966, 199-217.

——, Poème allégorique sur la secte rivale ("The Wiles of the Wicked Woman"), RQum V, 1964-1966, 361-374.

M. DELCOR, Recherches sur un horoscope en langue hébraïque provenant de Qumrân, RQum V, 1964-1966, 521-542.

N. DRAZIN, What can BeTALMUD prove ?, JQR 54, 1964, 333.

A. DUPONT-SOMMER, Observations sur le Commentaire de Nahum découvert près de la Mer Morte, Journal des Savants, 1963, 201-227.

——, Deux documents horoscopiques esséniens découverts à Qumrân près de la Mer Morte, CRAIBL, 1965, 239-253.

——, La secte des Esséniens et les horoscopes de Qumrân, Archeologia no. 15, mars-avril 1967, 24-31.

I. H. EYBERS, Notes on the Texts of Samuel found in Qumran Cave 4, Papers read at 3rd Meeting of Die OT Werkgemeenskap in Suid-Afrika, 1960, 1-17.

J. A. FITZMYER, A Bibliographical Aid to the Study of the Qumrân Cave IV Texts 158-186, CBQ 31, 1969, 59-71.

S. B. HOENIG, What is the Explanation for the Term "Betalmud" in the Scrolls ?, JQR 53, 1962-1963, 274-276.

——, BeTALMUD and TALMUD, JQR 54, 1963-1964, 334-339.

——, Dorshé Ḥalakot in the Pesher Nahum Scrolls, JBL 83, 1964, 119-138.

——, The Pesher Nahum "Talmud", JBL 86, 1967, 441-445.

K. G. KUHN, Phylakterien aus Höhle 4 von Qumran, Heidelberg, 1957.

Z. WACHOLDER, A Qumran Attack on the Oral Exegesis ? The Phrase 'šr btlmwd šqrm in 4Q Pesher Nahum, RQum V, 1964-1966, 575-578.

S. ZEITLIN, The Expression BeTALMUD in the Scrolls militates against the View of the Protagonists of their Antiquity, JQR 54, 1963-1964, 89-98.

——, 'ASHER BeTALMUD, JQR 54, 1963-1964, 340-341.

——, The Word BeTALMUD and the Method of Congruity of Words, JQR 58, 1967-1968, 78-80.

k. *Other Texts, chiefly from Cave* 11

M. BAILLET, Remarques sur le manuscrit du livre des Jubilés de la grotte 3 de Qumrân, RQum V, 1964-1966, 423-433.

W. H. BROWNLEE, The 11Q Counterpart to Psalm 151,1-5, RQum IV, 1963-1964, 379-389.

M. DELCOR, Zum Psalter von Qumran, BZ 10, 1966, 15-29.

A. Dupont-Sommer, David et Orphée, Paris, 1964.

——, Le Psaume CLI dans 11 QPsᵃ et le problème de son origine essénienne, Sem 14, 1964, 25-62.

——, Notes quomrâniennes: 1) sur 11QtJob, col. XXXIII (this should be XXXVIII); 2) sur 11QPsᵃ, col. XXII, Sem 15, 1965, 71-78.

R. Y. Ebied, A Triglot Volume to the Epistle to the Laodiceans, Psalm 151 and other Biblical Materials, Bibl 47, 1966, 243-254.

O. Eissfeldt, Eine Qumran-Textform des 91. Psalms, Bibel und Qumran (Festschrift Bardtke), 82-85.

G. Fohrer, 4QOrNab, 11QtgJob und die Hioblegende, ZAW 75, 1963, 93-97.

M. H. Goshen-Gottstein, The Psalms Scroll (11QPsᵃ): A Problem of Canon and Text, Textus 5, 1966, 22-33.

C. E. l'Heureux, The Biblical Sources of the "Apostrophe to Zion", CBQ 29, 1967, 60-74.

A. Hurvitz, Observations on the Language of the Third Apocryphal Psalm from Qumran, RQum V, 1964-1966, 225-232.

M. de Jonge, A. S. van der Woude, 11Q Melchizedek and the New Testament, NTSt 12, 1965-1966, 301-326.

B. Jongeling, Publication provisoire d'un fragment provenant de la grotte 11 de Qumrân (11Q JérNouv ar), JSJ 1, 1970, 58-64.

——, Note additionnelle, JSJ 1, 1970, 185-186.

——, Een belangrijke Dode-Zeerol: Job in het Aramees, Rondom het Woord 13, 1971, 282-293.

D. Lührmann, Ein Weisheitspsalm aus Qumran (11QPsᵃ XVIII), ZAW 80, 1968, 87-97.

J. van der Ploeg, Le Targum de Job de la grotte 11 de Qumran, Mededelingen der Koninklijke Nederlandse Akademie van Wetenschappen, afd. Letterkunde, Nieuwe Reeks deel 25, no. 9, Amsterdam, 1962.

——, Un targum du livre de Job. Nouvelle découverte dans le désert de Judah, BiVieChr no. 58, 1964, 79-87.

——, Le Psaume XCI dans une recension de Qumrân, RB 72, 1965, 210-217.

——, Lév. IX, 23-X, 2 dans un texte de Qumran, Bibel und Qumran (Festschrift Bardtke), 153-155.

——, Un petit rouleau de psaumes apocryphes (11QPsApᵃ), Tradition und Glaube, Göttingen, 1971, 128-139.

I. Rabinowitz, The Alleged Orphism of 11QPss 28,3-12, ZAW 76, 1964, 193-300.

J. A. Sanders, The Dead Sea Psalms Scroll, New York, 1967.

P. W. Skehan, The Apocryphal Psalm 151, CBQ 25, 1963, 407-409.

——, A Broken Acrostic and Psalm 9, CBQ 27, 1965, 1-5.

J. Strugnell, More Psalms of "David", CBQ 27, 1965, 207-216.

——, Notes on the Text and Transmission of the Apocryphal Psalms 151, 154 (= Syr. II) and 155 (= Syr. III), HThR 59, 1966, 257-281.

E. W. Tuinstra, Hermeneutische aspecten van de Targum van Job uit grot XI van Qumrân, diss. Groningen, 1970.

A. S. van der Woude, De handschriften uit grot 11 van Chirbet Qumrân, Phoenix (Leiden) 9, 1963, 33-37.

——, Das Hiobtargum aus Qumran Höhle XI, Congress Volume, Bonn 1962, Suppl. to VT 9, Leiden, 1963, 322-331.

——, Melchisedek als himmlische Erlösergestalt in den neugefundenen eschatologischen Midraschim aus Qumran Höhle XI, OTS 14, Leiden, 1965, 354-373.

——, Ein neuer Segensspruch aus Qumran (11QBer), Bibel und Qumran (Festschrift Bardtke), 253-258.

——, Nieuwe gegevens over de handschriften uit grot 11 van Chirbet Qumran, Phoenix (Leiden) 12, 1966, 300-306.

——, Fragmente des Buches Jubiläen aus Qumran Höhle XI, Tradition und Glaube, Göttingen, 1971, 140-146.

——, vide M. de Jonge.

Y. Yadin, Another Fragment (E) of the Psalms Scroll from Qumran Cave 11 (11QPsᵃ), Textus 5, 1966, 1-10 and pl. I-V.

1. *Murraba'at, Masada etc.*

E. Koffmahn, Die Doppelurkunden aus der Wüste Juda, STDJ V, Leiden, 1968.

M. R. Lehmann, Studies in the Murabba'at and Naḥal Ḥever Documents, RQum IV, 1963-1964, 53-81.

J. T. Milik, Deux documents inédits du Désert de Juda, Bibl 38, 1957, 245-268. [The second document is an Aramaic deed of sale probably from Murabba'at].

——, Les documents de Murabba'at, BiTerS 33, 1960, 16-18.

——, Un fragment mal placé dans l'édition du Siracide de Masada, Bibl 47, 1966, 425-426.

S. Segert, Zur Orthographie und Sprache der aramäischen Texte von Wadi Murabba'at, ArOr 31, 1963, 122-137.

H. Stegemann, J. Becker, Zum Text von Fragment 5 aus Wadi Murabba'at, RQum III, 1961-1962, 443-448.

Y. YADIN, New Discoveries in the Judean Desert, BiAr 24, 1961, 34-50.
——, More on the Letters of Bar Kochba, BiAr 24, 1961, 86-95.
——, De nouveaux documents sur la révolte de Bar Kokhéba, BiTerS 58, 1963, 6-8; 13-17.
——, Les documents récemment découverts dans le désert de Juda, CRAIBL, 1963, 150-152.
——, The Nabataean Kingdom, Provincia Arabia, Petra and En-Geddi in the Documents from Naḥal Ḥever, JEOL VI (no. 17), 1959-1966, 227-241.
——, The Ben Sira Scroll from Masada. With Introduction, Emendations and Commentary, Jerusalem, 1965.
R. YARON, The Murabba'at Documents, JJS 11, 1960, 157-171.
S. ZEITLIN, The Ben Sira Scroll from Masada, JQR 56, 1965-1966, 185-190.

G. ARCHAEOLOGY AND HISTORY

The General Publications and the Studies on various manuscripts give also many archaeological and historical data.

A. ADAM, Antike Berichte über die Essener, Berlin, 1961.
J. M. ALLEGRO, Further Light on the History of the Qumran Sect, JBL 75, 1956, 89-95.
——, Thrakidan, the "Lion of Wrath" and Alexander Jannaeus, PEQ 91, 1959, 47-51.
M. BLACK, The Essene Problem, London, 1961.
S. G. F. BRANDON, Jesus and the Zealots. A Study of the Political Factor in Primitive Christianity, Manchester, 1967.
Chr. BURCHARD, Pline et les Esséniens, RB 69, 1962, 533-569.
J. CARMIGNAC, Les éléments historiques des "Hymnes" de Qumrân, RQum II, 1959-1960, 205-222.
J. COPPENS, Allusions historiques de la Genèse apocryphe, La Secte de Qumrân et les origines du christianisme (RechBib 4), Bruges, 1959, 109-112.
G. R. DRIVER, The Judaean Scrolls. The Problem and a Solution, Oxford, 1965.
A. DUPONT-SOMMER, Lumières nouvelles sur l'arrière-plan historique des écrits de Qoumran, Eretz-Israel 8. E. L. Sukenik Memorial Volume, Jerusalem, 1967, 25-36.

E. KOFFMAHN, Die staatsrechtliche Stellung der essenischen Ver-
einigungen in der griechisch-römischen Periode, Bibl 44, 1963,
46-61.

H. KOSMALA, Hebräer-Essener-Christen. Studien zur Vorgeschichte
der frühchristlichen Verkündigung, Leiden, 1959.

E. M. LAPERROUSAZ, Étude de quelques problèmes concernant "L'archéologie et les manuscrits de la Mer Morte. À propos d'un livre
récent, Sem 12, 1962, 67-104. [Referring to R. DE VAUX, L'archéologie ...].

H. E. DEL MEDICO, Le mythe des Esséniens des origines à la fin du
moyen âge, Paris, 1958.

K. G. PEDLEY, The Library at Qumran, RQum II, 1959-1960, 21-41.

J. VAN DER PLOEG, Les Esséniens et les origines du monachisme
chrétien, Il Monachesimo Orientale (Orientalia Christiana Analecta 153), Rome, 1959, 321-339.

E. J. PRYKE, The Identity of the Qumran Sect. A Reconsideration,
NT 10, 1968, 43-61.

J. R. ROSENBLOOM, Notes on Historical Identifications in the Dead
Sea Scrolls, RQum I, 1958-1959, 265-272.

C. ROTH, The Historical Background of the Dead Sea Scrolls, Oxford,
1958.

——, Qumran and Massadah: A Final Clarification Regarding the
Dead Sea Sect, RQum V, 1964-1966, 81-87.

H. H. ROWLEY, The History of the Qumran Sect, BJRL 49, 1966-
1967, 203-232.

P. SACCHI, Il problema degli anni 390 nel Documento di Damasco I,
5-6, RQum V, 1964-1966, 89-96.

M. H. SEGAL, The Qumran War Scroll and the Date of its Composition, ScrHier 4, 138-143.

H. SEIDEL, Erwägungen zur Frage des geistigen Ursprungsortes der
Erweckungsbewegung von Qumran, Bibel und Qumran (Festschrift Bardtke), 188-197.

H. SÉROUYA, Les Esséniens, Paris, 1959.

S. SZYSZMAN, Das Karäertum in seinen Beziehungen zum Essänertum
in der Sicht einiger Autoren des 17. und 18. Jahrhunderts, Bibel
und Qumran (Festschrift Bardtke), 226-231.

J. L. TEICHER, Archeology and the Dead Sea Scrolls, Antiquity 37,
1963, 25-30. [Largely versus R. DE VAUX].

W. TYLOCH, The History of the Qumran Community, Warszawa, 1964.
[Polish].

R. DE VAUX, L'archéologie et les Manuscrits de la Mer Morte (The Schweich Lectures of the British Academy 1959), London, 1961.
——, Esséniens ou Zélotes? À propos d'un livre récent, RB 73, 1966, 212-235. [Referring to G. R. DRIVER, The Judaean Scrolls].
——, Essenes or Zealots?, NTSt 13, 1966-1967, 89-104. [= Preceding paper in English].
G. VERMES, The Etymology of "Essenes", RQum II, 1959-1960, 427-443.
N. WALKER, Concerning the 390 Years and the 20 Years of the Damascus Document, JBL 76, 1957, 57-58.
N. WIEDER, The Judean Scrolls and Karaism, London, 1962.
Y. YADIN, Masada, Herod's Fortress and the Zealots' Last Stand, London, 1966; Dutch translation, Bussum, 1971.

H. RELIGION AND CULT. THEOLOGY. ORGANIZATION. THE MESSIAH(S). THE TEACHER OF RIGHTEOUSNESS

G. W. AHLSTRÖM, Hammôreh liṣdāqāh in Joel II, 23, Congress Volume 1968, Suppl. to VT 17, Leiden, 1969, 25-36.
J. BECKER, Das Heil Gottes. Heils- und Sündenbegriffe in den Qumrantexten und im Neuen Testament, Göttingen, 1964.
O. BETZ, Offenbarung und Schriftforschung in der Qumransekte, Tübingen, 1960.
H. BIETENHARD, Sabbatvorschriften von Qumrān im Lichte des rabbinischen Rechts und der Evangelien, Qumran-Probleme, 53-74.
R. E. BROWN, J. Starcky's Theory of Qumran Messianic Development, CBQ 28, 1966, 51-57.
F. F. BRUCE, Holy Spirit in the Qumran Texts, AnLeeds 6, 1966-1968, 49-55.
A. CAQUOT, Ben Sira et le Messianisme, Sem 16, 1966, 43-86.
J. CARMIGNAC, Le Docteur de Justice et Jésus-Christ, Paris, 1957; English edition: Christ and the Teacher of Righteousness. The Evidence of the Dead Sea Scrolls, Baltimore-Dublin, 1962.
——, Le retour du Docteur de Justice à la fin des jours?, RQum I, 1958-1959, 235-248.
——, La théologie de la souffrance dans les Hymnes de Qumrân, RQum III, 1961-1962, 365-386.

——, MWRH ḤṢDQ. Peut-on traduire par "le Docteur de Justice"?, RQum III, 1961-1962, 529-533.

N. CASERTA, La Congregazione qumranica e la prima Comunità di Gerusalemme, Asprenas 6, 1959, 14-46.

J. COPPENS, La piété des Psalmistes à Qumrân, La secte de Qumrân et les origines du christianisme (RechBib 4), Bruges, 1959, 149-161.

M. DELCOR, Le Docteur de Justice, Nouveau Moïse, dans les Hymnes de Qumrân, Le Psautier. Études présentées aux 12es Journées Bibliques 1961, Louvain, 1962, 407-423.

——, Le vocabulaire juridique, cultuel et mystique de l'"initiation" dans la secte de Qumrân, Qumran-Probleme, 109-134.

A. M. DENIS, Les thèmes de connaissance dans le Document de Damas, Louvain, 1967.

I. H. EYBERS, Aspekte van die organisasie en rites van die Joodse Qoemraansekte, I, II, Pretoria, 1961.

C. T. FRITSCH, The So-Called "Priestly Messiah" of the Essenes, JEOL VI, 1959-1966, 242-248.

J. C. G. GREIG, Gospel Messianism and the Qumran Use of Prophecy, Studia Evangelica. Papers presented to the International Congress on "The Four Gospels in 1957" held at Christ Church Oxford 1957, Berlin, 1959, 593-599.

W. GRUNDMANN, Die Frage nach der Gottessohnschaft des Messias im Lichte von Qumran, Bibel und Qumran (Festschrift Bardtke), 86-111.

J. HEMPEL, Die Stellung des Laien in Qumran, Qumran-Probleme, 193-215.

A. J. B. HIGGINS, The Priestly Messiah, NTSt 13, 1966-1967, 211-239.

C. H. HUNZINGER, Beobachtungen zur Entwicklung der Disziplinarordnung der Gemeinde von Qumran, Qumran-Probleme, 231-247.

H. W. HUPPENBAUER, Der Mensch zwischen zwei Welten. Der Dualismus der Texte von Qumran (Höhle I) und der Damaskusfragmente. Ein Beitrag zur Vorgeschichte des Evangeliums, Zürich, 1959.

G. JEREMIAS, Der Lehrer der Gerechtigkeit, Göttingen, 1963.

J. JEREMIAS, Die theologische Bedeutung der Funde am Toten Meer, Göttingen, 1962.

M. DE JONGE, The use of the word "anointed" in the time of Jesus, NT 8, 1966, 132-148.

A. S. KAPELRUD, Die aktuellen und die eschatologischen Behörden der Qumrangemeinde, Qumran-Probleme, 259-268.

——, Der Bund in den Qumranschriften, Bibel und Qumran (Festschrift Bardtke), 137-149.

S. T. KIMBROUGH, The Concept of Sabbath at Qumran, RQum V, 1964-1966, 483-502.

——, The Ethic of the Qumran Community, RQum VI, 1967-1969, 483-498.

H. W. KUHN, Enderwartung und gegenwärtiges Heil. Untersuchungen zu den Gemeindeliedern von Qumran, Göttingen, 1966.

W. S. LaSOR, The Messianic Idea in Qumran, Studies and Essays in Honor of A. Neuman, Leiden, 1962, 343-364.

R. B. LAURIN, The Problem of Two Messiahs in the Qumran Scrolls, RQum IV, 1963-1964, 39-52.

J. LICHT, An Analysis of the Treatise of the Two Spirits in DSD [= Manual of Discipline], ScrHier 4, 88-100.

J. LIVER, The "Sons of Zadok the Priests" in the Dead Sea Sect, RQum VI, 1967-1969, 3-30.

G. MAIER, Mensch und freier Wille nach den jüdischen Religionsparteien zwischen Ben Sira und Paulus, Tübingen, 1971.

J. Murphy-O'CONNOR, La "vérité" chez Saint Paul et à Qumrân, RB 72, 1965, 29-76.

J. NEUSNER, The Fellowship (ḤBWRH) in the Second Jewish Commonwealth, HThR 53, 1960, 125-142.

B. NOACK, The Day of Pentecost in Jubilees, Qumran and Acts, ASTI 1, 1962, 73-95.

E. NIELSEN, La Guerre considérée comme une religion et la Religion comme une Guerre, StTh 15, 1961, 93-112.

F. NÖTSCHER, Vom Alten zum Neuen Testament. Gesammelte Aufsätze, Bonn, 1962.

P. VON DER OSTEN-SACKEN, Gott und Belial. Traditionsgeschichtliche Untersuchungen zum Dualismus in den Texten aus Qumran, Göttingen, 1969.

J. VAN DER PLOEG, The Belief in Immortality in the Writings of Qumran, BiOr 18, 1961, 118-124.

J. PRYKE, "Spirit" and "Flesh" in the Qumran Documents and Some New Testament Texts, RQum V, 1964-1966, 345-360.

——, The Sacraments of Holy Baptism and Holy Communion in the Light of the Ritual Washings and Sacred Meals at Qumran, RQum V, 1964-1966, 543-552.

H. RINGGREN, Tro och liv enligt Döda-Havsrullarna, Stockholm, 1961.

——, The Faith of Qumran: Theology of the Dead Sea Scrolls, Philadelphia, 1963. [Translation of preceding work].

C. ROTH, The subject matter of Qumran exegesis, VT 10, 1960, 51-68.

——, The Teacher of Righteousness and the Prophecy of Joel, VT 13,
1963, 91-95.

J. SCHREINER, Geistbegabung in der Gemeinde von Qumran, BZ 9,
1965, 161-180.

K. SCHUBERT, Die Gemeinde vom Toten Meer. Ihre Entstehung und
ihre Lehren, München-Basel, 1958.

——, Das Problem der Auferstehungshoffnung in den Qumrantexten
und in der frührabbinischen Literatur, WZKM 56, 1960, 154-167.

——, Die Entwicklung der Auferstehungslehre von der nachexilischen
bis zur frührabbinischen Zeit, BZ 6, 1962, 177-214.

O. J. F. SEITZ, Two Spirits in Man: an Essay on Biblical Exegesis,
NTSt 6, 1959-1960, 82-95.

C. SPICQ, Une allusion au Docteur de Justice dans Matthieu XXIII,
10 ?, RB 66, 1959, 387-396.

J. STARCKY, Les quatre étapes du messianisme à Qumran, RB 70,
1963, 481-505.

P. STUHLMACHER, Gerechtigkeit Gottes bei Paulus, Göttingen, 1965.

E. F. SUTCLIFFE, The Monks of Qumran as Depicted in the Dead Sea
Scrolls, London-Westminster, 1960.

W. TYLOCH, Quelques remarques sur le caractère social du mouve-
ment de Qumran, Qumran-Probleme, 341-351.

G. VERMES, The Qumran Interpretation of Scripture in its Historical
Setting, AnLeeds 6, 1966-1968, 85-97.

P. WALLENDORF, Rättfärdighetens Lärare, diss., Helsinki, 1964.

E. A. WCELA, The Messiah(s) of Qumran, CBQ 26, 1964, 340-349.

J. WEINGREEN, The Title Môrēh Ṣedek, JSS 6, 1961, 162-174.

K. WEISS, Messianismus in Qumran und im Neuen Testament, Qumran-Probleme, 353-368.

P. WERNBERG-MØLLER, A Reconsideration of the Two Spirits in the
Rule of the Community (1Q Serek III, 13-IV, 26), RQum III,
1961-1962, 413-441.

——, The nature of the Yaḥad according to the Manual of Discipline
and related Documents, AnLeeds 6, 1966-1968, 56-81.

A. S. VAN DER WOUDE, Die messianischen Vorstellungen der Gemeinde
von Qumran, Assen, 1957.

——, Le Maître de Justice et les deux Messies de la Communauté
de Qumrân, La secte de Qumrân et les origines du christianisme
(RechBib 4), Bruges, 1959, 121-134.

I. QUMRAN AND THE OLD TESTAMENT

F. I. ANDERSON, The Dead Sea Scrolls and the Formation of the Canon, BullEThS 1, 1958, 1-7.

(H. BARDTKE), Bibel und Qumran. Beiträge zur Erforschung der Beziehungen zwischen Bibel- und Qumranwissenschaft, Hans Bardtke zum 22.9.1966, Berlin, 1968.

D. BARTHÉLEMY, Les découvertes de Qumrân et la critique textuelle de l'Ancien Testament, BullComÉt 3, 1958-1959, 424-434.

O. BETZ, Offenbarung und Schriftforschung in der Qumransekte, Tübingen, 1960.

W. H. BROWNLEE, The Meaning of the Qumrân Scrolls for the Bible with Special Attention to the Book of Isaiah, New York, 1964.

F. F. BRUCE, Biblical Exegesis in the Qumran Texts (Exegetica III,1), The Hague, 1959; British edition, completely reset, London, 1960.

J. CARMIGNAC, Les citations de l'Ancien Testament et spécialement des poèmes du Serviteur, dans les Hymnes de Qumrân, RQum II, 1959-1960, 357-394.

J. CONRAD, Die Entstehung und Motivierung alttestamentlicher Paraschen im Licht der Qumranfunde, Bibel und Qumran (Festschrift Bardtke), 47-56.

F. M. CROSS Jr., The Ancient Library of Qumran and Modern Biblical Studies, New York, 1958; German edition, revised and enlarged: Die antike Bibliothek von Qumran, Neukirchen, 1967.

——, The History of the Biblical Text in the Light of the Discoveries in the Judaean Desert, HThR 57, 1964, 281-299.

——, The Contribution of the Qumrân Discoveries to the Study of the Biblical Text, IEJ 16, 1966, 81-95.

A. DÍEZ-MACHO, El texto bíblico del comentario de Habacuc de Qumran, Lex Tua Veritas (Festschrift H. Junker), Trier, 1961, 59-64.

I. H. EYBERS, The Book of Ezekiel and the Sect of Qumran, Papers read at 4th Meeting of Die OT Werkgemeenschap in Suid-Afrika, 1961, 1-9.

——, Some Light on the Canon of the Qumran Sect, Papers read at 5th Meeting of Die OT Werkgemeenschap in Suid-Afrika, 1962, 1-14.

——, Enkele gedagtes oor die Ou-Testamentiese Kanon, Theologia Evangelica 1, 1968, 9-15.

J. A. FITZMYER, The Use of Explicit Old Testament Quotations in

Qumran Literature and in the New Testament, NTSt 7, 1960-1961, 297-333.

M. H. GOSHEN-GOTTSTEIN, The Psalms Scroll (11 QPsª): A Problem of Canon and Text, Textus 5, 1966, 22-23.

——, Hebrew Biblical Manuscripts. Their History and Their Place in the Hebrew University Bible Project Edition, Bibl 48, 1967, 243-290.

S. LOWY, Some Aspects of Normative and Sectarian Interpretation of the Scriptures, AnLeeds 6, 1966-1968, 98-163.

R. MAYER, J. REUSS, Die Qumranfunde und die Bibel, Regensburg, 1959.

——, Dodezeerollen en Bijbel, Leiden, 1960. [Dutch edition of preceding work].

R. E. MURPHY, The Dead Sea Scrolls and the Bible, Westminster Md., 1956, 1957²; French edition: Le Couvent de la Mer Morte et la Bible, Abbaye de Maredsous (Belgium), 1957.

F. NÖTSCHER, Gotteswege und Menschenwege in der Bibel und in Qumran, Bonn, 1958.

J. VAN DER PLOEG, Bijbelverklaring te Qumrân, Mededelingen der Kon. Ned. Akademie van Wetenschappen, afd. Letterkunde, Nieuwe Reeks 23, 1960, 207-229.

P. SACCHI, Il testo dei Settanta nella problematica più recente, Atene e Roma, nuova serie 9, 1964, 145-158.

P. W. SKEHAN, The Biblical Scrolls from Qumran and the Text of the Old Testament, BiAr 28, 1965, 87-100.

A. SZÖRÉNYI, Das Buch Daniel, ein kanonisierter Pescher?, Congress Volume, Genève, 1965, Suppl. to VT 15, Leiden, 1966, 278-294.

S. TALMON, DSIa as a Witness to Ancient Exegesis of the Book of Isaiah, ASTI 1, 1962, 62-72.

——, Aspects of the Textual Transmission of the Bible in the Light of Qumran Manuscripts, Textus 4, 1964, 95-132.

J. C. TREVER, The Qumran Covenanters and their Use of Scripture, Personalist 39, 1958, 127-138.

G. VERMES, The Qumran Interpretation of Scripture in its Historical Setting, AnLeeds 6, 1966-1968, 85-97.

R. WEISS, A Comparaison between the Massoretic and the Qumran Texts of Nahum III: 1-11, RQum IV, 1963-1964, 433-439.

It stands to reason that much material regarding Qumran and the Old Testament is to be found in the General Works and in the studies

on Bible Texts and Commentaries from the Judean desert, vide
E. Translations and Commentaries, and F. Studies on various Manuscripts.

J. APOCRYPHAL AND PSEUDEPIGRAPHICAL LITERATURE

Chr. Burchard, Untersuchungen zu Joseph und Aseneth, Tübingen,
    1965.
J. Carmignac, Les affinités qumrâniennes de la Onzième Ode de
    Salomon, RQum III, 1961-1962, 71-102.
——, Les rapports entre l'Ecclésiastique et Qumrân, RQum III,
    1961-1962, 209-218.
——, Un Qumrânien converti au christianisme: l'auteur des Odes de
    Salomon, Qumran-Probleme, 75-108.
——, Recherches sur la langue originelle des Odes de Salomon, RQum
    IV, 1963-1964, 429-432.
M. Delcor, Cinq nouveaux psaumes esséniens ?, RQum I, 1958-1959,
    85-102.
——, Le testament de Job, la prière de Nabonide et les traditions
    targoumiques, Bibel und Qumran (Festschrift Bardtke), 57-74.
P. Grelot, L'eschatologie des Esséniens et le livre d'Hénoch, RQum I,
    1958-1959, 113-131.
M. de Jonge, The Testaments of the Twelve Patriarchs and the New
    Testament, Studia Evangelica. Papers presented to the Inter-
    national Congress on "The Four Gospels in 1957" held at Christ
    Church Oxford 1957, Berlin, 1959, 546-556.
——, Christian Influence in the Testaments of the Twelve Patriarchs,
    NT 4, 1960, 182-235.
——, Once more: Christian Influence in the Testaments of the Twelve
    Patriarchs, NT 5, 1962, 311-319.
——, Testamenta XII Patriarchorum, Leiden, 1964.
E. Kutsch, Der Kalender des Jubiläenbuches und das Alte und das
    Neue Testament, VT 11, 1961, 39-47.
——, Die Solstitien im Kalender des Jubiläenbuches und in äth.
    Henoch 72, VT 12, 1962, 205-207.
M. R. Lehmann, Ben Sira and the Qumran Literature, RQum III,
    1961-1962, 103-116.
A. A. di Lella, The Hebrew Text of Sirach. A Text-critical and
    Historical Study, London-The Hague-Paris, 1966.

J. Mejía, Posibles contactos entre los manuscritos de Qumran y los Libros de los Macabeos, RQum I, 1958-1959, 51-72.

——, Contribución de Qumrân a la exégesis de los libros de Los Macabeos, Sacra Pagina. Miscellanea biblica Congressus Internationalis Catholici de re biblica II, Paris-Gembloux, 1959, 20-27.

J. O'Dell, The Religious Background of the Psalms of Solomon, RQum III, 1961-1962, 241-257.

M. Philonenko, Les interpolations chrétiennes des Testaments des Douze Patriarches et les Manuscrits de Qumrân, Paris, 1960.

——, e.a., Pseudépigraphes de l'Ancien Testament et Manuscrits de la Mer Morte I, Paris, 1967.

M. Testuz, Les idées religieuses du livre des Jubilés, Genève-Paris, 1960.

Y. Yadin, The Ben Sira Scroll from Masada, Jerusalem, 1965; modern Hebrew edition: Eretz-Israel VIII, Jerusalem, 1967, 1-45.

K. QUMRAN AND JUDAISM. THE CALENDAR

J. Amusin, Spuren antiqumranischer Polemik in der talmudischen Tradition, Qumran-Probleme, 5-27.

W. Beilner, Der Ursprung des Pharisäismus, BZ 3, 1959, 235-251.

M. Black, The Patristic Accounts of Jewish Sectarianism, BJRL 41, 1958-1959, 285-303. [Also to be found in M. Black, The Scrolls and Christian Origins, New York, 1961, 48-74].

E. Ettisch, Die Gemeinderegel und der Qumrankalender, RQum III, 1961-1962, 125-133.

——, Der grosse Sonnenzyklus und der Qumrankalender, ThLZ 88, 1963, col. 185-194.

J. van Goudoever, Biblical Calendars, Leiden, 1959; 2nd revised ed. 1961; French translation: Fêtes et calendriers bibliques, Paris, 1967.

M. Hengel, Die Zeloten. Untersuchungen zur jüdischen Freiheitsbewegung in der Zeit von Herodes I. bis 70 n.Chr., Leiden-Köln, 1961. [= Diss. Tübingen, 1959].

A. Jaubert, Le calendrier des Jubilés et les jours liturgiques de la semaine, VT 7, 1957, 35-61.

——, Aperçus sur le calendrier de Qumrân, La secte de Qumrân et les origines du christianisme (RechBib 4), Bruges, 1959, 113-120.

——, La notion d'alliance dans le Judaïsme aux abords de l'ère chrétienne, Paris, 1963.

——, Le Judaïsme aux abords de l'ère chrétienne, InfHist 27, 1965, 29-32.

E. KUTSCH, Der Kalender des Jubiläenbuches und das Alte und das Neue Testament, VT 11, 1961, 39-47.

M. R. LEHMANN, Talmudic Material relating to the Dead Sea Scrolls, RQum I, 1958-1959, 391-404.

——, Midrashic Parallels to Selected Qumran Texts, RQum III, 1961-1962, 545-551.

G. MAIER, Mensch und freier wille nach den jüdischen Religionsparteien zwischen Ben Sira und Paulus, Tübingen, 1971.

J. MEYSING, L'énigme de la chronologie biblique et qumrânienne dans une nouvelle lumière, RQum VI, 1967-1969, 229-251. [Dealing with K. STENRING, The Enclosed Garden].

C. ROTH, The Zealots and Qumran: the basic issue, RQum II, 1959-1960, 81-84.

——, The Zealots — A Jewish Sect, Judaism 8, 1959, 33-40.

——, A Talmudic Reference to the Qumran Sect?, RQum II, 1959-1960, 261-265.

H. H. ROWLEY, The Qumran Sectaries and the Zealots. An examination of a Recent Theory, VT 9, 1959, 379-392.

G. G. SCHOLEM, Jewish Gnosticism, Merkabah Mysticism, and Talmudic Tradition, New York, 1960.

M. SIMON, Les sectes juives au temps de Jésus, Paris, 1960; Dutch translation: De Joodse sekten ten tijde van Jezus, Amsterdam, 1965 (Carillon-reeks no. 43).

K. STENRING, The Enclosed Garden, Stockholm, 1966. [Study on Biblical Calendars].

S. TALMON, The Calendar Reckoning of the Sect from the Judaean Desert, ScrHier 4, 162-199.

G. VERMES, Essenes and Therapeutai, RQum III, 1961-1962, 495-504.

——, Scripture and Tradition in Judaism, SP-B 4, Leiden, 1961.

N. WIEDER, The Judean Scrolls and Karaism, London, 1962.

L. QUMRAN AND THE NEW TESTAMENT

1. GENERAL PUBLICATIONS. THE GOSPELS. THE ACTS. THE EPISTLES. THE REVELATION

S. Chr. AGOURIDÉS, Ta cheirographa tès nekras thalassès kai hè Kainè Diathèkè, Athens, 1959.

W. F. ALBRIGHT, New Horizons in Biblical Research, Oxford, 1963. [Chapter 3: New Testament Research after the Discovery of the Dead Sea Scrolls].

(H. BARDTKE), vide *sub* section I.

D. BARTHÉLEMY, La sainteté selon la communauté de Qumrân et selon l'Évangile, La secte de Qumrân et les origines du christianisme (RechBib 4), Bruges, 1959, 203-216.

G. BAUMBACH, Qumrân und das Johannes-Evangelium. Eine vergleichende Untersuchung der dualistischen Aussagen der Ordensregel von Qumrân und des Johannes-Evangeliums mit Berücksichtigung der spätjüdischen Apokalypsen, Berlin, 1958. [Summary of dissertation, Berlin, 1956].

J. BECKER, Das Heil Gottes. Heils- und Sündenbegriffe in den Qumrantexten und im Neuen Testament. Göttingen, 1964. [= Diss. Heidelberg, 1961: Ṣedaḳa. Heils- und ...].

M. BLACK, The Scrolls and the New Testament, NTSt 13, 1966-1967, 81-90. [Referring to G. R. DRIVER, The Judaean Scrolls ...].

O. BÖCHER, Der johanneische Dualismus im Zusammenhang des nachbiblischen Judentums, Gütersloh, 1965. [= Diss. Mainz, 1963].

F. M. BRAUN, L'arrière-fond du 4e Évangile, L'Évangile de Jean. Études et Problèmes (RechBib 3), Bruges ,1958, 179-196.

H. BRAUN, Qumran und das Neue Testament, I, II, Tübingen, 1966.

J. CARMIGNAC, Recherches sur le "Notre Père", Paris, 1969.

L. CERFAUX, Influence de Qumrân sur le Nouveau Testament, La secte de Qumrân et les origines du christianisme (RechBib 4), Bruges, 1959, 233-244.

J. H. CHARLESWORTH (ed.), John and Qumran, London, 1972.

M. A. CHEVALIER, L'Esprit et le Messie dans le Bas Judaïsme et le Nouveau Testament, Paris, 1958. [Diss. Strasbourg].

J. COPPENS, Le Don de l'Esprit d'après les textes de Qumrân et le 4e Évangile, L'Évangile de Jean. Études et Problèmes (RechBib 3), Bruges, 1958, 209-223.

——, Le "Mystère" dans la théologie paulinienne et ses parallèles qumrâniens, Littérature et Théologie pauliniennes (RechBib 5), Bruges, 1960, 148-165.

——, Les affinités qumrâniennes de l'épître aux Hébreux, NRT 84, 1962, 128-141, 257-282; deuxième édition complétée, ALBO IV, 1962, fasc. 1.

E. Dabrowski, The Discoveries at Qumran near the Dead Sea and the New Testament, Poznán-Warszawa-Lublin, 1960. [Polish].

C. Daniel, Une mention essénienne dans un texte syriaque de l'Apocalypse, Mus 79, 1966, 155-164.

——, Une mention paulinienne des Esséniens de Qumrân, RQum V, 1964-1966, 553-567.

——, Les "Hérodiens" du Nouveau Testament sont-ils des Esséniens ?, RQum VI, 1967-1969, 31-53.

——, Les Esséniens et "ceux qui sont dans les maisons des rois" (Matthieu 11:7-8 et Luc 7:24-25), RQum VI, 1967-1969, 261-277.

——, Esséniens et Eunuques (Matthieu 19:10-12), RQum VI, 1967-1969, 353-390.

——, Les Esséniens et l'arrière-fond historique de la parabole du Bon Samaritain, NT 11, 1969, 71-104.

——, "Faux prophètes": surnom des Esséniens dans le Sermon sur la Montagne, RQum VII, 1969-1971, 45-80.

——, Nouveaux arguments en faveur de l'identification des Hérodiens et des Esséniens. RQum VII, 1969-1971, 397-402.

W. D. Davies, The Setting of the Sermon on the Mount, Cambridge, 1964.

G. R. Driver, The Number of the Beast, Bibel und Qumran (Festschrift Bardtke), 75-81.

J. Dupont, Les ptoochoi tooi pneumati et les 'NWY RWḤ de Qumrân, Neutestamentliche Aufsätze (Festschrift J. Schmid), Regensburg, 1963, 53-64.

J. A. Fitmyer, Essays on the Semitic Background of the New Testament, London, 1971.

D. Flusser, Blessed are the Poor in Spirit, IEJ 10, 1960, 1-13.

B. Gärtner, The Temple and the Community in Qumran and the New Testament. A Comparative Study in the Temple Symbolism of the Qumran Texts and the New Testament, Cambridge, 1965.

P. Geoltrain, Les études qoumraniennes et le Nouveau Testament, ÉgliseTh 23, 1960, 38-44. [Chronique bibliographique].

J. Gnilka, 2 Kor. 6:12-7:1 im Lichte der Qumrânschriften und der

Zwölf-Patriarchen-Testamente, Neutestamentliche Aufsätze (Festschrift J. Schmid), Regensburg, 1963, 86-99.

W. GRUNDMANN, Stehen und Fallen im qumranischen und neutestamentlichen Schrifttum, Qumran-Probleme, 147-166.

C. H. HUNZINGER, ... den Menschen (s)ein Wohlgefallen, BZion 72, 1957, 20-23.

——, Ein weiterer Beleg zu Lc 2:14 *anthroopoi eudokias*, ZNW 49, 1958, 129-130.

A. ISAKSSON, Marriage and Ministry in the New Temple. A Study with Special Reference to Mt 19:3-12 and 1 Cor. 11:3-16, Lund, 1965.

J. JEREMIAS, Abba. Studien zur neutestamentlichen Zeitgeschichte, Göttingen, 1966.

——, Le message central du Nouveau Testament, Paris, 1966. [Last chapter: Qumrân et la Théologie (= Die theologische Bedeutung der Funde am Toten Meer, Göttingen, 1962); The same paper in NRT 85, 1963, 674-690].

E. KAMLAH, Die Form der katalogischen Paränese im Neuen Testament, Tübingen, 1964.

A. R. C. LEANEY, The Scrolls and the New Testament, A Guide to the Scrolls (by Leaney, Hanson, Posen), London, 1958, 79-122.

G. MOLIN, Matthäus 5:43 und das Schrifttum von Qumran, Bibel und Qumran (Festschrift Bardtke), 150-152.

R. E. MURPHY, BŚR in the Qumrân Literature and *Sarks* in the Epistle to the Romans, Sacra Pagina. Miscellanea biblica Congressus Internationalis Catholici de re biblica II, Paris-Gembloux, 60-76.

J. MURPHY-O'CONNOR, La "vérité" chez Saint Paul et à Qumrân, RB 72, 1965, 29-76.

——, (ed.), Paul and Qumran. Studies in New Testament Exegesis, London-Dublin-Melbourne, 1968.

F. NÖTSCHER, Vom Alten zum Neuen Testament. Gesammelte Aufsätze, Bonn, 1962.

I. DE LA POTTERIE, L'arrière-fond du thème johannique de vérité, Studia Evangelica. Papers presented to the Intern. Congress on "The Four Gospels in 1957" held at Christ Church Oxford 1957, Berlin, 1959, 277-294.

P. RICCA, Die Eschatologie des vierten Evangeliums, Zürich-Frankfort aM., 1966.

K. ROMANIUK, La crainte de Dieu à Qumran et dans le Nouveau Testament, RQum IV, 1963-1964, 29-38.

H. H. Rowley, The Dead Sea Scrolls and the New Testament, London, 1960².

——, The Dead Sea Scrolls and the Gospels, Faith, Reason and the Gospels, edited by F. J. J. Heaney, Westminster Md., 1963, 183-210.

R. Schnackenburg, Die Erwartung des "Propheten" nach dem Neuen Testament und den Qumran-Texten, Studia Evangelica. Papers presented to the Intern. Congress on "The Four Gospels in 1957" held at Christ Church Oxford 1957, Berlin, 1959, 622-639.

K. Schubert, Die Bedeutung der Handschriftenfunde vom Toten Meer für das Neue Testament, Theologie heute, edited by L. Reinisch, München, 1959, 61-75.

L. R. Stachowiak, Die Antithese Licht-Finsternis: Ein Thema der paulinischen Paränese, ThQSchr 143, 1963, 385-421.

K .Stendahl (ed.), The Scrolls and the New Testament: An Introduction and a Perspective, New York, 1957; British edition: London, 1958.

K. Stendahl, The School of St. Matthew and its Use of the Old Testament, Lund, 1967². [First edition 1954, dissertation Uppsala University].

H. Vossberg, Die Funde am Toten Meer im Lichte des Neuen Testaments, Berlin, 1959.

J. de Waard, A Comparative Study of the Old Testament Text in the Dead Sea Scrolls and in the New Testament, STDJ IV, Leiden, 1961.

S. Wibbing, Die Tugend- und Lasterkataloge im Neuen Testament und ihre Traditionsgeschichte unter besonderer Berücksichtigung der Qumran-Texte, Berlin, 1959.

Y. Yadin, The Dead Sea Scrolls and the Epistle to the Hebrews, ScrHier 4, 36-55.

General works cited in section B often include one or more chapters dealing with the relations Qumrân-Bible, Qumrân-New Testament, Qumrân-Christianity.

2. Qumran and Christianity. John the Baptist. Jesus. The Date of the Last Supper

O. Betz, Die Proselytentaufe der Qumransekte und die Taufe im Neuen Testament, RQum I, 1958-1959, 213-234.

——, Le ministère cultuel dans la secte de Qumrân et dans le christianisme primitif, La secte de Qumrân et les origines du christianisme (RechBib 4), Bruges, 1959, 163-202.

——, Was wissen wir von Jesus, Stuttgart, 1965.

M. Black, The Scrolls and Christian Origins, New York, 1961.

——, The Dead Sea Scrolls and Christian Doctrine. A Discussion of Three Parallels to be found in the Dead Sea Scrolls: Sacerdotal Messianism, the Atonement, and Eschatology, London, 1966.

——, (ed.), The Scrolls and Christianity, London, 1969.

S. G. F. Brandon, Jesus and the Zealots. A Study of the Political Factor in Primitive Christianity, Manchester, 1967.

W. Brant, Wer war Jesus Christus? Verändern die Schriftrollenfunde vom Toten Meer unser Christusbild?, Stuttgart, 1957; French edition: Qui était Jésus-Christ?, Paris, 1958.

J. Carmignac, Comment Jésus et ses contemporains pouvaient-ils célébrer la Pâque à une date non officielle?, RQum V, 1964-1966, 59-79. [With a bibliography concerning the opinion of Miss A. Jaubert].

H. Chylinski, Wykopaliska w Qumran a pochodzenie chrześcijaństwa (= The Discoveries at Qumran and the Origins of Christianity), Warszawa, 1961.

E. Dabrowski, The Trial of Christ in Historio-critical Light, Poznań-Warszawa-Lublin, 1965. [Polish].

J. Daniélou, Les Manuscrits de la Mer Morte et les Origines du Christianisme, Paris, 1957; German edition: Qumran und der Ursprung des Christentums, Mainz, 1958; English edition: The Dead Sea Scrolls and Primitive Christianity, Baltimore Md., 1958.

W. D. Davies, Christian Origins and Judaism, Philadelphia-London, 1962.

R. Deichgräber, Gotteshymnus und Christushymnus in der frühen Christenheit, Göttingen, 1967.

A. Dupont-Sommer, Les manuscrits de la Mer Morte et l'histoire des origines chrétiennes, RUBruxelles 18, 1966, 168-189. [For the opinion of Dupont-Sommer vide also Les écrits esséniens ...].

W. Eiss, Qumran und die Anfänge der christlichen Gemeinde, Stuttgart, 1959.

A. Finkel, The Pharisees and the Teacher of Nazareth. A Study of Their Background, Their Halakhic and Midrashic Teachings, the Similarities and Differences, diss., Tübingen 1962, Leiden-Köln, 1964.

J. A. Fitzmyer, Jewish Christianity in Acts in Light of the Qumran Scrolls, Studies in Luke-Acts. Essays presented in Honor of Paul Schubert, Nashville (Tenn.), 1966, 233-257.

D. Flusser, The Dead Sea Sect and Pre-Pauline Christianity, ScrHier 4, 215-266.

M. García Cordero, Los descubrimientos del desierto de Judá y los orígines del Christianismo, CiTom 85, 1958, 59-137.

A. Giglioli, Il giorno dell'ultima cena e l'anno della morte di Gesù, RBibIt 10, 1962, 156-181.

J. Gnilka, Die essenischen Tauchbäder und die Johannestaufe, RQum III, 1961-1962, 185-207.

D. Howlett, The Essenes and Christianity. An Interpretation of the Dead Sea Scrolls, New York, 1957; French edition: Les Esséniens et le Christianisme. Une interprétation des Manuscrits de la Mer Morte, Paris, 1958.

A. Jaubert, La date de la Cène, calendrier biblique et liturgie chrétienne, Paris, 1957.

——, The Date of the Last Supper, ThDig 5, 1957, 67-72.

——, Aperçus sur le calendrier de Qumrân, La secte de Qumrân et les origines du christianisme (RechBib 4), Bruges, 1959, 113-120.

——, Jésus et le calendrier de Qumrân, NTSt 7, 1960-1961, 1-30.

——, Les séances du Sanhédrin et les récits de la passion, RHR 167, 1965, 1-33.

——, Une discussion patristique sur la chronologie de la passion, RechScR 54, 1966, 407-410.

——, Une lecture du lavement des pieds au mardi/mercredi saint, Mus 79, 1966, 257-286.

——, Le mercredi où Jésus fut livré, NTSt 14, 1967-1968, 145-164.

A. S. Kapelrud, Dødehavstekstene og urkristendommen, NTT 62, 1960, 113-127.

W. S. LaSor, Amazing Dead Sea Scrolls and the Christian Faith, Chicago, 1957, revised edition: 1959. [Parallel edition: The Dead Sea Scrolls and the Christian Faith, Chicago, 1962].

G. Lindeskog, Esséerna og Kristendomen, Annales Academiae Regiae Upsaliensis 5, 1961, 103-147.

F. M. López Melús, El cristianismo y los Esenios de Qumrán, Madrid, 1965.

J. Morgenstern, Some Significant Antecedents of Christianity, SP-B 10, Leiden, 1966.

L. Mowry, The Dead Sea Scrolls and the Early Church, Chicago, 1962; Notre Dame (Ind.)-London, 1966.

F. Nötscher, Voies divines et humaines selon la Bible et Qumrân, La secte de Qumrân et les origines du christianisme (RechBib 4), Bruges, 1959, 135-148.

——, Vom Alten zum Neuen Testament. Gesammelte Aufsätze, Bonn, 1962.

S. Pines, The Jewish Christians of the Early Centuries of Christianity according to a New Source, Jerusalem, 1966.

J. van der Ploeg (ed.), La secte de Qumrân et les origines du christianisme. Communications aux IXes Journées bibliques Louvain 1957 (RechBib 4), Bruges, 1959.

E. Repo, Der "Weg" als Selbstbezeichnung des Urchristentums. Eine traditionsgeschichtliche und semasiologische Untersuchung, Helsinki, 1964.

H. H. Rowley, The Baptism of John and the Qumrân Sect, New Testament Essays. Studies in Memory of T. W. Manson, Manchester, 1959, 218-229.

——, The Qumran Sect and Christian Origins, BJRL 44, 1961, 119-156. [Also to be found in H. R. Rowley, From Moses to Qumran. Studies in the Old Testament, London-New York, 1963, 239-279].

E. Ruckstuhl, Die Chronologie des Letzten Mahles und des Leidens Jesu, Einsiedeln-Zürich-Köln, 1963.

M. H. Scharlemann, Qumran and Corinth, New York, 1962.

K. H. Schelkle, Die Gemeinde von Qumran und die Kirche des Neuen Testaments, Düsseldorf, 1960.

M. H. Shepherd, Are both the Synoptics and John correct about the Date of Jesus' Dead?, JBL 80, 1961, 123-132.

J. Schmitt, L'organisation de l'Église primitive et Qumrân, La secte de Qumrân et les origines du christianisme (RechBib 4), Bruges, 1959, 217-231.

P. Seidensticker, Die Gemeinschaftsform der religiösen Gruppen des Spätjudentums und der Urkirche, StBFranc, LA 9, 1958-1959, 94-198.

E. Stauffer, Jesus und die Wüstengemeinde am Toten Meer, Stuttgart, 1960².

——, Jesus, Gestalt und Geschichte, Bern, 1957. [Has been translated in several languages].

J. Steinbeck, Das Abendmahl Jesu unter Berücksichtigung moderner Forschung, NT 3, 1959, 70-79.

K. STENDAHL (ed.), The Scrolls and the New Testament, New York, 1957-London, 1958.

A. STROBEL, Der Termin des Todes Jesu. Überschau und Lösungsvorschlag unter Einschluss des Qumrankalenders, ZNW 51, 1960, 69-101.

A. VÖGTLE, Chirbet Qumran und die Anfänge des Christentums, ObrhPastBl 59, 1958, 89-95, 120-132, 150-161. [Also separately available].

——, Das offentliche Wirken Jesu auf dem Hintergrund der Qumranbewegung, Freiburg i.Br., 1958.

N. WALKER, The Dating of the Last Supper, JQR 47, 1957, 293-295.

——, Concerning the Jaubertian Chronology of the Passion, NT 3, 1959, 317-320.

——, Jaubert's Solution of the Holy Week Problem, ET 72, 1960, 93-94.

——, Yet another Look at the Passion Chronology, NT 6, 1963, 286-289.

J. A. WALTHER, The Chronology of Passion Week, JBL 77, 1958, 116-122.

A. S. VAN DER WOUDE, De datum van het Laatste Avondmaal en de Oud-Priesterlijke kalender, VoxTheol 29, 1958-1959, 8-11.

M. SOME IMPORTANT MONOGRAPHS AND COLLECTIVE WORKS

H. BARDTKE (ed.), Qumran-Probleme. Vorträge des Leipziger Symposions über Qumran-Probleme 1961, Berlin, 1963.

(——), Bibel und Qumran. Beiträge zur Erforschung der Beziehungen zwischen Bibel- und Qumranwissenschaft, Hans Bardtke zum 22.9.1966, Berlin, 1968.

J. BECKER, Das Heil Gottes. Heils- und Sündenbegriffe in den Qumrantexten und im Neuen Testament, Göttingen, 1964.

O. BETZ, Offenbarung und Schriftforschung in der Qumransekte, Tübingen, 1960.

M. BLACK, The Scrolls and Christian Origins. Studies in the Jewish Background of the New Testament, London-Edinburgh-Paris-Melbourne-Johannesburg-Toronto (Ont.)-New York, 1961.

—— (ed.), The Scrolls and Christianity, London, 1969.

O. BÖCHER, Der johanneische Dualismus im Zusammenhang des nachbiblischen Judentums, Gütersloh, 1965.

H. Braun, Qumran und das Neue Testament I, II, Tübingen, 1966.

W. H. Brownlee, The Meaning of the Qumrân Scrolls for the Bible with Special Attention to the Book of Isaiah, New York, 1964.

F. F. Bruce, Biblical Exegesis in the Qumran Texts (Exegetica III,1), The Hague, 1959; British edition: London, 1960.

J. Carmignac, Recherches sur le "Notre Père", Paris, 1969.

J. H. Charlesworth (ed.), John and Qumran, London, 1972.

J. Daniélou, Les Manuscrits de la Mer Morte et Les Origines du Christianisme, Paris, 1957. [For translations vide section L, 2].

A. M. Denis, Les thèmes de connaissance dans le Document de Damas, Louvain, 1967.

I. H. Eybers, Aspekte van die organisasie en rites van die Joodse Qoemraansekte I, II, Pretoria, 1961.

J. A. Fitzmyer, Essays on the Semitic Background of the New Testament, London, 1971.

B. Gärtner, The Temple and the Community in Qumran and the New Testament. A Comparative Study in the Temple Symbolism of the Qumran Texts and the New Testament, Cambridge, 1965.

H. Goedhart, De slothymne van het Manual of Discipline. A Theological-Exegetical Study of 1 QS X,9-XI,22, Rotterdam, 1965.

H. W. Huppenbauer, Der Mensch zwischen zwei Welten. Der Dualismus der Texte von Qumran (Höhle 1) und der Damaskusfragmente. Ein Beitrag zur Vorgeschichte des Evangeliums, Zürich, 1959.

G. Jeremias, Der Lehrer der Gerechtigkeit, Göttingen, 1963.

E. Koffmahn, Die Doppelurkunden aus der Wüste Juda, STDJ 5, Leiden, 1968.

H. W. Kuhn, Enderwartung und gegenwärtiges Heil. Untersuchungen zu den Gemeindeliedern von Qumran, mit einem Anhang über Eschatologie und Gegenwart in der Verkündigung Jesu, Göttingen, 1966.

E. Y. Kutscher, The Language and Linguistic Background of the Complete Isaiah Scroll, Jerusalem, 1959. [Modern Hebrew]. English edition: Isaiah of the Dead Sea Scrolls. Its Language and its Linguistic Background, STDJ VI, Leiden, in the press.

F. M. López Melús, El cristianismo y los Esenios de Qumrân, Madrid, 1965.

M. Martin, The Scribal Character of the Dead Sea Scrolls I, II, Louvain, 1958.

R. MAYER, J. REUSS, Die Qumran-Funde und die Bibel, Regensburg, 1959; Dutch edition, Leiden, 1960.

G. MORAWE, Aufbau und Abgrenzung der Loblieder von Qumrân. Studien zur gattungsgeschichtlichen Einordnung der Hodajôth, Berlin, 1961.

J. MURPHY-O'CONNOR (ed.), Paul and Qumran. Studies in New Testament Exegesis, London-Dublin-Melbourne, 1968.

F. NÖTSCHER, Gotteswege und Menschenwege in der Bibel und in Qumran, Bonn, 1958.

——, Vom Alten zum Neuen Testament. Gesammelte Aufsätze, Bonn, 1962.

P. VON DER OSTEN-SACKEN, Gott und Belial. Traditionsgeschichtliche Untersuchungen zum Dualismus in den Texten aus Qumran, Göttingen, 1969.

J. VAN DER PLOEG (ed.), La secte de Qumrân et les origines du christianisme (RechBib 4), Bruges, 1959.

——, Bijbelverklaring te Qumran. Mededelingen der Kon. Ned. Ak. van Wetenschappen, Afd. Letterkunde, Nieuwe reeks, deel 23, no. 8, Amsterdam, 1960, (207-229).

Ch. RABIN (ed.), Essays on the Dead Sea Scrolls. In Memory of E. L. Sukenik, Jerusalem, 1961. [Modern Hebrew].

Ch. RABIN, Y. YADIN (edd.), Aspects of the Dead Sea Scrolls, ScrHier 4, Jerusalem, 1958, 1965[2].

H. RINGGREN, Tro och liv enligt Döda-havsrullarna, Stockholm, 1961; English edition: The Faith of Qumran. Theology of the Dead Sea Scrolls, Philadelphia, 1963.

E. RUCKSTUHL, Die Chronologie des letzten Mahles und des Leidens Jesu, Einsiedeln-Zürich-Köln, 1963.

K. H. SCHELKLE, Die Gemeinde von Qumran und die Kirche des Neuen Testaments, Düsseldorf, 1960.

S. H. SIEDL, Qumran. Eine Mönchsgemeinde im alten Bund. Studie über Serek ha-Yaḥad, Rome-Paris-Tournai-New York, 1963.

E. STAUFFER, Jesus, Gestalt und Geschichte, Bern, 1957.

K. STENDAHL (ed.), The Scrolls and the New Testament, New York, 1957-London, 1958.

R. DE VAUX, L'archéologie et les manuscrits de la Mer Morte (Schweich Lectures 1959), London, 1961.

J. DE WAARD, A Comparative Study of the Old Testament Text in the Dead Sea Scrolls and in the New Testament, Leiden, 1965.

M. Weise, Kultzeiten und kultischer Bundesschluss in der "Ordensregel" vom Toten Meer, SP-B 3, Leiden, 1961.

N. Wieder, The Judean Scrolls and Karaism, London, 1962.

A. S. van der Woude, Die messianischen Vorstellungen der Gemeinde
von Qumrân, Assen, 1957.

Y. Yadin, Masada, Herod's Fortress and the Zealots' Last Stand,
London, 1966; Dutch edition, Bussum, 1971.

In this section we have not mentioned the commentaries on the various
scrolls. These can be found in section E.

IV. MISHAIC AND TALMUDICAL HEBREW

COMPILED BY

T. de BRUIN

General Works

Encyclopaedia Judaica, 16 vols, Jerusalem 1972.

Jewish Encyclopedia, I. Singer ed., 12 vols., New York-London,
1901-1906, repr. 1967.

Encyclopedia Judaica, J. Klatzkin ed., 10 vols., (Up to "Lyra" only),
Berlin, 1928-34.

האנציקלופדיה העברית, כללית, יהודית וארץ ישראלית Jerusalem-Tel Aviv,
1949 ff.

The Universal Jewish Encyclopedia, I. Landman ed., 10 vols., New
York, 1939-43, repr. 1948.

S. Shunami, Bibliography of Jewish Bibliographies, Jerusalem, 1965.

M. Steinschneider, Catalogus librorum hebraeorum, 3 vols., Berlin-
Leipzig, 1852-94, repr. Hildesheim, 1964.

——, Bibliographisches Handbuch über die theoretische und prak-
tische Literatur für hebräische Sprachkunde, Leipzig, 1859-1917,
repr. Hildesheim, 1969.

P. Thomsen, Die Palaestina Literatur, eine internationale Bibliographie in systematischer Ordnung, 5 vols., Leipzig, 1903-38.

Paleography, Codicology

C. Bernheimer, Paleografia ebraica, Firenze, 1924.

S. A. BIRNBAUM, The Hebrew Scripts, London, 1954 ff.

S. A. BIRNBAUM, The Hebrew Scripts, 2 prts, Leiden 1971.

M. STEINSCHNEIDER, Vorlesungen über die Kunde hebräischer Handschriften, deren Sammlungen und Verzeichnisse, Leipzig, 1897,
repr. Hildesheim, 1966.

——, (Hebr. transl. of "Vorlesungen …") הרצאות על כתבי יד עבריים
Jerusalem, 1965 (with additional notes by A. M. HABERMAN).

A. LINGUISTICS*

1. GRAMMARS

a. *Hebrew*

K. ALBRECHT, Neuhebräische Grammatik auf Grund der Mišna,
München, 1913.

E. PORATH, לשון חכמים לפי מסורות בבליות שבכתבי יד ישנים Jerusalem, 1938, repr. 1971.

M. H. SEGAL, A Grammar of Mishnaic Hebrew, Oxford, 1926, repr.
1957.

b. *Aramaic*

G. DALMAN, Grammatik des jüdisch-palästinischen Aramäisch, Leipzig, 1905², repr. Darmstadt, 1960.

J. N. EPSTEIN, דקדוק ארמית בבלית, Jerusalem-Tel-Aviv, 1960.

M. L. MARGOLIS, Lehrbuch der aramäischen Sprache des babylonischen Talmuds, München, 1910.

H. ODEBERG, Short Grammar of Galilaean Aramaic, Lund, 1939.

W. B. STEVENSON, Grammar of Palestinian Jewish Aramaic, Oxford,
1924, repr. 1962.

2. DICTIONARIES

E. BEN YEHUDA, מילון הלשון העברית הישנה והחדשה, 8 vols., Berlin-
Jerusalem, 1908-1959, repr. New York, 1960.

G. DALMAN, Aramäisch-neuhebräisches Handwörterbuch zum Targum,
Talmud und Midrash, Göttingen, 1938³, repr. Hildesheim, 1967.

---

* Works on Aramaic are mentioned in this bibliography as far as they are useful for
the texts mentioned in section B. Cf. also the bibliography on Aramaic by H. J. W. DRIJ-
VERS.

M. Jastrow, A Dictionary of the Targumin, the Talmud Babli and Yerushalmi, and the Midrashic Literature, 2 vols., New York, 1903, repr. 1950.

A. Kohut, ספר הערוך השלם, 9 vols., Wien, 1878-1892, repr. New York, 1950.

S. Krauss, Griechische und lateinische Lehnwörter im Talmud, Midrasch und Targum, 2 vols., Berlin, 1898-99, repr. Hildesheim, 1966.

J. Levy, Wörterbuch über die Talmudim und Midraschim, 4 vols., Berlin-Wien, 1924², repr. Darmstadt, 1963.

——, Chaldäisches Wörterbuch über die Targumim und einen grossen Theil des rabbinischen Schrifttums, Leipzig, 1867-68, repr. Köln, 1959.

3. Concordances

H. J. Kasovsky, אוצר לשון המשנה, 4 vols., Frankfurt a.M., 1928, repr. Jerusalem, 1960.

——, אוצר לשון התוספתא, 6 vols., Jerusalem, 1941-1961.

——, אוצר לשון התלמוד Jerusalem, 1954 ff.

——, אוצר לשון האונקלוס, 2 vols., Jerusalem, 1940.

B. Kosovsky, אוצר לשון התנאים, מכילתא דרבי ישמעאל, 4 vols., Jerusalem, 1965-66.

——, אוצר לשון התנאים, ספרא, 4 vols., Jerusalem, 1967-68.

4. Linguistic Studies, Monographies

a. *Hebrew*

A. Ben David, לשון המקרא ולשון חכמים, Tel-Aviv, 1968.

Ch. B. Friedmann, Zur Geschichte der ältesten Mischna-Überlieferung, Frankfurt a.M., 1927.

E. Y. Kutscher, Mittelhebräisch und jüdisch Aramäisch im neuen Köhler-Baumgartner, Festschr. W. Baumgartner, Leiden, 1967, 158-175.

——, לשון חז"ל in ספר חנוך ילון, Jerusalem, 1961, 246-280.

H. Yalon, מבוא לניקוד המשנה, Jerusalem 1962.

——, פרקי לשון, Jerusalem 1971.

See also indices of JQR, MGWJ, Leshonenu, Tarbiz, REJ.

b. *Aramaic*

E. Y. KUTSCHER, מחקרים בארמית הגלילית, Tarbiz 21, 1951, 192-205;
2, 1952, 53-63, 185-192; 23, 1953, 36-60.

——, מחקר הארמית של התלמוד הבבלי, Leshonenu 26, 1962,149-183.

F. ROSENTHAL, Die Aramäistische Forschung, Leiden, 1939, repr. 1964.

——, An Aramaic Handbook, 4 vols., Wiesbaden, 1967.

See also indices of JQR, MGWJ, Leshonenu, Tarbiz, REJ.

B. LITERATURE

1. GENERAL INFORMATIONAL WORKS

J. N. EPSTEIN, מבואות לספרות התנאים, Jerusalem-Tel-Aviv, 1957.

——, מבואות לספרות האמוראים, Jerusalem-Tel-Aviv, 1962.

W. O. E. OESTERLY, G. H. Box, A Short Survey of the Literature of
Rabbinical and Mediaeval Judaism, London, 1920.

M. STEINSCHNEIDER, Jewish Literature from the eight to the eighteenth
century, with an Introduction on Talmud and Midrash, London,
1857, repr. Hildesheim, 1967.

H. L. STRACK, Einleitung in Talmud und Midraš, München, 1921,
repr. = Introduction in Talmud and Midrash, New York, 1959.

2. TEXTS AND THEIR TRANSLATIONS

a. *Mishna*

"TEXTUS RECEPTUS" with commentary by Obadyah BERTINORO and
Tosafot YOM TOB, Lipmann Heller, many times reprinted at
various places.

Ch. ALBECK, ששה סדרי משנה מפורשים ומנוקדים, 6 vols., Jerusalem-Tel-
Aviv, 1958.

G. BEER, O. HOLTZMANN, a.o., The so-called "Giessener Mishna",
Giessen, 1912 ff.

G. BEER, Faksimile Ausgabe des Mischnacodex Kaufmann A 50,
Den Haag, 1929, repr. Jerusalem, 1968.

W. H. LOWE, מתניתא דתלמודא דבני מערבא, Cambridge, 1883, repr.
Jerusalem, 1968.

Cod. Parma, משנה כ"י פארמה "ב", דברי מבוא מ. בן אשר, Jerusalem 1971.

tr.   H. DANBY, The Mishnah, Oxford, 1933, repr. 1964.

b. *Tosefta*

S. Lieberman, תוספתא ע״פ כ״י ווינא, New York, 1955 ff.

M. Zuckermandel, תוספתא ע״פ כתב יד ערפורט וווינה, Pasewalk, 1880,
    repr. Jerusalem, 1963.

tr. D. W. Windfuhr, Die Tosefta, Übersetzung und Erklärung,
    Stuttgart, 1960 ff.

c. *Mekhilta*

H. S. Horovitz (ed.), Mechilta d'Rabbi Ismael, Breslau, 1930, repr.
    Jerusalem, 1960.

J. Z. Lauterbach (ed.), Mekilta de-Rabbi Ishmael, 3 vols., (text +
    trad.), Philadelphia, 1949.

J. N. Epstein, E. Z. Melamed (edd.), Mekhilta de Rabbi Shim'on
    bar Yoḥai, Jerusalem, 1955, repr. 1960.

d. *Sifra*

J. H. Weiss (ed.), ספרא דבי רב הוא ספר תורת כהנים, Wien, 1862,
    repr. New York, 1946.

M. Friedmann (ed.), ספרא דבי רב כולל מדרשי התנאים לספר ויקרא,
    Breslau, 1915, repr. Jerusalem, 1967.

tr. J. Winter, Sifra, Halachischer Midrasch zu Leviticus, Breslau,
    1938.

e. *Sifre*

H. S. Horovitz (ed.), ספרי על ספר במדבר וספרי זוטא, Leipzig, 1971,
    repr. Jerusalem, 1965.

L. Finkelstein (ed.), Siphre zu Deuteronomium, Breslau, 1935-39.

M. Friedmann (ed.), ספרי דבי רב עם תוספות מאיר עין, Wien, 1864,
    repr. Jerusalem, 1968.

tr. K. G. Kuhn, Sifre zu Numeri, Stuttgart, 1959.

H. Ljungman, Sifre zu Deuteronomium, Stuttgart, 1964 ff.

f. *Midrash rabba*

"Textus receptus" with commentary Mattenat Kehuna, 'Eṣ Yosef
    and 'Anaf Yosef, many times reprinted at various places.

J. Theodor, Ch. Albeck (edd.), Bereschit Rabba, mit kritischem
    Apparat und Kommentar, 3 vols., Berlin, 1912-31, repr. Jeru-
    salem, 1965.

M. MARGULIES (ed.), Midrash Wayyikra Rabba, based on mss, and Genizah fragments, 5 vols., Jerusalem, 1953-60, repr. 1966.

S. LIEBERMAN (ed.), Midrash Debarim Rabba, ed. for the first time from the Oxford ms. no. 147, Jerusalem, 1940, repr. 1964.

S. BUBER (ed.), Midrash Echa Rabbati, herausg. nach einer Hs. aus der Bibl. zu Rom, Wilna, 1899, repr. Tel-Aviv, 1964.

tr. H. FREEDMAN, M. SIMON, Midrash Rabbah translated into English, 10 vols., London, 1939, repr. 1951.

g. *Pesiqta*

S. BUBER (ed.), Pesikta, die älteste Hagada, herausg. nach einer in Zefath vorgefundenen und in Ägypten copirten Handschrift, Lemberg, 1868, repr. Jerusalem, 1963.

B. MANDELBAUM (ed.), Pesikta de Rav Kahana, according to an Oxford Manuscript, 2 vols., New York, 1962.

M. FRIEDMANN (ed.), Pesikta Rabbati, Midrash für den Festcyclus, Wenen, 1880, repr. Tel-Aviv, w.d.

tr. W. G. BRAUDE, Pesikta Rabbati transl. from the Hebrew, 2 vols., New-Haven-London, 1968.

h. *Other frequently quoted midrashim*

מדרש תנחומא על חמשה חומשי תורה עם הפירושים המפורסמים עץ יוסף ועֵנֵף יוסף textus receptus many times reprinted at various places.

S. BUBER (ed.), Midrasch Tanchuma, ein agadischer Commentar zum Pentateuch, Wilna, 1885, repr. Jerusalem, 1964.

———, מדרש תהלים המכונה שוחר טוב Wilna, 1891, repr. Jerusalem, 1966.

tr. W. G. BRAUDE, The Midrash on Psalms, 2 vols., New Haven, 1959.

ילקוט שמעוני, אוסף מדרשי חז״ל לכ״ד ספרי תנ״ך textus receptus many times reprinted at various places.

D. HOFFMANN (ed.), Midrasch Tannaim zu Deuteronomium, 2 vols., Berlin, 1909, repr. Tel-Aviv, w.d.

A. JELLINEK (ed.), Bet ha-Midrasch Sammlung kleiner Midraschim, 6 vols., Leipzig-Wien, 1853-1877, repr. Jerusalem, 1966.

tr. A. WÜNSCHE, Aus Israels Lehrhallen, 6 vols., Leipzig, 1907-09, repr. Hildesheim, 1967.

S. SCHECHTER (ed.), Midrash hag-Gadol, forming a collection of ancient Rabbinic Homilies to the Pentateuch (Genesis), Cambridge, 1902.

M. MARGULIES (ed.), Midrash Haggadol on the Pentateuch, Genesis, Jerusalem, 1956, repr. 1967.

——, Midrash Haggadol on the Pentateuch, Exodus, Jerusalem, 1967.

Z. RABINOVITZ (ed.), Midrash Hag-gadol on the Pentateuch, Numbers, Jerusalem, 1967.

S. FISCH (ed.), Midrash hag-Gadol on the Pentateuch, Numbers, Manchester, 1940.

——, Midrash hag-Gadol on the Pentateuch, 2 vols., London, 1957.

H. LICHTENSTEIN (ed.), Megillat Ta'anit, (text + tr.), HUCA 8-9, 1931-32, 318-351.

B. Z. LURIE (ed.), Megillat Ta'anit, (text + tr.), Jerusalem, 1964.

B. RATNER (ed.), Seder 'Olam Rabba, Wilna, 1897, repr. New York, 1965.

M. FRIEDMANN (ed.), Seder Eliahu Rabba we-Seder Eliahu Zuṭa (= Tanna deBe Eliahu), Wien, 1902, repr. Jerusalem, 1960.

PIRQE DE RABBI ELI'EZER, textus receptus, reprinted at various places.

tr. G. FRIEDLÄNDER, Pirke de Rabbi Eliezer, London, 1916, repr. New York, 1965.

S. SCHECHTER (ed.), Abot de Rabbi Natan, Wien, 1887, repr. Jerusalem, 1966.

tr. J. GOLDIN, The Fathers according to Rabbi Nathan, New-Haven, 1955.

i. *Babylonian Talmud*

TEXTUS RECEPTUS, with commentary of RASHI and TOSAFOT, frequently quoted acc. to the edition "Romm", Wilna, 1902-03, and reprinted.

L. GOLDSCHMIDT (ed.), Der babylonische Talmud, (text + tr.), 9 vols., Berlin-Den Haag, 1897-1935.

H. STRACK (ed.), Der babylonische Talmud, nach der einzigen vollständigen Hs. München Cod. 95, 2 vols., Leiden, 1912, repr. Jerusalem 1971.

tr. L. GOLDSCHMIDT, Der babylonische Talmud, 12 vols., Berlin, 1930-37, repr. Darmstadt, 1966.

I. EPSTEIN (ed.), The Babylonian Talmud, 18 vols., London, 1946-49, repr. 1961.

j. *Palestinian Talmud* (*Yerushalmi*)

TEXTUS RECEPTUS, mostly reprint of the edition Krotoschin, 1886.

תלמוד ירושלמי...עם פירושים וביאורים מאת גאוני ישראל Jerusalem, 1960.

Cod. Vatican, ‏תלמוד ירושלמי כ״י וטיקאן ... דברי מבוא מאת שאול ליברמן.‎
Jerusalem 1970.

Cod. Leiden, Cod. Scal. 3 ‏תלמוד ירושלמי כ״י ליידן‎ Jerusalem 1971.

tr. M. Schwab, Le Talmud de Jérusalem, 7 vols., Paris, 1871-90, repr. 1960.

k. *Targum*

A. Sperber, The Bible in Aramaic, 4 vols., Leiden, 1959 ff.

M. Ginzburger, Das Fragmententhargum zum Pentateuch, Berlin, 1899, repr. Jerusalem 1966.

——, Thargum Jonathan den Usiel zum Pentateuch nach der Londoner Handschrift, Berlin, 1903, repr. Hildesheim, 1969, Jerusalem 1966.

P. Kahle, Masoreten des Westens II, Stuttgart, 1930, repr. Hildesheim, 1967.

A. Diez-Macho, Neophyti 1, tomo I: Genesis, Madrid-Barcelona, 1968.

Targum Yerushalmi, Facs. of cod. Neofiti 1 on the Pentateuch, 2 vols, Jerusalem 1971.

3. Monographies, Studies, Introductions and Manuals to the Mentioned Texts

a. *Mishna*

Ch. Albeck, Untersuchungen über die Redaktion der Mischna, Berlin, 1923.

——, ‏מבוא למשנה‎, Jerusalem-Tel-Aviv, 1959.

J. N. Epstein, ‏מבוא לנוסח המשנה‎ , Jerusalem, 1948, repr. 1962.

Z. Frankel, ‏דרכי המשנה‎, Leipzig, 1860, repr. Tel-Aviv, 1959.

L. Palache, Inleiding in de Talmoed, Haarlem, 1922, repr. 1954.

b. *Tosefta*

J. H. Dünner, Die Theorien über Wesen und Ursprung der Tosephta kritisch dargestellt, Amsterdam, 1874.

S. Lieberman, ‏תוספתא כפשוטה, באור ארוך לתוספתא‎, New York, 1949 ff.

A. Schwarz, Tosefta, Mischna und Baraitha in ihrem Verhältnis zu einander, 2 vols., Frankfurt a.M., 1908.

A. Spanier, Die Toseftaperiode in der tannaitischen Literatur, Berlin, 1936.

c to k. (*Midrash*) *in general*

W. BACHER, Die Agada der Tannaiten, 2 vols., Strassbourg, 1884-1890, repr. Berlin, 1965-66.

——, Die Agada der palästinensischer Amoräer, 3 vols., Strassbourg, 1892-99, repr. Berlin, 1968.

——, Die Agada der babylonischen Amoräer, Strassbourg, 1878, repr. Hildesheim, 1967.

——, Die exegetische Terminologie der jüdischen Traditionsliteratur, 2 vols., Leipzig, 1899-1905, repr. Darmstadt, 1965.

——, Tradition und Tradenten in den Schulen Palästinas und Babyloniens, Leipzig, 1914, repr. Berlin, 1966.

L. GINZBERG, The Legends of the Jews, 7 vols., Philadelphia, 1909, repr. 1954.

M. D. GROSS, אוצר האגדה, 3 vols., Jerusalem, 1955, repr. 1965.

I. HEINEMANN, דרכי האגדה, Jerusalem, 1953.

A. HYMAN, אוצר דברי החכמים ופתגמיהם 3 vols., Tel-Aviv, 1956.

M. M. KASHER, ספר תורה שלמה New York, 1949 ff.

L. ZUNZ, Die gottesdienstlichen Vorträge der Juden historisch entwickelt, Berlin, 1832, repr. Hildesheim, 1966 from ed. Frankfurt a.M., 1892.

——, הדרשות בישראל (trad. of 1892, ed. by Ch. ALBECK with add. notes), Jerusalem, 1947, repr. 1954.

i. *Babylonian Talmud*

Ch. ALBECK, מבוא לתלמודים, Tel-Aviv 1969.

E. A. MELAMED, אשנב התלמוד, Jerusalem, 1965'.

M. MIELZINER, Introduction to the Talmud, Cincinnati, 1894[1], New York, 1969[3].

R. RABBINOVICZ, ספר דקדוקי סופרים 16 vols., München, 1867-1897, repr. New York, 1960.

——, M. S. FELDBLUM, ספר דקדוקי סופרים, גיטין, New York, 1966.

j. *Palestinian Talmud*

Z. FRANKEL, מבוא הירושלמי, Breslau, 1870, repr. Jerusalem, 1967.

L. GINZBERG, פירושים וחידושים בירושלמי 4 vols., NewYork, 1941-61.

S. LIEBERMAN, הירושלמי כפשוטו, Jerusalem, 1935.

D. B. RATNER, אהבת ציון וירושלים (coll. variant readings), Wilna, 1901-1917, repr. Jerusalem, 1967.

k. *Targum*

R. Le Déaut, Introduction à la littérature targumique, vol. I, Rome, 1966.

C. HISTORY

1. General Bibliographies

J. Neusner, A Life of Rabban Yohanan ben Zakkai, Leiden, 1962, 181-194.

E. Schürer, A History of the Jewish People in the Time of Jesus, abridged ed. by N. N. Glatzer, New York, 1961, repr. 1963, 409-416.

2. Cultural History

M. Avi-Yonah, Geschichte der Juden im Zeitalter des Talmud, Berlin, 1962.

S. W. Baron, A Social and Religious History of the Jews, Philadelphia, 1953[2] ff.

B. Z. Dinur, תולדות ישראל מסופרות ע״י מקורות ותעודות Tel-Aviv, 1958 ff.

S. Dubnow, Weltgeschichte des jüdischen Volkes, 10 vols., Berlin, 1925-29.

L. Finkelstein, The Jews, their History, Culture and Religion, 2 vols., New York, 1949, repr. 1961.

H. Graetz, Geschichte der Juden von den ältesten Zeiten bis auf die Gegenwart, 11 vols., 1863-70.

A. Hyman, תולדות התנאים והאמוראים, London, 1909.

J. Klausner, היסטוריה של הבית השני, 5 vols., Jerusalem, 1953.

J. Neusner, A History of the Jews in Babylonia, 5 vols., Leiden, 1965- .

C. Roth (ed.), The World History of the Jewish People, London, 1964- .

H. H. ben Sassoon ed., תולדות עם ישראל, Tel -Aviv 1969.

E. Schürer, Geschichte des jüdischen Volkes im Zeitalter Jesu Christi, 3 vols., Leipzig, 1898-1902[3], repr. Hildesheim, 1964.

S. Zeitlin, The Rise and Fall of the Judean State, 2 vols., Philadelphia, 1962-67.

3. Archeology, Art, Numismatics

E. R. Goodenough, Jewish Symbols in the Greco-Roman period, 13 vols., New York, 1953-65.

S. Krauss, Talmudische Archäologie, 3 vols., Leipzig, 1910-12, repr. Hildesheim, 1966.

——, Synagogale Altertümer, Berlin, 1922, repr. Hildesheim, 1966.

L. A. Mayer, A Bibliography of Jewish Numismatics, Jerusalem, 1966.

——, A Bibliography of Jewish Art, ed. O. Kurz, Jerusalem, 1967.

4. Geography

M. Avi-Yonah, גיוגרפיה הסטורית של ארץ ישראל, Jerusalem, 1951.

——, S. Safrai, אטלם קרטא לתקופת הבית השני, Jerusalem, 1967.

5. Theology

I. Elbogen, Der jüdische Gottesdienst in seiner geschichtlichen Entwicklung, Frankfurt a.M., 1924, repr. Hildesheim, 1962.

M. Kadushin, The Rabbinic Mind, New York, 1952.

E. G. Montefiore, H. Loeve, A Rabbinic Anthology, Philadelphia, 1959.

G. F. Moore, Judaism in the First Centuries of the Christian Era, 3 vols., Cambridge (Mass.), 1927, repr. 1962.

S. Schechter, Some Aspects of Rabbinic Theology, New York, 1909, repr. 1961.

G. Scholem, Major Trends in Jewish Mysticism, Jerusalem, 1941, repr. New York, 1954.

E. E. Urbach, חז״ל, פרקי אמונות ודעות, Jerusalem 1971.

D. PERIODICALS

ErIs	= (Eretz Yisrael). (ארץ ישראל)
HB	= Hebräische Bibliographie.
HUCA	= Hebrew Union College Annual.
IEJ	= Israel Exploration Journal.
JQR	= Jewish Quarterly Review.

JJS = Journal of Jewish Studies.
JSS = Journal of Semitic Studies.
JSJ = Journal for the Study of Judaism.
KirSeph = קרית ספר, רבעון ביבליוגרפי (Kirjat Sefer).
לשוננו = (Leshonenu).
MGWJ = Monatschrift für die Geschichte und Wissenschaft des Judentums.
PAAJR = Proceedings of the American Academy for Jewish Research.
REJ = Revue des Études Juives.
Semitica.
סיני = (Sinai).
תרביץ = (Tarbiz).
ZfHB = Zeitschrift für hebräische Bibliographie.
ציון = (Zion).

V. HEBREW OF THE MIDDLE AGES

COMPILED BY

M. BOERTIEN

General Works

G. WIGODER (ed.), Encyclopedia Judaica, 14 vols., Jerusalem, 1971.

C. ROTH, G. WIGODER, The New Standard Jewish Encyclopedia, revised ed., London, 1970.

J. F. OPPENHEIMER (ed.), Lexicon des Judentums, Gütersloh, 1971[2].

Z. WERBLOWSKY, G. WIGODER, The Encyclopedia of the Jewish Religion, Jerusalem-Tel Aviv, 1966 (cp. review by L. H. FELDMAN in BiOr XXVI (1969), 397-406).

H. J. SCHOEPS, Jüdische Geisteswelt, Zeugnisse aus zwei Jahrtausenden, Darmstadt, 1953.

A. E. MILLGRAM, An Anthology of Medieval Hebrew Literature, London-New York-Toronto, 1961.

I. ABRAHAMS, Jewish Life in the Middle Ages, 2nd. revised ed., London, 1932.

J. R. MARCUS, The Jew in the Medieval World, repr. New York, Philadelphia, 1960.

C. ROTH, History of the Jews, repr. New York, 1961, 135-232.

A. BIBLIOGRAPHIES

Systematische Catalogus van de Judaica der Bibliotheca Rosenthaliana, 9 vols., Amsterdam, 1936-1966.

I. JOEL, Index of articles on Jewish Studies, No. 1 to ..., Jerusalem, 1969-   , (Issued by the Editorial Board of "Kiryath Sefer").

Bibliographical notes in:

S. W. BARON, A Social and Religious History of the Jews, 2nd ed., vols. III-X, New York, 1957-1965 (vols. III-VII: High Middle Ages, 500-1200; vols. IX-X: Late Middle Ages and Era of European Expansion, 1200-1650). Cp. Index to vols. I-VIII, New York, 1960.

S. FINKELSTEIN (ed.), The Jews, their History, Culture and Religion, 2 vols., 3rd ed., New York, 1960.

E. L. DIETRICH, Die hebräische Literatur der nachbiblischen Zeit, in: Handbuch der Orientalistik, 3. Band: Semitistik, Leiden, 1954, 80-122.

B. LINGUISTICS

1. GENERAL

S. W. BARON, Vol. VII: Hebrew Language and Letters, New York, 1958.

W. CHOMSKY, Hebrew the Eternal Language (Hebr.), Jerusalem, 1967, 158-211.

G. E. WEIL, Elie Lévita, humaniste et masorète (Studia Post-Biblica, vol. VII), Leiden, 1963.

2. SELECTED LEXICOGRAPHICAL WORKS

Elieser BEN IEHUDA, Thesaurus totius hebraitatis et veteris et recentioris, 15 vols., Berlin-Jerusalem-New York, 1911-1959.

Y. AVINERI, Genuzim megullim, 'Oṣar millim 'atikot ..., Tel Aviv, 1968.

R. LEVY, Contribution à la lexicographie française selon d'anciens textes d'origine juive, Syracuse, 1960.

3. A Selection of Text Editions

I. Davidson, Thesaurus of Medieval Hebrew Poetry (Hebr.), 4 vols.,
New York, 1924-1933.

——, Supplement, Cincinnati, 1937-38. Offprint from HUCA, XII-
XIII.

Ch. Schirmann, Hebrew Poetry in Spain and in the Provence (Hebr.),
4 vols., Jerusalem-Tel Aviv, 1954-60.

——, New Hebrew Poems from the Genizah (Hebr.), Jerusalem, 1965.

——, Anthologie der hebräischen Dichtung in Italien (Hebr.), Berlin,
1934.

Ch. Brody, M. Wiener, A. M. Habermann, Anthology of Hebrew
Poetry (Hebr.), 2 vols., Jerusalem, 1963-65.

Y. Avineri, Hekhal Rashi (Hebr.), 5 vols., Tel Aviv, 1949.

A. Darom, Kimchi's Commentary on the Book of Psalms (Hebr.),
Jerusalem, 1967.

Ch. D. Shevel, Ramban's Commentary on the Torah (Hebr.), Jerusalem, repr. 1972.

C. HISTORY AND HISTORY OF LITERATURE

S. W. Baron, Vol. VI: Laws, Homilies, and the Bible, New York,
1958.

——, Vol. VII: Hebrew Language and Letters, New York, 1958.

——, Vol. VIII: Philosophy and Science, New York, 1958.

J. Neusner, A History of the Jews in Babylonia, Vol. V: Later
Sasanian Times (Studia Post-Biblica, Vol. XV), Leiden, 1970.

Z. Ankori, Karaites in Byzantium, The Formative Years, 970-1100,
New York-Jerusalem, 1959.

A. A. Neuman, The Jews in Spain, 2 vols., Philadelphia, 1944.

Y. Baer, A History of the Jews in Christian Spain, 2 vols., Philadelphia, 1966. Reprint of the German edition with additional
bibliography: Berlin 1970.

H. J. Zimmels, Ashkenazim and Sephardim, Their relations, differences and problems as reflected in the rabbinical responsa,
London, 1958.

R. Renard, Sepharad; Le monde et la langue judéo-espagnole des
Séphardim, Mons, 1966.

M. Steinschneider, Jewish Literature from the 8th to the 18th
Century, 1857, repr. Hildesheim, 1965.
——, Die hebräischen Übersetzungen des Mittelalters, Berlin, 1893,
repr. Hildesheim, 1968.
M. Waxman, A History of Jewish Literature from the Close of the
Bible to our own Days, Vol. I, From the Close of the Canon to
the End of the 12th Century, New York, 1930, Book II: Medieval
Period, 155-469; Vol. II, From the 12th Century to the Middle
of the 18th Century, New York, 1933. Repr. 1968.
I. Zinberg, History of the Jewish Literature (revised Hebrew edition
of Di Geszichte fun der Literatur bej Idn, 2nd ed., Wilna, 1933),
vols. I-III, The Middle Ages, Tel Aviv, 1959-60.
A. M. Habermann, A History of Hebrew Poetry: see *sub* Liturgy.
J. L. Palache, De Hebreeuwsche litteratuur van den na-talmoedischen
tijd tot op onze dagen, Amsterdam, 1937, 5-368.

D. LITURGY

L. Zunz, Die gottesdienstlichen Vorträge der Juden, 2. Aufl., 1892;
revised Hebrew edition by Ch. Albeck, Jerusalem, 1954.
I. Elbogen, Der jüdische Gottesdienst in seiner geschichtlichen Ent-
wicklung, Frankfurt a.M., 1931, repr. Hildesheim, 1962.
L. Zunz, Die synagogale Poesie des Mittelalters, 2. Aufl., Frankfurt
a.M., 1920.
A. M. Habermann, A History of Hebrew Liturgical and Secular
Poetry; Eretz Yisrael, Babylonia, Spain and the Lands of Sefardi
Diaspora (Hebr.), Jerusalem, 1970.
M. Zulay, The Liturgical Poetry of Sa'adja Ga'on and his School
(Hebr.), Jerusalem, 1964.
J. Dov, Seder 'avodat Jisra'el, revised ed., Berlin, 1936.
D. Goldschmidt, Haggadah shel Pesah wetoldoteha, Jerusalem, 1969[3].
——, Seder ha-selihot, Jerusalem, 1965.
——, Seder ha-kinot le-tish'ah be-Av, Jerusalem, 1968.
——, Mahzor la-jamim ha-nora'im, 2 vols., Jerusalem, 1970.
J. Maier, Geschichte der Jüdischen Religion, Berlin, 1972.

E. PHILOSOPHY

J. Guttmann, Die Philosophie des Judentums, München, 1933,
Revised Hebr. ed., Jerusalem, 1951; English ed., London, 1964.

C. VAJDA, Introduction à la pensée juive du moyen-âge, Paris, 1947.
C. SINGER, D. W. SINGER, The Jewish factor in Medieval Thought, in: BEVAN and SINGER, The Legacy of Israel, Oxford, repr. 1953, 173-282.
C. SIRAT, Les théories des visions surnaturelles dans la pensée juive du moyen-âge, (Études sur le Judaisme médiéval, Tome I) Leiden, 1969.

VI. NEW AND MODERN HEBREW

COMPILED BY

M. BOERTIEN

Introductory Remark

More detailed information on abbreviated book titles is given in our chapter Hebrew of the Middle Ages.

A. HISTORY OF LITERATURE

M. WAXMAN, Vol. III: From the Middle of the 18th Century to the Year 1880, New York, 1936.
——, Vol. IV: From 1880 to 1935, New York, 1947.
——, Vol. V: From 1935 to 1960, New York-London, 1960.
J. ZINBERG, Vol. V: From 1780 to 1820 and the Haskala, Tel Aviv, 1959-60.
E. L. DIETRICH, Hebräische Literatur, 122-132.
S. HALKIN, Hebrew Literature, Trends and Values, New York, 1950 (French translation: Paris, 1958).
I. RABINOWICH, Major Trends in Modern Hebrew Fiction (Translated from the Hebr. ed.), Chicago, 1968.
M. KOHANSKY, The Hebrew Theatre, Its first fifty years, Jerusalem, 1969.
J. L. PALACHE, Hebreeuwsche litteratuur, 369-433.
Article: Hebrew Literature, Modern; in: Encyclopedia Judaica, Jerusalem, 1971, vol. 8. col. 175-214.

B. LANGUAGE AND GRAMMAR

H. B. ROSEN, A Textbook of Israeli Hebrew, Chicago, 1962.

G. ALSTER, B. M. MOSSEL, Hadachlil, Leerboek van het Israëlisch Hebreeuws, Assen, 1969.

D. COHEN et H. ZAFRANI, Grammaire de l'Hebreu vivant, Paris, 1968.

H. SIMON, Lehrbuch der modernen hebräischen Sprache, Leipzig, 1970.

W. CHOMSKY, Hebrew, 212-299.

Y. RADDAY, Course of Modern Hebrew: Ha-ṣa'ad ha-rishon; Sa'ad ṣa'ad; Ha-ṣa'ad ha-sheni, 4 vols., Jerusalem, 1960.

J. CAIS, P. ENOCH, Habet ushma (Audio-visual method), Parts I and II, Paris, 1966-71.

Article: Hebrew Grammar; in: Encyclopedia Judaica, Jerusalem, 1971, vol. 8, col. 77-175.

C. DICTIONARIES

Elieser BEN IEHUDA, Thesaurus.

A. EVEN-SHOSHAN, Millon ḥadash, 5 vols., Jerusalem, 1959.

——, Ha-millon hè-ḥadash, 7 vols., Jerusalem, 1966-70.

R. H. GROSSMANN, M. H. SEGAL, Compendious Hebrew-English Dictionary, 20th impr., Tel Aviv, 1960.

R. ALCALAY, The Complete Hebrew-English Dictionary, 4 vols., Tel Aviv, 1964-65. Repr. in one vol. Tel Aviv, 1970.

Ch. SCHACHTER, The New Universal Hebrew-English Dictionary, 2 vols., Tel Aviv, 1965.

A. ELMALEH, Nouveau dictionnaire hébreu-français, 5 tomes, Tel Aviv, 1950-57.

N. STUTCHKOFF, Thesaurus of the Hebrew Language, New York, 1968.

D. ANTHOLOGIES

1. HEBREW

S. BARUSHAW, T. CARMI, E. SPICEHANDLER, The Modern Hebrew Poem itself, 2nd ed., New York, 1966.

R. F. MINTZ, Modern Hebrew Poetry, A bilingual anthology, California, 1966.

E. SPICEHANDLER (ed.), Modern Hebrew Stories, Bantam Dual-Language Book, New York, 1971.

H. BARZEL (ed.), Ḥatané Peras Yisrael, Miḇḥar sippurim, Tel Aviv, 1970.

——, Shishshah Mesapperim. Tel Aviv, 1972.

2. FIRST READERS IN TRANSLATION

S. Y. PENUELI, A. UKHMANI, Anthology of Modern Hebrew Poetry, 2 vols., Jerusalem, 1966.

——, Hebrew Short Stories, An Anthology, 2 vols., Tel Aviv, 1965.

J. BLOCHER, A Selection of the Best Contemporary Hebrew Writing, New York, 1962.

F. SIERKSMA, L. MELKMAN, Eeuwig Israël, Zijn huidige plaats in de letterkunde, cultuur en wereld, 's Graveland, 1949.

E. HISTORY

C. ROTH, History of the Jews, 235-426.

S. GRAYZEL, A History of the Contemporary Jews, from 1900 to the Present, New York-Philadelphia, 1960.

A. HERZBERG, The Zionist Idea; A Historical Analysis and Reader, New York, 1960.

B. HALPERN, The Idea of the Jewish State, Cambridge/Mass., 1969².

XII. SYRIAC AND ARAMAIC

COMPILED BY

H. J. W. DRIJVERS

1. SYRIAC

General Works

A. BAUMSTARK, Geschichte der syrischen Literatur mit Ausschluss der christlich-palästinensischen Texte, Bonn 1922 (Bibliography up to 1922), reprint, Berlin, 1968).

J. T. CLEMONS, Un supplément américain au "Syriac Catalogue" de C. Moss, OrSyr 8, 1963, 469-484.

Elenchus Bibliographicus, Bibl.

P. MASSON, Éléments d'une Bibliographie française de la Syrie. Géographie, ethnographie, histoire, archéologie, langues, littératures, religions, Marseille, 1919.

C. MOSS, Catalogue of Syriac printed Books and related Literature in the British Museum, London, 1962.

E. NESTLE, art. "Syrische Kirche", RE, Vol. 19, Leipzig, 1907, 295-306.

I. ORTIZ DE URBINA, Patrologia Syriaca, sec. ed., Roma, 1965.

A. LINGUISTICS

1. GRAMMARS

T. ARAYATHINAL, Aramaic Grammar (method Gaspey-Otto-Sauer), 2 Vols., Mannanam, 1957-1959.

C. BROCKELMANN, Syrische Grammatik, 11th ed., Leipzig, 1968.

L. COSTAZ, Grammaire Syriaque, sec. ed., Beyrouth, 1955.

Th. NÖLDEKE, Kurzgefasste Syrische Grammatik, sec. ed., Leipzig, 1898, repr. Darmstadt, 1966.

A. UNGNAD, Syrische Grammatik mit Übungsbuch, sec. ed., München, 1932.

2. Lexica

Bar Bahlul, Lexicon Syriacum, ed. R. Duval, 5 vols., Paris, 1888-1901. Reprint Amsterdam 1970.

C. Brockelmann, Lexicon Syriacum, sec. ed., Halle, 1928, repr. Hildesheim, 1965.

R. Köbert, Addenda ad Vocabularium Syriacum, Romae 1956, Orientalia 39, 1970, 315-319.

P. Margoliouth, Supplement to the Thesaurus Syriacus of R. Payne Smith, Oxford, 1927.

R. Payne Smith, Thesaurus Syriacus, 2 vols., Oxford, 1879-1901.

——, P. Margoliouth, A Compendious Syriac Dictionary, Oxford, 1903, repr. Oxford, 1957.

J. Schleifer, Berichtigungen und Ergänzungen zum Supplement des Thesaurus Syriacus, Orientalia 8, 1939, 25-58.

Vocabularium Syriacum, Romae 1956.

3. Linguistic Monographies and Articles

K. Beyer, Der reichsaramäische Einschlag in der ältesten syrischen Literatur, ZDMG 116, 1966, 242-254.

H. Birkeland, The Syriac Phonematic Vowel Systems, Festskrift til Prof. Olaf Broch, Oslo, 1947, 13-39.

J. Blau, The origins of open and closed e in Proto-Syriac, BSOAS 32, 1969, 1-9.

M. M. Bravmann, Syriac dalmā, "lest", "perhaps", and some related Arabic pronomina, JSS 15, 1970, 189-204.

M. M. Bravmann, The infinitive in the function of "psychological predicate" in Syriac, Le Muséon 89, 1971, 219-223.

S. P. Brock, Greek Words in the Syriac Gospels (VET and PE), Mus 80, 1967, 389-426.

A. Denz, Strukturanalyse der pronominalen Objektsuffixe im Altsyrischen und klassischen Arabisch, Diss. München, 1962.

A. Dihle, Die Anfänge der griechischen akzentuierenden Verskunst, Hermes 82, 1954, 182-199.

A. Guillaumont, Détermination et indétermination du nom en syriaque, GLECS 5, 1948-51, 91-94.

——, La Phrase dite „nominale" en syriaque, GLECS 5, 1948-51, 31-33.

E. Jenni, Altsyrische Inschriften, ThZ 21, 1965, 371-385.

S. Moscati, Lo stato assoluto nell'aramaico orientale, AIUON 4, 1962, 79-83.

T. Muraoka, Remarks on the syntax of some types of noun modifier in Syriac, JNES 31, 1972, 192-194.

J. Pirenne, Aux origines de la graphie syriaque, Syria 40, 1963, 101-137.

F. Rosenthal, Die aramaistische Forschung, 179-211.

F. Rundgren, Das altsyrische Verbalsystem, UUÅ 1960: 11, 49-75.

——, Aramaica I, OrientSuec. 14/15, 1966, 75-89.

A. Schall, Studien über griechische Fremdwörter im Syrischen, Darmstadt, 1960.

J. B. Segal, The diacritical point and the accents in Syriac, Oxford, 1953.

F. Vattioni, Appunti sulle iscrizioni siriache antiche, Augustinianum II, 1971, 433-446.

Th. Weiss, Zur ostsyrischen Laut- und Akzentlehre auf Grund der ostsyrischen Massorah-Handschrift des Britischen Museums, Bonner Orient. Studien 5, Stuttgart, 1933.

4. Palaeography

J. Assfalg, Syrische Handschriften (syrische, karšunische, christlich-palästinische, neusyrische und mandäische Handschriften). Verzeichnis der orientalischen Handschriften in Deutschland. Band V, Wiesbaden 1963.

J. T. Clemons, A Checklist of Syriac Manuscripts in the United States, OrChrP 32, 1966, 224-251; 478-522.

W. H. P. Hatch, An Album of dated Syriac manuscripts, Boston, 1956.

A. van Lantschoot, Inventaire des manuscrits syriaques des fonds Vatican (490-631), Barberini oriental et Neofiti, Roma, 1965.

J. Leroy, Les manuscrits syriaques à peintures conservés dans les bibliothèques d'Europe et d'Orient. Contribution à l'étude de l'iconographie des églises de langue syriaque. I, II. Paris 1964.

W. F. Macomber, New Finds of Syriac Manuscripts in the Middle East, ZDMG, Suppl. I, 2, 1969, 473-482.

I. Ortiz de Urbina, Patrologia Syriaca, sec. ed., Roma, 1965, 19-23: a survey of catalogues of syriac manuscripts and related literature.

H. Zotenberg, Catalogues des manuscrits syriaques et sabéens (mandaïtes) de la bibliothèque nationale, Paris 1874.

B. LITERATURE

1. EDITIONS OF SYRIAC TEXTS

a. *Inscriptions*

J.-B. CHABOT, Inscriptions syriaques de Bennaouī, Syria 10, 1929, 252-256.

H. J. W. DRIJVERS, Old-Syriac (Edessean) inscriptions, Leiden 1972.

J. LEROY, Mosaiques funéraires d'Édesse, Syria 34, 1957, 306-342.

A. MARICQ, Les plus anciennes inscriptions syriaques, Syria 34, 1957, 303-305 = Classica et Orientalia, Paris, 1965, 33-35.

H. POGNON, Inscriptions sémitiques de la Syrie, de la Mésopotamie et de la région de Mossoul, Paris, 1907.

J. B. SEGAL, Some Syriac Inscriptions of the 2nd-3rd Century A.D., BSOAS 16, 1954, 13-37.

——, New Syriac Inscriptions from Edessa, BSOAS 22, 1959, 23-41.

——, Four Syriac Inscriptions, BSOAS 30, 1967, 293-304.

See further:

E. JENNI, Die altsyrische Inschriften, 1.-3. Jahrhundert n. Chr., ThZ 21, 1965, 371-385.

F. ROSENTHAL, Aramaistische Forschung, 195-199.

b. *The Bible*

For editions of the Old and New Testament in Syriac see:

C. BROCKELMANN, Syrische Grammatik, 10th ed., Leipzig, 1965, 155-159.

J. A. EMERTON, The Peshitta of the Wisdom of Solomon, Leiden 1959.

I. ORTIZ DE URBINA, Patrologia Syriaca, sec. ed., 224-229.

J. H. HOSPERS, The present-day state of research on the Pešitta since 1948, Verbum. Essays on some aspects of the religious function of words dedicated to Dr. H. W. Obbink, Utrecht, 1964, 148-157.

The Old Testament in Syriac, according to the Peshiṭta version ... ed. by the Peshiṭta Institute, Sample Edition: Song of Songs, Tobit, IV Ezra, Leiden, 1966.

General Preface (P. A. H. DE BOER & W. BAARS), Leiden 1972.

Part IV, 6: Prayer of Manasseh, Apocryphal Psalms, Psalms of Solomon, Tobit, I (3) Esdras, Leiden 1972.

W. BAARS, New Syro-hexaplaric Texts. Edited, commented upon and compared with the Septuagint, Leiden, 1968.

P. B. DIRKSEN, The transmission of the text in the Peshiṭta manuscripts of the Book of Judges, Leiden 1971.

c. *The oldest literature*

J. H. CHARLESWORTH, Les Odes de Salomon et les manuscrits de la Mer Morte, RB 77, 1970, 522-549.

W. CURETON, Spicilegium Syriacum, London, 1855.

——, Ancient Syriac Documents relative to the earliest establishment of Christianity in Edessa, London, 1874, repr. Amsterdam, 1967.

F. C. CONYBEAR, J. RENDEL HARRIS, A. SMITH LEWIS, The Story of Aḥiḳar, sec. ed., Cambridge, 1913.

R. DEGEN, Zwei Miszellen zur Chronik von Se'ert OC 54, 1970, 76-95.

H. J. W. DRIJVERS, The Book of the Laws of Countries. Dialogue on Fate of Bardaiṣan of Edessa, Assen, 1965.

J. A. GOLDSTEIN, The Syriac Bill of Sale from Dura-Europos, JNES 25, 1966, 1-16.

R. GRAFFIN (ed.), Patrologia Syriaca, 3 vols., Paris, 1904-1926.

L. HALLIER, Untersuchungen über die Edessenische Chronik, TU 9, 1, Leipzig, 1892.

G. PHILLIPS, The Doctrine of Addai, the apostle, now first edited in a complete form in the original syriac with an english translation and notes, London, 1876.

J. RENDEL HARRIS, A. MINGANA, The Odes and Psalms of Solomon, 2 vols., Manchester, 1916-1920.

W. STROTHMANN, Makarios und die Makariosschriften in der syrischen Literatur, OC. 54, 1970, 96-105.

W. WRIGHT, Apocryphal Acts of the Apostles, 2 vols., London, 1871.

d. *The later literature*

All editions of syriac texts can be found in the existing histories of syriac literature. There are two great series, i.e. Corpus Scriptorum Christianorum Orientalium (CSCO), Scriptores Syri and Patrologia Orientalis (PO), ed. R. GRAFFIN, F. NAU.

2. History of Literature

A. Baumstark, Geschichte der syrischen Literatur mit Ausschluss
    der christlich-palästinensischen Texte, Bonn, 1922, repr. Berlin,
    1968.

——, A. Rücker, Die syrische Literatur, Handbuch der Orientalistik
    III, 2/3, Leiden, 1954, 168-207.

J. B. Chabot, Littérature syriaque, Paris 1934.

R. Duval, La littérature syriaque, 3rd ed., Paris, 1907. Reprint
    Amsterdam 1970.

M. I. Moosa, Studies in Syriac Literature, The Muslim World 58, 1968,
    105-119; 194-217; 317-333.

I. Ortiz de Urbina, Patrologia Syriaca, sec. ed., Roma, 1965.

W. Wright, A Short History of Syriac Literature, London, 1894
    (reprint 1967).

C. HISTORY AND RELIGION

A great bibliography on the history of the churches of Syria can be
found in:

I. Ortiz de Urbina, Patrologia Syriaca, sec. ed., Roma, 1965, 14-17.

W. Bauer, Rechtgläubigkeit und Ketzerei im ältesten Christentum,
    BHTh 10, Tübingen, 1934.

S. P. Brock, The Syriac version of the Pseudo-Nonnos mythological
    Scholia, Univ. Cambridge Orient. Publ. 20, Cambridge Uni-
    versity Press 1971.

F. C. Burkitt, Urchristentum im Orient, Tübingen, 1907.

R. Dussaud, Topographie de la Syrie antique et médiévale, Paris,
    1927.

A. J. Festugière, Antioche païenne et chrétienne, Paris, 1959.

J.-M. Fiey, Assyrie chrétienne, 3 vols., Beyrouth, 1965-1968.

F. Haase, Altchristliche Kirchengeschichte nach orientalischen Quel-
    len, Leipzig, 1925.

W. Hage, Die syrisch-jakobitische Kirche in frühislamischer Zeit,
    Wiesbaden, 1966.

Ph. K. Hitti, History of Syria including Lebanon and Palestine,
    sec. ed., London, 1957.

J. Joseph, The Nestorians and their Muslim Neighbours. A Study of Western Influence on their Relations, Princeton Orient. Series 20, Princeton, 1961.

R. Köbert, Bemerkungen zu den syrischen Zitaten aus Homer und Platon im 5. Buch der Rhetorik des Anton von Tagrit und zum syrischen Περὶ ἀσκήσεως angeblich von Plutarch, Or. 40, 1971, 438-447.

J. Labourt, Le christianisme dans l'empire perse sous la dynastie sassanide, sec. ed., Paris, 1904.

J. Leroy, Une copie syriaque du Missale Romanum de Paul III et son arrière-plan historique, MUSJ 46, 1970-71, 355-382.

B. Ludger, Die Chronologie der Syrer, Sitz. Ber. Osterr. Akad. d. d. Wiss. Phil.-hist. Kl. 264, Bd. 3. Abh. 1969.

P. Narsi, L'Histoire des Églises chaldéenne et syrienne, 2 vols., Mossul s.d.

F. Nau, Les arabes chrétiennes de Mésopotamie et de Syrie du VIIe et VIIIe siècle, Paris, 1933.

J. B. Segal, Mesopotamian Communities from Julian to the Rise of Islam, Proceedings British Acad., Vol. XLI, London, 1955, 109-139.

——, Edessa, the Blessed City, Oxford, 1970.

B. Spuler, Die Nestorianische Kirche, Die Westsyrische Kirche, Handbuch der Orientalistik VIII, 2, Leiden, 1961, 120-216.

A. Vööbus, History of Ascetism in the Syrian Orient. A Contribution to the History of Culture in the Near East, vol. I, II, III, ..., Leuven, 1958-   .

G. Wiessner, Zur Märtyrerüberlieferung aus der Christenverfolgung Schapurs II. Untersuchungen zur syrischen Literaturgeschichte I, AAWG, Phil.-Hist. Klasse III, 67, Göttingen, 1967.

D. IMPORTANT JOURNALS

AnBoll, Bibl, BSOAS, ByZ, JA, Mus, MUSJ, OrChr, OrChrP, OS, Proche-Or.Chr, RSO, RSR, Syria, ZDMG.

2. ARAMAIC

General works with bibliographies or many bibliographical references

C. Brockelmann, Das Aramäische, einschliesslich des Syrischen, Handbuch der Orientalistik III 2/3, Leiden, 1954, 135-162.

J. B. Chabot, Les langues et les littératures araméennes, Paris, 1910.

Ch. Clermont-Ganneau, Recueil d'archéologie orientale, 8 vols., Paris, 1888-1924.

G. A. Cook, A Textbook of North-Semitic Inscriptions, Oxford, 1903.

Corpus Inscriptionum Semicarum II, Paris, 1889-   . (= CIS).

H. Donner, W. Röllig, Kanaanäische und Aramäische Inschriften, 3 vols., sec. ed., Wiesbaden, 1966-1969 (= KAI).

A. Dupont-Sommer, Littérature araméenne, Histoire des Littératures I, ed. R. Quenau, Paris, 1955, 631-646.

Elenchus Bibliographicus, Bibl.

C. F. Jean, J. Hoftijzer, Dictionnaire des inscriptions sémitiques de l'Ouest, Leiden, 1965.

J. Hoftijzer, Kanttekeningen bij het onderzoek van de westsemitische epigraphie, JEOL XV, 1957-1958, 112-125.

——, Religio Aramaïca, Godsdienstige verschijnselen in aramese teksten, MVEOL 16, Leiden, 1968.

J. J. Koopmans, De literatuur over het Aramees na 1940, JEOL XV, 1957-58, 125-132.

——, Aramäische Chrestomathie, 2 vols., Leiden, 1962.

E. Y. Kutscher, Aramaic, in: Current trends in linguistics, ed. by Th. A. Sebeok, Vol. 6, Linguistics in South West Asia and North Africa, The Hague-Paris 1970, 347-412.

M. Lidzbarski, Handbuch der Nord-Semitischen Epigraphik nebst ausgewählten Inschriften, 2 vols., Weimar, 1898.

——, Ephemeris für semitische Epigraphik, 3 vols., Giessen, 1900-1915.

Répertoire d'épigraphie sémitique, Paris, 1900-   . (= RÉS).

F. Rosenthal, Die aramaistische Forschung seit Th. Nöldeke's Veröffentlichungen, Leiden, 1939, repr. 1964.

—— (ed.), An Aramaic Handbook, 4 vols., Wiesbaden, 1967.

S. Segert, Aramäische Studien I. ArOr 24, 1956, 383-403.

S. Segert, Aramäische Studien III-V. ArOr 26, 1958, 561-584.

J. Teixidor, Bulletin d'épigraphie sémitique, Syria XLIV, 1967, 163-195; XLV, 1968, 353-389 (is continued).

OLD ARAMAIC

General Works

J. NAVEH, Old Aramaic Inscriptions, AIUON 16, 1966, 19-36.
J. NAVEH, Early Aramaic inscriptions, Lešonénu 29, 1964-65, 183-197.
J. NAVEH, Addenda to Early Aramaic inscriptions, Lešonénu 30, 1965-66, 157-160.

A. LINGUISTICS

1. GRAMMARS

R. DEGEN, Altaramäische Grammatik der Inschriften des 10.-8. Jh. v. Chr., AKM 38, 3, Wiesbaden, 1969.
G. GARBINI, L'Aramaico Antico, Roma, 1956.
——, Il Semitico di Nord-Ovest, Napels, 1960.

2. LEXICON

C.-F. JEAN, J. HOFTIJZER, Dictionnaire des inscriptions sémitiques de l'Ouest, Leiden, 1965 (= DISO).

3. LINGUISTIC MONOGRAPHIES AND ARTICLES

K. AARTUN, Zur Frage des bestimmten Artikels im Aramäischen, AcOr 24, 1959, 5-14.
C. BROCKELMANN, Neuere Theorien zur Geschichte des Akzents und des Vokalismus im Hebräischen und Aramäischen, ZDMG NF 19, 1940, 332-371.
F. M. CROSS, D. N. FREEDMAN, Early Hebrew Orthography. A Study of the Epigraphic Evidence, Am.Or.Ser. 36, New Haven, 1952.
R. DEGEN, Zur Schreibung des Kaška-Namens in ägyptischen, ugaritischen und altaramäischen Quellen, WO 4/1, 1967, 48-60.
——, Die Präfixkonjugationen des Altaramäischen, ZDMG, Suppl. I/2, Wiesbaden, 1969, 701-706.
J. A. FITZMYER, The Aramaic Inscriptions of Sefîre, Biblica et Orientalia 19, Roma, 1967, 139-181: Appendix. The Grammar of the Sefîre Inscriptions.

J. FRIEDRICH, Kanaanäisch und Westsemitisch, Scientia 84, 1949, 220-223.

——, Phönizisch-punische Grammatik, AnOr 32, Roma, 1951 (Addendum).

——, Der Schwund kurzer Endvokale im Nordwestsemitischen, AfO 18, 1957, 3-14.

——, Zur passivischen Ausdrucksweise im Aramäischen, AfO 18, 1957, 124-125.

——, Zur Bezeichnung des langen ā in den Schreibweisen des Aramäischen, Or N.S. 26, 1957, 37-42.

——, Zur Stellung des Jaudischen in der Nordwestsemitischen Sprachgeschichte, Studies in Honor of Benno Landsberger on his seventy-fifth Birthday April 21, 1965, Ass.Stud. 16, Chicago, 1965, 425-429.

G. GARBINI, Nuovo materiale per la grammatica dell'Aramaico antico, RSO 34, 1959, 41-54.

——, Unité et variété des dialectes araméens anciens, Akten des XXIV. Internationalen Orientalisten-Kongresses 1957, Wiesbaden, 1959, 242-244.

——, Semitico Nord-Occidentale e Aramaico, G. LEVI DELLA VIDA (ed.), Linguistica Semitica: Presente e Futuro, Studi Semitici 4, Roma, 1961, 59-90.

——, I dialetti dell'aramaico antico e lo yaudico, AIUON 19, 1969, 1-8.

——, Le matres lectiones e il vocalismo nell'aramaico antico, AIUON 19, 1969, 8-15.

H. L. GINSBERG, Aramaic Dialect Problems, AJSL 50, 1933-34, 1-9; AJSL 52, 1935-36, 95-103.

——, The Classification of the North-West Semitic Languages, Akten des XXIV. Internationalen Orientalisten-Kongresses 1957, Wiesbaden, 1959, 256-257.

J. C. GREENFIELD, Dialect traits in Early Aramaic, Lešonénu 32, 1968, 359-368.

Z. S. HARRIS, The Development of the Canaanite Dialects, New Haven, 1939.

M. HELTZER, Some North-West Semitic Epigraphic Gleanings from the XI'VI Centuries B.C., AIUON 21, 1971, 183-198.

W. B. HENNING, Ein persischer Titel im Altaramäischen, BZAW 103, Berlin, 1968, 136-143.

A. JEPSEN, Kleine Bemerkungen zu drei westsemitischen Inschriften, MIO 15, 1969, 1-5.

E. Y. KUTSCHER, Contemporary Studies in North-Western Semitic, JSS X, 1965, 21-51.

M. LIVERANI, Antecedenti dell'onomastica aramaica antica, RSO 37, 1962, 65-76.

S. MOSCATI, Preistoria e storia del consonantismo ebraico antico, Roma, 1954.

——, Sulla posizione linguistica del semitico nord-occidentale, RSO 31, 1956, 229-234.

——, Il Semitico di Nord-Ovest, Studi Orientali in onore di Giorgio Levi della Vida II, Roma, 1956, 201-221.

J. NAVEH, The Development of the Aramaic Script, The Israel Academy of Sciences and Humanities, Proceedings V, 1, Jerusalem 1970.

A. POEBEL, Das appositionell bestimmte Pronomen der 1. Pers. Sing. in den westsemitischen Inschriften und im Alten Testament, Chicago, 1932.

H. B. ROSÉN, Zur Vorgeschichte des Relativsatzes im Nordwestsemitischen, ArOr 27, 1959, 186-198.

F. ROSENTHAL, Die aramaistische Forschung seit Th. Nöldeke's Veröffentlichungen, Leiden, 1939 (reprint 1964).

S. SEGERT, Aramäische Studien I, ArOr 24, 1956, 383-403.

——, Aramäische Studien III-V, ArOr 26, 1958, 561-584.

——, Altaramäische Schrift und Anfänge des griechischen Alphabets, Klio 41, 1963, 38-57.

——, Zur Schrift und Orthographie der altaramäischen Stelen von Sfire, ArOr 32, 1964, 110-126.

——, Ugaritisch und Aramäisch, Studia semitica Ioanni Bakoš dicata, Bratislava 1965, 215-226.

——, Contribution of Professor I. N. Vinnikov to Old Aramaic Lexicography, ArOr 35, 1967, 463-466.

W. VON SODEN, Zur Einteilung der semitischen Sprachen, WZKM 56, 1960, 177-191.

——, Aramäische Wörter in neuassyrischen und neu- und spätbabylonischen Texten I (aga-muš), Or 35, 1966, 1-20; II (n.-z. und Nachträge), Or 37, 1968, 261-271.

R. STIEHL, Kanaanäisch und Aramäisch, AAW I, Berlin, 1964, 213-236.

A. J. WENSINCK, Het oudste Arameesch, Utrecht, 1909.

B. LITERATURE

1. PRINCIPAL EDITIONS OF OLD-ARAMAIC TEXTS

CIS.

G. A. COOK, A Textbook of North-Semitic Inscriptions, Oxford, 1903.
F. M. CROSS, The stele dedicated to Melcarth by Ben-Hadad of Damascus, BASOR 205, 1972, 36-42.
H. DONNER, W. RÖLLIG, KAI.
J. A. FITZMYER, The Aramaic letter of king Adon to the Egyptian Pharaoh, Biblica 46, 1965, 41-55.
——, The Aramaic Inscriptions of Sefîre, Biblica et Orientalia 19, Roma, 1967.
J. J. KOOPMANS, Aramäische Chrestomathie, 2 vols., Leiden, 1962.
M. LIDZBARSKI, Ephemeris für semitische Epigraphik, 3 vols., Giessen, 1900-1915.

RÉS.

F. VATTIONI, Epigrafia aramaica, Augustinianum 10, 1970, 493-532.

2. LITERARY AND STYLISTIC STUDIES

A. CAQUOT, Une inscription araméenne d'époque assyrienne, Hommages à André Dupont-Sommer, Paris 1971, 9-16.
T. COLLINS, The Kilamuwa inscription — a Phoenician poem. Die Welt des Orients 6, 1971, 183-188.
R. DEGEN, review of H. DONNER - W. RÖLLIG, KAI, sec. ed. Wiesbaden 1966-1969, ZDMG 121, 1971, 121-139.
——, Zum Ostrakon CIS II, 138, Neue Ephemeris für Semitische Epigraphik, Wiesbaden 1972, 23-27.
——, Der Räucheraltar aus Lachisch, Neue Ephemeris für Semitische Epigraphik, Wiesbaden, 1972, 39-48.
——, Die aramäische Tontafeln vom Tell Halaf, Neue Ephemeris f. Semitische Epigraphik, Wiesbaden 1972, 49-57.
G. R. DRIVER, Aramaic names in Accadian texts, RSO 32, 1957, 41-57.
J. A. FITZMYER, A further note on the Aramaic inscription Sefire III. 22, JSS 14, 1969, 197-200.
J. FRIEDRICH, Zu der altaramäischen Stele des ZKR von Hamat, AfO 21, 1966, 83.

——, Nochmals die phönizische Inschrift von Pyrgi, Festschrift F. ALTHEIM, Berlin 1969, 205-209.

S. GEVIRTZ, West-Semitic Curses and the Problem of the Origins of Hebrew Law, VT 11, 1961, 137-158.

J. C. GREENFIELD, Studies in West Semitic Inscriptions I. Stylistic Aspects of the Sefire Treaty Inscriptions, AcOr 29, 1965-1966, 1-18.

Z. BEN-HAYYIM, Comments on the inscriptions of Sfire. Lešonénu 35, 1971, 243-253.

D. R. HILLERS, Treaty Curses and the Old Testament Prophecy, Biblica et Orientalia 16, Roma, 1964.

S. KAUFMAN, Si'gabbar, Priest of Sahr in Nerab, JAOS 90, 1970, 270-271.

M. LIVERANI, Antecedenti dell'onomastica aramaica antica, RSO 37, 1962, 65-76.

D. J. McCARTHY, Treaty and Covenant, Analecta biblica 21, Roma, 1963.

J. Naveh, Early Aramaic Inscriptions, Lešonénu 29, 1964-65, 183-197.

——, Addenda to Early Aramaic Inscriptions, Lešonénu 30, 1965-66, 157-160.

C. HISTORY AND RELIGION

W. F. ALBRIGHT, The Amarna Letters from Palestine-Syria, The Philistines and Phoenicians, CAH II, rev. ed., Cambridge, 1966, 46-53.

A. ALT, Die syrische Staatenwelt vor dem Einbruch der Assyrer, ZDMG 13, 1934, 233-258 = Kleine Schriften III, 1959, 214-232.

R. D. BARNETT, The Gods of Zinjirli, Compte Rendu de l'Onzième Rencontre assyriologique international, Leiden, 1964, 59-87.

R. A. BOWMAN, Arameans, Aramaic, and the Bible, JNES 7, 1948, 65-90.

G. BUCCELLATI, Cities and Nations of Ancient Syria, Studi Semitici 26, Roma, 1967.

M. DIETRICH, Die Aramäer Südbabyloniens in der Sargonidenzeit (700-648), Neukirchen, 1970.

A. DUPONT-SOMMER, Les Araméens, Paris, 1949.

——, Sur les débuts de l'histoire araméenne, Suppl. VT I, Leiden, 1953, 40-49.

296 LANGUAGES OF THE ANCIENT NEAR EAST

K. F. Euler, Königtum und Götterwelt in den altaramäischen Inschriften von Nordsyrien, ZAW 56, 1939, 272-313.

J. Hoftijzer, Religio Aramaïca. Godsdienstige verschijnselen in aramese teksten, MVEOL 16, Leiden, 1968.

B. Landsberger, Sam'al. Studien zur Entdeckung der Ruinenstätte Karatepe, Ankara, 1948.

M .Liverani, Introduzione alla storia dell'Asia anteriore, Roma, 1963.

J .R. Kupper, Les nomades en Mésopotamie au temps des rois de Mari, Bibliothèque de la faculté de philosophie et lettres de l'Université de Liège, fasc. 112, Paris, 1957.

A. Malamat, The Aramaeans in Aram Naharayim and the Rise of their States, Jerusalem, 1952 (in Hebrew); cf. idem, BA 21, 1958, 96-102.

M. McNamara, De populi Aramaeorum primordiis, Verbum Domini 35, 1957, 129-142.

S. Moscati, Sulle origine degli Aramei, RSO 26, 1951, 16-22.

——, The Aramaean Aḫlamu, JSS 4, 1959, 303-307.

M. Noth, Der historische Hintergrund der Inschriften von Sefīre, ZDPV 77, 1961, 118-172.

R. T. O'Callaghan, Aram Naharaim. A Contribution to the History of Upper Mesopotamia in the second Millennium B.C., AnOr 26, Roma, 1948.

J. F. Ross, Prophecy in Hamath, Israel and Mari, HThR 63, 1970, 1-28.

P. Sacchi, Per una storia di Aram, La Parola del Passato 14, 1959, 124-134.

——, Osservazioni sul problema degli Aramei, Atti et Memorie dell' Accademia Toscana di Scienze e Lettere, La Colombaria 25, 1960-61, 85-142.

S. Schiffer, Die Aramäer, Leipzig, 1911.

M. Unger, A History of Damascus from the earliest Times until its Conquest by Assyria, Baltimore, 1946-47.

G. Widengren, Aramaica et Syriaca, Hommages à André Dupont-Sommer, Paris 1971, 221-231.

H. J. Zobel, Das Gebet um Abwendung der Not und seine Erhörung in den Klageliedern des Alten Testaments und in der Inschrift des Königs Zakir von Hamat VT 21, 1971, 91-99.

D. IMPORTANT JOURNALS

AcOr, AfO, AIUON, ArOr, BA, BASOR, IrAnt, JAOS, JNES, JSS, MIO, MUSJ, Or, OA, RA, RSO, VD, VT, WO.

OFFICIAL ARAMAIC

General works with many bibliographical references

F. ALTHEIM, R. STIEHL, Die aramäische Sprache unter den Achaimeniden I. Geschichtliche Untersuchungen, Frankfurt a.M., 1963.
——, Supplementum Aramaicum. Aramäisches aus Iran. Anhang: Das Jahr Zarathustras, Baden-Baden, 1957.
F. ROSENTHAL, Die aramaistische Forschung seit Th. Nöldeke's Veröffentlichungen, Leiden, 1939, repr. 1964.

A. LINGUISTICS

1. GRAMMARS

H. BAUER, P. LEANDER, Grammatik des Biblisch-Aramäischen, Halle, 1927, repr. Hildesheim, 1962.
——, Kurzgefasste Biblisch-Aramäische Grammatik, Halle, 1929, repr. Hildesheim, 1965.
A. DAMMRON, Grammaire de l'Araméen biblique, Strasbourg, 1961.
J. J. KOOPMANS, Arameese Grammatica, sec. ed., Leiden, 1957.
P. LEANDER, Laut- und Formenlehre des Aegyptisch-Aramäischen, Göteborg, 1928, repr. Hildesheim, 1966.
L. PALACIOS, Grammatica Aramaico-Biblica, sec. ed., Roma-Tournay-Paris, 1955.
F. ROSENTHAL, A Grammar of Biblical Aramaic, sec. ed., Wiesbaden, 1963.
H. L. STRACK, Grammatik des Biblisch-Aramäischen, 6th ed., München, 1921.

2. LEXICA

C.-F. JEAN, J. HOFTIJZER, Dictionnaire des inscriptions sémitiques de l'Ouest, Leiden, 1965.
L. KOEHLER, W. BAUMGARTNER, Lexicon in Veteris Testamenti Libros, sec. ed., with Supplementum, Leiden, 1958.
E. VOGT, Lexicon linguae aramaicae veteris testamenti documentis antiquis illustratum. Romae 1971.

3. LINGUISTIC MONOGRAPHIES AND ARTICLES

K. AARTUN, Zur Erklärung des aramäischen Adverbs kaddû, Oriens
18/19, 1965-1966, 347-351.

F. ALTHEIM, R. STIEHL, Supplementum Aramaicum. Aramäisches aus
Iran. Anhang: Das Jahr Zarathustras, Baden-Baden, 1957.

——, Philologia Sacra, Tübingen, 1958.

——, Die aramäische Sprache unter den Achaimeniden I. Geschichtliche Untersuchungen, Frankfurt a.M., 1963.

——, Aramäisch als Weltsprache, AAW I, Berlin, 1964, 181-236.

——, Spirantisierung der Emphaticae. Aramäische Inschriften aus
Šīmbār, AAW III, Berlin, 1966, 59-73.

W. BAUMGARTNER, Das Aramäische im Buche Daniel, ZAW N.F. 4,
1927, 81-133 = Zum Alten Testament und seiner Umwelt,
Leiden, 1959, 68-123.

E. BENVENISTE, Termes et noms achéménides en araméen, JA 225,
1934, 177-193.

——, La construction passive du parfait transitif. BSL 48, 1952, 52-63.

——, Éléments perses en araméen d'Égypte, JA 242, 1954,
297-310.

F. R. BLAKE, Studies in Semitic Grammar. The Etymology of the
Aramaic Particle 't, 'yty, JAOS 35, 1915-1917, 377-381.

——, A Resurvey of Hebrew Tenses. Appendix: Hebrew Influence on
Biblical Aramaic, Scripta Pont. Inst. Bibl. 103, Roma, 1951.

——, Studies in Semitic Grammar V, JAOS 73, 1953, 7-16.

M. M. BRAVMANN, The Aramaic nomen agentis qātōl and some similar
phenomena of Arabic, BSOAS 34, 1971, 1-4.

B. COUROYER, Termes égyptiens dans les papyri araméens du Musée
de Brooklyn, RB 61, 1954, 554-559.

F. M. CROSS, D. N. FREEDMAN, Early Hebrew Orthography. A Study
of the Epigraphic Evidence, AmOr.Ser. 36, New Haven, 1952.

W. EILERS, Iranisches Beamtentum in der keilinschriftlichen Überlieferung, AKM 25, 1940.

J. A. FITZMYER, The Syntax of kl, kl' in the Aramaic Texts from
Egypt and in Biblical Aramaic, Bibl 38, 1957, 170-184.

G. GARBINI, Sull'alternativa h > ' in semitico, AIUON, 1, 1959,
47-52.

B. GEIGER, Zu den iranischen Lehnwörtern im Aramäischen, WZKM
37, 1930, 195-203.

H. L. Ginsberg, Aramaic Dialect Problems, AJSL 50, 1933-1934, 1-9; 52, 1935-1936, 95-103.

——, Aramaic Studies Today, JAOS 62, 1942, 229-238.

——, Notes on some Old Aramaic Texts, JNES 18, 1959, 143-149.

J. C. Greenfield, Studies in Aramaic Lexicography I, JAOS 82, 1962, 290-299.

——, The "periphrastic" imperative in Aramaic and Hebrew, IEJ 19, 1969, 199-210.

P. Grelot, Le waw d'apodose en araméen d'Egypte, Semitica 20, 1970, 33-39.

——, Notes d'onomastique sur les textes araméens d'Égypte, Semitica 21, 1971, 95-117.

——, Études sur les textes araméens d'Éléphantine, RB 78, 1971, 515-544.

P. Joüon, Notes grammaticales, lexicographiques et philologiques sur les papyrus araméens d'Égypte, MUSJ 18, 1934, 1-89.

K. A. Kitchen, The Aramaic of Daniel, Notes on some problems in the Book of Daniel, London, 1965, 31-79.

E. Y. Kutscher, The Hermopolis Papyri, Israel Oriental Studies I, 1971, 103-119.

S. J. Liebermann, The Aramaic Argillary Script in the seventh Century, BASOR 192, 1968, 25-31.

R. Macuch, Gesprochenes Aramäisch und aramäische Schriftsprache in F. Altheim/R. Stiehl, Christentum am Roten Meer I, Berlin 1971, 537-557.

J. L. Malone, Wave Theory, Rule Ordening and Hebrew-Aramaic Segolation, JAOS 91, 1971, 44-66.

J. de Menasce, Mots d'emprunt et nommes propres iraniens dans les nouveaux documents araméens, BiOr 11, 1954, 161-166.

S. Morag, The Vocalization Systems of Arabic, Hebrew and Aramaic, The Hague, 1962.

——, Biblical Aramaic in Geonic Babylonia, Studies in Egyptology and Linguistics in Honour of H. J. Polotsky, ed. by H. B. Rosén, Jerusalem, 1964, 117-131.

T. Muraoka, Notes on the Syntax of Biblical Aramaic, JSS 11, 1966, 151-168.

J. Naveh, The Paleography of the Hermopolis Papyri, Israel Oriental Studies I, 1971, 120-122.

P. Nober, El significado de la palabra aramea 'asparnā' en Esdras, EstBib 16, 1957, 393-401.

——, 'adrazdā' (Esdras 7, 23), BZ 2, 1958, 134-138.

——, Lexicalia irano-biblica, VD 36, 1958, 102-105.

E. Puech, Sur la racine "ṣlḫ" en hébreu et en araméen, Semitica 21, 1971, 5-19.

C. Rabin, The Nature and Origin of the šafʿel in Hebrew and Aramaic, Erets Israel 9, 1969, 148-158 (in Hebrew).

J. J. Rabinowitz, The Susa Tablets, The Bible and the Aramaic Papyri, VT 11, 1961, 55-77.

——, Grecisms and Greek Terms in the Aramaic Papyri, Bibl 39, 1958, 77-82.

——, More on Grecisms in Aramaic Documents, Bibl 41, 1960, 72-74.

H. B. Rosén, On the Use of the Tenses in the Aramaic of Daniel, JSS 6, 1961, 183-203.

H. H. Rowley, The Aramaic of the Old Testament. Grammatical and Lexical Study of its Relations with other early Dialects, Oxford, 1929.

F. Rundgren, Zur Bedeutung von šršw-Ezra VII, 26, VT 7, 1957, 400-404.

H. H. Schaeder, Iranische Beiträge I, Halle, 1930.

G. Schuttermayer, RḤM- Eine lexikalische Studie, Biblica 51, 1970, 499-525.

S. Segert, Aufgaben der biblisch-aramäischen Grammatik, Communio Viatorum 1, 1958, Heft 2, 127-134.

——, Concerning the Methods of Aramaic Lexicography, ArOr 30, 1962, 505-506.

M. H. Silverman, Jewish Personal Names in the Elephantine Documents. A Study in onomastic development, University Microfilms, Ann Arbor, 1967.

——, Aramean Name-Types in the Elephantine Documents, JAOS 89, 1969, 691-709.

——, Onomastic Notes to "Aramaica Dubiosa", JNES 28, 1969, 192-196.

A. Spitaler, Zur Frage der Geminatendissimilation im Semitischen. Zugleich ein Beitrag zur Kenntnis der Orthographie des Reichsaramäischen, Indogermanische Forschungen 61, 1952, 257-266.

——, Zum Problem der Segolisierung im Aramäischen, Stud. Orient. C. Brockelmann, Halle, 1968, 193-199.

R. Stiehl, Wörterverzeichnis aramäischer Inschriften und sonstiger Urkunden aus parthischer Zeit, F., Altheim, Geschichte der Hunnen 5, Berlin, 1962, 110-125.

W. F. STINESPRING, The Active Infinitive with Passive Meaning in Biblical Aramaic, JBL 81, 1962, 391-394.

M. WAGNER, Die lexikalischen und grammatikalischen Aramaismen im alttestamentlichen Hebräisch, BZAW 96, Berlin, 1966.

J. G. WILLIAMS, A Critical Note on the Aramaic Indefinite Plural of the Verb, JBL 83, 1964, 180-183.

H. WUTHNOW, Die semitischen Menschennamen in griechischen Inschriften und Papyri des vorderen Orients, Studien zur Epigraphik und Papyruskunde I/4, Leipzig, 1930.

B. LITERATURE

1. PRINCIPAL EDITIONS OF OFFICIAL ARAMAIC TEXTS

N. AIMÉ-GIRON, Textes araméens d'Égypte, Cairo, 1931.

——, Adversaria Semitica, BIFAO 38, 1939, 1-63.

——, Adversaria Semitica III, ASAE 40, 1941, 433-460.

F. ALTHEIM, R. STIEHL, Aramäische Inschriften, AAW V/1, Berlin, 1968, 72-84.

——, Ostraka aus Nisā, AAW II, Berlin, 1965, 204-229.

N. AVIGAD, Aramaic inscriptions in the Tomb of Jason, IEJ 17, 1967, 101-111.

H. BAUER, B. MEISSNER, Ein aramäischer Pachtvertrag aus dem 7. Jahre Darius I, SPAW, Phil.-hist. Kl., Berlin, 1936.

E. BENVENISTE, A. DUPONT-SOMMER, Une inscription indo-araméenne d'Aśoka provenant de Kandahar (Afghanistan), JA 254, 1966, 437-465.

A. D. H. BIVAR, A rosette phialē inscribed in Aramaic, BSOAS 24, 1961, 189-199.

——, S. SHAKED, The inscriptions at Shīmbār, BSOAS 27, 1964, 265-290.

R. A. BOWMAN, An Aramaic religious text in Demotic script. JNES 3, 1944, 219-231.

R. A. BOWMAN, Aramaic Ritual Texts from Persepolis, Chicago 1970.

E. BRESCIANI, Un papiro aramaico da El Hibeh del Museo Archeologico di Firenze, Aegyptus 39, 1959, 3-8.

——, Papiri aramaici egiziani di epoca persiana presso il Museo Civico di Padova, RSO 35, 1960, 11-24.

——, M. KAMIL, Le lettere aramaiche di Hermopoli, Atti della Acc.

Naz. dei Lincei, Cl. d. Sc. morali, storiche et filol., Serie VIII, vol. XII, fasc. 5, Roma, 1966.

G. CARDASCIA, Les Archives de Murašu, une famille d'hommes d'affaires babyloniens à l'époque Perse 455-403 av.J.-C., Paris, 1951.

C. P. CARRATELLI, G. GARBINI, A bilingual graeco-aramaic edict by Aśoka. The first Greek inscription discovered in Afghanistan. Serie orientale Roma, Roma 1964.

B. COUROYER, A propos de la stèle de Carpentras, Semitica 20, 1970, 17-21 (P. GRELOT, Post-Scriptum, 21-22).

A. COWLEY, Aramaic Papyri of the Fifth Century B.C., Oxford, 1923, repr. Osnabrück, 1967.

R. DEGEN, The Aramaic Inscription from Taxila, Lešonénu 34, 1970, 314-317.

——, Ein neuer aramäischer Papyrus aus Elephantine, P. Berol. 23001, Neue Ephemeris f. Semitische Epigraphik, Wiesbaden 1972, 9-22.

L. DELAPORTE, Épigraphes araméens, Paris, 1912.

M. DELCOR, Une inscription funéraire araméenne, trouvée à Daskyleion, Mus 80, 1967, 301-313.

I. M. DIAKONOFF, W. A. LIWŠIC, Dokumenty iz Nisy, Moscow, 1960.

H. DONNER, W. RÖLLIG, KAI.

G. R. DRIVER, Aramaic Documents of the Fifth Century B.C., sec. ed., Oxford, 1957 (first ed. with facsimiles, Oxford, 1954).

A. DUPONT-SOMMER, La tablette cunéiforme araméenne de Warka, RA 39, 1942-1944, 35-62.

——, Un ostracon araméen inédit d'Éléphantine adressé à Ahutab, Revue des Études Sémitiques et Babyloniaca, 1942-1945, fasc. 2, 65-75.

——, Un contrat de métayage égypte-araméen de l'an 7 de Darius I, MAI 14, Paris, 1944, 61-106.

——, La doctrine gnostique de la lettre "Waw" d'après une lamelle araméenne inédite, Paris, 1946.

——, Une stèle araméenne d'un prêtre de Ba'al trouvée en Égypte, Syria 33, 1956, 79-87.

——, Trois inscriptions araméennes inédites sur des bronzes du Luristan. Collection de M. Foroughi, IrAnt IV, 1964, 108-118.

——, Une plaquette d'argent à inscription araméenne. Collection de M. Foroughi, IrAnt IV, 1964, 119-132.

——, E. BENVENISTE, Une inscription indo-araméenne d'Aśoka provenant de Kandahar (Afghanistan) JA 254, 1966, 437-466.

——, Une nouvelle inscription araméenne d'Aśoka trouvée dans la vallée du Laghman (Afghanistan), CRAI, janvier-mars 1970, 158-173.

E. EBELING, Das aramäisch-mittelpersische Glossar Frahang-i-Pahlavik im Lichte der assyriologischen Forschung, MAOG 14/1, Leipzig, 1941.

P. H. L. EGGERMONT, J. HOFTIJZER, The Moral Edicts of King Aśoka, Textus minores 29, Leiden, 1962.

J. A. FITZMYER, The Padua Aramaic Papyrus Letters, JNES 21, 1962, 15-24.

G. GOYON, Nouvelles inscriptions rupestres du Wadi Hammamat, Paris, 1957, 117 ff. (an aramaic alphabet).

P. GRELOT, Sur la stèle de Carpentras. Semitica 17, 1967, 73-75.

——, Essai de restauration du papyrus A.P. 26, Semitica 20, 1970, 23-31.

R. S. HAWSON, Aramaic Funerary and Boundary Inscriptions from Asia Minor, BASOR 192, dec. 1968, 3-11.

J. P. HAYES - J. HOFTIJZER, Notae Hermopolitanae, VT 20, 1970, 98-106.

H. HUMBACH, Die aramäische Inschrift von Taxila, Wiesbaden, 1969.

H. HUMBACH, Additional notes on the Aramaic Inscription from Taxila, JSS 26, 1969, 39-42.

J. J. KOOPMANS, Aramäische Chrestomathie, 2 vols., Leiden, 1962.

W. KORNFELD, Aramäische Sarkophagen in Assuan, WZKM 61, 1967, 9-16.

E. G. KRAELING, The Brooklyn Museum Aramaic Papyri. New Documents of the Fifth Century B.C. from the Jewish Colony at Elephantine, New Haven, 1953.

E. Y. KUTSCHER-J. NAVEH-S. SHAKED, The Aramaic inscriptions of Aśoka, Lešonénu 34, 1970, 125-138.

——, The bilingual inscription from Armazi, Lešonénu 34, 1970, 309-313.

M. LIDZBARSKI, Phönizische und aramäische Krugaufschriften aus Elephantine, AAB, Berlin, 1912.

——, Altaramäische Urkunden aus Assur, WVDOG 38, Leipzig, 1921.

H. LOZACHMEUR, Un ostracon araméen inédit d'Eléphantine (collection Clermont-Ganneau no. 228), Semitica 21, 1971, 81-93.

R. MEYER, Ein aramäischer Papyrus aus den ersten Jahren Nebukadnezars II, Festschrift für Friedrich Zucker zum 70. Geburtstag, Berlin, 1954, 251-262.

J. T. MILIK, Lettre araméen d'el-Hibeh, Aegyptus 40, 1960, 79-81.

J. NAVEH, Aramaica Dubiosa, JNES 27, 1968, 317-325.

J. NAVEH-S. SHAKED, A recently published Aramaic papyrus, JAOS 91, 1971, 379-382.

J. NAVEH, The Aramaic inscriptions of boundary stones in Armenia, Die Welt des Orients 6, 1971, 42-46 (= Lešonénu 35, 1971, 155-160).

A. PERIKHANIAN, Une inscription araméenne du roi Artašēš trouvée à Zanguézour (Siwnikʿ), RÉArmén, N.S. 3, 1966, 17-29.

B. PORTEN-J. C. GREENFIELD, The Aramaic Papyri from Hermopolis. ZAW 80, 1968, 216-231.

C. PUBLIESE-CARRATELLI, G. LEVI DELLA VIDA, Un editto bilingue greco-aram. di Aśoka ... Testo, Traduzione e Note, con Prefazione di G. TUCCI e Introduzione di U. SCERRATO, Roma, 1958.

I. RABINOWITZ, Aramaic Inscriptions of the Fifth Century B.C.E. from a North-Arab Shrine in Egypt, JNES 15, 1956, 1-9.

——, Another Aramaic Record of the North-Arabian Goddess Han-'Ilat, JNES 18, 1959, 154-155.

E. SACHAU, Drei aramäische Papyrusurkunden aus Elephantine, Berlin, 1908.

——, Aramäische Papyrus und Ostraka aus einer jüdischen Militär-kolonie zu Elephantine, 2 vols., Leipzig, 1911.

A. H. SAYCE, A. E. COWLEY, Aramaic Papyri discovered at Assuan, London, 1906.

D. SCHLUMBERGER, L. ROBERT, A. DUPONT-SOMMER, E. BENVENISTE, Une bilingue gréco-araméenne d'Aśoka, JA 248, 1958, 1-48.

J. B. SEGAL, Miscellaneous fragments in Aramaic, Iraq 31, 1969, 170-173.

S. SHAKED, Notes on the New Aśoka inscription from Kandahar, JRAS 1969, 118-122.

W. Th. IN DER SMITTEN, Eine aramäische Inschrift in Pakistan aus dem 3. Jhdt. v.Chr. BiOr 28, 1971, 309-311.

J. STARCKY, Une tablette araméenne de l'an 34 de Nabuchodonosor (AO 21.063), Syria 37, 1960, 99-115.

M. SZNYCER, Ostraca d'époque parthe trouvés à Nisa (U.S.S.R.), Sem V, 1955, 65-98.

——, Nouveaux ostraca de Nisa, Sem XII, 1962, 105-126.

——, Les inscriptions araméennes de Tang-i-Butan, JA 253, 1965, 1-9.

J. TEIXIDOR, Un nouveau papyrus araméen du règne de Darius II, Syria 41, 1964, 285-290.

C. HISTORY AND RELIGION

A. AYAD BOULOS, The Topography of Elephantine according to the Aramaic Papyri, Publications of the Institute of Coptic Studies, Dept. of Semitic Studies, Cairo, 1967.

F. ALTHEIM, R. STIEHL, Aramäisch als Weltsprache, AAW I, Berlin, 1964, 181-236.

E. BRESCIANI, La satrapia d'Egitto, Studi classici e orientali 7, 1958, 132-188.

A. DUPONT-SOMMER-L. ROBERT, La déesse de Hiérapolis Castabala (Cilicie). Bibliothèque archéologique et historique de l'institut français d'archéologie d'Istanbul, XVI, Paris 1964, 7-15.

J. HARMATTA, Irano-Aramaica. Zur Geschichte des frühhellenistischen Judentums in Aegypten, Acta Antiqua 7, Budapest, 1959, 337-409.

E. C. B. MACLAURIN, Date of the Foundation of the Jewish Colony at Elephantine, JNES 27, 1968, 89-96.

J. T. MILIK, Les papyrus araméens d'Hermoupolis et les cultes syrophéniciens en Égypte perse, Bibl 48, 1967, 546-622.

——, Le couvercle de Bethphagé, Hommages à André Dupont-Sommer, Paris 1971, 75-94.

Y. MUFFS, Studies in the Aramaic Legal Papyri from Elephantine, Studia et Documenta ad Iura Orientis antiqui pertinentia VIII, Leiden, 1969 (with a large bibliography).

B. PORTEN, Archives from Elephantine. The Life of an ancient Jewish Military Colony, Berkeley-Los Angeles, 1968 (with large bibliography).

——, The Religion of the Jews of Elephantine in the Light of the Hermopolis Papyri, JNES 28, 1969, 116-121.

——, J. C. GREENFIELD, The Aramaic Papyri from Hermopolis, ZAW 80, 1968, 216-231.

J. J. RABINOWITZ, The Susa tablets, the Bible and the Aramaic papyri, VT 11, 1961, 55-77.

H. H. SCHAEDER, Esra der Schreiber, BHTh 5, Tübingen, 1930 = Studien zur orientalischen Religionsgeschichte, Darmstadt, 1968, 162-241.

A. VERGER, Ricerche giuridiche sui papiri aramaici di Elefantina, Studi Semitici 16, Roma, 1965 (with "bibliografia dei papiri e degli ostraca aramaici di Elefantina" — 324 items).

A. Vincent, La religion des Judéo-Araméens d'Éléphantine, Paris, 1937.
A. Volterra, 'YHWDY' e "RMY' nei papiri aramaici del V secolo provenienti dall'Egitto, RCL 1963, 131-173.
R. Yaron, Introduction to the Law of the Aramaic Papyri, Oxford, 1961.

D. IMPORTANT JOURNALS

AcOr, Aegyptus, AfO, AIUON, ArOr, ASAE, BAIBL, BA, BASOR, Bibl, BibOr, BSOAS, BZ, CBQ, ChrE, CRAIBL, EstBib, EW, GLECS, HUCA, IEJ, IIJ, JA, JAOS, JBL, JEA, JNES, JPOS, JRAS, JSS, MUSJ, MIO, OA, OLZ, PEQ, RA, RB, REJ, RSO, Syria, VD, VT, WO, WZKM, ZA, ZAW, ZDMG, ZDPV.

Palmyrene

General Works with Bibliographies

CIS II, Tom 3, Paris, 1932.
J. G. Février, La religion des Palmyréniens, Paris, 1931.
——, Essai sur l'histoire politique et économique de Palmyre, Paris, 1931.
F. Rosenthal, Die Sprache der palmyrenischen Inschriften und ihre Stellung innerhalb des Aramäischen, MVÄG 46/1, Leipzig, 1936.
——, Die aramäistische Forschung, Leiden, 1939, 300-301: 'Nachweis der palmyrenischen Inschriften' (cf. pp. 93-103).
J. Starcky, art. "Palmyre", SDB VI, 1960, 186-192.

A. LINGUISTICS

1. Grammars

J. Cantineau, Grammaire du Palmyrénien épigraphique, Cairo, 1935.
F. Rosenthal, Die Sprache der palmyrenischen Inschriften und ihre Stellung innerhalb des Aramäischen, MVÄG 46/1, Leipzig, 1936.

2. Lexicon

Jean, Hoftijzer, DISO.

3. Linguistic Monographies and Articles

A. Caquot, Sur l'onomastique religieuse de Palmyre, Syria 39, 1962, 231-256.
——, Quelques nouvelles données palmyréniennes, GLECS 7, 1954-57 77-78.
W. Goldmann, Die palmyrenischen Personennamen. Beitrag zur semitischen Namenkunde, Leipzig, 1937.
Th. Nöldeke, Beiträge zur Kenntnis der aramäischen Dialekte III. Über Orthographie und Sprache der Palmyrener, ZDMG 24, 1870, 85-109.
E. Y. Kutscher, The Language of the Genesis Apocryphon, Scripta Hierosolymitana IV, 1957, 1-35.
J. K. Stark, Personal names in Palmyrene inscriptions, Oxford 1971.

B. LITERATURE

1. Principal Editions of Palmyrene Texts

A. Bounni, Inscriptions palmyréniennes inédites, AAS 11, 1961, 145-162.
——, N. Saliby, Six nouveaux emplacements fouillés à Palmyre (1963-1964), AAS 15, 1965, 121-138.
J. Cantineau, Textes funéraires palmyréniens, RB 39, 1930, 520-551.
——, Inscriptions Palmyréniennes, Damas-Chalon-sur-Saône, 1930.
——, Textes palmyréniens provenants de la fouille du temple de Bêl, Syria 12, 1931, 116-142.
——, Tadmorea, Syria 14, 1933, 169-202; 17, 1936, 267-282; 346-355; 19, 1938, 72-82; 153-171.
——, J. Starcky, J. Teixidor, Inventaire des Inscriptions de Palmyre, fasc. 1-11, Beyrouth, 1930-1965 (is continued).
J. B. Chabot, Choix d'inscriptions de Palmyre, Paris, 1922.
CIS II, 3.
C. Dunant, Une nouvelle inscription caravanière de Palmyre, Mus. Helv.: 13, 1956, 216-225.

C. Dunant, Le sanctuaire de Baalshamin à Palmyre III. Les inscriptions, Rome 1971.

M. Gawlikowski, Nouvelles inscriptions du Camp de Dioclétien, Syria 47, 1970, 313-325.

——, Inscriptions de Palmyre, Syria 48, 1971, 407-426.

H. Ingholt, Deux inscriptions bilingues de Palmyre, Syria 13, 1932, 278-292.

——, Inscriptions and Sculptures from Palmyra I, Berytus 3, 1936, 83-127; II, Berytus 5, 1938, 93-140.

——, Five dated tombs from Palmyra, Berytus 2, 1935, 57-120.

——, Palmyrene Inscription from the Tomb of Malkū, MUSJ 38, 1962, 99-119.

——, H. Seyrig, J. Starcky, Recueil de tessères de Palmyre, Paris, 1955.

R. du Mesnil du Buisson, Inventaire des inscriptions palmyréniennes de Doura-Europos, Paris, 1939.

——, Les tessères et les monnaies de Palmyre, 2 vols., Paris, 1944-1962.

——, Inscriptions sur jarres de Doura-Europos, MUSJ 36, 1959, 3-49.

K. Michalowski, Palmyre. Fouilles Polonaises, 3 vols., Warsaw-The Hague, 1960-1964.

RÉS.

M. Rodinson, Une inscription trilingue de Palmyre, Syria 27, 1950, 137-142.

M. Rostovtzeff, Les inscriptions caravanières de Palmyre, Mélanges Glotz, 1932, 793-811.

——, Une nouvelle inscription caravanière de Palmyre, Berytus 2, 1935, 143-148.

F. Safar, Inscriptions from Wadi Hauran, Sumer 20, 1964, 9-27.

D. Schlumberger, La Palmyrène du Nord-Ouest, suivi d'un Recueil épigraphique (H. Ingholt, J. Starcky, G. Ryckmans), Paris, 1951.

M. Sobernheim, Palmyrenische Inschriften, MVÄG 10, 2, 1905.

J. Starcky, Autour d'une dédicace palmyrénienne à Sadrafa et à Du'anat, Syria 26, 1949, 43-85.

——, Trois inscriptions Palmyréniennes, MUSJ 28, 1949-50, 47-58.

——, Inscriptions palmyréniennes conservées au musée de Beyrouth, BMB 12, 1955, 29-44.

——, Inscriptions archaïques de Palmyre, Studi orientalistici in onore di Giorgio Levi della Vida II, Roma, 1956, 509-528.

——, Deux inscriptions palmyréniennes, MUSJ 38, 1962, 121-139.
——, Une inscription palmyrénienne trouvée près de l'Euphrate, Syria 40, 1963, 47-55.
J. TEIXIDOR, Deux inscriptions palmyréniennes du musée de Bagdad, Syria 40, 1963, 33-46.

C. HISTORY, RELIGION, ART AND ARCHITECTURE

A. ABDUL-HAK, L'hypogée de Taâi à Palmyre, AAS II, 1952, 193-251.
F. ALTHEIM, R. STIEHL, Odainat und Palmyra, AAW II, 1965, 251-273.
A. BOUNNI, Antiquités palmyréniennes dans un texte arabe du Moyen Age, MUSJ 46, 1970-71, 331-339.
A. CHAMPDOR, Les ruines de Palmyre, third ed., Paris, 1953.
P. COLLART, Le sanctuaire de Baalshamîn à Palmyre. Fouilles suisses, 1954, 1955, 1956, Rapport préliminaire, AAS VII, 1957, 67-90.
——, J. VICARI, Le Sanctuaire de Baalshamin à Palmyre, I, II. Topographie et Architecture. Bibliotheca Helvetica Romana X, 1, 2, Rome, 1969.
R. DUSSAUD, Topographie historique de la Syrie antique et médiévale, Paris, 1927.
——, La Palmyrène et l'exploration de M. Alois Musil, Syria 10, 1929, 52-62.
——, La pénétration des Arabes en Syrie avant l'Islam, Paris, 1955.
O. EISSFELDT, Tempel und Kulte syrischer Städte in hellenistisch-römischer Zeit, AO 40, Leipzig, 1941.
——, Zu syrischen Tempeln und Kulten in hellenistisch-römischer Zeit, OLZ 44, 1941, Sp. 433-441 = Kleine Schriften II, Tübingen, 1963, 309-316.
R. FELLMANN, Le Sanctuaire de Baalshamin à Palmyre. Vol. V. Die Grabanlage. Bibliotheca Helvetica Romana, X, 5, Rome 1970.
J.-G. FÉVRIER, Essai sur l'histoire politique et économique de Palmyre, Paris, 1931.
——, La religion des Palmyréniens, Paris, 1931.
M. GAWLIKOWSKI, Monuments funéraires de Palmyre, Warszawa 1970.
——, Palmyrena, Berytus 19, 1970, 65-86.
Dj. AL-HASSANI, J. STARCKY, Autels palmyréniens découverts près de la source Efqa, AAS III, 1953, 145-164; VII, 1957, 95-122.
J. HOFTIJZER, Religio Aramaico, Godsdienstige verschijnselen in aramese teksten, MVEOL 16, Leiden, 1968.

H. INGHOLT, Studier over Palmyrensk Skulptur, Copenhagen, 1928.

——, The Sarcophagus of Be'elai and other sculptures from the tomb of Malkû, Palmyra, MUSJ 46, 1970-71, 173-200.

O. KLÍMA, Zum Palmyrenischen Zolltarif, Studia Semitica Ioanni Bakoš dicata, Bratislava, 1965, 147-151.

F. MELLINGHOF, Ein Relief aus Palmyra. Untersuchungen zu seiner geschichtlichen Einordnung und Deutung, AAW V/2, 1969, 58-164.

R. DU MESNIL DU BUISSON, Les tessères et les monnaies de Palmyre. Un art, une culture et une philosophie grecs dans les moules d'une cité et d'une religion sémitiques, Paris, 1962.

——, Les origines du Panthéon palmyrénien, MUSJ 39, 1963, 169-195.

——, Première Campagne de fouilles à Palmyre, CRAIBL 1966, 158-190.

K. MICHALOWSKI, Mélanges offerts à K. M., Warszawa, 1966.

R. MOUTERDE, A. POIDEBARD, La voie antique des caravanes entre Palmyre et Hit au IIe s. ap. J.-C., Syria 12, 1931, 101-115.

I. A. RICHMOND, Palmyra under the Aegis of the Romans, JRS 53, 1963, 431-454.

J. SABEH, Sculptures palmyréniennes inédites, AAS III, 1953, 17-26.

D. SCHLUMBERGER, Études sur Palmyre I. Le développement urbain de Palmyre, Berytus 2, 1935, 149-162.

——, La Palmyrène du Nord-Ouest, Paris, 1951.

——, Le prétendu camp de Dioclétien à Palmyre, MUSJ 38, 1962, 77-97.

——, Les quatre tribus de Palmyre, Syria 48, 1971, 121-133.

H. SEYRIG, Antiquités syriennes, 6 vols., Paris, 1934-1966.

——, Le repas des morts et le "banquet funèbre" à Palmyre, AAS I, 1951, 32-41.

J. STARCKY, Palmyre, Paris, 1952.

——, art. "Palmyre", SDB VI, 1960, col. 1066-1103.

——, S. MUNAJJED, Palmyre, Damas, 1948.

E. WILL, Le relief de la tour de Kithot et le banquet funéraire à Palmyre, Syria 28, 1951, 70-100.

——, Marchands et chefs de caravanes à Palmyre, Syria 34, 1957, 262-277.

——, La tour funéraire de Palmyre, Syria 26, 1949, 87-116.

D. IMPORTANT JOURNALS

AAS, ADAJ, BASOR, Berytus, BMB, IEJ, MUSJ, PEQ, RB, Syria, ZDMG, ZDPV.

NABATAEAN

General Works with Bibliographies

J. CANTINEAU, Le Nabatéen II. Choix de textes-lexique, Paris, 1932, 181-202 (Bibliography).
N. GLUECK, Deities and Dolphins, The Story of the Nabataeans, London, 1966, 559-570 (Bibliography).
J. STARCKY, Pétra et la Nabatène, SDB VII, 1966, col. 886-1018.
F. ROSENTHAL, Die aramäistische Forschung, Leiden, 1939, 299 (Nachweis der nabatäischen Inschriften).

A. LINGUISTICS

1. GRAMMAR

J. CANTINEAU, Le Nabatéen I. Notions générales-écriture, grammaire, Paris, 1930.

2. LEXICON

J. CANTINEAU, Le Nabatéen II. Choix de textes-lexique, Paris, 1932.
JEAN, HOFTIJZER, DISO.

3. LINGUISTIC MONOGRAPHIES AND ARTICLES

F. ALTHEIM, R. STIEHL, Spirantisierung der *bgdkpt*, AAW III, 1966, 39-58.
J. CANTINEAU, Nabatéen et Arabe, Annales de l'Institut d'études orientales I, 1934-1935, 77-97.
J. STARCKY, Pétra et la Nabatène, SDB VII, 1966, col. 924-937.
F. ROSENTHAL, Die aramäistische Forschung, Leiden, 1939, 83-92.

B. LITERATURE

1. PRINCIPAL EDITIONS OF NABATAEAN TEXTS

G. W. AHLSTRÖM, A Nabatean inscription from Wadi Mukatteb, Sinai, Festschrift G. WIDENGREN I, 1972, 323-331.

J. CANTINEAU, Le Nabatéen II. Choix de textes-lexique, Paris, 1932. CIS II, 2.

Ch. CLERMONT-GANNEAU, Les Nabatéens en Égypte, RHR 80, 1919, 1-29.

G. DALMAN, Neue Petra-Forschungen und der heilige Felsen von Jerusalem, Leipzig, 1912.

R. DUSSAUD, F. MACLER, Voyage archéologique au Ṣafa et dans le Djebel ed-Drûz, Paris, 1901.

——, Missions dans les religions désertiques de la Syrie Moyenne, Paris, 1903.

O. EISSFELDT, Neue Belege für nabatäische Kultgenossenschaften, MIO. 15, 1969, 217-227.

J. A. JAUSSEN, R. SAVIGNAC, Mission archéologique en Arabie, 3 tomes (6 vols.), Paris, 1909-1922.

E. LITTMANN, Syria. Publications of the Princeton University Archaeological Expeditions to Syria in 1904-1905 and 1909, IV/A, Nabataean Inscriptions, Leiden, 1914.

——, Nabataean Inscriptions from Egypt, BSOAS 15, 1953, 1-28; 16, 1954, 211-246.

——, D. MEREDITH, Nabataean Inscriptions from Egypt II, BSOAS 16, 1954, 496-503.

J. T. MILIK, Nouvelles inscriptions nabatéennes, Syria 35, 1958, 227-251.

A. NEGEV, Nabataean Inscriptions from 'Avdat (Oboda), IEJ 11, 1961, 127-138; 13, 1963, 113-124.

——, New dated Nabataean Graffiti from the Sinai, IEJ 17, 1967, 250-255. RÉS.

F. SAFAR, Inscriptions from Wadi Hauran, Sumer 20, 1964, 9-27.

J. STARCKY, Un contrat nabatéen sur papyrus, RB 61, 1954, 161-181.

——, Nouvelle épitaphe nabatéenne donnant le nom sémitique de Pétra, RB 72, 1965, 95-97.

——, J. STRUGNELL, Deux nouvelles inscriptions nabatéennes, RB 73, 1966, 236-247.

——, Une inscription nabatéenne de l'an 18 d'Arétas IV, Hommages à André DUPONT-SOMMER, Paris 1971, 151-159.

C. J. M. DE VOGUÉ, Syrie centrale. Inscriptions sémitiques. Paris 1868-1877.

F. V. WINNETT-W. L. REED, Ancient Records from North Arabia, Toronto 1970. (141-160: Nabatean inscriptions (J. T. MILIK).

Y. YADIN, Expedition D — The Cave of Letters, IEJ 12, 1962, 227-257.

C. HISTORY, RELIGION, ART AND ARCHITECTURE

F. ALTHEIM, R. STIEHL, Berichte über die Anfänge der Nabatäer, AAW I, Berlin, 1964, 31-39.

W. BACHMANN, C. WATZINGER, Th. WIEGAND, Petra, Berlin, 1921.

R. E. BRÜNNOW, A. VON DOMASZEWSKI, Die Provincia Arabia, 3 vols., Strasbourg, 1904-1909.

Ch. CLERMONT-GANNEAU, Recueil d'archéologie orientale, 8 vols., Paris, 1888-1924.

G. DALMAN, Petra und seine Felsheiligtümer, Leipzig 1908.

——, Neue Petra-Forschungen und der heilige Felsen von Jerusalem, Leipzig 1912.

L. DIEZ MERINO, Origen de los signos que acompanan a las inscripciones nabateas del Sinai, Liber Annuus. Studi Bibli Franciscani 19, 1969, 264-304.

R. DUSSAUD, La pénétration des Arabes en Syrie avant l'Islam, Paris, 1955.

N. GLUECK, Explorations in Eastern Palestine I, AASOR 14, 1934; II, AASOR 15, 1935; III, AASOR 18-19, 1939; IV, AASOR 25-28, 1951.

——, The Other Side of the Jordan, New Haven, 1940.

——, Rivers in the Desert, New York, 1959.

——, Deities and Dolphins. The Story of the Nabataeans, London, 1966.

G. Lankester HARDING, The Antiquities of Jordan, London, sec. ed., 1967.

J. HOFTIJZER, Religio Armaica. Godsdienstige verschijnselen in aramese teksten, MVEOL 16, Leiden, 1968.

A. KAMMERER, Pétra et la Nabatène. L'Arabie Petrée et les Arabes du Nord dans leur rapports avec la Syrie et la Palestine avant l'Islam, 2 vols., Paris, 1929-1930.

A. B. W. KENNEDY, Petra. Its History and Monuments, London, 1925.

J. NAVEH, Some notes in Nabatean Inscriptions from 'Avdat, IEJ 17, 1967, 187-189.

A. NEGEV, The Nabatean Necropolis of Mampsis (Kurnub), IEJ 21, 1971, 110-129.

P. J. PARR, G. R. H. WRIGHT, J. STARCKY, C. M. BENNETT, Découvertes récentes au sanctuaire du Qasr à Petra: I Compte rendu des dernières fouilles. II Quelques aspects de l'architecture et de la sculpture. III Les inscriptions du téménos. Syria 45, 1968, 1-66 (= QDAP 12/13: 1967-68, 5-50).

P. J. PARR, Petra, London, 1969.

Petra und das Königreich der Nabatäer, hrsg. v. Naturhistorischen Gesellschaft Nürnberg, München, 1970.

D. SOURDEL, Les cultes du Hauran à l'époque romain, Paris, 1952.

J. STARCKY, Palmyréniens, Nabatéens et Arabes du Nord avant l'Islam in M. BRILLANT et R. AIGRAIN, Hist. des Religions IV, Paris 1956, 201-237.

——, Petra et la Nabatène, SDB VII, 1966, col. 886-1018.

——, Nouvelles stèles funéraires à Pétra, ADAJ 10, 1965, 43-49.

——, Le Temple Nabatéen de Khirbet Tannur. A propos d'un livre récent, RB 65, 1968, 206-235.

Y. YADIN, The Nabataean Kingdom, Provincia Arabia, Petra and En-geddi in the Documents of Naḥal Ḥever, JEOL 17, 1963, 227-241.

Y. ZAHRAN, La civilisation nabatéenne à l'époque impériale romaine en Transjordanie, Thèse lettres, Paris, 1961.

D. IMPORTANT JOURNALS

AAS, AASOR, ADAJ, BA, BASOR, Berytus, BMB, IEJ, JPOS, MUSJ, PEQ, QDAP, RB, Syria, ZDPV.

ARAMAIC OF HATRA

A. LINGUISTICS

1. LEXICON

JEAN, HOFTIJZER, DISO.

2. Grammar and Syntax

A. Caquot, L'araméen de Hatra, GLECS IX, 1960-1963, 87-89.
R. Degen, Die Genitivverbindung im Aramäischen der Hatra-Inschriften, Orientalia 36, 1967, 76-80.

B. LITERATURE

1. Principal Editions of Inscriptions of Hatra

B. Aggoula, Remarques sur les inscriptions hatréennes, Berytus 18, 1969, 85-104.
F. Altheim, R. Stiehl, Hatra und Nisā, AAW II, Berlin, 1965, 191-204.
——, R. Stiehl, Hatra, AAW IV, Berlin, 1967, 243-305.
W. Andrae, P. Jensen, Aramäische Inschriften aus Assur und Hatra aus der Partherzeit, MDOG 60, Leipzig, 1920.
A. Caquot, Nouvelles inscriptions araméennes de Hatra I, Syria 29, 1952, 89-118; II, Syria 30, 1953, 234-246; III, Syria 32, 1955, 49-59; IV, Syria 32, 1955, 261-272; V, Syria 40, 1963, 1-16; VI, Syria 41, 1964, 251-272.
R. Degen, Neue aramäische Inschriften aus Hatra (Nr. 214-230), WO 5, 1970, 222-236.
O. Krückmann, Die neuen Inschriften von Hatra, AfO 16, 1952-53, 141-148.
J. T. Milik, A propos d'un atelier monétaire d'Adiabène: Natounia, Revue Numismatique, VIᵉ Série, Tome IV, 1962, 51-58.
F. Safar, Inscriptions of Hatra, Sumer 7, 1951, 170-184; 8, 1952, 183-195; 9, 1953, 240-249; 11, 1955, 314; 17, 1961, 9-35; 18, 1962, 21-64; 21, 1965, 31-44; 24, 1968, 3-32.
J. Teixidor, Aramaic Inscriptions of Hatra, Sumer 20, 1964, 77-82.

C. HISTORY, RELIGION, ART AND ARCHITECTURE

W. Andrae, Hatra, nach Aufnahmen von Mitgliedern der Assur-Expedition der Deutschen Orient-Gesellschaft I, WVDOG 9, Leipzig, 1908; II, WVDOG 21, Leipzig, 1912.

A. Caquot, Note sur le "semeion" et les inscriptions araméennes de Hatra, Syria 32, 1955, 59-69.

S. Downey, Cult Banks from Hatra, Berytus 16, 1966, 97-109.

——, Notes sur une stèle de Hatra, Syria 45, 1968, 105-109.

S. Fukai, The Artifacts of Hatra and Parthian Art, EW 11, 1960, 135-181.

D. Harnack, Parthische Titel, vornehmlich in den Inschriften aus Hatra. Ein Beitrag zur Kenntnis des parthischen Staates, in: F. Altheim, R. Stiehl, Geschichte Mittelasiens im Altertum, Berlin, 1970, 492-549.

J. Hoftijzer, Religio Aramaica. Godsdienstige verschijnselen in aramese teksten, MVEOL 16, Leiden, 1968.

D. Homès-Fredericq, Hatra et ses sculptures parthes. Étude stylistique et iconographique. Uitgaven van het Nederlands Historisch-Archaeologisch Instituut te Istanbul XV, Istanbul, 1963.

H. Ingholt, Parthian Sculptures from Hatra. Orient and Hellas in Art and Religion, Memoirs of the Connecticut Academy of Art and Sciences 12, New Haven, 1954.

H. J. Lenzen, Ausgrabungen in Hatra, AA 70, 1955, 334-375.

——, Gedanken über den grossen Tempel in Hatra, Sumer 11, 1955, 93-106.

A. Maricq, Hatra de Sanatrouq, Syria 32, 1955, 273-288.

——, Classica et Orientalia 2. Les dernières années de Hatra: L'alliance romaine, Syria 34, 1957, 288-296.

W. al-Salihi, Hercules-Nergal at Hatra, Iraq 33, 1971, 113-115.

J. Teixidor, Notes hatréennes, Syria 41, 1964, 273-284; 43, 1966, 91-97.

——, The Altars Found at Hatra, Sumer, Vol. 21, 1965, 85-93.

——, The Kingdom of Adiabene and Hatra, Berytus 17, 1967-1968, 1-11.

J. Walker, The Coins of Hatra, NumChron 18, 1958, 167-172.

D. IMPORTANT JOURNALS

Berytus, Sumer, Syria.

Jewish Aramaic

General Works with Bibliographies or Many Bibliographical References

R. Le Déaut, Introduction à la littérature targumique I., Rome, 1966.

P. NICKELS, Targum and New Testament. A Bibliography together
with a New Testament Index, Rome, 1967.

F. ROSENTHAL, Die aramäistische Forschung, 106-132.

H. L. STRACK, Einleitung in Talmud und Midraš, München, 1930.

A. LINGUISTICS

1. GRAMMARS

G. DALMAN, Grammatik des Jüdisch-Palästinischen Aramäisch nach
den Idiomen des palästinischen Talmud, des Onkelostargum und
Prophetentargum und der Jerusalemischen Targume, sec. ed.,
Leipzig, 1905, repr. Darmstadt, 1960 (+ Aramäische Dialektproben).

J. A. FITZMYER, The Genesis Apocryphon of Qumran Cave I, Biblica
et Orientalia 18, Rome, 1966, Appendix II: A Sketch of Qumran
Aramaic, 173-206.

H. ODEBERG, I: The Aramaic Portions of Bereshit Rabba with Grammar of Galilaean Aramaic; II: Short Grammar of Galilaean
Aramaic, Leipzig-Lund, 1939.

W. STEVENSON, Grammar of Palestinian Jewish Aramaic, sec. ed.,
by J. Emerton, Oxford, 1966.

2. LEXICA

G. DALMAN, Aramäisch-Neuhebräisches Handwörterbuch zu Targum,
Talmud und Midrasch, third ed., Göttingen, 1938.

M. JASTROW, A Dictionary of the Targumim, the Talmud Babli and
Yerushalmi, and the Midrashic Literature, 2 vols., New York,
1950.

J. LEVY, Neuhebräisches und Chaldäisches Wörterbuch über die
Talmudim und Midrashim, sec. ed., 4 vols., Leipzig, 1924, repr.
Darmstadt, 1963.

——, Chaldäisches Wörterbuch, Köln, 1959.

3. LINGUISTIC MONOGRAPHIES AND ARTICLES

W. BACHER, Die exegetische Terminologie der jüdischen Traditionsliteratur, 2 vols., Leipzig, 1899-1905, repr. Darmstadt, 1965.

H. BIRKELAND, The Language of Jesus, Oslo, 1954.

M. Black, An Aramaic Approach to the Gospels and Acts, third ed., Oxford, 1966.

——, Aramaic Studies and the language of Jesus, In Memoriam Paul Kahle, BZAW 103, Berlin, 1968, 17-28.

A. Diez Macho, La lengua hablada por Jesu Cristo, OA 2, 1963, 95-132.

M. C. Doubles, Indications of Antiquity in the Orthography and Morphology of the Fragment Targum, In Memoriam Kahle, BZAW 103, Berlin, 1968, 79-89.

A. Dupont-Sommer, Remarques linguistiques sur un fragment araméen de Qoumrân (Prière de "Nabonide") GLECS 8, 1959, 48-50.

J. A. Fitzmyer, The languages of Palestine in the first century A.D., CBQ 32, 1970, 501-531.

B. A. Fletcher, The Aramaic Sayings of Jesus. Discovering the Language Jesus spoke, 1967.

S. Fränkel, Die aramäischen Fremdwörter im Arabischen, Leiden, 1886, repr. 1962.

M. Z. Kadari, The use *of* ‏-ד‎ *clauses* in the language of Targum Onkelos, Textus III, 1963, 36-59.

C. J. Kasowski, A Concordance of the Targum of Onkelos, Jerusalem, 1940.

P. Kahle, Masoreten des Ostens, Die ältesten punktierten Handschriften des Alten Testaments und der Targume, Leipzig, 1913, repr. Hildesheim, 1966.

——, Masoreten des Westens I/II, Leipzig, 1927-1930, repr. Hildesheim, 1967.

——, The Cairo Geniza, sec. ed., Oxford, 1959.

——, Das palästinische Pentateuchtargum und das zur Zeit Jesu gesprochene Aramäisch, ZNW 49, 1958, 100-116.

E. Y. Kutscher, Studies in Galilean Aramaic, Jerusalem, 1952 (in Hebrew).

——, The Language of the Genesis Apocryphon: A Preliminary Study. Aspects of the Dead Sea Scrolls, ScrHier 4, Jerusalem, 1958, 1-35.

——, Das zur Zeit Jesu gesprochene Aramäisch, ZNW 51, 1960, 46-54.

——, The Language of the Hebrew and Aramaic Letters of Bar Cochba and his Contemporaries, Lešonenu 25, 1961, 117-133; 26, 1962, 7-23.

——, Mittelhebräisch und Jüdisch-Aramäisch im neuen Köhler-Baumgartner, Hebräische Wortforschung, Festschrift f. W. Baumgartner, Suppl. VT 16, Leiden, 1967, 158-175.

S. KRAUSS, Griechische und Lateinische Lehnwörter in Talmud, Midrash und Targum, 2 vols., Berlin, 1898-1899.

J. L. MALONE, Juncture in the Aramaic Verb of the Onkelos and Jonathan Targums, JNES 31, 1972, 156-166.

M. L. MARGULIS, Hebrew and Aramaic in the Talmud and Midrash, Leshonénu 27, 1963, 20-33.

S. MORAG, The vocalization Systems of Arabic, Hebrew and Aramaic, The Hague, 1962.

L. PRIJS, Ergänzungen zum talmudisch-aramäischen Wörterbuch, ZDMG 117, 1967, 266-287.

H. H. ROWLEY, Notes on the Aramaic of the Genesis Apocryphon, Hebrew and Semitic Studies presented to G. R. Driver, ed. D. Winton THOMAS, W. D. McHARDY, Oxford, 1963, 116-129.

S. SEGERT, Aramäische Studien II. Zur Verbreitung des Aramäischen in Palästina zur Zeit Jesu, ArOr 25, 1957, 21-37.

——, Die Sprachenfragen in der Qumrângemeinschaft, Qumrân-Probleme, Berlin, 1963, 315-339.

——, Zur Orthographie und Sprache der aramäischen Texte von Wadi Murabba'at, ArOr 31, 1963, 122-137.

——, Sprachliche Bemerkungen zu einigen aramäischen Texten von Qumran, ArOr 33, 1965, 190-206.

C. C. TORREY, Studies in the Aramaic of the first Century A.D., ZAW 65, 1953, 228-247.

J. VAN ZIJL, The root prq in Targum Isaiah, Journal of Northwest Semitic Languages II, 1972, 60-73.

B. LITERATURE

1. PRINCIPAL EDITIONS OF JEWISH ARAMAIC TEXTS

F. ALTHEIM, R. STIEHL, Inscriptions of the Synagogue of Dura-Europos. East and West N.S. 9, 1958, 7-28.

——, Im Umkreis Daniel's, AAW V/2, Berlin, 1969, 3-23. (Edition and translation of 4 QOrNab).

N. AVIGAD, Aramaic Inscriptions in the Tomb of Jason, IEJ 17, 1967, 101-111.

——, Y. YADIN, A Genesis Apocryphon. A Scroll from the Wilderness of Juda, Jerusalem, 1956.

M. BAILLET, Fragments araméens de Qumrân 2. Déscription de la Jérusalem Nouvelle, RB 62, 1955, 222-245.

——, J. T. MILIK, R. DE VAUX, Discoveries in the Judaean Desert of Jordan III. Les 'Petites Grottes' de Qumran, Oxford, 1962.

D. BARTHÉLÉMY, J. T. MILIK, Discoveries in the Judaean Desert I. Qumran Cave I, Oxford, 1955.

P. BENOIT, J. T. MILIK, R. DE VAUX, Discoveries in the Judaean Desert II. Les Grottes de Muraba'ât, Oxford, 1961.

A. BERLINER, Targum Onkelos. Herausgegeben und erläutert, Berlin 1884, (repr.: Jerusalem 1968).

G. DALMAN, Aramäische Dialektproben, sec. ed., Leipzig, 1927, repr. Darmstadt, 1960.

R. LE DÉAUT-J. ROBERT, Targum des Chroniques, 2 Vols, Analecta Biblica 51, Rome 1971.

A. DÍEZ MACHO, Nuevos fragmentos del Targum palestinense, Sefarad 15, 1955, 1-39.

——, Deux nouveaux fragments du Targum palestinien à New York, Studi G. Rinaldi, Genova, 1967, 175-189.

——, NEOPHYTI 1. Targum Palestinense. Ms de la Biblioteca Vaticana. Tomo 1: Genesis, Edición príncipe, introduccion general y versión castellana. Tomo 2: Éxodo, Edición príncipe etc. Tomo 3 : Levítico, Edición príncipe etc. Consejo Superior de Investigaciones Cientificas, Seminario Filologico "Cardenal Cisneros" Textos y Estudios 7 and 8, Madrid-Barcelona 1968, 1970 and 1971.

J. A. FITZMYER, The Aramaic "Elect of God" Text from Qumran Cave IV, CBQ 27, 1965, 348-372.

——, The Genesis Apocryphon of Qumran Cave I. A Commentary, Biblica et Orientalia 18, Rome, 1966.

J.-B. FREY, Corpus Inscriptionum Judaicarum. Recueil des inscriptions juives qui vont du IIIe siècle avant Jésus-Christ au VIIe siècle de notre ère, 2 vols., Roma, 1936-1952.

M. GINSBURGER, Das Fragmententhargum, Berlin, 1899. reprint n.d.

——, Thargum Jonathan ben Usiël zum Pentateuch, Berlin, 1903. reprint n.d.

P. KAHLE, Masoreten des Ostens. Die ältesten punktierten Handschriften des Alten Testaments und der Targume, Leipzig, 1913, repr. Hildesheim, 1966.

——, Masoreten des Westens I/II, Leipzig, 1927-1930, repr. Hildesheim, 1967.

P. DE LAGARDE, Prophetae Chaldaice, Leipzig, 1872. repr. Osnabrück 1967.

——, Hagiographa Chaldaice, Leipzig, 1873. repr. Osnabrück 1967.

S. LIEBERMANN, Midrash Debarim Rabbah, sec. ed., Jerusalem, 1964.

M. L. MARGULIES, Midrash Wayyikra Rabba, 5 vols., Jerusalem, 1953-1960.

A. MERX, Chrestomathia Targumica, Berlin, 1888.

R. MEYER, Das Gebet des Nabonid, Sitzungsberichte der Sächsischen Akad. d. Wiss. zu Leipzig, Phil.-Hist. Kl. 107/3, Berlin, 1962.

J. T. MILIK, Un contrat juif de l'an 134 après J.-C., RB 61, 1954, 182-190.

——, Le Testament de Lévi en araméen. Fragment de la grotte 4 de Qumrân, RB 62, 1955, 398-406.

——, 'Prière de Nabonide' et autres écrits d'un cycle de Daniel. Fragments de Qumrân 4, RB 63, 1956, 407-415.

——, Deux documents inédits du désert de Juda, Bibl 38, 1957, 245-268.

——, Hénoch au pays des Aromates, RB 65, 1958, 70-77.

——, Parchemin judéo-araméen de Doura-Europos, an 200 après J.-C., Syria 45, 1968, 97-104.

A. NEUBAUER, The Book of Tobit. A chaldee Text from an unique ms. in the Bodleian Library, Oxford, 1878.

J. OBERMANN, Inscribed Tiles from the Synagogue of Dura, Berytus 7, 1942, 89-117.

H. ODEBERG, The Aramaic Portions of Bereshit Rabba I. Text with Transcription, Lund-Leipzig, 1939.

J. P. M. v.d. PLOEG, A. S. v.d. WOUDE (avec la collaboration de B. JONGELING, Le Targum de Job de la grotte XI de Qumrân, Leiden, 1971.

A. SPERBER, The Bible in Aramaic, based on old manuscripts and printed texts, 4 Vols. in 5 Parts, Leiden, 1959-   .

J. STARCKY, Un texte messianique araméen de la grotte 4 de Qumrân, École des langues orientales anciennes de l'Institut Catholique de Paris: Mémorial du cinquantenaire 1914-1964, Paris, 1964, 51-66.

J. F. STENNING, The Targum of Isaiah, Oxford, 1949.

M. TESTUZ, Deux fragments inédits des manuscrits de la Mer Morte, Semitica 5, 1955, 37-38.

L. H. VINCENT, Les épigraphes judéo-araméens postexiliques, RB 56, 1949, 274-294.

2. History of Literature and Literary Studies

R. Bloch, Note méthodologique pour l'étude de la littérature rabbinique, RSR 43, 1955, 194-227.

J. W. Bowker, Haggadah in the Targum Onkelos, JSS 12, 1967, 51-66.

——, The Targums and rabbinic literature. An introduction to Jewish Interpretations of Scripture. Cambridge, 1969.

F. M. Cross, The Discovery of the Samaria Papyri, BiAr 26, 1963, 110-121.

G. Dalman, Grammatik des jüdisch-palästinischen Aramäisch nach den Idiomen des palästinischen Talmud, des Onkelostargum und Prophetentargum und der Jerusalemischen Targume, sec. ed., Leipzig, 1905, repr. Darmstadt, 1960 (+ Aramäische Dialektproben), 6-39.

R. Le Déaut, Introduction à la Littérature Targumique I, Roma, 1966.

——, Lévitique XXII 26-XXIII 44 dans le Targum Palestinien. De l'importance des gloses du Codex Neofiti 1, VT 18, 1968, 458-471.

——, Les études targumiques. État de la recherche et perspectives pour l'exégèse de l'AT, EL 44, 1968, 5-34.

A. Díez Macho, The recently discovered Palestinian Targum. Its Antiquity and Relationship with the other Targums, Suppl. VT 7, Leiden, 1960, 222-245.

M. C. Doubles, Toward the Publication of the Extant Texts of the Palestinian Targum(s), VT 15, 1965, 16-27.

P. Grelot, Les Targums du Pentateuque. Étude comparative d'après Gen. 4, 3-16, Sem 9, 1959, 59-88.

P. Grelot, Remarques sur le second Targum du livre d'Esther, RB 77, 1970, 230-239.

P. Kahle, The Cairo Geniza, sec. ed., Oxford, 1959.

E. Koffmahn, Die Doppelurkunden. Studies on the Texts of the Desert of Judah 5, Leiden, 1968.

G. J. Kuiper, A Study of the Relationship between a Genesis Apocryphon and the Pentateuchal Targumin in Genesis 14:1-12, In Memoriam Kahle, BZAW 103, 1968, 149-161.

M. McNamara, Targumic Studies, CBQ 28, 1966, 1-19.

——, The New Testament and the Palestinian Targum to the Pentateuch, AnalBibl 27, Roma, 1966.

——, Some Early Rabbinic Citations and the Palestinian Targum to the Pentateuch, RSO 41, 1966, 1-15.

J. Malfroy, L'Utilisation du vocabulaire sapientiel du Deutéronome dans le Targum palestinien (Codex Neofiti), Sem 17, 1967, 81-97.

M. Mielziner, Introduction to the Talmud, third ed., New York, 1925.

J. T. Milik, Problèmes de la littérature Hénochique à la lumière des fragments araméens de Qumran, HThR 64, 1971, 333-378.

M. P. Miller, Targum, Midrash and the Use of the Old Testament in the New Testament, Journal for the Study of Judaism 2, 1971, 29-82.

S. Schulz, Die Bedeutung der neuen Targumforschung für die synoptische Tradition, Abraham unser Vater, Festschrift für O. Michel, Leiden, 1963, 425-436.

H. L. Strack, Einleitung in Talmud und Midraš, München, 1930.

G. Vermès, The Targumic Versions of Genesis IV, 3-16, AnLeeds 3, 1961-62, 81-114.

——, Scripture and Tradition in Judaism, Leiden, 1961.

A. G. Wright, The literary genre Midrash, 1968.

J. van Zijl, Errata in Sperber's edition of Targum Isaiah, ASTI 4, 1965, 189-192.

J. van Zijl, A second list of errata in Sperber's edition of Targum Isaiah, Annual of the Swedish Theological Institute VII, 1968-69, Leiden 1970.

C. HISTORY AND RELIGION

F. M. Abel, Histoire de la Palestine depuis la conquête d'Alexandre jusqu'à l'invasion Arabe, 2 vols., Paris, 1952.

W. Bousset, H. Gressmann, Die Religion des Judentums in spathellenistischen Zeit, Fourth ed., Tübingen, 1966.

A. Marmorstein, The old rabbinic Doctrine of God, 2 vols., London, 1927-1937.

G. F. Moore, Judaism in the first Centuries of the Christian Era, ninth ed., 3 vols., Cambridge, 1962.

J. Neusner, A History of the Jews in Babylonia, 5 vols., Leiden, 1965- .

B. Reicke, Neutestamentliche Zeitgeschichte, Berlin, 1965.

E. Schürer, Geschichte des jüdischen Volkes im Zeitalter Jesu Christi, third and fourth ed., 4 vols., Leipzig, 1901-1911.

D. IMPORTANT JOURNALS

AASOR, ADAJ, ArOr, BA, BASOR, Bibl, CBQ, EstBíb, HUCA,
IEJ, JAOS, JBL, JJS, JQR, JSS, Lĕšonénu, MUSJ, OA, PEQ, RB,
REJ, RQum, RSO, Sefarad, Sem, Textus, VT, ZAW, ZDMG, ZNW.

SAMARITAN ARAMAIC

General Works

L. A. MAYER, Bibliography of the Samaritans, ed. by D. Broadribb,
Suppl. to Abr. Nahrain I, Leiden, 1964.
F. ROSENTHAL, Die aramaistische Forschung, 133-143.

A. LINGUISTICS

1. GRAMMARS

H. PETERMANN, Grammatik der samaritanischen Sprache, Leipzig,
1873.
I. ROSENBERG, Lehrbuch der samaritanischen Sprache und Literatur,
Wien-Pest-Berlin, 1901.
A. E. COWLEY, The Samaritan Liturgy, 2 vols., London, 1909, Vol. II:
Glossary.

2. LEXICON

Z. BEN-ḤAYYIM, A Hebrew-Arabic-Aramaic-Samaritan Glossary in
Hebrew and Aramaic I, 440-616, Jerusalem 1957.
M. JASTROW, A Dictionary of the Targumim, the Talmud Babli and
Yerushalmi, and the Midrashic Literature, 2 vols., New York,
1950.
J. LEVY, Neuhebräisches und Chaldäisches Wörterbuch über die
Talmudim und Midrashim, sec. ed., 4 vols., Leipzig, 1924, repr.
Darmstadt, 1963.

3. LINGUISTIC MONOGRAPHIES AND ARTICLES

F. ALTHEIM, R. STIEHL, Erwägungen zur Samaritanerfrage, AAW IV,
Berlin, 1967, 204-223.

A. E. Cowley, The Samaritan Liturgy, 2 vols., Oxford, 1909, Vol. I, pp. xxxv-xlii.

J. R. Díaz, Arameo Samaritano, EstBíb 18, 1959, 171-182.

J. C. Greenfield, Samaritan Hebrew and Aramaic in the Work of Z. ben Ḥayyim, Bibl 45, 1964, 261-268.

Z. Ben-Ḥayyim, On the study of the Samaritan language, Tarbiz 10. 1939, 81-89.

——, The literary and oral tradition of Hebrew and Aramaic amongst the Samaritans, 3 Vols., Jerusalem 1957-67.

P. Kahle, Textkritische und lexikalische Bemerkungen zum samaritanischen Pentateuchtargum, Diss. Halle, Leipzig, 1898.

S. Kohn, Zur Sprache, Literatur und Dogmatik der Samaritaner, AKM 5/4, 1876.

Z. Ben-Ḥayyim, The Literary and Oral Tradition of Hebrew and Aramaic amongst the Samaritans, 2 vols., Jerusalem, 1957 (in Hebrew).

B. LITERATURE

1. Principal Editions of Samaritan Aramaic Texts

A. E. Cowley, The Samaritan Liturgy, 2 vols., Oxford, 1909.

P. Kahle, Fragmente des samaritanischen Pentateuchtargums, ZA 16, 1902, 79-101; ZA 17, 1903, 1-12.

J. Macdonald, Memar Marqah. The Teaching of Marqa, ed. and transl., 2 vols., Beiheft ZAW 84, Berlin, 1963.

S. J. Miller, The Samaritan Molad Mosheh, New York, 1949.

H. Petermann, C. Vollers, Pentateuchus Samaritanus, 2 vols., Berlin, 1872-1891.

2. Literary Studies

F. M. Cross Jr., The discovery of the Samaria papyri, The Biblical Archaeologist 26, 1963, 110-121.

J. R. Díaz, Ediciones del Targum samaritano, EstBíb 15, 1956, 105-108.

——, Los fragmentos del Targum samaritano publicados, EstBíb 15, 1956, 297-300.

L. Goldberg, Das samaritanische Pentateuchtargum. Eine Unter-

suchung seiner handschriftlichen Quellen, Bonner Orient. Stud. 11,
1935.
P. Kahle, Die zwölf Marka Hymnen aus den "Defter" der samaritanischen Liturgie, Opera Minora, Leiden, 1956, 186-212.
D. Rettig, Memar Marqa. Ein samaritanischer Midrash zum Pentateuch, Bonner Orient. Stud. 8, 1934.

C. HISTORY AND RELIGION

J. Bowman, Samaritanische Probleme. Studien zum Verhältnis von
Samaritanertum, Judentum und Urchristentum, Stuttgart, 1967.
M. Gaster, The Samaritans. Their History, Doctrines and Literature,
London, 1925.
H. G. Kippenberg, Garizim und Synagoge. Traditionsgeschichtliche
Untersuchungen zur samaritanischen Religion der aramäischen
Epoche. RGVV 30, Berlin 1971.
J. Macdonald, The Theology of the Samaritans, London, 1964.
J. A. Montgomery, The Samaritans, The Earliest Jewish Sect.
Their History, Theology and Literature, Philadelphia, 1907.
reprint New York 1968.
J. D. Purvis, The Samaritan Pentateuch and the Origins of the
Samaritan Sect, Harvard Semitic Monographs 2, Cambridge, 1968.

Syro-Palestinian Christian Aramaic

General Works with Bibliographies or Many Bibliographical References

F. Rosenthal, Die aramaistische Forschung, 144-159.
F. Schulthess, Grammatik des christlich-palästinischen Aramäisch,
hrsg. v. E. Littmann, Tübingen, 1924, repr. Hildesheim, 1965.

A. LINGUISTICS

1. Grammars

Th. Nöldeke, Über den christlich-palästinischen Dialekt, ZDMG 22,
1868, 443-527.
F. Schulthess, Grammatik des christlich-palästinischen Aramäisch,
hrsg. v. E. Littmann, Tübingen, 1924, repr. Hildesheim, 1965.

2. Lexica

R. Payne-Smith, Thesaurus Linguae Syriacae, 2 vols., Oxford, 1879-1901.

F. Schulthess, Lexicon Syropalaestinum, Berlin, 1903.

3. Linguistic Monographies and Articles

A. Baumstark, Das Problem des christlich-palästinischen Penta-teuchtextes, OrChr 3, 10, 1935, 201-224.

J. W. Bowman, The Term 'Gospel' and its Cognates in the Palestinian Syriac, New Testament Essays in Memory of T. W. Manson, Manchester, 1959, 54-67.

F. Rosenthal, Die aramaistische Forschung, 149-153.

B. LITERATURE

1. Principal Editions of Syro-Palestinian Christian Aramaic Texts

W. Baars, A Palestinian Syriac Text of the Book of Lamentations, VT X, 1960, 224-227.

——, Two Palestinian Syriac Texts identified as parts of the Epistle of Jeremy, VT XI, 1961, 77-81.

M. Baillet, Un livret magique en christopalestinien à l'Université de Louvain, Mus 76, 1963, 375-400.

M. Black, Rituale Melchitarum, Bonner Orient. Stud. 22, 1938.

——, A Palestinian Syriac Palimpsest leaf of Acts XXI, 14-26, BJRL 23, 1939, 201-214.

——, A Christian Palestinian Syriac Horologion, Cambridge, 1954.

F. C. Burkitt, The Palestinian Syriac Lectionary, JThS 6, 1905, 91-98.

H. Duensing, Christlich-palästinisch-aramäische Texte und Fragmente nebst einer Abhandlung über den Wert der palästinischen Septuaginta, Göttingen, 1906.

——, Zwei christlich-palästinisch-aramäische Fragmente aus der Apostelgeschichte, ZNW 37, 1938, 42-46.

——, Neue christlich-palästinisch-aramäische Fragmente, NAWG, Phil.-Hist. Kl., 1944, 215-227.

——, Nachlese christlich-palästinisch-aramäischer Fragmente, NAWG, Phil.-Hist. Kl., 1955, 115-191.

G. H. GWILLIAM, Anecdota Oxoniensia. Semitic Series I/5, Oxford, 1893, The Palestinian Version of the Holy Scriptures. Five more fragments etc.

——, F. C. BURKITT, J. F. STENNING, Anecdota Oxoniensia. Semitic Series I/9, Oxford, 1896, Biblical and Patristic Relics of the Palestinian Literature.

P. KOKOWZOFF, Nouveaux fragments syro-palestiniens de la Bibliothèque Imperiale de Saint-Pétersbourg, St.-Petersbourg, 1906.

P. DE LAGARDE, Evangeliarium Hierosolymitanum. Bibliothecae Syriacae quae ad Philologiam Sacram pertinent, Göttingen, 1892, 257-402.

J. P. N. LAND, Anecdota Syriaca IV, Leiden, 1875, 103-224 (Syriac text); 177-236 (Latin translation).

G. MARGOLIOUTH, The Liturgy of the Nile, JRAS 1896, 677-731.

——, The Palestinian Syriac Version of the Holy Scriptures, London, 1897.

——, More Fragments of the Palestinian Syriac Version of the Holy Scriptures, PSBA 18, 1896, 223-236; 19, 1896, 39-60.

J. T. MILIK, Une inscription et une lettre en araméen christo-palestinien, RB 60, 1953, 526-539 (cf. Biblica 42, 1961, 25).

N. V. PIGULEVSKAYA, Fragments syro-palestiniennes des Psaumes CXXIII-IV, RB 43, 1934, 519-527.

J. RENDEL HARRIS, Biblical Fragments from Mount Sinai, Cambridge, 1890.

F. SCHULTHESS, Christlich-palästinische Fragmente, ZDMG 56, 1902, 249-261.

——, Christlich-palästinische Fragmente aus der Omajjaden-Moschee zu Damaskus, Berlin, 1905.

A. SMITH LEWIS, A Palestinian Syriac Lectionary containing Lessons from the Pentateuch, Job, Proverbs, Prophets, Acts and Epistles, Studia Sinaitica VI, London, 1897.

——, Supplement to a Palestinian Syriac Lectionary, Cambridge, 1907.

——, Codex Climaci Rescriptus. Fragments of Sixth Century Palestinian Syriac Texts of the Gospels, of the Acts of the Apostles etc., Horae Semiticae 8, Cambridge, 1909.

——, The Forty Martyrs of the Sinai Desert and the Story of Eulogios. From a Palestinian Syriac and Arabic Palimpsest transcribed, Horae Semiticae 9, Cambridge, 1912.

——, M. Dunlop Gibson, The Palestinian Syriac Lectionary of the Gospels, re-edited from two Sinai Mss. and from P. de Lagarde's edition of the 'Evangeliarium Hierosolymitanum', London, 1899.

——, Palestinian Syriac Texts from Palimpsest Fragments in the Taylor-Schechter Collection, London-Cambridge, 1900.

2. Literary Studies

M. Black, The Palestinian Syriac Gospels and the Diatessaron, OrChr 36, 1941, 101-111.

F. C. Burkitt, Christian Palestinian Literature, JTS 2, 1901, 174-183.

L. Delekat, Die syropalästinische Übersetzung der Paulusbriefe und die Peshitta, NTSt 3, 1956-1957, 223-233.

——, Die syropalästinische Jesaja-Übersetzung, ZAW 77, 1959, 165-201.

M. J. Lagrange, L'Origine de la version syro-palestinienne des Évangiles, RB 34, 1925, 481-504.

C. IMPORTANT JOURNALS

JTS, NTS, OrChr, RB, VT, ZDMG, ZAW, ZNW.

Babylonian Talmudic Aramaic

General Works with Bibliographies or Many Bibliographical References

J. Neusner, A History of the Jews in Babylonia, 5 vols., Leiden, 1965-   .

F. Rosenthal, Die aramaistische Forschung, 212-223.

H. L. Strack, Einleitung in Talmud und Midraš, München, 1930, 150-194.

A. Linguistics

1. Grammars

J. N. Epstein, A Grammar of Babylonian Aramaic, Jerusalem, 1960 (in Hebrew).

C. Levias, A Grammar of the Aramaic Idiom contained in the Babylonian Talmud, Cincinnati, 1900.
H. L. Margolis, Lehrbuch der aramäischen Sprache des Babylonischen Talmuds, München, 1910.

2. Lexica

M. Jastrow, A Dictionary of the Targumin, the Talmud Babli and Yerushalmi, and the Midrashic Literature, 2 vols., New York, 1950.
J. Levy, Neuhebräisches und Chaldäisches Wörterbuch über die Talmudim und Midrashim, sec. ed., 4 vols., Leipzig, 1924, repr. Darmstadt, 1963.

3. Linguistic Monographies and Articles

J. N. Epstein, Notes on Post-Talmudic Aramaic Lexicography, JQR N.F. 5, 1914-15, 235-251; N.F. 12, 1921-22, 299-390.
——, Gloses babylo-araméennes, REJ 73, 1921, 27-58; 74, 1922, 40-72.
——, Babylonisch-aramäische Studien, Festskrift i anledning af Prof. D. Dimonsens 70-aarige Fødselsdag, Kopenhagen, 1923, 290-310.
S. Krauss, Talmudische Archaeologie, 3 vols., Frankfurt, 1911.
——, Griechische und Lateinische Lehnwörter in Talmud, Midrash und Targum, 2 vols., Berlin, 1898-1899.
E. Y. Kutscher, The research on the Aramaic of the Talmud Babli, Lešonénu 26, 1961-62, 149-183.
——, Neutralization of gender and number of the third person perfect of Babylonian Aramaic? Lešonénu 35, 1970, 36-38.
M. Schlesinger, Satzlehre der aramäischen Sprache des babylonischen Talmuds, Leipzig, 1928.

B. LITERATURE

1. Principal Editions of Babylonian Talmudic Aramaic Texts

L. Goldschmidt, Der Babylonische Talmud hrsg. und übers., 9 vols., Berlin-Leipzig-The Hague, 1897-1935.
C. H. Gordon, Aramaic Magical Bowls in the Istanbul and Baghdad Museum, ArOr 6, 1934, 319-334.

——, An Aramaic Exorcism, ArOr 6, 1934, 466-474.

——, An Aramaic Incantation, AASOR 14, 1933-34, 141-143.

——, Aramaic and Mandaic Magical Bowls, ArOr 9, 1937, 84-106.

——, Aramaic Incantation Bowls, Or 10, 1941, 116-141; 272-276; 278-289; 339-360.

——, Two Magic Bowls in Teheran, Or 20, 1951, 306-315.

W. S. McCullough, Jewish and Mandaean Incantation Bowls in the Royal Ontario Museum, Near and Middle East Studies 5, 1967.

M. Margalioth, Sepher ha-Razîm. A newly recovered Book of Magic from the Talmudic Period, Jerusalem, 1966.

J. A. Montgomery, Aramaic Incantation Texts from Nippur, University of Pennsylvania, The Museum, Publications of the Babylonian Section 3, Philadelphia, 1913.

J. Obermann, Two Magic Bowls. New Incantation Texts from Mesopotamia, AJSL 57, 1940, 1-31.

W. H. Rossell, A Handbook of Aramaic Magical Texts, New Yersey, 1953.

E. Yamauchi, Aramaic Magic Bowls, JAOS 85, 1965, 511-523.

M. Zulay, Zur Liturgie der babylonischen Juden, Bonner Orient. Studien 2, Stuttgart, 1933.

2. History of Literature

W. Bacher, Die Agada der babylonischen Amoräer, Frankfurt, 1913. reprint Hildesheim 1965.

——, Tradition und Tradenten in den Schulen Palaestinas und Babyloniens, Leipzig, 1914. reprint Berlin 1966.

M. Mielziner, Introduction to the Talmud, third ed., New York, 1925.

H. L. Strack, Einleitung in Talmud und Midraš, München, 1930.

J. Winter, A. Wünsche, Die jüdische Literatur seit Abschluss des Kanons, 3 vols., Trier, 1894, repr. Hildesheim, 1965.

C. HISTORY

M. Avi-Yonah, Geschichte der Juden im Zeitalter des Talmud, Studia Judaica II, Berlin, 1962.

J. Neusner, A History of the Jews in Babylonia, 5 vols., Leiden, 1965-   .

——, Jews and Judaism under Iranian Rule. Bibliographical Reflections, History of Religions 8, 1968, 159-177.

D. IMPORTANT JOURNALS

ArOr, HUCA, JA, JAOS, JJS, JQR, JRAS, Or, PAAJR, REJ, Textus, Tarbiẓ (hebrew), WZKM, ZDMG, ZNW.

MANDAIC

Bibliographies

E. S. DROWER, A Mandaean Bibliography, JRAS, 1953, 34-49.
C. H. KRAELING, Mandaic Bibliography, JAOS 46, 1926, 49-55;
    49, 1929, 281.
S. A. PALLIS, Essay on Mandaic Bibliography, 1560-1930, London-
    Kopenhagen, 1933.
K. RUDOLPH, Die Mandäer I. Das Mandäerproblem, FRLANT 74,
    Göttingen, 1960, 260-271.
——, Die Mandäer II. Der Kult, FRLANT 75, Göttingen, 1961, 428-
    436.
——, Theogonie, Kosmogonie und Anthropogonie in den mandäischen
    Schriften. Eine literarische und traditionsgeschichtliche Unter-
    suchung, FRLANT 88, Göttingen, 1965, 349-356.
——, Die Religion der Mandäer in Die Religionen Altsyriens, Alt-
    arabiens und der Mandäer von H. GESE, M, HÖFNER und K. RU-
    DOLPH, Stuttgart 1970, S. 459-462.
H. SCHLIER, Zur Mandäerfrage, ThRsch, N.R. 5, 1933, 1-34; 69-92.

A. LINGUISTICS

1. GRAMMARS

R. MACUCH, Handbook of classical and modern Mandaic, Berlin, 1965.
Th. NÖLDEKE, Mandäische Grammatik, Halle, 1875, repr. Darmstadt,
    1964 (with appendix by A. SCHALL).

2. LEXICON

E. S. DROWER, R. MACUCH, A Mandaic Dictionary, Oxford, 1963.

3. Linguistic Monographies and Articles

P. W. Coxon, Script Analysis and Mandaean Origins, JSS 15, 1970, 16-30.

M. Dietrich, Untersuchungen zum Mandäischen Wortschatz, Diss. Tübingen, 1958.

——, Zum Mandäischen Wortschatz, BiOr, vol. 24, 1967, 290-305.

G. Furlani, I nomi delle classi de demoni presso i Mandei, ANLA, Ser. 8, Vol. 9, Rome, 1954, 389-435.

——, I Termini mandei per tempio, santuario e chiesa, Studi Orient. in onore di G. Levi della Vida I, Roma, 1956, 341-360.

——, I significati di mand. raza = misterio, segreto, ANLA, Ser. 8, Vol. 7, Roma, 1957, 447-510.

J. L. Malone, Systematic Metathesis in Mandaic, Language 47, 1971, 394-415.

Th. Nöldeke, Mandäisches, ZA 30, 1915-16, 139-162.

F. Rosenthal, Die aramaistische Forschung, 226-254.

W. Sundberg, Mandaean textual cruces, Lund, 1961.

G. Widengren, Iranisch-semitische Kulturbegegnung in parthischer Zeit, Köln, 1960, 89-108; Parthische Lehnwörter im Mandäischen.

B. LITERATURE

1. Principal Editions and Translations of Mandaic Texts

W. Brandt, Mandäische Schriften übersetzt und erläutert, Göttingen, 1893.

A. Dillmann, Das christliche Adambuch des Morgenlandes, Göttingen, 1853.

G. R. Driver, A Magic Bowl, RA 27, 1930, 61-64.

E. S. Drower, Shafta ḏ Pishra ḏ Ainia, A Mandaean Magical Text, translated and transliterated, JRAS, 1937, 589-611; 1938, 1-20.

——, A Mandaean Phylactery (Qmaha ḏ bit mišqal ainia), Iraq 5, 1938, 31-54.

——, Three Mandaean Phylacteries, transliterated and translated, JRAS, 1939, 397-406.

——, A Mandaean Book of Black Magic, transliterated and translated, JRAS, 1943, 149-181.

——, Pišra ḏ-Šambra, a Phylactery of Rue (An invocation of the personified Herb), Or. N.S. 15, 1946, 324-346.

——, The Book of the Zodiac (Sfar Malwašia), London, 1949.

——, Šarḥ ḏ Qabin ḏ Šišlam Rba. Explanatory commentary of the marriage ceremony of the Great Šišlam, Biblica et Orientalia 12, Roma, 1950.

——, Diwan Abatur or Progress through the Purgatories, Text and Transl., Studi e Testi 151, Roma, 1950.

——, The Haran Gawaita and the Baptism of Hibil-Ziwa. The mandaic text reproduced with transl., notes and commentary, Studi e Testi 176, Roma, 1953.

——, The Canonical Prayerbook of the Mandaeans, Leiden, 1959.

——, The Thousand and Twelve Questions (Alf trisar šuialia), Berlin, 1960.

——, Mandaean Polemic, BSOAS 25, 1962, 438-448.

——, The Coronation of the Great Šišlam. Being a Description of the Rite of the Coronation of a Mandaean Priest according to the Ancient Canon, Leiden, 1962.

——, A Pair of Naṣoraean Commentaries (Two priestly documents), Leiden, 1963.

J. EUTING, Mandäischer Diwan, Strassbourg, 1904.

C. H. GORDON, Aramaic and Mandaic Magical Bowls, ArOr 9, 1937, 84-106.

M. LIDZBARSKI, Mandäische Zaubertexte, Ephemeris f. Sem. Epigraphik I, Giessen, 1902, 89-106.

——, Ein mandäisches Amulett, Florilegium ou recueil de travaux d'érudition dédiés à M. Melchior de Vogüé, Paris, 1909, 349-373.

——, Das Johannesbuch der Mandäer. Text und Uebersetzung, 2 vols., Giessen, 1905-1915.

——, Mandäische Liturgien AAWG, Phil.-Hist. Kl., N.F. 17/1 Berlin, 1920.

——, Ginzā. Der Schatz oder das grosse Buch der Mandäer, Quellen, der Religionsgeschichte 13, Göttingen, 1925.

W. S. McCULLOUGH, Jewish and Mandaean Incantation Bowls in The Royal Ontario Museum, Near and Middle East Studies 5, 1967.

R. MACUCH, Altmandäische Bleirollen, AAW IV, 91-203; V/1, 34-72.

J. A. MONTGOMERY, Aramaic Incantation Texts from Nippur, Philadelphia, 1913.

J. DE MORGAN, Textes Mandaïtes, Études Linguistiques V, Paris, 1904.

H. Pognon, Une incantation contre les génies malfaisants en mandaïte, Mém. de la Soc. de Ling. de Paris 8, Paris, 1894, 194-234.

——, Inscriptions mandaites des coupes de Khouabir, Paris, 1898.

M. Sokoloff, Notes on some Mandaic magical texts, Orientalia 40, 1971, 448-458.

E. M. Yamauchi, Aramaic Magic Bowls, JAOS 85, 1965, 511-523.

——, Mandaic Incantation Texts, AmOr Ser. 49, New Haven, 1967.

——, A Mandaic Magic Bowl from the Yale Babylonian Collection Berytus 17, 1967-1968, 49-63.

C. HISTORY AND RELIGION

P. W. Coxon, Script analysis and Mandaean origins, JSS 15, 1970, 16-30.

E. S. Drower, The Mandaeans of Iraq and Iran. Their cults, customs, magic, legends and folklore, Oxford, 1937, repr. Leiden, 1962.

——, The Secret Adam. A Study of Nasoraean Gnosis, Oxford, 1960.

I. Jeruzalmi, Les coupes magiques araméennes de Mésopotamie. Diss. Faculté des Lettres et Sciences Humaines, Paris, 1963.

R. Macuch, Anfänge der Mandäer, Versuch eines geschichtlichen Bildes bis zur frühislamischen Zeit, AAW II, Berlin, 1965, 76-190.

——, The origins of the Mandaeans and their script. JSS 16, 1971, 174-192.

J. Naveh, The origin of the Mandaic script, BASOR 198, 1970, 32-37.

K. Rudolph, Die Mandäer I. Das Mandäerproblem, FRLANT 74, Göttingen, 1960.

——, Die Mandäer II, Der Kult, FRLANT 75, Göttingen, 1961.

——, Theogonie, Kosmogonie und Anthropogonie in den mandäischen Schriften. Eine literarische und traditionsgeschichtliche Untersuchung, FRLANT 88, Göttingen, 1965.

——, Problems of a history of the development of the Mandaean religion, History of Religions 8, 1968, 210-235.

——, Die Religion der Mandäer in: H. Gese, M. Höfner, K. Rudolph, Die Religionen Altsyriens, Altarabiens und der Mandäer, Stuttgart, 1970, 403-469.

D. IMPORTANT JOURNALS

ArOr, JAOS, JNES, JRAS, OLZ, Or, ThR, WZKM, ZDMG.

XIII. EPIGRAPHIC SOUTH ARABIAN

COMPILED BY

A. J. DREWES

Introductory Remark

With few exceptions, this list is restricted to publications since 1943. Inscriptions published prior to that date have been included in *Corpus* or *Répertoire*, with bibliographical references for each inscription. A rich bibliography for the years 1716-1928 may be found in the *Répertoire*, vol. V; it will be continued in one of the next volumes of that publication. In order to avoid unnecessary duplication, the present list has not been compiled with a view to completeness. Section C, in particular, contains only a selection of the most important titles and, as a rule, reviews have been omitted. Periodicals such as *Bibliotheca Orientalis, Le Muséon, Orientalia, Palestinskij Sbornik* and *Syria* often publish important reviews as well as other contributions on the subject of ESA. The *Archiv für Orientforschung* regularly prints a survey of recent research and findings. The *Annales d'Éthiopie* reports in each volume on the results of the excavations in progress in northern Ethiopia and Eritrea.

The entries within each section of this list are arranged by authors' names, in alphabetical order. Whenever several publications by one and the same author are grouped together, the order is chronological. Articles constituting a series are listed according to the year of publication of the first article in the series. This applies also to those articles by A. Jamme which, while appearing under various titles, publish inscriptions bearing Jamme numbers; they are ordered according to the numbers of the inscriptions rather than chronologically.

A. LINGUISTICS

1. GRAMMARS

G. M. BAUER, Jazyk južnoaravijskoj pis'mennosti, Moscow, 1966.

A. F. L. Beeston, A Descriptive Grammar of Epigraphic South Arabian, London, 1962.
M. Höfner, Altsüdarabische Grammatik, Porta Linguarum Orientalium XXIV, Leipzig, 1943.

2. Grammatical Studies

A. F. L. Beeston, Phonology of the Epigraphic South Arabian Unvoiced Sibilants, Transactions of the Philological Society, 1951, 1-26.
——, The Syntax of the Adjective in Old South Arabian: Remarks on Jamme's Theory, JSS 3, 1958, 142-145.
W. K. Brzuski, Note sur les thèmes à seconde radicale graphiquement redoublée en sudarabique épigraphique, RO 25, 1961, 127-131.
J. Cantineau, La mutation des sifflantes en sud-arabique, in: Mélanges Gaudefroy-Demombynes, Cairo, 1935-1945, 313-323.
Ja. B. Gruntfest, Glagol v južnoarabskom jazyke, Leningrad, 1966.
——, O naklonenijah v jazyke južnoarabskih nadpisej, Voprosy grammatiki jazykov stran Azii, Leningrad, 1964, 92-99.
——, Infinitiv v južnoarabskom jazyke, Semitskie Jazyki 2, 1965, 1, 285-306.
——, Konsekutivnye konstrukcii v južnoarabskom jazyke, Kratkie Soobščenija Instituta Narodov Azii 86, Istorija i Filologija Bližnego Vostoka, Semitologija, 1965, 129-147.
A. Jamme, Le pronom démonstratif sabéen *mhn* et les conjonctions composites *lqbl(y)/ḏ(t)*, *kmhnmw* et *km'nmw*, Cahiers de Byrsa VI, 1956, 173-180.
——, Syntax of the Adjective in South Arabian, JSS 2, 1957, 176-181.
——, The Syntax of South-Arabian Adjectives again, JSS 4, 1959, 264-267.
W. S. LaSor, The Sibilants in Old South Arabic, JQR NS XLVIII, 1957-1958, 161-173.
P. Matthiae, Le *matres lectionis* dell' arabo preislamico, RSO XXXVIII, 1963, 231-234.
G. Ryckmans, Une grammaire des anciens dialectes de l'Arabie méridionale, Mus LVI, 1943, 137-145.
D. Stehle, Sibilants and Emphatics in South Arabic, JAOS 60, 1940, 507-543.

3. VOCABULARIES, INDICES

A. F. L. BEESTON, Sabaean Inscriptions, Oxford, 1937, 89-152, Index of Words.

C. CONTI ROSSINI, Chrestomathia arabica meridionalis epigraphica, Rome, 1931, 99-261, Glossarium, repr. Rome, 1958.

G. L. HARDING, An Index and Concordance of Pre-Islamic Arabian Names and Inscriptions. Near and Middle East Series 8, Toronto, 1971.

W. W. MÜLLER, Die Wurzeln Mediae und Tertiae Y/W im Altsüdarabischen, Tübingen, 1962.

J. PIRENNE, Répertoire d'épigraphie sémitique VIII, Paris, 1968, 117-258, Index des mots.

G. RYCKMANS, Les noms propres sud-sémitiques I, Répertoire analytique; II, Répertoires alphabétiques, Louvain, 1934.

4. LEXICOGRAPHICAL STUDIES

G. M. BAUER, Nekotorye social'nye terminy v drevnejemenskih tekstah, Semitskie Jazyki 2, 1965, 1, 313-335.

——, Termin *gwlm* v južnoaravijskoj epigrafike, Kratkie Soobščenija Instituta Narodov Azii 86, Istorija i Filologija Bližnego Vostoka, Semitologija, 1965, 205-219.

A. F. L. BEESTON, East and West in Sabaean Inscriptions, JRAS, 1948, 177-180.

——, Notes on Old South Arabian Lexicography I, Mus LXIII, 1950, 53-57; II, Mus LXIII, 1950, 261-268; III, Mus LXIV, 1951, 127-132; IV, Mus LXV, 1952, 139-147; V, Mus LXVI, 1953, 109-122; VI, Mus LXVII, 1954, 311-322.

——, Epigraphic South Arabian Calendars and Dating, London, 1956.

——, The Hebrew Verb *špt*, VT VIII, 1958, 216-217.

R. BORGER, Zwei ugaritologische Kleinigkeiten II, Eine ugaritisch-altsüdarabische Isoglosse, VT X, 1960, 72.

M. FORTE, Sull' origine di alcuni tipi di altarini sud-arabici, AIUON NS XVII, 1967, 97-120.

M. A. GHUL, Was the Ancient South Arabian *Mḏqnt* the Islamic *Miḥrāb*?, BSOAS XXV, 1962, 331-335.

M. HÖFNER, Über einige Termini in qatabanischen Kaufurkunden, ZDMG 105, 1955, 74-80.

——, Die altsüdarabischen Monatsnamen, in: K. SCHUBERT et. al. (Ed.), Vorderasiatische Studien, Festschrift für Prof. Dr. Viktor Christian, Vienna, 1956, 46-54.

——, War der sabäische Mukarrib ein "Priesterfürst"?, WZKM 54, 1957, 77-85.

——, Orts- und Götternamen in Südarabien, in: A. LEIDLMAIR (Ed.), Hermann von Wissmann-Festschrift, Tübingen, 1962, 181-185.

——, Altsüdarabische Stelen und Statuetten, in E. HABERLAND et. al. (Ed.), Festschrift für Ad. E. Jensen I, München, 1964, 217-232.

A. K. IRVINE, Some Notes on Old South Arabian Monetary Terminology, JRAS, 1964, 18-36.

A. G. LOUNDINE, "'Il Très-Haut" dans les inscriptions sud-arabes, Mus LXXVI, 1963, 207-209.

A. G. LUNDIN, Social'noe rassloenie v južnoj aravii VI v.n.e., PSb 4 (67), 1959, 97-111.

——, O titule mlk "car'" v južnoj Aravii serediny I tysjačeletija do n.e., Kratkie Soobščenija Instituta Narodov Azii 46, Drevnij Vostok, 1962, 202-212.

——, O značenii glagola ʿsy v drevnejemenskih nadpisjah, Semitskie Jazyki 2, 1965, 1, 306-313.

J. C. DE MOOR, Ugaritic ṮKḤ and South Arabian MṮKḤ, VT XIV, 1964, 371-372.

W. W. MÜLLER, Altsüdarabische Beiträge zum Hebräischen Lexicon, ZATW 75, 1963, 304-316.

J. PIRENNE, Le mur du temple sabéen de Mârib et ses inscriptions, AIBL, 1969, 80-91.

——, L'invective avant le combat ou le sens du verbe wśʿ-twśʿ en sud-arabe préislamique, in: R. STIEHL, H. E. STIER (Ed.), Beiträge zur Alten Geschichte und deren Nachleben, Festschrift für Franz Altheim zum 6.10.1968 II, Berlin, 1970, 27-34.

M. RODINSON, Ḫṣṣtn, royaume de Imru l-qays, GLECS VII, 1957, 114-116.

——, Notes de vocabulaire alimentaire sudarabique et arabe, GLECS IX, 1960-1963, 103-107.

——, Une phrase de style coranique dans une inscription sudarabique?, GLECS XIII, 1968-1969, 102-105.

E. ROSSI, Vocaboli sud-arabici nelle odierne parlate arabe del Yemen, RSO XVIII, 1940, 299-314.

G. RYCKMANS, Sabéen ḥbl = Accadien abullu?, L'inscription Fakhry 2, ArOr XVII, 1949, 310-312.

——, Heaven and Earth in the South Arabian Inscriptions, JSS 3, 1958, 225-236.

——, Notes épigraphiques 5e série, Mus LXXI, 1958, 125-139.

——, Le *Qayl* en Arabie méridionale préislamique, in: Hebrew and Semitic Studies presented to Godfrey Rolles Driver in Celebration of his Seventieth Birthday 20 August 1962, Oxford, 1962, 144-155.

——, Sud-arabe *mḏbḥt* = Hébreu *mzbḥ* et termes apparentés, in : E. Gräf (Ed.), Festschrift Werner Caskel, Leiden, 1968, 253-260.

J. Ryckmans, A propos du *m'mr* sud-arabe: RÉS 3884 bis, Mus LXVI, 1953, 343-369.

——, Le sens de *ḏ'l* en sud-arabe, Mus LXVII, 1954, 339-348.

R. B. Serjeant, Miḥrāb, BSOAS XXII, 1959, 439-453.

E. Ullendorff, South Arabian Etymological Marginalia, BSOAS XV, 1953, 157-159.

B. TEXTS

1. Classification, Concordances

M. Höfner, Die Sammlung Eduard Glaser, Verzeichnis des Glaser-Nachlasses, sonstiger südarabischer Materialbestände und einer Sammlung anderer semitischer Inschriften, SAWW 222, 5, 1944.

A. Jamme, Classification descriptive générale des inscriptions sud-arabes, Supplément à la Revue IBLA XI, 1948, 401-476, Tunis, 1948.

J. Pirenne, Répertoire d'épigraphie sémitique VIII, Paris, 1968, 17-115, Tables, Index I-XII.

G. Ryckmans, Les noms propres sud-sémitiques III, Concordance générale des inscriptions sud-sémitiques, Louvain, 1935.

2. Repertories

Corpus inscriptionum semiticarum, Pars quarta, Inscriptiones ḥimyariticas et sabaeas continens I, II, III, Paris, 1889-1929.

Répertoire d'épigraphie sémitique, especially V, VI, VII, Paris, 1929-1950.

3. Texts, Editions and Studies

a. *Works of major importance*

A. Jamme, Sabaean Inscriptions from Maḥram Bilqîs (Mârib), Publications of the American Foundation for the Study of Man III, Baltimore, 1962 [this book contains the inscriptions Ja(mme) 550-851, 853-855, 877-879].

A. G. Lundin, Die Eponymenliste von Saba (aus dem Stamme Ḫalîl), Sammlung Eduard Glaser V, SAWW 248, 1, 1965.

K. Mlaker, Die Hierodulenlisten von Maʿîn, nebst Untersuchungen zur altsüdarabischen Rechtsgeschichte und Chronologie, Sammlung orientalistischer Arbeiten 15, Leipzig, 1943.

Kh. Y. Nami, Našr nuqūš sāmiyya qadīma min janūb bilād al-ʿArab wašarḥuhā, Cairo, 1943.

G. Ryckmans, Epigraphical Texts, i.e. A. Fakhry, An Archaeological Journey to Yemen II, Cairo, 1952.

b. *Further publications*

[A photograph of] a Qataban (South Arabian) alabaster figure of a man, with incised inscription on the base, Archaeology 20, 1967, 73.

R. D. Barnett, South Arabian Sculptures, BMQ XVII, 1952, 47-48.

——, Department of Western Asiatic Antiquities, Acquisitions, 1961, BMQ XXVI, 1962-1963, 74 (no. 132932); Acquisitions, 1962, BMQ XXVI, 1962-1963, 136 (no. 132998).

——, A Review of Acquisitions, 1955-1962, of Western Asiatic Antiquities II, BMQ XXVII, 1964, 79-88.

G. M. Bauer, Sabejskaja nadpis' iz sobranija E. Glazera Nº 1210, Semitskie Jazyki, 1963, 135-147.

A. F. L. Beeston, Two Shabwa Inscriptions, Mus LX, 1947, 51-55.

——, The Ritual Hunt, Mus LXI, 1948, 183-196.

——, The Oracle Sanctuary of Jār al-Labbā, Mus LXII, 1949, 207-228.

——, A Sabaean Boundary Formula, BSOAS XIII, 1949, 1-3.

——, A Sabaean Penal Law, Mus LXIV, 1951, 305-315.

——, Old South Arabian Antiquities, JRAS, 1952, 20-23.

——, Four Sabaean Texts in the Istanbul Archeological Museum, Mus LXV, 1952, 271-283.

——, Remarks on the Ḥaḍrami Inscription Jamme 402, Or NS 22, 1953, 1-2.

——, Notes on the Mureighan Inscription, BSOAS XVI, 1954, 389-392.

——, The "Ta'lab Lord of Pastures" Texts, BSOAS XVII, 1955, 154-156.

——, Two Middle Sabaean Votive Texts, BO XVI, 1959, 17-18.

——, Qahtan, Studies in Old South Arabian Epigraphy I: The Mercantile Code of Qataban, London, 1959.

——, Epigraphic and Archaeological Gleanings from South Arabia, OA (Roma) I, 1962, 41-52.

——, A Sabaean Trader's Misfortunes, JSS XIV, 1969, 227-230.

G. BENARDELLI, A. E. PARRINELLO, Note su alcune località archeologiche del Yemen I, AIUON NS XX, 1970, 117-120; II, AIUON NS XXI, 1971, 111-118.

P. BONESCHI, L'inscription liḥyānite d'anciennes monnaies tenues pour sabéennes, RSO XXVI, 1951, 1-15.

——, Inscriptions humiliantes des monnaies sabéennes, RSO XXIX, 1954, 17-27.

——, La γλαῦξ athénienne et l'inscription liḥyānite de monnaies tenues pour sabéennes, RSO XXX, 1955, 229-234.

——, Le monogramme sud-arabe d'un vase antique à provisions, RSO XXXIII, 1958, 169-173.

——, Tres tituli sabaei iterum interpretati, RSO XXXIV, 1959, 27-32.

——, Duo tituli sabaei iterum interpretati, RSO XXXIV, 1959, 137-140.

——, Les inscriptions des vases à parfums et à cosmétiques du tombeau A 5 de Ḥureyda, RSO XL, 1965, 279-285.

G. J. BOTTERWECK, Altsüdarabische Glaser-Inschriften, Or NS 19, 1950, 435-444.

F. BRON, Une nouvelle inscription sabéenne, AIUON NS XIX, 1969, 264-265.

——, Note additionnelle à AION N.S. XIX, 1969, pp. 264-265, AIUON NS XIX, 1969, 567-568.

——, Inscriptions et gravures rupestres d'al-Uḫdūd (Naǧrān), AIUON NS XX, 1970, 259-262.

——, Antiquités sud-arabes dans les collections suisses, AION NS XX, 1970, 549-554.

W. L. BROWN, A. F. L. BEESTON, Sculptures and Inscriptions from Shabwa, JRAS, 1954, 43-62.

A. CAPUZZI, Yasir Yuhan'im in una nuova iscrizione sabea, AIUON NS XIX, 1969, 419-422.

A. CAQUOT, A. J. DREWES, Les monuments recueillis à Maqallé (Tigré), AE I, 1955, 17-41.

W. CASKEL, Entdeckungen in Arabien, Arbeitsgemeinschaft für Forschung des Landes Nordrhein-Westfalen, Geisteswissenschaften, Heft 30, Cologne and Opladen, 1954.

——, Der Sinn der Inschrift in Ḥiṣn al-Ġurāb, Folia Orientalia 12, 1970, 51-60.

H. DE CONTENSON, Trois sculptures de l'Arabie du Sud, Syria XLVI, 1969, 99-103.

C. CONTI ROSSINI, Ièha, Tsehùf Emni e Derà, RaStEt VI, 1947, 12-22.

A. DAVICO, Ritrovamenti sud-arabici nella zona di Cascasé, RaStEt V, 1946, 1-6.

F. DIAZ ESTEBAN, Inscripción sudarábiga en Madrid, Trabajos de Prehistoria, Instituto Español de Prehistoria del Consejo Superior de Investigaciones Científicas, Departamento de Prehistoria de la Universidad de Madrid, NS XXVI, 1969, 359-363.

D. B. DOE, The Site of 'Am'adiya near Mukeiras on the Audhali Plateau, South West Arabia, Aden Department of Antiquities Report, Bulletin 2, 1963, 1-12.

——, The Wadi Shirjan, Aden Department of Antiquities Report 1961-1963 and Bulletin 4, 1964, 1-3.

——, A. JAMME, New Sabaean Inscriptions from South Arabia, JRAS, 1968, 2-28 [Ja 2106-2120].

A. J. DREWES, Some Hadrami Inscriptions, BO XI, 1954, 93-94.

——, The Inscription from Dibdib in Eritrea, BO XI, 1954, 185-186.

——, Nouvelles inscriptions de l'Éthiopie, BO XIII, 1956, 179-182.

——, Les inscriptions de Melazo, AE III, 1959, 83-99.

——, Inscriptions de l'Éthiopie antique, Leiden, 1962.

——, R. SCHNEIDER, Documents épigraphiques de l'Éthiopie I, AE VII, 1967, 89-102; II, AE VIII, 1970, 57-72.

D. J. DUNCANSON, Girmaten — A New Archaeological Site in Eritrea, Antiquity XXI, 83, 1947, 158-163.

V. FRANCHINI, L. RICCI, Ritrovamenti archaeologici in Eritrea, RaStEt XII, 1953, 5-28.

G. GARBINI, Una nuova iscrizione di Šaraḥbi'il Ya'fur, AIUON NS XIX, 1969, 559-566.

——, Una bilingue sabeo-ebraica da Ẓafar, AIUON NS XX, 1970, 153-165.

——, Un oroscopo himyaritica, AIUON NS XX, 1970, 439-446.

——, Antichità yemenite I, AIUON NS XX, 1970, 400-404; II, AIUON NS XX, 1970, 537-548.

A. GAUDIO, Comunicazione sulla collezione archeologica sud-arabica del Museo archeologico dell' Asmara nel suo ordine di classificazione, Istituto di Studi Etiopici, Asmara, Bollettino I, 1953, 31-43.

M. A. GHUL, New Qatabāni inscriptions I, BSOAS XXII, 1959, 1-22; II, BSOAS XXII, 1959, 419-438.

M. HÖFNER, Drei sabäische Personenwidmungen, WZKM 51, 1948, 38-42.

——, Ta'lab als Patron der Kleinviehhirten, Die Inschriften Gl 1142, 1143, Serta Cantabrigiensia, Wiesbaden, 1954, 29-36.

——, Eine Qatabanische Weihinschrift aus Timna', Mus LXXIV, 1961, 453-459.

——, Bearbeitung der von Carl Rathjens in Sabaeica I und II in Abbildungen veröffentlichten altsüdarabischen Inschriften, sowie einiger sonstiger von ihm gesammelter Inschriftensteine, i.e. C. RATHJENS, Sabaeica III, Mitteilungen aus dem Museum für Völkerkunde in Hamburg XXVIII, Hamburg, 1966.

——, Eine altsüdarabische Sühne-Inschrift, in: Hebräische Wortforschung, Festschrift zum 80. Geburtstag von Walter Baumgartner, VT Supplement XVI, Leiden, 1967, 106-113.

——, J. M. SOLÁ SOLÉ, Inschriften aus dem Gebiet zwischen Mārib und dem Ǧōf, Sammlung Eduard Glaser II, SAWW 238, 3, Vienna, 1961.

A. M. HONEYMAN, The Letter-Order of the Semitic Alphabets in Africa and the Near East, Africa XXII, 1952, 136-147.

——, The Hombrechtikon Plaque, Iraq XVI, 1954, 23-28.

——, Epigraphic South Arabian Antiquities, JNES XXI, 1962, 38-43.

A. K. IRVINE, Homicide in pre-Islamic South Arabia, BSOAS XXX, 1967, 277-292.

M. AL-IRYANI, G. GARBINI, A Sabaean Rock-Engraved Inscription at Mosna', AIUON NS XX, 1970, 405-408.

A. JAMME, Pièces Anépigraphes Sud-Arabes d'Aden, Mus LXIV, 1951, 157-176 [Ja 1-57].

——, Pièces épigraphiques sud-arabes de la collection K. Muncherjee, Mus LXV, 1952, 95-137 [Ja 58-117].

——, Inscriptions Related to the House Yafash in Timna', in: R. LE-BARON BOWEN, Jr., F. P. ALBRIGHT, Archaeological Discoveries in South Arabia, Baltimore, 1958, 183-193 [Ja 118-122].

——, Pièces épigraphiques de Ḥeid bin 'Aqīl, la nécropole de Timna' (Hagr Koḥlân), Bibliothèque du *Muséon* 30, Louvain, 1952 [Ja 123-383].

——, Deux autels à encens de l'Université de Harvard, BO X, 1953, 94-95 [Ja 384-385].

——, Pièces qatabanites et sabéennes d'Aden, Anadolu Araştırmaları I, 1955, 117-126 [Ja 386-399].

——, Sabaean Inscriptions on Two Bronze Statues from Mārib (Yemen), JAOS 77, 1957, 32-36 [Ja 400-401].

——, Une inscription ḥaḍramoutique en bronze, Or NS 22, 1953, 158-165 [Ja 402].

——, Notes additionnelles à l'inscription Jamme 402, Or NS 23, 1954, 252.

——, Les inscriptions minéennes TaAM 4 et 5, Cahiers de Byrsa IV, 1954, 125-151 [Ja 403-404].

——, The She'b edh-Dhaqab Inscriptions, in: R. LeBaron Bowen, Jr., F. P. Albright, Archaeological Discoveries in South Arabia, Baltimore, 1958, 143-147 [Ja 405-406].

——, Les antiquités sud-arabes du Museo Nazionale Romano, Monumenti Antichi pubblicati per cura della Accademia Nazionale dei Lincei XLIII, Rome, 1956, col. 1-122 [Ja 411-482].

——, Antiquités funéraires épigraphiques qatabanites, Cahiers de Byrsa VII, 1957, 189-195 [Ja 483-488, 883-884].

——, Inscriptions on the Sabaean Bronze Horse of the Dumbarton Oaks Collection, Dumbarton Oaks Papers 8, 1954, 317-330 [Ja 489].

——, Note on the Dating of the Bronze Horse of the Dumbarton Oaks Collection, Washington, 1957.

——, Inscriptions du Musée de Ṣan'â' d'après les photographies de M. C. Ansaldi, Mus LXVII, 1954, 323-338 [Ja 490-505].

——, Trois plaques épigraphiques sabéennes du Musée de Ṣan'â', BO XI, 1954, 42-43 [Ja 506-508].

——, Inscriptions sud-arabes de la collection Ettore Rossi, RSO XXX, 1955, 103-130 [Ja 509-531].

——, Inscriptions de al-'Amâyid à Mâreb, Mus LXVIII, 1955, 313-324 [Ja 532-535].

——, An Archaic Dextrograde Sabaean Inscription from Mâreb, BASOR 134, April 1954, 25-26 [Ja 536].

——, Inscriptions des alentours de Mareb (Yemen), Cahiers de Byrsa V, 1955, 265-281 [Ja 538-549].

——, A Qatabanian Dedicatory Inscription from Hajar bin Ḥumeid, JAOS 75, 1955, 97-99 [Ja 852].

——, The Late Sabaean Inscription Ja 856, BO XVII, 1960, 3-5 [Ja 856].

——, South-Arabian Antiquities in the U.S.A., BO XII, 1955, 152-154 [Ja 857-862].

——, An Archaic South-Arabian Inscription in Vertical Columns, BASOR 137, February 1955, 32-38 [Ja 863].

——, Quatre inscriptions sud-arabes, Washington, 1957 [Ja 864-867].

——, Some Qatabanian Inscriptions Dedicating "Daughters of God", BASOR 138, April 1955, 39-47 [Ja 868-875].

——, La dynastie de Šaraḥbi'il Yakûf et la documentation épigraphique sud-arabe, Uitgaven van het Nederlands Historisch-Archaeologisch Instituut te Istanbul IX, Istanbul, 1961 [Ja 876].

——, Les pierres épigraphiques qatabanites Lyon 818 *bis* et *ter*, Cahiers de Byrsa VII, 1957, 205-217 [Ja 881-882].

——, Two New Hadrami Inscriptions from Zôfar, BO XXIV, 1967, 145-148 [Ja 885, 892].

——, Les trois antiquités qatabanites en bronze Ja 886-888, OA (Roma) II, 1963, 133-135 [Ja 886-888].

——, Inscription rupestre et graffites qatabanites photographiés par le Major M. D. VAN LESSEN, RSO XXXVII, 1962, 231-241 [Ja 889-891].

——, Documentation sud-arabe I et II, RSO XXXVIII, 1963, 303-322 [Ja 893-909, 408].

——, The Al-'Uqlah Texts (Documentation Sud-Arabe III), Washington, 1963 [Ja 910-1007, 409-410, 880].

——, Sabaean and Ḥasaean Inscriptions from Saudi Arabia, SS 23, Rome, 1966 [Ja 1008-1062].

——, The South-Arabian Collection of the University Museum (Cambridge, England), Documentation sud-arabe IV, RSO XL, 1965, 43-55 [Ja 1063-1092].

——, Inscriptions photographed at Qaryat al-Fa'w, RSO XLI, 1966, 289-301 [Ja 2099-2105].

——, New Ḥasaean and Sabaean Inscriptions from Saudi Arabia, OA (Roma) VI, 1967, 181-187 [Ja 2122-2127].

——, Liḥyanite, Sabaean and Thamudic Inscriptions from Western Saudi Arabia, RSO XLV, 1970, 91-113 [Ja 2147-2194].

——, A Qatabanian Bronze Votive Lamp Offering, BO XXVII, 1970, 178-179 [Ja 2195].

——, Les inscriptions rupestres de la région de Mukérâs, ARBB sér. 5 XXXVII, 1951, 307-320.

——, Aperçu général des inscriptions copiées à Mâreb (Yemen), ARBB sér. 5 XXXVIII, 1952, 289-306.

——, South-Arabian Inscriptions, in: J. B. PRITCHARD (Ed.), Ancient Near Eastern Texts Relating to the Old Testament, 2nd edition, Princeton, 1955, 506-513; 3rd edition, Princeton, 1969, 663-670.

——, Les albums photographiques de la collection Kaiky Muncherjee (Aden), Università di Roma, Studi orientali pubblicati a cura della scuola orientale III, Rome, 1955.

——, L'identification de Ta'lab au dieu lunaire et les textes sabéens Gl 1142 et 1143, BO XIII, 1956, 182-186.

——, Remarks on the South-Arabian Inscriptions Hamilton 3-13, JRAS, 1956, 146-156.

——, L'inscription ḥaḍramoutique Ingrams I et la chasse rituelle sud-arabe, Muséon LXIX, 1956, 99-108.

——, Un désastre nabatéen devant Nagran, Cahiers de Byrsa VI, 1956, 165-171.

——, Le faux sabéen RÉS 4964, Washington, 1956.

——, Les antiquités sud-arabes du Musée Borély à Marseille, Cahiers de Byrsa VIII, 1958-1959, 149-189.

——, La jarre épigraphique qatabanite de Haǧr bin Ḥumeid et son étude par Paulo Boneschi, RSO XXXIV, 1959, 127-136.

——, South Arabian Bronze Plaques of the Royal Asiatic Society, JRAS, 1962, 132-133.

——, Preliminary Report on Epigraphic Research in Northwestern Wâdî Ḥaḍramawt and at al-'Abar, BASOR 172, December 1963, 41-54.

——, Research on Sabaean Rock Inscriptions from Southwestern Saudi Arabia, Washington, 1965.

——, Documentation sud-arabe V, RSO XL, 1965, 287-299.

——, Notes on the Published Inscribed Objects Excavated at Ḥeid bin 'Aqîl in 1950-1951, Washington, 1965.

——, Les Listes Onomastiques Sabéennes De (?) Ṣirwâḥ en 'Arḥab, Washington, 1966.

——, The Sabaean Onomastic Lists from (?) Ṣirwâḥ in 'Arḥab (second half), RSO XLII, 1967, 361-406.

——, Minaean Inscriptions Published as Lihyanite, Washington, 1968.

——, Inscriptions from Hajar bin Ḥumeid, in: G. W. VAN BEEK, Hajar bin Ḥumeid, Baltimore, 1969, 331-352.

——, G. W. Van Beek, The South-Arabian Clay Stamp from Bethel again, BASOR 163, October 1961, 15-18.

W. I. Jones, A Pre-Islamic Site and a Sabean/Himyarite Inscription, TGUOS XIV, 1950-1952, 10-19.

W. E. N. Kensdale, Two South Arabian Antiquities, JRAS, 1953, 40-41.

——, Ḥaywʿaṭṭar Yadaʿ and the Nāʿiṭ Inscription, Mus LXVI, 1953, 371-372.

I. Ju. Kračkovskij, Dve južnoarabskie nadpisi v Leningrade, in: Izbrannye sočinenija I, Leningrad, 1955, 394-414.

A. G. Lundin, Južnoarabskaja istoričeskaja nadpis' VI v.n.e. iz Mariba, EV IX, 1954, 3-24.

——, Južnoarabskaja stroitel'naja nadpis' načala VI v., EV XIII, 1960, 78-94.

——, Nadpisi Jada'ila Ẓariḫa, syna Sumhuʿalaj, Mukarriba Saba', VDI, 1960, 3, 12-22.

——, Novye južnoarabskie nadpisi muzeja v Ṣanʿa I, EV XV, 1963, 36-50; II, EV XIX, 1969, 14-20.

——, O prave na vodu v sabejskom gosudarstve epohi mukarribov, PSb 11 (74), 1964, 45-57.

——, Nekotorye voprosy zemel'nyh otnošenij v drevnej Južnoj Aravii, Kratkie Soobščenija Instituta Narodov Azii 86, Istorija i Filologija Bližnego Vostoka, Semitologija, 1965, 148-154.

——, Novyj fragment sabejskoj nadpisi perioda mukarribov, PSb 15 (78), 1966, 47-53.

——, Sabejskie meževye nadpisi iz Džar al-Labba, V Vsesojuznaja sessija po drevnemu vostoku, 6-9 aprelja 1971, Tezisy dokladov, Akademija Nauk Gruzinskoj SSR, Otdelenie obščestvennyh Nauk, Tbilisi, 1971, 69-71.

T. C. Mitchell, A South-Arabian Tripod Offering said to be from Ur, Iraq XXXI, 1969, 112-114.

P. Moretti, Iscrizioni sabee aʿMàriya, AIUON NS XXI, 1971, 119-122.

Kh. Y. Nami, Nuqūš ʿarabiyya janūbiyya I, Majallat kulliyyat al-'ādāb, Cairo University, Bulletin of the Faculty of Arts 9, 1, May 1947, Arabic section 15-27; II, Majallat kulliyyat al-'ādāb 16, 2, December 1954, Arabic section 21-43; III, Majallat kulliyyat al-'ādāb 20, 1, May 1958, Arabic section 55-63; IV, Ḥawliyyāt kulliyyat al-'ādāb 22, 2, December 1960, Arabic section, 53-63; V, Ḥawliyyāt kulliyyat al-'ādāb 23, 1, May 1961, Arabic section,

1-9; VI, Ḥawliyyāt kulliyyat al-'ādāb 24, 1, May 1962, Arabic section, 1-8.

——, Nuqūš ḫirbat Ma'īn, majmū'at Muḥammad Tawfīq, Les monuments de Ma'īn (Yemen), Publications de l'Institut Français d'Archéologie Orientale du Caire, Études sud-arabiques II, Cairo, 1952.

——, Nuqūš ḫirbat Barāqiš 'alā ḍaw' majmū'at Muḥammad Tawfīq I, Majallat kulliyyat al-'ādāb, Cairo University, Bulletin of the Faculty of Arts 16, 1, May 1954, Arabic section, 1-21; II, Majallat kulliyyat al-'ādāb 17, 1, May 1955, Arabic section, 1-22; III, Majallat kulliyyat al-'ādāb 18, 2, December 1956, Arabic section, 1-36; IV, Majallat kulliyyat al-'ādāb 19, 2, December 1957, Arabic section, 93-124.

K. PETRÁČEK, Annotations aux inscriptions sud-arabes Ry 603-614 du Dār aḍ-Ḍiyāfa à Ṣan'ā', ArOr 29, 1961, 444-447.

——, Quelques faux sud-arabes de Ṣan'ā', AE IV, 1961, 125-127.

——, Südarabische Inschriften aus Ṣan'ā', ArOr 32, 1964, 358-364.

——, Drei südarabische Inschriften aus Ṣan'ā', ArOr 33, 1965, 65-66.

——, Südarabisches aus Bēt Ḥanḍal (Jemen), ArOr 33, 1965, 600-601.

H. St. J. B. PHILBY, Three new Inscriptions from Hadhramaut, JRAS 1945, 124-133.

——, A. S. TRITTON, Najran Inscriptions, JRAS, 1944, 119-129.

J. PIRENNE, Contribution à l'épigraphie sud-arabique, Semitica XVI, 1966, 73-99.

——, Une législation hydrologique en Arabie du Sud antique, l'inscription inédite du Djebel Khalbaṣ et le texte CIH 610, in: Hommages à André DUPONT-SOMMER, Paris, 1971, 117-135.

L. RICCI, Ritrovamenti archeologici in Eritrea, RaStEt XIV, 1955-1958, 48-68.

——, Note marginali: c) La statuetta di bovino in bronzo da Zĕbán Kutur, RaStEt XV, 1959, 112-113.

——, Iscrizioni rupestri dell' Eritrea I, RaStEt XV, 1959, 55-95; II, RaStEt XVI, 1960, 77-119.

——, Notizie archeologiche: Ritrovamenti a Meṭerá e Yeḥá — Der'á — Nuovi materiali da altri luoghi dell' Eritrea, RaStEt XVI, 1960, 120-123.

M. RODINSON, Conférences de M. Maxime Rodinson [I], École pratique des Hautes Études, IVᵉ Section, Sciences historiques et philologiques, Annuaire 1965/1966, Paris, 1965, 125-141; [II], Annuaire 1966/67, Paris, 1966, 121-139; [III], Annuaire 1968/1969, Paris,

1969, 97-118; [IV], Annuaire 1969/1970, Paris, 1970, 161-183;
[V], Annuaire 1970/1971, Paris, 1971, 161-165.

——, Sur une nouvelle inscription du règne de Dhoû Nowâs, BO
XXVI, 1969, 26-34.

G. RYCKMANS, Epigraphy, in: G. CATON THOMPSON, The Tombs and
Moon Temple of Hureidha (Hadhramaut), Oxford, 1944, 155-184.

——, Une inscription chrétienne sabéenne aux Musées d'Antiquités
d'Istanbul, Mus LIX, 1946, 165-172.

——, Notes épigraphiques, 4e série, Mus LX, 1947, 149-176.

——, Zuid-Arabische opschriftenfragmenten te Batavia, Tijdschrift
voor Ind. Taal-, Land- en Volkenkunde LXXXIII, 1949, 375-377.

——, Inscriptions Sud-Arabes, 8e série, Mus LXII, 1949, 55-124
[Ry 359-443]; 9e série, Mus LXIV, 1951, 93-126 [Ry 444;498];
10e série, Mus LXVI, 1953, 267-317 [Ry 499-519]; 11e série,
Mus LXVII, 1954, 99-119 [Ry 520-532]; 12e série, Mus LXVIII,
1955, 297-312 [Ry 533-534]; 13e série, Mus LXIX, 1956, 139-163
[Ry 535]; 14e série, Mus LXIX, 1956, 369-389 [Ry 536-539];
15e série, Mus LXX, 1957, 97-126 [Ry 540-556]; 16e série, Mus
LXXI, 1958, 105-119 [Ry 557-583]; 17e série, Mus LXXII,
1959, 159-176 [Ry 584-597]; 18e série, Mus LXXIII, 1960, 5-25
[Ry 598-617]; 19e série, Mus LXXV, 1962, 213-231 [Ry 618-661];
20e série, Mus LXXV, 1962, 441-453 [Ry 662-686]; 21e série,
Mus LXXVI, 1963, 419-423 [Ry 687-688]; 22e série, Mus
LXXVIII, 1965, 215-228 [Ry 689-735].

——, Graffites rupestres près du tombeau de Bin Hud, Mus LXVII,
1954, 181-185.

——, Graffites sabéens relevés en Arabie Saʻudite, in: Scritti in onore
di Giuseppe Furlani, RSO XXXII, 1957, 557-563.

——, Découvertes épigraphiques en Éthiopie, Mus LXXI, 1958,
141-148.

J. RYCKMANS, Himyaritica I, Mus LXIX, 1956, 91-98; II, Mus
LXXIX, 1966, 475-500.

——, Les corégents du roi himyarite Abūkarib Asʻad d'après le texte
Rossi 24, RSO XXXVII, 1962, 243-250.

——, Nouvelle interprétation d'un texte sabéen, BO XXV, 1968, 5-8.

——, La mancie par ḥrb en Arabie du Sud ancienne: l'inscription
Nami NAG 12, in: E. GRÄF (Ed.), Festschrift Werner Caskel,
Leiden, 1968, 261-273.

——, L'inscription sud-arabe Nami NAG 13-14, ErIs IX, 1969, 102-
108.

R. Schneider, Inscriptions d'Enda Čerqos, AE IV, 1961, 61-63.

——, Remarques sur les inscriptions d'Enda Čerqos, AE VI, 1965, 221-222.

——, Notes épigraphiques sur les découvertes de Maṭarā, AE VI, 1965, 89-92.

S. Smith, An Inscription from the Temple of Sin at Ḥuraiḏha in the Ḥaḏramawt, BSOAS 11, 1943-1946, 451-464.

J. M. Solá Solé, La inscripción Gl. 389 y los comienzos del monoteísmo en Sudarabia, Mus LXXII, 1959, 197-206.

——, Las dos grandes inscripciónes sudarábigas del dique de Mârib, Tübingen, 1960.

——, Inschriften aus Riyām, Sammlung Eduard Glaser IV, SAWW 243, 4, 1964.

H. Tschinkowitz, Kleine Fragmente (I. Teil), Sammlung Eduard Glaser VI, SAWW 261, 4, 1969.

G. W. Van Beek, A. Jamme, An Inscribed South Arabian Clay Stamp from Bethel, BASOR 151, October 1958, 9-16.

J. Walker, A New Type of South Arabian Coinage, Numismatic Chronicle, Fifth Series XVII, 1937, 260-279.

——, A South Arabian Inscription in the Baroda State Museum, Mus LIX, 1946, 159-162.

——, A Mysterious South Arabian Coin-Legend, Numismatic Chronicle, Sixth Series VIII, 1948, 39-42.

——, The Moon-God on Coins of the Ḥaḏramaut, BSOAS XIV, 1952, 623-626.

——, The Liḥyanite Inscription on South Arabian Coins, RSO XXXIV, 1959, 77-81.

——, A South Arabian Gem with Sabaean and Kufic Legends, Mus LXXV, 1962, 455-457.

——, A New Ḳatabanian Coin from South Arabia, ErIs VII, 1963, 127.

F. V. Winnett, A Himyarite Bronze Tablet, BASOR 110, April 1948, 23-25.

Y. Yadin, An Inscribed South-Arabian Clay Stamp from Bethel?, BASOR 196, December 1969, 37-45.

C. GENERAL

1. Bibliographies, Reference Works

Répertoire d'épigraphie sémitique V, Paris, 1929, pp. iii-lxxxiii,
Bibliographie.

A. Grohmann, Arabien, Kulturgeschichte des alten Orients, Handbuch
der Altertumswissenschaft III, 1, 3, 3, 4, München, 1963.

Y. Moubarac, Éléments de bibliographie sud-sémitique, REI XXIII,
1955, 121-176.

——, Les études d'épigraphie sud-sémitique et la naissance de l'Islam.
Éléments de bibliographie et lignes de recherches, REI XXV,
1957, 13-68.

J. Pirenne, Chronique d'archéologie sud-arabe 1955-1956, AE II,
1957, 37-68.

——, Un nouveau manuel des études sud-arabiques, BO XXIII,
1966, 3-15.

J. Ryckmans, Études d'épigraphie sud-arabe en russe 1 (année 1965),
BO XXIV, 1967, 271-273; 2 (année 1966), BO XXV, 1968,
153-156; 3 (année 1967, première partie), BO XXV, 1968, 283-
286; 4 (année 1967, 2ᵉ partie), BO XXVII, 1970, 3-4; 5 (année
1968), BO XXVII, 1970, 179; 6 (année 1969), BO XXVII, 1970,
179.

——, Bibliographie de Mgr G. Ryckmans, Mus LXXXIII, 1970,
13-40.

2. Archaeology, Geography, History, Religion

F. P. Albright, The Excavation of the Temple of the Moon at Mârib
(Yemen), BASOR 128, December 1952, 25-38.

——, The Himyaritic Temple at Khor Rory (Dhofar, Oman), Or
NS 22, 1953, 284-287.

W. F. Albright, The Chronology of Ancient South Arabia in the
Light of the First Campaign of Excavation in Qataban, BASOR
119, October 1950, 5-15.

——, The Chronology of the Minaean Kings of Arabia, BASOR 129,
February 1953, 20-24.

——, Review of J. Ryckmans, L'institution monarchique en Arabie
méridionale avant l'Islam (Maʿîn et Saba), JAOS 73, 1953, 36-40.

——, A Note on Early Sabaean Chronology, BASOR 143, October 1956, 9-10.

——, Zur Chronologie des vorislamischen Arabien, in: J. Hempel, L. Rost (Ed.), Von Ugarit nach Qumran, Beiträge zur alttestamentlichen und altorientalischen Forschung Otto Eissfeldt zum 1. Sept. 1957 dargebracht, Beihefte zur ZATW 77, Berlin, 1958, 1-8.

G. M. Bauer, Sabejskie nadpisi kak istočnik dlja issledovanija pozemel'nyh otnošenij v Sabe "epohi mukarribov", Moscow, 1964.

——, "Mukarrib" i "car'" (k voprosu o gosudarstvennom stroe drevnej Saby), VDI, 1964, 2, 17-36.

——, Nekotorye problemy eponimata v drevnej južnoj Aravii, VDI 100, 1967, 2, 124-147.

A. F. L. Beeston, Problems of Sabaean Chronology, BSOAS XVI, 1954, 37-56.

I. Ben-Zvi, Les origines de l'établissement des tribus d'Israel en Arabie, Mus LXXIV, 1961, 143-190.

H. Th. Bossert, Altsyrien, Kunst und Handwerk in Cypern, Syrien, Palästina, Transjordanien und Arabien von den Anfängen bis zum völligen Aufgehen in der Griechisch-Römischen Kultur, Die ältesten Kulturen des Mittelmeerkreises III, Tübingen, 1951.

R. LeBaron Bowen, Jr., F. P. Albright, Archaeological Discoveries in South Arabia, Publications of the American Foundation for the Study of Man II, Baltimore, 1958.

R. L. Cleveland, The 1960 American Archaeological Expedition to Dhofar, BASOR 159, October 1960, 14-26.

——, An Ancient South Arabian Necropolis, Objects from the Second Campaign (1951) in the Timna' Cemetery, Publications of the American Foundation for the Study of Man IV, Baltimore, 1965.

D. B. Doe, Southern Arabia, London, 1970.

A. Fakhry, An Archaeological Journey to Yemen I; II, Epigraphical Texts, by G. Ryckmans; III, Plates, Service des Antiquités de l'Égypte, Cairo, 1951-1952.

H. Goetz, An Indian Bronze from South Arabia, Archaeology 16, 1963, 187-189.

A. Grohmann, Göttersymbole und Symboltiere auf südarabischen Denkmälern, Denkschriften der K. Akademie der Wissenschaften in Wien, Ph.-H. Kl. 58, 1, 1914.

G. L. Harding, Archaeology in the Aden Protectorates, London, 1964.

M. Höfner, Südarabien, in: H. W. Haussig (Ed.), Wörterbuch der Mythologie, Stuttgart, 1962, 483-552.

——, Die vorislamischen Religionen Arabiens, in: H. Gese, M. Höfner, K. Rudolph, Die Religionen Altsyriens, Altarabiens und der Mandäer, Religionen der Menschheit 10, II, Stuttgart, 1970, 234-402.

A. K. Irvine, On the Identity of Habashat in the South Arabian Inscriptions, JSS 10, 1965, 178-196.

A. Jamme, Le panthéon sud-arabe préislamique d'après les sources épigraphiques, Mus LX, 1947, 57-147.

——, A New Chronology of the Qatabanian Kingdom, BASOR 120, December 1950, 26-27.

——, La religion sud-arabe pré-islamique, in: M. Brillant, R. Aigrain (Ed.), Histoire des religions 4, Paris, 1956, 239-307.

——, On a Drastic Current Reduction of South-Arabian Chronology, BASOR 145, February 1957, 25-31.

——, La paléographie sud-arabe de J. Pirenne, Washington, 1957.

——, Sabaean Inscriptions from Maḥram Bilqîs (Mârib), Publications of the American Foundation for the Study of Man III, Baltimore, 1962, 253-394, Part II, Historical Studies.

——, Une nouvelle chronologie des rois de Saba et de Raydân, BO XXII, 1965, 3-7.

——, A propos des rois ḥaḍramoutiques de al-'Uqlah, Washington, 1965.

K. Katz, A South Arabian Carving of Alabaster, Journal of the Walters Art Gallery XVII, 1954, 77-86.

A. G. Loundine, Yada'il Ḍariḥ, fils de Sumhu'alay, mukarrib de Saba', XXV Congrès International des Orientalistes, Conférences présentées par la délégation de l'URSS, Moscow, 1960.

——, Liste inédite des éponymes sabéens de la période des *mukarrib* de Saba', Mus LXXV, 1962, 131-137.

——, Éponymat sabéen et chronologie sabéenne, XXVI Congrès International des Orientalistes, Conférences présentées par la délégation de l'URSS, Moscow, 1963.

——, J. Ryckmans, Nouvelles données sur la chronologie des rois de Saba et ḏū-Raydān, Mus LXXVII, 1964, 407-427.

A. G. Lundin, Južnaja Aravija v VI veke, PSb 8 (71), Moscow-Leningrad, 1961.

——, Social'no ekonomičeskie dannye sabejskih posvjatitel'nih nadpisej perioda mukarribov, VDI, 1962, 3, 96-120.

——, Dopolnenija k spisku sabejskih eponimov, VDI 97, 1966, 3, 82-91.

——, K vozniknoveniju gosudarstvennoj organizacii v južnoj Aravii, PSb 17 (80), 1967, 50-73.

——, K diskussii o sabejskom eponimate, otvet G. M. BAUERU, VDI 101, 1968, 1, 120-126.

——, The List of Sabaean Eponyms again, JAOS 89, 1969, 533-541.

——, Carskaja vlast' v Južnoj Aravii v I tys. do n.e., VDI, 1970, 3, 3-16.

——, Gosudarstvo Mukarribov Saba' (Sabejskij Eponimat), Akademija Nauk SSSR, Institut Vostokovedenija, Moskva, Izdatel'stvo 'Nauka', glavnaja redakcija vostočnoj literatury, Moscow, 1971.

W. W. MÜLLER, Alt-Südarabien als Weihrauchland, Theologische Quartalschrift 149, 1969, 350-368.

U. OLDENBURG, Above the Stars of El. El in Ancient South Arabic Religion, ZATW 82, 1970, 187-208.

N. PIGULEVSKAJA, Les rapports sociaux à Nedjrān au début du VIe siècle de l'ère Chrétienne I, JESHO III, 1960, 113-130; II, JESHO IV, 1961, 1-14.

J. PIRENNE, La Grèce et Saba, une nouvelle base pour la chronologie sud-arabe, Extrait des Mémoires présentés par divers savants à l'Académie des Inscriptions et Belles-Lettres XV, Paris, 1955.

——, L'inscription "Ryckmans 535" et la chronologie sud-arabe, Mus LXIX, 1956, 165-181.

——, Paléographie des inscriptions sud-arabes, contribution à la chronologie et à l'histoire de l'Arabie du Sud antique I, Des origines jusqu'à l'époque himyarite, Verhandelingen van de Kon. Vlaamse Academie voor Wetenschappen, Letteren en Schone Kunsten van België, Kl. der Letteren 26, Brussels, 1956.

——, Le rinceau dans l'évolution de l'art sud-arabe, Syria XXXIV, 1957, 99-127.

——, Notes d'archéologie sud-arabe I, Stèles à la déesse Dhât Himyam (Hamîm), Syria XXXVII, 1960, 326-347; II, La statuette d'un roi de 'Awsân et l'hellénisation dans la statuaire sud-arabe, Syria XXXVIII, 1961, 284-310; III, Stèles à la déesse du Musée d'Aden, Syria XXXIX, 1962, 257-262; IV, La déesse sur des reliefs sabéens, Syria XLII, 1965, 109-136; V, Le trône de Dar El-Beida (Marib), Syria XLII, 1965, 311-341; VI, Le péristyle du temple de Mârib d'après les fouilles de 1951-52, Syria XLVI, 1969, 293-318.

——, Le Royaume Sud-Arabe de Qatabân et sa Datation d'après l'Archéologie et les Sources Classiques jusqu'au *Périple de la Mer Érythrée*, Bibliothèque du *Muséon* 48, Louvain, 1961.

——, Les phases de l'hellénisation dans l'art sud-arabe, VIIIe Congrès International d'Archéologie Classique: Le rayonnement des civilisations grecque et romaine sur les cultures périphériques, Paris, 1965, 535-541.

——, De la chronologie des inscriptions sud-arabes après la fouille du temple de Mârib (1951-52), BO XXVI, 1969, 303-311.

C. RATHJENS, Kulturelle Einflüsse in Südwest-Arabien von den ältesten Zeiten bis zum Islam, unter besonderer Berücksichtigung des Hellenismus, JKAF I, 1950, 1-42.

——, Sabaeica, Bericht über die archäologischen Ergebnisse seiner zweiten, dritten und vierten Reise nach Südarabien, Mitteilungen aus dem Museum für Völkerkunde in Hamburg XXIV, I, Der Reisebericht, Hamburg, 1953; II, Die unlokalisierten Funde, Hamburg, 1955; III, see above, p. 344, M. HÖFNER.

——, H. VON WISSMANN, Rathjens- v. Wissmannsche Südarabien-Reise 2, Vorislamische Altertümer, Hamburgische Universität, Abhandlungen aus dem Gebiet der Auslandkunde 38, B, 19, Hamburg, 1932; 3, Landeskundliche Ergebnisse, Hamburgische Universität, Abhandlungen aus dem Gebiet der Auslandkunde 40, B, 20, Hamburg, 1934.

G. RYCKMANS, Les inscriptions monotheistes sabéennes, in: Miscellanea Historica in honorem Alberti de Meyer I, Université de Louvain, Recueil de travaux d'histoire et de philologie, 3e série 22, 1946, 194-205.

——, L'Arabie antique et la Bible, in: L'Ancien Testament et l'Orient, Orientalia et Biblica Lovaniensia I, 1957, 89-109.

——, Les religions arabes préislamiques, 3e édition, in: M. GORCE, R. MORTIER (Ed.), Histoire générale des religions II, Paris, 1960, 200-228, 593-605.

J. RYCKMANS, L'institution monarchique en Arabie méridionale avant l'Islam (Ma'în et Saba), Bibliothèque du *Muséon* 28, Louvain, 1951.

——, Inscriptions historiques sabéennes de l'Arabie centrale, Mus LXVI, 1953, 319-342.

——, La persécution des Chrétiens himyarites au sixième siècle, Uitgaven van het Nederlands Historisch-Archaeologisch Instituut te Istanbul I, Istanbul, 1956.

——, Petits royaumes sud-arabes d'après les auteurs classiques, Mus LXX, 1957, 75-96.

——, Les "Hierodulenlisten" de Ma'īn et la colonisation minéenne, in: Scrinium Lovaniense, Mélanges historiques Étienne van Cauwenbergh, Louvain, 1961, 51-61.

——, Les rois de Hadramawt mentionnés à 'Uqla, BO XXI, 1964, 277-282.

——, La chronologie des rois de Saba et ḏū-Raydān, Uitgaven van het Nederlands Historisch-Archaeologisch Instituut te Istanbul XVI, Istanbul, 1964.

——, Le Christianisme en Arabie du Sud préislamique, in: Problemi attuali di scienza e di cultura, Atti del convegno internazionale sul tema: L'oriente cristiano nella storia della civiltà, Accademia Nazionale dei Lincei, quaderno 62, 1964, 413-453.

——, De quelques dynasties sud-arabes, Mus LXXX, 1967, 269-300.

——, Les confessions publiques sabéennes: le code sud-arabe de pureté rituelle, AIUON NS XXII, 1972, 1-15.

B. SEGALL, Sculpture from Arabia Felix: the Hellenistic Period, AJA 59, 1955, 207-214.

——, The Arts and King Nabonidus, AJA 59, 1955, 315-318.

——, Problems of Copy and Adaptation in the Second Quarter of the First Millennium, B.C., AJA 60, 1956, 165-170.

——, Notes on the Iconography of Cosmic Kingship, ArBu XXXVIII, 1956, 75-80.

——, Sculpture from Arabia Felix: the Earliest Phase, ArsOr II, 1957, 35-42.

A. H. SHARAFADDIN, Yemen, "Arabia Felix", Taiz, 1961.

——, Tārīḫ al-Yaman aṯ-ṯaqāfī, I, II, III, 1967.

S. SMITH, Events in Arabia in the 6th Century A.D., BSOAS 16, 1954, 425-468.

M. TAWFIK, 'Āṯār Ma'īn fī jawf al-Yaman, Les monuments de Ma'īn (Yemen), Publications de l'Institut Français d'Archéologie Orientale du Caire, Études sud-arabiques I, Cairo, 1951.

G. Caton THOMPSON, The Tombs and Moon Temple of Hureidha (Hadhramaut), Reports of the Research Committee of the Society of Antiquaries of London XIII, Oxford, 1944.

G. W. VAN BEEK, A Radiocarbon Date for Early South Arabia, BASOR 143, October 1956, 6-9.

——, Frankincense and Myrrh in Ancient South Arabia, JAOS 78, 1958, 141-152.

——, A New Interpretation of the So-Called South Arabian House Model, AJA 63, 1959, 269-273.

——, Frankincense and Myrrh, BibAr 23, 1960, 70-95.

——, South Arabian History and Archaeology, in: G. E. WRIGHT (Ed.), The Bible and the Ancient Near East, Essays in honor of William Foxwell Albright, New York, 1961, 229-248.

——, Hajar bin Ḥumeid: Investigations at a Pre-Islamic Site in South Arabia, Publications of the American Foundation for the Study of Man V, Baltimore, 1969.

——, G. H. COLE, A. JAMME, An Archeological Reconnaissance in Hadhramaut, South Arabia — A Preliminary Report, Smithsonian Report for 1963, 1964, 521-545.

F. V. WINNETT, The Place of the Minaeans in the History of Pre-Islamic Arabia, BASOR 73, February 1939, 3-9.

H. VON WISSMANN, Geographische Grundlagen und Frühzeit der Geschichte Südarabiens, Saeculum 4, 1953, 61-114.

——, De Mari Erythraeo, in: Lautensach-Festschrift, Stuttgarter Geographische Studien 69, 1957, 289-324.

——, Al-Barīra in Ǧirdān im Vergleich mit anderen Stadtfestungen Alt-Südarabiens, Mus LXXV, 1962, 177-209.

——, Zur Geschichte und Landeskunde von Alt-Südarabien, Sammlung Eduard Glaser III, SAWW 246, 1964.

——, Ḥimyar, Ancient History, Mus LXXVII, 1964, 429-497.

——, Zur Kenntnis von Ostarabien, besonders al-Qaṭīf, im Altertum, Mus LXXX, 1967, 489-508.

——, Zur Archäologie und antiken Geographie von Südarabien: Ḥaḍramaut, Qatabān und das ʿAden-Gebiet in der Antike, Uitgaven van het Nederlands Historisch-Archaeologisch Instituut te Istanbul XXIV, Istanbul, 1968.

——, M. HÖFNER, Beiträge zur historischen Geographie des vor-islamischen Südarabien, Akademie der Wissenschaften und der Literatur in Mainz, Abhandlungen der Geistes- und der Sozial-wissenschaftlichen Klasse, 1952, 4, Wiesbaden, 1953.

XIV. ETHIOPIAN LANGUAGES

COMPILED BY

J. H. HOSPERS

General Works

All the important materials can be found in:

W. LESLAU, An Annotated Bibliography of the Semitic Languages
of Ethiopia, The Hague, 1965.

The following publications from the years since 1965 must be enumerated here:

A. THE LANGUAGE

1. GRAMMARS

M. FRYDENLUND, K. SVENSEN, Amharic for Beginners, Leiden, 1967.
F. PRAETORIUS, Die Amharische Sprache, repr. Hildesheim, 1967.
——, Grammatik der Tigriña Sprache, repr. Hildesheim, 1968.

2. GRAMMATICAL STUDIES

D. L. APPLEYARD, /a-/ and /as-/ verb forms in Amharic, BSOAS
XXXV, 1972, 18-26.
G. GOLDENBERG, Kestanenna. Studies in a Northern Gurage Language
of Christians, OrSuec XVII, 1968, 61-102.
R. HETZRON, Internal labialization in the AA-group of outer South
Ethiopia, JAOS 91, 1971, 192-207.
——, Ethiopian Semitic Studies in Classification, JSS Monographs 2,
Manchester, 1972.
A. KLINGENHEBEN, Analogiebildungen im Amharischen, M. FLEISCH-
HAMMER, Studia Orientalia in memoriam C. Brockelmann[2],
Halle/S, 1970, 121-125.
W. LESLAU, An Amharic Conversation Book, Wiesbaden, 1965.
——, Hypothesis on a Proto-Semitic Marker of the Imperfect in
Gurage, JNES 26, 1967, 121-125.
——, The Jussive in Eža, JSS XII, 1967, 66-82.

——, An Archaic Vowel of the Jussive in Gurage, Gafat and Harari, Or 37, 1968, 90-93.

——, Toward a Classification of the Gurage Dialects, JSS XIV, 1969, 96-109.

——, The ma-clause in Harari, D. Cohen, Mélanges M. Cohen, Den Haag, 1970, 263-273.

——, Traces of laryngals in the Gurage dialect of Endegen, JNES 30, 1971, 218-224.

A. Murtonen, Early Semitic. A Diachronical Inquiry into the Relationship of Ethiopic to the Other So-Called South-East Semitic Languages, Leiden, 1967.

——, On Research into Early Semitic, GLECS XII, 1967-1968, 3-4.

H. J. Polotsky, Aramaic, Syriac and Geʿez, JSS IX, 1964, 1-10.

——, Le suffixe de la 3e personne pluriel en néo-éthiopien, D. Cohen, Mélanges M. Cohen, Den Haag, 1970, 286-289.

R. Richter, Einige Aspekte der Herausbildung des Amharischen als National- und Verkehrssprache Äthiopiens, MIO XVI, 1970, 597-601.

E. Ullendorff, The Challenge of Amharic, London, 1965.

——, Rässahu versus rassəččalähu, D. Cohen, Mélanges M. Cohen, Den Haag, 1970, 348-355.

3. Lexica

A. Dillmann, Lexicon Linguae Aethiopicae cum Indice Latino. Reprint: Osnabrück, 1969.

A. Klingenheben, Deutsch-Amharischer Sprachführer nebst einer grammatischen Einführung ins Amharische, Wiesbaden, 1966.

G. Troupeau, Un vocabulaire arabe-dialectal-éthiopien, D. Cohen, Mélanges M. Cohen, Den Haag, 1970, 333-342.

B. TEXTS

1. General

E. Hammerschmidt, Äthiopistik an deutschen Universitäten, Wiesbaden, 1968.

W. Leslau, Ethiopic and South Arabian, T. A. Sebeok, Current Trends in Linguistics, Vol. 6, The Hague-Paris, 1970, 467-527.

H. F. WIJNMAN, Ethiopia and Western Europe. The Origins and Development of Ethiopic Studies and Printings in the 16th Century, Leiden, 1972.

2. CHRESTOMATHIES

A. DILLMANN, Chrestomathia Aethiopica, Editio stereotypa. Addenda et corrigenda adiecit E. Littmann. Reprint: 1967.

W. LESLAU, Amharic Textbook, Wiesbaden, 1968.

E. ULLENDORFF, An Amharic Chrestomathy. Introduction, Grammatical Tables, Texts, Amharic-English Glossary, London, 1965.

3. TEXT EDITIONS

E. J. VAN DONZEL, 'Ënbāqom. Anqaṣa Amin (la porte de la foi), Apologie éthiopienne du Christianisme contre l'Islam à partir du Coran. Introduction, Texte critique, Traduction, Leiden, 1969.

W. LESLAU, A Short Chronicle on the Gafat, RSO XLI, 1966.

R. K. P. PANKHURST, The Ethiopian Royal Chronicles, London, 1967.

E. ULLENDORFF, The Anglo-Ethiopian Treaty of 1902, BSOAS XXX, 1967, 641-654.

——, Some Early Amharic Letters, BSOAS XXXV, 1972, 229-270.

——, A. DEMOZ, Two letters from the Emperor Yohannes of Ethiopia to Queen Victoria and Lord Granville, BSOAS XXXII, 1969, 135-142.

C. ARCHAEOLOGY, GEOGRAPHY, HISTORY, AND RELIGION

G. W. VAN BEEK, Monuments of Axum in the Light of South Arabian Archeology, JAOS 87, 1967, 113-122.

D. BUXTON, The Abyssinians, London, 1970.

E. HABERLAND, Untersuchungen zum äthiopischen Königtum, Wiesbaden, 1965.

C. R. HALLPIKE, The Konso of Ethiopia. A study of the values of a Cushitic people, London, 1972.

E. HAMMERSCHMIDT, Äthiopien: christliches Reich zwischen Gestern und Morgen, Wiesbaden, 1967.

A. H. M. JONES, E. MONROE, A History of Ethiopia[2], London, 1970.

M. KAMIL, Die amharische Dicht- und Verskunst, M. FLEISCHHAMMER, Studia Orientalia in memoriam C. Brockelmann², Halle/S, 1970, 105-119.

W. LESLAU, Ethiopians Speak. Studies in Cultural background, Berkeley-Los Angeles, 1965.

H. C. MARCUS, The Black Men who turned white: European attitudes towards Ethiopians, 1850-1900, ArOr 39, 1971, 155-166.

R. PANKHURST, Travellers in Ethiopia, London, 1965.

——, State and Land in Ethiopian History, Oxford, 1966.

M. POWNE, Ethiopian music. An introduction. Survey of Ecclesiastical and Secular Ethiopian music and instruments, London, 1968.

S. RUBENSON, King of Kings. Tewodros of Ethiopia, London, 1966.

W. SCHACK, The Gurage. A people of the Ensete Culture, London, 1966.

R. SCHNEIDER, Les titres des psaumes en éthiopien, D. COHEN, Mélanges M. Cohen, Den Haag, 1970, 424-428.

T. TAMRAT, Church and State in Ethiopia 1270-1527, London, 1972.

E. ULLENDORFF, The Ethiopians. An introduction to country and people², London, 1966.

——, Ethiopia and the Bible, London, 1968.

E. A. Wallis BUDGE, A History of Ethiopia (Nubia and Abessynia). According to the hieroglyphic inscriptions of Egypt and Nubia and the Ethiopian chronicles. Reprint: London, 1966.

B

COMPARATIVE SEMITICS

COMPARATIVE SEMITICS

COMPILED BY

J. H. HOSPERS

A. PUBLICATIONS WITH MANY BIBLIOGRAPHICAL REFERENCES

"Hamito-Semitic Languages" in the Linguistic Bibliography for the Year ...... published by the Permanent International Committee of Linguists under the auspices of the International Council for Philosophy and Humanistic Studies with the financial assistance of UNESCO, Utrecht-Antwerpen, 1951-   . Since the 2nd World War 17 numbers: 1951 (Linguistic Bibliography for the year 1948 and supplement for previous years) - 1970.

S. Moscati, A. Spitaler, E. Ullendorff, W. von Soden, An Introduction to the Comparative Grammar of the Semitic Languages. Phonology and Morphology, Wiesbaden, 1964. Reprint: Wiesbaden, 1969.

Important Reviews of the "Introduction" by Moscati c.s.:

D. Cohen, La linguistique sémitique et arabe à propos de quelques travaux récents, Revue des Études Islamiques XXXIII, 1965, 176-184.

S. Segert, Aim and Terminology of Semitic Comparative Grammar, RSO 40, 1965, 1-8.

M. Dahood, K. Deller, R. Köbert, Comparative Semitics. Some Remarks on a Recent Publication, Or NS 34, 1965, 35-44.

J. Blau, in Leshonenu 30, 1965-1966, 136-156.

H. Hirsch, Einige Bemerkungen zu einer vergleichenden Betrachtung der semitischen Sprachen, WZKM 61, 1967, 17-21.

W. Vycichl, in BiOr XXV, 1968, 26-34.

T. A. Sebeok (ed.), Current Trends in Linguistics, Vol. 6, Linguistics in South West Asia and North Africa, The Hague-Paris, 1970 (especially Part Three: Afroasiatic Languages, 237-661).

E. ULLENDORFF, Comparative Semitics, G. LEVI DELLA VIDA, Linguistica Semitica: Presente e Futuro, Roma, 1961, 13-32.

——, Comparative Semitics, T. A. SEBEOK, Current Trends in Linguistics, Vol. 6, The Hague-Paris, 1970, 261-273.

B. COMPARATIVE GRAMMARS

All the bibliographical material can be found in:

J. H. HOSPERS, A Hundred Years of Semitic Comparative Linguistics, Studia Biblica et Semitica Th. C. Vriezen dedicata, Wageningen, 1965, 138-151.

(There are by now reprints available of "Handbuch der Orientalistik", III. Band (articles by A. BAUMSTARK, C. BROCKELMANN and B. SPULER), Leiden, 1964, G. BERGSTRÄSSER's "Einführung", Darmstadt, 1963, C. BROCKELMANN's "Grundriss', Hildesheim, 1961 and 1966, M. COHEN's "Langues Chamito-Sémitiques", Paris, 1964, De Lacy Evans O'LEARY's "Comparative Grammar", Amsterdam, 1969, and L. H. GRAY's "Introduction to Semitic Comparative Linguistics", Amsterdam, 1971).

C. GENERAL WORKS

J. BARR, The Ancient Semitic Languages — The conflict between philology and linguistics, Transactions of the Philological Society 1968, Oxford, 1969, 37-55.

J. BARTH, Sprachwissenschaftliche Untersuchungen zum Semitischen, Leipzig 1907-1911 (Reprint: Amsterdam 1972).

H. BIRKELAND, Some Reflexions on Semitic and Structural Linguistics, Roman Jakobson Festschrift, Den Haag, 1956.

J. BLAU, Some Difficulties in the Reconstruction of "Proto-Hebrew" and "Proto-Canaanite", in Memoriam P. Kahle, BZAW 103, Berlin, 1968, 29-43.

——, Marginalia Semitica I, Israel Oriental Studies I, 1971, 1-35.

——, Marginalia Semitica II, Irael Oriental Studies II, 1972, 57-82.

C. BROCKELMANN, Stand und Aufgaben der Semitistik, R. HARTMANN, H. SCHEEL, Beiträge zur Arabistik, Semitistik und Islamwissenschaft, Leipzig, 1944, 3-41.

D. COHEN, Études de linguistique sémitique et arabe, Den Haag, 1970.

P. DHORME, Langues et écritures sémitiques, Paris, 1930.

I. M. DIAKONOFF, Problems of Root Structure in Proto-Semitic, ArOr 38, 1970, 453-480.

J. FRIEDRICH, Zur Stellung des Jaudischen in der Nord-West-Semitischen Sprachgeschichte, H. G. GÜTERBOCK, Th. JACOBSEN, Studies in Honor of Benno Landsberger, Chicago (Illin.), 1965, 425-429.

P. FRONZAROLI, Prospettive di metodo statistico nella classificazione delle lingue semitiche, ANLA Ser. 8, 16, 1961, 348-380.

G. GARBINI, Le lingue semitiche. Studi di storia linguistica, Ricerche IX, Napoli, 1972.

I. J. GELB, Sequential Reconstruction of Proto-Akkadian, Chicago (Illin.), 1969.

S. D. GOITEIN, Nicknames as Family Names, JAOS 90, 1970, 517-524.

J. H. GREENBERG, Patterning of Rootmorphemes in Semitic, Word VI, 1950, 162-181.

A. HALDAR, Bemerkungen zur frühen grammatikalischen Bearbeitung der semitischen Sprachen, M. A. BEEK, A. A. KAMPMAN, C. NIJLAND, J. RIJCKMANS, Symbolae Biblicae et Mesopotamicae F. M. Th. de Liagre Böhl Dedicatae, Leiden, 1972, 169-179.

P. JOÜON, Étude de philologie sémitique, MUSJ VI, 2, 1913, Beyrouth, 1913.

E. Y. KUTSCHER, Comparative Studies in North-Western Semitic, JSS 10, 21-51.

M. LAMBERT, Le groupement des langues sémitiques, Paris, 1921.

B. LANDSBERGER, Prinzipienfragen der semitischen, speziell der hebräischen Grammatik, OLZ XXIX, 1926, 967-979.

——, Probleme der akkadischen und semitischen Sprachen, ZDMG 81, 1927, 42-43.

W. LESLAU, Semitic Languages, Encyclopaedia Brittanica 20, 1961, 314-317.

——, Observations on Semitic Cognates in Ugaritic, Or 37, 1968, 347-366.

——, Comparative Semitic Studies, Den Haag (in preparation).

J. MACDONALD, New Thoughts on a Biliteral Origin for the Semitic Verb, AnLeeds V, 1963-1965, Leiden, 1966, 63-85.

L. MATOUŠ, Semitischer Cercle IV, ArOr 36, 1968, 468-481. — See also the preceding articles in the numbers 34-36.

S. MOSCATI, Sulla ricostruzione del proto-semitico, RSO 35, 1960, 1-10.

——, Sulla più antica storia delle lingue semitiche, ANLA Ser. 8, 15, 1960, 79-101.

368   COMPARATIVE SEMITICS

C. Rabin, The Origin of the Subdivisions of Semitic, Hebrew and Semitic Studies presented to G. R. Driver, Oxford, 1963, 104-115.

K. H. Schmidt, Historische Sprachvergleichung und ihre typologische Ergänzung, ZDMG 116, 1966, 8-22.

G. M. Schramm, The Semitic Languages: an Overview, in: T. A. Sebeok (ed.), Current Trends in Linguistics, Vol. 6, The Hague-Paris, 1970, 257-260.

S. Segert, Tendenzen und Perspektiven der vergleichenden semitischen Sprachwissenschaft, M. Fleischhammer, Studia Orientalia in memoriam C. Brockelmann, Halle, 1968, 167-173.

W. von Soden, Zur Einteilung der semitischen Sprachen, WZKM 56, 1960, 177-191.

E. Ullendorff, What is a Semitic Language?, Or 27, 1958, 66-75.

A. Ungnad, Das Wesen des Ursemitischen. Eine sprachgeschichtlich-psychologische Untersuchung, Leipzig, 1925.

D. PHONOLOGY

F. R. Blake, Studies in Semitic Grammar IV. The "Emphatic" consonants in Semitic, JAOS 66, 1946, 212-215.

J. Blau, The Origins of Open and Closed e in Proto-Syriac, BSOAS XXXII, 1969, 1-9.

M. M. Bravmann, The Semitic Causative Prefix š/sa, Mus 82, 1969, 517-522.

——, The West-Semitic Conditional Conjunction 'im, 'in and Some Related Particles of Arabic and Akkadian, Mus 83, 1970, 241-248.

J. Cantineau, La voyelle de secours i dans les langues sémitiques, Sem II, 1949, 51-67.

——, A Propos des sons g, k, q dans les langues Sémitiques, BSLP 46, 1950, pp. xxv-xxvii.

——, Le consonantisme du sémitique, Sem IV, 1953, 79-94.

W. T. Claassen, The Role of /ṣ/ in the North-West Semitic Languages, AION XXI, 1971, 285-302.

F. C. Corriente, A Survey of Spirantization in Semitic and Arabic Phonetics, JQR LX, 2, 1969, 147-171.

W. Fischer, Die Position von ض im Phonemsystem des Gemeinsemitischen, M. Fleischhammer, Studia Orientalia in Memoriam C. Brockelmann, Halle, 1968, 55-63.

G. Garbini, The Phonetic Shift of Sibilants in North-Western Semitic in the First Millennium B.C., JNSL I, 1971, 32-38.

A. Haudricourt, La mutation des emphatiques en Sémitique, GLECS 5, 1948-1951, 49-50.

W. Leslau, The Semitic Phonetic System, L. Kaiser, Manual of Phonetics, Amsterdam, 1957, 325-329.

A. Martinet, Remarques sur le consonantisme sémitique, BSLP 49, 1953, 67-78.

S. Morag, The Vocalization Systems of Arabic, Hebrew and Aramaic. Their phonetic and phonemic principles, Den Haag, 1962. (Reprint : 1972).

S. Moscati, Il sistema consonantico delle lingue semitiche, Roma, 1954.

A. Murtonen, The Semitic Sibilants, JSS 11, 1966, 135-151.

G. Olinder, Zur Terminologie der semitischen Lautähnlichkeiten, Lund, 1934.

K. Petráček, Die Phonologie und ihre Verwendung in der Semitistik, ArOr 24, 1956, 631-634.

——, Das Problem des ġain im Südsemitischen, M. Fleischhammer, Studia Orientalia in Memoriam C. Brockelmann, Halle, 1968, 139-145.

A. Spitaler, Zur Frage der Geminatendissimilation im Semitischen. Zugleich ein Beitrag zur Kenntnis der Orthographie des Reicharamäischen, IF LXI, 1952, 257-266.

W. Watson, Shared Consonants in Northwest Semitic, Bibl 50, 1969, 525-533.

——, More on Shared Consonants, Bibl 52, 1971, 44-50.

E. MORPHOLOGY

K. Aartun, Übber die Parallelformen des selbständigen Personalpronomes der I. Person Singular im Semitischen, UF 3, 1971, 1-8.

J. Aro, Die Vokalisierung des Grundstammes im semitischen Verbum, StOr XXXI, Helsinki, 1964.

——, Parallels to the Akkadian Stative in the West Semitic Languages, Studies in honor of B. Landsberger, Chicago (Illin.), 1965, 407-411.

J. Blau, Hyper-Correction and Hypo-Correction in Pseudo Correct Features, Mus LXXVI, 1963, 363-367.

——, Some Problems of the Formation of the Old Semitic Languages in the Light of Arabic Dialects, Proceedings of the International Conference on Semitic Studies in Jerusalem, 1965, Jerusalem, 1969, 38-44.

——, On Pseudo-Corrections in Some Semitic Languages, Jerusalem-Leiden, 1970.

G. R. Castellino, Di alcuni valori particolari del causativo semitico, A. F. Gabrieli, Studi orientalistici offerti etc., Roma, 1964, 51-60.

D. Cohen, Remarques sur la dérivation nominale par affixes dans quelques langues sémitiques, Sem XIV, 1964, 73-93. Also in: D. Cohen, Études de Linguistique Sémitique et Arabe, Den Haag, 1970, 31-48.

F. C. Corriente, On the Functional Yield of Some Synthetic Devices in Arabic and Semitic Morphology, JQR LXX, 1971, 20-50.

V. Christian, Das Wesen der Semitischen Tempora, ZDMG N.F. 6, 1927, 232-258.

G. R. Driver, Some Uses of QTL in the Semitic Languages, Proceedings of the International Conference on Semitic Studies in Jerusalem 1965, Jerusalem, 1969, 49-64.

W. Eilers, Zur Funktion von Nominalformen. Ein Grenzgang zwischen Morphologie und Semasiologie, WO III, 1964, 80-145.

H. Fleisch, Les verbes à allongement vocalique interne en Sémitique, Paris, 1944.

——, Yaqtula canaanéen et subjonctif arabe, M. Fleischhammer, Studia Orientalia in Memoriam C. Brockelmann, Halle, 1968, 65-76.

C. Fontinoy, Le duel dans les langues sémitiques, Paris, 1969.

G. Garbini, Il tema pronominale p i Semitico, AION XXI, 1971, 245-248.

I. J. Gelb, Morphology of Akkadian, a Comparative and Historical Sketch, Chicago, 1952.

G. Goldenberg, Tautological Infinitive, Israel Oriental Studies I, 1971, 36-85.

M. H. Goshen-Gottstein, The System of Verbal Stems in the Classical Semitic Languages, Proceedings of the International Conference on Semitic Studies in Jerusalem 1965, Jerusalem, 1969, 70-91.

R. Hetzron, Third Person Singular Pronoun Suffixes in Proto-Semitic, OrSuec XVIII, 1969, 101-127.

——, The Evidence for Perfect *yáqtul and Jussive *yaqtúl in Proto-Semitic, JSS 14, 1969, 1-21.

G. Janssens, The Present-Imperfect in Semitic, BiOr XXIX, 1972, 3-7.

J. Kurylowicz, L'Apophonie en Sémitique, Den Haag, 1962.

A. Murtonen, Broken Plurals. Origin and development of the system, Leiden, 1964.

F. A. Pennacchietti, Studi sui pronomi determinativi semitici, Napoli, 1968.

——, La classe degli aggettivi denotativi nelle lingue semitiche e nelle lingue berbere, AION XX, 1970, 285-294.

C. Rabin, The Structure of the Semitic System of Case-Endings, Proceedings of the International Conference on Semitic Studies in Jerusalem 1965, Jerusalem, 1969, 190-204.

O. Rössler, Verbalform und Verbalflexion in den semitohamitischen Sprachen, ZDMG 100, 1950, 461-514.

F. Rundgren, Das Verbalpräfix yu- im Semitischen und die Entstehung der faktitiv-kausativischen Bedeutung des D-Stammes, OrSuec XII, 1963, 99-115.

——, Erneuerung des Verbalaspektes im Semitischen. Funktionell-diachronische Studien zur semitischen Verblehre, Uppsala, 1963.

——, Ablaut und Apothematismus im Semitischen, OrSuec XIII, 1964, 48-83.

——, À propos d'une hypothèse nouvelle concernant la provenance du morphème qatal-a, OrSuec XIV-XV, 1965-1966, 62-74.

W. von Soden, Tempus und Modus im Semitischen, Akten des XXIV. Intern. Orientalistenkongresses, München, 1959, 263.

——, Die Zahlen 20-90 im Semitischen und der status absolutus, WZKM 57, 1961, 24-28.

——, n als Wurzelaugment im Semitischen, M. Fleischhammer (ed.), Studia Orientalia in Memoriam C. Brockelmann, Halle, 1968, 175-184.

E. Ullendorff, The Form of the Definite Article in Arabic and Other Semitic Languages, Arab and Islamic Studies in honor of H. A. R. Gibb, Leiden, 1965, 631-637.

J. W. Wevers, Semitic Bound Structures, Canadian Journal of Linguistics 7, 1961, 9-14.

A. Zaborski, Root-Determinatives and the Problem of Biconsonantal Roots in Semitic, Folia Orientalia 11, 1969, 307-313.

F. LEXICOGRAPHY

J. Aro, Gemeinsemitische Ackerbauterminologie, ZDMG 113, 1963, 471-480.

M. M. Bravmann, North-Semitic Hayyîm/n „Life" in the Light of Arabic, Mus 83, 1970, 551-557.

D. Cohen, Dictionnaire de Racines Sémitiques ou attestées dans les langues sémitiques, Fasc. I; '/H-'TN, Den Haag, 1970.

——, Le vocabulaire de base sémitique et le classement des dialectes du sud, D. Cohen, Études de linguistique sémitique et arabe, Den Haag, 1970, 7-30.

H. Dreyer, The Root h-p-ṯ in the Semitic Languages, Leiden, 1970.

H. Dürbeck, Zur Methode des Semasiologen bei der Bedeutungs-bestimmung von Farbenbezeichnungen, ZDMG 118, 1968, 22-28.

F. C. Fensham, The Son of a Handmaid in North-West Semitic, VT XIX, 1969, 312-321.

P. Fronzaroli, Studie sul lessico commune semitico, ANLA, S. VIII, Vol. XIX, Firenze, 1964. 6. La natura domestica, id., 1969, 285-320.

A. Guillaume, Hebrew and Arabic Lexicography. A comparative study, Leiden, 1965.

M. Held, Studies in Comparative Semitic Lexicography, Studies in honor of B. Landsberger, Chicago (Illin.), 1965, 395-406.

——, The Root zbl/sbl in Akkadian, Ugaritic and Biblical Hebrew, JAOS 88, 1968, 90-96.

I. Hrbek, ḫg und verwandte Wurzeln in den Semitischen Sprachen, M. Fleischhammer, Studia Orientalia in Memoriam C. Brockel-mann, Halle, 1968, 95-104.

G. Krotkoff, Lahm "Fleisch" und leḥem "Brot", WZKM 62, 1969, 76-82.

P. Lacau, Les noms des parties du corps en égyptien et en sémitique, Paris, 1970.

W. Leslau, Observations on Semitic Cognates in Ugaritic, Or 37, 1968, 347-366.

F. Rundgren, Semitische Wortstudien, OrSuec 10, 1961, 99-136.

S. Segert, Considerations on Semitic Comparative Lexicography, ArOr 28, 1960, 470-487.

——, A Preliminary Report on a Comparative Lexicon of North-West Semitic Languages, Acta d. 25. Or.-Kongr. 1960, 383-385.

——, Hebrew Bible and Semitic Comparative Lexicography, VTS XVII (Congress Vol., Rome, 1968), Leiden, 1969, 204-211.

——, Die Arbeit am vergleichenden Wörterbuch der semitischen Sprachen mit Hilfe des Computer IBM 1410, ZDMG, Supple-menta I, 2, Wiesbaden, 1969, 714-717.

Apart from the above named publications useful material can be found in lexica as:

L. KOEHLER, W. BAUMGARTNER, Hebräisches und Aramäisches Lexicon zum Alten Testament. Dritte Auflage neu bearbeitet von W. BAUMGARTNER unter Mitarbeit von B. HARTMANN und E. Y. KUTSCHER, Leiden, 1967- .

C. BROCKELMANN, Lexicon Syriacum², Halle, 1928.

G. HAMITO-SEMITICS

G. R. CASTELLINO, The Akkadian Personal Pronouns and Verbal System in the Light of Semitic and Hamitic, Leiden, 1962.

M. COHEN, Essai comparatif sur le vocabulaire et la phonétique du chamito-sémitique, Paris, 1947.

——, Langues chamito-sémitiques et linguistique historique, Scientia 86, 1951, 304-310. (Also in: M. COHEN, Cinquante années de recherche, Paris, 1955, 210-217).

——, Langues chamito-sémitiques, A. MEILLET, M. COHEN, Les langues du monde², Paris, 1952, 81-181. (Reprint: Paris. 1964).

——, Sémitique, égyptien, libycoberbère, couchitique et méthode comparative, BiOr X, 1953, 88-90.

——, Vue générale du verbe Chamito-Sémitique, Proceedings of the International Conference on Semitic Studies in Jerusalem 1965, Jerusalem 1969, 45-48.

I. M. DJAKONOFF, Semitic-Hamitic Languages. An essay in classification, Moscow, 1965.

D. O. EDZARD, Die semitohamitischen Sprachen in neuer Sicht, Revue d'Assyriologie et d'Archéologie Orientale 61, 1967, 137-149. — Review of I. M. DJAKONOFF's book.

J. FRIEDRICH, Semitisch und Hamitisch, BiOr IX, 1952, 154-157.

C. H. GORDON, Egypto-Semitica, Scritti in onore di Giuseppe Furlani, RSO 32, 1957, 269-277.

J. H. GREENBERG, The Afro-Asiatic (Hamito-Semitic) Present, JAOS 72, 1952, 1-9.

——, An Afro-Asiatic Pattern of Gender and Number Agreement, JAOS 80, 1960, 317-321.

C. T. HODGE, Afroasiatic. A Survey, Den Haag, 1971.

J. H. HOSPERS, A Hundred Years of Semitic Comparative Linguistics, Studia Biblica et Semitica Th. C. Vriezen dedicata, Wageningen, 1966, 138-151.

G. JANSSENS, Belang van de Hamitische talen voor de Semietische

vergelijkende taalkunde, Handelingen van het XXIVde Vlaams
Filologencongres te Leuven, 1961, 123-127.

——, Contribution to the Verbal System in Old Egyptian. A new approach to the reconstruction of the Hamito-Semitic Verbal
System, Or Gand VI, Leuven, 1972.

A. KLINGENHEBEN, Die Präfix- und die Suffix Konjugationen im
Hamitosemitischen, MIO 4, 1956, 211-277.

P. LACAU, Egyptien et Sémitique, Syria 31, 1954, 286-306.

——, Les noms des parties du corps en égyptien et en sémitique,
Paris, 1970.

W. LESLAU, The Rainbow in the Hamito-Semitic Languages, Orbis 5,
1956, 478-483.

——, Semitic and Egyptian Comparisons, JNES 21, 1962, 44-49.

J. LUKAS, Über Nunation in afrikanischen Sprachen, ZDMG Suppl. I,
3, 1092-1095.

H. G. MUKAROVSKY, Langues apparentées au chamito-sémitique,
GLECS 11, 1966-1967, 83-91. — With a critical note of D. COHEN.

G. D. NEWBY, The Dependent Pronoun in Semitic and Egyptian,
JQR LXII, 1972, 193-198.

K. PETRÁČEK, Die Grenzen des Semitohamitischen. Zentralsaharanische
und Semitohamitische Sprachen in phonologischer Hinsicht,
ArOr 40, 1972, 6-50.

M. RODINSON, Le chamito-sémitique à la lumière d'un nouvel ouvrage,
JA 238, 1950, 151-160.

O. RÖSSLER, Verbalbau und Verbalflexion in den semito-hamitischen
Sprachen, ZDMG 100, 1950, 461-514.

——, Akkadisches und Libysches Verbum, Or 20, 1951, 101-107 and
366-373.

——, Der semitische Charakter der libyschen Sprache, ZA 50, 1952,
212-250.

——, Libysch-Hamitisch-Semitisch, Oriens 17, 1964, 199-216.

A. ROTH-LALY, Lexique des parlers arabes tchado-soudanais, I,
Paris, 1969.

W. VON SODEN, Zur Methode der semitisch-hamitischen Sprachvergleichung, JSS 10, 1965, 159-177.

T. W. THACKER, The Relationship of the Semitic and Egyptian Verbal
Systems, Oxford, 1954.

——, Compound Tenses Containing the Verb "be" in Semitic and
Egyptian, Hebrew and Semitic Studies presented to G. R. Driver,
Oxford, 1963, 156-171.

G. W. TSERETELI, Zur Frage der Beziehungen zwischen den semitischen
und hamitischen Sprachen, MIO 16, 1970, 271-280.

J. Vergote, De verhouding van het Egyptisch tot de Semietische talen. — Le rapport de l'Égyptien avec les langues sémitiques, Brussel, 1965.

W. Vycichl, Ein passives Partizip qatīl im Ägyptischen und Semitischen, ZDMG 109, 1959, 253-257.

——, Is Egyptian a Semitic Language ?, Kush 7, 1959, 27-44.

——, Gedanken zur ägyptisch-semitischen Sprachverwandtschaft, Mus 73, 1960, 173-176.

——, Die 2-radikaligen Verben des Ägyptischen und der Berbersprachen, BiOr XXIII, 1966, 247-248.

——, Das hamitosemitische Nomen Agentis Qattâl in den Berbersprachen, Mus 83, 1970, 541-545.

H. SEMITIC WRITING

1. General Handbooks and Parts of Handbooks
with Many Bibliographical References

K.-H. Bernhardt, Die Umwelt des Alten Testaments. I, Die Quellen und ihre Erforschung, par. 6, Schriften und Sprachen, Gütersloh, 1967, 279-362.

E. Buchholz, Schriftgeschichte als Kulturgeschichte, Bellenhausen, 1965.

M. Cohen, La grande invention de l'écriture et son évolution. 3 tomes, Paris, 1958.

P. Dhorme, Langues et écritures sémitiques, Paris, 1930.

E. Doblhofer, Zeichen und Wunder. Die Entzifferung verschollener Schriften und Sprachen, München, 1964.

G. R. Driver, Semitic Writing from Pictograph to Alphabet[3]. London, 1970.

J. G. Février, Histoire de l'Écriture, Nouvelle édit., Paris, 1959.

K. Földes-Papp, Vom Felsbild zum Alphabet. Die Geschichte der Schrift von ihren frühesten Vorstufen bis zur modernen lateinischen Schreibschrift, Stuttgart, 1966.

J. Friedrich, Entzifferung verschollener Schriften und Sprachen[2], Berlin, 1966.

——, Die Parallel-Entwicklung der drei alten Schrift-Urschöpfungen, OrAnt III, 1959, 95-101.

——, Geschichte der Schrift. Unter besonderer Berücksichtigung ihrer geistigen Entwicklung, Heidelberg, 1966.

I. J. GELB, Von der Keilschrift zum Alphabet. Grundlagen einer Schriftwissenschaft, Stuttgart, 1958. — Translation of the following work.

——, A Study of Writing. The foundations of grammatology. Revised edition, Chicago-London, 1963.

U. HAUSMANN (ed.), Handbuch der Archäologie, I. Band: Allgemeine Grundlagen der Archäologie. Begriff und Methode, Geschichte, Problem der Form, Schriftzeugnisse; Zweiter Teil: Die Schrift und die Schriftzeugnisse, München, 1969, 205-389.

E. HERING, Rätsel der Schrift², Leipzig, 1961.

H. JENSEN, Die Schrift in Vergangenheit und Gegenwart², Berlin, 1958. (English translation by G. UNWIN: Sign, Symbol and Script, London, 1970).

V. MAAG, Die Schrift, H. SCHMÖKEL (ed.), Kulturgeschichte des alten Orient III, VIII, Stuttgart, 1961, 519-544.

J. MOUNTFORD, Writing, in: Encyclopaedia of Linguistics, Information and Control, Oxford-London-New York, 1969.

K. SETHE, Vom Bilde zum Buchstaben. Die Entstehungsgeschichte der Schrift. (Mit einem Beitrag von S. SCHOTT, Leipzig, 1939).

J. TSCHICHOLD, Geschichte der Schrift in Bildern, Basel, 1940.

K. WEULE, Vom Kerbstock zum Alphabet. Urformen der Schrift², Stuttgart, 1928.

2. CUNEIFORM WRITING

F. BAYER, Die Entwicklung der Keilschrift, Roma, 1927.

A. FALKENSTEIN, Die Entzifferung der Keilschrift. Die Keilschrift, Handbuch der Orientalistik, Erste Abt., Zweiter Band, Erster und Zweiter Abschnitt, Lief. 1: Das Sumerische, Leiden, 1959, 1-13.

I. J. GELB, Old Akkadian Writing and Grammar², MAD II, Chicago, 1961.

Ph. H. J. HOUWINK TEN CATE, Computer en spijkerschrift, Phoenix 14, 1968, 159-165.

K. JARITZ, Schriftarchäologie der altmesopotamischen Kultur, Graz, 1967.

M. LAMBERT, Écritures idéographiques et syllabiques en Mesopotamie et en Islam, GLECS 11, 1966-1967, 74-82.

B. MEISSNER, K. OBERHUBER, Die Keilschrift³, Berlin, 1967.

P. MERIGGI, Altsumerische und proto-elamische Bilderschrift,

W. Voigt (ed.), XVII. Deutscher Orientalistentag, Teil 1, ZDMG Suppl. I, Wiesbaden, 1969, 156-161.

3. Hieroglyphic Writing

a. *Ancient Egyptian Scripts*

H. P. Blok, De ontcijfering van het oud-Aegyptische schrift, De Nieuwe Gids 39, 1924, 414-426.

H. Brunner, Hieratisch, Handbuch der Orientalistik, Erste Abt., Erster Band (H. Kees, Ägyptologie), Erster Abschnitt (Ägyptische Schrift und Sprache), Leiden, 1959, 40-47.

——, Demotisch, Handbuch der Orientalistik, Erste Abt., Erster Band (H. Kees, Ägyptologie), Erster Abschnitt (Ägyptische Schrift und Sprache), Leiden, 1959, 48-51.

——, Änigmatische Schrift (Kryptographie), Handbuch der Orientalistik, Erste Abt., Erster Band (H. Kees, Ägyptologie), Erster Abschnitt (Ägyptische Schrift und Sprache), Leiden, 1959, 52-61.

J. Capart, Je lis les hiéroglyphes, Bruxelles, 1946.

N. M. Davies, Picture Writing in Ancient Egypt, London, 1958.

A. Erman, O. Krückmann, Die Hieroglyphen[3], Berlin, 1968.

E. Iversen, The Myth of Egypt and its Hieroglyphs in European Tradition, Copenhagen, 1961.

J. M. A. Janssen, Hiëroglyphen. Over lezen en schrijven in Oud-Egypte, Leiden, 1952.

A. Scharff, Archäologische Beiträge zur Frage der Entstehung der Hieroglyphenschrift, München, 1942.

A. Schmitt, Die Vokallosigkeit der ägyptischen und semitischen Schrift, IF LXI, 1952, 216-227.

S. Schott, Hieroglyphen. Untersuchungen zum Ursprung der Schrift, Wiesbaden, 1951.

——, Die Erfindung der Ägyptischen Schrift, Handbuch der Orientalistik, Erste Abt., Erster Band (H. Kees, Ägyptologie), Erster Abschnitt (Ägyptische Schrift und Sprache), Leiden, 1959, 18-21.

——, Das Schriftsystem und seine Durchbildung, Handbuch der Orientalistik, Erste Abt., Erster Band (H. Kees, Ägyptologie), Erster Abschnitt (Ägyptische Schrift und Sprache), Leiden, 1959, 22-31.

——, Abhängigkeit und Einwirkung, Handbuch der Orientalistik, Erste Abt., Erster Band (H. Kees, Ägyptologie), Erster Abschnitt (Ägyptische Schrift und Sprache), Leiden, 1959, 32-39.

W. TILL, Vom Wesen der ägyptischen Schrift, Die Sprache 3, 1956, 207-215.

B. VAN DER WALLE, Autour des Hieroglyphica d'Horapollon, ChrE 36, 1961, 106-113.

b. *Hittite Hieroglyphics*

Ph. H. J. HOUWINK TEN CATE, De ontcijfering van de Hittitische Hieroglyphen, Phoenix IX, 1963, 11-20.

E. LAROCHE, Les hiéroglyphes hittites, I: L'écriture, Paris, 1960.

4. THE ALPHABET

a. *General*

L. A. BANGE, A Study of the Use of vowel-Letters in Alphabetic-consonantal writing, München, 1971.

H. BAUER, Der Ursprung des Alphabets, Leipzig, 1937.

K. BEYER, Die Problematik der semitischen Konsonantenschrift, "Ruperto-Carola" XIX, 42, 1967, 12-17.

D. DIRINGER, The Alphabet. A Key to the History of Mankind, 2 vols., 3rd ed. completely reviewed with the collaboration of R. REGENSBURGER, London, 1968. — The book is full of quite up-to-date bibliographical references.

———, The Alphabet in the History of Civilization, in: W. A. WARD (ed.), The Role of the Phoenicians in the Interaction of Mediterranean Civilizations, Beirut, 1968, 33-41.

G. GARBINI, Considerazioni nell'origine dell' alfabeto, AION XVI, 1966, 1-18.

C. H. GORDON, The Accidental Invention of the Phonemic Alphabet, JNES 29, 1970, 193-197.

W. RÖLLIG, Die Alphabetschrift, in: U. HAUSMANN (ed.), Allgemeine Grundlagen der Archäologie (Handbuch der Archäologie, I), München, 1969, Zweiter Teil: Die Schrift und die Schriftzeugnisse, Erster Abschnitt, Erster Kap., F, 289-302.

K. SETHE, Der Ursprung des Alphabets, Nachr. d. götting. Gesellsch. d. Wiss., Gesch. Mitt., 1916, 88-161.

TODDI, L'Alfabeto parla di sé, Roma, 1951.

H. TUR-SINAI, The Origin of the Alphabet, JQR XLI, 1950, 83-109; 159-179; 277-301.

b. *Proto-Sinaitic*

W. F. ALBRIGHT, The Proto-Sinaitic Inscriptions and their Decipherment, Cambridge, Mass., 1966.

H. BAUER, Zur Entzifferung der neuentdeckten Sinaischrift und zur Entstehung des semitischen Alphabets, Halle, 1918. (Reprint: Osnabrück, 1966).

A. VAN DEN BRANDEN, Le déchiffrement des inscriptions protosinaïtiques, Almachriq 52, 1958, 361-395.

——, L'origine des alphabets protosinaïtiques, arabes préislamiques et phéniciens, BiOr XIX, 1962, 198-206.

——, Les inscriptions protosinaïtiques, OrAnt 1, 1962, 197-214.

A. H. GARDINER, The Egyptian Origin of the Semitic Alphabet, JEA 3, 1916, 1-16.

——, T. E. PEET, The Inscriptions of Sinai², London, 1952.

M. SPRENGLING, The Alphabet: Its Rise and Development from the Sinai Inscriptions, Chicago, 1931.

c. *Pseudo-Hieroglyphic (Gublitic)*

E. DHORME, Déchiffrement des inscriptions pseudo-hiéroglyphiques de Byblos, Syria XXV, 1946-1948, 1-35.

M. DUNAND, Byblia grammata: Documents et recherches sur le développement de l'écriture en Phénicie, Beyrouth, 1945.

G. JANSSENS, Contribution au déchiffrement des inscriptions pseudo-hiéroglyphiques de Byblos, Bruxelles, 1957.

A. JIRKU, Entzifferung der gublitischen Schrift durch E. Dhorme, FuF 26, 1950, 90-92.

M. MARTIN, A Preliminary Report after Reexamination of the Byblian Inscriptions, Or 30, 1961, 46-78.

——, Revision and Reclassification of the Proto-Byblian Signs, Or 31, 1962, 250-271 and 339-383.

H. SOBELMANN, The Proto-Byblian Inscriptions: A Fresh Approach, JSS 6, 1961, 226-245.

d. *Proto-Canaanite*

W. F. ALBRIGHT, Some observations on the New Material for the History of the Alphabet, BASOR 134, 1954, 26.

A. VAN DEN BRANDEN, Anciennes inscriptions sémitiques, BiOr XVII, 1960, 218-222.

F. M. CROSS, The Evolution of the Proto-Canaanite Alphabet, BASOR 134, 1954, 15-24.

——, An Archaic Inscribed Seal from the Valley of Aijalon, BASOR
    168, 1962, 12-18.

——, The Origin and Early Evolution of the Alphabet, ErIs VIII,
    1967, 8*-24*.

A. GOETZE, A Seal Cylinder with an Early Alphabetic Inscription,
    BASOR 129, 1953, 8-11.

G. MANSFELD, Deux "Ostrakons" incisés à écriture paléocanaanéenne
    du Tell de Kamid el-Loz, BMB XXII, 1969, 67-75.

W. RÖLLIG, G. MANSFELD, Zwei Ostraka von Tell Kamid el-Loz und
    ein neuer Aspekt für die Entstehung des kanaanäischen Alphabets,
    WO V, 1970, 265-270.

B. ROSENKRANZ, Zu einigen Tafeln mit unbekannter Schrift in der
    Sammlung De Liagre Böhl in Leiden, BiOr XXIII, 1966, 235-238.

H. SCHMÖKEL, Zur Vorgeschichte des Alphabets, FF 26, 1950, 153-155.

e. Deir 'Allā

A. VAN DEN BRANDEN, Essai de déchiffrement des inscriptions de
    Deir 'Allā, VT 15, 1965, 129-150.

H. CAZELLES, Deir Alla et ses tablettes, Sem XV, 1965, 1-21.

——, Nouvelle écriture sur tablettes d'argile trouvées à Deir Alla
    (Jordanie), GLECS 10, 1963-1966, 66-67.

H. J. FRANKEN, Clay Tablets from Deir 'Allā, Jordan, VT XIV, 1964,
    377-379.

——, A Note on How the Deir 'Allā Tablets were Written, VT XV,
    1965, 150-152.

G. SAUER, Die Tafeln von Deir 'Allā, ZAW 81, 1969, 145-155.

M. WEIPPERT, Archäologischer Jahresbericht, ZDPV 80, 1964, 169-
    172.

——, Archäologischer Jahresbericht, ZDPV 82, 1966, 299-310.

G. E. WRIGHT, Fresh Evidence for the Philistine Story, BiAr XXIX,
    1966, 70-86.

f. Alphabetic Cuneiform Writing

W. F. ALBRIGHT, The Beth-Shemesh Tablet in Alphabetic Cuneiform,
    BASOR 173, 1964, 51-53.

H. BAUER, Entzifferung der Keilschrifttafeln von Ras Schamra,
    Osnabrück, 1968. — Reprint of the 1930 edition.

F. M. CROSS, The Canaanite Cuneiform Tablet from Taanach, BASOR
    190, 1968, 41-46.

——, Th. O. Lambdin, An Ugaritic Abecedary and Origins of the Proto-Canaanite Alphabet, BASOR 160, 1960, 21-26.

O. Eissfeldt, Ein Beleg für die Buchstabenfolge unseres Alphabets aus dem 14. Jh. v. Chr., FF 26, 1950, 217-220.

J. Friedrich, Der Wert semitischer Versionen in Entzifferungs-Bilinguen, Ugaritica VI, 1969, 229-234.

C. H. Gordon, The Ugaritic "ABC", Or 19, 1950, 374-376.

D. R. Hillers, An Alphabetic Cuneiform Tablet from Taanach, BASOR 173, 1964, 45-50.

P. W. Lapp, The 1966 Excavations at Tell Ta'annek, BASOR 185, 1967, 2-39.

E. A. Speiser, The Syllabic Transcription of Ugaritic (h) and (ḫ), BASOR 175, 1964, 42-47.

M. Weippert, Archäologischer Jahresbericht, ZDPV 82, 1966, 311-328.

G. L. Windfuhr, The Cuneiform Signs of Ugarit, JNES 29, 1970, 48-51.

g. *Phoenician Alphabet*

D. Diringer, Problems of the Present Day on the Origin of the Phoenician Alphabet, CHM 4, 1957-1958, 40-58.

M. Dunand, Nouvelle inscription phénicienne archaique, RB 39, 1930, 321-331.

J. B. Peckham, The Development of the Late Phoenician Scripts, Cambridge, Mass., 1968.

h. *Old Hebrew Alphebet*

J. D. Amusin, M. L. Heltzer, The Inscription from Meṣad Ḥasha-vyahu. Complaint of a Reaper of the Seventh Century B.C., IEJ 14, 1964, 148-157.

S. A. Birnbaum, The Hebrew Scripts. 2 vols., Leiden, 1971.

F. M. Cross, The murabba'at Papyrus and the Letter found near Yabne-Yam. Epigraphical notes on the Hebrew document of the 8-6th century B.C., II: BASOR 165, 1962, 34-46.

——, The Inscribed Jar Handles from Gibeon. Epigraphical notes on the Hebrew documents of the 8-6th centuries B.C., III: BASOR 168, 1962, 18-23.

R. S. Hanson, Paleo-Hebrew Scripts in the Hasmonean Age, BASOR 175, 1964, 26-42.

S. H. Horn, An Inscribed Seal from Jordan, BASOR 189, 1968, 41-43.

J. T. Milik, F. M. Cross, Inscribed Javelin-heads from the period of the Judges, BASOR 134, 1954, 5-15.

J. Naveh, A Palaeographic Note on the Distribution of the Hebrew Script, HThR 61, 1968, 68-74.

W. L. Reed, F. V. Winnett, Fragment of an Early Moabite Inscription from Kerak, BASOR 173, 1963, 1-8.

i. *Old Aramaic Alphabet*

N. Avigad, Aramaic Inscription in the Tomb of Jason, IEJ 17, 1967, 101-111.

J. Naveh, The Date of the Deir 'Allā Inscription in Aramaic Script, IEJ 17, 1967, 256-258.

——, The Development of the Aramaic Script, Jerusalem, 1970.

J. Pirenne, Aux origines de la graphie syriaque, Paris, 1963.

j. *Arabic Alphabet*

N. Abbott, Rise of the North Arabic Script, Chicago, 1939.

M. Aksel, Das Schrift-bild in der Türkischen Kunst, Anatolica I, 1967, 110-117.

W. F. Albright, The Chaldaean Inscriptions in Proto-Arabic Script, BASOR 128, 1952, 39-45.

A. Alparslan, L'art de la calligraphie en Turquie au XVe et XVIe siècles, REI XXXV, 1967, 219-224.

A. S. Arif, Arabic Lapidary Kūfic in Africa. A study of the development of the Kūfic script (3rd-6th century A.H.), London, 1967.

A. Grohmann, Arabische Paläographie. 2 vols. Graz-Wien-Köln, 1967-1971.

E. Kühnel, Islamische Schriftkunst, Berlin-Leipzig, 1942.

F. A. Rice, The Classical Arabic Writing System, Cambridge, Mass., 1959.

A.-M. Schimmel, Islamic Calligraphy, Leiden, 1970.

X. I. H. Semaan, A Linguistic View of the Development of the Arabic Writing System, WZKM 61, 1967, 22-40.

J. Sourdel-Thomine, Les origines de l'écriture arabe, à propos d'une hypothèse récente, REI XXXIV, 1966, 151-157.

G. Vajda, Album de paléographie arabe, Paris, 1958.

k. *South-Arabic and Ethiopic Alphabet*

W. F. Albright, On the Early South-arabic Inscription in Vertical Columns, BASOR 138, 1955, 50.

R. D. Biggs, A Chaldean Inscription from Nippur, BASOR 179, 1965, 36-38.

A. Jamme, An Archaic South-Arabian Inscription in Vertical Columns, BASOR 137, 1955, 32-38.

——, Preliminary Report on Epigraphic Research in North-Western Wâdî Ḥadramawt and at al-'Abar, BASOR 172, 1963, 41-54.

E. Ullendorf, The Origin of the Ethiopic Alphabet, BiOr XII, 1955, 217-218.

I. PERIODICALS

Comparatistic studies and studies on Semitic writing can be found in all periodicals that are dealing with the study of the Ancient Near East. Beside it sometimes studies in the field of Comparative Semitics are published in periodicals dealing with General Linguistics. A list of the most important periodicals is given here below:

Abhandlungen der Gesellschaft der Wissenschaften zu Göttingen (AGWG).

Abhandlungen für die Kunde des Morgenlandes (AKM).

Abr-Nahrain (AbN).

Acta Linguistica Hafniensia. International Journal of Structural Linguistics (ALH).

African Abstracts. Quarterly Review of the International African Institute.

Der Alte Orient (AO).

American Journal of Archaeology (AJA).

American Journal of Semitic Languages and Literature (AJSL).

Annali dell'Istituto (Universitario) Orientale di Napoli (AI[U]ON).

Annual of the American Schools of Oriental Research (AASOR).

Annual of Leeds University Oriental Society (AnLeeds).

Annual of the Swedish Theological Institute (ASTI).

Archiv für Orientforschung (AfO).

Archiv Orientalni (ArOr).

Archivum Linguisticum. A Review of Comparative Philology and General Linguistics (ArchLing).

Atti dell' Academia Nazionale dei Lincei (Memorie) ([A]ANL[M]).

Beiträge zur Assyriologie und Semitischen Sprachwissenschaft.

Biblica (Bibl).

Biblical Archaeological (BiAr).

Bibliotheca Orientalis (BiOr).

Biblische Zeitschrift (BZ).
Bulletin of the American Schools of Oriental Research (BASOR).
Bulletin d'Études Orientales (BEO).
Bulletin of the Jewish Palestine Exploration Society (BJPES).
Bulletin du Musée de Beyrouth (BMB).
Bulletin de la Société de Linguistique de Paris (BSLP).
Bulletin of the School of Oriental and African Studies (BSOAS).
Cahiers d'Histoire Mondiale (CHM).
Canadian Journal of Linguistics (CJL).
Comptes Rendus du Groupe Linguistique d'Études Chamito-Sémitiques
    (GLECS).
Comptes Rendus des Séances de l'Académie des Inscriptions et Belles
    Lettres (CRAIBL).
Chronique d'Égypte (ChrE).
Ephemerides Theologicae Lovanienses (ETL).
Eretz Israel (ErIs).
Folia Linguistica. Acta Societatis Linguisticae Europaeae.
Forschungen und Fortschritte (FF).
Foundations of Language.
General Linguistics.
Glossa.
Indogermanische Forschungen (IF).
International Journal of American Linguistics (IJAL).
Israel Exploration Journal (IEJ).
Jewish Quarterly Review (JQR).
Journal of the American Oriental Society (JAOS).
Journal of the Ancient Near Eastern Society of Columbia University
    (JANES).
Journal Asiatique (JA).
Journal of Biblical Literature (JBL).
Journal of Cuneiform Studies (JCS).
Journal of Egyptian Archaeologie (JEA).
Journal of Jewish Studies (JJS).
Journal of Linguistics.
Journal of Near Eastern Studies (JNES).
Journal of the Royal Asiatic Society (JRAS).
Journal of the Society of Oriental Research (JSOR).
Journal of Semitic Studies (JSS).
Kush (Ks).
Language. Journal of the Linguistic Society of America.

Leipziger Semitische Studien (LSS).
Leshonenu.
Lingua. International Review of General Linguistics.
Linguistics. An International Review.
La Linguistique.
Linguistische Berichte. Forschung, Information, Diskussion.
Materials for the Akkadian Dictionary (MAD).
Mélanges de l'Université Saint Joseph (MUSJ).
Mitteilungen der Altorientalischen Gesellschaft (MAOG).
Mitteilungen der Deutschen Orientgesellschaft (MDOG).
Mitteilungen des Instituts für Orientforschung (MIO).
Mitteilungen der Vorderasiatischen Gesellschaft (MVAG).
Le Muséon (Mus).
Nachrichten der Akademie der Wissenschaften in Göttingen (NAWG).
Nachrichten von der Gesellsśhaft der Wissenschaften zu Göttingen (NGWG).
De Nieuwe Gids.
Orbis.
Oriens.
Oriens Antiquus (OA).
Oriental Institute Publications (OIP).
Orientalia (Or).
Orientalia Gandensia (OrGand).
Orientalia Lovaniensia Periodica (OLP).
Orientalia Suecana (OrSuec).
Orientalistische Literaturzeitung (OLZ).
Orient Press. Bollettino Bibliografico di Studi Orientalistici
Palestine Exploration Fund Quarterly Statement (PEFQS).
Palestine Exploration Quarterly (PEQ).
Phoenix.
Proceedings of the Society of Biblical Archaeology (PSBA).
Rassegna di Studi Etiopici (RSE).
Rendiconti dell' Accademia Nazionale dei Lincei (ANLA).
Revue d'Assyriologie et d'Archéologie Orientale (RA).
Revue Biblique (RB).
Revue des Études Islamiques (REI).
Revue des Études Sémitiques (RES).
Revue Sémitique (RS).
Rivista degli Studi Orientali (RSO).
Scientia.

Semitica (Sem).

Semitic Journal of Linguistics (SJL).

Sitzungsberichte der Preussischen Akademie der Wissenschaften (SPAW).

Die Sprache. Zeitschrift für Sprachwissenschaft.

Studia Linguistica. Revue de Linguistique générale et comparée.

Studia Orientalia (StOr).

Syria.

Transactions of the Philological Society.

Vetus Testamentum (VT).

Die Welt des Orients (WO).

Wiener Zeitschrift für die Kunde des Morgenlandes (WZKM).

Word.

Zeitschrift der Alttestamentlichen Wissenschaft (ZAW).

Zeitschrift für Assyriologie (ZA).

Zeitschrift der Deutschen Morgenlandschen Gesellschaft (ZDMG).

Zeitschrift des Deutschen Palästina Vereins (ZDPV).

Zeitschrift für Phonetik, Sprachwissenschaft und Kommunikations-forschung.

Zeitschrift für Semistik und Verwandte Gebiete (ZS).

LIST OF PERIODICALS, SERIES,
COLLECTIVE WORKS AND MANUALS

AA	Artibus Asiae.
AAA	Annals of Archaeology and Anthropology.
AAB	Abhandlungen der Deutschen Akademie der Wissenschaften zu Berlin.
AAS	Annales Archéologiques de Syrie.
AASOR	Annual of the American Schools of Oriental Research.
AAW	Anzeiger für die Altertumswissenschaft.
AAWG	Abhandlungen der Akademie der Wissenschaften in Göttingen.
AB	Assyriologische Bibliothek.
ABAW	Abhandlungen der Bayrischen Akademie der Wissenschaft.
AbN	Abr Nahrain.
AcAn	Acta Antiqua Academiae Scientiarum Hungaricae.
AcAr	Acta Archaeologica Academiae Scientiarum Hungaricae.
AcOr (Bud)	Acta Orientalia Academiae Scientiarum Hungaricae.
AcOr(K)	Acta Orientalia Havniae.
AcOr(L)	Acta Orientalia Lugduni Batavorum.
ADAJ	Annual of the Department of Antiquities of Jordan.
AE	Annales d'Éthiopie.
Aeg	Aegyptus.
AfAb	African Abstracts.
AfO	Archiv für Orientforschung.
Afr	Africa.
AGSU	Arbeiten zur Geschichte des Spätjudentums und Urchristentums.
AGWG	Abhandlungen der Gesellschaft der Wissenschaften zu Göttingen.
AHDO	Archives d'Histoire du Droit Orientale.
AIPHOS	Annuaire de l'Institut de Philologie et d'Histoire Orientales et Slaves.
AI(U)ON	Annali dell'Istituto (Universitario) Orientale di Napoli.
AJA	American Journal of Archaeology.
AJSL	American Journal of Semitic Languages and Literatures.
AJT	American Journal of Theology.
AKAW	Abhandlungen der Königlichen Preussischen Akademie der Wissenschaften zu Berlin.
AKM	Abhandlungen für die Kunde des Morgenlandes.
AL	Acta Linguistica.
ALBO	Analecta Lovaniensia Biblica et Orientalia.
ALH	Acta Linguistica Hafniensia.
	Almachriq.
	Altertum.
ALZ	Allgemeine Literaturzeitung.
AMI	Archäologische Mitteilungen aus Iran.

	Anadolu.
	Anatolia.
AnBoll	Analecta Bollandiana.
ANEP	The Ancient Near East in Pictures relating to the Old Testament[2] (J. B. Pritchard, London, 1969).
ANET	Ancient Near Eastern Texts relating to the Old Testament[3] (J. B. Pritchard, London, 1969).
ANLA	Atti della Academia Nazionale dei Lincei.
AnLeeds	Annual of the Leeds University Oriental Society.
AnOr	Analecta Orientalia.
AnSt	Anatolian Studies.
AnStEbr	Annuario di Studi Ebraici.
AnSur	Antiquity and Survival.
	Antiquity.
AO	Der Alte Orient.
AOAT	Alter Orient und Altes Testament.
AOS	American Oriental Series.
AP	American Papyri of the Fifth Century B.C. (A. Cowley, Oxford 1923, Reprint: Osnabrück, 1967).
APAW	Abhandlungen der Preussischen Akademie der Wissenschaften zu Berlin.
AQR	Asiatic Quarterly Review.
ArBu	The Art Bulletin.
	Archaeologia.
	Archéologie Vivante.
ArchLing	Archivum Linguisticum.
ArchLitg	Archiv für Liturgiewissenschaft.
ArOr	Archiv Orientâlnî.
ArRW	Archiv für Religionswissenschaft.
ArSK	Archiv für Schriftkunde.
ArsOr	Ars Orientalis.
AS	Assyriological Studies.
ASAE	Annales du Service des Antiquités de l'Égypte.
ASAW	Abhandlungen der Sächsischen Akademie der Wissenschaften.
ASGW	Abhandlungen der Philologisch-Historischen Klasse der Königlichen Sächsischen Gesellschaft der Wissenschaften.
ASSF	Acta Societatis Scientiarum Fennicae.
	Asprenas.
ASTI	Annual of the Swedish Theological Institute.
	Atene e Roma.
AThR	Anglican Theological Review.
	Atiqôt.
Atti e Memorie	Atti e Memorie dell'Accademia Toscani di Scienze e Lettere.
	Augustianum.
AUP	Annales de l'Université de Paris.
BusBiR	Australian Biblical Review.
AA	Beiträge zur Assyriologie und Semitischen Sprachwissenschaft.
BAIBL	Bulletin de l'Académie des Inscriptions et Belles Lettres.

BANE	The Bible and the Ancient Near East (Essays W. F. Albright, New York, 1961).
BASOR	Bulletin of the American Schools of Oriental Research.
BASOR SS	Bulletin of the American Schools of Oriental Research. Supplementary Series.
BBB	Bonner Biblische Beiträge.
BBK	Berliner Beiträge zur Keilschriftforschung.
BBM	Bulletin of the Brooklyn Museum.
BCH	Bulletin de Correspondance Hellénique.
BDB	Brown-Driver-Briggs, A Hebrew and English Lexicon of the Old Testament (Oxford, 1929; Reprint: Oxford, 1968).
BE	The Babylonian Expedition of the University of Pennsylvania.
BEA	Bulletin d'Études Arabes.
Bell	Belleten.
BEO	Bulletin d'Études Orientales.
BEOD	Bulletin des Études Orientales, Damas.
	Berytus.
BES	J. Teixidor, Bulletin d'Epigraphie Sémitique (Syria 44-, 1967-).
BHK³	Biblia Hebraica³ (R. Kittel, Stuttgart, 1937).
BHTh	Beiträge zur Historischen Theologie.
BiAr	The Biblical Archaeologist.
Bibel und Qumran	Bibel und Qumran. Beiträge zur Erforschung der Beziehungen zwischen Bibel- und Qumranwissenschaft (Festschrift H. Bardtke, Berlin, 1968).
Bibl	Biblica.
	The Bible Translator.
BiblRes	Biblical Research. Papers of the Chicago Society of Biblical Research.
BibOr	Bibbia e Oriente.
BIES	Bulletin of the Israel Exploration Society.
BIFAO	Bulletin de l'Institut Français d'Archéologie Orientale du Caire.
BiOr	Bibliotheca Orientalis.
BiTerS	Bible et Terre Sainte.
BiVieChr	Bible et Vie Chrétienne.
BiWelt	Die Bibel in der Welt.
BJPES	Bulletin of the Jewish Exploration Society.
BJRL	Bulletin of the John Rylands Library.
BLOT	Booklist of the Society for Old Testament Studies.
BM	Baghdader Mitteilungen.
BMAP	The Brooklyn Museum Aramaic Papyri (E. G. Kraeling, New Haven 1953, Reprint: Arno Press, 1969).
BMB	Bulletin du Musée de Beyrouth.
BMQ	British Museum Quarterly.
BOR	Babylonian and Oriental Record.
BSAW	Berichte über die Verhandlungen der Sächsischen Akademie der Wissenschaften.
BSGW	Berichte über die Verhandlungen der Sächsischen Gesellschaft der Wissenschaften.

BSLP	Bulletin de la Société de Linguistique de Paris.
BSOAS	Bulletin of the School of Oriental and African Studies.
BullComÉt	Bulletin du Comité des Études.
BullEThS	Bulletin of the Evangelical Theological Society.
BWANT	Beiträge zur Wissenschaft vom Alten und Neuen Testament.
ByZ	Byzantinische Zeitschrift.
BZ	Biblische Zeitschrift.
BZAW	Beihefte zur Zeitschrift für die Alttestamentliche Wissenschaft.
BZion	Der Bote aus Zion.
CAD	The Assyrian Dictionary of the University of Chicago.
CAH	The Cambridge Ancient History.
	Cahiers de Byrsa.
CanJTh	Canadian Journal of Theology.
CBQ	The Catholic Biblical Quarterly.
CCER	Cahiers du Cercle Ernest Renan.
CHM	Cahiers d'Histoire Mondiale.
ChQR	The Church Quarterly Review.
ChrE	Chronique d'Égypte.
CIH	Corpus Inscriptionum Himyariticum.
CIS	Corpus Inscriptionum Semiticarum.
CiTom	La Ciencia Tomista.
CJL	Canadian Journal of Linguistics.
CollBrugGand	Collationes Brugenses et Gandavenses.
CRAIBL	Comptes Rendus de l'Académie des Inscriptions et Belles Lettres.
DBS	Dictionnaire de la Bible. Supplément.
DJD	Discoveries in the Judaean Desert (III, IV, V: + of Jordan), Oxford.
DISO	Dictionnaire des Inscriptions Sémitiques de l'Ouest (Ch. F. Jean & J. Hoftijzer, Leiden 1965).
DLZ	Deutsche Literaturzeitung.
DMOA	Documenta et Monumenta Orientis Antiqui.
EA	El-Amarna.
EgliseTh	Église et Théologie.
EL	Ephemerides Lovanienses.
ErIs	Eretz Israel.
EstBib	Estudios Biblicos.
EstOr	Estudios Orientales.
ET	Expository Times.
ETL	Ephemerides Theologicae Lovanienses.
EV	Epigrafika Vostoka.
EvQ	The Evangelical Quarterly.
EW	East and West.
FF	Forschungen und Forschritte.
FL	Foundations of Language.
FO	Folia Orientalia.
FolLing	Folia Linguistica.
FRLANT	Forschungen zur Religion und Literatur des Alten und Neuen Testaments.

GGA	Göttingische Gelehrte Anzeige.
GlasgOrTrans	Glasgow University Oriental Society Transactions.
GLECS	Comptes Rendus du Groupe Linguistique d'Études Chamito-Sémitiques.
Greg	Gregorianum.
GTT	Gereformeerd Theologisch Tijdschrift.
HB	Hebräische Bibliographie.
	Hespéris.
HO	Handbuch der Orientalistik (B. Spuler (ed), Leiden).
HT	Hespéris Tamuda.
HThR	Harvard Theological Review.
HTS	Hervormde Teologische Studies.
HUCA	Hebrew Union College Annual.
IBHR	International Bibliography of the History of Religions.
IEJ	Israel Exploration Journal.
IF	Indogermanische Forschungen.
IIJ	Indo-Iranian Journal.
IJAL	International Journal of American Linguistics.
IM	Istanbuler Mitteilungen.
InfHist	Information Historique.
	International Journal of Middle East Studies.
IrAnt	Iranica Antiqua.
	Iraq.
Isl	Der Islam.
	Israel Oriental Studies.
IZBG	Internationale Zeitschriftenschau für Bibelwissenschaft und Grenzgebiete.
JA	Journal Asiatique.
JAL	Journal of African Languages.
JANES	Journal of the Ancient Near Eastern Society of Columbia University.
JAOS	Journal of the American Oriental Society.
JBL	Journal of Biblical Literature.
JCS	Journal of Cuneiform Studies.
JEA	Journal of Egyptian Archeology.
JEOL	Jaarbericht van het Vooraziatisch-Egyptisch Genootschap "Ex Oriente Lux".
JESHO	Journal of Economic and Social History of the Orient.
JESt	Journal of Ethiopian Studies.
JJP	Journal of Juristic Papyrology.
JJS	Journal of Jewish Studies.
JKAF	Jahrbuch für Kleinasiatische Forschung.
JL	Journal of Linguistics.
JNES	Journal of Near Eastern Studies.
JNSEL	Journal of Northwest Semitic Languages.
	Journal des Savants.
JPOS	Journal of the Palestine Oriental Society.
JQR	Jewish Quarterly Review.

JRAfS	Journal of the Royal African Society.
JRAS	Journal of the Royal Asiatic Society.
JRel	The Journal of Religion.
JRS	Journal of Roman Studies.
JSA	Journal de la Société des Africanistes.
JSJ	Journal for the Study of Judaism in the Persian, Hellenistic and Roman Periods.
JSOR	Journal of the Society of Oriental Research.
JSS	Journal of Semitic Studies.
JTS	Journal of Theological Studies.
JTVI	Journal of the Transactions of the Victoria Institute.
Jud	Judaica.
	Judaism.
KAF	Kleinasiatische Forschungen.
KAI	Kanaanäische und Arämäische Inschriften[2] (H. Donner, W. Röllig, Wiesbaden, 1966-1969).
	Kairos.
KBL	Lexicon in Veteris Testamenti Libros (L. Köhler, W. Baumgartner, Leiden, 1958; Third Edition: W. Baumgartner, B. Hartmann, E. Y. Kutscher, Hebräisches und Aramäisches Lexikon zum Alten Testament, I-, Leiden, 1967-).
KirSeph	Kirjath Sepher (קרית ספר).
	Klio.
Ks	Kush.
KZ	Kuhns Zeitschrift für Vergleichende Sprachforschung.
Lěšonénu	Leshonenu (לשוננו).
	Levant.
Lg	Language. Journal of the Linguistic Society of America.
LibAnt	Libya Antiqua.
MAD	Materials for the Akkadian Dictionary.
MAI	Mémoires présentés par les divers savants à l'Académie des Inscriptions et Belles Lettres de l'Institut de France.
MAOG	Mitteilungen der Altorientalischen Gesellschaft Leipzig.
MAW	Mededelingen der Koninklijke Academie van Wetenschappen.
MCS	Manchester Cuneiform Studies.
MDOG	Mitteilungen der Deutschen Orientgesellschaft in Berlin.
MDP	Memoires de la Délégation en Perse.
MDVS	Det Kgl. Danske Videnskabernes Selskab, Historisk-filologiske Meddelelser.
MEA	Middle Eastern Affairs.
MEAH	Miscelanea de Estudios Arabes y Hebraicos.
MélPhLJ	Mélanges de Philosophie et de la Littérature Juives.
MGWJ	Monatschrift für Geschichte und Wissenschaft des Judentums.
MIDEO	Institut Dominicain d'Études Orientales du Caire, Mélanges.
MIO	Mitteilungen des Instituts für Orientforschung.
MLVS	Mededelingen uit de Leidse Verzameling van Spijkerschrift Inscripties.
MO	Le Monde Oriental.

MRS	Mission de Ras-Shamra.
MSL	Materialien zum Sumerischen Lexikon.
MSLP	Mémoires de la Société Linguistique de Paris.
MSOS	Mitteilungen des Seminars für Orientalischen Sprachen zu Berlin.
MSS	Münchener Studien zur Sprachwissenschaft.
Mus	Le Muséon.
MusHelv	Museum Helveticum.
MUSJ	Mélanges de l'Université Saint-Joseph.
MVAG	Mitteilungen der Vorderasiatisch-Ägyptischen Gesellschaft.
MVEOL	Mededelingen en Verhandelingen van het Vooraziatisch-Egyptisch Genootschap "Ex Oriente Lux".
MW	The Muslim World.
NAWG	Nachrichten der Akademie der Wissenschaften in Göttingen.
NBG	Nieuwe Vertaling Nederlands Bijbelgenootschap.
NedTT	Nederlands Theologisch Tijdschrift.
NESE	Neue Ephemeris für Semitische Epigraphik (R. Degen, W. W. Müller, W. Röllig, Wiesbaden, 1972-).
NGWG	Nachrichten von der Gesellschaft der Wissenschaften zu Göttingen.
	De Nieuwe Taalgids.
	La Nouvelle Clio.
NRT	Nouvelle Revue Théologique.
NT	Novum Testamentum.
NTS	Norsk Tidsskrift for Sprogvidenskap.
NTSt	New Testament Studies.
NTT	Norsk Teologisk Tidsskrift.
NumChron	Numismatic Chronicle.
	Numen.
OA	Oriens Antiquus.
OB	Orientalische Bibliographie.
ObrhPastBl	Oberrheinisches Pastoralblatt.
OIP	Oriental Institute Publications.
OLP	Orientalia Lovaniensia Periodica.
OLZ	Orientalistische Literaturzeitung.
OM	Oriente Moderno.
Or	Orientalia.
	Orbis.
OrChr	Oriens Christianus.
OrChrP	Orientalia Christiana Periodica.
OrGand	Orientalia Gandensia.
	Oriens.
OrSuec	Orientalia Suecana.
OS	L'Orient Syrien.
OTS	Oud Testamentische Studiën.
PAAJR	Proceedings of the American Academy for Jewish Research.
PalCl	Palestra del Clero.
PAOS	Proceedings of the American Oriental Society (in JAOS).
PAPS	Proceedings of the American Philosophical Society.
PASb	Per erdneaziatskij Sbornik Voprosij chattologii i churritologii.

PC	De Heilige Schrift ("Petrus Canisius" Vertaling).
PEFQS	Palestine Exploration Fund Quarterly Statement.
PEQ	Palestine Exploration Quarterly.
Personalist	The Personalist.
	Phoenix.
PJB	Palästina-Jahrbuch des Deutschen Evangelischen Instituts für Altertumswissenschaft.
Proche-OrChr	Proche-Orient Chrétien.
PRU	Le Palais Royal d'Ugarit.
PSb	Palestinskij Sbornik.
PSBA	Proceedings of the Society of Biblical Archaeology.
QDAP	Quarterly of the Department of Antiquities in Palestine.
QumranProbleme	Qumran-Probleme. Vorträge des Leipziger Symposions über Qumran-Probleme 1961 (H. Bardtke (ed), Berlin, 1963).
RA	Revue d'Assyriologie et d'Archéologie Orientale.
RAA	Revue de l'Académie Arabe.
RAfr	Revue Africaine.
RAI	Rencontre Assyriologique Internationale.
RAIt	Rendiconti della (Reale) Accademia d'Italia.
RaStEt	Rassegna di Studi Etiopici.
RB	Revue Biblique.
RBI	Revue Biblique Internationale.
RBibIt	Rivista Biblica (Italiana).
RÉ	Revue d'Egyptologie.
REArmén	Revue des Etudes Arméniennes.
RechBib	Recherches Bibliques.
RechScR	Recherches de Science Religieuse.
REI	Revue des Études Islamiques.
RÉJ	Revue des Études Juives.
RÉNLO	Revue de l'École Nationale des Langues Orientales.
RES	Revue des Études Sémitiques.
RestQ	Restoration Quarterly.
	Revue d'Archéologie Africaine.
RFLHGA	Revue de la Faculté de Langues, d'Histoire et de Géographie, Université d'Ankara.
RGG	Die Religion in Geschichte und Gegenwart.
RHA	Revue Hittite et Asianique.
RHPhR	Revue d'Histoire et de Philosophie Religieuses.
RHR	Revue de l'Histoire des Religions.
RLV	Reallexikon der Vorgeschichte.
ROC	Revue de l'Orient Chrétien.
Rondom het Woord	Rondom het Woord. Theologische Etherleergang van de Nederlandse Christelijke Radiovereniging (Hilversum).
RQum	Revue de Qumran.
RS	Revue Sémitique d'Épigraphie et d'Histoire Ancienne.
RSO	Rivista degli Studi Orientali.
RSR	Recherches de Sciences Religieuses.
RSV	Revised Standard Version.

RT	Recueil de Travaux relatifs à la philologie et à l'archéologie égyptiennes et assyriennes.
RThPh	Revue de Théologie et de Philosophie.
RUBruxelles	Revue de l'Université de Bruxelles.
	Saeculum.
SAOC	Studies in Ancient Oriental Civilization.
SAWM	Sitzungsberichte der Akademie der Wissenschaften zu München.
SAWW	Sitzungsberichte der Akademie der Wissenschaften zu Wien.
SBAW	Sitzungsberichte der Bayerischen Akademie der Wissenschaften.
SBOT	Sacred Books of the Old Testament.
SbWak	Sitzungsberichte der Wiener Akademie.
	Scientia.
ScJTh	Scottish Journal of Theology.
ScrHier 4	Aspects of the Dead Sea Scrolls. Scripta Hierosolymitana 4. (Jerusalem, 1958, 1965²).
SDAW	Sitzungsberichte der Deutschen Akademie der Wissenschaften zu Berlin.
SDB	Supplément au Dictionnaire de la Bible.
SEÅ	Svensk Exegetisk Årsbok.
Sef	Sefarad.
Sem	Semitica.
	Semitics.
SHAW	Sitzungsberichte der Heidelberger Akademie der Wissenschaften.
Sinai	Sinai (סיני).
SJL	Semitic Journal of Linguistics.
SL	Studia Linguistica. Revue de linguistique générale et comparée.
SPAW	Sitzungsberichte der Preussischen Akademie der Wissenschaften.
SP-B	Studia Post-Biblica.
	Die Sprache.
SS	Studi Semitici.
SSAW	Sitzungsberichte der Sächsischen Akademie der Wissenschaften.
StBFrancLA	Studii Biblici Franciscani Libri Annui.
STDJ	Studies on the Texts of the Desert of Judah.
StIslam	Studia Islamica.
StOr	Studia Orientalia.
StTh	Studia Theologica.
	Studi Etruschi.
	Studi Maghrebini.
	Sumer.
SWAW	Sitzungsberichte der Wiener Akademie der Wissenschaften.
	Syria.
TAPA	Transactions of the American Philological Association.
Tarbiz	Tarbiz (תרביץ).
	Textus.
ThDig	Theology Digest.
Theologia Evangelica	Theologica Evangelica. Journal of the Faculty of Theology/ University of South-Africa.
ThL	Theologisches Literaturblatt.

ThLZ	Theologische Literaturzeitung.
ThQSchr	Theologische Quartalschrift.
ThRsch	Theologische Rundschau.
ThZ	Theologische Zeitschrift.
TPS	Transactions of the Philological Society.
Tradition und Glaube	Tradition und Glaube. Das frühe Christentum in seiner Umwelt. Festgabe für K. G. Kuhn (Göttingen, 1971).
TS	Theological Studies.
TU	Texte und Untersuchungen zur Geschichte der altchristlichen Literatur.
UF	Ugarit Forschungen.
	Ugaritica.
UUÅ	Uppsala Universitets Årsskrift.
VAB	Vorderasiatische Bibliothek.
VD	Verbum Domini.
VDI	Vestnik Drevnej Istorii.
VoxTheol	Vox Theologica.
VS	Vorderasiatische Schriftdenkmäler der Königlichen Museen zu Berlin.
VT	Vetus Testamentum.
VTS	Supplements to Vetus Testamentum.
WI	Die Welt des Islams.
WO	Die Welt des Orients.
	Word.
WVDOG	Wissenschaftiche Veröffentlichungen der Deutschen Orient-gesellschaft.
WZJ	Wissenschaftliche Zeitschrift der Friedrich Schiller Universität Jena.
WZKM	Wiener Zeitschrift für die Kunde des Morgenlandes.
ZA	Zeitschrift für Assyriologie.
ZÄS	Zeitschrift für Ägyptische Sprache und Altertumskunde.
ZAW	Zeitschrift für die Alttestamentliche Wissenschaft.
ZDMG	Zeitschrift der Deutschen Morgenländischen Gesellschaft.
ZDPV	Zeitschrift des Deutschen Palästina-Vereins.
ZfHb	Zeitschrift für Hebräische Bibliographie.
Zion	Zion (ציון).
ZK	Zeitschrift für Keilschriftforschung und verwandte Gebiete.
ZKM	Zeitschrift für die Kunde des Morgenlandes.
ZNW	Zeitschrift für die Neutestamentliche Wissenschaft und die Kunde der älteren Kirche.
ZPh	Zeitschrift für Phonetik und Allgemeine Sprachwissenschaft.
ZS	Zeitschrift für Semitistik und verwandte Gebiete.
ZTK	Zeitschrift für Theologie und Kirche.
ZVS	Zeitschrift für Vergleichende Sprachforschung.

J. H. Hospers
B. Jongeling

ADDITIONS

Additions to I. Akkadian

p. 3 P. Garelli, L'assyriologie. Que sais-je ? Nr. 1144, Paris, 1964.
V.K. Afanasieva, a.o., Cuneiform Studies, USSR Acad. of
Sciences, Inst. of the peoples of Asia, fifty years of Soviet
oriental studies, « Nauka », Moscow, 1968.

p. 5 G. Castellino, Grammatica accadica introduttiva, Rome,
1970.

p. 6 For the history of Akkadian grammatical research cf. E.
Reiner, Akkadian, in : Th. Sebeok (ed.), Current trends in
linguistics 6, The Hague, 1970, 274-303.

p. 12, l. 7 from bottom : ... AASF B 166, Helsinki, 1970.

p. 13 AMSAS;

p. 14 LDN; LSC; SP; Spldiv.; SSA.
M. Birot; J. Bottéro; J.N. Postgate;

p. 16 K.A. al-A'dami, A new lu. sha text in the Iraq Museum,
including women's professions, Sumer 25, 1969, 97-98.

p. 17 B. Meissner, Supplement zu den assyrischen Wörterbüchern,
Leyden, 1898.

p. 19, l. 6 from top KMI;

p. 20 MAOG 6/1-2; 7/1-2; MKJ;

p. 21 A.K. Grayson, Assyrian royal inscriptions 1, Wiesbaden, 1972.

p. 23 M. Dietrich; O. Loretz; W. Mayer, Nuzi-Bibliographie,
AOATS 11, Kevelaer; Neukirchen-Vluyn, 1972.

p. 24 W.W. Hallo; W.K. Simpson, The Ancient Near East. A history
New York; Chicago; San Francisco; Atlanta, 1971.

p. 25 R. Bogaert, Les origines antiques de la banque de dépôt. Une
mise au point accompagnée d'une esquisse des opérations de
banque en Mésopotamie, Leyden, 1966.

p. 26 B. Brentjes, Land zwischen den Strömen. Kulturgeschichte
alten Zweistromlandes Irak, Heidelberg, 1963.
G. Castellino, Le civiltà mesopotamiche, Le civiltà asiatiche 4,
Venice, 1962.
H. Klengel (ed.), Beiträge zur sozialen Struktur des Alten
Vorderasien, Berlin, 1971.

p. 27   J.C. DE MOOR, Mondelinge overlevering in Mesopotamië, Ugarit en Israël, Leyden, 1965.

p. 29   R. LABAT, Les grands textes de la pensée babylonienne, in : Les religions du Proche-Orient asiatique, Paris, 1970, 13-349.
P.T. PAFFRATH, Zur Götterlehre in den altbabylonischen Königsinschriften, Paderborn, 1913, reprint 1967.

p. 30   J.J.M. ROBERTS, The earliest Semitic pantheon. A study of the Semitic deities attested in Mesopotamia before Ur III, Baltimore; London, 1972.
R. MacC. ADAMS, The study of Ancient Mesopotamian settlement patterns and the problem of urban origins, Sumer 25, 1969, 111-124.
——; H.J. NISSEN, The Uruk countryside. The natural setting of urban societies, Chicago, 1972.

p. 31   R.S. ELLIS, A bibliography of Mesopotamian archaeological sites, Wiesbaden, 1972.
McGUIRE GIBSON, Umm El-Jīr, a town in Akkad, JNES 31, 1972, 237-294.

p. 35   J. VAN SETERS, The terms « Amorite » and « Hittite », VT 22, 1972, 64-81.

p. 12   E. SALONEN, Glossar zu den altbabylonischen Urkunden aus Susa, StOr 36, Helsinki, 1967.

ADDITIONS TO II. SUMERIAN

p. 40   G. GRAGG, Observations on grammatical variation in Sumerian literary texts, JAOS 92, 1972, 204-213.
I.T. KANEVA, Participles in Sumerian, MIO 16, 1970, 541-565.

p. 41   A. POEBEL, The tenses of the intransitive verb in Sumerian, AJSL 50, 1933-'34, 143-170.

p. 42   M. CIVIL, The Anzu-Bird ans scribal whimsies, JAOS 92, 1972, 271.
J.S. COOPER, g ì r - KIN « to stamp out, trample », RA 66, 1972, 81-83.

p. 45   A. ZAKAR (with comments by other scholars and reply by the author), Sumerian Ural-Altaic affinities, Current Anthropology 12/2, Glasgow, 1971, 215-225.

p. 47   N.W. FORDE, Nebraska cuneiform texts of the Sumerian Ur III dynasty², Lawrence, 1972.

p. 48   For Sumerian royal inscriptions of the early Old Babylonian period cf. further Å. Sjöberg, JCS 24, 1972, 72-73; D. Arnaud, RA 66, 1972, 33-36.

p. 52 C.B.F. Walker, a.o., Cuneiform texts from Babylonian tablets in the British Museum 51, London, 1972, Nr. 105-112; 141; 180-186; 189; 191.

p. 53 F.A. Ali, Three Sumerian letters, Sumer 26, 1970, 145-178.

B. Alster, A Sumerian incantation against gall, Or 41, 1972, 349-358.

——, Ninurta and the Turtle, UET 6/1, 2, JCS 24, 1972, 120-125.

D. Arnaud, Quelques nouvelles briques inscrites de Larsa, RA 66, 1972, 33-38.

p. 54 R.D. Biggs, Notes brèves 2, RA 62, 1968, 95-96.

p. 55 G. Castellino, Two Šulgi hymns (BC), SS 42, Rome, 1972.

p. 56 J.S. Cooper, Bilinguals from Boghazköi II, ZA 62, 1972, 62-81.

p. 60 I.J. Gelb, The Arua institution, RA 66, 1972, 1-32.

p. 62 L.W. King, The letters and inscriptions of Hammurabi, King of Babylon 3 vol., London, 1898-1900.

J. Klein, Šulgi D : a neo-Sumerian royal hymn, Philadelphia, 1969 (Univ. Microfilms Ltd., High Wycombe, England, nr. 9-131; xerocopy).

p. 65, l. 6 from top add : W. Heimpel, JAOS 92, 1972, 288-291.

p. 68 H. Limet, Le poème épique « Inanna et Ebiḫ », une version des lignes 123-182, Or 40, 1971, 11-28.

D.I. Owen, A unique letter-order in the University of North Carolina, JCS 24, 1972, 133-134.

——, Neo-Sumerian texts from American collections, I, JCS 24, 1972, 137-173.

P.A. Parr, A letter of Ur-Lisi, governor of Umma, JCS 24, 1972, 135-136.

p. 69 D.D. Reisman, Two neo-Sumerian royal hymns, Philadelphia, 1970 (Univ. Microfilms Ltd., High Wycombe, England, nr. 70, 16, 201, xerocopy).

F. Reschid, Ein im neuen Iraq Museum ausgestellter Text, Sumer 23, 1967, 133-143.

p. 70 H. Sauren, Zu den Wirtschaftsurkunden des Musée d'Art et d'Histoire I, AION 30, 1, 1970, 1-19.

p. 70, l. 5-3 from bottom read : A. Shaffer, Sumerian sources of tablet XII of the Epic of Gilgameš, Philadelphia, 1963 (Univ.

Microfilms Ltd., High Wycombe, England, nr. 63-7085,
xerocopy).

p. 71, l. 13 form top add : ZA 62, 1972, 35-61; W. Heimpel, JAOS 92,
1972, 285-288).

p. 71   Å. Sjöberg, A commemorative inscription of King Šūsîn,
JCS 24, 1972, 70-73.

——, « He is a good seed of a dog » and « Engardu the Fool »,
JCS 24, 1972, 107-119.

——, In praise of the scribal art, JCS 24, 1972, 126-131.

p. 73   C. Wilcke, Der aktuelle Bezug der Sammlung der sumerischen
Tempelhymnen und ein Fragment eines Klageliedes, ZA 62,
1972, 35-61.

G.D. Young, Utu and Justice : a new Sumerian proverb, JCS
24, 1972, 132.

p. 76, l. 4 from bottom read : ... Ann Arbor, 1965 (Univ. Microfilms
Ltd., High Wycombe, England, nr. 65-7915, xerocopy).

p. 77   H.T. Wright, a.o., The administration of rural production in
an early Mesopotamian town, Ann Arbor, 1969.

p. 78   B.J. Siegel, Slavery during the Third Dynasty of Ur, AmAn,
n.s., 49, I, 2, New York 1947, reprint 1969.

p. 81, l. 11 from bottom : ... AfO 23, 1970, 71-72.

p. 82   Th. Jacobsen, A survey of the Girsu (Telloh) region, Sumer 25,
1969, 103-109.

p. 40   W. Heimpel, Observations on rhythmical structure in Sumerian
literary texts, Or 39, 1970, 492-495.

28-2-1973.   W. H. Ph. Römer

Additions to XI. Hebrew

p. 180   G. Schramm, Hebrew Reference Grammar, Den Haag, 1973.

p. 184   J. Barr, The Verb ‚Be’ in the Biblical Languages, The Verb
‚Be’ and its Synonyms, Vol. 7 Foundations of Language Supplementary Series, Dordrecht, in prep.

p. 195   C. Rabin, Hebrew zaḥal, Israel Oriental Studies II, 1972,
362-368.

E.J. Revell, Studies in the Palestinism vocalization of Hebrew, J.W. Wevers, D.B. Redford, Essays on the Ancient
Semitic World, Toronto, 1970, 51-100.

p. 199   J.W. Wevers, Heth in Classical Hebrew, J.W. Wevers,
         D.B. Redford, Essays on the Ancient Semitic World, Toronto,
         1970, 101-112.
         R.J. Williams, The Passive Qal Theme in Hebrew, J.W.
         Wevers, D.B. Redford, Essays on the Ancient Semitic
         World, Toronto, 1970, 43-50.
p. 202   A. Diez Macho, Manuscritos hebreos y arameos de la Biblia.
         Contribución al estudio de las diversas tradiciones del texto
         del Antiguo Testamento, Roma, 1971.
p. 206   R.C. Culley, Metrical Analysis of Classical Hebrew Poetry,
         J.W. Wevers, D.B. Redford, Essays on the Ancient Semitic
         World, Toronto, 1970, 12-28.
p. 208   P.W. Skehan, Studies in Israelite Poetry and Wisdom,
         Washington D.C., 1971.
         J. Bright, A History of Israel², Philadelphia, 1972.
p. 209   A.H.J. Gunneweg, Geschichte Israels bis Bar Koahba,
         Stuttgart, 1972.
         H.M. Orlinsky, Understanding the Bible through History
         and Archaeology (New Ed. of « Ancient Israel »), New York,
         1972.

2-3-1973   J. H. Hospers